CONTROVERSIES IN VOTING BEHAVIOR

CONTROVERSIES IN VOTING BEHAVIOR

Fifth Edition

✦ ✦ ✦

Edited by

RICHARD G. NIEMI
University of Rochester

HERBERT F. WEISBERG
The Ohio State University

DAVID C. KIMBALL
University of Missouri–St. Louis

CQ PRESS

A Division of SAGE
Washington, D.C.

CQ Press
2300 N Street, NW, Suite 800
Washington, DC 20037

Phone, 202-729-1900; toll-free, 1-866-427-7737 (1-866-4CQ-PRESS)

Web: www.cqpress.com

Copyright © 2011 by CQ Press, a division of SAGE. CQ Press is a registered
trademark of Congressional Quarterly Inc.

Cover design: Paula Goldstein
Composition: C&M Digitals (P) Ltd.

⊗ The paper used in this publication exceeds the requirements of the American
National Standard for Information Sciences—Permanence of Paper for Printed
Library Materials, ANSI Z39.48-1992.

Printed and bound in the United States of America

14 13   2   3   4   5

Library of Congress Cataloging-in-Publication Data

Controversies in voting behavior / edited by Richard G. Niemi, Herbert F.
Weisberg, David C. Kimball. — 5th ed.
    p. cm.
 Includes bibliographical references and index.
 ISBN 978-0-87289-467-9 (alk. paper)
1. Elections. 2. Voting. I. Niemi, Richard G. II. Weisberg, Herbert F. III.
Kimball, David C. IV. Title.

JF1001.C575 2011
324.9—dc21

                                                        2010011803

To our wives,

Shirley Niemi
Judy Weisberg
Laura Arnold

Contents

✧ ✧ ✧

Preface

✧ ✧ ✧

What we have come to realize more and more through editing multiple editions of this book is how much our understanding of voting behavior depends heavily on developments in the real world. There is perhaps stability at the broadest level—candidates, parties, and issues continuously underlie people's voting choices. But beyond that ethereal notion, the real world changes in ways that demand new explanations and interpretations as well as attention to topics that were previously not even on the radar screen. Rising voter turnout over the past three elections, changes in the media environment for campaigns and for news dissemination more broadly, intense partisanship in Washington, and the changing geography of election results are matters that have risen to prominence since the previous edition was published. They are also topics that researchers could not and have not ignored.

There is also, however, continuity of sorts in the topics considered and the controversies they spawn. Thus, readers will again find a concern with political participation; what voters know about and how they conceptualize politics; what determines people's votes; the relationship between partisanship, issues, and voting; and partisan realignment. Yet how each of these topics is approached is different from how it was tended to in the past. The authors of the works included bring to each item a fresh perspective that requires us to update our understanding of voters, both in America and in democracies throughout the world.

While new controversies develop, old ones do not always disappear, at least not entirely. A good example is the concern with long-term perspectives on voter turnout. In the mid-1970s, when we put together the first edition, there was a great deal of concern with nineteenth-century voter turnout and decision making. Since then, there have been some new contributions, but it is clearly not enough of a contemporary controversy for us to write a new interpretation of it. Nonetheless, it remains an interesting topic. Consequently, some readers—especially graduate students wanting to get an understanding of the full sweep of the field of voting behavior—might wish to consult certain of our essays in previous editions. In our current essays, we make occasional references to the past to signal where readers might find this especially useful.

Unlike in previous editions, we have included some original work in this volume. Because of our sense of how quickly things can change (witness again the reversal of voter turnout since 2000), we thought it worthwhile to ask a number of authors to update their analyses to substantiate their continued relevance and validity. That the analyses have withstood such a test speaks to the choice of these articles as worthy of inclusion here and of continued study by voting researchers. For those who read these articles when they first appeared, we note that the original points they made have not changed; new readers and old, however, should benefit from knowing that they have withstood analysis with the most recent data now available.

We are especially grateful to the authors who have contributed new pieces or updated material. This includes Mike McDonald's explanation of the calculation of Voting-Eligible Population (VEP) turnout rates, Paul Goren's updating of his article on political sophistication, Marc Hetherington's updating of his article on resurgent partisanship, Alan Abramowitz on the one hand and Mo Fiorina and Samuel Abrams on the other hand updating their controversy on political polarization through the 2008 election, and M. V. Hood, Quentin Kidd, and Irwin Morris updating their research on the Republican Party in the South.

We would like to thank the people at CQ Press for prodding us, waiting for us, and then assisting us in the steps needed to produce a volume such as this. Charisse Kiino bore the bulk of this work and did it with patience and thoughtfulness. Lorna Notsch handled the production process efficiently. Larry Baker carried out the copy editing with skill and speed. We are grateful to Michael Hanmer for his critique of one of the introductions. David Campbell of the University of Notre Dame and Lynn Vavreck of UCLA reviewed the manuscript as a whole; their comments resulted in a number of improvements. Finally, Kimball thanks the University of Missouri Research Board for supporting this research.

R.G.N.
H.F.W.
D.C.K.

INTRODUCTION

1. The Study of Voting and Elections

Another presidential election, this time with the first African-American nominee facing a war hero, during a severe economic downturn, with the winner succeeding a president whose popularity had waned. The scenario is that of the United States in November 2008, with elements that are very different from a typical election year. But, as in those other years, the public looked forward to the election as a solution to its problems but all too soon realized that it could not solve all the nation's problems.

At some point the public wonders why such election excitement exists. And then one remembers other elections around the world, as in mid-2009, when the people of Iran protested in the streets when the reelection of the incumbent president was announced more quickly than it would have been possible to hand-count the ballots. The protestors in Iran probably recognized that the challengers were not all that different politically from the incumbent, but they still were willing to risk their lives protesting an election that made a travesty of democracy. Like other peoples around the world, they recognized the essential truth of the comment of Britain's wartime prime minister, Winston Churchill, that "it has been said that democracy is the worst form of government except all those other forms that have been tried from time to time." Democracy and free elections might not solve all problems, but their absence can be an even more serious problem.

What are the functions of elections in a democracy? They allow citizens to choose the government, and they restrain political leaders who wish to maximize their chances of reelection. Elections are thus one means of linking public attitudes with governmental policy. In addition, electing a government is a way of legitimizing its authority. Elections provide a peaceful means for political change and conflict resolution. Along with this view of elections is a corresponding view of voters as choosing intelligently among the candidates, largely on grounds of the policies they advocate. Although no one would argue that all voters are well informed, underlying this perspective is the assumption that voters as a whole make careful and informed choices.

An opposite view holds that elections are just symbolic in character. Elections are a secular ritual of democracy, and voting makes citizens think of themselves as participants in the nation's governance. Voters feel they have fulfilled their civic duty by voting, even if the chance that a single vote affects the election outcome is nearly nil and even if the election outcome is not really going to alter future public policy. Correspondingly, according to this view voters do not necessarily make

1

intelligent, informed decisions—nor do they need to. Few know anything about the candidates, and what they do know is often irrelevant to governance. Consequently, election results are uninterpretable. This view of elections emphasizes that voting does more to make citizens feel good than to alter political outcomes.

Those who view elections as symbolic usually emphasize the limited effectiveness of elections as instruments of popular control. One reason is that institutional structures are sometimes created to limit majority rule, often with the purpose of protecting minority rights. For example, bicameral legislatures slow down the passage of bills; super-majority rules, common in many state legislatures, and the filibuster in the U.S. Senate can likewise frustrate majority rule. Second, centrist, establishment political parties do not offer voters a full range of choices. Additionally, policymaking in some areas is "depoliticized," as when the Federal Reserve Board makes decisions on monetary policy, government bureaucrats make de facto policy in many areas, and the judiciary's rulings control policy on such issues as abortion and gay rights.[1] As a result, elections do not necessarily affect the course of government policies.

The controversy concerning the role of voting and elections turns to a considerable extent on the actual effects of elections. Do elections matter? In the United States, do Democratic and Republican administrations pursue different polices? In other nations, is public policy different under left-wing and right-wing governments? To some extent, these are subjective questions. A Libertarian would perceive little difference between Democratic and Republican policies in the United States. A Marxist in Europe might regard policies of both left-wing and right-wing governments with equal disdain.

Fortunately, whether elections matter is also partly an empirical question. Government policy outputs under Democratic and Republican administrations can be compared, as can those under left-wing and right-wing governments. There is, in fact, an increasing body of such studies, and they nearly always find policy differences between governments. A variety of research, for example, shows a relationship between party leadership of government and spending on social welfare (Bartels 2008; Erikson, MacKuen, and Stimson 2002; see Hicks and Swank 1992, and the references cited therein). Increasingly, researchers are trying to relate policy decisions directly to public opinion, usually finding a close connection between the two (Stimson 2004; Erikson, MacKuen, and Stimson 2002; Hetherington 2005).

Scholarly studies are not required to reveal the consequences of elections. In 1964, U.S. senator Barry Goldwater of Arizona ran for president of the United States as a conservative candidate offering "a choice and not an echo." When he lost in a landslide, President Lyndon B. Johnson instituted liberal Great Society programs such as the War on Poverty. In 1980 former California governor Ronald Reagan ran on virtually an antigovernment platform, and he turned his large victory margin over President Jimmy Carter into a mandate for conservative action by restraining the growth of the government's domestic programs and lowering taxes. President George W. Bush's 2004 election over U.S. senator John Kerry of

Massachusetts was clearly a choice in favor of the strong leadership he had demonstrated in the War on Terrorism. Margaret Thatcher's 1979 victory over James Callaghan in Britain led to the denationalization of some industries that previous Labour governments had nationalized, and the reelection of Conservative governments in 1983, 1987, and 1992 reinforced that decision, whereas Tony Blair's election in 1997 resulted in careful movements toward increased cooperation with the European Union. These are policy consequences of elections that voters will notice. The election of black mayors in a number of U.S. cities in the 1980s—though not a policy shift as such—suggests another important kind of change; the extensive voting along racial lines in many of those mayoral elections is also prima facie evidence that voters are aware of at least some differences in candidates, and it shows as well a presumption that who gets elected makes a difference.[2]

A more difficult question is whether even these consequences make a difference in the long run. Does it really matter if there is a war on poverty, restrained growth of federal programs, or denationalization of industry? Problems seem to remain in any case. From the early 1980s through the early 1990s, the United States has seemed to be on an economic roller coaster, going from severe inflation to harsh unemployment and then back again to inflation. In the later 1990s, there was unprecedented economic well-being along with budget surpluses, leading to discussion of a New Economy fueled by technological advances in the information age. And this was followed in the first decade of the new century by the most severe set of economic disruptions since the Great Depression. The result was that voters lined up behind a return to Democratic rule in the 2008 election, though there was continued skepticism about government in general and about many government-run programs.

Significantly, the electorate has had a reaction, if not an answer, to these possibly unanswerable questions. There seems to be a trend toward voting on the basis of perceived candidate competence or other candidate traits. Carter's defeat in 1980 was less a mandate for Reagan's conservative polices than a rejection of Carter's inability to handle inflation, the American hostages in Tehran, and other problems (Miller and Wattenberg 1981). Thatcher's reelection in 1983 reflected public satisfaction with Britain's successful victory over Argentina in the Falkland Islands war as well as simultaneous dismay over the Labour Party's extreme and sometimes incoherent disarmament policy. Despite the success of the U.S.-led coalition forces in the Persian Gulf War in early 1991, President George H. W. Bush was in trouble with the U.S. electorate a year later because he was not perceived as able to translate his foreign policy successes into domestic economic solutions. President Bill Clinton's reelection in 1996 signaled a desire to go with successful economic solutions, while George W. Bush's victory in 2004 signaled satisfaction with his leadership style. At the state level, the election in 2008 of talk show host and comedian Al Franken as a senator from Minnesota was a vote in favor of a new personality who was decidedly not a traditional politician. In the end, it may be that there are no solutions that work, but the public knows enough to reject leaders who cannot deliver and keep those who achieve some success.

The public does not always reward politicians if times are good, but it punishes them if times are not good enough, which keeps politicians on their toes, even if they are not always responsible for prevailing conditions.

Whether in terms of policy consequences or leadership choices, elections retain their importance in democracies. They do make a difference, at least in the short run. And voters to some degree make choices on the basis of this difference. At the same time, it must be admitted that nobody fully understands voting and elections. The understanding of these topics has changed a great deal in the past few decades, paralleling changes in the ways they are studied. Yet to our frequent dismay, many of the major questions in the field are not yet settled, despite the considerable attention that has been paid to them. Nevertheless, the answers to some of these questions are becoming clearer.

How to Study Voting

Methodology

Modern voting studies rely heavily on survey research. There are certainly other ways of studying elections, but the most direct and often the most valid way of understanding why people vote as they do is to ask them. Of course, not all surveys provide reliable results. Indeed, one might wonder why one should accept any results based on surveys of perhaps fifteen hundred voters out of an electorate of millions. A complete explanation would require a lengthy statistical explanation (see, for example, Weisberg 2005b), but some brief points can be made, especially to underscore the point that reliable polls are not conducted haphazardly but according to scientific principles. Most important in conducting a survey is the way in which the sample is selected. Surveys that interview a few "typical" voters, that interview people at a single street corner, or that rely on "call-ins" to a television program should not be taken seriously, for there is no reason to believe that the people interviewed are typical of the electorate. By contrast, the best scientific sampling procedures give everyone in the population an equal (or at least a known) probability of being part of the sample. Probability theory can then be used to estimate how close results for the sample are to those for the population of interest. For example, using conventional sampling techniques, a sample of about fifteen hundred people will give results that are generally (95 percent of the time) within 3 percent of the true result. Thus, a survey finding that 65 percent of the electorate supports a particular party can be interpreted as meaning that its level of support in the population as a whole is (almost certainly) between 62 and 68 percent.

There is inevitable error, of course, in attempting to describe a population with just a sample, but such error is generally tolerable. For example, it does not matter for predicting election outcomes if a party's support really is as low as 62 percent or as high as 68 percent. Moreover, the 3 percent error margin could be reduced, though that would generally not be cost-effective, since cutting the error to, say, 1.5 percent would require the expense of about 4,500 interviews. Only when trying to predict a very close election might greater accuracy be necessary, and in such cases the pollsters prefer to admit that the election is "too close to call." Note, by the way, that the size of the sample is what matters for most purposes, not the size of the population. Thus, one would want about 1,500 interviews for a national sample or for a sample of the New Hampshire electorate.

Aside from these sampling issues, the validity of a survey depends on the wording of the questions that are asked, and for this task mathematical principles are of less help. Different language obtains different results, often only marginally different but occasionally very much so. At best, researchers "pretest" question wording to make sure it is valid before using it in an actual survey. Sometimes, though, researchers gradually realize that a standard wording that has been used for years is no longer ideal and opt to change it, which can lead to problems in over-time comparisons. In any case, there is no perfect wording for survey questions, so dependence on wording is always important to acknowledge.

Experiments also are increasingly being used in voting studies. Researchers as different in their orientations as political psychologists and formal theorists now use experiments to test their theories of voter decision making. These studies often use small numbers of participants and may even rely on student participants. As examples, political psychologists have shown participants campaign brochures and ads and have used their recollection of topics in those materials as tests between different theories of the process of candidate evaluation (Lodge, McGraw, and Stroh 1989; Lau and Redlawsk 2006) and to determine the effects of campaign material in general (Lodge, Steenbergen, and Brau 1995) and TV ads in particular (Valentino, Hutchings, and White 2002; Brader 2006). Formal theorists have used experiments to test whether participants who are given particular incentives vote in predictable ways (Feddersen, Gailmard, and Sandroni 2009) as well as how voters respond to candidates taking ambiguous positions (Tomz and Van Houweling 2009). Studies of voter turnout—especially how it can be increased—also rely on field experiments, with get-out-the-vote appeals applied to random samples of registered voters in real elections rather than in a laboratory (Green and Gerber 2004; Gerber, Green, and Larimer 2008).

Surveys and experiments each have advantages and disadvantages. Surveys excel in their representativeness, which allows ready generalization from samples to the mass public. They are also the most direct way to get at people's motivations, though many political psychologists give more credence to statistical analyses of motivations than to respondents' self-reports of their reasons for voting for one candidate rather than another (Nisbett and Wilson 1977; Rahn, Krosnick, and Breuning 1994; Kessel and Weisberg 1999). And they can provide information about almost any topic, including some—such as how people voted—that are impossible to know on an individual level without asking people. At the same time, many individuals think about politics only casually, causing problems of response instability, sensitivity to question wording, and various kinds of "response effects" (Zaller 1992, chap. 2). Surveys can also mismeasure political reality, as when post-election surveys find exaggerated turnout rates (Silver, Anderson, and Abramson 1986; Duff, Hanmer, Park, and White 2007) and overstated votes for winning candidates (Wright 1993). And surveys may misrepresent attitudes on sensitive issues because individuals choose "don't know" rather than revealing a politically incorrect response (Berinsky 1999).[3] Finally, it is also difficult to assess causation in surveys, since all variables are measured simultaneously (though panel surveys can help in this regard).

Experiments are better able to establish causation, as the researcher manipulates the experimental variable and controls (or randomizes) for the effects of extraneous variables. However, experiments are often based on limited groups of participants who are not representative of the entire population, especially experiments using student participants. The choice of participants may not matter for some topics, but using college students limits results to people who are used to dealing with abstract concepts. Because of this, it is also becoming common to perform "survey experiments" as part of telephone or Internet surveys, for example by giving different "lead-ins" to issue questions to random halves of a sample so as to assess the effect of issue "framing" on responses (Kuklinski, Quirk, Jerit, and Rich 2001). Even so, some scholars are beginning to note the limits of survey experiments (Gaines, Kuklinski, and Quirk 2007). All in all, experiments are a very useful addition to the toolbox of voting researchers, though political surveys will likely remain the dominant mode of studying elections because they can employ representative samples in a real-world setting.

In addition to surveys and experiments, voting studies make use of several other types of data. Aggregate election data have been analyzed from the earliest voting studies. Logical difficulties in making statements about individual-level behavior on the basis of aggregate data have limited the usefulness of this approach—though some studies have demonstrated the usefulness of new statistical procedures for dealing with the "ecological fallacy" in analyzing racial voting patterns (Tomz and Van Houweling 2003) and split-ticket voting (Burden and Kimball 2002; Elff, Gschwend, and Johnston 2008). Shaw (1999a, 348) also notes some advantages to the use of aggregate data to study campaign effects. State legislative research has also relied heavily on aggregate data because of the sheer number of races involved and the variability of institutional settings, which is absent in congressional elections.[4] Aggregate economic data are often used as well; when combined with aggregate election data or data on presidential or prime ministerial approval, they provide useful insight into the influence of economic conditions on voting and leadership evaluation (see the introduction and readings in Part III). Those studies often are historical, covering lengthy time periods, sometimes including the period before surveys were widely taken.

Yet another important type of data is written and electronic material, including party platforms, campaign information, newspaper articles on campaigns, and television ads. Methods of content analysis help digest these large volumes of material. For example, several scholars have used party platforms and other texts to estimate the policy positions of political parties and others (Laver, Benoit, and Garry 2003; Klingemann et al. 2006; Monroe and Schrodt 2008). Geer (2006) has content-analyzed presidential campaign ads, and Goldstein and colleagues (Goldstein and Freedman 2002; Franz et al. 2007) use what may now be a standard source of data on the content, timing, and market location of televised campaign ads. The study of campaign effects often utilizes events data (Shaw 2006). The availability of newspaper archives on the Internet through LexisNexis is particularly important in facilitating the use of these materials in studying elections (Nadeau, Niemi, Fan, and Amato 1999). The use of aggregate data and written and electronic documents should continue, even while political surveys remain the dominant mode of studying elections.

The Data Base

The articles in this book are generally based on special surveys rather than on commercial polls, such as the Gallup Poll. The main reason for this involves what each is studying. The Gallup organization must forecast election results for its newspaper customers. Newspapers want to publish interesting stories, and predictions of election outcomes are certainly that. Gallup does very well in this prediction game. However, political scientists are typically studying the last election rather than the next. This is because they do not want to predict *who* will win a particular election so much as to understand *why* someone won. Explaining election outcomes requires asking people many more questions than the commercial pollsters do. Voters cannot just be asked who they will vote for. They must be asked their feelings about each candidate, each party, each issue, how they obtained information on the election, how they voted in the past, and so on. This requires separate polls.

Some academic political polls were reported in the 1920s, but the first important voting surveys were not conducted until the 1940s (see Table 1-1). Continuous national political surveys began with the formation of the University of Michigan's well-known Institute for Social Research. The Survey Research Center (and more recently the Center for Political Studies) section of the Institute has continued surveying up to the present day. The Michigan surveys are now administered by the American National Election Studies (ANES) under a continuing grant from the National Science Foundation, with researchers from universities across the country able to participate in preparing questions for the surveys and in analyzing the results. The ANES surveys are currently being conducted by a collaboration of the University of Michigan and Stanford University. Special surveys have sometimes been conducted to study particular topics, but the ANES surveys, with their hundreds of questions about the parties, the candidates, and the issues, have become the standard data base for the study of U.S. elections. Many of the studies reported in this book are based on these ANES surveys.

The usual pattern for the ANES surveys in presidential election years has been to interview the same people before and after the election. A desire to focus on

Table 1-1 Major Columbia and American National Election Studies (ANES) Surveys (national face-to-face surveys unless otherwise stated)

Year	Study*	Survey Design
1940, 1948	Columbia University, Bureau of Applied Social Research	Single-county panel surveys
1944	National Opinion Research Center (University of Chicago)	Post-election survey
1948–2008 presidential election years	University of Michigan SRC; later American National Election Studies (ANES)	Pre-election respondents, reinterviewed post-election (except post-election only in 1948); half of the interviews were by telephone in 2000; minorities over-sampled in some years.
1950	Columbia University, Bureau of Applied Social Research	Four-state study
1954–1998 congressional election years	University of Michigan SRC; later American National Election Studies (ANES)	Post-election surveys, except for 1954 pre-election survey
1956–58–60; 1972–74–76; 1990–91–92; 2000–02–04	University of Michigan SRC; later American National Election Studies (ANES)	Panel surveys
1980	University of Michigan ANES	Four-wave panel survey
1984	University of Michigan ANES	Continuous monitoring survey
1988	University of Michigan ANES	16 state "Super Tuesday" presidential primary survey
1988–90–92	University of Michigan ANES	Pooled Senate study
2008	ANES	Internet panel survey

*Major published reports based on these studies through 1996 are listed in the fourth edition of *Controversies in Voting Behavior,* 8–10.

Note: All the above studies involve post-election interviews, except for the 1954 pre-election study. The presidential-year studies (except for 1944 NORC and 1948 SRC) also involve one or more pre-election interviews.

The ANES surveys are available through www.electionstudies.org.

electoral change, however, has led to some other study designs. An important variation is repeated pre-election interviews with the same person to analyze changes in vote intentions, as was done in the 1940 and 1948 Columbia studies, the 1980 ANES study, and the 2008 ANES Internet survey. Another important variant is interviewing the same people across election years so that voting change between elections can be examined, as was done in the 1956–58–60, the 1972–74–76, 1990–91–92, and the smaller 2000–02–04 ANES "panel" studies. A final variation for presidential elections is weekly interviewing of different people throughout the election year, as was done in the 1984 ANES "rolling thunder" (continuous monitoring) study. The above studies all focus on the presidential election itself, though in 1988 ANES conducted a major study of presidential primary voting on "Super Tuesday."

A simpler study design has been used for ANES studies in congressional election years, with interviews conducted only after the election has taken place. The first major ANES study of a congressional election was in 1958, which included interviews with the congressional candidates in those districts where voters had been interviewed. There were minor ANES studies of the 1962, 1966, 1970, and 1974 congressional elections. By 1978 congressional scholars had begun doubting many of the findings from the 1958 study and were developing new theories of congressional voting. The 1978 survey became a major study of congressional voting and resulted in a vast explosion of work on the topic. Similarly, a specially designed study in 1988–1992 focused attention on elections to the U.S. Senate.[5] Data from all the ANES surveys are also freely downloadable from its Web site, www.electionstudies.org.

The most significant trend, begun by the early 1980s, was an expansion of the number and variety of large-scale data sets and therefore in the subject matter covered. There are several explanations for these developments. For one, the shift from door-to-door interviews to telephone interviews and, more recently, Internet surveys has made it easier to conduct national surveys from a single site, without the difficulty of training separate teams of interviewers in multiple communities. As a result, the national news media, political parties, and academic political scientists are able to conduct more frequent national surveys. Another reason for the growth of available studies is greater cooperation between academic and commercial organizations; studies that once might have sat unused in the electronic equivalent of file drawers are now easily available to researchers through the Inter-University Consortium for Political and Social Research (www.icpsr. umich.edu) and other data archives.

While telephone and Internet election surveys are now ubiquitous, the ANES still relies on face-to-face surveys for its "bread-and-butter" standard pre- and post-election surveys. For one thing, response rates are much higher in face-to-face surveys, upwards of 60 percent in the 2004 ANES survey, compared to response rates of 20 percent or much lower in the other modes. The interviewer is able to generate more rapport with the respondent in face-to-face interviews, leading to higher quality data, and studies show that respondents enjoy face-to-face interviews more. The 2000 ANES survey was conducted half through face-to-face and half through telephone interviewing, but the results of the two were very different (Fogarty, Kelly, and Kilburn 2005), leading to the decision to revert to face-to-face interviewing for the future in order to maintain comparability with the time series of studies dating back to 1948.

Additionally, as Table 1-2 indicates, there are important political surveys conducted outside of the ANES aegis. For example, the National Black Election Study was conducted in 1984, 1988, and 1996, the Latino National Political Survey was taken in 1989–90, and the National Latino Study was completed in 2006.[6] The National Opinion Research Center's General Social Survey (GSS) often contains questions on political issues. Also, the National Election Pool (NEP) (previously Voter News Service and, before that, various separate news organizations) conducts "exit polls" after presidential primaries and presidential and off-year general elections. These polls focus mostly on how people just voted, but they include a few additional questions that are increasingly used in academic studies. Wright, Erikson, and McIver (1985), for example, used the CBS News/*New York Times* exit polls to establish rankings of the states in terms of their Republican-Democrat and liberal-conservative balances. More recently, exit poll data have been used to study topics as diverse as the gender gap in voting (Schaffner 2005), turnout effects (Citrin, Schickler, and Sides 2003), ethnic voting patterns (Barreto et al. 2006), and the racial gap in voided ballots (Tomz and Van Houweling 2003). Frequent polling by some of these organizations (especially GSS, Gallup, and, more recently, various Pew research centers) has led to long time series on political indicators; these time series document stability and change in a wide array of political attitudes.[7] The political parties have also sponsored some polls of these types, though, unfortunately, their data are generally less accessible to academics.

The most interesting new surveys of the 2000–2008 period were telephone and Internet-based. The National Annenberg Election Study (NAES) has conducted large-scale nightly phone surveys throughout the election year, adding up to more than 100,000 interviews in total. This enabled NAES analysts to determine when candidate fortunes changed in the campaign period (Johnston, Hagen, and Jamieson 2004; Johnston, Thorson, and Gooch 2009). By 2004, there was also a national Internet survey, conducted by Knowledge Networks (Hillygus and Shields 2008). In 2006, several universities banded together to conduct the Internet-based Cooperative Congressional Election Study (CCES), with each participant group having access to a common core of questions plus the questions that it submitted. Similarly, in 2008, several universities joined the Cooperative Campaign Analysis Project (CCAP), which conducted a multiwave Internet panel survey, with each participant group having its own questions in addition to a common core of questions. The 2008 ANES panel survey also used the Internet, but panel attrition led to its having a nonrepresentative sample by the postelection wave (showing John McCain winning), whereas CCES and CCAP used propensity-scoring methods to weight their data to yield results that closely approximate probability-based phone samples.

These newer survey approaches have led to controversy regarding the choice of survey modes and sampling procedures. While face-to-face surveys have long been considered the "gold standard," that view is weakening because of cost (millions of dollars for national surveys) and the increased difficulty of obtaining high response rates. Telephone surveys are far less expensive, but their response rates are considerably lower and face new challenges as people abandon landlines

Table 1-2   Other Major U.S. Election Surveys (national samples unless otherwise indicated)

Year	Study*	Survey Design
1961	Negro Political Participation Study (a)	Face-to-face survey of the South
1967	Political Participation in America (a)	Face-to-face survey
1968	Comparative State Elections Project (a)	Face-to-face survey of thirteen states
1972, 1976	Presidential Campaign Impact on Voters (a)	Face-to-face panel surveys of 1–2 cities
1984, 1988, 1996	National Black Election Study (a)	Face-to-face/telephone surveys; panel study, 1984–1988
1984	Presidential Election Campaign Study (a)	Face-to-face panel survey of neighborhoods in one city
1990	American Citizen Participation Study (a)	Face-to-face survey
1989–1990	Latino National Political Study (a)	Face-to-face survey
2000–04–08	National Annenberg Election Study (NAES) (b)	Telephone continuous monitoring/panel survey
2002, 2004, 2006, 2008	Surveys on Congress (c)	Telephone survey 2002–2004; Internet survey 2006–2008
2004	Knowledge Networks (d)	Internet survey
2004	National Politics Study (a)	Telephone survey, oversamples of minority populations
2006	Latino National Survey (a)	Telephone survey
2006–2010	YouGov/Polimetrix, Cooperative Congressional Election Study (CCES) (e)	Internet survey
2008	YouGov/Polimetrix, Cooperative Campaign Analysis Project (CCAP)	Six-wave Internet survey
2008	National Annenberg Election Study (NAES) (b)	Five-wave online panel survey
2008	AP-Yahoo News Election Survey	Eleven-wave online, probability-based panel study
Ongoing	Gallup Poll; CBS/*New York Times*; ABC/*Washington Post*; Voter News Service, National Election Pool (f)	Surveys over many years; face-to-face/telephone/self-administered; cross-section surveys; exit polls; special surveys

*Major published reports based on these studies, through 1996, are listed in the fourth edition of *Controversies in Voting Behavior*, 12–13.

Note: The General Social Survey (GSS), conducted by the National Opinion Research Center at the University of Chicago since 1972, is not an election survey per se, but it includes questions about political issues along with measures of liberal-conservative self-identification and party identification.

(a) Available at the Inter-University Consortium for Political and Social Research, www.icpsr.umich.edu.

(b) See www.annenbergpublicpolicycenter.org and Romer et al. (2006).

(c) Available at www.centeroncongress.org (click on Learn about Congress, Surveys on Congress).

(d) Available upon request from the users (Hillygus and Shields 2008).

(e) The 2006 study is available at web.mit.edu/polisci/portl/cces/commoncontent.html.

(f) Many of these surveys are available at the Roper Center: www.ropercenter.uconn.edu.

in favor of cell phones. Internet surveys are not only less expensive, but they can have many more respondents at low cost. It is also easier to add new questions to both telephone and Internet surveys to keep up with changing real-world events, which is not possible with large-scale, national face-to-face surveys, as was exemplified by ANES's inability to add questions about the economic meltdown and about Sarah Palin to its 2008 pre-election survey. The counter-argument has always been that the ANES use of probability sampling is more scientifically valid, but the use of propensity-scoring matching can mitigate the use of nonprobability sampling for Internet surveys. Specifically, the weighting adjustments used in face-to-face surveys to correct for varying respondent cooperation patterns among age and gender groups is no different logically from the model-based adjustments used for nonprobability Internet surveys (Vavreck and Rivers 2008). Nonetheless, as panel-based Internet surveys ultimately rest on a volunteer ("opt in") base, there is concern that they may in fact not be representative of the underlying population, at least for some populations and some subjects (Malhotra and Krosnick 2007; Niemi, Portney, and King 2008).

There also has been an increasing use of sophisticated analysis methods in election studies, such as "matching" techniques to estimate causal effects (Ho et al. 2007; Kousser and Mullin 2007). In addition, there is greater use of multilevel models for data where observations (such as voters or survey respondents) are nested within higher-level units of aggregation (such as districts or nations). These methods often incorporate contextual data with surveys that cross national or district boundaries. For example, Duch and Stevenson (2005) examined the impact of economic considerations on voters in several countries while Gelman (2008) studied voting behavior in the American states. Structural equation models and panel data continue to be used to study the stability of attitudes over time and estimate the impact of different attitudes on voting decisions (Goren 2004; Evans and Andersen 2006; Lewis-Beck, Nadeau, and Elias 2008). What is surprising is that this greater methodological sophistication is not necessarily leading to greater consensus on the leading controversies in the field. Instead, the more sophisticated techniques frequently require arbitrary decisions and untestable assumptions. As a result, the debates become more methodologically advanced without necessarily leading to incontestable conclusions.

Surveys about elections are also used extensively outside the United States. In countries where the election date is not fixed (such as Britain, Japan, and a number of others), prime ministers and party leaders now consult these polls before deciding on the timing of the election (see the references in Smith 2009). The media poll extensively during the campaigns, so much so that there are almost daily reports of new polls in countries (again such as Britain) that have short election campaigns. In some situations, especially when multiple parties are competing, polls have also been important in suggesting to citizens how to maximize the impact of their vote.[8]

Some of the early cross-national academic polls represented attempts to replicate the Michigan surveys in other countries, often by collaboration between some of the original Michigan researchers and investigators from the country in question (e.g., Butler and Stokes 1969; Converse and Pierce 1986). These early studies frequently found that the concepts and questions developed in the American surveys were not applicable in other countries (e.g., Thomassen 1976). As a result, later election studies have been conducted by native researchers based on their understanding of their countries.[9]

There are also important initiatives for taking comparable election surveys across countries. The Comparative National Elections Project (CNEP, at www .cnep.ics.ul.pt/index1.asp) uses similar surveys across more than twenty countries to study the role of intermediaries in voting, especially personal discussants, mass media, and organizations such as political parties. The Comparative Study of Electoral Systems (CSES, at www.cses.org) is a collaborative program that has resulted in fairly comparable post-election survey data (and additional contextual data) for more than fifty countries.

How to Understand Voting

The Theories

There are countless ways to understand voting. Two potential paradigms were explored by an early Columbia University research team, but neither had a lasting impact. The 1940 Columbia study was based on a consumer preference model: each party was seen as presenting a product to the public, the campaign was seen as an advertising campaign during which the competing products were weighed by the public, and the voters were seen as recording their final choices when they stepped into the booth on election day. The problem with this model was that most people knew how they would vote even before the national conventions were held, particularly since President Franklin D. Roosevelt was running for a third term in office in 1940. People knew whether or not they were going to vote for him without listening attentively to the campaign.[10] In the end, the Columbia researchers explained the 1940 election with a sociological model, relating voters' socioeconomic status (education, income, and class), religion, and place of residence (urban or rural) to their vote. These social group factors accounted for most of the observed differences in voting in their study of a single county, but it did not explain why those social group differences appeared; nor did it hold when applied by the University of Michigan scholars to their national sample in 1948. More complex consumer preference and sociological models might have been useful (and indeed have received attention in recent years), but the time had come for a sharp break with these early models.

The Michigan researchers analyzed the 1952 election using a social-psychological model, which developed into one of the dominant paradigms in the field. The major emphasis was on three attitudes: the person's attachment to a party, the person's orientation toward the issues, and the person's orientation toward the candidates. The emphasis on parties, candidates, and issues explicitly incorporated political variables into the voting model. A theory mapping how these three factors interrelate in their effects on the vote came in the landmark Michigan report on the presidential elections of the 1950s, *The American Voter* (Campbell, Converse, Miller, and Stokes 1960). A person's identification with a party became the core of the model. It in turn affected the person's attitude toward candidates and issues. The authors describe this in terms of a "funnel of causality." The phenomenon to be explained—voting—is at the tip of the funnel, but it is preceded by, and dependent on, a variety of factors. The funnel's axis is time. Events follow one another, converging in a series of causal chains and moving from the mouth of the funnel to its tip. Thus a multitude of causes narrows into the voting act. At the mouth of the funnel are sociological background character-istics (ethnicity, race, region, religion, and the like), social status characteristics (education, occupation, class), and parental characteristics (class, partisanship). All affect the person's choice of party identification, which is the next item in the funnel. Party identification in turn influences the person's evaluation of the can-didates and the issues, which again proceeds further into the funnel. The next part of the funnel features incidents from the campaign itself, as these events are reported by the media. Even closer to the tip are conversations the voter has with family and friends about the election. Finally comes the vote itself. While each of the prior factors affects the vote, the Michigan group concentrated on parties, candidates, and issues, rather than on the early social characteristics or the later communications network.

This remains the basic Michigan model (Beck 1986), with a more explicit division today between what are designated long-term and short-term factors. Party identification is an important long-term factor affecting the vote. Issues and especially candidates are short-term factors specific to the election. (Even if the issues and/or candidates are carry-overs from previous elections, they are inter-preted by voters in a new context in the given election.) This social-psychological model of the vote has affected virtually all later research, serving as the prime paradigm of the vote decision through most of the post-1950 period. And it continues to affect research in other countries, even though it was eventually decided that a different model was more applicable for those settings. *The Amer-ican Voter Revisited* (Lewis-Beck, Jacoby, Norpoth, and Weisberg 2008) reapplied *The American Voter* model and analysis to the 2000 and 2004 elections, showing that replication yielded results remarkably similar to those for the 1950s.

Another model of voting became popular by the 1970s: the rational voter model. According to this model, voters decide whether or not to vote and which candidate to vote for on some rational basis, usually on the basis of which action gives them greater expected benefits. They vote only if they perceive greater gain from voting than the cost (mainly in time) of voting. In the usual formulation, they vote for the candidate closest to them on the issues. A major contribution of this approach is that it provides a more explicit and precise theoretical basis for voting decisions and for their analysis than do other approaches. If voters are rational in the sense indicated, then we can expect certain types of behavior in specific circumstances. In addition, the rational voter model lends itself more than others to predicting what effects changes in external conditions will have. The early work was more mathematical than empirical, but increasingly surveys became a mechanism for testing some of the conclusions of the rational voter model. Substantively, the major contribution of the rational voter approach has been to emphasize the role of issues, which were submerged in most readings of the early findings of the Michigan researchers (see, for example, Fiorina 1981). The early antagonism between the social-psychological and rational voter approaches has long since declined, and most studies now bridge the approaches. Increasingly, rational voter models are tested with the same empirical data used to test social-psychological models, and this has lessened the barriers between the two.

A third approach has formed around what might be termed "modern political psychology." Social psychology has developed considerably since the 1950s when *The American Voter* was written. In particular, that field has experienced what is often referred to as a "cognitive revolution," as psychologists have achieved better understandings of the basis of human thoughts. Simultaneously, the field has given greater attention to human emotions and their effects on behaviors. These developments have been applied widely across the social sciences, with one result being a new field of political psychology. Given the basis of this approach in psychology, many of the studies following this approach use experimental methods. The political psychology perspective has been particularly powerful in dealing with the problem of decision-making under limited information, which is one way of conceptualizing the voting task. Rational choice and political psychology perspectives were originally seen as at odds with one another, but it is now more common to view them as complementary, with political psychology dealing with the origin of preferences and rational choice with strategic behavior once individual preferences are chosen.

All in all, the articles reprinted in this book reflect a variety of theories about voting. They are based most heavily on the social-psychological approach, but often modify and adapt the Michigan model of the 1950s to accommodate later elections and new interpretations of voting. Several of the pieces are strongly influenced by the rational voter perspective or the political psychology approach. While there has been a good deal of convergence between these underlying theories of voting behavior, disagreements remain over what the focus of future election studies should be and therefore over how best to design future empirical work, including whether to continue the basic structure of national election surveys and all of the specific design elements that are a part of that structure (Franklin and Wlezien 2002).[11]

A Note on Studies outside the United States

It is apparent from our listing of election surveys as well as our recollection of early voting studies that our emphasis is on voting in the United States. The basis for this is more one of practicality than of principle. Were we to include

studies from other countries, we would surely have to identify personalities, anno-
tate party names, prepare election calendars, and provide explanations of differences in election laws and traditions. Doing so would detract from our focus on
the substantive matters that form the core of our volume while not, we believe,
adding greatly to our understanding of fundamental aspects of public opinion and
voting behavior.

While behavior of all sorts responds to the institutional (as well as temporal)
context in which it occurs, there are many ways in which the attitudes and behavior of the mass public are the same the world-over. Highlighting findings from
one context should not obscure the degree to which these same findings—and the
same controversies—characterize electorates elsewhere. In moving from one
country to another, we may have to adjust the means (such as the absolute level
of turnout), but not our understanding of what motivates behavior and how it
varies across a populace.

The first edition of this volume was called *Controversies in American Voting
Behavior*. For the second edition, with more studies from an ever-increasing set
of countries documenting the communalities in political behavior, we dropped
"American" from the title. Still, there is the matter of practicality. Consequently,
the studies included here are, with one exception (chap. 10) based on American
data. That we chose to include one study from elsewhere, despite differences in
context, serves to underscore the belief we have articulated that voting behavior
(within functioning democracies, at any rate) has many similarities, wherever it
takes place.

In the Further Readings section at the end of this chapter, we list a number
of books about public opinion and voting behavior across multiple countries as
well as election studies and reports from around the globe. Many countries also
now have their own national election studies, and there are numerous books and
articles based on them. We urge readers to consult these not only to learn about
those countries but also to broaden their knowledge of voting behavior generally.

The Controversies

We organize this book around a series of substantive controversies in the
voting behavior literature. We begin with voter turnout and political participation
more broadly. The focus is on whether participation has declined in recent years
or simply changed from traditional to newer forms. There is a major emphasis on
both measurement and conceptual issues. How exactly one measures the number
of people eligible to vote, for example, is a disarmingly simple question that, once
answered, yields a considerably altered picture of recent voter turnout. Other
questions are about the meaning of community service and online activities.
Looking ahead, what do current trends in participation, especially among the
youth population, have to say about the future?

The second controversy has to do with the electorate's ability to deal
with political matters. This used to be phrased in terms of the public's level of

ideological thinking and their level of political sophistication (for example, in our chapters in the early editions of this book), but this debate now emphasizes a more fundamental matter: the public's ability to process political information, taking for granted their relatively low level of knowledge. This controversy has important ramifications throughout the voting behavior field. One of the most important findings of the early voting studies was that the electorate had limited information about the issues of the day. V. O. Key Jr. (1966) felt compelled to respond to that view, mustering evidence to demonstrate that "voters are not fools," but this evidence did not challenge the limited information level of voters. The rational choice perspective has been useful in showing that voters can make rational decisions even with limited information, as by judging past performance of the parties rather than having to pay attention to their promises for the future. However, the political psychology approach has tackled the matter head on, showing that there are ways that people make good decisions with limited information.

Just how good those decisions are, however, is now subject to debate. There is also a focus on where and when voters obtain information, how reliable that information is, and whether changing technology has resulted in greater knowledge and sophistication throughout the electorate or, perversely, whether its primary contribution has been greater inequalities in information acquisition. Finally, this controversy examines whether low levels of information among segments of the public contribute to political inequality.

The third part of this book turns directly to vote determinants. Given the early view of voters as having limited capacities to deal with political matters, the scholarly controversy in the 1970s involved whether issue-voting occurs. By the 1980s the debate had turned to what kind of issues affect voting, and by the 1990s it involved the relative importance of issue-voting versus voting on the basis of candidates. In the early 2000s, the controversy turned to the more basic question of whether election outcomes should be seen as largely predetermined or as affected by issues, candidates, and the media in election campaigns (for example, Niemi and Weisberg 2001). In this edition we turn to the lively controversy as to the relative importance of cultural and economic issues in contemporary voting. Underlying this controversy are lingering and difficult methodological questions of how best to measure attitudes as well as how to measure the influence of various attributes in the face of possible endogeneity between all these features and the vote itself.

One of the most important variables in our modern understanding of voting is party identification. Early debates involved the role and stability of partisanship, including how much politics affects partisanship. In this edition, we turn to partisan and attitudinal polarization: to what extent has the country polarized politically? The popular press has made a lot of American politics becoming very polarized, but we shall see that there is a vibrant debate in the scholarly literature as to the meaning of polarization, its extent, and its causes. Once again, measurement and definitional issues are at the fore, but that makes the debates no less engaging or meaningful.

The final part of this book focuses on party system change. There has long been debate as to whether the American party system is realigning, dealigning, or even being reinvigorated. In this edition we focus attention on the realignment that occurred in the second half of the twentieth century in the South. We examine a controversy as to whether that realignment was primarily economic, racial, or cultural.

The controversies examined in this book thus play off earlier scholarly debates, but often with some new twist in how the debate is now framed. At times this is virtually stylistic, as when the old controversy about information levels in the mass public is turned into a debate over how the public gets by with what information it has. More often the controversy is now phrased in more complex terms. For example, instead of just arguing whether issues influence voter decisions, the question now is about the kinds of issues that influence voters and the conditions under which they are more or less effective. Perhaps the largest change has to do with the reemphasis on partisan behavior and the debate over the causes of and extent of polarization in the general public.

While there remain controversies in the field, it is also important to acknowledge that we have learned much about voting behavior over the years. Voter turnout in the United States is low by international standards but not as low as is sometimes reported. It has also varied widely over the nation's history. Information levels among the public are generally low but vary enormously. Many citizens decide how to vote before the campaign really begins, often on the basis of long-standing partisan attachments. Contrary to initial beliefs, however, party identification is not fully stable. The party system of today is not the same as the system that developed out of the New Deal era of the 1930s. Voting behavior is much more complex than it was viewed when *The American Voter* was written.

The persistence of controversies in this field is in itself important. One might expect that the combination of sophisticated methodology, high-quality data, and effective theories would yield a commonly accepted understanding of voting and elections. This has not been the case. Controversy remains: over whether political participation is declining; over the implications of limited citizen information; over which issues are affecting the vote; over the extent of partisan polarization; over the causes of changes in the party system in the South. Controversy remains, but what could be more appropriate in the elections field? Elections are about controversy, and the study of elections will always evoke controversy.

Notes

1. That does not mean, of course, that such decisions are free from political influences, as congressional in-fighting over the confirmation of Supreme Court nominees makes patently clear.
2. Elections can affect the electorate as well. Hajnal (2006), for example, argues that the election of black mayors has made white Americans more tolerant of black political leadership.

3. Lodge et al. (1995 318, 321) also argue that surveys give biased results about the significance of recall of campaign events and that experiments are a better method for determining this.

4. Additionally, surveys—both of state legislators themselves and of citizens about their legislators—have become more common. See, for example, Kurtz, Cain, and Niemi (2007) and Sarbaugh-Thompson et al. (2004).

5. In addition to these studies, ANES has conducted several "pilot studies" that were designed to test new survey questions. Complete information on these studies is available at the ANES Web site.

6. Additionally, in 2008 the ANES conducted approximately three hundred extra interviews each with African-Americans and with Latinos.

7. Compilations of over-time data can be found on the Web sites of Gallup (www .gallup.com), GSS (www.norc.org/GSS+Website), and Pew Research Centers (www .pewtrusts.org). A handy compilation for a variety of measures and attitudes is Stanley and Niemi (2010).

8. See Crewe and Harrop (1989) on the role of polls and the media in advertising "tactical voting" in the British general election of 1987.

9. See Mochmann, Oedegaard, and Mauer (1998) for an extensive listing of non-U.S. academic surveys and published reports on those surveys through 1995. The number of national and cross-national election studies is now very large. One can locate many of them by searching archives cited at the end of this chapter under Election Studies/ Reports Web Sites.

10. Between 1952 and 2004, an average of 63 percent of voters in presidential elections said they made their vote decision before or during the nominating conventions (Campbell 2008a).

11. Indeed, we have witnessed considerable expansion over the past decade or so in the design and focus of election studies broadly conceived. In addition to greater use of a variety of survey designs—continuous monitoring surveys, within- and between-election panel surveys, and experimental surveys—there has been more frequent use of contextual data in the form of "hard" economic numbers, information about the allocation of campaign resources, figures about both media production and consumption, and so on. There have also been substantially rejuvenated areas of investigation, such as the study of election administration.

Further Readings

The Role of Elections

Powell, G. Bingham, "Election Laws and Representative Governments: Beyond Votes and Seats." *British Journal of Political Science* 36 (2006): 291–315. Finds that governments and policy-making configurations emerging from bargaining after PR elections are significantly closer to their citizens than those created by SMD elections.

Powell, G. Bingham, *Elections as Instruments of Democracy: Majoritarian and Proportional Visions* (New Haven, Conn.: Yale University Press, 2000). Policy consequences of majority and proportional election systems.

Voting Technology and Election Administration

Alvarez, R. Michael, and Thad E. Hall, *Electronic Elections: The Perils and Promises of Digital Democracy* (Princeton, N.J.: Princeton University Press, 2008). Balanced treatment of the pros and cons of electronic voting and how it can best be implemented.

Ewald, Alec C., *The Way We Vote: The Local Dimension of American Suffrage* (Nashville, Tenn.: Vanderbilt University Press, 2009). Balanced discussion of pros and cons of decentralization of election administration—both historically and currently.

Herrnson, Paul S., Richard G. Niemi, Michael J. Hanmer, Benjamin B. Bederson, Frederick G. Conrad, and Michael W. Traugott, *Voting Technology: The Not-So-Simple Act of Casting a Ballot* (Washington, D.C.: Brookings, 2008). Experimental studies of usability of varying kinds of ballots and electronic voting systems.

Massicotte, Louis, André Blais, and Antoine Yoshinaka, *Establishing the Rules of the Game* (Toronto: University of Toronto Press, 2004). Sourcebook about election laws around the world.

Percy, Herma. *Will Your Vote Count? Fixing America's Broken Electoral System.* Westport, CT: Praeger, 2009). Review of numerous complaints about and potential problems involving contemporary voting.

Saltman, Roy G., *The History and Politics of Voting Technology* (New York: Palgrave Macmillan, 2006). Comprehensive coverage through 2005.

Public Opinion and Public Policy

Bartels, Larry M., *Unequal Democracy: The Political Economy of the New Gilded Age* (New York: Russell Sage Foundation, and Princeton, N.J.: Princeton University Press, 2008). Growing inequality in America is the result of policy choices attributable to Republican administrations.

Erikson, Robert S., Michael B. MacKuen, and James A. Stimson, *The Macro Polity* (New York: Cambridge University Press, 2002). A careful examination of the relationship between public opinion and government performance and policy.

Hetherington, Marc J., *Why Trust Matters* (Princeton, N.J.: Princeton University Press, 2005). Argues that declining public trust in government is partly responsible for a more conservative direction in government policy.

Stimson, James A., *Tides of Consent* (New York: Cambridge University Press, 2004). The interpretability of the public's "mood," and the importance of movement in public opinion on elections and public policy.

Election Studies/Reports Web Sites

American National Election Studies: www.electionstudies.org. See especially the Guide to Public Opinion.

Comparative Study of Electoral Systems (CSES): www.cses.org. The "about" page lists numerous other comparative studies as well.

Compendia of election and related archives: www.intute.ac.uk/cgi-bin/search. pl?term1=election+data&limit=0 and www.gesis.org/en/research/networks/ data-infrastructure/ifdo.

Council of European Social Science Data Archives: www.cessda.org.

International Foundation for Electoral Systems (IFES): www.aceproject.org (on elections) and www.electionguide.org (on election administration).

Inter-university Consortium for Political and Social Research (ICPSR): www .icpsr.umich.edu

National Annenberg Election Survey (NAES): www.annenbergpublicpolicycenter.org/ProjectDetails.aspx?myId=1.

Roper Center for Public Opinion Research: www.ropercenter.uconn.edu. See especially its U.S. Elections and Presidential Elections pages.

World Values Survey: www.worldvaluessurvey.org

Books Studying Voting across a Series of U.S. Elections

Abramson Paul R., John H. Aldrich, and David W. Rohde, *Change and Continuity in the 2008 Elections* (Washington, D.C.: CQ Press, 2010). Factors affecting voting in the 2008 election.

Flanigan, William H., and Nancy H. Zingale, *Political Behavior of the American Electorate*, 12th ed. (Washington, DC: CQ Press, 2010). Textbook treatment of issues, candidates, and elections.

Niemi, Richard G., and Herbert F. Weisberg, eds. *Classics in Voting Behavior*. (Washington, DC: CQ Press, 1993). Reprints of numerous classic voting studies along with summary introductions.

Books on Recent Elections

Hillygus, D. Sunshine, and Todd G. Shields, *The Persuadable Voter: Wedge Issues in Presidential Campaigns* (Princeton, N.J.: Princeton University Press, 2008). Cross-cutting issue preferences occur frequently, resulting in voters changing preferences.

Lewis-Beck, Michael S., William G. Jacoby, Helmut Norpoth, and Herbert F. Weisberg, *The American Voter Revisited* (Ann Arbor: University of Michigan Press, 2008). Applies the theory and analytical methods of *The American Voter* to examine the 2000 and 2004 presidential elections.

Shaw, Daron R., *The Race to 270* (Chicago: University of Chicago Press, 2006). Examines the strategic decisions and the impact of presidential campaigns in the 2000 and 2004 elections. Compares how political scientists and campaign professionals study elections.

Books Emphasizing a Political Psychology Approach

Brader, Ted, *Campaigning for Hearts and Minds* (Chicago: University of Chicago Press, 2006). Examines the psychological impact of emotional appeals in campaign advertising.

Lau, Richard R, and David P. Redlawsk, *How Voters Decide*. (New York: Cambridge University Press, 2006). Examines how voters process information and make candidate choices, and seeks to determine how many people correctly choose the candidate most aligned with their preferences.

Books on Public Opinion and Voting Behavior across Multiple Countries
Dalton, Russell J., *Citizen Politics: Public Opinion and Political Parties in Advanced Industrial Democracies*, 5th ed. (Washington, D.C.: CQ Press, 2008). Political attitudes, behavior, and party systems in France, Great Britain, Germany, and the United States.
Dalton, Russell J., *Democratic Challenges, Democratic Choices* (Oxford: Oxford University Press, 2004). Excellent, well-grounded discussion of the causes and consequences of declining trust in countries around the globe.
Inglehart, Ronald, *Modernization and Postmodernization: Cultural, Economic, and Political Change in 43 Societies* (Princeton, N.J.: Princeton University Press, 1997). Sweeping overview of changes in attitudes and values across the contemporary world.
LeDuc, Lawrence, Richard G. Niemi, and Pippa Norris, eds., *Comparing Democracies 3: Elections and Voting in the 21st Century* (London: Sage, 2010). Wide-ranging coverage of election systems, the media, campaign finance, the outcome of elections, and other election-related topics.

PART I
POLITICAL PARTICIPATION

2. Is Political Participation Declining or
Simply Changing Form?

That citizen engagement is important to the life of a democratic polity is considered almost a given: it is thought to improve the quality of government, provide legitimacy for governments and their policies, and enrich individuals' lives (Macedo et al. 2005, 4–5); it is regarded as a fundamental aspect of education for democracy, recommended as a component of civics instruction from an early age (National Standards for Civics and Government 1994). Thus, when voter turnout, the most basic and widely engaged-in kind of political participation, appeared to be in free-fall in the years after 1972, the search was on for probable causes (Brody 1978; Teixeira 1987; Miller 1992; Rosenstone and Hansen 1993). When widespread declines were observed in other forms of political and social participation and were found to be generational in nature (Putnam 2000), alarm bells were sounded by academics (e.g., Macedo et al. 2005; Wattenberg 2008), blue-ribbon commissions (e.g., "America's Civic Health Index" 2006) and popular commentators (e.g., Mindich 2005).[1]

Yet some researchers have argued that these are false alarms—that the observed declines miss the point. It may be true that people are participating less in "conventional" political activities; but participation in newer kinds of activities—be it boycotting, buycotting, directly contacting politicians, protesting, or blogging—is taking up the slack (Dalton 2009). Civic engagement, more broadly conceived to include all sorts of community activities, is also up ("Volunteer Growth in America" 2006; Zukin et al. 2006). Moreover, voting itself may not be in decline (in the United States), an argument made by some even before the obvious increases observed in the last three presidential elections (McDonald and Popkin 2001; McDonald, this volume, chap. 4).

The arguments revolve in part around measurement issues. How exactly do we measure the denominator—i.e., the number of people who could have voted—in calculating voter turnout? Is some data unreliable, and should it therefore be discounted? Have we failed adequately to observe certain kinds of involvement, including relatively new online activities? The debate also involves questions of definition and interpretation. Is community service really political engagement? Is motivation relevant, as when young people engage in service largely to pad their resumes in order to get into better colleges? And, of course, how and to what degree do observed trajectories predict future levels of involvement?

In this chapter we summarize the arguments and evidence on both sides of the debate. The first side has been in play for somewhat longer, so the evidence is somewhat more developed. Only now, for example, are researchers beginning to pay close attention to use of the newer forms of media and electronic interaction (see, for example, Hindman 2009; Boulianne 2009; Perlmutter 2008; Davis 2005, 2009), and this could alter our understanding of what it means to be politically involved in the twenty-first century. Still, enough points have been made on both sides to make this a lively controversy.

Americans (and Other Electorates) Have Become Disengaged from Politics

Signs of disengagement from politics go back to the 1960s.[2] In the middle of that decade, the percentage of independents (including leaners) suddenly jumped from about 27–28 percent to about 35 percent and later to as much as 40 percent of the electorate. Other indicators of a more candidate-centered politics, such as increased split-ticket voting and heightened neutrality toward the parties, occurred about the same time (Aldrich and Niemi 1996; Wattenberg 1998). Simultaneously, trust in government declined sharply (Hetherington 2005; Dalton 2008, 242–43). It is true that attitudes toward the parties have reverted somewhat to their earlier levels (Bartels 2000; Hetherington 2001, Born 2008; Prior 2007, 16). Yet the percentage of independents has remained high, the incumbency effect is undiminished, and trust, while moving up and down with the changing political environment, has never reached its highs from the 1950s.[3]

In any event, it is the decline in voter turnout that has garnered the most attention and, perhaps more than anything else, suggests that Americans are turning away from politics. Turnout in U.S. presidential elections declined steadily from about 63 percent (of the voting-age population) in 1960 to about 51 percent in 1988; after an upturn in 1992, it declined to less than 50 percent in 1996 (see chapter 4). Attempts to account for the decline pointed to other factors that were themselves indicators of declining political engagement—weakened partisanship, declining political efficacy, less frequent newspaper reading (Teixeira 1987), a drop in civic duty (Campbell 2006, 187–192), lower levels of mobilization by the parties (Rosenstone and Hansen 1993), and the disappearance of more effective, face-to-face mobilization (Gerber and Green, 2000).[4]

Turnout in recent elections (and a shift in focus to the voting-*eligible* population) has altered somewhat the weight of this evidence. The percentage voting jumped up in 1992—probably due to the excitement caused by the three-way race involving businessman Ross Perot—fell back in 1996 but then it climbed in three straight elections, reaching a level in 2008 (of the voting-eligible population) that nearly matched the level in 1960.[5] Still, as researchers have noted, the decline and apparent return to prior levels occurred at a time when education levels (a prime mover behind high turnout) advanced greatly, poll taxes and other impediments to voting by African Americans were removed, and registration laws were significantly relaxed.[6]

Among the changes in registration practices, the so-called Motor Voter Law, passed in 1993, was the most significant, requiring states to make voter registration readily available when individuals applied for or renewed a driver's license or when they applied for public assistance, providing for universal mail registration, and prohibiting the purging of nonvoters from voter rolls. It had the effect of increasing the number of registered individuals, but turnout itself was largely unchanged (Highton and Wolfinger 1998; Knack 1999; Martinez and Hill 1999; Hanmer 2009).

In the past decade, efforts have been made to ease the process of voting itself, but these efforts, too, have met with mixed results. The ability to register to vote as late as Election Day itself is now the law in eight states;[7] its effects are perhaps bigger than those of other reforms, but they are still in the single-digit range (Brians and Grofman 2001) and may only apply to states that adopted the reform early and enthusiastically (Hanmer 2004). In Oregon and most of Washington's counties, voting is by mail only. No-excuse and permanent absentee voting, along with various forms of early voting, have become common practice in a number of states (Fortier 2006). These reforms have generated higher turnout in certain instances such as low-level elections, but the general conclusion is that they help retain inconsistent voters but do little to stimulate new voters (Traugott 2004; Berinsky 2005).[8]

Thus, despite favorable changes in demographics and the law, other changes—in demographics (an increase in single persons), the law (lowering the voting age to 18), and perhaps above all in attitudes—mean that voter turnout in the United States remains low by world standards and is, at best, just back to where it was sixty years ago. Moreover, in assessing changes in turnout, we need not limit ourselves to the American electorate. To the extent that common factors are driving changes in political behavior worldwide, changes observed elsewhere may provide a clue about behavior in the United States and the pattern it is likely to undergo in the future.

If we thus broaden our scope, we find that turnout is declining in nations around the world. Even including countries such as Australia and Belgium, where voting is compulsory, turnout has dropped by about 10 percentage points between peak turnout levels in the 1960s or 1970s and the 2000s (Blais 2010; see also Dalton 2008, 36–38).[9] In a few cases, turnout in recent elections has declined precipitously. In Canada, for example, turnout since 2000 has averaged only 61 percent, down from highs of about 80 percent in the late 1950s and early 1960s and from 75 percent as recently as 1988. In the United Kingdom, turnout in the 2001 and 2005 parliamentary elections was about 60 percent, down from an average of more than 75 percent through 1992.[10]

Withdrawal from politics is not limited to voting. Some of the steepest declines are in what is sometimes referred to as passive participation, or processes of becoming informed. (Another term is cognitive engagement.) Reading a daily newspaper is one such indicator. On this measure the evidence is unmistakable. In the 1950s, three-quarters of the American public read at least one newspaper daily (a quarter read two or three papers daily). By 2004, the percentage reading a paper daily had dropped to just above 40 percent. The percentages claiming to read specifically about the presidential campaign dropped equally precipitously. Similarly, television viewership of national network evening news shows has dropped to the point that the programs are in danger of disappearing altogether. Likewise, the percentages watching the national party conventions and presidential debates have fallen off.[11]

Participation in various sorts of "conventional" political behavior (political party and campaign activity) has also fallen off. Putnam (2000, 39) cites National Election Studies data to show that the percentage attending political meetings and working for a political party dropped significantly (though not always steadily) between about 1970 and the mid-1990s. Data from the same source reveals a large drop in the percentage of individuals wearing a button or having a bumper sticker (Dalton 2009, 63). Drawing on Roper data, Putnam (2000) also shows large declines in political rally attendance and political party work but also in other political activities, including committee service, membership in a "better government group," and newspaper letter-writing.[12] The election of 2004 was an exception, with substantially greater participation in all campaign activities than in the recent past (Dalton 2009, 63), but it would take several such years to establish a turnaround from the general decline.

As with voting, declines in campaign activity are not restricted to the United States. Dalton, McAllister, and Wattenberg (2000, 57–59) examined trends in election campaign activities in nine countries over varying periods between 1964 and 1996. The trend was downward in almost every instance, leading them to conclude that the "direction of change is clear. Contemporary electorates are becoming less likely to participate in elections, and they are becoming more likely to be spectators." (58).

Americans' disengagement from politics extends to a wide range of social interaction and civic involvement, including church attendance, workplace connections, and club meeting attendance (Putnam, chaps. 3–7). Some of these, such as card-playing (105), social visiting (99), and league bowling (112), are related to politics only in the vaguest of senses—though even they may be symptoms of a more individualistic and less cooperative culture in which we are less trusting of others (Putnam 2000, chap. 8). Other kinds of interaction, such as union membership, PTA membership, and attendance at religious services, all of which showed sharp declines in the second half of the twentieth century, bear a more direct relationship to political behavior. Union membership and religious attendance, for example, have long been related to one's partisan affiliation (Stanley and Niemi 2006). Again, the trends described by Putnam are at least to some extent mirrored abroad. Scarrow (2007), for example, notes that membership in political parties has declined markedly in democracies around the world (see also Mair and van Biezen 2001).

The withdrawal from politics shows up in one other significant way. Americans, at best, appear to be no more knowledgeable about politics than fifty years ago (Delli Carpini and Keeter 1996, chap. 3; Neuman 1986; Bennett 1988, 1989; Smith 1989). This lack of movement flies in the face of enormous increases in education over this time along with the tremendous technological advancements that have made it possible to access news in ways that were never available before.

It may be, however, that television, cable, and even newer methods of getting the news have simply substituted for the information flows that in a previous era came via newspapers and radio. Moreover, by various measures, the quality of news coverage has deteriorated (Gilens, Vavreck, and Cohen 2007, 1164).

That the growth in alternative news sources has not resulted in knowledge gains may be attributable to the way in which modern media are used. Markus Prior (in work included in chapter 3) observes that in an earlier era users had little choice about what to take in, as news was interspersed with entertainment. With the development of numerous, specialized cable channels and the infinitely differentiated world of Web sites, following politics can become a full-time preoccupation, but equally well, political news can be avoided altogether. Individuals inclined toward the latter are now less likely to pick up news by accident, as it were.

Not only do news differentiation and preferences for news possibly explain the aggregate stability of political knowledge, they may result in greater knowledge gaps between those inclined toward political news versus entertainment. Prior finds support for this effect both in a year-long panel study and in cross-sectional analyses. Moreover, he finds that news preferences bear a similar relationship to turnout. Those who shy away from political news turn out to vote at lower levels, thus contributing to a kind of participation gap.

An important feature of Americans' disengagement from politics is that it is generational in origin. That is, the declines in turnout and other forms of participation and in knowledge are particularly notable among young people. Of course it has long been true that young people vote at lower rates than older citizens (for example, Tingsten 1937). In the 1960s, at a time now viewed as the high point of U.S. voter turnout in the past one hundred years, Converse (1971) wrote a report for an organization concerned about "the problem of non-voting among young adults in the United States." But age gaps in all sorts of participation have opened up since then. We show one among many striking examples of this in Table 2-1. The table shows that in 1960, a slightly greater proportion of young people than people over 65 reported reading newspapers about the presidential campaign. Over time, reading the newspaper dropped among people of all ages, but much more so among younger generations; in recent elections, the gap between old and young readers has been nearly 30 percentage points.

Similar patterns occur for voter turnout, general political interest, aspects of television viewing, and various forms of active participation (such as signing petitions, attending public meetings, and so on) (Wattenberg 2008, Putnam 2000, 252). Regarding political knowledge, Wattenberg (2008, 77) expresses the

Table 2-1 Newspaper Reading about the U.S. Presidential Campaign, by Age, 1960–2008

	Percent reading about the campaign				Difference between 65+ & <30
	18–29	30–44	45–64	65+	
1960	84	80	81	74	+10
1964	75	80	80	77	−2
1968	68	81	76	72	−4
1972	49	59	62	61	−11
1976	68	78	77	70	−2
1980	56	78	76	72	−16
1984	66	82	82	77	−11
1988	50	61	71	74	−24
1992	51	63	72	73	−22
1996	40	47	64	71	−31
2000	41	50	62	69	−28
2004	56	62	70	80	−24
2008	46	57	67	80	−34

Source: American National Election Studies.

Note: Question wording, 1952–1976: "We're interested in this interview in finding out whether people paid much attention to the election campaign this year. Take newspapers for instance—did you read about the campaign in any newspaper?" 1980–1984: "Did you read about the campaign in any newspapers?" 1988–2008: "How many days in the past week did you read a daily newspaper? (If the respondent has read a daily newspaper:) "Did you read about the campaign in any newspaper?

relationship with age in terms of correlations, but the point is the same. In the 1960s, age and political knowledge were nearly uncorrelated; young and old knew about the same amount. But the correlation has grown over time and is now close to .30, prompting Wattenberg to ask "Is this the least politically knowledgeable generation of American youth ever?"[13]

Further, to the extent that increases in volunteer work and unconventional political behavior are characteristic of younger individuals, they have increased as much as or more so among older people (Wattenberg 2008, chap. 8). This undercuts the argument (see below) that youths have turned away from conventional behavior but have disproportionately taken up these new forms. Relatively speaking, even with respect to unconventional participation, young people are no more likely to be engaged than are older people.

Once again, the same sorts of generational patterns that are found in the United States characterize other electorates. Turnout by age, which showed relatively small differences in many countries in the early 1970s, now show substantial gaps between turnout of those under thirty and those over sixty-five (Wattenberg 2008, 107). Wattenberg documented similar changes for newspaper reading, television viewing, and political knowledge.[14] Dalton (2004, 93) notes that "the long-term decrease of political support [in a half-dozen nations] has been disproportionately greater among the young." With respect to party membership, there is evidence that declining numbers in European parties come especially from a drop in youth enrollments (Offe and Fuchs 2002, 216; Rothstein 2002, 294).

In general, concern over the apparent lack of political interest and involvement among young people has spread throughout much of the democratic world. What Henn, Weinstein, and Forrest (2005, 558) write about Britain could be said of many other countries in addition to the United States:

> . . . the general message that youth in Britain today are politically disengaged is one that seems to hold particular sway within academic and policy circles alike. . . . Consequently, there is concern amongst politicians and officials that this age group has a disaffection from politics that is deeply entrenched; that in the medium to long term, the more civic-oriented older generations will be replaced by this younger skeptical generation; and that the legitimacy of the political system is itself therefore under threat.

Two final points should be made. First, exactly what caused the observed changes in political outlooks and behavior is not known with any degree of precision. Some political events, such as the fall of communism, might have played a role, but researchers usually point to broad societal shifts such as changes in the role of women and the rise in single-parent families; the development of television, cable, and now of the Internet; increasing secularization; globalization of markets and the workforce; and growing recognition of climate and other environmental changes (though it is very difficult to include these kinds of factors in empirical tests). In any event, the fact that changes are so widespread diminishes the role of country-specific factors, such as particular candidates or elections or institutional changes.[15] The generational character of the change may be due simply to the general tendency of young people to react more readily to changing conditions along with the speed and coincidence of large-scale changes during the second half of the twentieth century.

The other remaining point is that patterns can be altered and trends reversed quickly, especially within any single country. Turnout in the United States is a case in point, as it increased in 2000, 2004, and then in 2008, reaching nearly the high-water mark of 1960. Similarly, party mobilization in 2004 and 2008 reached levels not previously seen, and participation in 2008 caucuses was at record levels.[16] But the underlying cause of this spurt in voter turnout may have been the contentiousness and closeness of the presidential race in these three elections. Does this short-term pattern foreshadow a general reversal of the decades-long downward trend? Not necessarily. Exceptions and temporary reversals will occur, but if disengagement is indeed related to societal changes that are themselves not likely to be reversed (for example, globalization, secularization, or media dispersion), the patterns described above are likely to continue, especially as the inevitable process of generational replacement occurs.

Disengagement of Americans (and Others)
from Politics Is a Myth

The world has unquestionably changed in the past half-century in ways that affect how Americans relate to the political world. One of the most significant changes is in the way we communicate with each other and with government. The quintessential civic duty of "calling or writing to your congressman" has become far easier with the advent of cheap long-distance calls and e-mail. The same goes for circulating and signing petitions, especially across large, spread-out populations. One can still put a bumper sticker on one's car proclaiming one's candidate preferences, but that seems old-fashioned and likely to reach far fewer people than posting messages on Web sites.

Likewise, the way we get news and information has changed dramatically. In the 1950s, newspapers—often available in both morning and afternoon editions—and radio were the predominant way of keeping abreast of national and world events. In the 1960s, network news programs on television began to dominate—more so as technology permitted the airing of live broadcasts from around the world. More recently, cable channels and now the Internet have begun to replace network television as the prime source of news.

Attitudes and underlying values have also changed dramatically. As Dalton (2009) has recently documented, there has been a movement away from a view of citizenship as duty toward one of engagement. The former emphasizes behavior such as obeying laws, voting, paying taxes, and serving in the military. The latter emphasizes individual autonomy but also the idea that one should help others both at home and abroad; it emphasizes political behavior in the form of non-electoral activities such as community service and direct action to help others.[17] Unsurprisingly, younger people have been the most eager to adopt the norms of engaged citizenship.

These changes in modes of communication, news dissemination, and values have naturally caused changes in some kinds of political behavior. Reliance on newspapers is a prime example. Many people find newspapers less useful when television and the Internet can update news from anywhere in the world almost instantaneously; in addition, despite what researchers tend to see as superior coverage by newspapers, television better conveys information to some individuals (or on some topics) because it is less cognitively demanding (Neuman, Just, and Crigler 1992; Kwak 1999; Eveland and Scheufele 2000). Thus, declining readership of newspapers is to be expected and is hardly an indication that Americans have lost interest in politics.

Consider instead a more direct measure. The American National Election Studies have asked how often "you follow what's going on in government and public affairs." It is true that the percentage replying "most of the time" has dropped off from what it was in the 1960s and early 1970s (when the civil rights movement and then the Vietnam War were very salient). Since 1978, however, there has been little movement in this indicator. Another measure, asking about interest in the campaign then underway, also shows high values in most (though not all) of the elections through 1976; but the previous peak value was tied in the election of 1992 and exceeded by one point in 2004. And yet another measure shows high percentages in recent years of voters who say they care who wins the presidential election.[18] The 2008 election also produced high values on both measures, although not quite as high as 2004.

Insofar as partisanship is an indication of connectedness with politics, the evidence does not point to any serious withdrawal, and surely not recently. As noted above, the percentage of independents remains higher than in the 1950s, but it has remained relatively steady since the mid-1970s. Other indicators, such as recognition of party differences (Born 2008), the relationship between party, ideology, and issue positions (Abramowitz and Saunders 1998; Jacobson 2008, 21–33), party-based voting at both the presidential and U.S. House levels (Bartels 2000; Born 2008), and split-ticket voting (Stanley and Niemi 2010, 128) have all moved in the past two or even three decades in a direction suggesting a greater influence of parties.

What about measures of active participation, beginning with voter turnout? The argument that Americans are disengaged from politics took a direct hit with the publication of McDonald and Popkin's (2001) analysis of turnout data through 2000. Their argument is straightforward. Turnout is usually calculated using voting age population (VAP) as the base. Since the 1970s, however, an increasing proportion of the adult population is not eligible to vote—mostly because of the presence of non-citizens (legal or otherwise), but also because of an increasing number of felons and ex-felons who have lost the right to vote.[19] If one calculates turnout using the voting eligible population (VEP) as the base, the path of turnout after 1972 shows only a slight decline. If one adds the results of the 2004 and 2008 elections, one would have to conclude that turnout is (at least temporarily) on the rise (see this volume, Figure 4.1).[20] McDonald's original chapter in this volume explains the VEP calculation in some detail.

Moving beyond turnout, the argument about disengagement turns largely on the kinds of participation measures that are considered. Evidence of declining involvement, some argue, reflects a fixation on old measures that do not tap the kinds of participation that are most relevant today. What has heretofore been referred to as conventional political behavior—activity often related to political campaigns—has admittedly become less frequent in the last decade or more. Working for a party or candidate, for example, though never engaged in by more than a small percentage of the population, fell by half between its height in 1960 (6 percent) and 1988 and beyond (3 percent). Wearing a button or displaying a bumper sticker declined similarly—from about 20 percent to about 10 percent in the 1990s and 2000 (though remarkably it jumped back to 21 percent in 2004 and 18 percent in 2008). Giving money dropped off as well (though it, too, reversed course in 2004 and 2008). One such item, however, showed no decline; throughout the entire period from the 1950s on, people remained equally inclined to try to persuade others how to vote—if anything, this indicator also increased in 2004 and 2008.[21]

These kinds of activities, however, are only a part of the story. Direct contacting, communal activity, and protesting and contentious action[22]—still often referred to collectively as unconventional political behavior—reveal quite a different picture. Many of these activities were considered sufficiently unusual enough in the 1950s and into the 1960s that survey respondents were not asked about them. Yet even foreshortened trends, beginning in the 1970s, show increasing levels of activity. Signing petitions, joining in boycotts, taking part in lawful demonstrations, and participating in unofficial strikes all show an increase over earlier years (Dalton 2008, 51; Listhaug and Grønflaten 2007; for contrary evidence about petitions, see Putnam 2000, 45).[23] Researchers have even coined a new term—buycotts—to describe the act of purchasing a particular product or brand because one likes the company that produces it (Zukin et al. 2006, 60; see also Stolle, Hooghe, and Micheletti 2005).[24] Community service has also increased.

It is not only that specific acts are now more frequent. The targets of contacting and protesting have changed as well. Norris (2002, 193) explains this eloquently:

> These [state-oriented] activities remain important, but today the diffusion of power resulting from both globalization and decentralization means that this represents an excessively narrow conceptualization, one that excludes some of the most common targets of civic engagement. *Non-state-oriented* activities are directed toward diverse actors in the public, nonprofit, and private sectors . . . [including] international human rights organizations, women's NGOs, transnational environmental organizations, anti-sweatshop and anti-land mines networks, the peace movement, and anti-globalization and anticapitalist forces.

"Because of these developments," she adds (193–194), "it has become more difficult for citizens to use conventional state-oriented channels of participation, exemplified by national elections, as a way of challenging those in power, reinforcing the need for alternative avenues and targets of political expression and mobilization." In short, in thinking about political engagement, we have to change our entire perspective as well as our vocabulary. What was once unconventional is now quite normal. Activities that were once infrequent and regarded as of dubious legitimacy are now considered part of the standard repertoire.

The same difference of focus and vocabulary may account for perceived declines in communal activity. Participation in some kinds of organizations and activities has unquestionably dropped off, as Putnam (2000) so clearly demonstrates. But when one considers the change from membership associations to advocacy groups that took place in the 1960s and after, the picture is very different (Skocpol 1999). And when one adds in various forms of community involvement, whether through membership in organizations or through episodic "service" activities, the picture changes yet again. The diversity of organizations and the unstructured nature of these activities make it difficult to assess participation accurately, but over-time comparisons suggest growth rather than decline. Verba, Schlozman, and Brady (1995, 72), for example, report small increases in group involvement in communities between 1967 and 1987, with another growth by 2000 (Dalton 2008, 46). Data from the World Values Survey indicate dramatic growth over a twenty-year period in "membership in civic associations, environmental groups, women's groups, or peace groups" (Dalton 2008, 46).

The trends described here are largely repeated when we look abroad. Dalton, McAllister, and Wattenberg (2000, 57), for example, report that political interest, as measured over varying periods of time in the national election studies of nearly a dozen countries, almost uniformly trended upward. Campaign activity, in contrast, was largely downward (59). As in the United States, participation shifted to newer kinds of activities. Across eight post-industrial democracies, signing petitions went from 32 percent in the mid-1970s to 60 percent in the mid-1990s; demonstrating went from 9 to 17 percent; and boycotting jumped from 5 to 15 percent (Norris 2002, 198; see also Dalton 2008, 51; Inglehart 1997, 312–315; see also Listhaug and Grønflaten 2007). Over-time data do not exist for advanced non-European countries, but levels of protest activities in 1999–2002 matched those in Europe (Rucht 2007, 714).

Finally, we also need to revise our views about generational change. With respect to turnout, young people in the United States improved their voting rate in 2004 and again in 2008 (McDonald 2010). Turnout among voters eighteen to twenty-nine years old was up by eleven points over 2000, matching the levels of thirty years earlier and reducing the gap between themselves and older voters. Participation was also up substantially in the 2008 presidential primaries and caucuses (Kirby, Marcelo, Gillerman, and Linkins 2008). Concerns about ever-decreasing turnout due to generational replacement are misplaced.[25]

More broadly, the young participate differently, not necessarily less. It is true that they are less active in campaign activities. With respect to civic activities, however, they are about as active as older individuals (Zukin et al., 2006). They may be even more active when it comes to activities such as boycotting and protesting (Dalton 2009, 71). It is important to recognize, of course, that unconventional behavior began to be adopted by the young some years ago. This makes the current generation of youths less distinct from middle-aged citizens and truly distinct only from the relatively elderly (Wattenberg 2008, 191–194; Zukin et al. 2006, 188). But that makes the transition from an emphasis on conventional to unconventional behavior no less important.

As noted above, we do not know exactly why these changes in modes of participation occurred. Clearly, however, they are associated with opinion changes that are less compatible with the older kinds of behavior and more compatible with the new. When asked what makes a good citizen, older generations are inclined to respond in terms of duty, including such things as paying taxes and voting, whereas younger generations focus more on non-electoral engagement (Dalton 2009, chap. 2–3; Zukin et al. 2006, 97–103; Campbell 2006, 192). In turn, people who adhere to distinctive views on citizenship display different attitudes and behavior (Dalton 2009; Campbell 2006).

Conclusion

However one evaluates the research discussed in this chapter, there is no doubt that political participation is not the same now as it was a half-century ago. Voter turnout has been variable, tending toward the low side (with a recent uptick in the United States); membership in what were traditional civic and political organizations is down markedly while new types of organizations have sprung up in large numbers; what were thought of as conventional (mainly campaign) acts have given way to a broader array of activities, including more that are focused on direct action; and the media themselves and media consumption have changed in ways that were not even conceived of five or six decades ago. Political attitudes have changed as well, in ways related to participation. Views of what constitutes good citizenship have evolved toward greater challenging of and less outright deference to authority and toward newer forms of direct action.

Changes of this magnitude inevitably raise questions about likely consequences. Underlying much of the writing about participation declines is a sense that democracy is at risk, to paraphrase the title of a recent volume (Macedo et al. 2005; Skocpol 2003). Others focus on the young—citing their lack of engagement as evidence that "many young Americans may not be prepared to participate fully in our democracy now and when they become adults" (*The Civic Mission of Schools*, 2003, 4)—to project further declines in the future. Still others focus especially on voter turnout, asking whether declining numbers of voters will undercut the legitimacy of elected governments (for example, Lijphart 1997).

Counter-arguments are now being voiced more frequently. In this view, current levels of participation—even if they are lower than previously—are not a matter of concern, or at least not a grave concern. Some, as we have noted, argue that in any case it is the modes of participation that have changed greatly, not so much the level of involvement.[26] Others argue that people do not want more participation (Hibbing and Theiss-Morse 2002, chap. 8). Fiorina (1999), interestingly, adds a new twist. We have opened up the system to more engagement by more people, he argues, but citizens are less satisfied than they were. The only way forward, he suggests, is through still more involvement: "The relationship between political engagement and social welfare may well be U-shaped, with societies better off with either 'a little' or 'a lot' than with 'some.'" (418).

There is disagreement, finally, about what to do if we hold to the view that lack of participation is a problem. A number of "solutions" have been proposed: more and better civic education (*The Civic Mission of Schools* 2003; Levine 2007; Campbell 2006, chap. 8); changes to electoral and other institutions (Macedo et al. 2005; Donovan and Bowler 2004; Streb 2008), including possibly compulsory voting (Lijphart 1997); greater use of kinds of participation that may not require a physical presence (for example, electronic town halls) (Fiorina, 1999, 416); and use of deliberative polls and "deliberation day" (Fishkin 1995; Ackerman and Fishkin 2004). In the end, it is useful to recall that many of the conditions and changes that reformers are responding to are characteristic of countries around the world. It is tempting to think that it is *our* institutions and the attitudes of *our* young people that explain the changes we have observed. No doubt our institutions and our youth are a part of the explanation. But the commonality of developments here and elsewhere suggests that larger forces are also at work. Fully understanding changes in political participation—both their direction and their underlying causes—requires taking account of those forces as well.

Notes

1. Occasional concern was also voiced about *equality* of participation, most visibly by Arend Lijphart (1997) in his presidential address to the American Political Science Association. It was less newsworthy, however, because inequality is a perennial condition and "stratification in activity in the mid-1990s is not much different than it was in the mid-1970s" (Brady, Schlozman, Verba, and Elms 2002, 233).
2. We refer to the past fifty to sixty years because this period is especially well documented with survey data representative of the general public. A longer-term perspective might describe political interest and involvement in the nineteenth century and changes that occurred at the end of that century. See Burnham (1965) and the controversy surrounding his interpretation of the system of 1896, summarized in Niemi and Weisberg (1976).
3. A handy source for over-time numbers on partisanship, split-ticket voting, incumbency reelection levels and vote margins, and political trust (confidence in government) is Stanley and Niemi (2010). See also the "American National Election Studies Guide to Public Opinion and Electoral Behavior" at www.electionstudies.org/nesguide/nesguide.htm.
4. Leighley and Nagler (2007) also note that unions stimulated voter turnout and that that the large decline in union membership since the 1960s has contributed to the lower turnout levels.
5. We accept here McDonald's (2009) analysis that the turnout rate increased by 1.6 percentage points between 2004 and 2008 rather than the Census Bureau's Current Population Survey results that show a 0.2 percentage point decrease.
6. An excellent account of changes in the franchise and impediments to turnout, including those of the civil rights and post–civil rights periods, is Keyssar (2009).
7. In addition, North Dakota has not had a registration system since 1951 (Hanmer 2009) and, as of 2008, North Carolina has a provision for early voting with same-day registration (www.sboe.state.nc.us/content.aspx?ID=32).
8. Recently there has been a spate of well-executed experimental studies of get-out-the-vote campaigns, which show more and less successful ways of stimulating voter turnout (for example, Green and Gerber 2004). Most such studies reveal limited success (see, for example, the summary of mail experiments reported in Gerber, Green, and Larimer (2008). Green et al.'s recent study showed a surprisingly large effect of about 8 percent with only one mailing—though the method involved could raise ethical questions in that it involved telling people that a record of their having voted (or not) would be made public along with the records of others in their neighborhood.

9. In Blais's table, new democracies are included, so the number of countries varies from one decade to the next. If one limits the comparisons to countries that were rated 1 or 2 in 2008 on the Freedom House rating of political rights and held elections from the 1970s through the 2000s (N = 30), average turnout is as follows for the 1970s, 1980s, 1990s, and 2000–2008, respectively: 81.1, 80.7, 77.3, and 74.0. Twenty of these countries had free elections in the 1960s, with an average turnout of 84.5. Turnout is measured as the percentage of registered voters. In most cases, the percentage of registered voters is a very high percentage of the voting age population. The United States is excluded because of the lower proportion of eligible voters who are registered. For U.S. turnout figures, see chapter 4.

10. Turnout numbers for Canada and the UK are taken from www.elections.ca/content .asp?section=pas&document=turnout&lang=e and www.ukpolitical.info/Turnout45 .htm, respectively. More generally, turnout figures since World War II are shown for countries throughout the world on the International Institute for Democracy and Electoral Assistance's (IDEA) Web site, at www.idea.int.

11. The primary source for this paragraph, including the specific numbers, is Wattenberg (2008).

12. We mention the source of data because Dalton (2009, 214, note 24), whose perspective we convey more fully in the next section, criticizes Putnam's results as being based on less accurate samples. It is not clear, however, why *trends* would be misrepresented by the less accurate Roper data.

13. Various questions remain, most especially whether the observed declines are continuous or whether there are definable generations. Miller and Shanks (1996, chap. 3) argue that one can meaningfully divide the population into pre–New Deal (1920–1928), New Deal (1932–1964), and post–New Deal (1968–1992) generations (where the years refer to the year of first eligibility to vote for president). Lyons and Alexander (2000), partly for methodological reasons, opt for only two generations, defined by birth year (roughly equivalent to first being eligible to vote in the presidential election of 1954). Zukin et al. (2006) outline four generations by when they were born: before 1946, between 1946 and 1964, between 1965 and 1976, and after 1976. The analyses of Wattenberg and Putnam implicitly assume that changes are more or less continuous.

14. With respect to Canada, Blais, Gidengil, Nevitte, and Nadeau (2004) conclude that recent declines in turnout are due to "powerful generation effects" among post–baby boomers, and Howe (2003, 21) reports a "growing knowledge deficit." See also Gidengil et al. (2003).

15. Franklin (2004, chap. 7) argues that a number of countries lowered the voting age at roughly the same time and that this accounts for much of the decline in turnout between 1950 and 1999. Blais (2007, 629), however, argues that reductions in the voting age occurred well before turnout began its widespread decline.

16. See the percentage "contacted by either major party 1956–2004" in the Guide to Public Opinion section of the American National Election Studies Web site (www .electionstudies.org). For attendance at caucuses, see the numbers in various editions of Stanley and Niemi (2010).

17. As Dalton (2008b, 29) notes, there is overlap between his notion of engaged citizenship and post-materialist values that Inglehart (1990) has described as coming to dominate advanced industrial democracies.

18. These results (through 2004) are all found in the Guide to Public Opinion cited in note 16. For additional trend data on political interest, see Dalton (2008b, 59).

19. Since the 2000 election when the state of Florida engaged in questionable practices while trying to identify ex-felons who were not eligible to vote, the subject of felon disenfranchisement has been the subject of considerable research (Manza and Uggen 2006) and policy changes (see www.sentencingproject.org).

20. The dynamic for 2008 was unusual in that the turnout rate of white non-Hispanics declined by 1 percentage point, which was compensated by nearly a 5 percentage point increase among black non-Hispanics (McDonald 2009).

21. These are ANES data series. See note 16.

22. The terms are Dalton's (2008, 44–53). He adds the term "wired activism," though that often refers to how an activity (such as donating money) is carried out rather than to the kind of activity it is.

23. It should be pointed out that while protest activity was not *measured* in surveys in the 1950s and 1960s, it did occur on a large scale. One only has to think of sit-ins, marches, and other protest activities associated with the civil rights movement (which date at least to the Montgomery bus boycott in 1955–1956) and of the myriad anti-(Vietnam)war demonstrations beginning in 1965. "Protest behavior" was first measured systematically by political scientists in the mid-1970s in surveys that formed the basis for *Political Action* (Barnes, Kaase 1979). In this light it is instructive to read that "the waves of political protest that swept the advanced industrial democracies in the late 1960s startled scholars as well as politicians" (p. 13) and that protest *potential* was measured because actual protest behavior was (said to be) infrequent (pp. 57–58).

24. Inglehart (1997) refers to these newer modes of engagement as "elite challenging" (as opposed to "elite directed").

25. The matter of age or generation and turnout will continue to be hotly debated. While youth voting was up substantially in 2008, turnout among 18–29 year olds was still estimated to be 17 and 20 percentage points below those 45–59 and those 60 and over, respectively (McDonald 2010). Moreover, turnout in subsequent elections declined ("Massachusetts Senate Election"). One could also argue that the 52 percent turnout among 18–29 year olds in 2008 was not all that high considering the reported enthusiasm among the young for candidate Barack Obama.

26. In addition, apocalyptic writing about the extreme dangers of low turnout has declined in the United States since the 2004 election because turnout has been on the upswing.

Further Readings

Voter Turnout

Blais, André, *To Vote or Not to Vote: The Merits and Limits of Rational Choice Theory* (Pittsburgh: University of Pittsburgh Press, 2000). Explication and evaluation of a rational-choice perspective on turnout. Identifies system characteristics that contribute to differences in turnout across nations.

Campbell, David E., *Why We Vote: How Schools and Communities Shape Our Civic Life* (Princeton, N.J.: Princeton University Press, 2006). Curvilinear relationship between community homogeneity and turnout because civic norms foster turn-out in homogenous communities while people in heterogeneous communities hope to be the deciding voters.

Franklin, Mark N., *Voter Turnout and the Dynamics of Electoral Competition in Established Democracies since 1945* (Cambridge: Cambridge University Press, 2004). Institutional factors that explain turnout across countries; also explores recent turnout declines.

Green, Donald P., and Alan S. Gerber, *Get Out the Vote! How to Increase Voter Turnout* (Washington, D.C.: Brookings, 2004). Reviews and evaluates experiments on voter mobilization.

Keyssar, Alexander, *The Right to Vote: The Contested History of Democracy in the United States,* rev. ed. (New York: Basic Books, 2009). Comprehensive history of the evolution of suffrage in the United States.

Manza, Jeff, and Christopher Uggen, *Locked Out: Felon Disenfranchisement and American Democracy* (New York: Oxford University Press, 2006). History, politics, and effects of the disenfranchisement of felons and ex-felons.

Civic Engagement

Hibbing, John R., and Elizabeth Theiss-Morse, *Stealth Democracy: Americans' Beliefs about How Government Should Work* (Cambridge: Cambridge University Press, 2002), chaps. 7–8. Greater participation and more involvement in diverse settings do not have the benefits theorists claim.

Mutz, Diana, *Hearing the Other Side: Deliberative versus Participatory Democracy* (Cambridge: Cambridge University Press, 2006). Deliberation—holding discussions with people of diverse views—is inversely related to levels of political participation.

Putnam, Robert D., *Bowling Alone: The Collapse and Revival of American Community* (New York: Simon & Schuster, 2000). Wide-ranging survey and aggregate data showing the decline of political, religious, and social organizations in the second half of the twentieth century.

Skocpol, Theda, *Diminished Democracy: From Membership to Management in American Civic Life* (Norman: University of Oklahoma Press, 2003). Since the 1960s, professionally managed organizations have replaced membership groups; many Americans now have fewer opportunities for involvement in community affairs.

Skocpol, Theda, and Morris P. Fiorina, eds., *Civic Engagement in American Democracy* (Washington, D.C.: Brookings; New York: Russell Sage, 1999). Casts a critical and insightful eye on the history, dynamics, and future of organizational structures and involvement.

Verba, Sidney, Kay Lehman Schlozman, and Henry E. Brady, *Voice and Equality: Civic Voluntarism in American Politics* (Cambridge, Mass.: Harvard University Press, 1995). An enduring treatment of numerous aspects of political and civic participation.

Participation of Young People

Center for Information & Research on Civic Learning & Engagement. www
.civicyouth.org. Reports and data about turnout and other participation, with
an emphasis on young people.

Dalton, Russell J., *The Good Citizen: How a Younger Generation is Reshaping American Politics,* rev. ed. (Washington, D.C.: CQ Press, 2009). Describes a shift
over time from a duty-based to a participant view of good citizenship and
related differences in attitudes and modes of participation.

Wattenberg, Martin P., *Is Voting for Young People?* (New York: Pearson/Longman,
2008). Highly readable presentation of declining political engagement among
young people, both in the United States and abroad; argues that civic participation has not picked up the slack.

Zukin, Cliff, Scott Keeter, Molly Andolina, Krista Jenkins, and Michael X. Delli
Carpini, *A New Engagement? Political Participation, Civic Life, and the Changing American Citizen* (Oxford: Oxford University Press 2006). A description of
new modes of political and civic participation in the early 21st century, with a
focus on generational changes.

Gender, Race, Religion, and Participation

Burns, Nancy, Kay Lehman Schlozman, and Sidney Verba, *The Private Roots of
Public Action: Gender, Equality, and Political Participation* (Cambridge, Mass.:
Harvard University Press, 2001). Apart from voting, women participate less
than men; men's and women's experiences in school, families, workplace, and
elsewhere determine their political involvement.

Campbell, David E. ed., *A Matter of Faith: Religion in the 2004 Presidential Election* (Washington, D.C.: Brookings, 2007). Chiefly about direction of the vote,
but briefly touches on mobilization.

Harris, Fredrick C., Valeria Sinclair-Chapman, and Brian D. McKenzie, *Countervailing Forces in African-American Civic Activism, 1973–1994* (New York:
Cambridge University Press, 2006). How national political, economic, and
social conditions shaped black civic and political participation.

Equality/Stratification of Participation

American Democracy in an Age of Rising Inequality (Washington, D.C.: Task Force
on Inequality and American Democracy, American Political Science Association, 2004). Wealth has become more concentrated, and the wealthy participate
more than others. Racial/ethnic and gender disparities continue. Government
is more responsive to the privileged.

Hindman, Matthew, *The Myth of Digital Democracy* (Princeton, N.J.: Princeton
University Press, 2009). Elites dominate how political material is presented and
accessed on the Web; participation is not concentrated among the young and
has not been greatly democratized.

Prior, Markus, *Post-Broadcast Democracy: How Media Choice Increases Inequality in Political Involvement and Polarizes Elections* (New York: Cambridge University Press, 2007). Experimental and survey evidence that the growth of specialized media allows the uninterested to avoid politics, thus increasing inequality of information and participation.

Consequences of Low vs. High Turnout

Hajnal, Zoltan, *America's Uneven Democracy: Race, Turnout, and Representation in City Politics* (Cambridge: Cambridge University Press, 2010). Lower turnout among Latinos and Asian Americans leads to underrepresentation in local government, with significant consequences for election outcomes and government policies.

Participation around the World

Inglehart, Ronald, *Modernization and Postmodernization: Cultural, Economic, and Political Change in 43 Societies* (Princeton, N.J.: Princeton University Press, 1997), chap. 10. Analysis of participation in conventional and unconventional activities in some twenty countries in 1981 and 1990.

Norris, Pippa, *Democratic Phoenix: Reinventing Political Activism* (Cambridge: Cambridge University Press, 2002). Analysis of turnout, party membership, and political participation in numerous countries, with an emphasis on new modes of activism.

Van Deth, Jan W., José Ramón Montero, and Anders Westholm, *Citizenship and Involvement in European Democracies: A Comparative Analysis* (London: Routledge, 2007). Citizenship views, organizational involvement, control over daily life, and conventional and unconventional political participation in twelve European democracies.

Turnout Studies/Reports Web Site

International Institute for Democracy and Electoral Assistance (International IDEA): www.idea.int/elections. Turnout figures for individual countries since 1945. Turnout by age and gender (selected countries). Information on compulsory voting.

3. News vs. Entertainment: How Increasing Media Choice Widens Gaps in Political Knowledge and Turnout

Markus Prior

The rise of new media has brought the question of audience fragmentation and selective exposure to the forefront of scholarly and popular debate. In one of the most widely discussed contributions to this debate, Sunstein (2001) has proposed that people's increasing ability to customize their political information will have a polarizing impact on democracy as media users become less likely to encounter information that challenges their partisan viewpoints. While this debate is far from settled, the issue which precedes it is equally important and often sidestepped: as choice between different media content increases, who continues to access *any type* of political information? Cable television and the Internet have increased media choice so much in recent decades that many Americans now live in a high-choice media environment. As media choice increases, the likelihood of "chance encounters" (Sunstein) *with any political content* declines significantly for many people, as this study will demonstrate. Greater choice allows politically interested people to access more information and increase their political knowledge. Yet those who prefer nonpolitical content can more easily escape the news and therefore pick up less political information than they used to. In a high-choice environment, lack of motivation, not lack of skills or resources, poses the main obstacle to a widely informed electorate.

As media choice increases, content preferences thus become the key to understanding political learning and participation. In a high-choice environment, politics constantly competes with entertainment. Until recently, the impact of content preferences was limited because media users did not enjoy much choice between different content. Television quickly became the most popular mass medium in history, but for decades the networks' scheduling ruled out situations in which viewers had to choose between entertainment and news. Largely unexposed to entertainment competition, news had its place in the early evening and again before the late-night shows. Today, as both entertainment and news are available around the clock on numerous cable channels and web sites, people's content preferences determine more of what those with cable or Internet access watch, read, and hear.

Distinguishing between people who like news and take advantage of additional information and people who prefer other media content explains a puzzling empirical finding: despite the spectacular rise in available political information, mean levels of political knowledge in the population have essentially remained

Source: American Journal of Political Science 49, 3 (July 2005): 577–592.

constant (Delli Carpini and Keeter 1996; Gilens, Vavreck, and Cohen 2004). Yet the fact that average knowledge levels did not change hides important trends: political knowledge has risen in some segments of the electorate, but declined in others. Greater media choice thus widens the "knowledge gap" (Tichenor, Donohue, and Olien 1970). Following Tichenor and colleagues' formulation of the knowledge gap hypothesis, numerous studies have examined the diffusion of information in the population and the differences that emerge between more and less informed individuals (for reviews see Gaziano 1997; Viswanath and Finnegan 1996). According to some of these studies, television works as a "knowledge leveler" (Neuman 1976, 122) because it presents information in less cognitively demanding ways (Eveland and Scheufele 2000; Kwak 1999). To reconcile this effect with the hypothesis that more television widens the knowledge gap, it is necessary to distinguish the effect of news exposure from the effect of the medium itself. In the low-choice broadcast environment, access to the medium and exposure to news were practically one and the same, as less politically interested television viewers had no choice but to watch the news from time to time (more on this below). As media choice increases, exposure to the news may continue to work as a "knowledge leveler," but the distribution of news exposure itself has become more unequal. Access to the medium no longer implies exposure to the news. Television news narrows the knowledge gap *among its viewers.* For the population as a whole, more channels widen the gap.

The consequences of increasing media choice reach beyond a less equal distribution of political knowledge. Since political knowledge is an important predictor of turnout and since exposure to political information motivates turnout, the shift from a low-choice to a high-choice media environment implies changes in electoral participation as well. Those with a preference for news not only become more knowledgeable, but also vote at higher rates. Those with a stronger interest in other media content vote less.

This study casts doubt on the view that the socioeconomic dimension of the digital divide is the greatest obstacle to an informed and participating electorate. Many casual observers emphasize the great promise new technologies hold for democracy. They deplore current socioeconomic inequalities in access to new media, but predict increasing political knowledge and participation among currently disadvantaged people once these inequalities have been overcome (for example, National Telecommunications and Information Administration 2002; Negroponte 1995). This ignores that greater media choice leads to greater *voluntary* segmentation of the electorate. The present study suggests that gaps based on socioeconomic status will be eclipsed by preference-based gaps once access to new media becomes cheaper and more widely available. Gaps created by unequal distribution of resources and skills often emerged due to circumstances outside of people's control. The preference-based gaps documented in this article are self-imposed as many people abandon the news for entertainment simply because they like it better. Inequality in political knowledge and turnout increases as a result of voluntary, not circumstantial, consumption decisions.

After presenting the theoretical framework that predicts changes in knowledge and turnout, two studies test this theory empirically. The first study is based on a nationally representative survey I designed specifically to measure content preferences and relate them to political knowledge and turnout. The second study relies on data collected by the National Election Studies and the Pew Research Center for the People and the Press. Although the preference measures are considerably weaker in the second study, they allow replication of the results for a longer time period and different modes of (survey) data collection.

Theory

The basic premise of this analysis is that people's media environment determines the extent to which their media use is governed by content preferences. According to theories of program choice, viewers have preferences over program characteristics (Bowman 1975; Lehmann 1971) or program types (Youn 1994) and select the program that promises to best satisfy these preferences. The simplest models distinguish between preferences for information and entertainment (Baum 2002; Becker and Schonbach 1989; Rubin 1984). In the low-choice broadcast environment, most people watched news and learned about politics because they were reluctant to turn off the set even if the programs offered at the time did not match their preferences. One study conducted in the early 1970s showed that 40% of the respondents reported watching programs because they appeared on the channel they were already watching or because someone else wanted to see them (LoSciuto 1972). Audience research has proposed a two-stage model according to which people first decide to watch television and then pick the available program they like best. Klein aptly called this model the "Theory of Least Objectionable Program" (1972, 77). If television viewers are routinely "glued to the box" (Barwise, Ehrenberg, and Goodhardt 1982) and select the best available program, we can explain why so many Americans watched television news in the 1960s and 70s despite modest political interest. Most television viewing in the broadcast era did not stem from a deliberate choice of a program, but rather was determined by convenience, availability of spare time, and the decision to spend that time in front of the TV set. And since broadcast channels offered a solid block of news at the dinner hour and again after primetime, many viewers were routinely exposed to news even though they watched television primarily to be entertained:

> Those viewers who can be counted on to watch a news program are not at all drawn to their set from their various pursuits by the appeal of the program; for the main part they are already watching television at that hour, or disposed to watch it then, according to the audience-research studies that networks have conducted over the years. (Epstein 1973, 90)

Once exposed to television news, people learn about politics (e.g., Neuman, Just, and Crigler 1992; Zhao and Chaffee 1995). Although a captive news audience does not exhibit the same political interest as a self-selected one and therefore may not learn as much, research on passive learning (Krugman and Hartley 1970) suggests that even unmotivated exposure can produce learning (Keeter and Wilson 1986; Zukin and Snyder 1984). According to Graber, "[p]eople who are exposed to large amounts of news will remember many stories despite lack of interest because mere exposure produces learning" (1988, 114). Hence, even broadcast viewers who prefer entertainment programs absorb at least basic political knowledge when they happen to tune in when only news is on.

I propose that such accidental exposure should become less likely in a high-choice environment because greater horizontal diversity (the number of genres available at any particular point in time) increases the chance that viewers will find content that matches their preferences. The impact of one's preferences increases, and "indiscriminate viewing" becomes less likely (Youn 1994). Cable subscribers' channel repertoire (the number of frequently viewed channels) is not dramatically higher than that of nonsubscribers (Heeter 1985), but their repertoire reflects a set of channels that are more closely related to their genre preferences. Two-stage viewing behavior thus predicts that news audiences should decrease as more alternatives are offered on other channels. Indeed, local news audiences tend to be smaller when competing entertainment programming is scheduled (Webster 1984; Webster and Newton 1988). Baum and Kernell (1999) show that cable subscribers, especially the less informed among them, are less likely to watch the presidential debates than otherwise similar individuals who receive only broadcast television. According to my first hypothesis, the advent of cable TV increased the knowledge gap between people with a preference for news and people with a preference for other media content.

Internet access should contribute to an increasing knowledge gap as well. Although the two media are undoubtedly different in many respects, access to the Internet, like cable, makes media choice more efficient. Yet, while they both increase media users' content choice, cable TV and the Internet are not perfect substitutes for each other. Compared at least to dial-up Internet service, cable offers greater immediacy and more visuals. The web offers more detailed information and can be customized to a greater extent. Both media, in other words, have unique features, and access to both of them offers users the greatest flexibility. For instance, people with access to both media can watch a campaign speech on cable and then compare online how different newspapers cover the event. Depending on their needs or the issue that interests them, they can actively search a wealth of political information online or passively consume cable politics. Hence, the effects of cable TV and Internet access should be additive and the knowledge gap largest among people with access to both new media.

There are several reasons why exposure to political information increases the likelihood that an individual will cast a vote on election day. Exposure increases political knowledge, which in turn increases turnout (e.g., Delli Carpini and Keeter 1996; Verba, Schlozman, and Brady 1995) because people know where, how, and for whom to vote. Furthermore, knowledgeable people are more likely to perceive differences between candidates and thus less likely to abstain due to indifference (Palfrey and Poole 1987). Independent of learning effects, exposure to political information on cable news and political web sites is likely to increase people's campaign interest (e.g., Bartels and Rahn 2000). Interest, in turn, affects turnout even when one controls for political knowledge (Verba, Schlozman, and Brady 1995). Entertainment fans with a cable box or Internet connection, on the other hand, will miss both the interest- and the information-based effect of broadcast news on turnout. My second hypothesis thus predicts a widening turnout gap in the current environment, as people who prefer news vote at higher rates and those with other preferences increasingly stay home from the polls.

Study I: The News and Entertainment Survey

Data and Measures

Demonstrating the assumed dynamic nature of widening gaps in knowledge and turnout with survey data requires a panel design, because only a panel design can show that knowledge levels changed over time. According to my theory, people with both a preference for news and access to cable and/or the Internet become more knowledgeable over time, while the opposite holds true for people who prefer entertainment programming and can choose between many different channels. According to a possible alternative hypothesis, more knowledgeable respondents who prefer news are more likely to have access to cable or the Internet in the first place than those who know less but are equally interested. If the reverse happens for respondents who prefer entertainment, an interaction effect of content preferences and media access emerges, but the knowledge gap would not in fact have widened as a result of greater media choice.

To evaluate these competing hypotheses, I designed the News & Entertainment (N&E) Survey, a panel survey of 2,358 randomly selected U.S. residents. It was conducted by Knowledge Networks in two waves in 2002 and 2003. Knowledge Networks interviews national probability samples over the Internet by providing a large panel, selected through Random Digit Dialing, with WebTV units and free Internet connections in exchange for taking surveys. The participants for this study constitute a randomly selected subset of the KN panel and are thus close to a random sample of the U.S. adult population.[1] The first survey wave was conducted in February and March 2002, the second wave in April 2003. Of the 2,358 first-wave respondents, the 1,957 who were still part of the Knowledge Networks panel in April 2003[2] were contacted again. Of these, 1,650 panelists were reinterviewed, generating a reinterview rate of 84%.

Each panel wave includes a large set of political knowledge questions about current political events, political officeholders, as well as institutions and processes. It is unclear if panel analyses of political learning should include the same items in both surveys. If different items are used, the two knowledge scales might tap different dimensions of knowledge. If the items are identical, the first interview might encourage panelists to find (or better remember) the answers. I exactly repeated a few items and used similar types of questions in the remaining cases. The appendix lists all knowledge questions and provides summary statistics for the resulting knowledge scales. Data on turnout come from the second panel wave of the N&E Survey. Respondents were asked whether or not they voted in the 2002 House elections. Cable access is coded as a dummy variable based on the question "Do you have either cable or satellite television?" Eighty-one percent of the respondents have cable access. Respondents are defined to have Internet access if they connect to the Internet using their home computers.[3] Thirty-eight percent fall in this category; 33% have access to both new media.

At any given time, television viewers must commit to one particular program. They can either watch entertainment or news, but not both. This notion implies that viewers evaluate the different programming options relative to each other. To assess respondents' preferences for news relative to other programming genres, they were shown a list of 10 genres and asked to select the one they liked best:

Science Fiction shows like *X-Files* or *Star Trek Voyager*
Comedy/Sitcoms like *Friends* or *The Simpsons*
Drama shows like *ER* or *Law and Order*
Soap Operas like *General Hospital* or *One Life to Live*
Reality TV shows like *Survivor* or *Cops*
Sports
Game shows like *Jeopardy* or *Who Wants to Be a Millionaire?*
News
Documentary programs on channels like History Channel or Discovery Channel
Music Videos

After respondents marked their favorite genre, the next screen showed them the remaining nine genres and again asked for the most-liked. This procedure was repeated twice more, yielding a ranking of respondents' four most-preferred television genres. Then, respondents were given a chance to mark all of the remaining genres that they "really dislike." For the purpose of this study, I am only interested in the ranking of news vis-á-vis all other genres. The appeal of news is greatest for respondents who select news as their favorite genre. At the opposite end are respondents who specifically mark news as one they dislike.[4] The measure of people's relative preferences for entertainment over news (to which I will refer as Relative Entertainment Preference or REP) is thus coded 5 if the respondent dislikes news, 4 if the respondent neither dislikes it nor selects it as one of her top four genres, and 3, 2, 1, and 0 if the respondent selects news as her fourth-, third-, second- or most-liked genre, respectively.[5] Exactly half of the respondents are indifferent to news, neither ranking it nor marking it as "disliked." Three percent dislike news explicitly and the remaining respondents rank it fourth (17%), third (14%), second (11%), or first (5%). The preference

Table 3-1 The Effect of Content Preferences on Political Knowledge (Study 1)

	(1)	(2)	(3)
Cable Access	.43 (.44)	.13 (.21)	.40* (.19)
Internet Access	.66* (.39)	.42* (.19)	.04 (.16)
Relative Entertainment Preference (REP)	.03 (.12)	−.05 (.06)	−.02 (.05)
REP × Cable	**−.23* (.14)**	**−.03 (.07)**	**−.10* (.06)**
REP × Internet	**−.22* (.11)**	**−.15** (.05)**	**−.03 (.05)**
Wave 1 Political Knowledge	.93** (.03)		
Civics Knowledge	−	.72** (.04)	.62** (.03)
Political Efficacy	.63* (.31)	.57** (.15)	.39** (.13)
Education	.15* (.06)	.10** (.03)	.17** (.03)
Income	.05** (.02)	.02* (.01)	.02** (.01)
R's primary language is English	2.39** (.43)	.22 (.25)	−.06 (.18)
Gender	−.34** (.14)	−.27** (.07)	−.33** (.06)
Age	.03** (.005)	.002 (.002)	.003 (.002)
TV Households, Nielsen 2002–03 (in 1,000,000)	.04 (.04)	.03 (.02)	.01 (.02)
R owns home computer	.15 (.19)	.01 (.10)	.13 (.08)
Constant	−3.98** (.71)	1.83** (.37)	2.01** (.30)
R^2	.48	.33	.30
N	1,571	1,577	2,250

**$p < .01$, *$p < .05$ (one-tailed).

Note: Cell entries are OLS coefficients and standard errors in parentheses.

distribution among second-wave respondents differs minimally (by no more than 1 percentage point per category) from the whole sample, indicating that respondents with a preference for entertainment were no more or less likely to complete the second survey. Similarly, the difference in political knowledge between first- and second-wave respondents is insignificant. With respect to the key variables, in other words, panel attrition is not a threat.

Analysis

When television viewers have a choice between different media content, their preferences should predict what programs they will select and, by extension, how much they will learn about politics. Relative Entertainment Preference (REP) should thus impact political knowledge significantly more among cable subscribers than among non-subscribers. Similarly, REP should have a stronger effect for Internet users. To test these hypotheses, political knowledge is regressed on cable and Internet access, REP, and the interaction between REP and media access.[6] The dependent variable in the first model shown in Table 3-1 is political knowledge as measured in the second wave of the N&E panel. All independent variables are from the first wave and were measured a year before the dependent

Figure 3-1   Political Knowledge and Relative Entertainment Preference

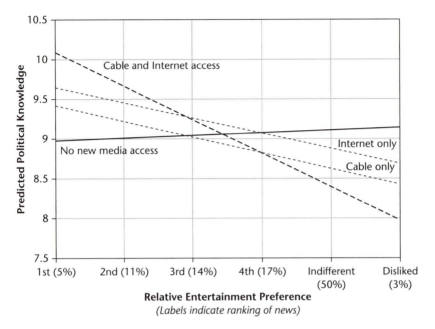

Note: The graph plots the predicted values based on model 1 in Table 3-1.

variable. The joint effect of preference and media access as of spring 2002 on political knowledge a year later is tested, while controlling for knowledge differences in 2002. Controlling for the lagged value of the dependent variable reduces problems of selection bias or reverse causation, because the change in knowledge between the two waves cannot affect first wave content preferences.

Model 1 provides clear support for the predicted effect of increased media choice. The two interactions of cable and Internet access with Relative Entertainment Preference are statistically significant in the predicted direction. The two main effects of media are sizable and positive, indicating that greater choice significantly increased political knowledge between the two panel waves for respondents with a weak entertainment preference. (Individually, only one of them reaches conventional levels of statistical significance, but their joint effect is different from zero at $p = .05$.) To illustrate the interactions, Figure 3-1 plots the predicted values for different levels of media choice. REP has little effect on political knowledge for respondents with neither cable nor Internet access. In a media environment where you cannot choose between entertainment and news, it does not matter very much if you prefer one or the other. Among those with access to both new media, on the other hand, the difference between highest and lowest REP amounts to a knowledge gain of about 27%. Compared to the modal category—indifference toward the news—new media users who rank news first or second are still 16% more knowledgeable.

The strong impact of content preferences is perhaps most clearly demonstrated by a comparison with the effect of education, typically one of the strongest predictors of political knowledge (Delli Carpini and Keeter 1996). Both variables have the same range (0–5 for REP, 1–6 for education) and similar distributions (their standard deviations are nearly identical at 1.26 for education and 1.27 for REP). The size of each interaction effect exceeds the impact of education. The change in knowledge associated with the difference between the most and the least educated respondents is about 9%, compared to the 27% change for the full range of REP among new media users.

In a high-choice environment, people's content preferences become better predictors of political learning than even their level of education.

By assessing the change in political knowledge compared to a baseline set by performance in the first panel wave, the panel design provides a very rigorous test of my hypotheses. A cross-sectional design still makes it possible to show static gaps in knowledge (rather than learning over time) among people with greater media access. In the cross-sectional case, however, the "baseline" cannot be knowledge assessed at an earlier point in time. Instead, I use knowledge that respondents presumably acquired earlier. Knowledge about governmental processes and institutions probably fits that description both because it is emphasized in civics education and because the correct answers do not change as frequently as for questions about current events. The dependent variable in columns 2 and 3 of Table 3-1 is thus Wave 1 knowledge of current affairs, while civics knowledge, also measured in Wave 1, serves as a control variable.[7] Column 2 includes only respondents who were also interviewed in Wave 2, while column 3 shows the same model for all Wave 1 respondents.

The results for the cross-sectional analysis are weaker than for the panel setup. Individually, only one of the two interaction effects is significant in each model. In both models, however, the addition of cable access, Internet access, and their interactions with REP increases the model fit significantly [$F(1,1562) = 3.5$, $p = .06$ for column 2, $F(1,2235) = 3.1$, $p = .08$ for column 3]. Bearing in mind later analyses in this article, it is useful to know that even cross-sectional data analysis can demonstrate the presence of wider knowledge gaps between news and entertainment fans in a high-choice media environment. Below, I take advantage of the greater availability of cross-sectional data to replicate the results obtained in this section.

Turnout

Increasing penetration of new media technologies should increase the difference in turnout rates between those who like news and those who prefer entertainment, both because political knowledge and turnout are tightly related and because exposure to political information motivates people to vote. People who do not like news should become less likely to go to the polls, while the reverse should happen among politically interested citizens with access to cable or the Internet. This proposition is tested by the models in Table 3-2 which regress turnout in the 2002 congressional election on Relative Entertainment Preference, access to cable and Internet, and their interactions (plus demographic controls). Consistent with the hypothesis, the logit coefficients for the interaction terms are negative and statistically significant (at $p < .01$ for Internet access and $p < .07$ for cable access). Including the lagged dependent variable (self-reported turnout in the 2000 House election, as measured in the first wave) in the model of 2002 turnout leaves the result largely unchanged (column 2). This is strong evidence against the alternative hypothesis that people with extreme content preferences were more likely (news-seekers) or less likely (entertainment-seekers) to turn out all along and just obtained access to cable or the Internet earlier or at higher rates than people with more moderate preferences.

Table 3-2   The Effect of Content Preferences on Turnout (Study 1)

	(1)	(2)
Cable access	.51 (.41)	.38 (.43)
Internet access	1.09** (.42)	1.09** (.43)
Relative Entertainment Preference (REP)	.09 (.11)	.06 (.12)
REP × Cable	**−.18# (.12)**	**−.17 (.13)**
REP × Internet	**−.30** (.12)**	**−.26* (.12)**
Turnout in 2000 House Election	—	1.05** (.16)
Wave 1 Political Knowledge	.16** (.03)	.16** (.03)
Sense of Civic Duty	.22 (.30)	.002 (.002)
Education	.23** (.06)	.22** (.06)
Gender	.22* (.13)	.15 (.14)
Age	.03** (.005)	.03** (.005)
Income	.04* (.02)	.04* (.02)
R is married	.41** (.14)	.36** (.14)
R's primary language is English	.41 (.005)	.50 (.48)
Racial Minority	.28 (.17)	.24 (.18)
TV Households, Nielsen 2002–3 (in 1,000,000)	−.01 (.04)	.00 (.04)
R owns home computer	.004 (.17)	−.06 (.17)
R owns VCR	.39** (.14)	.39** (.15)
R reports being registered to vote	3.38** (.33)	2.77** (.34)
Constant	−8.33** (.83)	−8.06** (.85)
Pseudo R^2	.26	.29
Log Likelihood	−762.8	−734.4
N	1,534	1,523

$**p < .01, *p < .05, \#p < .07$ (one-tailed).

Note: Cell entries are logit coefficients and standard errors in parentheses.

Figure 3-2 Turnout and Relative Entertainment Preference

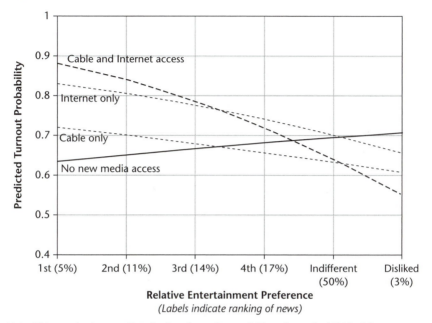

(Labels indicate ranking of news)

Note: This graph plots predicted values from the model in column 2 of Table 3-2.

Once people obtain access to new media, content preference becomes a powerful predictor of turnout, as shown by the predicted values in Figure 3-2 (derived from the second model in Table 3-2). Among respondents without either cable or Internet access, the relationship between content preference and turnout is not statistically different from zero. For cable subscribers and Internet users, in contrast, the effects of REP are sizable. Slightly more than half of the sample are indifferent toward news or dislike the genre. With access to cable and Internet, their probability of voting drops from about .69 to .64. Roughly a third of the sample ranks news among their top three genres. For them, cable and Internet access increases the probability of voting from about .65 to .82. Among new media users, in other words, moving from indifference to a fairly strong preference for news increases predicted turnout by almost 30%. Including Wave 2 political knowledge in the models reduces the magnitude of the effects by less than a third. This result could arise for two reasons: either because my measure of political knowledge does not capture the type of knowledge most relevant to encouraging turnout or because exposure to political information motivates people to vote even when it does not affect their political knowledge. Regardless of which reason is more important, this analysis shows that greater media choice makes content preference a major influence on turnout. As in the case of political knowledge, the effect of preference exceeds the effect of education, typically one of the strongest predictors.

Study 2: NES and Pew

The N&E Survey clearly supports the hypothesis that greater media choice increased inequality in the distributions of political knowledge and turnout. At the time of the survey, most Americans had enjoyed access to cable television for many years, and the Internet had reached about half of all households. The main purpose of replicating the analysis using additional (secondary) data—in addition to providing a general robustness check—is to determine if the results hold for different points in the diffusion process of cable TV and the Internet.

Data and Measures

Survey data for the replications come from the National Election Studies (NES) and the Media Consumption Surveys (MCS) conducted biannually by the Pew Center for the People and the Press. The NES conducts face-to-face (and, in 2000, telephone) interviews; Pew uses phone interviews. Unfortunately, the main drawback of secondary data is a big one. Neither the NES nor Pew's MCS include direct measures of the key concept, entertainment preference. Instead, only a few questions about exposure to entertainment shows are available. Hence, no measure derived from these data comes even close in construct validity to the measure in the N&E Survey. The two NES data sets that ask about cable and Internet access—the NES 1996 and 2000—include a variety of knowledge items. For each data set, a knowledge measure is created by summing the number of correct responses to 14 knowledge questions (listed in the appendix). Turnout in the NES 1996 is assessed by respondent's self-reported vote in the 1996 House election. Vote measures in the Pew surveys are based on questions about voting in the last presidential (and, in the MCS 1996, House) election.

Relative Entertainment Preference

Although secondary data sources provide no direct preference measures, it is possible to approximately infer respondents' relative preferences from the type of content they report watching. High entertainment exposure per se does not necessarily indicate a greater preference for entertainment. Respondents with high entertainment exposure may watch a lot of television in general, without necessarily preferring entertainment strongly to other genres. Hence, the mix of exposure to different genres, rather than absolute exposure to entertainment alone, should be a (very rough) indicator of underlying relative preference. Respondents who watch entertainment programs but little or no news probably do so out of a preference for entertainment. High news exposure and low entertainment exposure would reflect a preference for news. The ratio of entertainment viewing to overall viewing thus yields the best possible measure of relative entertainment preference in NES and Pew data. This ratio is defined as follows:

Relative Entertainment Preference (REP)

$$= \frac{\text{Entertainment Viewing}}{\text{Entertainment Viewing} + \text{News Viewing}}$$

News Viewing is the average number of days per week the respondent watched national and local news. The particular operationalization of entertainment viewing depends on the items in the surveys. For the NES 2000, entertainment viewing is average exposure to *Jeopardy, Wheel of Fortune,* and "television talk shows such as *Oprah Winfrey, Rosie O'Donnell,* or *Jerry Springer.*" The NES 1996 measures entertainment viewing as the average daily viewing of "*Jeopardy* or *Wheel of Fortune*" and *Dr. Quinn, Medicine Woman.* In the Pew data, entertainment viewing is operationalized as watching *Entertainment Tonight, Jerry Springer,* and *Oprah* (MCS 2000), watching *Entertainment Tonight* and MTV and reading *People* magazine (MCS 1998), and watching *Hardcopy, Jerry Springer,* and MTV (MCS 1996). All items used four-point response formats ("regularly," "sometimes," "hardly ever," "never"). REP cannot be computed for respondents who reported no information and entertainment viewing at all. These respondents are excluded from the analysis (2.4% in the MCS 1996, 2% in the MCS 1998, 4.5% in the MCS 2000, 5.8% in the NES 1996, and 9.9 in the NES 2000).

The resulting REP measures range from 0 to 1 and have means of between .21 (NES 1996) and .28 (MCS 2000) with standard deviations between .19 and .28. Evidently, the ratio measures are skewed toward news preference. This is not surprising because the surveys asked about very few entertainment programs and—with the exception of the NES 2000 talk show item—only about specific programs rather than genres. Many respondents surely reported low entertainment exposure not because they do not like entertainment, but because they were not asked about their favorite shows. Yet even though the REP measures built from NES and Pew data underestimate people's preference for entertainment, they still identify a set of respondents to whom entertainment programming is relatively more attractive. To verify that measures of REP are roughly comparable for the different data sets, I examined the relationship between demographics and REP for each data source. Demographics have very similar effects on the more precise REP measure in the N&E Survey and on the somewhat noisier ones in NES and Pew surveys.

Analysis

As before, political knowledge (Table 3-3) and turnout (Table 3-4) are regressed on access to cable TV and the Internet, Relative Entertainment

Preference, and the respective interactions. Overall, the replications clearly support the hypothesis that greater media choice makes content preferences better predictors of people's political knowledge and turnout. All interactions of cable access and REP are in the predicted direction and six of the seven are statistically significant. The conditioning effect of Internet access is evident for turnout only. To summarize the joint effect of preferences and media access in these replications, I use the average of the coefficients across the two knowledge models and the five turnout models, respectively, to graph predicted values for the range of REP in Figure 3-3. Political knowledge of respondents without access to cable or Internet is unrelated to their content preference. For those with access to cable TV, on the other hand, moving from low to high entertainment preference corresponds to a 20% drop in political knowledge. The effect of REP among Internet users is insignificant and not even in the predicted direction. This result is the only instance in this article in which a hypothesis is not supported. The turnout effects mirror the N&E analysis quite precisely. The likelihood of turnout among people without access to cable or Internet is just above chance regardless of their

Table 3-3   The Effect of Content Preferences on Political Knowledge (Study 2)

	NES 1996	NES 2000
Cable Access	.26 (.22)	.04 (.23)
Internet Access	.15 (.22)	.39* (.21)
Relative Entertainment Preference (REP)	−.17 (.60)	.06 (.59)
REP × Cable	**−1.33* (.68)**	**−1.38* (.64)**
REP × Internet	**.80 (.68)**	**.09 (.52)**
Education	.44** (.05)	.58** (.05)
Gender	−.64** (.15)	−.88** (.14)
Age	.03** (.01)	.04** (.005)
Income (MV imputed)	.07** (.02)	.08** (.02)
Income was imputed	−.22 (.26)	−.14 (.19)
African American	−1.35** (.25)	−.78** (.24)
Hispanic or Latino	—	−.41 (.31)
Other Minority	−.15 (.45)	−.07 (.30)
R works 20+hours per week	.10 (.18)	−.38* (.17)
R lives in the South	−.31* (.16)	−.74** (.15)
Party ID	.02 (.03)	−.02 (.04)
Strength of Party ID	.37** (.08)	.43** (.07)
Frequency of political discussion with friends or family	1.60** (.24)	1.29** (.17)
Constant	3.52** (.46)	−.25 (.44)
R^2	.29	.40
N	1,284	1,334

$**p < .01, *p < .05$ (one-tailed).

Note: Cell entries are unstandardized OLS coefficients and standard errors in parentheses.

Table 3-4 The Effect of Content Preferences on Turnout (Study 2)

	NES 1996	Pew 2000	Pew 1998	Pew 1996	
	1996 House	1996 Pres.	1996 Pres.	1992 Pres.	1994 House
Cable	.49** (.21)	.25** (.11)	.18* (.10)	.59** (.15)	.36* (.14)
Internet	.21 (.21)	.62** (.11)	.54** (.12)	.58** (.18)	.34* (.17)
REP	**-1.28* (.61)**	.08 (.27)	.05 (.24)	-.84* (.38)	-.64 (.40)
REP × Cable	**-1.28* (.61)**	**-.57* (.29)**	**-.26 (.28)**	**-.99* (.44)**	**-1.15* (.46)**
REP × Internet	**.39 (.66)**	**-.67** (.28)**	**-.79** (.30)**	**-1.11* (.52)**	**-.10 (.53)**
Education	.31** (.05)	.22** (.02)	.26** (.02)	.23** (.03)	.22** (.03)
Income (MV imputed)	.07** (.01)	.10** (.02)	.11** (.02)	.08** (.02)	.15** (.02)
Income was imputed	.21 (.27)	-.91** (.09)	-.79** (.08)	-.60** (.14)	.07 (.14)
Gender	.19 (.14)	-.10 (.06)	.13* (.06)	-.21** (.08)	-.13* (.08)
Age	.04** (.005)	.04** (.002)	.04** (.002)	.04** (.003)	.05** (.003)
Employment Status	.09 (.17)	.19* (.07)	.17** (.07)	.26** (.08)	-.19* (.08)
Size of Town	—	-.07* (.03)	-.02 (.03)	-.02 (.04)	.05 (.04)
Party ID	.11** (.04)	—	—	—	—
Strength of Party ID	.61** (.08)	—	—	—	—
Constant	-4.87** (.46)	-3.25** (.21)	-3.19** (.18)	-2.45** (.26)	-3.70** (.27)
-2 Log-likelihood	1,354.9	6,219.8	7,121.8	4,180.4	4,179.3
N	1,410	2,910	2,856	1,674	1,620

**p < .01, *p < .05 (one-tailed).

Note: Cell entries are logit coefficients and standard errors in parentheses. Missing values on income were imputed.

Figure 3-3 Pew and NES Replications, Average Effects on Political
Knowledge and Turnout

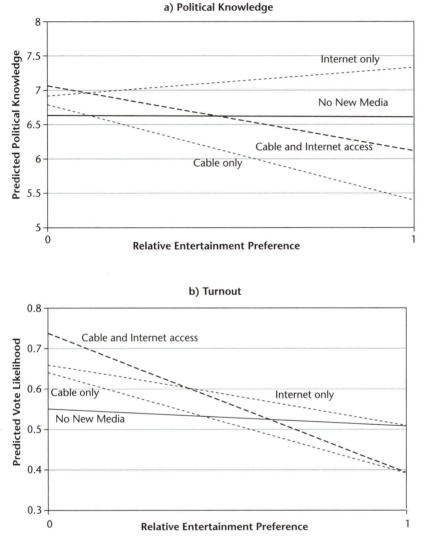

a) Political Knowledge

Internet only

No New Media

Cable and Internet access

Cable only

Predicted Political Knowledge

Relative Entertainment Preference

b) Turnout

Cable and Internet access

Cable only

Internet only

No New Media

Predicted Vote Likelihood

Relative Entertainment Preference

Note: This graph plots predicted values based on the average of the coefficients in Table 3-4.

entertainment preference. For those with cable and the Internet, the likelihood of casting a vote drops from a three-quarter chance among people with the least interest in entertainment to less than .4 among those with the strongest preference for entertainment.

Beyond replicating the N&E results, the analysis of NES and Pew data adds an important element by demonstrating that access to cable and Internet conditioned the effect of preferences as early as 1996 (the first year for which we have data to test the hypothesis). According to a competing hypothesis, respondents with strong content preferences may have had access to these media earlier. In that case, the finding that political knowledge and turnout are higher among news-seekers and lower among entertainment-seekers with greater media choice would not imply any changes in knowledge and turnout levels, only that these two segments were the most and least knowledgeable in the first place. The fact that Relative Entertainment Preference consistently had a sizable effect among cable viewers and Internet users between 1996 and 2003 makes this claim hard to sustain. During this period, the percentage of cable subscribers rose from 69% in 1996 (MCS 1996) to 81% in 2003 (N&E Survey), and the percentage of Americans with Internet access increased from a mere 21% in April of 1996 (MCS 1996) to 62% in 2000 (NES 2000). At some point in this diffusion process, even people with moderate content preferences would have obtained access to new media. Yet this analysis has shown significant effects both in 1996, when only 15% of population had access to both cable and the Internet, and in 2000, when 53% did. It thus becomes impossible to argue that over the period of this analysis, respondents with strong content preferences were always more likely to have greater media choice. The effect of increased choice appears to be quite stable over the past decade, even though more and more people gained access to cable TV and the Internet.

Successful replication minimizes concerns about one other methodological issue: Knowledge Networks, the company which conducted the N&E Survey, provides its respondents with WebTV to conduct periodic interviews. Strictly speaking, the N&E Survey therefore does not permit inferences about the effect of Internet access. Although WebTV is much less convenient than using a regular browser and a mouse, even N&E respondents with only WebTV access are not a genuine "no Internet" group. This is not a major concern here because if anything it would produce conservative estimates of the true effect. If respondents with WebTV as their only means of using the Internet did indeed behave just as Internet users with dial-up or broadband connections, then Internet access as I define it in the N&E Survey should not condition the effect of content preference at all. That Internet access does significantly boost the impact of content preference suggests that accessing the Internet on a television set is not quite the same thing as even a dial-up connection. Still, replicating results on data sets that include respondents with no Internet connection at all bolsters the robustness of my findings. Substantively, the more important point is that differences in the efficiency of media access probably matter as much as the difference between no access and presently typical dial-up connections. As Internet connections become faster, the impact of content preferences is likely to increase further.

In sum, replication using a number of different data sets was successful. The hypothesized conditioning effect of media choice has been shown for very different points in the diffusion process of cable TV and the Internet (1996–2003), for different interview modes (phone, face-to-face, and web-based) and political contexts (during election campaigns and mid-term), as well as for different measures of Relative Entertainment Preference.

Conclusion

When speculating about the political implications of new media, pundits and scholars tend to either praise the likely benefits for democracy in the digital age or dwell on the dangers. The optimists claim that the greater availability of political information will lead more people to learn more about politics and increase their involvement in the political process. The pessimists fear that new media will make people apolitical and provide mind-numbing entertainment that keeps citizens from fulfilling their democratic responsibilities. These two predictions are often presented as mutually exclusive. Things will either spiral upwards or spiral downwards; the circle is either virtuous or vicious. The analyses presented here show that both are true. New media do indeed increase political knowledge and involvement in the electoral process among some people, just as the optimists predict. Yet, the evidence supports the pessimists' scenario as well. Other people take advantage of greater choice and tune out of politics completely. Those with a preference for entertainment, once they gain access to new media, become less knowledgeable about politics and less likely to vote. People's media content preferences become the key to understanding the political implications of new media.

Analog cable systems and dial-up Internet connections—currently the most common ways of new media access—are only the first technological steps toward greater choice. Digital technology will multiply the number of choices and the efficiency of choosing, thereby further increasing the impact of content preferences on users' choices. This study has begun to show this impact, but it has also raised new questions: How are content preferences formed? How easily do they change? What changes them? A measure of content preferences not used in this study was included in both panel waves of the N&E Survey. Overtime correlations of .6 (Pearson's r) suggest considerable preference stability. In light of the powerful effects content preferences had in this study, the next logical step is to examine if and how political socialization, education, or the content and style of political news affect peoples preferences.

The decline in the size of news audiences over the last three decades has been identified as cause for concern by many observers who have generally interpreted it as a sign of waning political interest and a disappearing sense of civic duty. Yet changes in available content can affect news consumption and learning *even in the absence of preference* changes. People's media use may change in a modified media environment, even if their preferences (or political interest or sense of civic duty) remain constant. By this logic, the decreasing size of the news audience is not necessarily an indication of reduced political interest. Interest in politics may simply never have been as high as audience shares for evening news suggested. A combined market share for the three network newscasts of almost 90% takes on a different meaning if one considers that people had hardly any viewing alternatives. It was "politics by default" (Neuman 1996, 19), not politics by choice. Even the mediocre levels of political knowledge during the broadcast era (e.g., Delli Carpini and Keeter 1996), in other words, were partly a result of de facto restrictions of people's freedom to choose their preferred media content.

Ironically, we might have to pin our hopes of creating a reasonably evenly informed electorate on that reviled form of communication, political advertising. Large segments of the electorate in a high-choice environment do not voluntarily watch, read, or listen to political information. Their greatest chance for encounters with the political world occurs when commercials are inserted into their regular entertainment diet. And exposure to political ads can increase viewers' political knowledge (Ansolabehere and Iyengar 1995). At least for the time being, before recording services like TiVo, which automatically skip the commercial breaks, or subscriber-financed premium cable channels without advertising become more widespread, political advertising is more likely than news coverage to reach these viewers.

It might seem counterintuitive that political knowledge has decreased for a substantial portion of the electorate even though the amount of political information has multiplied and is more readily available than ever before. The share of politically uninformed people has risen since we entered the so-called "information age." Television as a medium has often been denigrated as "dumb," but, helped by the features of the broadcast environment, it may have been more successful in reaching less interested segments of the population than the "encyclopedic" Internet. In contrast to the view that politics is simply too difficult and complex to understand, this study shows that motivation, not ability, is the main obstacle that stands between an abundance of political information and a well- and evenly informed public.

When differences in political knowledge and turnout arise from inequality in the distribution of resources and skills, recommendations for how to help the information have-nots are generally uncontroversial. To the extent that knowledge and turnout gaps in the new media environment arise from voluntary consumption decisions, recommendations for how to narrow them, or whether to narrow them at all, become more contestable on normative grounds. As Downs remarked a long time ago, "[t]he loss of freedom involved in forcing people to acquire information would probably far outweigh the benefits to be gained from a better-informed electorate" (1957, 247). Even if a consensus emerged to reduce media choice for the public good, it would still be technically impossible, even temporarily, to put the genie back in the bottle. Avoiding politics will never again be as difficult as it was in the "golden age" of television.

APPENDIX

Description of Knowledge Measures

N&E Survey

Political Knowledge, Wave 1, 12-item index

"Which of the following countries shares a border with Afghanistan?"
(Russia/**Pakistan**/Iraq/Kazakhstan)

"In the war in Afghanistan, which of the following groups fought on the side of the coalition led by the United States and Britain?"
(The Islamic Jihad/The Taliban/**The Northern Alliance**/Al-Qaeda)

"Which of the following agencies was founded in the wake of the terrorist attacks on September 11?"
(**Office for Homeland Security**/Delta Force/National Security Agency/ Department of Civilian Defense)

"Would you say there is more, less, or about the same amount of crime in the United States today as compared to 10 years ago?"
(more/**less**/same)

"Please give me your best guess for this next question. For every dollar spent by the federal government in Washington, how much of each dollar do you think goes for foreign aid to help other countries?"
(following Gilens (2001), 5% or less is coded as correct)

"Do you happen to know which party currently has the most members in the House of Representatives in Washington?"
(Democrats/**Republicans**)

"Whose responsibility is it to determine if a law is constitutional or not?"
(President/Congress/**Supreme Court**)

"How much of a majority is required for the U.S. Senate and House to override a presidential veto?"
(one-half plus one vote/three-fifths/**two-thirds**/three quarters)

"How many four-year terms can the president of the United States serve?"
(1/**2**/3/unlimited number of terms)

"In general, thinking about the political parties in Washington, would you say that Democrats are more conservative than Republicans, or Republicans are more conservative than Democrats?"
(Democrats more conservative/**Republicans more conservative**)

"On this page, you see four photographs. Do you happen to know which of the photographs shows John McCain?"

"On this page, you see four photographs. Do you happen to know which of the photographs shows Vladimir Putin?"
Cronbach's alpha = .70, mean—8.0, s.d. = 2.4

Political Knowledge, Wave 2, 15-item index

"Who is the current secretary of defense?"
(**Donald Rumsfeld**/John Ashcroft/George Tenet/Colin Powell)

"Who is the current Senate majority leader?"
(**Bill Frist**/Trent Lott/Dick Gephardt/John Kerry)

"Who is the Chief Justice on the U.S. Supreme Court?"
(**William Rehnquist**/Clarence Thomas/Antonin Scalia/Anthony Kennedy)

"What office is currently held by Condoleezza ("Condi") Rice?"
(U.S. Attorney General/**National Security Adviser**/Secretary of Defense/ White House Chief of Staff)

"What position is currently held by Ari Fleischer?"
(White House Chief of Staff/**White House Press Secretary**/Education Secretary/Senior Presidential Campaign Advisor)

"What position is currently held by Alan Greenspan?"
(Director of the Central Intelligence Agency/Treasury Secretary/**Chairman of the Federal Reserve**/Commerce Secretary)

"For each of the following politicians, please indicate to which party they belong: Tom Daschle, Christine Todd Whitman, Howard Dean, Ralph Nader."
(Republican, Democrat, Green Party, Reform Party)

"Do you happen to know which party currently has the most members in the House of Representatives in Washington?"
(Democrats/**Republicans**)

"Do you happen to know which party currently has the most members in the Senate?"
(Democrats/**Republicans**)

"Whose responsibility is it to determine if a law is constitutional or not?"
(President/Congress/**Supreme Court**)

"How much of a majority is required for the U.S. Senate and House to override a presidential veto?"
(one-half plus one vote/three-fifths/**two-thirds**/three quarters)

"In general, thinking about the political parties in Washington, would you say that Democrats are more conservative than Republicans, or Republicans are more conservative than Democrats?"
(Democrats more conservative/**Republicans more conservative**)

Note: One half of the respondents were randomly assigned to a visual condition in which photographs of the politicians instead of their names were shown on screen. For the purpose of this study, I simply average across this (random) variation.

Cronbach's alpha = .83, mean—8.3, s.d. = 3.8

NES 2000

Political Knowledge, 14-item index

Knows which party had majority in the House before election

Knows which party had majority in the Senate before election

Correctly responds that Trent Lott's current job is Senate majority leader (open-ended)

Correctly responds that William Rehnquist's current job is chief justice of the Supreme Court (open-ended)

Correctly responds that Tony Blair's current job is prime minister of England/Great Britain (open-ended)

Correctly responds that Janet Reno's current job is attorney general (open-ended)

Correct recall of incumbent/challenger

Correct recognition of incumbent/challenger (rated on feeling thermometer)

Correctly identifies incumbent in the district

Remembers something about incumbent in district

Gives response other than "Don't Know" to "Do you happen to know about how many years [incumbent] has been in the House of Representatives?"

Gives response other than "Don't Know" to "How good a job would you say U.S. Representative [NAME] does of keeping in touch with the people in your district?"

mean = 4.97, s.d. = 3.18

NES 1996

Political Knowledge, 14-item index

Knows which party had majority in the House before election

Knows which party had majority in the Senate before election

Correctly responds that Al Gore's current job is vice-president (open-ended)

Correctly responds that William Rehnquist's current job is chief justice of the Supreme Court (open-ended)

Correctly responds that Boris Yeltsin's current job is president (leader) of Russia (open-ended)

Correctly responds that Newt Gingrich's current job is Speaker of the House (open-ended)

Correct recall of incumbent/challenger

Correct recognition of incumbent/challenger (rated on feeling thermometer)

Correctly identifies incumbent in the district

Gives response other than "Don't Know" to "Did Representative [NAME] vote for or against the welfare reform bill?"

Gives response other than "Don't Know" to "How often has Representative [NAME] supported President Clinton's legislative proposals?"

Gives response other than 'Don't Know' to "How good a job would you say U.S. Representative [NAME] does of keeping in touch with the people in your district?" mean = 8.43, s.d. = 3.07

Notes

1. The household cooperation rate during the period of the two surveys was 53%. The survey completion rate for the first wave was 85%. For details on the sampling mechanism used by Knowledge Networks, see Krotki and Dennis (2001). In a comparison of KN data to an RDD telephone survey, Krosnick and Chang (2009) found the KN sample to be representative of the U.S. population in terms of demographics and political attitudes.
2. Almost all of the remaining 400 respondents had voluntarily withdrawn from the KN panel by the time of the second survey wave. Since few of the surveys KN panelists complete cover politics, this panel attrition should not be of great concern for my analysis. Empirically, respondents who withdrew did not differ significantly on key variables from respondents who remained active (see below).
3. As Knowledge Networks conducts interviews through WebTV, all respondents in the N&E Survey have basic Internet access on their television. Study 2 uses samples that include respondents without any web access. I discuss the implications of this difference below.
4. This measure assumes that people either have preferences over genres or can generalize from particular program examples for each genre. I designed a second measure of content preferences that asked about liking of news and entertainment in general without mentioning genres or programs. The different measures of the same concept are strongly correlated and yield essentially the same results.
5. I use a linear specification for simplicity. My theory does not necessarily imply linear effects, and quadratic or logarithmic transformations of REP indeed produce similar results.
6. I include control variables to account for alternative explanations of political learning. As cable is not affordable for all Americans, access is correlated with demographic

variables, notably income and education. Also included are measures of the respondent's media environment that do not directly affect media choice (e.g., the size of the respondent's media market).

I excluded 23 respondents who revealed a lack of effort from all analyses of the N&E Survey. These respondents were identified by checking response set on two other measures of content preferences. Respondents answered five or six questions arranged on two screens in grid form. The 23 respondents were excluded because they selected the same response for all items on a screen (even though the orientation of questions varied). I also excluded six respondents who answered all or all but one current events question correctly in Wave 1, but only one or none at all in Wave 2. These dramatic differences probably arise because respondents lacked the motivation to complete the knowledge items in the second wave.

7. The civics knowledge index is the number of correct responses to the questions about judicial review, presidential veto, maximum number of presidential terms, and the more conservative party (see appendix).

4. Voter Turnout: Eligibility Has Its Benefits

Michael P. McDonald

A democracy's health is often measured by the civic participation of its citizens. Having observed what appeared to be declining voter turnout for a quarter century or more, elections scholars had by the turn of the millennium become increasingly alarmed that America's democracy was on life support. Rosenstone and Hansen (1993, 57) described this downward drift as "the most important, most familiar, most analyzed, and most conjectured trend in recent American political history." Book titles suggested American voters were "vanishing" (Patterson 2002), "disappearing" (Teixeira 1992), and unable to be found (e.g., Avey 1989; Doppelt and Shearer 1999; Hadley, Steeper, and Swayze 1978; Ladd 1992; Piven and Cloward 1988; Wattenberg 2002). Numerous scholars proposed explanations, including a decline in civic society (Putnam 2000), the rise of cable television (Baum and Kernell 1999), negative advertising (Ansolabehere and Iyengar 1995), generational replacement (Miller and Shanks 1996), divided government (Franklin and de Mino 1998), diminishing partisan attachment (Abramson and Aldrich 1982), weakened voter mobilization efforts (Rosenstone and Hansen 1993), and others (e.g., Cassel and Luskin 1988; Cavanagh 1981; Shaffer 1981). Front-page stories appeared in prominent newspapers such as the *Washington Post* (Morin and Deane 2000), the *New York Times* (Johnson 1998), *USA Today* (Hampson 1998), and the *Christian Science Monitor* (Sneider 1996). These extensive citations barely do justice to the breadth of the scholarly and popular media angst over declining turnout rates.

In 2001, Samuel Popkin and I published a watershed article in the *American Political Science Review* that demonstrated that turnout rates were not going down; rather, the number of those ineligible to vote was going up (McDonald and Popkin 2001). Those who lamented voter turnout declines were basing their concerns on an increasingly poor measure of voter turnout. The ineligible population had grown so large, so fast, that it was creating misperceptions about American citizens' civic engagement.

Turnout rates were previously commonly calculated as a percentage of the domestic voting-age population (VAP), which prior to the passage of the Twenty-sixth Amendment in 1971 was age twenty-one in most states, and after, age eighteen. We coined the term voting-eligible population (VEP), and showed that turnout rates for those eligible to vote were not in long-term decline. Ineligible persons included in the VAP, particularly noncitizens, but also ineligible felons, were increasing faster than the citizen population. Changes in the overseas citizen

Source: This piece is an original essay commissioned for this volume.

population contributed slightly to misperceptions of declining turnout rates; following the end of the Cold War, military personnel (who could cast absentee ballots) returning from overseas were increasingly counted among the domestic VAP. The Census Bureau's increasingly accurate count of the entire population further contributed to misperceptions; past VAP estimates were artificially too low and turnout rates thus too high.[1] Finally, the drop in turnout from 1968 to 1972 was overstated since lower-voting propensity 18–20 year olds granted voting rights in most states by the Twenty-sixth Amendment were now included in the voting-age population.

At the time of publication of our article, we showed that presidential election turnout rates for those eligible to vote were essentially flat from 1972 to 2000. This directly challenged theories seeking to explain long-term voter turnout rate declines by correlating trends in society with trends in turnout. Updated turnout rate numbers described below suggest a slight decline of -0.2 percentage points per presidential election from 1972 to 2000 (Figure 4-1). However, after reaching their modern low of 51.7 percent in 1996, turnout rates have increased for three consecutive elections and are now increasing 0.5 percentage points per presidential election from 1972 to 2008. The 2008 turnout rate of 61.7 percent is on par with turnout rates in the low 60-percent range during the golden age of turnout of the 1950s and 1960s, which many scholars who wrote about turnout rate declines used as their basis for comparison. Indeed, the trend line for the entire 1948–2008 post–World War II era is only -0.2 percentage points per presidential election. (All of these trend estimates are almost certainly the lower bound since they do not include corrections for the Twenty-sixth Amendment, the increasing accuracy of the census, and the inability to historically correct for permanently disfranchised felons). Without the VEP correction, the 2008 VAP turnout rate of 56.8 percent would be the highest since 1968, but still substantially below the 1960 turnout rate of 63.8 percent, which might therefore perpetuate the research agenda of explaining declining voter turnout rates. What appears from these data to be more theoretically interesting is explaining turnout *variation,* rather than *decline.*

Why did no one think of estimating the VEP before? Walter Dean Burnham deserves much credit for producing painstaking historical calculations of turnout rates among those eligible to vote, but because he went on a hiatus in the mid-1980s (Burnham 1987; 2007), he missed the rapid increase in noncitizens and the smaller increase among ineligible felons among the VAP in the 1980s and 1990s. Others long recognized VAP as an inaccurate measure of those eligible to vote (for example, Andrews 1966; Plissner and Mitofsky 1981; Wolfinger and Rosenstone 1980). Scholars used them on the grounds that since VAP was readily available from the Census Bureau, it afforded "consistency and comparability" (Gans 1997, 46) and that constructing the VEP was "difficult and imprecise" (Teixeira 1992, 6). Burnham, however, showed that it is possible to construct the VEP with hard work. Indeed, modern students of American politics may take for granted how accessible the necessary data to construct the VEP are since they are now

Figure 4-1 Voting-eligible (VEP) and Voting-age (VAP) Presidential
Turnout Rates, 1948–2008

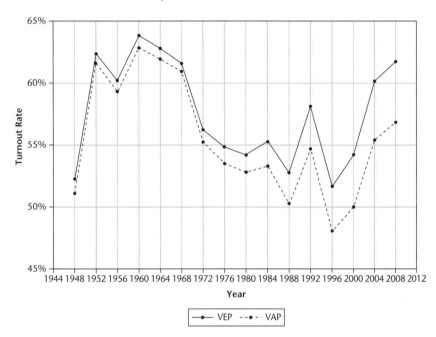

often available online, whereas before they often required extensive library research and hand data entry.

Teixeira (1992, 6) argues that the VAP is the correct denominator to use on normative grounds: "at the most basic level . . . , the voting-age population *is* the eligible electorate." Federal amendments extend voting suffrage to all persons age eighteen and older regardless of their race or gender. States otherwise decide who is eligible to vote. If a state wished, it could extend voting rights to noncitizens, as was the case during the United States' first century (Keyssar 2000). Even today, a handful of localities grant noncitizens residents' voting rights for their local elections. Eighteen is not a special age, either, as many states allow eligible seventeen year olds to vote in primaries. In addition, the percentage of the VAP that is eligible to vote may be a meaningful statistic for those advocating changing voting eligibility requirements, such as repealing felony disfranchisement laws.

Regardless of whether one prefers VAP to measure the turnout rate, a poor theory explaining voter turnout *variability* would fail to account for voting *eligibility*. Consider the case of vote over-report bias in the American National Election Studies (ANES). A greater percentage of survey respondents report voting than either VAP or VEP turnout rates indicate. This well-studied phenomenon is known as vote over-report bias (e.g., Abelson et al. 1992; Presser and Traugott

1992). Survey methodologists are concerned by vote over-report bias since it may be a symptom of error for many other attitudinal and behavioral questions where no yardstick exists to measure against. The universe from which the ANES survey sample of respondents is drawn is roughly the domestic non-institutional citizen-VAP, which is substantially similar to the VEP (McDonald 2003). Although the ANES is prone to vote over-report bias, the ANES turnout rate tracks the VEP turnout rate. Yet, some scholars analyzed the ANES to explain turnout rate declines (for example, Miller and Shanks 1996). One scholar concluded that since the ANES turnout rates were not going down, something must be wrong with the ANES (Burden 2000). This example demonstrates how tortured scholars' logic had become. The ANES turnout rate was not decreasing along with the VAP turnout rate, so the ANES must be faulty. The most conjectured trend in recent American political history was leading an entire field of political research down the wrong path, wasting able scholars' intellect on solving false problems.

Measurement Improvements

Updating turnout rates is challenging. New data continuously become available, both new election results and new data used to construct the voting-eligible population. For this reason, all turnout-rate estimates are subject to revision. Updated numbers are posted at www.elections.gmu.edu, with all data sources and methods used to construct these estimates presented as transparently as possible. New data and methods to improve measurement are welcome. The common goal should be to construct the best possible measure of voter turnout to guide public education, research, and policymaking.

The number of ballots cast. Surprisingly, the number of people who cast a ballot in a given American national election is not known with precision. There is a difference between ballots *cast* and ballots *counted* in that hundreds of thousands of people cast an invalid ballot that is not counted, perhaps because they cast a provisional ballot when they were not properly registered to vote, did not follow correct procedures in casting their absentee ballot, or cast multiple ballots.[2] Those who cast a ballot at least participated in the democratic process, and reducing casting errors may be an election administration goal. Yet, as the recent United States Election Assistance Commission Election Day Surveys show, many states or the local jurisdictions within them fail to report detailed information on the number of ballots cast, and a handful of states do not report total number of ballots counted.[3] Occasionally, local election officials report a different number than their state counterparts. And occasionally, some states do not report election results for uncontested elections or report slightly revised numbers when a recount occurs. The quality and availability of data becomes significantly worse and scarce for more historical data.

The best comparable historical turnout statistic is the number of votes cast statewide for the presidential office in a presidential election year and the highest statewide vote for U.S. senate, state governor, or sum of U.S. House of Representatives in a midterm election. In some elections, particularly midterm, another office may attract more voters because of differing levels of electoral competition. In some recent elections, I report votes for such alternative offices as the vote for highest office. I also report the total number of ballots cast in the many states where it is available. The difference between the total ballots cast and the votes cast for highest office is known as the residual vote and is another measurement of voting errors; it may occur when voters select more candidates than allowed for an office or fail to record a vote for any office (for example, Ansolabehere and Stewart 2005b).

Election statistics may reasonably be expected to be available immediately following an election, but this is often not the case. Some states, particularly those that process millions of absentee and provisional ballots, take nearly a month to report their official election results, which can be delayed further by recounts. But the media want to report the turnout rate the day after an election, so a projection is needed. I adjust the number of votes counted for the highest office as reported by the Associated Press on election night by the percentage of votes counted by election night in past elections. This estimate is imprecise, and I continually revise turnout numbers as election officials update their reports on the number of uncounted absentee and provisional ballots.[4]

The voting-age population. The voting-eligible population (VEP) is also challenging to construct. The base for the VEP is the voting-age population (VAP). The domestic VAP is available as of April 1 at the beginning of a decade from the decennial census. Between censuses, Census Bureau demographers estimate the VAP as of July 1 in a given year by estimating population changes. I project the November 1 VAP using these estimates. The VAP estimate becomes more error-prone as the decade progresses. When a new census reveals the "true" VAP, the Census Bureau adjusts the population estimates for the previous decade to align them with the new census.[5] For example, following publication of our original article (McDonald and Popkin 2001), updated population estimates for the previous decade were released and I updated the 1990–2000 turnout rates accordingly.

Noncitizens. The domestic VAP is adjusted to create an estimate of the VEP by removing estimates of those ineligible to vote and to adding eligible citizens living overseas. The largest segment of the ineligible population nationally is noncitizens, which has increased as a share of VAP from 2.6 percent in 1972 to 8.6 percent in 2008. This adjustment alone is sufficient to demonstrate no long-term post-1972 voter turnout decline.

I have changed the methodology to calculate the VAP percentage of noncitizens. Previously, I used the November Current Population Surveys (CPS) from 1964 to the present, and I interpolated decennial census data prior to 1964. Now, I use the interpolation method solely. One reason for this methodology change is that I became less confident that the 1982–1992 CPS surveys provide reliable noncitizen estimates. The CPS reports a puzzling decline in noncitizens from 1992 to 1994 (McDonald and Popkin 2001, 971). Further investigation reveals that the 1982–1992 CPS noncitizen estimates are uniformly higher than estimated using an interpolation between the 1980 and 1990 censuses. While there are several CPS survey methodology changes during this period, a likely source of this apparent overestimation of noncitizens is that the CPS surveys during this period are weighted to population estimates that have the 1980 census as a base. A more in-depth understanding of this puzzling CPS pattern may be relevant to many voting studies that analyze CPS data over time.

A second reason for this methodology change is that the Census Bureau now conducts an annual survey known as the American Community Survey (ACS) that is meant to replace the decennial census long form, which is the source for citizenship on past censuses.[6] The ACS sample size is substantially larger than the CPS, so it is more reliable from a sampling standpoint. Using the ACS is also most consistent with the between-census interpolation method.

Other adjustments: ineligible felons and overseas citizens. Two other adjustments are possible using publicly available data sources, as described in McDonald and Popkin (2001, 971–972). The number of ineligible felons may be estimated by cross-referencing Department of Justice reports on the prison, probation, and parole populations with state felon disfranchisement laws.

The number of overseas citizens can be estimated using various government data sources. Starting in 2008, I began estimating the number of overseas citizens in each state, using Department of Defense reports that detail overseas deployment by state of origin and apportioning estimates of civilian population proportional to states' citizen-VAP. I believe this latter adjustment is sound because the thousands of voter registration applications generated through the Overseas Vote Foundation (OVF) are roughly proportional to states' citizen-VAP.[7]

I do not make two possible corrections. I do not estimate the number of permanently disfranchised felons in some states, which is likely a substantial number of otherwise eligible voters (Manza and Uggen 2006). I do not estimate the number of persons who are disfranchised because they have been found mentally incompetent by a court of law.

Why not use registration as the turnout rate denominator? This is my most frequently asked question from reporters and the general public. All states except North Dakota require eligible persons to register before they are truly eligible to vote. This is true even for Election Day registration states; voters must first register before they are allowed to vote. Voter registration turnout rates might thus seem a reasonable denominator for a turnout rate, and nearly all election officials report turnout as a percentage of the registered voters in their jurisdiction. This statistic may be meaningful for election administration purposes, such as the allocation of voting machines to polling places.

However, there are good reasons why registration is not a consistent denominator for turnout rates, between states and over time. A persistent problem with voter registration is what is known as *deadwood*, people who are registered at an address but no longer live there (McDonald 2007). As an indicator of the magnitude of deadwood, according to the 2008 CPS 71.0 percent of citizen-VAP reported being registered, while aggregate statistics indicate that the total number of voter registrations was 87.9 percent of the VEP.[8] It is unknown whether vote over-report bias extends to reported registration. States, and even localities within states, vary how they purge deadwood from their voter registration rolls. Jurisdictions may change their administrative practices, particularly in response to federal voter list maintenance mandates found in the National Voter Registration Act of 1993 and the Help America Vote Act of 2002. There is anecdotal evidence from election officials that the voter registration rolls have become increasingly inflated over time, because it is now more difficult to purge deadwood and because some nonvoters register at their driver's license office without an intention to vote (on this latter point, see Knack 1995). The result is that registration turnout rates may be artificially lowered over time as they accumulate more deadwood and more casual motor voter registrants.

State and Lower-Level Turnout Rates

In addition to national turnout rates from 1787 to the present, state-level turnout rates from 1980 to the present are available on my Web site (see also McDonald 2002). Scholars most frequently ask me for turnout rate estimates at lower levels of geography. Estimates of the VEP for other elections, such as those at the county or municipal level, may be constructed following these recommendations.

Citizenship data is generally available from the decennial census, and now the ACS. At a minimum, citizen-VAP should be computed where data are available, since citizenship is the largest component of the VEP adjustment and will likely be correlated with Hispanic ethnicity and socioeconomic status. Failing to make a citizenship adjustment may lead to misperceptions of trends and cross-unit comparisons, resulting in estimation bias.

Complete Department of Justice reports on prisoners, parolees, and probationers are only available from 1980 to the present. Prior prisoner statistics are available from the Inter-university Consortium for Political and Social Research's Study 8912, "Historical Statistics on Prisoners in State and Federal Institutions, Year End 1925–1986." National and regional numbers of parolees and probationers may be estimated from 1948 to 1978 by applying the ratio to the number of prisoners for years where all statistics are available. A scholar interested in state-level numbers may adjust for prisoners only, or apply a similar state-specific estimation method to make a further adjustment for parolees and probationers.

At lower levels of aggregation, including congressional districts, there is a way to account for prisoners with current census data. The census identifies the number of individuals incarcerated in prisons or jails, though the type of facility is not identified. A reasonable assumption to identify prisons, where felons are located, may be to classify a facility with more than twenty-five incarcerated persons as a prison. Starting in 2010, the Census Bureau will identify group quarters populations, which will enable a more direct method of counting prisoners.

Assumptions are needed to project forward population estimates from the last decennial census. The Census Bureau releases total population estimates for counties and municipalities, which may be reasonably used to estimate their VAP. Another data source are the three-year and five-year ACS estimates, which provide an estimate for citizen voting-age population for counties, municipalities, and even congressional districts. There is a censoring issue for citizenship estimates among smaller jurisdictions, as the Census Bureau does not report statistics with high sampling error. A reasonable estimation method applies the three-year or five-year ACS citizenship estimates where available and apportions the difference in citizenship between the statewide and sum of available counties (or other geography) among the counties without reported data.

Concluding Remarks

The rise of American presidential turnout rates in the new millennium to the relatively "high levels" experienced half a century ago challenges voting behavior scholars. What caused a resurgence of civic participation within the last decade? Increased campaign mobilization efforts, in sophistication and in scale, and the rise of early voting are two recent electoral innovations (McDonald and Schaller 2009). If mobilization efforts are the primary cause, then Rosenstone and Hansen's (1993) postulation that campaigns' decreasing mobilization efforts were to blame for voter turnout declines deserves a reexamination as it may be a factor in the observed variability of turnout rates.

Caution should be exercised before anointing a theory to explain recent turnout rate increases, however, since simple correlations between perceived voter turnout declines and other societal and political phenomenon led to a proliferation of theories to explain declining turnout rates. An important lesson is that correlation is not causation. Most likely, there are multiple explanations for variation in voter turnout rates over time: campaign mobilization efforts, interest among voters, the ease of voting, and the capacity for citizens to process information are likely explanations, among others. Hopefully, scholars will now seek to explain this variation in presidential elections, rather than focus on explaining declines. A difficulty is that there are few presidential elections to generalize from, which is why a unified theory to explain voter participation in all elections is needed. I suspect that such a theory will be a hybrid of rational choice and political psychology theories that explain why individuals take political action.

Recently, comparative scholars have become concerned about declining turnout rates across many developed democracies (for example, Franklin 2004). In some instances, recent American turnout rates now exceed those in other countries, such as Canada, France, and the United Kingdom,[9] whose comparatively higher turnout rates had previously led some to explain American citizens' comparatively lower participation (for instance, Powell 1986). My first reaction is to question the assumption that these international turnout rates are indeed falling, as they are calculated using countries' VAP or voter registration. The ways by which countries conduct their censuses, changes in their voting-ineligible populations, and how these countries administer their voter registration may affect the comparability of international turnout rates across counties and over time. Research by scholars familiar with various countries is needed to develop VEP estimates elsewhere in the world.

Voter turnout is a motivating example in a popular introductory research methods textbook of how measurement of concepts matters to political research (Johnson and Reynolds 2008, 9). Sometimes, simple measurement issues can trip up even the most esteemed professors. I hope that the American voter turnout example inspires students of the social sciences to aggressively challenge even the most basic theoretical assumptions, as occasionally surprising new insights can dramatically change the research agenda of an entire field.

Notes

1. The U.S. General Accounting Office (1997) reported the net undercoverage of the census total population was 5.8 percent in 1940 and 1.8 percent in 1990. The undercount could be contributing as much as 1.3 percentage points to an apparent decline in the turnout rate. The reliability of the historical undercoverage estimates, how to apply them to the voting-age population, and how to distribute them across states is unknown. For this reason, no adjustment is made for census undercoverage (McDonald and Popkin 2001, 965).

2. In nearly all cases, the casting of multiple ballots is not intentional fraud. Rather, they can arise when a ballot is spoiled and a new ballot is issued. Sometimes, people attempt to both cast an absentee ballot and vote in person because they fear their ballot was lost. In this latter situation, voters are often permitted to cast a provisional ballot. Such multiple ballots are easily detectable by election administrators and these ballots are not counted. However, election officials often do not separately report these multiple ballots in provisional ballots statistics. Furthermore, they often do not report the number of people who cast a provisional ballot, but were not eligible to vote (they do not have the resources to determine if a person was indeed eligible, beyond their voter registration status). These issues, among others, confound using the total number of provisional ballots cast to construct an estimate of the total number of eligible people who tried to vote. There are further sources of error, too, such as absentee ballots lost in the mail or voters who are checked off the wrong line in poll books.

3. Various reports of recent election statistics are available at www.eac.gov. Care must be taken in consuming these data since all jurisdictions do not report all election statistics, and definitions of statistics of seemingly simple concepts such as an absentee ballot can vary across jurisdictions.

4. Knowledgeable election scholars have queried me during the counting period to ask why I estimate more votes than reported by the media. The media's count is typically

based on actual counted ballots, which excludes absentee and provisional ballots that have not been counted, while I include in my estimates a projection of how many of the uncounted ballots are valid. Unfortunately, the media often report these lower numbers, and draw inferences about voting behavior in the election, without fully understanding the election administration process for counting ballots.

5. This is known as the intercensial adjustment. The "true" population does not include adjustments for undercounting or overcounting segments of the population, which in the past have generally produced a net undercount of the entire population.

6. See www.census.gov/acs/www/index.html.

7. I am on OVF's advisory board and monitor state-level voter registration statistics through OVF's website.

8. Some jurisdictions manage their deadwood by placing registrants who have not recently voted or responded to a mailed notice on a list of inactive voters. Among these jurisdictions, some may report the total of active and inactive registrations as their total voter registrations and some may report active registrations only. Further complicating matters is that some jurisdictions have changed their reporting method.

9. International voter turnout statistics provided by the International Institute for Democracy and Electoral Assistance are available at www.idea.int.

PART II
POLITICAL INFORMATION

5. How Important Are Informational Differences among Voters?

Despite being in the United States' second war in Iraq since 1991, many Americans in 2006 still had trouble finding Iraq on a map or reciting basic facts about the country (GfK Roper Public Affairs 2006). Many Americans also lack basic knowledge about their own political system, such as First Amendment rights, membership on the Supreme Court, or which of the two major political parties is more ideologically conservative. And shockingly, political knowledge has remained about the same over a half-century or more despite major growth in education levels (Delli Carpini and Keeter 1996; Wattenberg 2008, 75–80).

There is a long-standing controversy over whether a lack of political information matters for voting behavior and for democracy generally (Converse 1964; Key 1966; Niemi and Weisberg 2001, chap. 6). Do voters make reasonable decisions despite their lack of knowledge? Are informational differences exacerbated or mitigated by changes in media and campaign environments? Does political information modify the impact of vote determinants? Would voters make different decisions if they were more fully informed? And, as we asked in the previous edition and repeat now, does a healthy democracy depend on a well-informed electorate?

This controversy continues, although in modified form. In earlier incarnations of this debate, revisionist streams in the literature sought to redeem voters, arguing that individuals make good decisions by means of shortcuts, or "heuristics," and that collective decisions are sensible, even if individual decisions are suspect (e.g., Popkin 1994; Lupia and McCubbins 1998; Page and Shapiro 1992). More recently, other researchers have reacted by pointing out what they see as weaknesses in both the theory and evidence supporting these arguments. In addition, new fronts have opened in this debate. Recent research has focused more on the information environment in elections, with numerous studies of the content of campaign advertising, candidate speeches, and news coverage of campaigns. At the same time, scholars have asked whether informational inequalities contribute to inequalities of income as well as differences in influence on a range of policy outputs. Here we review the various strands of the controversy over the political knowledge of the public, focusing especially on the newer arguments.

Informational Differences among Voters Are
Large and Consequential

A long line of research notes that there is significant variation in levels of political sophistication among the mass public. Many Americans do not interpret politics in terms of a left-right ideological spectrum. Many do not use, or even understand, the terms "liberal" or "conservative" when discussing politics and, many do not hold issue positions that could be grouped together as part of a liberal or conservative ideology (Converse 1964; Lewis-Beck et al. 2008). In addition, many people do not know basic facts about the nation's political leaders, parties, and political institutions (Converse 1964; Luskin 2002; Zaller 1992; Delli Carpini and Keeter 1996; Althaus 2003; Lewis-Beck et al. 2008; Highton 2009).[1]

A reaction to these observations, developed largely in the 1990s and described more fully in the next section, is that voters turn to heuristics that allow them to vote in sensible, even rational, ways. Yet other researchers see this as a kind of a false hope. There are two common critiques of the literature on voting heuristics. First, while few would dispute the claim that many decision-making shortcuts are available to voters, it is difficult to document how many voters, or which voters, use a particular heuristic. Second, in studies examining the question, it is unclear whether heuristics improve voter decision-making. Kuklinski and colleagues, for example, identify circumstances where heuristics may mislead voters (Kuklinski and Hurley 1994; Kuklinski and Quirk 2001). In general, do heuristics help voters make better decisions than if they relied on other information decision-making strategies? As Bartels (1998, 198) aptly put it, "it is easier to assume than to demonstrate that cues and shortcuts do, in fact, allow relatively uninformed voters to behave as if they were fully informed."

Coming at it from a different direction, Lau and Redlawsk find that information and memory are important components in voter reasoning. In an article reprinted here, Lau and Redlawsk (2001a) find evidence of heuristic use by almost all voters. However, more informed voters are more likely to rely on heuristics based on endorsements and ideology and less likely to use party or candidate appearance heuristics. Lau and Redlawsk also attempt to measure "correct voting," in which people vote for the candidate closest to their preferences. In their most common experimental measure, subjects witness a simulated campaign on a computer screen, clicking on the headlines (about candidates, endorsements, issues, etc.) they want to investigate. By observing this information-seeking behavior, Lau and Redlawsk are able to measure the importance each subject attaches to different types of information. They then average together the issue positions, group endorsements, party affiliations, and personality and appearance ratings for each candidate, weighted by the importance of each subject attached to each piece of information. The candidate with the highest total rating is the presumed "correct" choice.[2]

Using this measure, Lau and Redlawsk find that while heuristic decision-making often leads to more "correct" voting decisions by highly informed people, heuristics tend to produce less "correct" voting by low information voters. As a result, more informed voters are significantly more likely to vote correctly (Lau and Redlawsk 2006; Lau, Andersen, and Redlawsk 2008). While there are likely disagreements about how to measure correct voting, Lau and Redlawsk provide a fundamental challenge to the low-information rationality paradigm, which is justified partly on the basis of its advantages for less knowledgeable voters.

Many other studies find that informational differences affect voting behavior in important ways. For example, one's ideological orientation is a stronger predictor of voting choices and other policy positions for more knowledgeable voters than for less knowledgeable voters (Sniderman, Brody, and Tetlock 1992; Zaller 1992; Goren, forthcoming). Models of vote choice, using standard predictors such as party identification, issues, and candidate evaluations, tend to find that the choices of less informed voters are less predictable than the choices of highly informed voters (Bartels 2008; Zaller 2004; Potthoff and Munger 2005). Political information is a key moderating variable that enables voters to link specific policies and candidate choices with more general principles or policy preferences.

More recent voting studies find other information effects. Gomez and Wilson (2001; 2006), for example, find that political sophistication regulates the nature of economic voting. Based on a theory of attribution of responsibility, they hypothesize that well-informed people vote more on the basis of their own financial situation, while less informed voters are more influenced by evaluations of the national economy. Politically informed voters are more able to connect their own economic status to specific government policies while less knowledgeable voters are apt to think that the economy is entirely in the hands of the president. Gomez and Wilson find evidence in the United States and four other countries to support this thesis.[3] Significantly, this difference in reasoning suggests that the economic interests of informed voters are more likely to be transmitted to elected public officials.

Informational differences also mean that certain voters are more aware of political developments generally and election campaigns specifically, and high- and low-information voters respond to them differently. For example, knowledgeable voters are more aware of campaign activity and the nature of political competition (Huckfeldt et al. 2007). Low-information voters are more likely to be "floaters" in presidential elections, switching parties from one election to the next. This, in turn, means that low-information voters are more responsive to changes in economic conditions, government performance, and the ideological positions of the candidates, while more informed voters tend to be strongly partisan and relatively impervious to changes in candidates and policies (Zaller 2004). More informed voters also show both greater levels of ideological polarization and a stronger correlation between ideology and party identification (Abramowitz and Saunders 2008).[4] As a consequence, more educated and informed people are more responsive to the growing elite level polarization in the United States (Hetherington 2001 and in this volume; also see Zaller 1992;

Delli Carpini and Keeter 1996; Box-Steffensmeier and De Boef 2001), thus contributing disproportionately to the polarization of American politics.

Perhaps the most important effect of informational differences is that some voters may not act in their own best interests. That is, poorly informed voters may choose policies or candidates that they would not prefer if they had more information. Previous studies by Althaus (1998), Bartels (1996) and Delli Carpini and Keeter (1996) make this point. More recent studies continue to raise these concerns. For example, Gilens (2001) uses a similar methodology to estimate the policy positions of a fully informed public. Rather than relying solely on general measures of political sophistication, he also measures public knowledge of policy-specific facts, such as whether crime rates have declined. He finds that many Americans lack factual knowledge relevant to specific policy proposals and that the absence of policy-specific information leads many people to hold different positions than if they were better informed. In fact, the absence of policy-specific information has a greater impact on public opinion than a lack of general political knowledge. Finally, Gilens (2001) concludes that people with higher levels of general political knowledge are more likely to make use of new policy-specific information when making political evaluations.

Althaus (2003) extends his previous research arguing that public opinion surveys may not accurately reflect the opinions of less knowledgeable people. Low information respondents are significantly less likely to give an opinion on several different public policy questions. More importantly, a fully informed public would have different policy preferences—often more liberal policy preferences—than the relatively ill-informed public. On a more positive note, Althaus finds that information effects on public opinion are smaller for highly salient issues that receive a lot of media attention. In addition, information effects did not seem to change dramatically over time.

Bartels (2008) also expands on some of his previous work and, like Gomez and Wilson, finds that highly informed people are more likely to connect economic inequality to specific governmental policies. Thus, more informed people, especially among Democrats, were more likely to oppose the 2001 Bush tax cuts. In general, had the public been better informed, there would have been more opposition to these tax cuts. Thus, the studies by Gilens (2001), Althaus (2003) and Bartels (2008) similarly conclude that an uninformed public contributes to a less egalitarian society.[5]

There are several other consequences of low levels of political information, including low levels of political participation (e.g., Wattenberg 2008; Prior, chapter 3 in this volume), public support for antidemocratic views (e.g., Delli Carpini and Keeter 1996, 221–223), and susceptibility to manipulation by political elites (e.g., Page and Shapiro 1992, chap. 9). These concerns remain. In addition, recent studies make a connection between political information and representation. For example, information is a predictor of voter turnout (Delli Carpini and Keeter 1996; Lassen 2005), and others have found that paying attention to politics has its rewards. Martin (2003) finds that areas with high voter turnout receive a larger share of federal appropriations than areas with low turnout. Griffin and Newman (2005) find that the policy preferences of voters predict the roll-call voting records of U.S. senators but the preferences of nonvoters do not. Hajnal (2010), with an unusual focus on local elections, finds that low voter turnout skews policy toward less redistributive and more allocative spending. In short, the preferences of less informed, nonvoters are underrepresented in government.

Recent research also links a lack of political information to income inequality, since income and political knowledge are correlated. Low-income voters are less politically informed than high-income voters (Althaus 2003; Bartels 2008). One implication is that low-income voters may behave differently than high-income voters and are underrepresented as a result. Bartels (2008) finds that there is an income bias in economic voting, where low- and middle-income voters are most responsive to income growth among the wealthiest Americans rather than to growth in their own income group. This works to the benefit of Republican presidential candidates and presumably against the economic interests of many low-income voters. Furthermore, Bartels (2008) finds that legislators are responsive to the preferences of high-income constituents but not low-income constituents, although the disparity in responsiveness is not entirely attributed to information differences. Gilens (2005) finds that American policy change is more representative of the preferences of high-income citizens than low-income citizens. Furthermore, on issues where high- and low-income groups have opposing preferences, actual policy change is responsive to high-income preferences but not the preferences of poor or middle-class Americans. In a similar vein, Jacobs and Page (2005) find that public opinion has less influence on American foreign policy than the preferences of more informed business leaders and experts.

Overall, these studies indicate a number of consequences of lack of knowledge. A lack of information leads to different methods of evaluating and choosing candidates. In addition, a lack of information contributes to low levels of political participation. As a result, there is a connection between low information and political inequality, with public policy less responsive to the preferences of voters who are uninformed. These are serious concerns. While decision-making aids may help low-information voters make reasonable decisions, it is not at all clear that they are a sufficient substitute for more information. Above all, it appears that they do not mitigate political inequality the way a more knowledgeable electorate would.

Informational Differences Are Exaggerated and Have Little Effect on Voters

A vigorous revisionist literature has challenged the characterization of an unsophisticated electorate since shortly after the publication of Converse's (1964) classic treatise. One response focuses on what Converse (1990) has termed the "miracle of aggregation." That is, statistical aggregation of survey respondents in public opinion polls and voters in election returns overcomes the deficiencies of individuals. Errors based on lack of information will tend to be random and thus cancel out when the opinions or votes of many people are totaled. As a result, aggregate public opinion is relatively stable over time and only changes in response to important events (Page and Shapiro 1992). More recent studies continue this theme. For example, MacKuen, Erikson, and Stimson (2002) find that the "public mood" for liberal or conservative policies responds predictably to national conditions and government performance. In addition, election outcomes also clearly reflect the public mood. Other recent studies examine public voting intentions and evaluations of presidential candidates over the course of a campaign and find similar patterns (Linn, Moody, and Asper 2009; Johnston, Hagen, and Jamieson 2004).

Revisionists generally agree that many voters have little interest in or knowledge about politics. However, they argue that the ability to rank and choose between candidates does not require detailed political knowledge (Popkin 2006). Furthermore, some scholars argue that studies of political information should focus more attention on the knowledge needed to make effective decisions rather than what is typically measured in surveys (Popkin 1994; Lupia 2006; Druckman 2005; Druckman and Nelson 2003). Other researchers note that voters make use of a number of heuristics, or decision-making cues, to make well-reasoned voting choices. Several scholars note elements of the voting environment that ease the information burden on voters. For example, extensive media coverage of politics, including even entertainment forums such as MTV and Comedy Central, along with highly publicized campaigns, help inform voters, particularly those who are less attentive to politics. Summarizing this perspective, Popkin (2006, 235) states, "A focus on what voters don't know and can't do misses much of what they do know and can do."

According to this perspective, voters do not need to be fully informed to make reasonable decisions.[6] Decision-making shortcuts help voters choose a candidate without knowing a lot about alternative candidates or about the political system. Partisanship is arguably the most common voting heuristic, and it conveys a great deal of information. Voters can rely on a candidate's party affiliation or stated ideology to make inferences about a candidate's issue positions and the groups supporting the candidate. As a result, it is no surprise that partisanship is a strong vote predictor (Campbell et al. 1960; Bartels 2000) and structures political conflict when a candidate's party affiliation is included on the ballot (Wright and Schaffner 2002).

Endorsements by interest groups or individual politicians also serve as decision-making aids for voters. Group endorsements can be especially useful in ballot initiative contests (Lupia 1994; Lupia and McCubbins 1998; Gerber and Phillips 2003). Recent studies also argue that endorsements are a critical factor in presidential nomination contests (Cohen, Karol, Noel, and Zaller 2008). Other studies note that voters apply candidate or group stereotypes based on a candidate's personal traits, such as race or gender, or groups that support a candidate (Sanbonmatsu 2002; Valentino et al. 2002; Cutler 2002). McDermott (2005) reports on candidate occupations as yet another decision-making aid used by voters in the few states that include those cues on ballots. Listing occupations on the ballot reduces ballot roll-off and provides an advantage to the candidate with a perceived qualification advantage.

Lau and Redlawsk (1997; 2001a; 2006) address some of these issues, using experiments to simulate and manipulate how voters discuss and incorporate campaign information into voting decisions. They test a low-information decision-making model of voting against others that presume a more informed electorate. They also examine whether people "vote correctly," that is, whether they select the candidate most in accord with their own policy and candidate preferences. In their experiments, approximately 70 percent of the subjects voted correctly. Using ANES data, they find that, on average, 75 percent of people vote correctly in presidential elections.[7]

One element of this controversy that has received less attention involves the role of core values in voter decision-making. In research that is partially reprinted here with an update, Goren (2004; forthcoming) makes two important arguments. First, he argues that a small number of core values are held by all voters. Regardless of their level of knowledge, all voters develop and use these core values to evaluate public figures and policy choices.[8] He primarily examines the values of economic liberalism, moral conservatism, and foreign policy militarism. Goren argues that people apply these values to evaluate debates and assess candidates with respect to economic policy, cultural issues, and foreign affairs, respectively. Second, Goren (forthcoming) finds that core values have a strong impact on voting decisions, regardless of the voter's level of political information. This stands in contrast to other studies, described above, that find informational differences in the degree to which voters rely on ideological views, economic evaluations, or certain heuristics to make voting decisions.

The role of the news media is often misinterpreted as well. The media, especially television, often come in for criticism regarding the informational content in news coverage of politics. Coverage of presidential campaigns has declined in volume and has arguably shifted away from the issue positions of candidates toward poll results and other elements of the horse race (Patterson 1993; Farnsworth and Lichter 2007; Gilens, Vavreck, and Cohen 2007).[9] Traditional television news organizations have reduced their coverage of "hard news," such as public policy debates, and shifted toward entertainment fare due to increased competition from "soft news" programming, such as *Oprah Winfrey* (Hamilton 2003). However, others see a silver lining in this last trend. In a series of studies, Baum (2002; 2003; 2005) argues that soft news programs, such as entertainment news and talk shows, contain a fair amount of political content, particularly of foreign crises. Since these programs have drawn many viewers away from traditional news sources, soft news programs can inform many people who are otherwise inattentive to politics. Baum found that soft news viewers were more aware of a series of major news events than nonviewers. In addition, the information boost of soft news programming was strongest for those with low levels of general political knowledge (Baum 2002; 2003). In addition, TV talk shows now feature many appearances by presidential candidates. These appearances tend to soften their image among viewers of the opposite political party, particularly those with low levels of political information.

One may wonder, of course, whether soft news programming can mislead voters. In a study reprinted here, Baum and Jamison (2006) find that exposure to soft news programs increases the chances that less knowledgeable voters will choose a presidential candidate consistent with their issue preferences. As their dependent variable, Baum and Jamison use a measure very similar to the "correct voting" measure developed by Lau and Redlawsk (2006). While hard news consumption improves the chances of voting correctly among highly informed voters, soft news consumption is more important for less informed voters. Thus, the growth of soft news programming may serve as an information equalizer for American voters. In addition, Jerit, Barabas, and Bolsen (2006) find that while increased print media coverage of an issue exacerbates educational differences in political information (as highly educated people become more informed with a significantly smaller boost for less educated people), increased television coverage of an issue increases knowledge for all levels of education. The decline of newspapers may also have an equalizing effect on political information.[10]

A number of recent studies of political campaigns move beyond the impact on voting decisions to examine the informational contributions of campaigns (for instance, Johnston, Hagen, and Jamieson 2004; Fournier 2006). These studies often find that political campaigns help equalize informational differences among voters. For example, Gilens, Vavreck, and Cohen (2007) note that while there has been a significant decline in news coverage of presidential campaigns over the last fifty years, campaigns have become more informative during that same period, and as a result public knowledge of presidential candidates has remained steady over time. Kam (2006; 2007) argues that campaigns encourage open-minded thinking about politics and reduce pro-incumbent biases among voters. Nicholson (2003; 2005) finds that ballot initiative campaigns, and media coverage of them, increase public awareness of issues and prime those issues as voting criteria in candidate elections. Geer (2006) provides a spirited and well-supported defense of negative campaign advertising. He finds that negative campaign ads are more likely to include issue-based content than positive ads. As a result, the growing frequency of negative ads in presidential elections is a positive development for informing voters.

Goldstein, Freedman and colleagues (Freedman, Franz, and Goldstein 2004; Franz et al. 2007) examine a vast database of the content, timing and volume of all televised advertisements in congressional and presidential campaigns in media markets around the country. They argue that campaign advertisements are "multivitamins" that help inform voters and motivate them to participate in politics (Freedman, Franz, and Goldstein 2004, 725). In particular, the informational and motivational effects of political advertising tend to be most pronounced for the least informed voters.[11]

On another front, there are some recent studies indicating that common measures of political sophistication and issue attitudes underestimate public knowledge and competence. This continues a previous line of debate and some of the initial reactions to Converse's work on "non-attitudes" (Achen 1975). For example, Mondak (2001) criticizes the features of many common political knowledge questions, such as the convention of offering a "don't know" response option. By doing so, common measures may understate levels of political knowledge for some respondents.[12] Mondak (2001) finds more pronounced effects of political knowledge on other attitudes when knowledge is measured differently.[13] In addition, Davis and Silver (2003) report effects of the race of the interviewer that may produce a downward bias in survey questions assessing political knowledge.

In another important measurement study, Ansolabehere, Rodden, and Snyder (2008) revisit the measurement of issue attitudes (Converse 1964; Achen 1975). They note that when multiple survey questions are incorporated into measures of issue attitudes, a good deal of measurement error is eliminated. Using up to thirty-four survey items to create issue scales, they find that issue attitudes are relatively stable over time (and they are strong predictors of presidential voting, rivaling the effect of party identification). In addition, while the issue preferences of high-information voters are more stable over time than for low-information voters, the differences are not that large. Finally, they find little evidence that issue attitudes are a stronger predictor of vote choice for more informed voters, contrary to previous studies (Delli Carpini and Keeter 1996; Zaller 1992). While some may dispute the methodological choices of Ansolabehere et al. (2008), such as imputing a significant amount of missing data in the survey questions they examine, it is hard to ignore their fundamental point about the impact of measurement error in measures of political attitudes.

Finally, some challenge the claim that more sophisticated voters make more rational choices and thus would be better for democracy. A growing literature on biases in information processing raises interesting concerns about voter decision-making that tend to cast highly informed voters, or at least the seemingly highly informed, in an unfavorable light. Mistaken beliefs, such as about the portion of the federal budget devoted to welfare programs, are not only common (Kuklinski et al. 2000), but also are often confidently held and influence policy preferences (see also Gilens 2001).[14] Moreover, people are often unwilling to change mistaken beliefs, even when confronted with correct information. Intriguingly, increasing media exposure increases the chances of faulty memory of one's past political preferences (Joslyn 2003). In another example, even though people maintained fairly accurate factual beliefs about casualty levels in the Iraq War, partisans adjusted their interpretations of whether casualty levels were too high to conform to their prior level of support for the war (Gaines et al. 2007). Similarly, Taber and Lodge (2006) found that people tend to uncritically accept new information that supports their preexisting preferences but discount evidence that contradicts their policy preferences, what they call a "disconfirmation bias"— and more knowledgeable people tend to exhibit this bias more frequently (see also Redlawsk 2002). Furthermore, people who are more informed may actually have less accurate political perceptions, as on the performance of the economy, especially when accurate perceptions may reflect poorly on their political party (Achen and Bartels 2006; Shani 2006; Zaller 2004). A more polarized media environment, with MSNBC and Fox News catering to different partisan tastes, may exacerbate these effects. Paradoxically, this recent work implies that a more informed electorate will be more partisan and less open-minded (Friedman 2006; Kuklinski, Quirk, and Peyton 2008).

Conclusion

The controversy over the level and meaning of informational differences has not been resolved, although the focus has changed. Previously, revisionists had shifted the debate to more favorable terrain by arguing that citizens often make reasonable decisions based on very limited information. By noting predictable patterns in aggregate opinion, as well as decision-making shortcuts and other cognitive devices available to low-information voters, revisionists put the onus on critics of public sophistication to demonstrate the consequences of lack of knowledge. Over the last ten years, scholars have done just that, citing instances in which cues are inadequate or misleading as well as showing that knowledge matters for how people process new information, the criteria they use to evaluate candidates, and the correlates of their voting choices. There is also evidence of two more important consequences of political knowledge. First, people with high levels of information are more likely to choose candidates who reflect their policy preferences. Second, lack of information is linked to inequality of outcomes; public officials and public policy seem to reflect the preferences of the highly informed more than those of the uninformed.

The outlook for reducing inequality in political information is not favorable. Mainstream media organizations, such as newspapers and network television, have sharply reduced their coverage of public affairs. And contrary to initial hopes, the growing number of media choices on the Internet and cable television may well exacerbate differences between the informational haves and have-nots (Prior 2007). Furthermore, despite significant gains in education over several decades, there has been only a modest increase in ideological sophistication among American voters and very little change in levels of political information (see above). These findings lead some to question whether more education, particularly college education, actually improves political awareness (Highton 2009). Indeed, the likelihood that the public will become more informed in the near future is so low that Bendor and Bullock (2008) argue that the competence of public officials is a more important subject of scholarly attention than public competence.

In some respects, the ball is in the court of the revisionists in the political information controversy. We know that voters can rely on a number of decision-making shortcuts. But do these heuristics help low-information voters make better decisions, and do heuristics help to mitigate the inequality that derives in part from a lack of information? In addition, both sides in the controversy need to provide clearer theoretical and empirical definitions of citizen performance. By what standards do we judge voter decision-making (Druckman 2005)? Are there other criteria besides a fully informed electorate? Recent examples include studies of "correct" voting (Lau and Redlawsk 2006), trade-offs between different policy goals (Kuklinski et al. 2001), and susceptibility to manipulation (Druckman 2001). We expect scholars to continue in this direction.

We end by noting that the information level of the citizenry as a whole may be more important than the qualities of individual voters. More than a half-century ago, Berelson told us that there existed a variety of types of individuals—some interested in politics and having all the characteristics we attribute to the ideal citizen of yore and others uninterested in politics and possessing few of these characteristics—and he argued that this might be just what is needed for successful democratic governance (Berelson, Lazarsfeld, and McPhee 1954, chap. 14). System requirements, in other words, may be met not with a single mold for its citizens but with a continuum that accommodates a wide range of citizen types. Thus, our real concern might be how best to use the *range* of citizen characteristics to better govern twenty-first century societies.

Notes

1. See *Critical Review* (2006, numbers 1–3, and 2008, numbers 1–2) for reflections on Converse's original research on belief systems and citizen competence. Low levels of political knowledge and sophistication are not an exclusive preserve of Americans (see, for example, Butler and Stokes 1969, Part II; Gidengil, Blais, Nevitte, and Nadeau 2004, chap. 3), though comparisons focusing on understanding of the left-right dimension and on international affairs suggest that Americans are at the low end of the distribution (Barnes and Kaase 1979; Milner 2002, 55–59), Americans are in the middle of the pack in terms of the percentage of the public that can position themselves on a left-right scale (Dalton 2010). Party and election system characteristics explain some of the variation across nations (Gordon and Segura 1997).

2. A modified version of the measure is applied to ANES survey data (Lau and Redlawsk 1997; Lau, Andersen, and Redlawsk 2008).

3. There is some debate, however, about the conditions under which sophistication moderates economic voting (Godbout and Bélanger 2007; Gomez and Wilson 2007).

4. Surprisingly, however, more informed voters were found to be more responsive to emotional appeals in campaign advertising (Brader 2006), perhaps because they are more aware of campaign activity in general.

5. Some may question the methodology of these studies (for instance, Kuklinski, Quirk, and Peyton 2008). Lupia (2006), for example, raises the question of whether researchers can presume to estimate how a fully informed public will behave. Specifically, these models tend to assume that the effects of other predictors on policy preferences remain unchanged when people become fully informed. A few exceptions (Gilens 2001; Luskin, Fishkin, and Jowell 2002; Sturgis 2003) include experimental manipulations of information and yield similar results.

6. In explaining low levels of political knowledge, some revisionists cite models of "on-line" information processing (Lodge, McGraw, and Stroh 1989), in which people continuously incorporate new information into their opinions of politicians or issues but then quickly forget those bits of information while remembering their summary evaluation. However, one recent test (Redlawsk 2001) finds that the on-line model does not entirely explain voter decision-making.

7. Lau and Redlawsk's results can admittedly be interpreted in a positive or negative light. On the negative side, perhaps a quarter of the population does not vote correctly, despite the use of heuristics. On the positive side, low-information decision-making processes seem to improve the likelihood of voting correctly. In addition, they find that the typical (in the United States) campaign environment influences the ability of people to vote correctly. Correct voting is more common in two-candidate contests, when opposing candidates are ideologically distinct and when campaigns are more intense (Lau and Redlawsk 2006; Lau, Andersen, and Redlawsk 2008). Thus, voters depend on campaigns that offer "a choice, not an echo," a point that was made forcefully by Key (1966) in an early rejoinder to Converse's work.

8. Jacoby (2006) reaches a somewhat different conclusion, arguing that sophistication moderates the impact of core values on public opinion.

9. Conflicting evidence is found in content analyses that cover one hundred or more years of campaigning (Sigelman and Bullock 1991; Antista et al. 2010).

10. Of course others have a less positive assessment of recent developments in the media marketplace and the ability of the media to inform all citizens. As discussed in section 2, Prior (2005) argues that increasing entertainment options available to consumers exacerbates informational differences among citizens (also, see Wattenberg 2008).

11. However, the effects they document are modest. The multivitamin metaphor is appropriate to describe the informational contribution of campaigns. Just as a vitamin does not provide the nourishment of three square meals a day, political campaigns are limited in meeting the informational needs of citizens.

12. ANES staff is reviewing its coding of some political knowledge questions, which may reveal somewhat higher levels of political knowledge among American adults (Krosnick et al. 2008). For a broader critique of political knowledge measures, see Lupia (2006). Also relevant is Delli Carpini and Keeter's (1996, 95–98) discussion of "contested truths, close calls, and lagged attention."

13. However, Mondak's recommendations are disputed by Sturgis, Allum, and Smith (2008).

14. For public misperceptions of economic concepts, see Caplan (2007).

Further Readings

Information Limits

Bartels, Larry M., *Unequal Democracy: The Political Economy of the New Gilded Age*. (Princeton, N.J.: Princeton University Press, 2008). Examines voting behavior and policy preferences by levels of income and knowledge. These differences contribute to political and economic inequality.

Critical Review 18 (2006) No. 1-3. The issue features several articles evaluating the classic study on "The Nature of Belief Systems in Mass Publics" by Philip Converse.

Delli Carpini, Michael X., and Scott Keeter, *What Americans Know about Politics and Why It Matters* (New Haven, Conn.: Yale University Press, 1996). Classic work on how much Americans know about politics and how that has varied over time and subject matter. Also examines the consequences of unequal knowledge.

Gilens, Martin, "Political Ignorance and Collective Policy Preferences," *American Political Science Review* 95 (2001): 379–396. A fully informed public would have different policy preferences.

Hall, Crystal C., Amir Goren, Shelly Chaiken, and Alexander Todorov, "Shallow Cues with Deep Effects: Trait Judgments from Faces and Voting Decisions." In *The Political Psychology of Democratic Citizenship*, eds. Eugene Borgida, Christopher M. Federico, and John L. Sullivan (Oxford: Oxford University Press, 2009). Judgments of competence based solely on candidates' facial appearance predict the outcomes of elections.

Kuklinski, James H., and Norman L. Hurley, "On Hearing and Interpreting Political Messages: A Cautionary Tale of Citizen Cue-Taking," *Journal of Politics* 56 (1994): 729–751. An example of the shortcomings of decision-making cues.

Kuklinski, James H., Paul J. Quirk, Jennifer Jerit, and Robert F. Rich, "The Political Environment and Citizen Competence," *American Journal of Political Science* 45 (2001): 410–424. Performance in making trade-offs depends on the political environment; favorable conditions, while hard to obtain, can eliminate individual differences in sophistication.

Lau, Richard R., David J. Andersen, and David P. Redlawsk, "An Exploration of Correct Voting in Recent U.S. Presidential Elections," *American Journal of Political Science* 52 (2008): 395–411. Individual political sophistication and the campaign environment are important predictors of voting correctly.

Lau, Richard R., and David P. Redlawsk, *How Voters Decide: Information Processing during Election Campaigns* (New York: Cambridge University Press, 2006). Examines prominent theories of voter decision-making using experimental methods and survey data. Provides a measure of voting correctly.

Zaller, John R., *The Nature and Origins of Mass Opinion* (New York: Cambridge University Press, 1992). Influential study that examines the impact of information on public opinion and voting behavior.

Informational Awareness and Shortcuts

Ansolabehere, Stephen, Jonathan Rodden, and James M. Snyder Jr., "The Strength of Issues: Using Multiple Measures to Gauge Preference Stability, Ideological Constraint, and Issue Voting," *American Political Science Review* 102 (2008): 215–232. Using a large number of items eliminates measurement error; the impact of issues, properly measured, rivals that of party identification.

Cohen, Marty, David Karol, Hans Noel, and John Zaller, *The Party Decides: Presidential Nominations before and after Reform* (Chicago: University of Chicago Press, 2008). Individual and interest-group endorsements have powerful effects on presidential nominations.

Gerber, Elisabeth R., and Justin H. Phillips, "Development Ballot Measures, Interest Group Endorsements, and the Political Geography of Growth Preferences." *American Journal of Political Science* 47 (2003): 625–639. Interest group endorsements are important determinants of voting behavior on ballot measures.

Goren, Paul, *On Voter Competence* (New York: Oxford University Press, forthcoming). Examines several core political values and their impact on voting decisions.

Jones, David R., and Monika L. McDermott, *Americans, Congress, and Democratic Responsiveness* (Ann Arbor: University of Michigan Press, 2009). Argues that the public is able to evaluate the performance of Congress in ideological terms. Public approval of Congress is an important factor in voting behavior and policy making.

Lupia, Arthur, and Matthew D. McCubbins, *The Democratic Dilemma: Can Citizens Learn What They Need to Know?* (Cambridge: Cambridge University Press, 1998). People can and often do make reasoned choices in the absence of full information, and political institutions can influence public reasoning.

Nicholson, Stephen P., *Voting the Agenda: Candidates, Elections, and Ballot Propositions* (Princeton, N.J.: Princeton University Press, 2005). Ballot measures often shape the issue agenda in candidate campaigns on the same ballot.

Decision-Making Biases

Gaines, Brian J., James H. Kuklinski, Paul J. Quirk, Buddy Peyton, and Jay Verkuilen, "Same Facts, Different Interpretations: Partisan Motivation and Opinion on Iraq," *Journal of Politics* 69 (2007): 957–974. Partisanship influences how people interpret the same set of facts.

Taber, Charles S., and Milton Lodge, "Motivated Skepticism in the Evaluation of Political Beliefs," *American Journal of Political Science* 50 (2006): 755–769. People tend to evaluate new information in ways that confirm their prior beliefs.

Aggregate Public Opinion

Erikson, Robert S., Michael B. MacKuen, and James A. Stimson, *The Macro Polity* (New York: Cambridge University Press, 2002). The public mood responds to political events and is a predictor of election outcomes and policy change.

Page, Benjamin I., and Robert Y. Shapiro, *The Rational Public: Fifty Years of Trends in Americans' Policy Preferences* (Chicago: University of Chicago Press, 1992). Classic defense of the sensibility of the electorate. Aggregate opinion is generally stable and changes sensibly.

The Information Environment in Campaigns and the Media

Franz, Michael M., Paul B. Freedman, Kenneth M. Goldstein, and Travis N. Ridout, *Campaign Advertising and American Democracy* (Philadelphia: Temple University Press, 2007). Campaign advertising helps inform and mobilize less knowledgeable voters.

Geer, John G., *In Defense of Negativity: Attack Ads in Presidential Campaigns* (Chicago: University of Chicago Press, 2006). Argues that negative advertisements help inform voters.

Gilens, Martin, Lynn Vavreck, and Martin Cohen, "The Mass Media and the Public's Assessments of Presidential Candidates, 1952–2000." *Journal of Politics* 69 (2007): 1160–1175. Media coverage of presidential campaigns has declined but campaigns have become more informative.

Jerit, Jennifer, Jason Barabas, and Toby Bolsen, "Citizens, Knowledge, and the Information Environment." *American Journal of Political Science* 50 (2006): 266–282. Examines the relationship between media coverage and public knowledge on a series of issues.

6. The *Oprah* Effect: How Soft News Helps Inattentive Citizens Vote Consistently

Matthew A. Baum and Angela S. Jamison

Democratic theorists have long argued that a prerequisite for representative democracy is for citizens to vote in their own, subjectively determined, interests (Banfield 1961; Dahl 1961). To do so, of course, they must have sufficient information to determine which candidates will best represent their interests. But since markets, rather than statesmen, govern the provision of information in democracies, the "proper" role of the press in helping citizens fulfill their civic duties remains open to debate (Bennett and Entman 2000; Norris 2000; Schudson 1998; Zaller 2003). This is particularly true for political campaigns, voting behavior, and the primary link between them—news coverage. While many claim the media have an *obligation* to inform citizens sufficiently to enable them to judge which candidate best matches their own, self-defined, preferences (e.g., L. Bennett 1997; Patterson 2000), others observe that because news content is determined by the vicissitudes of the marketplace, the news media are not well suited for such a role (Baum 2003; Hamilton 2003; Norris 2000; Zaller 2003).[1]

For many in the former camp, the current state of political news, and thus of citizens' political knowledge—as well as, by extension, their competence as democratic citizens—is bleak (L. Bennett 2003; S. Bennett N.d.; Patterson 1993, 2000). But others (e.g., Popkin 1994; Schudson 1998; Zaller 2003) counter that a press that provides limited quantities of political information is not necessarily dysfunctional, arguing that such concerns underestimate citizens' capacity to make reasoned voting decisions based on relatively small quantities of information. By employing information shortcuts, they argue, typical individuals may act as competent democratic citizens—at least with respect to voting—even if the political information they consume is imperfect and they consume it in small quantities (Lupia and McCubbins 1998; Popkin 1994).

Advocates of the former perspective frequently cite the proliferation of soft news as evidence of the news media's failure to equip citizens with proper or sufficient information (L. Bennett 2003; Patterson 2000, 2003). Patterson (2000), for instance, implicitly argues that, ceteris paribus, hard news—defined as coverage of breaking events involving top leaders, major issues, or significant disruptions in the routines of daily life—is of higher quality than soft news, which lacks a public policy component, featuring instead sensationalized presentation, human-interest themes, and dramatic subject matter. As Zaller states, "soft news is information that is either personally useful or merely entertaining" (2003, 129). In short, a

Source: *Journal of Politics* 68, 4 (November 2006): 946–959.

prevalent scholarly critique of the contemporary news media is thus that they offer too little *hard* news and too much *soft* news, thereby making it difficult for citizens to obtain sufficient information to make informed vote choices.

Zaller reframes this debate, observing: "the question of news quality is whether news provides a *sufficiently* rich and engaging ration of political information to make democracy work" (2003, 111; emphasis added). We agree, and we suspect that, with the issue framed in this manner, the aforementioned soft news critics would agree as well, albeit continuing to question whether soft news provides *enough* political information "to make democracy work." Yet, this begs the central questions motivating the present study: (1) How do we know how much information is *sufficient*? and (2) Can citizens extract *sufficient* information from *soft* news to make reasoned vote choices and thus to make democracy work?

As the preceding definition suggests, most prior research (e.g., L. Bennett 2003; Patterson 2000, 2003; Prior 2003) assesses the political utility of news—implicitly or explicitly equated with normative notions of news "quality"—primarily in terms of its content. That is, scholars have focused more on the *supply* of political information than on the nature of citizens' *demands*, or what it is that citizens *do* with the news they consume.

This emphasis, however, conflicts with predominant theories of political participation, which trace the decision to vote to utility maximization (Downs 1957; Riker and Ordeshook 1968). Given that rational individuals employ heuristic cues to compensate for incomplete information, citizens with different information needs will vary in what they require to fulfill their civic duties successfully. One of the most fundamental such duties is (arguably) voting for the candidate whose economic, social and/or public policy preferences most closely match a voter's own—self-defined and subjectively determined—preferences (henceforth "voting consistently").[2]

In deciding which candidate better matches their preferences, different voters prioritize different things. Some emphasize their economic well-being; others prioritize candidates' values or policy positions. Regardless, every voter must assess, in *some* manner, which candidate best matches her own preferences on whatever dimensions are most salient to her. *Voting consistently* merely requires voting for the candidate who really *does* best match one's self-defined preferences.

But how can we assess citizens' capacity to vote consistently while recognizing that rational individuals expose themselves to varying *kinds* and *levels* of political information? Rather than focusing exclusively on the *content* of political news, we investigate how, in making their vote choices, different kinds of *consumers* use different kinds of *news*.[3] Some may need the *New York Times* to determine which candidate they "ought" to favor; others may do just as well with *Oprah*.

Soft News and Voting Behavior

Virtually all media outlets that present at least *some* information about public affairs offer a mix of "soft" and "hard" news content; most have offered ever more of the former. Yet some clearly offer more than others. Elsewhere, Baum (2002, 2003) refers to those media outlets that focus *primarily* on such material—including entertainment and tabloid news shows, network newsmagazines, and daytime and late night talk shows—as the *soft news media*. These outlets differ in many respects. Yet, in contrast to traditional, hard news outlets—such as the *New York Times* or network evening newscasts—they all focus primarily on soft news themes like crime, disaster, or scandal, and they all cover political issues similarly to one another (Baum 2003). Their audiences also tend to have comparatively little education or interest in politics (Baum 2003; Hamilton 2003).

For a combination of instrumental and conceptual reasons, which we discuss below, we focus our empirical investigation on one prominent type of soft news outlet: daytime talk shows. While not "news" shows in the traditional sense, a vast majority of these programs' content is explicitly intended to be "either personally useful or merely entertaining" (Zaller 2003, 129).

To be sure, some potential voters consume hard news out of an intrinsic interest in politics or public affairs. But do less politically engaged individuals, who do not seek out traditional hard news, manage to extract *quality* information from different media outlets, like daytime talk shows, that maximize their utility as consumers? We argue that, for these latter individuals, the answer is *yes*.

Different people place different values on political news. For individuals who neither understand nor care about politics, consuming political news can be costly—in terms of the effort required to comprehend the information, as well as the lost opportunities to spend one's time on more appealing endeavors—while offering little expected benefit (e.g., entertainment). All else equal, such individuals are relatively unlikely to consume much hard news. If they *do* encounter any traditional news programs, they are unlikely to pay much attention to or understand the relatively more complex information such shows present (Baum 2002; Hamill and Lodge 1986; Hamilton 2003). Before relatively apolitical individuals will attend to political information, the expected benefit must outweigh the expected cost. This is only likely if such information is cheap to consume.

Why would an individual who is uninterested in and does not understand politics pay attention to political news? Baum (2002, 2003) argues soft news can, under some circumstances, render political information cost-effective for even apolitical individuals. His "incidental by-product" model shows that if substantive political information is presented in an entertaining context, it can be piggy-backed (i.e., attached) to information intended primarily to entertain, and hence consumed incidentally, effectively at no extra cost. An apolitical individual may therefore be willing to consume even relatively low-benefit political information, as doing so becomes essentially costless. Since the soft news media make information accessible and entertaining, they are ideally suited for piggybacking. The net effect is that low-awareness individuals who typically ignore most political information are less likely to do so in a soft news context.

Voting consistently, in turn, is not of overwhelming importance to an individual who does not care about politics. If such an individual votes, she would presumably prefer the candidate who best matches her personal preferences. Yet, by definition, doing so is not among her top priorities. Hence, she will be willing to accept a greater risk of error than an individual who cares deeply about her vote choice. For a politically inattentive individual, soft news is of "high quality"—by our definition—if it increases the probability of voting consistently to a degree acceptable to her, such that the expected benefit of the improvement outweighs the expected cost of gaining it. In the aggregate, we should thus observe a greater likelihood of consistent voting among politically unaware soft news consumers, relative to their counterparts who consume no soft news.

All else equal, hard news is better suited for enhancing the probability of voting consistently. After all, gathering more information should reduce the likelihood of inadvertently voting for the "wrong" candidate. Yet, for most political sophisticates, hard news media are both *intrinsically* appealing and, due to their relatively more information-intensive coverage of politics, more efficient information sources than soft news outlets. For such individuals, hard news may also be more entertaining, regardless of whether it enhances their probability of voting consistently. In fact, because highly aware individuals *already* possess substantial political knowledge (Zaller 1992), exposure to campaign coverage via either the soft or hard news media is likely to have a limited effect on their vote choices. However, to the extent doing so has any effect at all, it seems likely to raise their probability of voting consistently, at least somewhat. After all, they possess a sufficient knowledge base to comprehend hard news and integrate it into their overall candidate evaluations. Our first two hypotheses follow.

> H1: Among highly politically aware individuals, consuming soft news will have little, if any, effect on the propensity to vote consistently.
> H2: Among highly politically aware individuals, consuming hard news will increase the propensity to vote consistently.

In contrast, low-awareness individuals are less likely to be willing to expend significant time and energy to enhance their probability of voting consistently. Since these individuals do not find hard news intrinsically enjoyable, they will typically avoid it. Their real choice is frequently *not* whether to consume hard or soft news, but rather whether to consume soft news or *no* news. Consequently, we argue that low-awareness individuals are better off consuming soft news than no news at all. After all, research (Baum 2003, 2005; Young 2006) has shown that soft news outlets—including daytime talk shows—*do* cover presidential politics. And they do so in ways that make such information interesting for their relatively apolitical audiences.

Many low-awareness voters, in turn, base their vote choices more on the candidates' personal qualities—as an information shortcut—than their policy positions (Baum 2005). By assessing the candidates' "likeability" (Sniderman,

Brody, and Tetlock 1991), voters can often figure out which candidate best represents their interests, even absent substantial knowledge of their policy positions. Consequently, entertainment-oriented talk show (henceforth "E-talk show") candidate interviews can help viewers vote consistently even absent significant discussion of policy issues. Nevertheless, despite their "soft" approach to political interviews, E-talk show interviews do address public policy, albeit far less so than campaign coverage by traditional news outlets.

For instance, Baum (2005) content analyzes TV interviews with presidential candidates during the 2000 campaign. Four daytime E-talk shows (*The Oprah Winfrey Show, The Rosie O'Donnell Show, Live with Regis and Kelly,* and *The Queen Latifah Show*) interviewed the major party candidates. These interviews averaged about 27 minutes and included, on average, slightly more than one mention of a campaign-related policy issue per minute.[4] The corresponding averages for candidate interviews on traditional network and cable news shows, and for a random sample of national news campaign reports not involving candidate interviews, were about 2.5 and 2.6 mentions per minute, respectively.

Given the aforementioned relatively greater complexity of information presented by hard news outlets (Hamilton 2003), we further argue that if the choice *is* between soft or hard news, low-awareness individuals may *still* be better off consuming soft news. Even if a low-awareness individual is exposed to hard news campaign coverage, she is less likely than her more politically aware counterparts to attend to or comprehend it. Consequently, consuming political information via soft news should enhance low-awareness individuals' propensity to vote consistently more than consuming no news at all, or consuming hard news alone. This suggests four additional hypotheses.

H3: Politically unaware individuals who consume soft news will be more likely to vote consistently than their counterparts who do not consume soft news.

H4: The consistent-vote-enhancing effect on high-awareness individuals associated with consuming hard news will be smaller than that associated with consuming soft news among low-awareness individuals.

H5: Among politically unaware individuals, consuming hard news will have a weaker effect than consuming soft news on the propensity to vote consistently.

H6: Among politically unaware individuals, consuming hard news will have a relatively weak effect on the relationship between soft news consumption and voting consistently.

The 2 × 2 matrix below summarizes our theoretical predictions, from which we derive our hypotheses. It presents the predicted magnitude and direction of the effects of exposure to different types of news by different types of consumers on the likelihood of voting consistently.

	Consumer Characteristics	
News Characteristics	Low Political Awareness	High Political Awareness
Complex (Hard News)	Small Effect	Medium Increase
Simple/Accessible (Soft News)	Large Increase	Small Effect

Dependent Variable: Voting Consistently

To test our hypotheses, it is necessary to measure the consistency between a voter's preferences and her vote. This, of course, presupposes the existence of some objective standard by which we can evaluate whether a voter *has*, in fact, voted consistently. After all, to at least some extent, a voter's political preferences are subjective. Voters weigh issues differently; some prioritize candidates' personal ethics or values, while others care more about their policy positions. Different voters care more or less about different policies. While we cannot calculate *perfectly* which candidate best matches a voter's preferences, we believe a useful approximation is possible. For this purpose, following Lau and Redlawsk (1997), we rely on a semi-objective, experimentally derived measure of voting "correctly." (We have replaced the term "correctly" with "consistently," which we believe carries fewer normative implications.) Lau and Redlawsk experimentally tested a measure of "correct" voting based on the congruence of each voter's chosen candidate with her own stated issue preferences, weighted by the intensity of those preferences. They found that their measure *outperformed*—that is, the subjects were more likely to vote "correctly" than—those same voters in a mock election where they were constrained to select limited amounts of campaign information.

Lau and Redlawsk tested their "correct vote" concept against all NES surveys between 1972 and 1988. They developed an algorithm measuring respondents' issue preferences and their self-reported "closeness" to a series of societal groups (e.g., "labor unions" or "business"), where respondents' closeness to a given group was statistically significantly related to their probability of voting for one or the other candidate. Their algorithm also incorporated respondents' perceptions concerning the major party candidates' stances on the issues, as well as respondent and candidate ideologies and party identification. Finally, their algorithm employed the "directional" method (Rabinowitz and Macdonald 1989) in order to take into account the *intensity* (i.e., magnitude) and valence of the differences between the candidates' "true" issue positions—as determined by the model—and the issue positions of the respondent. (For a detailed discussion of how the algorithm is calculated, see Lau and Redlawsk [1997, 596–97]. For a summary of factors included in the algorithm, see our online appendix located at www .journalofpolitics.org.)

The Lau and Redlawsk algorithm produces a summary statistic for each candidate, where a positive value indicates that voting for a given candidate is "correct" for a given respondent. The statistics for the two candidates are then combined into a single summary indicator, where a negative (positive) value represents a predicted "correct" vote for one (the other) candidate. We compared these predictions against respondents' actual self-declared vote choice. Based on this comparison, we created a dichotomous dependent variable, called "Consistent Vote," scored 1 whenever the predicted and actual vote cohered, and 0 otherwise.[5]

We apply Lau and Redlawsk's model to the 2000 NES. We replicate their algorithm, with three exceptions. First, to estimate the candidates' actual issue positions, Lau and Redlawsk rely on the opinions of NES respondents whose political knowledge—based on a battery of factual knowledge questions—exceed the overall mean in the survey. We employ alternative means of calculating the candidates' actual policy positions. Our models interact media consumption with respondents' political awareness. Hence, factual knowledge would be endogenous to Lau and Redlawsk's estimate of candidates' "true" issue positions, as highly aware individuals would, by definition, tend to vote more correctly according to the algorithm. After all, their opinions form much of the basis for determining what constitutes a correct vote. We also believe that defining as "experts" all respondents who exceed the overall survey mean is too lenient, particularly given that the mean respondent answered correctly only about one-third of the political knowledge questions.

Consequently, we employ two alternative measures of the candidates' "true" policy positions. First, we surveyed a group of actual experts. We asked about 80 political scientists with expertise in American politics to rate the candidates on the issue scales employed by the NES survey. We received 40 replies and employed the mean ratings of these 40 experts as our first estimate of the candidates' "true" issue positions. Notably, the standard deviation on our experts' assessments is far smaller than that for the estimates of Lau and Redlawsk's NES "expert" respondents: .64 for our experts versus 1.02 for NES respondents whose factual political knowledge exceeded the survey mean. *Our* experts were thus in greater agreement on the candidates' positions.[6]

For our second alternative assessment of the candidates' true issue positions, we relied on the judgments of *fully informed* researchers. We asked five undergraduates and one graduate student to read literally everything the candidates said during the 2000 campaign. All candidate speeches, advertisements, press releases, and other statements are available on a CD-ROM ("In their Own Words: Sourcebook for the 2000 Presidential Election"). After our researchers read all of its contents, we asked them to rate the candidates' positions on each pertinent issue area.

Figure 6-1 summarizes the estimates of our American politics experts and student researchers on each issue dimension included in the "correct vote" algorithm. Each question asked respondents to rate the candidates' issue positions on a 1–5 or 1–7 scale. For instance, the "Services vs. Spending" question asked respondents whether each candidate would like the government to provide fewer

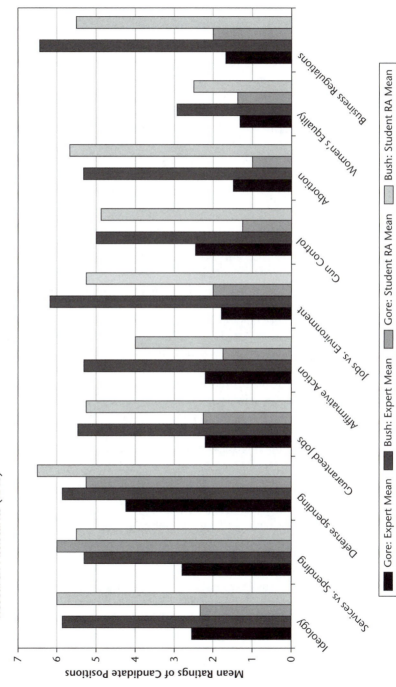

Figure 6-1 Mean Ratings of Candidates' "True" Positions by American Politics Experts and "Fully Informed" Student Research Assistants (RA's)

Legend: Gore: Expert Mean | Bush: Expert Mean | Gore: Student RA Mean | Bush: Student RA Mean

Categories: Ideology | Services vs. Spending | Defense spending | Guaranteed Jobs | Affirmative Action | Jobs vs. Environment | Gun Control | Abortion | Women's Equality | Business Regulations

Y-axis: Mean Ratings of Candidate Positions (0 to 7)

services in order to reduce spending, provide more services even if it meant an increase in spending, or keep spending at about the same level as in 2000. Respondents rated the candidates on a 1–5 scale, where 1 represented "reduce spending and services a great deal," and 5 represented "increase spending and services a great deal." We normalized all scales to a 1–7 interval. (The complete survey questionnaire is available in our online appendix.)

The evaluations of our "fully informed" researchers correlate at .87 with those of our "experts."[7] For the students, the overall standard deviation across all issue dimensions was .65, again far smaller than that of the NES "expert" respondents, and nearly identical to the political scientists.[8] Despite significant differences between the ratings of the two groups on several issue dimensions, there were *no* instances where switching from one to the other indicator altered the algorithm's summary prediction for a respondent. Hence, we report only the results based on the estimates from our expert survey. (Results using the latter estimates are available from the authors.)

The second difference between Lau and Redlawsk's algorithm and ours concerns approval of the incumbent president. They add a small constant derived from the incumbent's approval rating among NES "experts" to the estimate of the "correctness" of voting for Gore, but not for Bush. In our view, approving of the incumbent in a situation where his vice president is on the ballot ought to influence equally the "objective" appropriateness of voting for either candidate. Hence, we include this factor in our estimation of the "consistency" of voting for Bush.[9]

Finally, Lau and Redlawsk derived their final summary estimates of each respondent's "correct" vote in two different ways, calculating: (1) the overall mean value across the various factors included in the summary estimate, and (2) the total sum of all factors included in the summary estimate. These methods correlate at over .98. Lau and Redlawsk employ the first method. At the margins, we prefer and hence report results employing the second, as it preserves the full ranges of variation in the original variables. However, the two methods produce comparable results.

Independent Variables

The 2000 NES includes a series of questions concerning media consumption habits, one of which asks respondents how often they watch daytime talk shows. We investigate the implications of watching these programs, as well as traditional hard news shows (including national network news and newspapers), for respondents' voting behavior. Our key causal variable is based on the following question: "How many times in the last week have you watched daytime television talk shows such as 'Oprah Winfrey,' 'Rosie O'Donnell,' or 'Jerry Springer'?" Because only 9% of respondents reported watching more than three such shows, we collapse this indicator into four categories, coded: 0 = none, 1 = one time, 2 = two times, and 3 = three or more times. Overall, 28% of respondents indicated that they had watched at least one daytime talk show during the prior week. (For the recoded scale, m = .61 and s = 1.07.)

While this indicator does not explicitly measure exposure to *presidential politics* on daytime talk shows, we believe that, in addition to being the best—to our knowledge, the *only*—available indicator for testing our hypotheses in close proximity to a presidential election, it is also reasonably valid. There are two reasons for this. First, Baum (2005) reports that the major party presidential candidates made six appearances on daytime talk shows during the 2000 campaign (plus four on late-night talk shows).[10] The more an individual watched daytime talk shows during the fall of 2000, the more likely she was to have been watching when a candidate appeared. Second, the NES asks respondents about their talk show viewing *in the week prior to the interview.* All but one of the candidates' daytime talk show appearances took place during the pre-election wave—beginning on September 5, 2000. Hence, the relationship between watching daytime talk shows and encountering candidate interviews while doing so was far higher during this period than at any other time.

Nevertheless, to compensate, at least in part, for the imprecision of our key causal variable, we replicate our results with a modified version of the talk show consumption indicator, weighted by the number of days, at the time of a given respondent's NES interview, since the last candidate appearance on an E-talk show:

$$\left(\frac{\text{\# of E-talk shows watched in prior week}}{\text{days since last candidate E-talk show appearance}} \right)^{11}.$$

We base this weight factor on two assumptions: (1) as the proximity of a candidate E-talk show interview to a given NES interview increases, so too will the relationship between talk show viewing and the probability of encountering a candidate interview while viewing, and (2) the more recent a respondent's media consumption, the more accurate her recollections of that consumption. We further discuss and report the results from this robustness test below, in our investigation of possible selection effects.

The control variables fall into four categories and include many of the most widely employed variables in the study of American voting behavior (e.g., Rosenstone and Hansen 1993, 273–275) and in Baum's (2005) investigation of E-talk show effects on vote choice. These are: (1) demographics (age, education, gender, race, religiosity), (2) political attitudes (strength of partisanship, ideology, participation in the campaign, preference for divided government, intent to vote for opposition party candidate), (3) political disaffection (trust in government, external efficacy), and (4) media consumption (national network TV news, local TV news, newspapers, political talk radio, politics on the internet, cable access, TV campaign ads, morning TV news shows).[12]

Following Baum (2005), we also create an indicator of respondents' political awareness. Zaller defines political awareness as "the extent to which an individual pays attention to politics and understands what he or she has encountered" (1992, 21). In order to capture both parts of Zaller's definition (attention and understanding), we create a scale derived from four elements: (1) interest in government and public affairs, (2) attention to the 2000 election, (3) level of political information, as estimated by the interviewer,[13] and (4) factual political knowledge, derived from a series of ten questions. We collapsed each element to a 0–1 interval and then summed them to create our political awareness indicator. The resulting variable, which combines objective measures with respondents' self-assessments, runs from 0 to 4 ($\mu = 2.5$ and $\sigma = 1.0$).[14] To determine whether consuming talk shows and hard news have differing effects on different types of respondents, we separately interact daytime talk show and traditional news consumption with political awareness.[15] To estimate traditional news consumption we create a scale based upon respondents' self-declared frequency of watching national network TV newscasts and reading daily newspapers during the prior week.[16] (See online appendix for question wording and coding.)

Statistical Results

Table 6-1 presents the results from five logit analyses testing our six hypotheses. Model 1 excludes all but two controls—strength of candidate preferences and political participation—both of which are potentially critical factors influencing the probability of a consistent vote as well as of willingness to reevaluate one's vote choice based upon new information.[17] We include this preliminary model to determine whether any of our results are artifacts of model specification. In fact, the key coefficients in the basic model, though not identical to the fully specified models, are nonetheless similar in magnitude and significance. Hence, we can proceed more confidently to the fully specified models.

Table 6-1 Logit Analyses of Correlates of Consistent Voting

	Model 1	Model 2	Model 3	Model 4	Model 5
Media Consumption					
Daytime TV Talk Shows	.364	.513	.494	.082	1.226
	(.202)^	(.240)*	(.240)*	(.084)	(.578)*
Hard News[a]	−.124	−.076	−.066	−.072	−.066
	(.107)	(.128)	(.130)	(.125)	(.127)
Local TV News	—	−.036	−.037	−.038	−.036
		(.020)^	(.020)^	(.020)^	(.020)^
Morning News TV Shows	—	−.133	−.135	−.129	−.128
		(.068)*	(.068)*	(.067)^	(.067)^
TV Campaign Ads	—	−.349	−.365	−.122	−.358
		(.232)	(.234)	(.639)	(.230)
Talk Radio	—	.052	.070	.059	.052
		(.073)	(.074)	(.072)	(.073)
Cable Access	—	−.358	−.370	−.363	−.367
		(.215)^	(.214)^	(.215)^	(.214)^
Campaign News on Web	—	.191	.188	.181	.188
		(.190)	(.191)	(.190)	(.191)

Table 6-1 *(continued)*

	Model 1	Model 2	Model 3	Model 4	Model 5
Demographics					
Education	—	.042	.048	.041	.041
		(.039)	(.039)	(.039)	(.039)
Age	—	.006	.004	.005	.005
		(.006)	(.006)	(.006)	(.006)
Male	—	−.129	−.114	−.138	−.122
		(.180)	(.182)	(.180)	(.179)
White	—	−.447	−.386	−.453	−.445
		(.348)	(.349)	(.347)	(.347)
Black	—	−.314	−.445	−.277	−.270
		(.426)	(.434)	(.426)	(.427)
Guidance from Religion	—	−.018	−.008	−.025	−.021
		(.074)	(.075)	(.074)	(.074)
Political Knowledge & Attitudes					
Political Awareness	−.238	.095	.098	.096	.065
	(.152)	(.179)	(.180)	(.245)	(.178)
Cross-party Vote Intention	—	−.685	−.657	−.632	−.668
		(.364)^	(.383)^	(.366)^	(.364)^
Strength of Candidate Preferences	.672	.458	.448	.457	.469
	(.160)***	(.192)*	(.191)	(.192)*	(.192)*
Strength of Partisanship	—	.299	.280	.290	.293
		(.093)***	(.093)**	(.093)**	(.093)**
Campaign Participation	.212	.247	.242	.243	.286
	(.447)	(.482)	(.480)	(.484)	(.487)
Ideology	—	.005	.002	.005	.005
		(.003)*	(.003)	(.003)*	(.003)*
Party Identification	—	—	−.106	—	—
			(.053)*		
Prefer Divided Government	—	−.384	−.398	−.386	−.386
		(.203)^	(.204)*	(.203)^	(.203)^
External Political Efficacy	—	.208	.229	.198	.201
		(.223)	(.222)	(.222)	(.222)
Trust in Government	—	−.271	−.289	−.267	−.251
		(.100)**	(.100)**	(.100)**	(.100)**
Interaction Terms					
Pol. Awareness × Talk Shows	−.127	−.165	−.164	—	−.357
	(.073)^	(.084)*	(.084)*		(.205)^
Pol. Awareness × Hard News	.039	.049	.048	.049	.046
	(.038)	(.044)	(.044)	(.043)	(.044)
Pol. Awareness × Campaign Ads	—	—	—	−.086	—
				(.232)	
Constant	.083	1.531	1.856	1.621	1.580
	(.403)	(.960)	(.971)^	(1.044)	(.952)^
χ^2	40.37***	77.66***	80.54***	74.03***	78.36***
Pseudo R^2 (N)	.033	.076	.081	.073	.076
	(1081)	(988)	(988)	(988)	(988)

^$p \leq .10$, *$p \leq .05$, **$p \leq .01$, ***$p \leq .001$; Heteroskedasticity-consistent standard errors in parentheses.

[a]National Network News + Daily Newspapers.

In Model 2, we add all control variables, except Party ID, which is also included in the "correct vote" algorithm. Including it as a control effectively places it on both sides of the equation. Model 3 replicates Model 2, with Party ID as a separate control variable. Presumably because it *is* included in the algorithm, including or excluding party ID makes virtually no difference for the results. Hence, we focus our discussion on Model 2, excluding Party ID as a control variable.

Turning to our hypothesis tests, we begin with Hypothesis 3 (H3), which predicts that politically unaware soft news consumers will be more likely to vote consistently than their counterparts who do not consume soft news. For ease of interpretation, we employ a simulation technique (King, Tomz, and Wittenberg 2000) to transform the key coefficients from Model 3 into probabilities, as well as to estimate the statistical significance of the predicted effects. The two top quadrants in Figure 6-2 illustrate the results, separately presenting the effects of talk show consumption among respondents who do and do not consume hard news (top-left graphic) and the effects of hard news consumption among respondents who do and do not consume soft news (top right graphic), as respondents' political awareness varies from one standard deviation below, to one standard deviation above, the mean.[18]

These relationships support H3. The thick lines in the figure denote statistically significant curves ($p < .05$ for the talk show graph and $p < .10$ for the hard news graph), while the thinner lines represent insignificant relationships. Among low-awareness respondents who report consuming *no* hard news, as talk show consumption increases from its minimum to maximum values, the probability of voting consistently increases by 13 percentage points, from .72 to .85 ($p < .05$). As predicted by H6, variations in hard news consumption have virtually no effect on this relationship. The corresponding increase among low-awareness respondents who consume the *maximum* quantity of hard news is 14 percentage points, from .70 to .84 ($p < .05$).

The top-right graphic in Figure 6-2 also supports H1, which predicts at most modest effects of consuming soft news among highly aware individuals. Among these latter respondents, a maximum increase in talk show consumption is associated with small and statistically insignificant effects on the propensity to vote consistently, regardless of hard news consumption.

We turn next to Hypotheses 2, 4, and 5. Model 3 in Table 6-1 also tests these hypotheses. The top-right graphic in Figure 6-2 illustrates the results. Beginning with H5, among low-awareness respondents who do not consume talk shows, a maximum increase in hard news consumption is associated with a small and statistically insignificant decline of 2 percentage points (from .72 to .70) in the probability of voting consistently. The corresponding effect among low-awareness maximum talk show consumers is a statistically insignificant decline of one percentage point (from .85 to .84). Consistent with H5, these effects are far smaller than those associated with consuming soft news.

Figure 6-2 Probability of Voting Consistently as Daytime Talk Show or Hard News Consumption and Political Awareness Vary

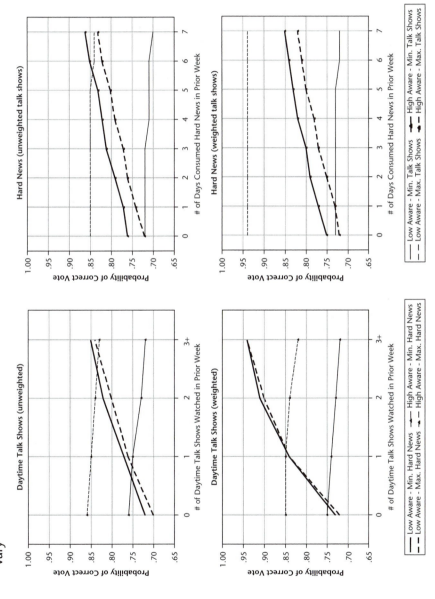

Note: Statistically significant curves shown in bold.

H2 and H4 predict that consuming hard news will increase the propensity of highly aware individuals to vote consistently, but less so than the corresponding effect of consuming soft news on low-awareness consumers. The two bolded curves shown in the bottom graphic of Figure 6-2 indicate that among highly aware respondents, a maximum increase in hard news consumption is associated with increases of 10 (from .76 to .86) or 11 (from .72 to .83) percentage points, respectively, among respondents who consume minimum or maximum quantities of daytime talk shows ($p < .10$).

Looking across the top two graphics in Figure 6-2, we see that, as also predicted by H4, consuming talk shows has a modestly stronger effect among low-awareness respondents than the corresponding effects of consuming hard news among highly aware respondents. Taken together, these results are largely supportive of H2 and H4—though more strongly so in the former case.

Finally, Model 4 of Table 6-1 indirectly tests the incidental exposure model underlying our news quality framework. This table includes an interaction between exposure to campaign ads on TV and political awareness in place of the interaction between daytime talk shows and political awareness. If low-awareness respondents consume political information in the soft news media largely via piggybacking, then viewing campaign ads should not affect their probability of voting consistently. After all, campaign ads are unambiguously political—and recognizable as such—rather than being geared primarily toward entertainment. Hence, low-awareness individuals should tend to either avoid or ignore them. TV ads also seem unlikely to influence highly aware individuals, who typically will not view partisan political messages as credible unless the source is a fellow partisan (Lupia and McCubbins 1998; Miller and Krosnick 2000). In fact, our results support the model. No meaningful interaction arises between consuming TV campaign ads and the probability of voting consistently, regardless of respondents' levels of political awareness.

Possible Selection Effects

Our talk show exposure indicator could be capturing some internal characteristic(s) of viewers having little to do with exposure to campaign information. For instance, compared to no viewers, daytime talk show viewers tend to be less politically aware or engaged and to hold weaker candidate preferences (Baum 2005). Even though we control for these and other factors, it remains possible that a disproportionate number of individuals interested in the election but undecided about the candidates, who typically do not watch daytime talk shows, elected to tune in to help resolve their uncertainty. This would call into question the incidental by-product model underlying our hypotheses. To test this possibility, we employ the weighted variant of our talk show variable. If our results are driven by the differing internal characteristics of E-talk show viewers relative to nonviewers, we should not find a systematic relationship between the timing of E-talk show interviews relative to NES interviews and the probability of voting consistently. Instead, weighting the talk show indicator ought to *weaken*, rather than *strengthen*, its utility as a proxy for any such internal characteristics.

If, however, our interview subjects *are* responding to the *content* of E-talk shows, then the shorter the time gap between candidate appearances on such shows and their NES interviews, the *stronger* ought to be the relationship between talk show consumption and the probability of voting consistently. After all, previous research (e.g., Druckman and Nelson 2003; Iyengar and Kinder 1987; Luskin, Fishkin, and Jowell 2002) has shown that, like the precision of people's memories, the effects of exposure to new information, including media effects, tend to erode over time.[19] Consequently, all else equal, the closer the proximity of the hypothesized stimulus (i.e., the candidate E-talk show interview) to the response (i.e., the NES interview), the greater the extent to which variations in our talk show indicator will capture the likelihood of consuming E-talk show candidate interviews and the more accurate ought to be the respondents' recollections regarding their media consumption.

To test these possibilities, Model 5 in Table 6-1 replicates Model 2, employing the weighted talk show consumption indicator. The results, shown in the bottom half of Figure 6-2, indicate that the effects of consuming daytime talk shows, weighted by the proximity of the NES interview to the most recent candidate appearance on an E-talk show, are even *stronger* than the corresponding effects associated with the unweighted daytime talk show indicator. A maximum increase in daytime talk show consumption by a respondent interviewed on the day following a candidate appearance is associated with 21 and 22 percentage point increases in the probability of voting consistently, for respondents who consumed the minimum and maximum amounts of hard news, respectively (from .73 to 0.94 and from .72 to 0.94, respectively, $p < .05$). The effects of variations in hard news consumption are virtually unchanged from Model 2.[20]

In the latter model, the maximum probability of voting consistently for low-awareness frequent daytime talk show viewers is actually higher than for their highly aware counterparts who consumed the maximum quantity of hard news. Though counterintuitive, this is likely an artifact of the extreme range of the distribution represented by frequent daytime talk show consuming respondents interviewed *just* after a candidate appearance on an E-talk show.

If the internal characteristics of respondents were driving our results, we would also expect that during weeks in which the candidates appeared on daytime talk shows, the audiences for such shows would be at least somewhat different than in periods in which the candidates made no appearances. In particular, candidate-attracted audience members might be *more* politically aware and engaged— after all, they would have gone out of their way to find campaign information in a relatively improbable place—but *less* strongly committed to their party's candidate.

The maximum number of candidate appearances on daytime talk shows in any single week was two. Hence, respondents who reported watching *more* than two such shows during the prior week *could not* have done so exclusively to see candidates. To determine whether candidate-seeking, occasional viewers differed materially from regular talk show viewers, we divided talk show viewers into four subgroups, based upon whether: (1) they reported watching *one or two* versus *three or more* daytime talk shows in the prior week, and (2) their interviews took place within seven days of a candidate appearance on a daytime talk show. For each subgroup, we calculated averages for political awareness, strength of partisanship, campaign participation, probability of having "strong" candidate preferences, and probability of caring about the election outcome. The results (see online appendix) indicate that there are *no* statistically significant differences for any of these five factors regardless of frequency of talk show viewing or timing of the interview.

As a final test for selection effects (see online appendix), we replicated our models, substituting game shows (*Wheel of Fortune* and *Jeopardy*) for talk show consumption. Like daytime talk shows, game shows are entertainment oriented. Yet they are virtually devoid of political content. Once again, if the *internal* characteristics of viewers who prefer entertainment-oriented media—net of the factors in our models—account for the reported patterns, then we might anticipate similar patterns associated with consuming game shows and talk shows. If, however, the relationships are attributable to the *content* of daytime talk shows, then game show consumption should not influence the propensity to vote consistently. In fact, regardless of their political awareness, game show viewers were not more likely than non-viewers to vote consistently. This further suggests that self-selection into daytime talk show audiences is not driving these relationships.[21]

Conclusion

Citizens' ability to vote consistently depends on the information they consume, but not in the manner that many scholars have assumed. Our finding that some individuals derive civic-oriented "quality" from news consumed primarily for entertainment should give at least some pause to those who decry the proliferation of soft news in the media marketplace. The apparent quality of these citizens' vote choices, given their media consumption, also suggests significant resourcefulness among the less politically engaged segments of the public.

Looking to the interaction of political behavior and news consumption, we render an understanding of quality that extends to hard or soft news, and thereby focuses our analysis on the conditions under which quality results from the interaction of citizens' news consumption and their political decision making. As much as possible, this places the assessment of news quality in the hands of citizens we understand to be rational. Upon doing so, we discover that, at least with respect to voting, most citizens are able to act in their own interests, even if their predilection is for Oprah Winfrey instead of Jim Lehrer.

Patterson calls for a standard of news quality that "requires the non-elite press, and not just the elite press, to contribute to an informed public" (2003, 141). Our understanding of news quality serves this agenda. We found that for some voters, one of the least "elite" press outlets—daytime talk shows—does "do good" among the very voters who cause most worry for many democratic theorists: the politically unengaged.

Indeed, a democratic theory which takes seriously the proposition that individuals act to maximize their utility, and which grants that citizens need not retain reams of information in their heads in order to be good citizens (Zaller 2003), does not need to rely on elite prescriptions for news consumption. Rather, low-awareness voters' ability to maximize their personal utility extends not only to their media-consumption choices but also, in the narrow case of soft news consumers, to their low-information vote choices.

We found that low-awareness talk show consumers enhanced their propensity to vote consistently to such an extent that they effectively caught up—in this admittedly narrow sense—to their highly aware counterparts (see Figure 6-2).[22] While we by no means conclude from this that soft news can transform a low-awareness voter into a political sophisticate, voting consistently does not require that it do so. In U.S. presidential elections, the vote choice is typically dichotomous. Relative to some democratic electoral institutions that ask voters to decide between literally dozens of candidates, the American two-party, plurality-rule electoral system greatly simplifies the work of typical voters. Most of the time, and for the vast majority of Americans, "voting consistently" merely requires weighing two candidates to determine who is likely to best represent their interests.

Given, in turn, that low-awareness voters tend to be among the least strongly wedded to their political attitudes and preferences (Zaller 2004), they are most likely to be willing to alter their vote choice in response to new information, conditional on receiving it (Baum 2005; Zaller 1992). The soft news media are well suited—indeed, expressly intended—to capture the attention of these relatively apolitical voters (Baum 2003, 2005).

Consequently, for low-awareness individuals, even a relatively small increase in information may enhance the ability of low-awareness voters to figure out which of the two major-party candidates best represents their interests, thereby resulting in a switch from an inconsistent to a consistent vote. Indeed, our findings suggest that less politically aware citizens can act reasonably effectively in the voting booth without much hard news, presumably because alternative sources, such as daytime talk shows, provide them with sufficient political cues to vote in their own interests.

Even though E-talk shows focus far more on candidates' personalities than their policy positions (Baum 2005), there is no reason to believe that the political information contained in these programs, however limited in scope or personality oriented, is fundamentally inaccurate. This suggests that, in the context of U.S. elections, a little information may indeed go a long way, particularly for the least politically aware voters. It further suggests that when low-awareness Americans tune in to Oprah, Regis, or Leno, democracy may well be strengthened, rather than weakened.

Notes

1. Due to voters' subjective weighting of different considerations, one's *preferences* over values or public policies might diverge from her "objective" *self-interests*. For our purposes, a voter's *inherently* subjective preferences are essentially equivalent to her *self-defined and subjectively determined* interests. Hence, a voter's determination of her own self-interest, while arguably *conceptually* prior to, is *observationally* indistinguishable from, her preferences. We employ these terms interchangeably.

2. Assessment of self-interest may be an information shortcut for some voters, many of whom lack sufficient political knowledge to understand how policy proposals relate to societal effects (Delli Carpini and Keeter 1996). Yet they *do* understand their own circumstances and values and so can extrapolate from these to the state of the nation.

3. News serves purposes other than provision of political information, and facilitating consistent voting is only one of many potential measures of quality. Yet voting is a fundamental democratic civic duty, and, in our view, information provision is among the most important functions of news.

4. Late-night E-talk show (e.g., *Tonight Show*) candidate interviews (not addressed in the 2000 NES) averaged about 17 minutes and included about .56 issue mentions per minute, for a total of approximately 9.5 total mentions of campaign-related issues per interview.

5. We exclude nonvoters and those who reported voting for an independent or third-party candidate, as the algorithm makes no predictions in this regard. Theoretically, a respondent could receive a score of zero, in which case the algorithm would make no prediction. However, none did so.

6. The mean ideological score for our 40 experts was 4.75 on a 1–7 scale, where 7 represented "extremely liberal" and 1 "extremely conservative." The corresponding average among NES "expert" respondents was 3.55. Hence, our experts were more liberal than Lau and Redlawsk's. Our liberal and conservative experts might disagree on the candidates' issue positions, which might influence our estimates of the candidates' "true" positions. In fact, among our experts, the average difference between liberals and conservatives was only about 7%, while the standard deviations are nearly identical. Among liberal NES "experts," the standard deviation remains virtually unchanged, at 1.0. This suggests that even after controlling for ideological differences, our experts converged more than the NES "expert" respondents. Hence, our experts' estimated issue positions are likely more reliable than those of the NES "expert" respondents, as defined by Lau and Redlawsk.

7. A t-test indicates that the differences between the two groups are statistically insignificant.

8. The mean ideological score across our six research assistants was 4.83 on the identical 1–7 scale.

9. Presidential approval is closely related to partisanship, which is a strong predictor of vote choice. Thus one could argue that this factor ought not to be included in an algorithm intended to test the exogenous influence of short-term information flows. However, excluding incumbent approval from the algorithm has no material effect on our reported results (see our online appendix).

10. This pattern continued unabated in 2004. For instance, John Kerry and George W. Bush appeared on *Live with Regis and Kelly* and *Dr. Phil* (as well as *The Late Show*

with David Letterman, The Tonight Show with Jay Leno, and *The Daily Show with Jon Stewart*), while John McCain campaigned for Bush on *The View*.

11. For the weight, $\mu = 16.7$, while the median is six days. For NES interviews between September 5 and 11, the most recent prior E-talk show interview (a June Gore appearance on *Live with Regis and Kelly*) occurred between 88 and 94 days prior to the NES interview. This inflates the mean relative to the median.

12. Price and Zaller (1993) find that survey respondents tend to overstate their media consumption when asked about their "typical" consumption of broad media categories. The questions employed herein ask respondents to recall their consumption of specific programs during the prior week, thereby, according to Price and Zaller, partially mitigating this problem. Moreover, differences in the probabilities of holding an attitude, as media exposure varies, should not be affected by systematic overreporting of the level of exposure. Along these lines, Price and Zaller point out that self-reported media consumption questions are appropriate for studies (similar to ours) aimed at showing that exposure to different media have different attitudinal consequences.

13. Zaller (1992, 338) reports that the interviewer's assessment performed as well as most scales constructed from 10 to 15 direct knowledge questions. He also (Zaller 1985) looked for, but failed to find, any evidence of a systematic bias in favor of higher-status individuals, such as white males.

14. Self-reports of interest in politics or public affairs can be somewhat unreliable. Yet, the alpha reliability score for the four items included in the summary scale is .70, indicating that the scale is fairly reliable. A factor analysis indicates that the four items load strongly on a common underlying factor, with factor loadings ranging from .61 to .80. Moreover, the 4-item scale correlates more strongly with a variety of other factors related to political awareness—including "hard" news exposure, intent to vote (preelection) or having voted (post-election), caring about the outcome of the presidential election, political trust, external political efficacy, strength of partisanship, campaign participation, and campaign attention via national TV news—than do any of the individual items, or any other combination of them. (See our online appendix for reliability and validity test results.)

15. Among respondents who report consuming no daytime talk shows, 180 scored at least one standard deviation below the mean on our political awareness scale, while 229 scored at least one standard deviation above the mean. Among those who report consuming three or more daytime talk shows during the prior week, the corresponding numbers are 49 and 20 respondents below and above the mean level of political awareness, respectively.

16. For the hard news consumption scale, which is normalized to a 0–7 interval, $\mu = 3.37$ and $\sigma = 2.24$. We tested our hard news index using a variety of media consumption indicators, including local and morning TV news. None performed as well as our specification.

17. Excluding political participation modestly weakens the relationships. The only control variable that significantly affects the key relationships is strength of candidate preferences. This suggests that voters who feel strongly about a candidate have a relatively "strong" reason for doing so, and hence are unlikely to vote inconsistently, even if they are not particularly knowledgeable about politics.

18. For all reported results, we vary political awareness in the identical manner.

19. Some research—the so-called "sleeper effect" literature (see Gillig and Greenwald 1974)—suggests that individuals forget their own assessments of source unreliability

(i.e., discounting cues) more quickly than the actual content of media messages (or at least disassociate the former from the latter). If so, media effects would increase over time, net of the erosion of the discounting cue. Yet, psychologists have found these effects hold only when discounting cues are received *after* the message (Kumkale and Albarracin 2004), which is not the case in our study. (See online appendix for additional discussion of the sleeper effect argument.)

20. A similar weighting on the hard news indicator performed poorly, presumably because campaign coverage is virtually ubiquitous in the traditional news media.

21. We have not accounted for all possible correlates of voting consistently or all factors potentially related to the decision to consume talk shows, some of which may correlate with consistent voting. We have, however, sought to account for the *most likely* correlates of talk show viewing and consistent voting. All have proven either insignificant or largely orthogonal to our predicted relationships.

22. If we reformulate our political awareness scale to include only the two knowledge items (excluding interest and attention), while the overall pattern remains similar, low-awareness talk show consumers no longer fully "catch up" (see online data appendix). This may result from excluding the motivation element of our indicator, which presumably moderates the gap between "low" and "high" awareness.

7. Advantages and Disadvantages of Cognitive Heuristics in Political Decision Making

Richard R. Lau and David P. Redlawsk

The "cognitive revolution" may not have revolutionized research in political science to the extent it has in psychology, but it did provide a pat answer to one of the most troubling and persistent questions in the field: how a public that is notoriously uninterested and largely "innocent" of political matters can provide any control over public policy. The widespread ignorance of the general public about all but the most highly salient political events and actors is one of the best documented facts in all of the social sciences (e.g., Converse 1975; Delli Carpini and Keeter 1996; Kinder and Sears 1985). While almost everyone in the United States knows who the president is, barely half of the public can name even the most prominent members of the cabinet, and only a third can name their two senators or their representative in Congress.[1] Bare majorities know the simplest facts about how government works, and fewer still hold "real" attitudes toward even the most important political issues of the day (Converse 1964).

Yet this widespread ignorance flies in the face of what is required of citizens by classic democratic theory, which assumes that an informed and attentive public is necessary for democracy to work effectively. The problem is that democracy seems to be working pretty well, despite the "hands off" approach of most of its citizens. Lau and Redlawsk (1997) estimate that in recent U.S. presidential elections, about 75 percent of the voting public (which admittedly is barely half of the eligible electorate) voted "correctly," by which they mean "in accordance with what their fully informed preferences would be." And if we look not at individual opinions but at "aggregate" public opinion, that opinion appears far more stable and reasonable than the "minimalist" view of public opinion would suggest (Page and Shapiro 1989).

These seemingly contradictory findings are typically reconciled in one of two ways. Aggregate opinion can be much more stable and apparently "rational" than individual opinions, as long as error in individual opinions is assumed to be random (see Miller 1986; Wittman 1989). Even large proportions of random error "cancel out" in the aggregate, resulting in fairly efficient "collective choices." The benefits of aggregate decision making disappear once nonrandom error is introduced, however (Althaus 1998). Well-known biases in both what gets reported in the press (e.g., Gans 1979; Patterson 1980) and how people selectively perceive political information (Graber 1984; Kinder and Sears 1985) mean that a great deal of the error in individual opinions must be nonrandom.

Source: American Journal of Political Science 45, 4 (October (2001): 951–971.

The second, and in our opinion, more compelling way that widespread political ignorance can be reconciled with the view that democracies work reasonably well is by referring to the psychological literature on "cognitive heuristics" (e.g., Kahneman, Slovic, and Tversky 1982; Nisbett and Ross 1980). This literature is predicated on the view of humans as "limited information processors" or "cognitive misers" (Fiske and Taylor 1991; Lau and Sears 1986; Simon 1957, 1985) who have become quite adept at applying a variety of information "shortcuts" to make reasonable decisions with minimal cognitive effort in all aspects of their lives. Indeed, one of the reasons this line of argument is so compelling is that it explains the low levels of political information to begin with: it is not just in politics that people are faced with making decisions with far less than full information, and it is only reasonable to assume that people will apply to politics the same information shortcuts they have learned to use throughout life (see also Downs 1957).

This line of argument presumes two essential points. The first is that just about everyone can (and does) employ cognitive shortcuts in thinking about politics—that is, heuristic use is not limited to political experts, say, or any other nonrepresentative sample of the public—just as everyone must at times rely upon cognitive heuristics to comprehend nonpolitical aspects of their lives. The second point is that heuristic use at least partially *compensates for* a lack of knowledge about and attention to politics, so that citizens who are largely unaware of events in Washington nonetheless can make reasonably accurate political judgments. This view is so pervasive now in political science that we could probably refer to it as the new conventional wisdom.

As Bartels (1996) warns, however, it is far easier to *assume* that information shortcuts allow uninformed voters to act as if they were fully informed, than to demonstrate that in fact they do (see also Kuklinski and Quirk 2000, for a recent critique of this literature). Indeed, it is far easier to assume that voters use cognitive heuristics in the first place than to carefully define and actually demonstrate their use. In some real sense, "low information rationality" (Popkin 1991) has become a catch-all term, a *verbal* solution to tricky analytic problems that is consistent with certain stylized facts about the electorate, a verbal solution which allows researchers to move on to other problems they find more tractable (see also Sniderman 1993). Bartels' (1996) recent demonstration of very real and politically consequential effects of information per se on the political preferences of otherwise similar individuals illustrates the dangers of merely assuming that cognitive shortcuts somehow overcome most of the problems of cognitive limitations and political ignorance. Bartels' findings should also remind us of a possible liability of cognitive heuristics, one emphasized much more by psychologists than by political scientists: heuristics can sometimes introduce serious *bias*, along with cognitive efficiency, into decision making.

Believing that information matters is not inconsistent with believing that cognitive heuristics also matter, however. While we should not simply assume that cognitive heuristics are used (or are used effectively) by everyone, they may nonetheless be an important part of the decision-making processes of most voters. Heuristics may even improve the decision-making capabilities of some voters in some situations but hinder the capabilities of others. The trick is not assuming or guessing, but providing hard evidence. The proof, as they say, is in the pudding.

The remainder of this article is divided in four sections. The first will carefully define five cognitive heuristics that are widely used by voters during an election. By "heuristics," we mean problem-solving strategies (often employed automatically or unconsciously) which serve to "keep the information processing demands of the task within bounds" (Abelson and Levi 1985, 255). The reader should not expect any surprising "discoveries" here, for none of these heuristics will be new to students of voting behavior. Rather, discussion will focus on the extent to which various familiar influences on the vote decision act as heuristics, as cognitive shortcuts, the ways they provide cognitive "savings," and how their use might result in biased decision making.

Then we will present a relatively new research technique, a "dynamic process-tracing methodology," that is ideally suited for studying information processing and decision making during an election. Next, a series of experiments that we have conducted using this technique will be briefly described. Data from several of these experiments will then be used to address two major empirical questions: (1) What are the individual and contextual determinants of heuristic use? and (2) Does the use of heuristics affect (without prejudging whether it improves or hinders) the quality of political decision making? Our own expectations are expressed in the guise of formal hypotheses. The final section of the article will summarize what we have learned, try to place it in the context of related work within political science and psychology, and set out a research agenda for the future.

Five Common Cognitive Heuristics Employed by Voters

Political scientists have considered a number of different heuristics that citizens can employ to help make sense of politics (Brady and Sniderman 1985; Hamill, Lodge, and Blake 1985; Iyengar 1990; Jervis 1986; Lodge and Hamill 1986; Lupia 1994; Ottati 1990; Ottati, Fishbein, and Middlestadt 1988; Scholz 1998; Sniderman, Brody, and Tetlock 1991; Sniderman et al. 1986). We have grouped these into five major categories. The first and perhaps most important political heuristic is relying on a candidate's party affiliation (Lodge and Hamill 1986; Rahn 1993); a closely related heuristic is relying on a candidate's *ideology* for cognitive savings (Conover and Feldman 1986, 1989; Hamill, Lodge, and Blake 1985; Sniderman et al. 1986). Party and ideological stereotypes or schemata are among the richest and most widely shared in American politics. If the salient characteristics of a particular politician are consistent with or representative of the prototypic Republican, say, then voters may readily infer that she is for a strong defense, low taxes, against government intervention in the economy, against abortion, and so on; and will probably have a readily-available affective response (what Fiske 1986, calls a schema-based affective response) to the party label. Relying on stereotypes or schemata provides an obvious cognitive saving, to the extent that particular attributes (e.g., issue stands) are assumed "by default" rather than learned individually in each specific instance. They can also lead to obvious biases or errors, most dramatically when a particular candidate is mistakenly categorized as liberal when he is really moderate, say, but more subtly (and probably more frequently) when a general categorization is more or less correct but the presumed default values are not true in all instances (e.g., a pro-choice Republican like former Governor Whitman of New Jersey). Although these two heuristics are quite similar, party cues are somewhat simpler to grasp, and noticeably more prevalent on the American political scene. For theoretical reasons it will be convenient to treat them as distinct.[2]

Endorsements are another type of political information that has obvious heuristic value. In contrast to carefully considering each candidate's stands on all policies that affect women in a particular election, say, a voter could instead simply learn a relevant interest group's endorsement (like NOW) as a summary of all of the difficult candidate- and issue-specific information processing. In essence, voters who rely on endorsements defer the tough cognitive effort to trusted others. All that is necessary is to learn the candidate endorsed by a group, and one's own attitude toward the endorsing group, and an obvious and cognitively-efficient inference can be made (see Brady and Sniderman 1985; Sniderman, Brody, and Tetlock 1991). The more candidates in an election, and the larger the number of issues that should be considered, the greater the cognitive savings. Potential biases or errors in influence are introduced when the reason for the endorsement is different from what the voter expects, or when the actual candidate endorsed is unclear. Although we have no examples of them in our experiments, exactly the same cognitive efficiency is gained when voters rely on the endorsements or recommendations of respected individuals like former party leaders, prominent politicians or political commentators, or the editorial boards of trusted newspapers (see Carmines and Kuklinski 1990; Mondak 1993; Sniderman et al. 1986; Sniderman, Brody, and Tetlock 1991).[3]

Although it is typical to derogate political polls as merely "horse race" information, poll results provide another very important type of cognitive savings. Here the heuristic cues are coming from the electorate as a whole rather than a particular subsample of the electorate, and as such provide less specific information. But the information that is provided can produce tremendous reductions in cognitive efforts. Polls provide "*viability*" information, and particularly early in the primary season when there are typically many candidates competing for a nomination, polls can help the voter eliminate several alternatives from consideration. Reducing the choice set from four candidates to two, say, immediately provides a 50 percent reduction in the amount of information that must be processed. Seeing a candidate leading in the polls provides a type of "consensus information" that could motivate a voter who had previously rejected or ignored a candidate to more closely consider that candidate (McKelvey and Ordeshook

1985; Mutz 1992). Errors can occur, however, if one candidate is ahead in the polls, and a brief consideration of this candidate proves him to be "satisfactory" (Simon 1957). In such cases voters might be willing to support this candidate and refrain from further political information processing, thus never actually locating the "best" candidate for them.

The final political heuristic to be considered here is possibly the most important (or at least most frequently employed): *candidate appearance.* This heuristic is so important because it is not restricted to the political realm but is used in all aspects of our social lives. Visual images are so pervasive in the social world that researchers rarely consider their heuristic value. A single picture or image of a candidate provides a tremendous amount of information about that candidate, including gender, race, and age, and often general "likableness," which immediately brings many social stereotypes into play (Riggle et al. 1992).[4] Visual images can also trigger emotions, which can have great impact on candidate evaluation (Marcus 1988; Marcus and MacKuen 1993). People who know absolutely nothing about politics nonetheless know a great deal about other people and make social judgments of all types using these social stereotypes with great cognitive efficiency (Rosenberg, Kahn, and Tran 1991). Moreover, most people have schemas or stereotypes for political leaders (Miller, Wattenberg, and Malanchuk 1986), just as they do for the political parties, and thus Kahneman and Tversky's (1972) representativeness heuristic can easily come into play. Of course one can legitimately question the appropriateness or reliability of making vote decisions on the basis of such "person" judgments, and when certain images become disproportionately available (e.g., Bush getting sick in Japan, Dukakis riding around in a tank), even otherwise reliable person judgments could be mistaken.

Hypotheses

The growing conventional wisdom within political science suggests that cognitive heuristics are used more or less effectively by virtually everyone to help them "tame the tide" (Graber 1984) of political information. Three primary hypotheses test this conventional wisdom and shape the analyses to follow. To begin with, and consistent with the conventional view, we expect most voters to employ at least some of the political heuristics identified above in trying to make sense of a political campaign and decide how to vote. Cognitive heuristics are made necessary by severe limitations in human information processing. This "prediction" seems so noncontroversial that we will not unduly glorify it by calling it a hypothesis. We will, however, be presenting a new method for determining or "observing" heuristic use, and we will examine our new measure in light of this baseline prediction.

Just because everyone uses some cognitive heuristics does not mean that everyone uses all of them, or uses all of them equally effectively. We will examine a variety of individual difference factors as predictors of heuristic use, the most theoretically interesting of which is political sophistication or expertise. Sniderman, Brody, and Tetlock (1991, 24–25; see also Brady and Sniderman 1985) clearly predict an interaction between political sophistication and the use of a "likability" heuristic (similar to our endorsement heuristic), on the one hand, and the use of abstract ideology (part of our political schemata heuristic), on the other. According to Sniderman, Brody, and Tetlock, use of these particular heuristics is limited to the more sophisticated portion of the public. Other common heuristics (viability and certainly candidate appearance) are less likely to be related to political sophistication, however, given the pervasiveness of "horserace" information during major elections and the importance of various person perception mechanisms in all aspects of our lives. Thus our first hypothesis states that virtually all voters employ some common political heuristics during political campaigns. Consequently, individual difference factors should not be strongly related to their use, with the exception of political sophistication. Sophistication should be related to the use of certain cognitive heuristics in political decision making, particularly the Ideological Schema heuristic and the Endorsement heuristic.

Situational or contextual factors should also influence heuristic use. Because heuristics provide cognitive efficiency, they should be relied upon more heavily in more cognitively complex situations and/or for decisions that involve more difficult choices. Bodenhausen and Wyer (1985), for example, find that stereotypes (similar to our two political schema heuristics) are more likely to be employed in complex judgment tasks (see also Bodenhausen and Lichtenstein 1987), and Abelson and Levi provide numerous examples of "informational biases that serve a simplifying function . . . [being] amplified under overload conditions" (1985, 287). When a choice is relatively easy, on the other hand, there is less need to use cognitive shortcuts. Hence our second hypothesis suggests the more complex the information environment, and the more difficult the choice, the more voters should rely on political heuristics, all else equal.

Most importantly, we hypothesize that the use of cognitive heuristics generally will be associated with higher quality decisions. Our reasoning is simple: if heuristics did not "work," at least most of the time, they would not be developed and utilized. Somewhat paradoxically, however, we expect heuristic use to be *most* efficacious for political experts. This is paradoxical because if heuristics serve to compensate for a lack of knowledge, they should be less necessary for the politically sophisticated. But as Sniderman, Brody, and Tetlock put it, the "comparative advantage [of experts] is not that they have a stupendous amount of knowledge, but that they know how to get the most out of the knowledge they do possess" (1991, 24). In other words, not only will experts be more likely to *employ* certain cognitive heuristics, but they should also be more likely to employ them *appropriately*. Thus our third hypothesis suggests that the use of cognitive heuristics will interact with political sophistication to predict higher quality decisions. In general, the decision making of relative experts will benefit most from political heuristic use.

Method

We have developed a new technique for studying political information processing, which we call a *dynamic processing tracing* methodology (see Lau 1995; Lau and Redlawsk 1997, 2001b; Redlawsk 2001a). Our technique is a revision of the classic "information board" developed by behavioral decision theorists for studying decision making (see Carroll and Johnson 1990, for an overview). The standard information board presents decision makers with an *m by n* matrix, where the columns of the matrix are headed by the different alternatives (e.g., candidates) and the rows of the matrix are labeled with different attributes (e.g., issue stands, past experience, and so forth). None of the specific information is actually visible, however, and decision makers must actively choose what information they want to learn by clicking a box on a computer screen. The researcher can record and analyze what information was accessed, the order in which it was accessed, how long it was studied, and so on. The basic premise of process tracing studies is that it is best to study decision making *while the decision is being made.* A growing literature in psychology, marketing, and the interdisciplinary field of behavioral decision theory employs information boards as a basic research tool.[5]

While the standard decision board is a reasonable model for studying certain types of decision making, it is a poor analog to the vote decision for a number of important reasons. With a decision board the decision maker can access any information any time he or she wants, while campaigns have a dynamic quality about them such that information easily available today might be harder to find tomorrow and almost completely gone by the following day. All information on a standard information board is equally easy to access, while in a political campaign certain types of information (e.g., hoopla and horse race) are much easier to find than others (e.g., detailed issue stands). Decision makers must actively choose to learn everything they find out about the alternatives with a standard information board, but much information during political campaigns (e.g., political commercials) comes to us without any active effort by the decision maker to learn that information. And most importantly, decision making with an information board is far too "manageable," too controllable, too easy; while during a typical high level political campaign (e.g., presidential elections and many statewide races in the U.S.), voters are overwhelmed by far more information than they can possibly process. In many ways the static information board represents an "ideal world" for decision making that can be contrasted to voting in an actual political campaign.

Our dynamic process-tracing methodology retains the most essential features of the standard information board while making it a better analog of an actual political campaign. Our guiding principle was to devise a technique that would mimic crucial aspects of an actual election campaign while still providing a detailed record of the search process employed by voters. If a standard information board is artificial because it is static and therefore too "manageable" we overwhelm subjects with information. If the standard information board is unrealistic by making all information available whenever a subject wants it, we mimic the ongoing flow of information during a campaign, where information available today might be much harder to find tomorrow. If the standard information board is artificial because all different types of information are equally available, we model in a realistic way the relative ease or difficulty of finding different types of information during a campaign. And if a standard information board only allows for information that is actively accessed by the decision makers, we provide our decision makers with a good deal of relevant information "free of charge," without any active decision on their part to learn that information.

We accomplished these goals by designing a radically revised information board in which the information about the candidates scrolls down a computer screen rather than being in a fixed location. There are only a limited number of attribute labels (six) visible on the computer screen—and thus available for access—at any given time. Most of these labels include a candidate's name and the particular information about that candidate that would be revealed if this label were "accessed" (e.g., "Martin's political experience;" "Walker's stand on defense spending"). The rate of scrolling is such that most people can read approximately two labels before the positions change. Subjects can "access" (i.e., read) the information behind the label by clicking a mouse. Thus this methodology combines the printed nature of information presentation in newspapers with the relatively uncontrollable order of information availability of electronic media. The scrolling continues while subjects process the detailed information they have accessed, so that typically there is a completely new screen when subjects return to the scrolling—thus mimicking the dynamic, ongoing nature to the political campaign.

The scrolling format of the information presentation achieves two of our goals, by making only a small subset of the information available at any one time, and by making the entire decision-making task much less "manageable." We also wanted to make some types of information "harder" to get than others and accomplished this by varying the probabilities that specific types of information would appear on the screen.[6] Finally, at periodic intervals the computer screen is taken over by a twenty-second political advertisement for one of the candidates in the campaign. Voters can carefully watch these commercials or avert their eyes while they are on the screen, but they cannot gather any other information relevant to the campaign while the commercial is on.[7]

Subjects

We have run four experiments with the dynamic process-tracing methodology described above, one of which also included a standard static information board. Three of the experiments used paid volunteers (most subjects were donating their $20 payment to a voluntary organization to which they belonged) and one used unpaid volunteers. All subjects had to be eligible voters (American citizens above the age of 18), with the only other restriction that no one currently attending college could participate in the experiment.

The 657 subjects who participated in the four experiments are not meant to be a representative sample, but they do comprise a broad pool of adult citizens. They ranged in age from 18 to 84 with a mean of 45. Fifty-four percent were female, and 16 percent were nonwhite; 28 percent had at most a high school degree, while 47 percent of the subjects were college graduates. Fifty-nine percent of the sample were currently employed, 5 percent unemployed, 23 percent retired, and 13 percent homemakers. In terms of religious preference, 35 percent were Catholics, 17 percent Jewish, 25 percent Protestants, and 11 percent professed some "other" religious preference. When it came to politics, 38 percent of the sample identified with the Democratic Party, and 27 percent identified with the Republican Party.

Procedure

The basic experimental paradigm has subjects "experience" and "vote in" a primary election involving multiple candidates in each party, and a subsequent general election involving one candidate from each party. We created a scenario for a mock presidential election involving 2–4 Democratic and 2–4 Republican candidates. Subjects "registered" to vote in either the Democratic or Republican primary, learned as much about any of the candidates as they wanted (or could, given the time and information available) during the primary campaign, "voted" for one of the candidates from their party, evaluated all candidates in the primary on a 100-point feeling thermometer, answered a few questions about the difficulty of the decision they had just made, learned which two candidates will be running in the fall campaign, gathered as much additional information about these two candidates as they wanted (or could) during the "general election" campaign, voted for one of them, evaluated the remaining candidates again on feeling thermometers, attributed a few issue stands to them, and answered the questions about the difficulty of the general election choice. Subjects also received an unexpected memory task where they were asked to recall as much as they could remember about the two candidates running in the general election campaign.

Before the campaigns began, subjects completed a fairly standard political attitudes questionnaire designed to measure their political preferences (crucial for determining which candidates they "should" support) and their general level of political sophistication. Figure 1 of Lau and Redlawsk (1997, 588) summarizes the typical experimental procedure, which on average lasted about one hour and forty-five minutes.

The candidates were all designed to be very realistic (e.g., they were dispersed along the ideological spectrum appropriate for their party, they were politically experienced, they were all at least 45 years old, etc.), although we were careful not to make any of the candidates appear too much like some actual individual.

Creating mock candidates provides crucial control over differences between subjects in prior knowledge of actual politicians. No one had any knowledge of any candidate before the mock campaign began, other than what might be inferred from, say, party affiliation.

Results

Direct Measures of Heuristic Use

Few studies of cognitive heuristics, whether in the political or any other realm, have direct measures of the use of the hypothesized heuristic. More typically, the availability of some cue is manipulated in a simple experiment, and heuristic use is inferred if hypothesized differences in some dependent variable occur (e.g., Carmines and Kuklinski 1990; Iyengar 1990; Mondak 1993; Quattrone and Tversky 1988). Alternatively, a significant regression weight in some model of impression formation or attitude change will be taken as evidence of heuristic processing (e.g., Brady and Sniderman 1985; Conover and Feldman 1986, 1989; Iyengar 1990; Lau 1986, 1989; Sniderman, Brody, and Tetlock 1991).

With process-tracing methodologies, however, hypothesized information-processing strategies can be *directly* observed and measured. We contend that *if a decision maker is employing a particular heuristic,* then in general *information relevant to that heuristic should be sought out early and often.* For example, if endorsements are to be of maximum use to a decision maker, they ought to be accessed as soon as they become available, and many of them ought to be examined. Particular types of information were determined a priori to be indicative of the use of a given heuristic, and we measured how early information within each category was accessed, the proportion of all available items within that category that were accessed, and the proportion of all accessed items that fell into that particular category, separately for information processing during the primary and general election campaigns.[8] We then formed summary scales of the use of the different types of political heuristics in the primary and general election campaigns by standardizing and then averaging together the three measures, after the priority measures were reversed so that early access of items within a category was scored high. We will have more to say about equating information search with heuristic use below.

The first four columns of Table 7-1 present various indicators of the extent to which voters in our experiments employed the five political heuristics discussed above. The first column shows the percent of subjects who examined at least two items categorized a priori as indicating heuristic use. This is a minimal standard of "use." The second column is perhaps the best indicator of the pervasiveness of heuristic use during our mock election campaigns, because it shows the average proportion of items actually selected during the mock campaigns that were examples of the different types of political heuristics. An average of

Table 7-1   Measures of Political Heuristic Use

	% Using Heuristic at All	Mean % of All Accessed Info. Coming from Category	% Unique Information from Category Ever Examined		Scale Reliability
			Mean	Std.Dev.	
Partisan Schema	98%	9.2%	83%	22%	.63
Ideology Schema	93%	4.6%	63%	31%	.77
Endorsement Heuristic	97%	10.4%	42%	23%	.82
Viability Heuristic (Polls)	98%	12.1%	37%	22%	.86
Candidate Appearance Heuristic	95%	6.7%	69%	29%	.73

Note: The first column reports the percent of all subjects accessing an item from the appropriate category (at least *twice,* to control for accidental accessing and "sampling"). The second column reports the percent of all accessed items that fell into a particular category, irrespective of how often any particular bit of information is accessed. The third column reports the mean percent of all relevant unique items within a category that were accessed at least once, while the fourth column reports the standard deviation of this measure. This last measure does not "double count" items that were accessed more than once, whereas data in the second column allows for such double counting. Table entries in the last column are Cronbach's alpha from the scales built to measure heuristic use. Data are limited to subjects in the more realistic dynamic scrolling conditions of the experiments. N varies between 550 and 555.

43 percent of the items selected came from one of the five categories of political heuristics. It is important to keep these numbers in perspective, however. One of the reasons the political heuristics we have identified here are so useful is that information relevant to them is so widely available—an availability modeled by the stochastic algorithm of our computer program. If all subjects had chosen information randomly, the data in the second column of Table 7-1 would not be very different. Nonetheless our baseline prediction is clearly supported: virtually all voters employ cognitive heuristics at least some of the time in making their vote decisions.

More indicative of how important the different heuristics were to individual subjects is data in the next two columns, which reports the mean percent and variability of the unique information considered within each category. On average subjects examined 42 percent of all of the group endorsements, for example, and 37 percent of the poll results that concerned candidates from their party in the primary and the two candidates during the general election. More important analytically, the variance of all five of these measures includes the full range of the potential scale, from not accessing *any* information relevant to a heuristic, to finding and accessing *all* of the relevant information. The internal consistency (Cronbach's alpha) of the summary scales of each type of heuristic use is reported in the last column of Table 7-1. The scale reliabilities vary between .63 and .86, very respectable numbers for relatively short scales.

Political Sophistication and Heuristic Use

It would certainly appear from the data reported in Table 7-1 that most voters in our experiments utilized the five political heuristics at least some time during their decision-making task. But a more complete investigation is warranted. In particular, Hypothesis 1 suggests that more politically sophisticated voters will be more likely to employ an Ideological Schema and the Endorsement Heuristic. The top panel of Table 7-2 shows the results of an analysis where the summary measures of use of each political heuristic are regressed on a comprehensive measure of political sophistication comprised of separate indicators of Political Knowledge, Political Behavior, Political Interest, Political Discussion, and Media Use (see Lau and Erber 1985); plus various demographic variables and standard political beliefs as controls. The bottom half of the table reports a similar analysis, keeping the different components of sophistication distinct.

As predicted by Hypothesis 1, political experts are more likely to use an Ideology Schema ($p < .05$, one-tailed) and the Endorsement Heuristic ($p < .001$). In the former case it is Political Knowledge and Following Politics in the Media which are particularly important, while in the latter case it is Political Knowledge and self-professed Political Interest.[9] Although we could find no prior literature suggesting this might be the case (and thus not formally specified in Hypothesis 1), it follows logically that if almost everyone uses political heuristics, but certain political heuristics are more likely to be employed by experts, then other political heuristics may be more the province of those low in political sophistication. Our data suggest two decent possibilities, the Candidate Appearance Heuristic and the Party Heuristic (although in the latter case the results are not quite statistically significant). All told, our data provide strong support for Hypothesis 1. We will control for the effects of political sophistication in the remainder of the analyses.

Situational Factors Determining Political Heuristics Use

The second hypothesis holds that voters will be more likely to employ cognitive heuristics in more difficult choice situations—that is, in situations with greater cognitive demands. The strongest test of this hypothesis comes from an experiment that varied the basic presentation format: in one condition the experiment utilized the classic static information board (which can be viewed as an ideal world for decision making), while the second condition used the much more challenging (and realistic) dynamic scrolling procedure described above. Our hypothesis clearly predicts greater use of cognitive heuristics with the dynamic rather than static procedure.[10]

To test this hypothesis we conducted a multivariate analysis of variance (MANOVA) in which the Static-Dynamic presentation format and Political Sophistication (dichotomized at its median) were the independent variables, and the five heuristic-use variables, summed across the primary and general election

Table 7-2 Effect of Political Sophistication on Use of Political Heuristics

Variable	Party Schema		Ideology Schema		Endorsement Heuristic		Viability Heuristic		Candidate Appearance Heuristic	
	B	SE B	B	SE B	B	SE B	B	SE B	B	SE B
Analysis 1										
Overall Measure of Sophistication	−5.31	(3.45)	9.87@	(5.34)	24.32***	(5.59)	4.30	(5.52)	−10.83*	(5.40)
Analysis 2										
Knowledge	−1.38	(3.26)	17.02***	(5.04)	14.38**	(5.32)	−2.97	(5.25)	−6.35	(5.16)
Behavior	.94	(2.25)	−.06	(3.49)	2.64	(3.68)	−2.56	(3.63)	−5.44	(3.57)
Discussion	−2.96	(2.44)	−2.39	(3.77)	−.48	(3.98)	−4.07	(3.93)	−1.52	(3.86)
Interest	−3.94	(2.61)	−3.40	(4.04)	9.49*	(4.27)	2.46	(4.21)	.43	(4.14)
Media Use	−1.19	(3.08)	10.56**	(4.76)	−.61	(5.03)	12.62**	(4.96)	−.88	(4.87)

@$p < .05$ (one-tailed) *$p < .05$ **$p < .01$ ***$p < .001$

Note: Table entries are unstandardized regression weights (with standard errors in parentheses), from two separate sets of analyses, the first where the summary measures of heuristic use are regressed on a comprehensive measure of political sophistication, the second where the same dependent variables are regressed on separate indicators of the constituent parts of political sophistication. All regressions also include controls for gender, race, age, education, family income, religiosity, and strength of partisanship and ideology. All variables have a 1-point range. Analyses are limited to the more realistic "dynamic scrolling" presentation format. N = 482.

Figure 7-1 Effect of Dynamic/Static Manipulation and Political Sophistication on Heuristic Use

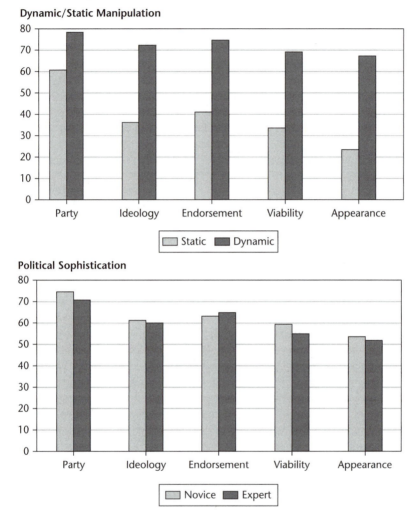

Dynamic/Static Manipulation

Political Sophistication

campaigns, were the dependent variables. The main effects of both the Static-Dynamic manipulation—multivariate $F(5,158) = 127.31, p < .001$—and Political Sophistication—multivariate $F(5,158) = 2.31, p < .05$—were statistically significant. As can be seen in the top half of Figure 7-1, all five of the political heuristics were much more likely to be employed when information was presented via the more realistic, and more cognitively difficult, dynamic scrolling format, compared to the ideal world of a static information board. All five of the univariate

Figure 7-2 Effect of Number of Candidates Manipulation on Heuristic Use

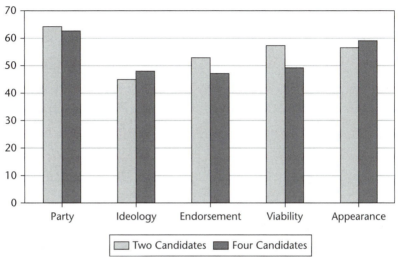

F tests were also highly significant. In contrast, differences in heuristic use between those high and low in political sophistication (displayed in the bottom half of Figure 7-1) were quite modest in magnitude and, as already seen in Table 7-2, mixed in direction. Only the Viability Heuristic produced a significant univariate *F* tests for sophistication.[11]

A second operationalization of task complexity is the number of alternatives in the choice set. Several of our experiments randomly manipulated the number of candidates running in the primary of the party in which the subject "registered" to vote. A choice is relatively simple with only two candidates, but much more complex with four candidates.[12] We again conducted a MANOVA with use of the five political heuristics during the primary election campaign as the dependent variables and Number of Candidates in the subject's party and Political Sophistication as the independent variables. The effect of Political Sophistication is essentially the same here as in Figure 7-1, albeit slightly weaker statistically. Of more immediate interest is the Number of Candidates manipulation, which was statistically significant, multivariate $F(5,356) = 4.71$, $p < .001$. An examination of the group means of the different dependent variables, however, shown in Figure 7-2, reflects a fairly complicated pattern of results. Subjects were slightly (and nonsignificantly) more likely to employ the Ideology and Candidate Appearance heuristics in the four candidate condition than the two candidate condition, but significantly more likely to employ the Endorsement and Viability heuristics in the two candidate condition. Clearly, something more than the need for cognitive efficiency is determining these results. Notice that there were only trivial differences in the use of the Party heuristic across conditions in this campaign—but of course party is of little use in distinguishing between candidates running in a primary election, at least after candidates belonging to the different parties are sorted out.

Together, these results are more complicated than Hypotheses 2 predicts. While voters of all stripes employ cognitive heuristics, they do not all equally appreciate the difficulty of the choice situation they face and revise their information-processing strategies to compensate for that difficulty. It is important to note that sophistication does *not* help explain any of these conflicting findings. More generally, the data on heuristic use suggest that cognitive heuristics may not be a panacea for the broad lack of information and interest in politics displayed by the average citizen they have been assumed to be. Heuristics may not be used in a cognitively most efficient manner by everyone, even the most politically sophisticated voters.

Is "Information Acquisition" the Same Thing as "Heuristic Use"?

We have argued that directly observing and measuring heuristic use is superior to indirectly inferring heuristic processing from some simple experimental manipulation or significant regression weight. Still one could ask with our operationalizations of heuristic use, is *gathering* relevant information the same thing as *using* a certain heuristic? At one level the answer is obvious: no one can "use" a heuristic if they do not know it is applicable, e.g., if they do not *know* the party affiliation of candidate(s). But we are not employing simple dichotomous operationalizations of heuristic use; frequency and time of information acquisition are also part of our measures. And even with simple information acquisition, how do we know the information is actually being *processed* and *used* in a heuristic manner?

The political science literature provides almost no guidance on this issue, and the psychology literature is little better. However, our experiments gathered a great deal of information that can be used to "flesh out" just what heuristic processing is (or ought to be), and to simultaneously validate our measures of heuristic use. We do not have the space to go into great detail here, but Table 7-3 provides a sense of the type of evidence we have gathered for three of our heuristics.[13] To begin with, heuristic use tends to be positively correlated with memory for relevant information. These positive correlations provide evidence that relevant information is at least *processed*. More telling for current purposes, however, would be evidence that employing heuristics allow voters to process information *efficiently*, to *reduce* information processing demands in some domains. That is the key.

After asking subjects to remember as much as they could about the two candidates in the general election campaign in our last experiment, we asked them to place the candidates on five different issue scales. Controlling on general Political Sophistication, both the Ideology and Endorsement heuristics—but not Party—are associated with more accurate placement of the two candidates on the issues in general. Even more telling (again controlling on Political Sophistication), all

Table 7-3 Further Validity Evidence for Measures of Political Heuristics

	Party Schema	Ideology Schema	Endorsement Heuristic
Memory for Relevant Items	r = .25***	r = .02	r = .22***
Accuracy of Perception of Issue Stands	NS	r = .16**	r = .17**
Accuracy of Inference Absent Actual Knowledge	b = 11.44**	b = 10.73**	b = 4.62*
Substitutes for Information Search in 4-Candidate Primary Condition	NS	b = -1.32**	b = -2.82***

*$p < .10$ **$p < .05$ ***$p < .01$

Note: Data in the first two rows of the table are partial correlations between the measure of heuristic use and the relevant criteria, controlling for Political Sophistication and Total Item Search. "Accuracy" in rows 2 and 3 is defined as agreement with experts' ratings of the candidates' actual issue stands. Data in the third row reports the regression weight for the interaction between the heuristic of interest and *not* actually accessing a candidate's issue stand, thus requiring inference. In the fourth row we report the regression weight for the interaction between heuristic use and the 2- or 4-candidate manipulation, where the dependent variable is the average number of issue stands accessed for in-party candidates. All regressions also controlled for Political Sophistication. Because these various criteria were not available in every experiment, N is 285 in the first row, 110 in the second and third rows, and 364 in the last row.

three of these heuristics were associated with more accurate placement of candidates on issues *in the absence of actually learning the candidates' stand on the issues.* Ideology and Endorsements—but again, not Party—also tend to *substitute* for accessing detailed issue information in the more taxing four-candidate primary condition, in that they were associated with less accessing of specific issue stands per candidate. Together, the data presented in Table 7-3 indicates that our measures of political heuristics truly are associated with heuristic processing of information. We know of no similar evidence in the political science literature.

Effect of Political Heuristics on Correct Voting

The third hypothesis states that use of political heuristics will be associated with higher quality decisions primarily among political experts. Defining "higher quality" decisions can be a very tricky matter. Fortunately, we can rely on the definitions presented earlier by Lau and Redlawsk (1997). We developed two techniques for determining whether subjects voted "correctly" in our experiments, one determined by the subjects themselves after a very thorough examination of all information available about the competing candidates (including much information the subjects had not actually seen when they made their vote choice); the second technique a more normative, objectively determined criteria. Because the subjective measure is only available for the primary election from two of the four experiments, but the normative measure is available for all elections in all experiments, we rely on the latter measure here.[14]

Our normative measure of correct voting is based on an approximation of how people could naively or intuitively go about making the vote decision. From the questionnaire filled out by subjects before the experiment began, we know where subjects stand on the issues, what groups they like, what party they identify with, and so on. We also know, objectively, where the candidates stand on the issues, what groups endorse which candidates, what party a candidate belongs to, and how attractive the candidates' appearance and personalities are.[15] We determine empirically what categories or types of information are important in the decision calculus of each voter by assuming that if a particular attribute (say, a candidate's stand on crime) was only considered for a single candidate, it was probably the product of simple curiosity, random error, or "sampling" but then rejection of this type of information, and therefore was not at all important in the voter's decision calculus. If a particular attribute was examined for two or more of the available candidates, on the other hand, we assume this type of information *was* an important part of the voter's decision calculus and is therefore a relevant consideration about every candidate. The favorableness of each individual attribute was rescaled to range between -1 at its most unfavorable (e.g., endorsement by a group the voter dislikes) to +1 at its most favorable (e.g., complete agreement with a candidate on an issue), and then a "normative naive" evaluation of each candidate was computed by averaging together the different considerations. This evaluation is "naive" in that it is based on the voter's *own* political values and preferences, and their *own* determination of what specific information is important to them. But this measure is "normative" in that it is also based on an objective, externally-determined evaluation of the candidates, and on the normative judgment that voters *should have* considered the same (important) information about all candidates in the choice set. A "correct" vote decision is then defined as a vote for the candidate with the highest "normative naive" evaluation. See the appendix of Lau and Redlawsk (1997) for more details on the construction of this measure.

There is one further complication. Although it is clear how to determine the "correct" choice with such a procedure, it is not so clear what to do about "incorrect" choices.[16] Should they all be treated equally, or should they somehow be scaled to reflect the egregiousness of the error? It does not seem right to treat voting for the worst possible candidate the same as voting for one that is only slightly inferior to the "best" possible candidate. We decided to employ a simple dichotomous "correct" or "not correct" dependent variable, but to create a "difficulty of choice set" independent variable to control for these other considerations. This control variable was created by computing the average difference between the naive normative evaluation of the best candidate in the choice set and the evaluation of each individual alternative in the choice set. When the alternatives are all evaluated very similarly, this average difference will be quite small, and it should be relatively difficult to pick out the best alternative. When the alternatives are evaluated quite differently, on the other hand, the average difference score will be much larger, and it should be relatively easier to pick out the best alternative. Our measure of the difficulty of the choice set is then the reciprocal of this average difference score, so that the more difficult choice sets have the highest scores on this control variable. This variable should be negatively correlated with the probability of a correct vote, all else equal.

We then specified logistic regression equations in which the dichotomous correct vote dependent variable was regressed on (1) the Difficulty of Choice Set control variable just described; (2) experimental manipulations of Task Complexity; (3) the comprehensive measure of Political Sophistication described above; (4) a summary measure of use of Political Heuristics,[17] dichotomized at its median; and finally (5) interactions between the last three factors. Because Hypothesis 3 argues that heuristic use will aid decision making primarily among politically sophisticated voters, we pay particular attention to the interaction between political sophistication and heuristic use on the probability of making a correct decision.

Our analysis considers the probability of a correct vote in the primary election of the experiments which manipulated the number of candidates in the choice set. The results of the logistic regression are shown in Table 7-4. As expected, subjects were much less likely to vote correctly in the more difficult four candidate condition than the two candidate condition ($p < .001$), and controlling on this manipulation, somewhat less likely to vote correctly when the choice set was more difficult ($p < .07$, one-tailed). Neither political sophistication nor heuristic use had a main effect in the analysis. But as predicted by Hypothesis 3, there was a significant two-way interaction between sophistication and heuristic use ($p < .01$). The nature of this interaction is shown in Figure 7-3. Cognitive heuristics are a great aid to the decision making of relatively sophisticated voters,

Table 7-4   Effect of Political Sophistication and Use of Heuristics on Correct Voting

Variable	B		S.E.
Constant	.40		.29
# of Candidates Manipulation	−2.04**		.42
Difficulty of Choice	−1.08		.71
Political Sophistication	−.21		.31
Heuristic Use	−.20		.38
Manipulation × Sophistication	.46		.37
Manipulation x Heuristics	.39		.60
Heuristics × Sophistication	.92*		.37
−2 * Log Likelihood		285.74	
Model Chi-Square (7 df)		56.21**	
Percent Correctly Classified		69.2%	
N		254	

$^*p < .01$ $^{**}p < .001$

Note: Table entries are logistic regression coefficients.

Figure 7-3   Effect of Political Sophistication and Heuristic Use on Correct Voting in Primary Election Campaign

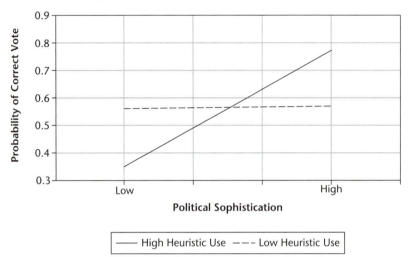

increasing the probability of their making a correct decision by 20 percent. But this advantage to the most sophisticated voters is almost exactly balanced by a comparable *disadvantage* for relatively unsophisticated voters, whose probability of making a correct vote decreases by almost 21 percent when they rely heavily upon cognitive heuristics. As Hypothesis 3 predicts, then, the decisions of more sophisticated voters are often helped by employing cognitive heuristics, but less sophisticated voters may actually end up making lower quality decisions if they employ those same heuristics (albeit, in a less efficient manner). Seen from another perspective, *political sophistication absent heuristic use contributes little to better decision making.* Only in combination with heuristic use does sophistication help improve decision making. What political sophistication brings a voter is knowledge of how the political world is typically structured, and the ability to make clear inferences from heuristic cues.[18]

*Dis*advantages of Heuristic Use

That very knowledge could work against sophisticated voters if the world (i.e., a political campaign) is not structured in the typical manner. One final manipulation varied the stereotypic nature of the outparty candidate (that is, the candidate from the party in which the subject did not "register") running in the general election campaign in one of our experiments. In the stereotypic condition this candidate was a moderate slightly to the left (if a Democrat) or right (if a Republican) of center. In the nonstereotypic condition the outparty candidate took a very liberal stand on some issues, a very conservative stand on others, and a moderate stand on the remaining issues. On average, the objective issue stands of the stereotypic and nonstereotypic candidates were indistinguishable (and their qualifications for the presidency on other dimensions were quite comparable), but the ideological range of views expressed by the nonstereotypic candidate was much greater—so much greater, in fact, that this candidate might very well take several issue stands that a voter preferred to the stands of the inparty candidate.[19]

Table 7-5 presents the results of an analysis in which correct voting is regressed on the difficulty of choice control variable, the nonstereotypic candidate manipulation, political sophistication, use of a party heuristic, and interactions between the last three factors. We focus on use of the party heuristic because the nonstereotypic candidate violated *partisan* stereotypes. The positive .72 interaction between Heuristic Use and Sophistication suggests that, as we have seen already, political heuristics are particularly efficacious for politically sophisticated voters—at least when the candidates conform to the expected norms of their parties. This interaction is not quite statistically significant at conventional levels ($p < .09$, one-tailed).[20] As shown by the significant three-way interaction between the experimental manipulation, political sophistication, and heuristic use, however, this advantage disappears when nonstereotypic candidates are running in the campaign. Now sophisticated voters who employ heuristics are noticeably less likely to vote correctly. As Figure 7-4 illustrates, when the outparty candidate is stereotypic (as is typically the case), using heuristics increases the probability of a correct vote among sophisticated voters from about .55 to .81. But when the outparty candidate is nonstereotypic, using heuristics

Table 7-5 Heuristic Use in Inappropriate Situations

Variable	B	S.E.
Constant	.41	.32
Nonstereotypic Manipulation	.29	.46
Political Sophistication	−.43	.38
Difficulty of Choice	.12	.72
Party Heuristic Use	−.27	.43
Nonstereotypic × Heuristic	.23	.65
Nonstereotypic × Sophistication	1.41*	.57
Heuristic × Sophistication	.72	.53
Nonstereotypic × Heuristic × Sophistication	−2.39*	.81
−2 × Log Likelihood	224.95	
Model Chi-Square (8 df)	12.75	
Percent Correctly Classified	62.9%	
N	178	

*$p < .01$

Note: Table entries are logistic regression coefficients. Dependent variable is voting correctly.

Figure 7-4   When Relying on Heuristics Hurts the Decision Making of Politically Sophisticated Voters

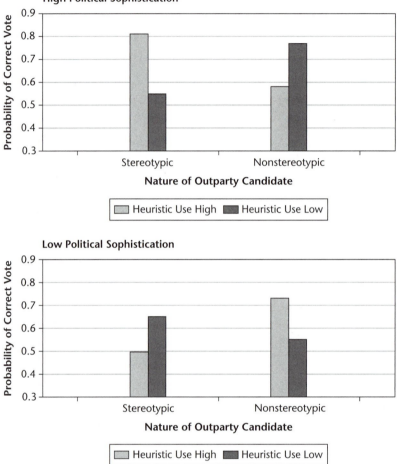

actually *decreases* the probability of a correct vote from .77 to .58 among sophisticated voters. The effects of heuristic use are opposite in direction, and noticeable smaller in magnitude, among unsophisticated voters.

Discussion

To summarize our most important findings, cognitive heuristics are not a panacea for all the ills of popular democracies. Although the five political heuristics considered here were used by almost everyone (at least outside of the "ideal world" of a static information board), they did not substitute for political sophistication in predicting correct voting. In fact, heavy reliance on political heuristics actually made decision making less accurate among those low in political sophistication. Only relative experts appear to be generally helped in their decision making by using heuristics. Thus our results should give pause to those who assert that heuristics are the answer to the problems of low information voting. We join in Bartels' (1996) skepticism that voters who are relatively unaware of politics can make decisions as if they had full information, simply by employing cognitive shortcuts. Ironically, heuristics are most valuable to those who might in fact need them least. Sophisticated voters, who understand the political environment, can use these shortcuts to their advantage. But even they can be misled when the political environment is not structured according to their prior expectations.

These conclusions are based on our being able to directly observe the information processing of voters. This increased observational power comes at a cost, however, in the realism of our experimental setting. While our simulation captures crucial aspects of modern election campaigns, we would not pretend that it captures all of them. As in any experiment, subjects in our "campaigns" knew they were being studied, which might alter their decision-making strategies in unknown ways. Voters were unfamiliar with all of the candidates before the election began, which at best is not the case when an incumbent is running for reelection. The "campaign" itself lasted little more than half an hour, leaving no time for reflection on any of the information learned about any of the candidates. All information about all of the candidates was obtained from a computer—a highly unusual experience for subjects (at least when we began running these experiments)—and all information was obtained in social isolation, without the opportunity to talk about the candidates and their views with other people. Thus in certain very important ways, the "mundane realism" of our campaign simulation was fairly low.

We would not argue with this assessment; our dynamic process-tracing methodology, as with any research technique, involves real tradeoffs between internal and external validity. On the other hand, we would argue that information boards are far less intrusive methods for conducting process tracing research than the alternatives ("think aloud" protocols, or monitoring eye movements; see Abelson and Levi 1985). As more and more people have access to computers and the internet at work and at home, and as more and more of us turn more regularly to internet sources for our political information, what five years ago was a relatively unusual manner of obtaining political information may soon become the norm. Furthermore, what our research design lacked in mundane realism, it made up for in *experimental realism* (Aronson, Wilson, and Brewer 1998). That is, with few exceptions subjects in our experiments truly cared about the mock election campaigns and took the task of deciding who to vote for quite seriously. Some subjects cheered if their candidate "won" their party's primary campaign, and many expressed disappointment when, at the end of the experiment, we did not tell them who "won" the general election campaign. During the debriefing we asked how realistic the candidates seemed, and only three subjects (of over 600 run) responded "Very Unrealistic."[21] Thus while we should never forget that our data come from subjects participating in a controlled laboratory experiment, we believe that our experimental procedure was sufficiently engaging, and the decision task facing voters sufficiently realistic, that our results should be take seriously. Certainly the great majority of our subjects took the task seriously.

Cognitive heuristics are not the only psychological mechanism used by people to "stem the tide" of political information, of course, and it would be remiss of us to not mention the work of Lodge and his colleagues at Stony Brook (Lodge, McGraw, and Stroh 1989; Lodge, Steenbergen, and Brau 1995). Lodge and colleagues argue that people typically form impressions of politicians by continually updating a "running tally" evaluation. Once any new information has been processed and the tally updated, the information itself can be (and often is) forgotten. Thus Lodge and his colleagues argue that the vote decision is often much better "informed" than would by inferred from the low levels of political information that can typically be recalled by everyday citizens. Although we do not agree with every aspect of the online model (see Lau and Redlawsk 2001b; Redlawsk 2001b), it seems clear that evaluations of political candidates are based on exposure to and the processing of much more information than can typically be recalled at some later date. Indeed, our dynamic process-tracing methodology is another technique for providing evidence to test the online model. The point we want to make here is to acknowledge that remembering the implications of some new information about a candidates (i.e., remembering the updated running tally) but forgetting the details of that new information is another way in which cognitively limited information processors cope with an overwhelmingly rich social environment.

We should also mention several relatively new theories within social psychology which distinguish between two largely distinct routes to attitude change (Chaiken 1980, 1987; Petty and Cacioppo 1986). Such theories should be of great relevance to political scientists, for what is a political campaign other than an elaborate, often quite expensive attempt at mass attitude change? According to these theories, when the recipient of a message is highly motivated (e.g., the message is personally relevant) and able (they have the intelligence and background knowledge to place the message in an appropriate context, and the immediate context is not too distracting) to think about the message, they will engage in relatively more effortful, systematic or "central route" processing of the message. This is the type of processing that most candidates (and most political scientists) wish citizens would engage in during a political campaign—but we know very few do. On the other hand, when motivation and/or ability are low, relatively more shallow, "heuristic," or "peripheral route" processing will occur. The latter process better describes most political information processing, and the simple heuristics that are studied in these attitude change experiments (e.g., experts are usually correct; someone arguing against her own self-interest really believes what she is saying) serve some of the same functions as the political heuristics examined in our study.

There is one important difference between how attitude theorists think about heuristic or peripheral route processing, however, and how we think about the political heuristics we have studied: how actively people seek out information relevant to the heuristics they do employ. Our method (with the exception of the candidate appearance heuristic) generally requires voters to actively decide to use any particular heuristic, while the attitude change theories under consideration here view heuristic processing as a much more automatic, almost unconscious "default" type of processing when motivation is low. This difference is more apparent than real, however, driven more by methodological than theoretical considerations. Even subjects in the "heuristic" or "peripheral route" conditions of these attitude change experiments must somehow learn that the communicator was attractive, say, or an expert. These experiments simply do not give subjects the option of not "accessing" this information, which from our perspective makes it appear much more "automatic" than in fact may be the case.

More recently political scientists have begun to examine the information environment in which processing occurs as a determinant of shifting processing modes. Whether the cause is the processor's emotional state of mind derived from an assessment of the relative familiarity and safety of the environment (Marcus, Neuman, and MacKuen 2000; Marcus and MacKuen, 1993) or the motivated reasoner's unexpected encounter with information that is affectively incongruent with previous expectations (Lodge and Taber 2000; Redlawsk 2001b), information processing may shift from routine, relatively thoughtless processing to processing under heightened awareness, where information is considered more carefully. In the agitated emotional state of mind as is characterized by anxiety, processors are expected to pay more attention to information, and would presumably be less likely to use heuristic-based processing. Thus, for some voters, our experimental environment might not represent the political environment in which they operate, in that it is not embedded in an environment of anxiety or uncertainty. We might expect that if the environment were emotionally challenging that heuristic use would be lessened. Likewise, encountering negative information about a liked candidate (or positive information about a disliked candidate) might also cause the voter to stop and think, at least temporarily focusing processing more carefully than otherwise would be the case, and thus decreasing reliance on heuristics. However, we believe that the political environment for most voters, most of the time, is not one of high emotional anxiety, given that the average citizen pays relatively little attention to politics in the first place. And the likelihood that motivated reasoners will actually encounter very much incongruent information is relatively low, since among other things, such processors are motivated toward preferential search for information that confirms rather than challenges existing evaluations. So while our findings may not apply in every environment all the time, we believe they are applicable to the peripheral route processing which represents the larger portion of political information processing voters carry out on a routine basis.

In conclusion, as a new technique for exploring political behavior, the experimental simulation described here—and its dynamic process-tracing methodology—offers an exciting new avenue for research. If political decisions are based at least in part on the information at hand when the decision is made, then it is time for political scientists to begin studying explicitly how information is gathered and how it is combined into a decision. Our answers to these questions have important implications for our theories of political behavior, and any practical recommendations we might make based on those theories.

For instance, the distinction between *using* a particular heuristic, and the apparent *effect* that use has on decision making, is important because the evidence from political science might lead policy makers to pursue very different courses of action if they were trying to improve voters' ability to make reasonable, coherent decisions. If we believed that cognitive shortcuts helped virtually everyone and consequently wanted to ensure that voters had sufficient heuristic cues available to make reasonable vote decisions, we might try to make sure that party and ideological labels, well-known group or elite endorsements, "characteristic images" of the candidates, and even reputable poll results were widely available before the election. This information is not too hard to come by in presidential elections,[22] at least for the politically motivated, but it is not nearly so prevalent for elections to lower offices. Although this idea would certainly require much more thought and research, some of this information could be provided in the voting booth when citizens go to the polls. Party labels already are a common part of the ballot for many types of elections; why not a picture of each candidate as well? Modern voting machines already have this capability, and it is currently employed in several countries around the world (e.g., Brazil). Why not provide the endorsements of a dozen broadly representative groups as well? Some states are already experimenting with internet voting, and consequently almost limitless information could be at voters' fingertips (mouse clicks?) as they make their web-based vote choices.

Our findings suggest, however, that were this path to be followed, it would aid the decision-making capabilities primarily of those already more interested and knowledgeable about politics. There is nothing wrong with aiding the decision making of this portion of the general public, as long as the capabilities of the remainder of the public are not harmed. Our findings raise an important cautionary flag here. But if the goal is to improve the decision making of less sophisticated voters, pursuing the road to cognitive shortcuts may prove to be a dead end. The political heuristics of all voters are not equal. "Republican" or "liberal" means one thing to a relatively naive citizen, and something much richer, more meaningful, and more nuanced to a politically sophisticated citizen. The cognitive revolution will not allow us to get away from the importance of civic engagement and attention to politics in the mind of a successful citizen.

Notes

1. This evidence is reviewed in Chapter 2 of Delli Carpini and Keeter (1996). Moreover, they note that because surveys' samples are not completely representative, and those who are not represented tend to have the least knowledge, these numbers undoubtedly overestimate the true figures.

2. We may be bucking the current tide in political science by employing the "schema" term. We agree with critics who claim the term has been used far too energetically and uncritically by political scientists, and that the older terms of "attitudes" or "stereotypes" could be substituted into much of the published work on political schemata with little loss of meaning (Kuklinski, Luskin, and Bolland 1991). If there are any areas in which this criticism does not hold true, however, it is in treating party and ideology as cognitive schemata. Researchers in these domains have carefully documented the memory, processing, and heuristic value of these two concepts (Conover and Feldman 1984, 1986, 1989; Hamill and Lodge 1986; Hamill, Lodge, and Blake 1985; Lau 1986, 1989; Lodge and Hamill 1986), and we feel on safe ground utilizing the "schema" concept here.

3. The term "endorsement" implies more formality than need be the case. A voter might easily infer that a particular candidate supports and is supported by a particular individual or social group by observing the individual with the candidate, or seeing many group members wildly cheering the candidate at a rally. The possibilities of mistaken inferences are greater with such "informal" endorsements, of course.

4. The psychology literature often treats these individual characteristics as distinct heuristics or stereotypes influencing person judgments. Because in practice these are all based on a person's appearance, however, we will combine them into a single heuristic.

5. For summaries of this literature, see Abelson and Levi 1985; Dawes 1988; Ford et al. 1989; Jacoby et al. 1987; Payne, Bettman, and Johnson 1992, 1993. For applications of information boards to political decision making by other researcher teams, see Herstein 1981; Mintz et al. 1997; and Riggle and Johnson 1996.

6. To make these probabilities realistic, we first conducted an elaborate study of the prevalence of different types of information in newspapers during the 1988 presidential campaign (Lau 1992) and modeled the probabilities after the actual prevalence of those types of information during the 1988 campaign.

7. Our typical experiment included ten twenty-second commercials during a twenty-two-minute primary campaign, and six twenty-second commercials during a twelve-minute general election campaign. Thus information from political commercials monopolized 17–22 percent of the total time during a campaign, with the remainder available for voters to access the information they wanted to learn (within the constraints of what was available, of course).

8. Candidates' "Party Affiliation," "Basic Social/Political Philosophy," and their "Basic Economic Philosophy" were deemed relevant to using a political schema heuristic; their pictures (e.g., "Picture of Gerry Singer") were relevant to the candidate appearance heuristic. The endorsements of any of fourteen interest groups were relevant to the endorsement heuristic; finally, any poll result was relevant to the viability heuristic. "*Non*heuristic" information was thus everything else available about the candidates, including specific issue stands, background information, and personality descriptions. What characterized this nonheuristic information was that it was candidate-specific and less prone to generalization than ideological or partisan labels.

Because the proportion of available items falling into the different categories differed widely, and because the order in which they appeared on the screen varied randomly, we could not simply consider how early during a campaign a particular item was accessed. Instead, the measure of early access was computed by noting whether the first available item within a category was accessed, the second accessed, and so on. This variable would be undefined if no items within a category were accessed during a campaign. To overcome this problem, in such instances we assigned a priority score of one more than the highest nonmissing priority score observed across subjects—in essence, assuming the subject *would have* accessed the next available item within that category if the campaign had lasted a little longer.

9. There is a scattering of significant effects among the control variables in these analyses, most strikingly a strong negative effect of age on use of all five of the political heuristics. This effect is probably an artifact of the timing of our experiments (older people in the 1990s being generally less familiar with personal computers) rather than a true difference in political heuristics use.

10. After subjects voted and evaluated the candidates in each election, they were asked how difficult the choice had been for them to make. These questions can be used as a manipulation check to determine if subjects perceived the static presentation format to be easier than the dynamic, scrolling format. Indeed they did: averaged across the two campaigns and all of our experiments, the choice was perceived as significantly more difficult in the dynamic, scrolling condition (M = 2.9) than the static condition (M = 2.3), $t(609) = 3.78$, $p < .001$

11. The general election campaign of that same experiment included, along with the presentation format, two further manipulations of the difficulty of the choice. The first manipulation involved the ideological distinctiveness of the two competing candidates, the second whether the candidate the voter supported in his or her party's primary had "won" the nomination and was running again in the general election campaign. The ideological distinctiveness manipulation had a significant effect on heuristic use, $F(5,147) = 2.54$, $p < .03$, albeit one which was much smaller than the effect of the static/dynamic manipulation. The prior rejection manipulation had no effect on heuristic use, however. The details of these analyses are available from the authors upon request.

12. The total number of candidates in the primary campaign was held constant at six, such that if there were two candidates running in the Democratic primary, there were four candidates running in the Republican primary, and vice versa. The manipulation check confirmed that subjects perceived the four-candidate primary to pose a more difficult choice than the two-candidate primary, $t(458) = 2.53$, $p < .02$.

13. Although we would argue that poll results generally have a great deal of heuristic value, particularly in campaigns with more than two candidates, the manipulations in several of the experiments required that it be possible for any of the candidates from the primaries to win their party's primary and advance to the general election campaign. To maintain plausibility across election campaigns, it was therefore necessary for all candidates to have roughly similar popular support during the primary campaign, as indicated in polls. In practice, then, there was little heuristic value to accessing poll results during our experiments, although of course no subjects knew this going into the experiment. Hence we cannot provide any validity evidence for the Viability Heuristic. Likewise candidate appearance can very efficiently provide a great deal of information to voters, although there is much less variance in the "type" of

people running for president than there is for lesser offices (a narrowness mirrored by our experiments), reducing in practice the heuristic value of the Appearance Heuristic for our experiments. Other than memory, none of the criteria examined in Table 7-3 were available for the Appearance Heuristic.

14. Moreover the two measures, when they are both available, produce very similar results; see Lau and Redlawsk (1997).

15. The "objective" stands of the candidates on the issues was determined by the mean ratings of every issue stand by seven experts. The attractiveness of the candidates' appearance and personalities was determined objectively by the mean ratings of sixty pretest subjects.

16. One possibility is Payne, Bettman, and Johnson's (1993) "optimal decision" measure. Their optimal choice formula equals the difference between the evaluation of the chosen alternative minus the evaluation of the worse alternative in the choice set, divided by the difference between the evaluations of the best and worst alternatives, or *(Chosen − Worst)/(Best − Worst)*.

   If the decision maker actually chooses the best alternative, this ratio equals 1.0; if the decision maker chooses the worst alternative, the ratio equals 0. The problem with this measure is that the best and worst alternatives in any choice set are always equated, irrespective of how difficult the choice was for the individual decision maker. To illustrate this problem, if for simplicity we reduce candidate evaluation to ideology, when a liberal is running against a conservative it is fairly easy for most voters to determine which candidate is better; but when two ideologically similar candidates are opposing each other, the correct choice is much more difficult for anyone to determine. Moreover, while a choice between a liberal candidate and a conservative candidate is easy for liberal and conservative voters to make, it is much more difficult from the point of view of moderates. Furthermore, when there are only two alternatives in the choice set, one is always the best choice and the other is always the worst choice. Somehow both the difficulty of the choice faced by a decision maker, and the "optimality" of the decision given that choice set, must be taken into consideration.

17. This summary measure combined our indicators of the Party Schema, Ideology Schema, and Endorsement Heuristic. As discussed in footnote 13 above, in practice there was little heuristic value associated with learning poll results or candidates' appearance in our experiments, and thus little reason they should be associated with correct voting.

18. Space precludes a detailed report on correct voting in the general election campaign experiments. Suffice it to say that the results conceptually replicate those just presented from the primary election. The crucial sophistication by heuristic use interaction is significant, $p < .05$. Again, the complete results are available from the authors upon request.

19. One item available for access about every candidate was their "Basic Social/Political Philosophy." For the stereotypic candidate from each party, this item read "[Candidate's name] is usually considered a moderate on most issues." For the two nonstereotypic candidates, this item read "It is difficult to label [candidate's name] as a traditional liberal or conservative."

20. The two-way interaction between the Nonstereotypic Candidate manipulation and Sophistication (which we did not predict) suggests that among voters who rarely use political heuristics, politically sophisticated voters are more likely than less sophisticated voters to vote correctly when the outparty candidate is nonstereotypic.

21. These three subjects were eliminated from the analysis. A somewhat larger number of subjects (eighteen) responded "Somewhat Unrealistic" to this question. These subjects' responses are included in the data reported here.

22. Indeed, one could argue that it is the role of each candidate's campaign to provide this information, and in presidential elections the major candidates have sufficient money to do just that. But in this case there is a huge heuristic cue for many voters to *disregard* the information—partisanship, which immediately suggests to many voters less trustworthy/objective information.

8. Political Sophistication and Policy Reasoning: A Reconsideration (Updated)

Paul Goren

The conventional wisdom in public opinion research holds that the ability to deduce specific policy preferences from abstract principles is conditional on political sophistication. Research shows that sophistication strengthens the relationship between liberal-conservative orientations and issue positions (Delli Carpini and Keeter 1996; Sniderman, Brody, and Tetlock 1991; Zaller 1992). However, the consensus makes the far broader claim that sophistication promotes reliance on all abstract beliefs and values. According to Zaller (1992, 25) "the impact of people's value predispositions always depends on whether citizens possess the contextual information needed to translate their values into support for particular policies." Delli Carpini and Keeter (1996, 229) posit that "the greater the store of information, the more often citizens will be able to connect their values with concrete matters of politics." Luskin (2002, 220) maintains that "[t]here are many reasons to think sophistication important, but perhaps its greatest importance lies in its conditioning of the relationship between values and policy and candidate preferences, which can be expected to be tighter among the more sophisticated."

This article examines critically whether the sophistication-interaction model of public opinion holds to the degree the consensus claims. I draw upon the work of Feldman (1988) and Hurwitz and Peffley (1987) to argue that political sophistication will neither affect the absorption of domain-specific principles from the broader political environment, nor strengthen the impact these principles have on policy preferences. My analysis of data from five American National Election Studies surveys yields two compelling findings. First, I demonstrate that beliefs about equal opportunity, self-reliance, and limited government in the social welfare domain and about militarism and anticommunism in the foreign policy domain are structured coherently and equivalently in the minds of citizens at different levels of sophistication. Second, I show that individuals are, for the most part, equally adept at grounding policy preferences in these principles. Simply put, all citizens hold genuine core beliefs and values and rely more or less equally on these when taking positions on many specific issues.

Source: American Journal of Political Science 48, 3 (July 2004): 462–478. The author slightly shortened the original, updated the analysis as shown in Tables 8-11 and 8-12, and added an epilogue.

Theoretical and Empirical Background

The domain-specific approach to the study of public opinion posits that everyone holds and uses abstract principles relevant to a given policy domain to constrain their policy preferences within that domain. These principles help people figure out what goes with what within, but not across, distinct issue areas (Feldman 1988; Hurwitz and Peffley 1987). For example, in the social welfare arena people deduce preferences from general beliefs about equality, while in the foreign policy domain attitudes toward defense issues are rooted in beliefs about militarism. Furthermore, beliefs about equality will not influence defense attitudes, nor will militarism affect social welfare preferences.

Why should everyone base his or her policy preferences on domain-specific principles? To begin with, public discourse in a policy domain is often shaped by a few general ideas. For instance, social welfare issues frequently reflect conflict between egalitarian and individualistic values, while foreign policy debates often center on how aggressive the United States should be in international affairs. Since these ideas are easy to recognize and understand, people can acquire them from the broader political environment with little effort. As Feldman states (1988, 418) "[i]t should not require a high degree of political sophistication for people to absorb the political norms of society when they are so ingrained in the political and social life of the nation."

Of course, possession does not guarantee use. There are two explanations as to why sophistication should not moderate the use of domain-specific principles. First, the information processing demands of doing so are quite low. While most people do not base policy preferences on liberal-conservative beliefs and know too little about politics to hold crystallized attitudes on most social and political issues (Converse 1964), they do adhere to a limited number of core principles from which such preferences may be readily constructed. That is, people can efficiently and effectively deduce preferences from the beliefs and values they hold. This is how cognitive misers process political information. Second, citizens are more capable of principle-based reasoning than is typically recognized. People use general beliefs and values to evaluate non-political aspects of their lives (e.g., work, school, and faith), and hence, can readily use these to reason about political issues when the need arises.

The sophistication-interaction theory of public opinion takes a much different view of the nature of mass-policy reasoning. Sophistication theories hold that people can connect values and preferences only if they already know a good deal about public affairs. Since many people lack such knowledge to begin with, large segments of the public will be unable to base issue positions on abstract principles. Thus, the sophistication-interaction approach posits that the highly informed will rely heavily on domain-specific principles to constrain their issue preferences, and that the uninformed cannot ground their attitudes in these principles (Converse 1964; Delli Carpini and Keeter 1996; Luskin 2002; Zaller 1992).

These competing theories of mass-policy reasoning are plausible, but both cannot be right. Surprisingly, little direct evidence supports either perspective. First, the seminal works in the domain-specific tradition demonstrate that general principles influence issue attitudes, but they fail to test whether sophistication moderates these relationships. It is possible that the least sophisticated third of the public fails to absorb these principles from the political environment or is unable to effectively use what they have. Whole sample estimates could easily obscure such heterogeneity. Thus, the claims of the domain-specific approach are not empirically corroborated in its leading works.

Two more recent studies address whether sophistication conditions the use of domain-specific principles. To begin with, in his comprehensive study of mass opinion change Zaller (1992) demonstrates that sophistication promotes reliance on partisan and ideological identifications, but there is little direct evidence that sophistication enhances the use of domain-specific principles. Zaller analyzes opinion change in periods where the ANES surveys lack relevant value measures; therefore, he utilizes ideology as a proxy indicator. Since ideology correlates with domain-specific principles only among the sophisticated, this strategy is invalid for drawing conclusions about whether the unsophisticated use domain-specific principles (see Goren 2001, 162–163). Goren (2001) tests for sophistication effects using valid measures of domain-specific principles in three policy domains. This work shows that sophistication promotes reliance on equal opportunity and self-reliance when citizens render social welfare preferences; does not condition the use of these principles when citizens evaluate affirmative action; and promotes reliance on moral traditionalism, but not equal opportunity, when people think about gay rights. That is, a sophistication effect emerges in three of six tests, a real, if not terribly robust, finding. Furthermore, and contrary to the predictions of sophistication theory, the unsophisticated rely on these principles. Overall, these studies suggest that sophistication matters to some extent, but they do not, and cannot, go very far toward resolving which theory better explains mass-policy reasoning.

The first problem lies in failing to test the assumption that the survey items measure domain-specific principles equivalently for citizens at different levels of sophistication. Conceptually, these works assume that the sophisticated and the unsophisticated hold coherently and identically structured principles. Attitude structure research shows that this assumption cannot be taken for granted (Converse 1964; Delli Carpini and Keeter 1996). Empirically, these works assume that measurement equivalence holds. Measurement equivalence exists when the relationships between positions on a psychological orientation and its corresponding indicators are the same in different populations. Conversely, measurement equivalence is absent when the relationships between positions on the latent orientation and the survey items differ across populations, or when one group translates a genuine orientation into meaningful survey responses while another lacks the orientation and responds randomly to the items designed to tap it (Drasgow and Kanfer 1985; Reise, Widaman, and Pugh 1993).

The second problem with the extant work is the underlying assumption that the explanatory variables are equally reliable at different levels of sophistication. The ability to draw inferences about coefficient differences across groups from standard regression estimates rests on the assumption that random measurement error contaminates the independent variables to an equally modest degree within each sample. The presence of random measurement error in two or more predictors biases all of the regression coefficients in a statistical model in unknowable ways: the biases can be upward, downward, or even directional (Achen 1983). If the reliabilities of the predictors differ across groups, regression coefficients may be biased differentially within groups. Thus, inferences based on statistical tests of group differences in the magnitudes of coefficients are uncertain. If cross-group reliability differences exist and an interaction test reveals that a regression coefficient differs significantly across the groups, it is unclear whether this reflects a genuine interaction in the population or an artificial one generated by sample bias differences. Similarly, an insignificant interaction test may indicate a lack of group differences in the population or different levels of within-sample bias. Since variables tend to be more reliable in more sophisticated samples, structural equation modeling techniques should be employed when testing for sophistication-interaction effects.

To sum up, the question of which theory better explains mass-policy reasoning is unsettled. Domain-specific works assume that sophistication does not affect the structure and use of core principles. Sophistication works rest on a narrow empirical base, ignore whether sophistication moderates belief structure, and ignore the potentially destructive consequences that cross-group reliability differences may have on statistical inference. Despite the empirical limits of the domain-specific work, the argument that everyone holds and uses these principles (see above) is compelling. Therefore, I predict that (H_1) domain-specific principles will be structured equivalently in the minds of sophisticated and unsophisticated citizens, and (H_2) the sophisticated and the unsophisticated will rely on these principles to the same degree to deduce their policy preferences.

Statistical Technique

I use structural equation modeling techniques to generate the statistical estimates for two reasons. First, the confirmatory factor analysis component of the general model can be used to test for measurement equivalence. If the factor loadings for the domain specific principle items are statistically identical, save for sampling variation, across sophistication-stratified samples, and the model-fit statistics are substantively acceptable within and comparable across the samples, measurement equivalence very likely holds. Second, the structural component of the general model estimates relationships between latent variables after accounting for random measurement error in the observed variables. This takes care of potential problems arising from cross-group reliability differences in the observed variables.[1]

Model fit is assessed as follows. I report the chi-square test, which tests the null hypothesis that the population covariation matrix for the observed variables equals the population covariance matrix implied by the hypothesized model. Given the limits of this test (see Bollen 1989, 266), I report three additional fit indices that describe how well the model fits the data: these are the chi-square/ degrees of freedom ratio, in which values of five or less indicate acceptable fit (Wheaton et al. 1977), and the adjusted goodness-of-fit index (AGFI) and the comparative fit index (CFI), where values of .90 or higher reflect good fit (Hu and Bentler 1995).

The Social Welfare Domain

Data and Model

The first set of analyses focuses on the issue of social welfare spending using data from the 1984, 1986, and 1990 ANES surveys.[2] Social welfare spending is one of the most important and enduring issues on the American political agenda, and it has received extensive attention in prior work on domain-specific reasoning (Feldman 1988; Goren 2001; Kinder and Sanders 1996). The dependent variables are latent attitudes toward government spending on social programs that benefit (1) the needy and (2) the elderly. In 1984 needy programs include "food stamps," "government jobs for the unemployed," and "assistance to blacks," while elderly programs include "Medicare" and "Social Security."[3] The 1986 and 1990 measures of each latent variable are similar.[4] Each factor is scaled so higher scores reflect pro-spending sentiment.

Equal opportunity, self-reliance, and limited government represent the key principles in the social welfare domain (Kinder and Sanders 1996). Equal opportunity reflects the idea that society should ensure that everyone has the same chance to get ahead in life (available all years). Strong egalitarians should favor more spending than weak egalitarians. Self-reliance is the belief that hard work leads to economic success (available in 1984 and 1986). Limited government indicates whether people favor a weak or strong federal government in domestic affairs (available in 1990). Support for individualistic values should be associated with a preference to cut spending. Party identification and ideology serve as control variables: Democrats and liberals should favor more spending than Republicans and conservatives, respectively. All explanatory variables are scaled so higher values reflect more left-wing responses; each should positively affect spending preferences. Finally, the models are estimated at three levels of sophistication, which I measure using political knowledge scales (see the appendix).

Statistical and Substantive Results

The first hypothesis maintains that each domain-specific principle is structured equivalently in the belief systems of citizens at different levels of

Table 8-1 1984 Confirmatory Factor Analysis Models for Social Welfare
Principles by Level of Sophistication, Unstandardized Estimates

	Low	Medium	High
Factor Loadings			
ξ_1 Equal opportunity (5-point scale)			
λ_1 Make sure everyone has equal opportunity to succeed	1.00	1.00	1.00
λ_2 Problem in country don't give everyone equal chance	3.33	2.67	4.27
λ_3 If people treated more equally have fewer problems	2.53	2.43	2.05
Cronbach's α	.54	.56	.59
ξ_2 Self-reliance (5-point scale)			
λ_4 People who don't get ahead should not blame system	1.00	1.00	1.00
λ_5 Hard work offers little guarantee of success	1.15	1.18	0.78
λ_6 If people work hard almost always get what want	2.07	2.00	1.14
λ_7 Person work hard has good chance of succeeding	1.35	1.54	0.87
Cronbach's α	.54	.61	.70
Factor Correlation	.10	.19	.66
Model Fit			
Robust χ^2	56.16**	74.09**	53.19**
Degrees of freedom	13	13	13
Robust χ^2/degrees of freedom	4.32	5.70	4.09
AGFI	.95	.93	.93
Robust CFI	.88	.88	.95
Number of cases	642	634	548

** $p < .01$.

Notes: Latent and observed variables are coded so higher scores reflect more left-wing sentiment;
therefore, each λ_1 should be positive. All factor loadings significant at $p < .01$. The metric of each factor
is defined by fixing the loading for the first item to 1.00. LM test of equal loadings for equal opportunity: $\chi^2_4 = 6.22$, $p = .18$. LM test of equal loadings for self-reliance: $\chi^2_6 = 19.63$, $p < .01$.

sophistication. It will be confirmed if the factor loadings for each principle are
statistically indistinguishable and the model-fit statistics are reasonable and substantively comparable across the groups. To illustrate for 1984, Table 8-1 shows
the loadings for the second and third equal opportunity items are as follows:
$\lambda_2^{low} = 3.33$, $\lambda_2^{med} = 2.67$, $\lambda_2^{high} = 4.27$ and $\lambda_3^{low} = 2.53$, $\lambda_3^{med} = 2.43$, $\lambda_3^{high} = 2.05$
(λ_1 equals 1.00 to scale the factor).[5] Are these loadings statistically comparable
across the groups? This can be determined using the Lagrange multiplier (LM)
test, which assesses the statistical effect adding free parameters has on a restricted
model. In the restricted model the factor loadings are constrained to be equal
across the samples (i.e. $\lambda_2^{low} = \lambda_2^{med} = \lambda_2^{high}$ and $\lambda_3^{low} = \lambda_3^{med} = \lambda_3^{high}$). The LM test

can be interpreted as the approximate increase in the model chi-square that results when all of the equality constraints are freed (degrees of freedom equal the number of constraints). A statistically insignificant LM test indicates that the constraints do not harm model fit, and thus, supports the inference that measurement equivalence holds (Bentler 1995, 126–128, 219–221). In short, an insignificant LM will support the conclusion that equal opportunity is structured the same way and to the same degree in the minds of individuals at different levels of awareness.

To return to the data at hand, Table 8-1 reveals that measurement equivalence holds generally, though not completely, for the domain-specific principles. First, the LM test for equal opportunity is statistically insignificant ($\chi^2_4 = 6.22$, $p = .18$), which means that model fit is not degraded when the loadings are constrained to be equal across the samples. In contrast, the LM test for self-reliance is statistically significant ($\chi^2_6 = 19.63$, $p < .01$), which shows that the loadings are not statistically equivalent across the samples (the loadings are somewhat weaker among the high sophistication group versus the medium/low groups). Lastly, model fit is adequate within each sample and differs marginally across the samples. The chi-square/degrees-of-freedom ratios are all around the 5.00 cut point and the AGFI and the CFI approach or surpass the .90 threshold of good fit. Overall, it appears that beliefs about equal opportunity are structured identically and beliefs about self-reliance are structured similarly across levels of sophistication.

The second hypothesis predicts that people rely on these principles to the same degree to construct their spending preferences. If the domain-specific hypothesis is right, then the γ_1 (equal opportunity) and γ_2 (self-reliance) coefficients should be positive and statistically significant in each group and statistically indistinguishable across the groups. If the sophistication-interaction model is right, then γ_1 and γ_2 should be positive and larger in higher groups ($\gamma_1^{high} > \gamma_1^{med} > \gamma_1^{low}$ and $\gamma_2^{high} > \gamma_2^{med} > \gamma_2^{low}$), significant in the high group and insignificant in the low group, and the differences in the magnitudes of γ_1 should be statistically significant. LM tests are used to determine if constraining the coefficients to be equal ($\gamma_1^{low} = \gamma_1^{med} = \gamma_1^{high}$ and then $\gamma_2^{low} = \gamma_2^{med} = \gamma_2^{high}$) leads to a statistically significant decrease in the model chi-square (degrees of freedom equals the number of constraints). Insignificant LM tests will support the conclusion that sophistication does not condition the use of these two principles.[6]

Table 8-2 reports the γ coefficients, robust standard errors, model-fit statistics, and LM tests for the 1984 needy and elderly spending models. The results clearly support the domain-specific theory of mass-policy reasoning. First, in both sets of models the equal opportunity variable is correctly signed and statistically significant at each level of sophistication, and its effect does not differ significantly across the samples (needy $\chi^2_2 = 0.99$, $p = .61$; elderly $\chi^2_2 = 0.38$, $p = .83$). Strong egalitarians consistently favor more social spending than weak egalitarians. Second, self-reliance has no effect, surprisingly, on spending attitudes in any sample. Third, party identification influences preferences as predicted in every

Table 8-2 1984 Structural Equation Models for Social Welfare Spending
Preferences by Level of Sophistication, Unstandardized Estimates

	Programs for the Needy			Programs for the Elderly		
	Low	Medium	High	Low	Medium	High
Structural Coefficients						
γ_1 Equal opportunity	0.678**	0.671**	0.930**	0.262**	0.352**	0.312*
	(.157)	(.137)	(.259)	(.105)	(.095)	(.176)
γ_2 Self-reliance	−0.067	−0.051	−0.074	0.110	0.034	−0.037
	(.092)	(.057)	(.056)	(.076)	(.049)	(.053)
γ_3 Party identification	0.097**	0.064 **	0.071 **	0.060 **	0.039 **	0.106**
	(.027)	(.019)	(.029)	(.021)	(.016)	(.027)
γ_4 Ideology	−0.017	0.001	0.083 *	−0.010	−0.019	0.008
	(.034)	(.030)	(.040)	(.026)	(.027)	(.039)
Model Fit						
Robust χ^2	96.74**	122.19**	154.68**	94.55**	101.51**	114.18**
Degrees of freedom	56	56	56	45	45	45
Robust χ^2/df	1.73	2.18	2.76	2.10	2.26	2.54
AGFI	.95	.95	.92	.95	.95	.93
Robust CFI	.95	.95	.96	.93	.95	.97
Number of cases	489	528	499	519	551	528

$^* p < .05; ^{**} p < .01.$

Notes: Higher values on the variables reflect more left-wing sentiment; therefore, each γ_i should be positive. CFA estimates omitted for clarity.

For the needy models:

The dependent variable is latent support for spending on social programs that benefit the needy (3-point scale). Robust standard errors are in parentheses. LM test of equal γ_1: $\chi^2_2 = 0.99, p = .61$.

For the elderly models:

The dependent variable is latent support for spending on social programs that benefit the elderly (3-point scale). Robust standard errors are in parentheses. LM test of equal γ_1: $\chi^2_2 = 0.38, p = .83$.

sample, ideology matters only for the sophisticated in the needy models, and model fit is excellent in each sample. In sum, political sophistication does not seem to moderate policy reasoning about social spending, at least in 1984.

For the 1986 data, the measurement model and structural equation estimates are presented in Tables 8-3 and 8-4, respectively. Table 8-3 shows that measurement equivalence holds for both equal opportunity and self-reliance. More specifically, the factor loadings are statistically comparable across the sophistication-stratified samples (equal opportunity $\chi^2_4 = 4.83$, $p = .31$; self-reliance $\chi^2_6 = 5.43$, $p = .49$), and the chi-square/degrees of freedom ratios and the AGFI and CFI indices reveal that model fit is good within and similar across all three samples. Thus, it appears that the process of translating beliefs about equal opportunity and self-reliance into survey responses is the same for everyone regardless of how much or little they know about public affairs.

Table 8-3 1986 Confirmatory Factor Analysis Models for Social Welfare
Principles by Level of Sophistication, Unstandardized Estimates

	Low	Medium	High
Factor Loadings			
ξ_1 Equal opportunity (5-point scale)			
λ_1 Make sure everyone has equal opportunity to succeed	1.00	1.00	1.00
λ_2 Problem in country don't give everyone equal chance	2.86	1.81	2.00
λ_3 If people treated more equally have fewer problems	2.32	2.32	1.90
Cronbach's α	.57	.64	.66
ξ_2 Self-reliance (5-point scale)			
λ_4 People who don't get ahead should not blame system	1.00	1.00	1.00
λ_5 Hard work offers little guarantee of success	0.90	1.05	1.00
λ_6 If people work hard almost always get what want	1.93	2.13	1.35
λ_7 Person work hard has good chance of succeeding	1.49	1.46	1.06
Cronbach's α	.51	.54	.65
Factor Correlation	−.09	.14	.30
Model Fit			
Robust χ^2	33.24**	25.34*	48.68**
Degrees of freedom	13	13	13
Robust χ^2/degrees of freedom	2.56	1.95	3.74
AGFI	.95	.96	.90
Robust CFI	.90	.95	.88
Number of cases	385	371	290

$^*p < .05;\ ^{**}p < .01.$

Notes: Latent and observed variables are coded so higher scores reflect more left-wing sentiment; therefore, each λ_i should be positive. All factor loadings significant at $p < .01$. The metric of each factor is defined by fixing the loading for the first item to 1.00. LM test of equal loadings for equal opportunity: $\chi^2_4 = 4.83, p = .31$. LM test of equal loadings for self-reliance: $\chi^2_6 = 5.43, p = .49$.

Next, the structural equation estimates in Table 8-4, while somewhat mixed, furnish more support for the domain-specific theory than for the sophistication-interaction approach. First, in both the needy and the elderly models, the equal opportunity variable is always positive, it is significant in five of the six samples, and its effect does not vary across the samples (needy $\chi^2_2 = 1.83, p = .40$; elderly $\chi^2_2 = 0.27, p = .87$). Strong egalitarians consistently favor more spending than weak egalitarians. Second, in the needy models the magnitude of the self-reliance coefficient increases monotonically as a function of sophistication, and it attains significance in the medium and high samples. Among these groups, a weaker commitment to self-reliance is associated with more support for spending on the needy. These differences, while impressive in substantive terms ($\gamma_2^{low} = 0.087$ vs. $\gamma_2^{high} = 0.274$), are not statistically significant ($\chi^2_2 = 1.50, p = .47$). However, in the elderly models self-reliance once again has no effect on spending preferences. Third, party identification is correctly signed and statistically significant while

Table 8-4 1986 Structural Equation Models for Social Welfare Spending
Preferences by Level of Sophistication, Unstandardized Estimates

	Programs for the Needy			Programs for the Elderly		
	Low	Medium	High	Low	Medium	High
Structural Coefficients						
γ_1 Equal opportunity	0.615**	0.383**	0.492**	0.303*	0.255**	0.210
	(.168)	(.088)	(.107)	(.131)	(.087)	(.141)
γ_2 Self-reliance	0.087	0.213**	0.274**	−0.152	0.142	−0.055
	(.119)	(.089)	(.082)	(.137)	(.087)	(.073)
γ_3 Party identification	0.073*	0.093**	0.067**	0.022	0.059**	0.082**
	(.032)	(.021)	(.026)	(.023)	(.021)	(.034)
γ_4 Ideology	0.014	0.097 **	−0.031	0.014	0.038	−0.031
	(.044)	(.040)	(.055)	(.035)	(.037)	(.060)
Model Fit						
Robust χ^2	68.15	78.33*	125.76**	48.76	57.32*	83.41**
Degrees of freedom	56	56	56	36	36	36
Robust χ^2/df	1.22	1.40	2.25	1.35	1.59	2.32
AGFI	.94	.94	.88	.95	.95	.90
Robust CFI	.98	.97	.93	.97	.96	.95
Number of cases	297	297	251	323	334	276

$^* p < .05;\ ^{**} p < .01.$

Notes: Higher values on the variables reflect more left-wing sentiment; therefore, each γ_i should be positive. CFA estimates omitted for clarity.

For the needy models:

The dependent variable is latent support for spending on social programs that benefit the needy (3-point scale). Robust standard errors are in parentheses. LM test of equal γ_1: $\chi^2_2 = 1.83, p = .40$. LM test of equal γ_2: $\chi^2_2 = 1.50, p = .47$.

For the elderly models:

The dependent variable is latent support for spending on Social Security (3-point scale). Robust standard errors are in parentheses. LM test of equal γ_1: $\chi^2_2 = 0.27, p = .87$.

ideology is insignificant in five of the six samples. Fourth, model fit is quite good across the board. Overall, the equal opportunity results for both issues strongly support the domain-specific approach, while the self-reliance effect from the needy models supports sophistication theory (but keep in mind that the differences in γ_2 are not statistically significant).

For the 1990 data, the confirmatory factor analysis and structural equation estimates appear in Tables 5 and 6 (in the original article), respectively. [In order to conserve space, these two tables are not reprinted here.] The first point to note, as Table 5 reveals, is that the LM tests for measurement equivalence for both principles are statistically insignificant (equal opportunity $\chi^2_4 = 8.03,\ p = .09;$

limited government $\chi_4^2 = 3.74$, $p = .44$) and that the hypothesized model fits the sample data very well within and across the groups. In other words, these principles are structured rationally and equivalently in the belief systems of citizens across the awareness spectrum.

For Tables 5 and 6, see Goren (2004)

Does political sophistication strengthen the relationship between these principles and attitudes toward social spending? The results reported in Table 6 are inconclusive. First, in the needy models, equal opportunity is positive and significant in each sample, and it manifests a stronger effect in the high group versus the low/medium groups ($\chi_2^2 = 6.37$, $p = .04$). However, in the elderly models, equal opportunity is positive and significantly larger in the low/high samples compared to the medium sample ($\chi_2^2 = 6.06$, $p = .05$). Second, in the needy models, all citizens rely the same amount on limited government to constrain their spending preferences ($\chi_2^2 = 0.73$, $p = .70$). Those who want a strong government favor spending more than those who want a limited government. This effect is not present in the elderly models, as the limited-government variable is correctly signed and statistically significant only in the least sophisticated sample. Third, neither party identification nor ideology matter much for policy reasoning about either type of social spending. Fourth, model fit is fine within and comparable across the samples for both issues. In sum, the limited government results from the needy models buttress the domain-specific theory; the equal opportunity results in the needy models support the sophistication-interaction theory to some extent (although the significant γ_1 in the low sample and the non-monotonic pattern of results weakens the case); and the equal-opportunity effect in the elderly models supports neither theory.

Summary of Social Welfare Results

Overall, the key findings are as follows. First, the confirmatory factor analysis models suggest that all citizens hold genuine and comparably structured beliefs about equal opportunity, self-reliance, and limited government. Measurement equivalence holds statistically in five of the six tests and substantively in all six. Second, the structural equation models imply that most people use these principles some of the time to guide their preferences on social spending, and that sophistication does not *systematically* condition these relationships. The domain-specific theory is supported by the findings that everyone relies on equal opportunity to the same degree in the 1984 and 1986 needy and elderly models, and on limited government in the 1990 needy models. The sophistication-interaction theory is supported by the findings that the highly aware rely more on self-reliance in the 1986 needy models and equal opportunity in the 1990 needy models (though there is some countervailing evidence in each case). Simply put, the results support domain-specific theory five times, sophistication-interaction theory twice, and neither theory once (the 1990 elderly models).

The Foreign Policy Domain

Data and Model

The next set of analyses focuses on foreign policy issues using ANES data from the 1988 survey and the 1987 pilot. I select foreign policy as the second domain to analyze because scholars disagree sharply over whether sophistication matters in this area (Hurwitz and Peffley 1987; Zaller 1992). In addition, foreign policy issues are further removed from the lives of citizens than domestic concerns; therefore, this issue area provides a difficult test for domain-specific theory. The dependent variables in the structural models are attitudes toward (1) defense spending (available both years), (2) aid to the contras (available both years), and (3) building more nuclear weapons (available in 1987). These variables are scaled so higher scores reflect more hawkish responses.

The key domain-specific principles in the foreign policy domain are militarism and anticommunism (Hurwitz and Peffley 1990, 1987). Militarism denotes whether people believe the United States should take a flexible or tough posture in dealing with foreign adversaries. Anticommunism reflects the degree of support for U.S. efforts to contain Soviet and communist influences abroad. Both variables are scaled so higher scores reflect more hawkish responses; hence, they should positively affect the policy-preference variables. Party identification serves as a control variable and is scaled so that higher values reflect Democratic affinities; it should negatively affect policy preferences. Estimates are generated at three levels of sophistication for 1988 and two for 1987.[7]

Statistical and Substantive Results

Do the politically aware and the unaware conceive of militarism and anticommunism in a similar fashion? The 1988 results suggest that, for the most part, they do. Table 8-7 shows that the LM tests for militarism ($\chi_4^2 = 1.46$, $p = .83$) and anticommunism ($\chi_2^2 = 2.37$, $p = .31$) are statistically insignificant, so we can conclude that measurement equivalence holds formally. Next, the model-fit results are substantively similar, with one exception. In the low sample the chi-square/degrees-of-freedom ratio falls below the 5.00 cut-point for acceptable fit, and the AGFI and CFI values exceed the desired .90 threshold. In the medium and high samples the chi-square ratios exceed 5.00, but the AGFI and CFI values are reasonable. Overall, the weight of the evidence suggests that foreign policy beliefs are structured similarly across levels of sophistication.

Do the aware and the unaware rely on militarism and anticommunism to the same degree to construct their defense spending preferences? The estimates in Table 8-8 reveal that this is the case. To begin with, the militarism coefficient is positive and significant in each sample and does not differ statistically across the samples ($\chi_2^2 = 3.13$, $p = .21$). Militarists want to spend more on defense than nonmilitarists, regardless of how much or little they know about politics. Second, anticommunism does not manifest the predicted effect in any sample. Third, as

Table 8-7 1988 Confirmatory Factor Analysis Models for Foreign Policy
Principles by Level of Sophistication, Unstandardized Estimates

	Low	Medium	High
Factor Loadings			
ξ_1 Militarism (3 point scale)			
λ_1 Better way to keep peace strong military/bargaining	1.00	1.00	1.00
λ_2 How important strong military for dealing w/enemies	1.28	1.29	1.13
λ_3 U.S. maintains power even if it means brink of war	2.02	1.84	1.75
Cronbach's α	.54	.64	.68
ξ_2 Anticommunism (5-point scale)			
λ_4 Any time country goes communist a threat to the U.S.	1.00	1.00	1.00
λ_5 U.S. do everything to prevent spread communism	0.84	0.98	1.04
Cronbach's α	.67	.77	.81
Factor Correlation	.67	.63	.73
Model Fit			
Robust χ^2	12.35*	31.68**	27.33**
Degrees of freedom	4	4	4
Robust χ^2/degrees of freedom	3.09	7.92	6.83
AGFI	.96	.92	.89
Robust CFI	.98	.96	.96
Number of cases	581	670	432

* $p < .05$; ** $p < .01$.

Notes: Latent and observed variables are coded so higher scores reflect more hawkish sentiment; therefore, each λ_i should be positive. All factor loadings significant at $p < .01$. The metric of each factor is defined by fixing the loading for the first item to 1.00. LM test of equal loadings for militarism: $\chi^2_4 = 1.46$, $p = .83$. LM test of equal loadings for anticommunism: $\chi^2_2 = 2.37$, $p = .31$.

expected, Democratic partisanship is inversely related to spending preferences. Fourth, the descriptive fit indices show that model fit is excellent within and differs trivially across the samples. To sum up, the domain-specific theory outperforms the sophistication-interaction theory in explaining how citizens reason about defense spending.

On the other hand, the sophistication approach does a better job accounting for mass-policy reasoning on the issue of contra aid. To start with, the militarism effect increases at each level of sophistication and reaches significance in the medium/high groups. Although the effect does not differ statistically across the samples ($\chi^2_2 = 2.59$, $p = .27$), the differences are impressive in substantive terms ($\gamma_1^{low} = 0.086$ vs. $\gamma_1^{high} = 0.450$). The estimates suggest that militarism is positively associated with support for Contra aid among highly and moderately sophisticated citizens, and that it is unrelated to attitudes toward Contra aid among the unsophisticated. Next, anticommunism again fails to influence foreign policy

Table 8-8   1988 Structural Equation Models for Foreign Policy Preferences by
Level of Sophistication, Unstandardized Estimates

	Defense Spending			Aid to Contras		
	Low	Medium	High	Low	Medium	High
Structural Coefficients						
γ_1 Militarism	2.213**	1.546**	1.253**	0.086	0.197*	0.450**
	(.479)	(.239)	(.267)	(.156)	(.099)	(.160)
γ_2 Anticommunism	−0.292*	0.067	0.133	0.081	0.112**	0.065
	(.173)	(.095)	(.101)	(.066)	(.039)	(.061)
γ_3 Party identification	−0.097*	−0.148**	−0.200**	−0.024	−0.114**	−0.103**
	(.042)	(.038)	(.055)	(.021)	(.017)	(.025)
Model Fit						
Robust χ^2	28.66*	46.39**	52.58**	20.09	41.96**	54.88**
Degrees of freedom	15	15	15	15	15	15
Robust χ^2/df	1.91	3.09	3.51	1.34	2.80	3.66
AGFI	.96	.95	.92	.98	.96	.92
Robust CFI	.98	.98	.97	.99	.98	.97
Number of cases	445	613	422	515	617	418

$^* p < .05; ^{**} p < .01.$

Notes: Higher values on the principle variables reflect more hawkish sentiment; therefore, γ_1 and γ_2 should be positive. Higher values on party identification reflect more Democratic leanings; therefore γ_3 should be negative. CFA estimates omitted for clarity.

For the defense spending models:

The dependent variable is latent support for defense spending (7-point scale). Robust standard errors are in parentheses. LM test of equal γ_1: $\chi_2^2 = 3.13, p = .21.$

For the aid to Contras models:

The dependent variable is latent support for federal spending on aid to the Contras (3-point scale). Robust standard errors are in parentheses. LM test of equal γ_1: $\chi_2^2 = 2.59, p = .27.$

preferences across the samples, while partisanship behaves as predicted in the two higher samples. Finally, model fit is fine within and across the samples.

Shifting attention to the 1987 models, we can see a comparable pattern of results. [Once again, to conserve space these tables are not reprinted here.] First, the confirmatory factor analysis models in Table 9 (in the original article) show that the politically aware and the unaware hold equivalently structured beliefs about militarism and anticommunism. The factor loadings are statistically indistinguishable (militarism $\chi_2^2 = 4.21, p = .12$; anticommunism $\chi_1^2 = 0.50, p = .48$) and model fit is substantively comparable in these samples. Second, Table 10 (in the original article) shows that for the defense spending issue everyone relies equally on militarism ($\chi_1^2 = 0.28, p = .60$), and that the sophisticated alone use it to construct preferences on Contra aid ($\gamma_1^{low} = 0.046, p = .40$ vs. $\gamma_1^{high} = 0.444, p < .01$; the coefficients do not differ significantly as the LM test shows: $\chi_1^2 = 2.46, p = .12.$).

On the issue of building more nuclear arms, sophistication is irrelevant: everyone uses militarism to the same extent ($\chi_1^2 = 0.41, p = .52$). Third, anticommunism and party identification have no effect whatsoever. Finally, model fit is uniformly excellent.

For Tables 9 and 10, see Goren (2004)

Summary of Foreign Policy Results

Overall, the foreign policy results yield some support for both theories, but the evidence comes down more in favor of the domain-specific approach. First, the four LM tests and model-fit comparisons indicate that all citizens possess genuine and similarly structured beliefs about militarism and anticommunism. Second, the structural models show that sophistication does not affect how citizens think about defense spending or nuclear arms, but that it seems to matter for Contra aid. Consistent with the domain-specific approach, people rely on militarism to the same degree when deducing attitudes toward defense spending and nuclear arms. On the more arcane issue of aiding the Contra rebels, only the sophisticated use militarism, as predicted by the sophistication interaction theory (cf. Zaller 1992, 144–147). In short, the results support the domain-specific theory three times and the sophistication-interaction theory twice.

Summary and Conclusions

This article posits that the domain-specific theory of mass-policy reasoning better reflects how citizens think about political issues than the sophistication-interaction theory that currently dominates the study of public opinion. I have drawn on the works of Feldman (1988) and Hurwitz and Peffley (1987) to argue that everyone can learn the political principles that animate public discourse and rely on these to the same degree to deduce policy preferences, because the information-processing demands of doing so are low and because citizens possess more ability to engage in value-based reasoning than is usually recognized. The findings presented above, which are based on a comprehensive set of analyses of public opinion data that span two policy domains, five issues, five domain-specific principles, and five ANES surveys, support these claims.

First, I have demonstrated that all citizens hold sensibly and comparably structured beliefs about equal opportunity, self-reliance, and limited government in the social welfare domain and militarism and anticommunism in the foreign policy domain. These findings show that the assumption that everyone holds genuine domain-specific principles is true and thereby corroborate the implicit claims made by Feldman (1988) and Hurwitz and Peffley (1987). While politically unsophisticated segments of the electorate are "innocent of ideology" (Converse 1964) we now know that this is not the case for core beliefs and values. Second, I have shown that the politically sophisticated do not *systematically* rely more on these principles to constrain their policy preferences than do the unsophisticated. Generally speaking, people rely to the same degree on equal opportunity and limited government to construct attitudes toward social spending and on militarism to guide positions on defense spending and nuclear arms. Thus, with the exception of a hard issue like Contra aid, political sophistication does not matter all that much. In the thirteen cases of significant principle-preference links, the results unequivocally support domain-specific theory eight times (equal opportunity on $needy_{84-86}$ and on $elderly_{84-86}$, limited government on $needy_{90}$, militarism on $defense_{88-87}$ and on nuclear $arms_{87}$); partly support sophistication-interaction theory four times (self-reliance on $needy_{86}$, equality on $needy_{90}$, and militarism on contra aid_{88-87}); and are inconclusive once (equality on $elderly_{90}$). In addition, the unsophisticated ground their preferences in domain-specific principles on every issue except aid to the contras.[8] Collectively, these findings rehabilitate the domain-specific theory of mass-policy reasoning and suggest that the sophistication-interaction model does not apply as broadly as the conventional wisdom presumes.

This conclusion requires qualification on several fronts. First, the guns-and-butter issues covered here are among the most important in the American political system, but they do not exhaust the universe of issues. Clearly, more research is needed to see if the patterns observed above hold for issues in domains such as race (e.g., affirmative action, equal treatment), civil liberties (e.g., freedom of speech, freedom of assembly), social policy (e.g., abortion, gay rights), and so on. Second, future research should pursue whether all citizens rely equally on other principles relevant to the social welfare and foreign policy domains. Does sophistication promote the use of humanitarianism when people evaluate the welfare state (Feldman and Steenbergen 2001)? Does sophistication enhance the use of cooperative internationalism when people ponder defense spending (Wittkopf 1990)? Third, the findings reported in this article rest on supporting a null hypothesis, a less-than-ideal research strategy. An alternative research design could seek to demonstrate that the sophisticated and the unsophisticated can be experimentally induced to ground policy preferences in broader principles to the same extent (see Lavine, Thomsen, and Gonzales, 1997 for supporting evidence).

What implications do my findings have for evaluating democratic citizenship in the American public? An optimistic reading of the evidence would stress that all people base attitudes toward social spending on broader beliefs about equal opportunity and attitudes toward defense spending and nuclear weapons on beliefs about militarism. Citizens do evaluate critical issues of the day using relevant principles rather than making up positions on the spot and quickly forgetting them (Converse 1964) or haphazardly drawing upon whatever considerations happen to be temporarily accessible in their minds (Zaller 1992). A more pessimistic reading of the evidence would focus on the fact that when constructing preferences people sometimes ignore self-reliance and limited government in the social welfare arena and entirely shun anticommunism in the foreign policy domain (at least in the late 1980s). Despite the prominence these principles have assumed in American political discourse and the ease with which they could be employed to construct preferences, most people do not use them. One could conclude, quite sensibly, that mass-policy reasoning is rather unsophisticated in a general sense (Luskin 2002). By grounding policy preferences in domain-specific principles, the mass public meets a criterion for approximating the standards of meaningful democratic citizenship. It does not exceed this criterion by much.

APPENDIX: QUESTION WORDING

For some items the question wording, format, and response options vary slightly across the surveys. The social welfare domain items, party identification, and ideology have been coded so that higher scores reflect more left-wing sentiment. The foreign policy domain items have been coded so that higher scores reflect more hawkish sentiment.

Programs for the needy: "Should federal spending on . . . be increased, decreased, or kept about the same?" 1984 and 1986 items: food stamps, government jobs for the unemployed, and assistance to blacks. 1990 items: food stamps, programs that assist blacks, government assistance for the homeless, and child care. Three-point scales.

Programs for the elderly: "Should federal spending on . . . be increased, decreased, or kept about the same?" 1984 items: Medicare and Social Security; 1986 and 1990 item: Social Security. Three-point scales.

Equal opportunity: (1) "Our society should do whatever is necessary to make sure that everyone has an equal opportunity to succeed." (2) "One of the big problems in this country is that we don't give everyone an equal chance." (3) "If people were treated more equally in this country, we would have many fewer problems." Five-point agree/disagree scales.

Self-reliance: (1) "Most people who don't get ahead should not blame the system; they have only themselves to blame." (2) "Hard work offers little guarantee of success." (3) "If people work hard they almost always get what they want." (4) "Any person who is willing to work hard has a good chance of succeeding." Five-point agree/disagree scales.

Limited government: (1) "One, the less government the better; or two, there are more things the government should be doing." (2) "One, we need a strong government to handle today's complex economic problems; or two, the free market can handle these problems without government being involved." (3) "One, the main reason government has become bigger over the years is because it has gotten involved in things that people should do for themselves; or two, government has become bigger because the problems we face today have become bigger." Three-point scales (includes volunteered middle option).

Party identification: Two measures are used. The first taps social identity with a party, the second taps the affective nature of that identification. (1) "Generally speaking, do you usually think of yourself as a Republican, a Democrat, an independent, or what?" [Partisan probe] "Would you call yourself a strong . . . or a not very strong . . . ?" [Non-partisan probe] "Do you think of yourself as closer to the Republican party or the Democratic party?" Seven-point scale. (2) (Democratic Party feeling thermometer—Republican Party feeling thermometer + 100)/25. Eight-point scale. Minor party identifiers/apoliticals on (1) and can't rate responses on (2) recoded to scale midpoints to preserve cases.

Ideology: Measured with the self-identification item and the follow-up probe for people who initially answer don't know/haven't thought much (this greatly reduces missing data). "We hear a lot of talk these days about liberals and conservatives. Here is a seven-point scale on which the political views that people hold are arranged from extremely liberal to extremely conservative. Where would you place yourself on this scale, or haven't you thought much about this?" [Probe] "If you had to choose, would you consider yourself a liberal or a conservative?" Three-point scale.

Defense spending: "Some people believe that we should spend much less money for defense. Others feel that defense spending should be greatly increased. Where would you place yourself on this scale, or haven't you thought much about this?" Seven-point scale for 1988 and five-point scale for 1987.

Aid to Contras: "Should federal spending on aid to the contras in Nicaragua be increased, decreased, or kept about the same." Three-point scale.

Nuclear weapons: "Would you strongly favor, not so strongly favor, not so strongly oppose, or strongly oppose the U.S. building more nuclear weapons?" Five-point scale.

Militarism: (1) "Which do you think is the better way for us to keep peace—by having a very strong military so other countries won't attack us, or by working out our disagreements at the bargaining table?" (2) "How important is it for the U.S. to have a strong military force in order to be effective in dealing with our enemies? Is it extremely important, very important, somewhat important, or not at all important?" (3) "The U.S. should maintain its position as the world's most powerful nation even if it means going to the brink of war." Three- to five-point scales.

Anticommunism: (1) "Any time a country goes communist, it should be considered a threat to the vital interests and security of the United States." (2) "The United States should do everything it can to prevent the spread of communism to any other part of the world." Five-point scales.

Political sophistication: The sophistication measure is a simple additive scale indicating the number of correct answers given to 14 or 15 knowledge items. Mondak

(2001) shows that such items are systematically biased by a guessing response set (i.e. guessers receive higher scores than nonguessers). To reduce this bias I adopt his recommended post hoc correction procedure for the multiple-choice items. This procedure is not utilized for the open-ended job/office holder items because some of these are too easy or too hard to assume a 50–50 chance of guessing correctly. These items are retained because their discriminatory power varies widely. 1984 items: correct placements for Reagan, Mondale, and the Democratic and Republican parties on ideology; correct placements for the parties on government spending, defense spending, and Central America involvement; and pre-/post-election party control of the House and Senate. 1986 and 1987 items: correct placements for both parties on ideology, government spending, and defense spending; party control of the House and Senate; and Bush, Weinberger, Rehnquist, Volcker, Dole, and O'Neill jobs. 1988 items: party placements and House and Senate control like the 1986 and 1987 items and Kennedy, Shultz, Rehnquist, Gorbachev, Thatcher, and Arafat jobs. 1990 items: party placements and House and Senate control like the 1986 and 1987 items and Quayle, Mitchell, Rehnquist, Gorbachev, Thatcher, Mandela, and Foley jobs.

Epilogue

My original article centers on two questions. First, does political sophistication affect systematically the relationship between latent political principles and responses to survey questions designed to measure those principles? Second, does sophistication augment the relationship between domain-specific principles and policy attitudes? I found that sophistication effects are the exception, not the rule. While the sophisticated offer more crystallized responses to the opinion items (see the Cronbach α estimates in the measurement model tables), the pattern of (largely) equivalent factor loadings suggests the less informed do as well as the more informed in translating latent principles into observable opinion reports. Regarding the structural models, while sophistication makes a difference on hard issues like Contra aid, it typically has little impact on the bread-and-butter issues of American politics.

There are three important questions my article did not address. The first is whether the measurement equivalence results generalize to other principles and years. The second centers on whether sophistication moderates the relationship between domain-specific principles and electoral choice. The third is what we should make of the aforementioned crystallization differences. I take these matters up here.

To begin with the first question, I make use of data from the 2008 ANES survey, which contains a rich array of measures necessary to address these points. I focus on three principles: equal opportunity, moral traditionalism, and family values. Although the survey contains multiple measures of attitudes toward specific foreign policy issues (e.g., the war in Iraq), it lacks good measures of militarism, which is why the principle is not included in what follows. Fortunately, the survey contains four measures that can be used to tap two dimensions of moral belief (Goren 2005). The first is moral traditionalism, which I define as the extent to which someone rejects tolerance of moral diversity because she believes ortho-dox moral views should prevail. The second principle is family values, which reflects support for traditional conceptions of family structure (i.e., heterosexual, two-parent households). Question-wording for the moral traditionalism items is as follows: (1) "The world is always changing and we should adjust our views of moral behavior to those changes" and (2) "We should be more tolerant of people who choose to live according to their own moral standards, even if they are very different from our own." The wording for the family values items is: (1) "The newer lifestyles are contributing to the breakdown of our society" and (2) "This country would have many fewer problems if there were more emphasis on tradi-tional family ties." There are five response options for each statement, ranging from "strongly agree" to "strongly disagree."

The first thing to do is determine whether the items tap latent principles to a comparable degree across sophistication-stratified samples. To measure sophis-tication I created a twelve-item political knowledge scale and broke the sample into low-, medium-, and high-knowledge groups.[9] I then estimated a confirma-tory factor analysis model for each sample. The model is specified so that responses to the three equality items, the two traditionalism items, and the two family-values items load on distinct factors. Put otherwise, I expect a three-factor solu-tion will emerge in all three samples. Critically, I also expect that the factor loadings will not differ across samples, save for sampling error.

Table 8-11 contains the statistical estimates. The key point to note is that measurement equivalence holds. As we can see, the hypothesized three-factor model fits the data exceptionally well in all groups, as evidenced by the model-fit statistics. The table further reveals that the factor loadings for each free item do not differ significantly across samples (see the LM test results reported in the note). These estimates dovetail nicely with what I reported in my article: the equal-opportunity results replicate those reported earlier while the moral tradi-tionalism and family-values results establish measurement-equivalence for two additional principles.[10] More broadly, my analysis of data from six ANES studies suggests that the politically aware and unaware hold genuine, equivalently struc-tured domain-specific principles.

On to the next question: do the politically aware and unaware rely on these principles to a similar degree when casting presidential votes? Theoretically, the arguments presented in the article about the ability of the sophisticated and unso-phisticated to ground their issue preferences in domain-specific principles applies here, though the specific mechanism underlying voter decision making differs to some extent.[11] I expect, once again, that the sophistication variable will prove inconsequential when it comes to the use of core principles. Of course, propo-nents of sophistication-interaction theory would posit that the relationship between general principles and electoral choice will depend on sophistication. I test these rival claims by modeling the 2008 presidential vote as a function of

Table 8-11 2008 Confirmatory Factor Analysis Models for Core Principles by Level of Sophistication, Unstandardized Estimates

	Low	Medium	High
Factor Loadings			
ξ_1 Equal opportunity (5-point scale)			
λ_1 Make sure everyone has equal opportunity to succeed	1.00	1.00	1.00
λ_2 Problem in country don't give everyone equal chance	1.85	2.06	1.56
λ_3 If people treated more equally have fewer problems	2.18	2.03	1.43
Cronbach's α	.56	.63	.70
ξ_2 Moral traditionalism (5-point scale)			
λ_4 World always changing and we should adjust	1.00	1.00	1.00
λ_5 Should be more tolerant of different moral standards	0.93	1.13	0.87
Cronbach's α	.44	.62	.64
ξ_3 Family Values (5-point scale)			
λ_6 New lifestyles contributing to breakdown of society	1.00	1.00	1.00
λ_7 Need more emphasis on traditional family ties	1.45	0.93	0.85
Cronbach's α	.43	.67	.73
Model Fit			
Robust χ^2	25.72 **	11.32	20.41*
Degrees of freedom	11	11	11
Robust χ^2/df	2.34	1.03	1.86
AGFI	.96	.98	.96
Robust CFI	.93	1.00	.99
Number of cases	688	715	658

$^* p < .05; ^{**} p < .01.$

Notes: Data weighted using ANES sampling weight. Latent and observed variables are coded so higher scores reflect more support for principle; therefore, each λ_i should be positive. All factor loadings significant at $p < .01$. The metric of each factor is defined by fixing the loading for the first item to 1.00. Scaled LM test of equal loadings for equal opportunity: $\chi_4^2 = 5.35, p = .25$. Scaled LM test of equal loadings for moral traditionalism: $\chi_2^2 = 2.51, p = .29$. Scaled LM test of equal loadings for family values: $\chi_2^2 = 2.07, p = .36$.

party identification, liberal-conservative identification, the three principles described above, political sophistication, and ideology x sophistication, equality x sophistication, traditionalism x sophistication, and family values x sophistication cross-product terms.[12]

Table 8-12 reports unstandardized logistic regression estimates for two vote-choice models. The dependent variable is coded so that the higher score denotes an Obama vote. Model 1 is the baseline, containing all variables except the domain-specific principle x sophistication cross-products. I anticipate that the party and equality variables will be positively related, and the moral value variables inversely related, to an Obama vote. The liberal-conservative constituent

Table 8-12 2008 Presidential Vote Choice Models

	Model 1	Model 2
Constant	−2.11* (0.99)	−4.55** (1.56)
Party identification (Hi = Dem)	0.63** (.06)	0.64** (.06)
Liberal-Conservative ID (Hi = lib)	−0.21+ (.13)	−0.21+ (.13)
Equal opportunity	0.16** (.05)	0.32** (.12)
Moral traditionalism	−0.11* (.05)	0.07(.12)
Family values	−0.22** (.06)	−0.15(.14)
Political sophistication	−0.37** (.09)	−0.04 (.19)
Liberal-conservative ID × sophistication	0.05** (.02)	0.05** (.02)
Equal opportunity x sophistication		−0.02+ (.02)
Moral traditionalism × sophistication		−0.03+ (.02)
Family values × sophistication		−.01 (.02)
Wald χ^2	248.44 **	257.81**
McFadden R^2	.64	.64
McKelvey-Zaviona R^2	.81	.81

$^+ p < .10;\ ^* p < .05;\ ^{**} p < .01;$

Notes: Data weighted using ANES sampling weight. Standard errors in parentheses. Wald test for three principle × sophistication terms in model 2: $\chi^2_3 = 5.12$, $p = .16$. N = 1,436.

variable should be insignificant, which would indicate that ideological leanings do not shape electoral choice among the least sophisticated. The liberal-conservative ID x sophistication term should be positive, which would show that ideology more strongly affects voter choice at higher levels of knowledge.

Turning to the results, we can see that the party and ideology x sophistication terms behave as predicted. Unsurprisingly, Democratic partisanship enhances the probability of casting an Obama ballot and liberal ideology has a comparable effect among informed voters. Most importantly for my purposes, the parameter estimate for each domain-specific principle is correctly signed and statistically significant. Since these coefficients are not directly interpretable, let us consider the predicted change in the probability of voting for Obama moving from minus one to plus one standard deviation on each principle (all other variables are held constant at their means). First, movement up the equal-opportunity scale raises the likelihood of an Obama vote by .21 (from .46 to .67). Second, increasing support for moral traditionalism lowers the probability of an Obama vote by .13 (from .63 to .50). Third, respondents one standard deviation above the family-values mean are far less likely to vote for Obama (.44) than those a standard deviation below the mean (.68). Put simply, domain-specific principles manifest strong effects on voter choice—at least in the 2008 presidential election.

What happens when the principle x sophistication terms are added to the baseline model? Not much, according to the model 2 estimates. The third column in Table 8-12 reveals a tendency for the less sophisticated to rely on beliefs about equality a bit more and for the more sophisticated to make somewhat greater use of beliefs about traditional morality (there is no hint of an effect in the family values x sophistication term). However, a Wald test of the null hypothesis that all three domain-specific principle x sophistication terms equal zero cannot be rejected ($\chi^2_3 = 5.12$, $p = .16$).[13] Finally, in terms of model fit, adding the principle x sophistication terms to the baseline does nothing for model fit. Overall, there is little evidence that sophistication strengthens the impact core principles have on voter decision making.

To sum up, my analysis of the 2008 data suggests that politically sophisticated and unsophisticated citizens are equally adept at (1) translating latent principles into meaningful responses on opinion items designed to tap those principles and (2) grounding their votes in said principles. Substantively, these results suggest, as did my original and current program of research (Goren forthcoming; 2001), that when it comes to the development and use of domain-specific principles, sophistication matters far less for political judgment and voter decision making than we have been led to believe.

The last question my original piece did not address was the relationship between political sophistication and the consistency of responses to the core principle items. Although the relevant information is presented in the confirmatory factor analysis tables—as evinced by the Cronbach α estimates—and referenced in footnote 1, the lack of discussion on this topic may have obscured the one area in which sophistication differences consistently emerged. To see why this is the case, I begin by noting that the alpha coefficients reported in each of my confirmatory factor analysis tables can be interpreted as estimates of the ratio of true score variance to observed scale variance for a given additive scale (Bollen 1989). That is, the higher the value alpha assumes in a given sample, the less the scale is contaminated by random errors of measurement. Scholars often assume that high levels of random measurement error in opinion reports reflect weakly developed attitudes or perhaps even nonattitudes. Hence, if the estimated alpha for an additive scale is very low (say .10), we conclude that citizens lack true attitudes or beliefs on the matter in question. Conversely, if the estimate alpha is very high (say .80) we conclude that the attitude or belief is genuine.

One of the most enduring findings in the study of electoral behavior is that the reliability of opinion reports is a positive function of sophistication. Accumulated research shows that the opinion responses of less sophisticated individuals are more heavily contaminated by random measurement error than responses provided by more sophisticated subsets of the public (Chong, McClosky, and Zaller 1983; Feldman 1989; Norpoth and Lodge 1985). Such results suggest that latent attitudes and beliefs held by the sophisticated are more developed or "crystallized" relative to those held by the less sophisticated. To put it another way, these results suggest that the political attitudes and beliefs held by the politically aware lie closer to the dispositional end of the attitude-nonattitude continuum (Converse 1970; Eagly and Chaiken 1993).

The results reported in my work are consistent with this finding.[14] Across the six CFA tables reported in the original article and in this epilogue, the Cronbach α estimates always increase monotonically as we move from the low- to medium- to high-sophistication groups. This holds for the social welfare principles of equal opportunity, self-reliance, and limited government (Tables 8-1, 8.3, 5) the foreign policy principles of militarism and anticommunism (Tables 8-7 and 9), and the moral principles of traditionalism and family values (Table 8-11). Some of the differences are rather modest, such as the .05 difference in the 1984 equal opportunity scale for low versus high respondents. Others are considerably larger, such as the .29 difference in the 2008 family values scales for low versus high respondents. Across the complete set of scales, the mean high-low difference is just under .16. Again, this suggests that politically aware respondents hold more fully crystallized principles relative to less sophisticated respondents. Such results make it plain that variance in political sophistication has important consequences for the consistency of survey responses (cf. Zaller 1992). On these grounds, sophistication matters.

But not terribly much. It is critical to recognize that while the responses of political experts reflect less noise than those of novices, this result does not imply that the latter lack genuine beliefs. A quick perusal of the alpha estimates for the less sophisticated across all the tables reveals immediately that the survey responses of the less sophisticated reflect much more than random noise. Despite the fact that I have only two to four items to tap each latent principle, the alpha estimate exceeds .50 in eleven of the thirteen cases (though a bit of this is probably attributable to shared method variance). The remaining two estimates are somewhat lower but not terribly so (moral traditionalism = .44 and family ties = .43), and they occur for two-item scales. More broadly, the mean alpha value across these thirteen scales equals .55 for the unsophisticated, meaning that latent true score variance accounts for over half of the observed score variance. The comparable mean is .70 for the sophisticated samples, clearly a more impressive figure, but one which suggests that crystallization differences are differences in degree rather than in kind. Finally, insofar as the reliability estimates for the most aware fall short of unity, we have grounds for suspecting that the survey questions bear some responsibility for the presence of random measurement error (see Norpoth and Lodge 1985).

In my judgment, the key point to take away from all this is that sophistication-based differences in attitude crystallization ultimately do not really affect the types of political judgment considered here. While the core principles held by the less sophisticated lie a bit further from the dispositional end of the attitude-nonattitude continuum than those held by their more sophisticated counterparts, they are crystallized sufficiently enough to shape preference formation and candidate choice to a comparable degree for these citizens (cf. Ansolabehere, Rodden, and Snyder 2008). This is an absolutely critical result because it shows that minor to moderate differences in attitude crystallization across levels of sophistication can be inconsequential when it comes to certain judgments rendered by people falling at different places along the sophistication continuum. Put simply, cognitively heterogeneous populations may differ systematically in terms of how developed their core principles are, but such differences do not affect their ability to ground political choices in these principles.

Notes

1. In the samples used here the principle items are more reliable at higher levels of sophistication (see the Cronbach α estimates in the measurement model tables below), which suggests that the attitude reports of the politically aware are more crystallized than those of the unaware (cf. Chong, McClosky, and Zaller 1983).

2. All models are estimated via maximum likelihood using the EQS program. ML estimation assumes that the observed variables are continuous and multivariate normally distributed. When these assumptions are violated chi-square tests and standard errors may be biased (Bollen 1989). To deal with this I report Satorra-Bentler (i.e., robust) chi-squares and robust standard errors, which are more accurate than the uncorrected ML statistics (Chou and Bentler 1995; Curran, West, and Finch 1997).

3. Needy and elderly programs are treated as separate dependent variables for two reasons. Conceptually, the elderly elicit more sympathy than people on welfare, blacks, and so on. Empirically, confirmatory factor analysis reveals that a two-factor solution in which the needy items load on one factor and the elderly items load on a second fits the data quite well across sophistication-stratified samples (see Goren 2004).

4. Question-wording and missing-data information for all items appear in the appendix.

5. I use only three of the six equality items on the ANES surveys for the following reasons. Americans equate equality with ensuring that people have the same opportunities to get ahead in life rather than having equal abilities or experiencing equal outcomes (Feldman and Zaller 1992). In terms of face validity, the items I employ (see Table 8-1 and appendix) more directly tap beliefs about equal opportunity than the items I exclude, which mention pushing equal rights (which alludes to civil rights for African Americans), worrying less about how equal people are, and if it is a problem that some people have more of a chance in life than others (the latter two seem to reference innate differences in ability). I ran a series of factor analyses on the full equality battery and found that the items I use load on one factor while the others load on a second (factor correlations are modest). Clearly, these are separate dimensions of equality, only one of which taps equal opportunity. Furthermore, in a parallel set of analyses, Sears, Henry, and Kosterman (2001, 97, 101, 105) find (1) comparable measurement model results; (2) that the non-opportunity items correlate with measures of biological and symbolic racism; and (3) that the equal opportunity items do not correlate with the racism measures. Thus, the items I use possess discriminant validity whereas the excluded items do not. Finally, note that I use four of the six available self-reliance items because my attempts to fit a model to all six yielded poor statistical fit.

6. Space limits preclude inclusion of the measurement model estimates that accompany the structural estimates.

7. Two further notes about the models. First, given the limited number of cases in the pilot study I split it into two rather than three groups. Second, ideology has little effect on the preference variables; therefore, it is excluded from the models.

8. The domain-specific theory posits that principles germane in one domain should not affect attitudes in unrelated domains. Such links would suggest that citizens use principles illogically and thereby undermine the theory. To see if citizens use these principles only in the relevant domains, I estimated structural models in which (1) equal opportunity and self-reliance or limited government were predictors of attitudes towards defense spending and Contra aid and (2) militarism and anticommunism served as predictors of attitudes toward spending on the needy and on the elderly (party identification and ideology were included as controls in all the models). I found that principles did not affect preferences in unrelated domains in twenty-nine of thirty-six tests. These analyses are available from the author upon request.

9. These items ask about placing Barack Obama, John McCain, the Democratic Party, and Republican Party on liberal-conservative scales and separate left-right scales; which party is more conservative at the national level; which party controls the House and Senate; and the interviewer rating of each respondent's apparent level of information about politics (alpha = .88).

10. I replicated these results using data from several additional ANES surveys that contain measures of equality, moral beliefs, and militarism. Some of these results will be reported in Goren (N.d).

11. My current program of research addresses this matter in much greater theoretical and empirical detail than is possible here (Goren N.d.).

12. I measure party ID with a simple additive scale comprised of the standard seven-point self-placement item and a feeling thermometer difference measure. Liberal-conservative identification is measured via a simple additive scale based on the pre- and post-election seven-point self-placement items. Both variables are coded so that higher scores denote stronger left-leaning sentiments.

13. In contrast, for model 1 a test of the null hypothesis that all three core principle coefficients equal zero can be rejected ($\chi^2_3 = 31.87$, $p < .001$).

14. In my current research I find a comparable pattern of results using data from the 1984–2008 ANES surveys (Goren forthcoming).

PART III
VOTE DETERMINANTS

9. Are Economic Factors Weakening as
Vote Determinants?

Ultimately, studies of voting behavior attempt to explain the determinants of voting choices. Common explanations of voting decisions have touched on party identification (Campbell et al. 1960), retrospective evaluations of the government (Key 1966; Fiorina 1981), issues and ideology (Downs 1957; Enelow and Hinich 1984; Petrocik 1996), as well as candidate characteristics (Stokes 1966b; Weisberg and Rusk 1970). Is voting mainly a function of party loyalties? Is voting based primarily on popularity of the outgoing government, or on the major issues of the day? Are characteristics of candidates (such as their experience or appearance) most important to voters? There is evidence that all of the factors listed above influence voters, but that consensus on the relative importance of partisanship, issues, and candidate traits is unlikely (Niemi and Weisberg 2001, chap. 9).

Other debates delve into a more specific concern by examining the influence of campaigns on voting decisions. Are election outcomes determined before the campaign even begins, by long-term forces such as partisanship, the economy, and incumbency? Alternatively, do campaigns and the media shape voter perceptions and influence election results? Recent research continues to indicate, that while each election does not begin from scratch, media and campaign events have more than a minimal influence on voters and elections (Niemi and Weisberg 2001, chap. 10; Shaw 2006; Hillygus and Shields 2008; Vavreck 2009).

More recently, the question of what determines the vote has reemerged, renewing and expanding a focus on the importance of economic factors. One type of economic consideration has been a staple of voting studies in the United States and other democracies—that is, that social class is a reliable predictor of voting, with middle-class and wealthy voters favoring conservative political parties while poor and working-class voters tending to support leftist parties. A second fundamental hypothesis of voting studies is that evaluations of economic performance shape voting decisions, with voters rewarding the incumbent party in good times and punishing the governing party in bad times. Now, however, a revisionist literature is challenging both presumptions, arguing that economic influences have been overstated and are being matched or eclipsed by other vote determinants. Some arguments suggest that rising partisan polarization has reduced the impact of economic evaluations on voters for at least the past decade. Others argue that "economic voting" is generally limited as to time and place. And still others argue that new social cleavages based partly on cultural values have displaced class divisions.

Class Voting Is in Decline; Social Issues Are on the Rise

The first economic factor under siege in voting studies is class. A long-standing perspective views politics in terms of class conflict, with economic self-interest being a primary motivator for voters. For example, wealthy voters tend to favor low taxes and less government involvement in the economy while low-income voters tend to prefer taxes to support redistributive government programs. Economic issues especially important to this class conflict include taxes, unemployment, and government regulation of the economy. In the United States in the middle of the twentieth century, class divisions provided the main basis for the New Deal coalition in the Democratic Party and its opposition in the Republican Party (Lazarsfeld, Berelson, and Gaudet 1948). Class politics also was an important source of party conflict in other democracies during that period and for some time after (Alford, 1963; Butler and Stokes 1969; Lipset 1981).

Studies of class voting have relied heavily on occupation as a key measure of class, usually pitting working-class manual laborers against business owners and middle-class white-collar employers (Alford 1963). The class voting cleavage hypothesizes that working-class voters support left-leaning parties much more than middle-class voters. However, using occupation-based measures, studies starting at least two decades ago identify a decline in class voting in the United States and other industrialized democracies (Franklin, 1985; Knutsen 2007; Dalton 2008, chap. 8; Lewis-Beck et al. 2008, 342–343; Abramson, Aldrich, and Rohde 2007, chap. 5). In the United States., the working-class coalition of the Democratic Party has gradually eroded over the past fifty years (Stanley and Niemi 2006). For the most part, the scholarly consensus is that class voting has declined. Brooks, Nieuwbeerta, and Manza (2006), using more extensive occupational class categories, find that class voting is undiminished in some countries, but they still observe a drop in class voting in countries such as Britain and the United States.

There is more debate about why class voting has declined and what has taken its place. Some point to changes in the economies of industrial democracies that have altered the class structure. The growth of the service economy in many countries has produced a large group of white-collar service workers, what some call a "new middle class" (Dalton 2008; Knutsen 2007). In fact, Dalton (2008) describes traditional class divisions as "old politics" and argues that the new middle class is defining a "new politics" in many countries. Several scholars have followed the work of Inglehart (1990), who argues that as industrialized nations have satisfied the basic material needs of many citizens, "post-material" (quality of life) considerations have grown in importance as vote determinants.

Post-material issues can include environmental protection, civil rights for both women and minorities, and disputes over religious and cultural values (such as abortion, gun control, and now gay marriage). For example, Dalton (2008) compares materialists (who care more about pocketbook issues and security) with post-materialists (who care more about environmental protection and social equality). He finds voting differences between materialists and post-materialists that rival or exceed class differences. In addition, post-material values are more prevalent among younger and more educated voters. Dalton goes so far as to predict that issue cleavages will gain in importance in explaining voting behavior at the expense of demographic differences, such as class (Dalton 2008, 168). Studies find that post-materialist attitudes are important predictors of voting behavior in other countries as well (Palmer 1995; Lusztig and Wilson 2005).[1]

In American politics, common post-material issues tend to involve conflicts over social issues tinged with religious and moral considerations. Some observers posit a growing "culture war" in which social issues are displacing class differences as vote determinants (see this volume, chap. 12). Miller and Schofield (2003) argue that party activists have created a second, cultural issue dimension in American politics during the last forty years (see also Shafer and Claggett 1995). In addition, the cultural dimension has reduced the power of the economic cleavage as low-income, but socially conservative, "populists" have shifted their voting support toward the Republican Party and high-income socially liberal "cosmopolitans" increasingly vote for Democratic candidates. As a result, each party needs to negotiate a balance between economic and social-issue activists in its coalition (Schofield and Miller 2007). In the popular press, Frank (2004) argues that GOP politicians have skillfully used social issues to induce low-income voters to support Republican candidates and vote against their economic interests. A recent study by Hillygus and Shields (2008) notes that voters are more likely to be cross-pressured (that is, hold issue positions inconsistent with their partisanship) on moral issues than economic issues. As a result, moral issues are appealing to party strategists as "wedge" issues in campaigns.[2] Finally, they find that cultural issues have been an important source of Democratic Party defection among southern white voters in several recent elections (see this volume, chap. 21).

More generally, religion, moral values, and social issues have received increasing attention in studies of voting behavior during the last twenty years. Several scholars examine religious affiliation and commitment as predictors of vote choice (White 2003; Layman 2001; Layman and Green 2006; Green 2007). While voting differences between faith traditions have diminished, religious beliefs and religious commitment are frequently examined as voting predictors. Studies of religious beliefs often focus on divisions over doctrinal orthodoxy and the authoritative nature of religious texts, pitting traditionalists against modernists (Hunter 1991; Layman and Green 2006). Religious commitment focuses more on behavior, such as how often one prays or attends worship services. Across several faith traditions, voters with more traditional religious beliefs and higher levels of religious commitment are more likely to support Republican candidates and conservative views (Wald and Calhoun-Brown 2006; Layman and Green 2006). However, researchers generally find that political cleavages defined by religious beliefs and behavior are most sharply defined for issues closely linked to moral values, such as abortion and gay marriage, and to voters who are most aware of those issues.

Some voting studies examine white evangelical Protestants as a key religious voting bloc (Layman 2001; Layman and Green 2006). Evangelical voters tend to be on the traditional side of the orthodoxy divide and tend to have high levels of religious commitment. Consequently, white evangelical voters have become a critical part of the Republican Party coalition (Wald and Calhoun-Brown 2006). In addition, Campbell (2006) argues that "religious threat" is another feature of culture-war politics in the United States. He finds that evangelical voters are more likely to vote for Republican presidential candidates when they live in the presence of more secular people in their community.

Other studies move beyond religion to identify moral values and other cultural orientations as predictors of voting behavior. Leege and colleagues (2002) argue that cultural conflicts over a range of such issues inform campaign strategy and influence voting behavior in the United States. Weisberg (2005a) examines two dimensions of moral values: moral traditionalism refers to a preference for traditional family values and structures; moral judgment refers to one's willingness to condemn alternative lifestyles, such as cohabitation or homosexuality. Weisberg provides evidence that the two concepts are distinct dimensions of moral attitudes and that they are related to opinions on issues such as abortion. Barker and Tinnick (2006) test ideas of Lakoff (2002) about parenting values as metaphors for political parties in the United States. People who favor "nurturant" parenting roles are more likely to hold liberal positions on many issues and vote for Democratic candidates. Voters who favor "disciplinarian" parenting roles are more likely to hold conservative issue positions and support Republican candidates (Barker and Tinnick 2006).

In a similar vein, Hetherington and Weiler (2009) identify authoritarianism, a desire to maintain order, as a critical value in political disputes over cultural and foreign policy issues and, hence, a key predictor of voting behavior. Those with an authoritarian view of the world are increasingly likely to vote for Republican candidates while those with a less authoritarian and more nuanced view tend to vote for Democrats. They find that authoritarianism is more prevalent among whites with low levels of education and income, fueling a cultural conflict that appeared in the 2008 Democratic presidential nominating contest between U.S. Senators Barack Obama and Hillary Clinton. Most importantly, because a growing number of issue debates, including gay marriage, immigration, civil rights, and the use of military force, are informed by an authoritarian worldview, a political cleavage defined by authoritarianism may rival the traditional economic cleavage that has historically separated the two main parties in the United States.

The scholarly emphasis on moral and religious values may have peaked after the 2004 presidential election. Several months before the election, the Massachusetts Supreme Judicial Court ruled that a ban on gay marriage violated the state constitution, leading to gay wedding ceremonies in Massachusetts. In an effort designed partly to mobilize religious voters, conservative groups placed initiatives to ban gay marriage on the ballot in several states, including the battleground states of Florida and Ohio. The National Election Pool exit polls indicated that a plurality (22 percent) of voters selected "moral values" as the most important issue facing the country, and roughly 80 percent of those moral values voters selected President George W. Bush. These facts heavily shaped post-election interpretations of the election among journalists, with many concluding that moral values were a strong influence on voting (Mulligan 2008).

Political science research was less conclusive. Some argued that the ballot initiatives in 2004 increased the importance voters attached to the issue (Donovan, Tolbert, and Smith 2008) and mobilized white evangelical Protestants to support President Bush (Campbell and Monson 2008). As a result, attitudes toward gay marriage were a strong influence on voters (Lewis 2005; Mulligan 2008). Others argued that attitudes toward gay marriage did not predict the votes of Independents or voters in swing states and were outweighed by opinions on the economy and foreign affairs (Burden 2004; Hillygus and Shields 2005). In addition, Hillygus and Shields (2008, chap. 6) observe that the direct-mail campaigns of both Bush and his Democratic opponent, U.S. Senator John Kerry, featured much more discussion of economic and foreign policy issues than moral issues. Langer and Cohen (2005) also argue that any effect of moral values in the 2004 election is overstated. They show that voter concerns about moral values had not increased over previous elections and that the moral values item in exit polls was less predictive of voting than other issues, especially the economy and terrorism. Nevertheless, the fact that this scholarly debate is taking place indicates that researchers are considering religion and moral values more seriously as vote determinants.[3]

Of course there are frequently short-term noneconomic factors that affect election outcomes. In addition to gay marriage in 2004, for example, the Iraq War was an important issue in the election, with the Republicans portraying it as an essential part of the larger War on Terrorism and the Democrats claiming it was a diversion from that larger war. While attitudes toward the Iraq War were generally negative, several studies show that the war helped bolster President Bush's image as a strong leader, which was a key factor in his victory (Weisberg and Christenson 2007; Norpoth and Sidman 2007; Abramson et al. 2007). A very different noneconomic issue was relevant in the 2008 election—racial attitudes, activated by the nomination of the first African-American major party presidential candidate. Analysis shows that racial attitudes affected voting in 2008 (Tesler and Sears 2009; Weisberg and Devine 2009; Clarke et al. 2009; Barreto and Segura 2009), mobilizing the Democratic vote among African Americans, increasing it among white racial liberals, and decreasing it among white racial conservatives.

The 2004 and 2008 examples point to one other important noneconomic vote determinant: how the public perceives the candidates. Political psychologists (Kinder 1986; Funk 1999) have distinguished several basic candidate traits: their leadership, competence, integrity, and empathy. Studies repeatedly find perceived leadership to be significant in affecting the vote, while competence is, interestingly, not significant under multivariate controls. Integrity and empathy are each significant in some elections but not others. Other political psychologists (Marcus, Neuman, and MacKuen 2000) instead emphasize the emotions that candidates elicit from voters, such as whether the candidate makes voters feel angry or hopeful. Obviously campaigns develop television ads that try to play to these findings—emphasizing their candidate's leadership ability and empathy and trying to make people feel hopeful about their candidate while challenging the other candidate's experience and integrity and trying to make people feel afraid of the opposition party candidate (Brader 2006).

Economic Voting Effects Are Overstated

The second attack on economic factors is on economic voting per se. By 2007, more than four hundred published studies had examined economic evaluations and voting (Lewis-Beck and Stegmaier 2007). Traditionally, researchers have identified two important dimensions of economic evaluations. One involves the time perspective of the voter. As articulated by Key (1966), some posit that economic evaluations are retrospective, focusing on past events and a candidate or party's prior performance in handling the economy. If economic conditions have been good, the incumbent party tends to be rewarded. If the economy has deteriorated, then the incumbent party tends to be defeated (Fiorina 1981; Kiewiet 1983). Others follow Downs (1957) and argue that voters consider how a candidate or party is expected to handle the economy in the future (Lockerbie 2007; MacKuen, Erikson, and Stimson 1992).

Another dimension of economic voting involves the locus of economic conditions considered by the voter. "Egotropic" evaluations focus on personal or household finances, while "sociotropic" evaluations focus on national economic conditions (Kinder and Kiewiet 1981). Studies of presidential elections tend to find more evidence for sociotropic voting than for egotropic voting (Lewis-Beck and Stegmaier 2007; Kiewiet 1983). Gomez and Wilson (2001, 2006) refine the argument, theorizing that well-informed people vote more on the basis of egotropic economic evaluations, while less informed voters are more influenced by sociotropic evaluations. They find evidence in the United States and four other countries to support this thesis. Importantly, this suggests that the economic interests of informed voters are more likely to be received by public officials (see also Bartels 2008).

However, there is a debate about the degree to which economic voting is a function of partisanship rather than an independent vote determinant. As we note in Part IV, there is evidence of resurgent partisanship in the United States.

As the authors of *The American Voter* theorized, party identification "raises a perceptual screen through which the individual tends to see what is favorable to his partisan orientation" (Campbell et al. 1960, 133; see also Bartels 2002). More recent studies in political psychology elaborate on this theory. For example, Taber and Lodge (2006) find evidence of a "disconfirmation bias" in political reasoning—people tend to argue against evidence contrary to their beliefs and uncritically accept evidence that supports their beliefs. If we think of these effects in terms of economic evaluations, those who identify with the governing party want to believe their party is improving the nation's economy, while those who identify with the out-party tend to believe the governing party is hurting the economy, all in spite of objective evidence. Thus, survey-based measures of economic evaluations may be heavily influenced by partisanship rather than actual economic conditions. As a result, the impact of economic evaluations on voting is exaggerated.

In an article reprinted here, Evans and Andersen (2006) argue that voters' economic perceptions are strongly influenced by their partisan preferences, and they examine a case that does not conform to the expectations of retrospective economic voting theory. They note that public support for the governing Conservative Party of Britain declined as the nation's economy improved noticeably during the 1990s. In addition, using panel data Evans and Andersen find that retrospective economic evaluations are influenced by prior opinions of the Conservative Party. Once those effects are controlled, economic evaluations have a weaker impact on support for the governing party (also, see Anderson et al. 2004).

Other studies using different data and methods also note a relationship between partisanship and economic evaluations (Duch, Palmer, and Anderson 2000; Ladner and Wlezien 2007; Gerber and Huber 2009; Wlezien, Franklin, and Twiggs 1997; Johnston, Thorson, and Gooch 2010).[4] Using panel survey data, Bartels (2002) finds that prior partisanship has a powerful effect on current economic evaluations, while prior economic evaluations have almost no impact on current partisanship. In addition, Bartels notes several examples of sharp partisan differences in evaluations of economic conditions when objective indicators provide pretty clear answers about the economy. Wilcox and Wlezien (1993) use a survey experiment to show that other political attitudes have a strong impact on economic evaluations (see also Conover, Feldman, and Knight 1986). Rudolph (2006) finds evidence of partisan bias in citizens' evaluations of a governor's responsibility for budget deficits. Another study finds that consumer confidence, a common economic indicator, is influenced by political factors such as media coverage of the economy, the party of the president, evaluations of the president, and political events (De Boef and Kellstedt 2004).[5]

Collectively, these studies raise questions about the validity and reliability of some economic evaluation measures, and they suggest that economic evaluations are endogenous to vote choice (that they are influenced by more powerful causes of voting behavior such as partisanship). Other studies raise additional measurement concerns about survey-based measures of economic performance. One concern is measurement error. Some posit that most measurement error in survey questions about economic evaluations is random. Therefore, aggregating survey-based data produces a valid macro-level measure of economic performance (Page and Shapiro 1992; Erikson, MacKuen, and Stimson 2004). Duch, Palmer, and Anderson (2000) challenge this claim, finding systematic error in survey measures of the national economy as a function of political sophistication, media exposure and other factors. Thus, they argue that aggregated, survey-based measures of economic performance are biased as well. The net result of these studies is to raise questions about the impact of economic evaluations on voting, as measured by public opinion surveys.

The Decline of Economic Factors Is Exaggerated and Premature

The apparent decline of class voting along with questions about whether economic evaluations are caused by rather than causing political preferences has provoked a vigorous defense of the importance of economic interests and evaluations as determinants of the vote. There is, for example, a strong push back against the conclusion that class voting is in decline. While there is evidence that occupational differences have lost power as vote predictors, several studies suggest the continuing importance of other measures of class differences. In particular, many recent voting studies suggest that income rather than occupation is the most relevant measure of economic self-interest.[6] Given that wealth may vary substantially within the same occupation, income is a more direct measure of a voter's economic interests. Bartels (2006, 2008), Brewer and Stonecash (2007), and McCarty, Poole, and Rosenthal (2006) present evidence of increasing, rather than decreasing, income differences between Republicans and Democrats (see also this volume, Part V on the GOP realignment in the South). Gelman (2008) provides a more nuanced view, arguing that there are important political differences between rich and poor voters, but also important cultural differences between wealthy voters from different regions of the country. As a result, voting differences between low-income and high-income citizens are most pronounced in relatively poor states. Finally, Grafstein (2005) argues that unemployment status is an important measure of the influence of class politics, with unemployed people more likely to vote for Democratic presidential candidates. Given the decline in manufacturing jobs and the growth of service and knowledge-based occupations in many advanced democracies, one can argue that income and unemployment should replace occupation as a measure of class differences and fundamental economic interests of voters.

Another response to the argument that economic factors are in decline comes from burgeoning efforts to document the content of campaign appeals made by the major parties and their leading candidates. These studies tend to find that economic issues still comprise the bulk of partisan campaign messages.

Contrary to arguments about a growing moral/culture war in the United States, Smith (2007) argues that Republican Party rhetoric has increasingly focused on economic issues. The growth of conservative think tanks and magazines capitalized on growing public anxiety about economic issues and pushed economic rhetoric into elite policy debates after the 1960s. During the same period, Republican politicians increased their reliance on economic arguments in speeches and campaigns. As a result, the GOP was perceived as better at handling the economy for many of the last forty years. These perceptions helped Republican presidential candidates gain voter support, even after controlling for objective economic conditions. Similarly, studies of presidential campaign messages in televised advertisements and direct mailings find that economic issues are mentioned more often than moral issues (Hillygus and Shields 2008; Geer 2006). And despite declining news coverage and changing content, increasing numbers of campaign ads may have helped to assure that voters hear about candidates' policy positions (Gilens, Vavreck, and Cohen 2007). Even in recent elections, when cultural issues have been relatively prominent, people more frequently mention economic or foreign policy issues than moral issues when asked what they like or dislike about the political parties and their presidential candidates (Lewis-Beck et al. 2008; Brewer 2009).[7]

Yet more evidence for the continuing importance of economic voting comes from scholarly efforts weighing the relative impact of economic and moral considerations on voting decisions. These studies tend to find that economic attitudes are stronger predictors of voting behavior than cultural attitudes.[8] In one such article, reprinted here, Ansolabehere, Rodden, and Snyder (2006) create comprehensive measures of economic and moral issue positions. They first report that most voters have moderate positions on moral issues, contrary to the claims of a culture war in the United States (see Part 5 on party polarization). More to the point here, they find that economic attitudes have a stronger impact than moral issues on voting in presidential elections (see also Ansolabehere, Rodden, and Snyder 2008). Bartels (2008) finds a similar pattern over twenty years of presidential voting in the United States. Goren (forthcoming) examines "core values" rather than issue attitudes and finds that economic liberalism has a greater impact than moral values on voting decisions. Similarly, Lewis-Beck and colleagues (2008) find that social welfare opinions (along with defense attitudes) are more closely related to partisanship than lifestyle attitudes, which include abortion and gay marriage.

In the same vein, some scholars have revisited the claim by Frank (2004) that the Republican Party has become more adept at wooing low- and middle-income white voters with religious and cultural appeals, to the exclusion of economic appeals. Bartels (2008; 2006) effectively debunks many of Frank's arguments. Low-income white voters have not defected from the Democratic Party. If anything, these voters have become more supportive of Democratic presidential candidates, particularly outside the South. Brewer (2009) also finds that low-income voters have a substantially more favorable view of the Democratic Party than high-income voters. In addition, economic issues still outweigh cultural issues in explaining the votes of low-income and middle-income Americans. If anything, it is high-income voters with liberal social attitudes who have been moving toward the Democratic Party in recent years (also see Gelman 2008; Brewer and Stonecash 2009).

There is no consensus yet in the debate over the endogeneity of economic evaluations. However, there is some agreement that studies using panel data are needed to better sort out the causal impact of partisanship and economic evaluations on each other and on voting (Evans and Andersen 2006; Lewis-Beck and Stegmaier 2007). As noted above, some of these studies conclude that economic evaluations are influenced by partisanship and vote intentions. Lewis-Beck, Nadeau, and Elias (2008) examine panel data from the United States and argue, contrary to Evans and Andersen, that economic evaluations are not much influenced by partisanship. In addition, they find that economic evaluations still serve as important independent predictors of vote choice. However, in comparing the statistical models and use of panel data in articles by Evans and Andersen (2006) and Lewis-Beck and colleagues (2008), one finds that they use different measures of party support and they make different assumptions in constructing their causal models of voting. In particular, Lewis-Beck and colleagues (2008) make assumptions in their causal model that others would dispute. Nevertheless, we expect more studies using panel data from other countries and time periods to bring more evidence to bear on this controversy.

There is less controversy in a growing research agenda that examines the contexts in which economic voting may be stronger or weaker, with an emphasis on the clarity of government responsibility for the economy. In these studies, economic voting is theorized to be stronger in countries and situations where voters clearly understand the responsibility of the national government. For example, Anderson (2006) finds that economic voting is weaker in countries with multilevel governance, which tends to obscure the role of the national government. Hellwig (2001) finds that economic voting is weaker in countries with more globalized economies. Nadeau, Niemi, and Yoshinaka (2002) find that a number of institutional features that reduce the clarity of responsibility (including the number of parties in the governing coalition) also reduce the impact of economic voting and that clarity of responsibility can vary across time within individual countries as well as between countries. Finally, Duch and Stevenson (2008) provide the most comprehensive study of comparative economic voting, with further evidence to support the clarity of responsibility thesis. An important point, however, is that none of these studies suggests that the effect of the economy is in general decline; the economy often has a large impact on the vote—it simply varies in response to identifiable institutional parameters.

Defenders of economic voting also point to a growing election-forecasting literature that relies heavily on retrospective voting theory. Most of the forecasting models use economic conditions and presidential approval as important predictors of election outcomes. These are measures that can be observed well before the campaign (see the *International Journal of Forecasting*, April-June 2008, and *PS: Political Science & Politics*, October 2008; Fair 2009), leading some to question whether campaigns have much influence on presidential elections. With the exception of the 2000 presidential election, forecasting models have been successful at predicting recent U.S. presidential elections. In a series of forecasting studies published before the 2008 election, eight of nine correctly predicted an Obama victory and six of nine correctly predicted a comfortable Obama margin (Campbell 2008b). In another series of forecasts published before the 2004 election, six of seven correctly predicted a clear victory in the popular vote for President Bush (Campbell 2004; see also Fair 2002, 59–66). However, as a series of post-election assessments in the March 2001 issue of *PS* indicate, forecasting models were less successful at predicting vote share in the 2000 presidential election. Seven separate forecasts made in August of 2000 all incorrectly predicted a healthy popular vote victory for Al Gore (Wlezien 2001).

The failure of forecasting models in the 2000 presidential election led to a debate about whether forecasting models accurately captured the impact of economic factors or whether the "flaw" was that the Gore campaign failed to emphasize the Clinton administration's economic record. Bartels and Zaller (2001) take the former position, arguing that many forecasting models fail to adequately measure the impact of economic change on voters. They argue that change in real disposable income is a better economic variable than change in gross domestic product. Other forecasting models have been modified to include a job creation measure (Lewis-Beck and Tien 2008). Bartels and Zaller (2001) are also relatively early advocates of the power of model aggregation. They find that averaging among many models produces a more reliable forecast than relying on a single forecasting model. The aggregation principle has also been used in other election forecasting studies (Graefe, Armstrong, Cuzàn, and Jones 2009) and in popular Web sites like Pollster.com.

Finally, Bartels (2008) also seeks to modify forecasting models but focuses on the time horizon and the type of economic growth that best predicts presidential voting. In terms of the time horizon, the results can be summed up by the phrase "What have you done for me lately?" Bartels finds that voters tend to use a very short time horizon for making retrospective economic evaluations, largely basing evaluations on economic growth in the presidential election year rather than over the entire four-year term. In addition, he points to an income bias in economic voting whereby even low- and middle-income voters are most responsive to income growth among the wealthiest Americans.

In contrast to efforts to modify forecasting models, Vavreck (2009) argues that the Gore campaign failed in 2000 because it underemphasized the economy. She notes that the incumbent party has an incentive to tout the economy in good times while the challenging party has an incentive to concentrate on an economic message in bad times. When not facing either of those conditions, presidential candidates should focus their campaign messages on noneconomic issues. In examining presidential campaign communications, she reports that candidates who follow this strategy are more successful than those who do not. More generally, she argues that researchers must be careful to observe whether or not campaigns amplify existing economic conditions. Thus, the economy could appear to be weak in a given instance, but the "problem" is not so much faulty reasoning about the factors that underlie presidential campaigns as it is about the choices candidates make about what to emphasize.

In the end, it is important to note that all of the various qualifications to economic voting models as well as all of the modifications to forecasting models reaffirm that economic factors are crucial vote determinants even if economic voting is not completely understood. All of these approaches call for refining—not abandoning—the economy as a major factor in vote determinants models.

Conclusion

One part of the controversy over economic voting has, we think, been settled. That is, the debate over the decline of class voting in the United States has been resolved, at least to a degree. Class voting, based on self-reports, is no longer highly correlated with voter preferences. Occupation, on which self-reports have historically been based, no longer appears to be an adequate measure of class differences or economic interests. When income is used as a measure of class differences, there is no evidence of a decline in class voting. If anything, voting is more stratified than in the past. More studies may be needed to determine whether the apparent decline in class voting in other nations vanishes when income is used as the class measure. But in the United States, income, not self-reported class, is what is crucial.

Another part of the controversy may also have been settled. There seems to be agreement that economic voting occurs to different degrees depending on institutional characteristics as well as the specific economic conditions that exist at any given time. There is even agreement at a broad level that characteristics that clarify and amplify the government's responsibility for the economy are a crucial determinant of the economy's impact on voters.

Apart from these points, however, the debate goes on. Are economic evaluations sufficiently determined by partisanship and other evaluations that economic views are more effect than cause? How frequently does clarity of responsibility allow the economy to rise to a major determinant of the vote? Can we specify conditions under which other issues predominate? In fact, can we really determine which factors are *most* crucial? Even in 2008, one might point out, when the U.S. economy was shattered and evaluations of the national economy were more pessimistic than in any presidential year that American National Election Studies surveys asked the question (Holbrook 2009), not all analyses have concluded that it was the primary factor in Obama's victory.[9]

Studies of vote determinants, while having focused heavily on the economy for the past decade, will continue to consider other factors as well—including episodic issues such as wars as well as other *classes* of issues, including moral, cultural, and religious matters. Nor will candidate characteristics (e.g., race, ethnicity, gender) and perceived candidate competence be ignored. In the long run, we anticipate that the broad categories first identified by the authors of *The American Voter*—parties, issues, and candidates—will frame discussions of what determines voter decisions and election outcomes, rising and falling in their salience depending on institutional factors and the influx of particular events and individuals. As has been the case for the past half-century, the task for political scientists is to make sense of what sometimes seem like random patterns, establishing connections to institutional factors and to strategic party and candidate decisions that underlie our individual and collective votes.

Notes

1. Post-materialism is also seen as a driver of attitudes toward government (more critical of authority but supportive of democracy) and of political behavior (more elite-challenging as opposed to elite-directed). See this volume, chap. 2 and Inglehart, 1997; 1999).

2. Wedge issues are social or political issues that are especially divisive, particularly those that tend to split supporters of one group or party.

3. In 2008, the economy and the war in Iraq (and possibly racial attitudes) were considered the dominant influences. Yet Hillygus and Henderson (2010) found that social issues (in the form of an additive scale of policy questions about abortion, gay marriage, stem cell research, and school prayer) were an important predictor of general-election voting even in the face of controls for the economy, war, and race.

4. In a recent study Gerber and Huber (2009) find that partisan differences in economic evaluations are related to economic behavior. After a presidential election consumption increases more in counties that had strongly supported the winning candidate.

5. It should be noted that there is a debate about how similar the economic evaluations of Democrats and Republicans should be to support the contention that public evaluations are influenced by objective economic indicators. Green, Palmquist, and Schickler (2002) argue that economic evaluations of Democrats, Republicans, and Independents tend to move in a parallel pattern. They interpret this to mean that, despite some evidence of partisan influence on economic evaluations, voters still use objective evidence to update their economic evaluations (see also Gerber and Green 1999). In contrast, Bartels (2002) argues that if there is true Bayesian updating of economic evaluations, then the economic evaluations of Republicans and Democrats should converge, which does not happen.

6. See Stonecash (2000, App.) and Bartels (2008, 66–72) for discussions of these measurement issues.

7. Duch and Stevenson (2008, chap. 6) argue that voters need to know about *changes* in economic variables if economic voting is to occur; they report that changes in

economic indicators are associated with greater news coverage of these topics and that voters, in turn, are affected by this coverage.

8. One exception is Brewer and Stonecash (2007), who find that abortion attitudes and affect toward gays and lesbians have become more closely associated with presidential and congressional voting than income. However, they also note that the impact of income on voting has not declined. It would have been more illuminating to include other issue attitudes, particularly economic issues, as part of the comparison.

9. Johnston, Thorson, and Gooch (2010) examine the timing of the reversal of fortune for Obama's candidacy in an effort to link it to the collapse of Lehman Brothers and other specific events over the course of the 2008 campaign. As obvious as the connection might sound, the data do not seem to support such a connection. Clarke et al. (2009), in contrast, find that the economic meltdown and views that the Democrats were best able to deal with it were important to Obama's victory. Linn, Moody, and Asper (2009) find that adverse economic events in the fall of 2008 boosted Obama's standing in trial-heat polling. But Hillygus and Henderson (2010) argue that concern over the economy worked against Obama in the primaries. See also the discussion above of noneconomic factors that were important in the 2004 and 2008 elections.

Further Readings

Class and Economic Voting—United States

Ansolabehere, Stephen, Jonathan Rodden, and James M. Snyder Jr., "The Strength of Issues: Using Multiple Measures to Gauge Preference Stability, Ideological Constraint, and Issue Voting," *American Political Science Review* 102 (2008): 215–232. Using a large number of items eliminates measurement error; the impact of issues, properly measured, rivals that of party identification.

Bartels, Larry M., "Beyond the Running Tally: Partisan Bias in Political Perceptions," *Political Behavior* 24 (2002): 117–150. Argues that economic evaluations are influenced by partisanship.

Bartels, Larry M., *Unequal Democracy: The Political Economy of the New Gilded Age* (Princeton, N.J.: Princeton University Press, 2008). Argues that economic evaluations are important vote determinants, but many voters are short-sighted in applying them, resulting in an advantageous electoral environment for Republican presidential candidates and policies that exacerbate income inequality.

Gerber, Alan S., and Gregory A. Huber, "Partisanship and Economic Behavior: Do Partisan Differences in Economic Forecasts Predict Real Economic Behavior?" *American Political Science Review* 103 (2009): 407–426. Partisan differences in economic evaluations influence consumer spending patterns after presidential elections.

Goren, Paul, *On Voter Competence* (New York: Oxford University Press, forthcoming). Examines several core political values and their impact on voting decisions. Economic liberalism has a larger impact on voters than other values.

Grafstein, Robert, "The Impact of Employment Status on Voting Behavior," *Journal of Politics* 67 (2005): 804–824. Argues for the use of unemployment status in voting studies and finds that unemployed voters are more supportive of Democratic candidates.

Hillygus, D. Sunshine, and Todd G. Shields, *The Persuadable Voter: Wedge Issues in Presidential Campaigns* (Princeton, N.J.: Princeton University Press, 2008). Large numbers of voters are persuadable, and parties take advantage of that by emphasizing divisive (wedge) issues.

Vavreck, Lynn, *The Message Matters: The Economy and Presidential Campaigns.* (Princeton, N.J.: Princeton University Press, 2009). Scholars need to study how presidential campaigns reinforce the impact of economic conditions. Candidates who do not respond strategically to the environment created by economic conditions tend to lose.

Class and Economic Voting—Comparative Studies

Clarke, Harold D., David Sanders, Marianne C. Stewart, and Paul Whiteley, *Political Choice in Britain* (New York: Oxford University Press, 2004). Finds that economic evaluations had a strong impact on voting in the 2001 British election.

Duch, Raymond M., and Randolph T. Stevenson, *The Economic Vote: How Political and Economic Institutions Condition Election Results* (New York: Cambridge University Press, 2008). Using data from nineteen countries, the authors argue that the degree of economic voting is a function of the clarity of the government's responsibility for economic conditions.

Nadeau, Richard, Richard G. Niemi, and Antoine Yoshinaka, "A Cross-National Analysis of Economic Voting: Taking Account of the Political Context across Time and Nations," *Electoral Studies* 21 (2002): 403–423. The extent of economic voting varies as clarity of government responsibility varies across nations and across time within nations.

Religious or Cultural Factors in Elections

De La O, Ana L., and Jonathan A. Rodden, "Does Religion Distract the Poor? Income and Issue Voting around the World," *Comparative Political Studies* 41 (2008): 437–476. A comparative study finds that the votes of the religious are better explained by their positions on moral than economic issues.

Green, John C., *The Faith Factor: How Religion Influences American Elections* (Westport, Conn.: Praeger, 2007). A primer on the impact of religion on American voters.

Hetherington, Marc J., and Jonathan Weiler, *Authoritarianism and Polarization in American Politics* (New York: Cambridge University Press, 2009). Authoritarianism, a core value defined by one's desire to maintain order, informs many political debates between the two major political parties in the United States.

Layman, Geoffrey C., *The Great Divide: Religious and Cultural Conflict in American Party Politics* (New York: Columbia University Press, 2001). A careful examination of a partisan cleavage in the United States based on religious and cultural issues, affecting elected officials, party activists, and the mass public.

Layman, Geoffrey C., and John C. Green, "Wars and Rumours of Wars: The Contexts of Cultural Conflict in American Political Behaviour" *British Journal of Political Science* 36 (2006): 61–89. Provides a detailed definition of orthodox religious beliefs and religious commitment and their impact on voting behavior and public opinion. The culture war is confined to issues that tap into moral values and voters who are most aware of them.

10. The Political Conditioning of Economic Perceptions

Geoffrey Evans and Robert Andersen

Proponents of economic voting models argue that economic performance, or at least voters' perceptions of the economy, provides a central explanation of electoral change. As a recent comprehensive review concludes:

> The powerful relationship between the economy and the electorate in democracies the world over comes from the economic responsiveness of the electors, the individual voters. Among the issues on the typical voter's agenda, none are more consistently present, nor generally has a stronger impact, than the economy. Citizen dissatisfaction with economic performance substantially increases the probability of a vote against the incumbent. (Lewis-Beck and Stegmaier 2000, 211)

An opposing view treats economic perceptions as endogenous variables, suggesting that the public's grasp of economic performance is generally weak and strongly influenced by other aspects of its political belief systems. In this view, one's political orientation influences how one responds to questions about the performance of the economy. In other words, the causal arrow between the economy and politics is reversed.

The mechanisms through which political beliefs might impact economic perceptions are various: an expression of partisan loyalty, cognitive consistency needs, or simply a desire to maintain the appearance of consistency in the interview context are all possibilities. More importantly, it could derive from the role of the party as a source of trusted information on the basis of which people assess the economy. Some, if not all, of these mechanisms are present in Campbell et al.'s influential notion of the party as a filter through which economic performance is assessed: "Identification with a party raises a perceptual screen through which the individual tends to see what is favorable to his partisan orientation" (Campbell et al. 1960, 133). This emphasis continued with Stokes' observations on the "capacity of party identification to color perceptions" (1966, 127), Converse's (1964) seminal article that emphasized the centrality of partisan attachments for voters' political belief systems, and Miller's (1991; Miller and Shanks 1996) reaffirmation of partisanship as a categorical rather than gradualist conception.

More recently, studies by authors such as Markus (1982) and Zaller have concluded that: "people tend to accept what is congenial to their partisan values and to reject what is not" (1992, 241). Similarly, other studies have demonstrated the role of partisan cues in political information processing (i.e., Conover and

Source: The Journal of Politics 68, 1 (February 2006): 194–207.

Feldman 1989; Jacoby 1988; Lodge and Hamill 1986; Rahn 1993). The role of partisanship in explaining how "observers with different preconceptions interpret the same piece of evidence in ways that conform to their initial views" (Gerber and Green 1999, 197) has led researchers to draw on psychological models of attitude change and persistence which emphasize the cognitive costs of holding inconsistent views (Abelson 1968) or cognitive biases in information processing (Nisbett and Ross 1980). In the last few years the role of partisanship in political perceptions and behavior has thus received renewed advocacy and dispute (see the ten articles in Geer 2002) in relation to its measurement (Greene 2002) and effects on other aspects of political orientations such as issues (Bartels 2002; see also Evans and Andersen 2004). Using a multiple-indicator approach to error estimation, Green, Palmquist, and Schickler (2002; Green and Palmquist 1990; Schickler and Green 1997) provide the most persuasive case for treating party identity as an enduring social identity that is learned during formative political socialization. Bartels' (2000) study demonstrates the increasing predictive power of party loyalties on voting behavior, particularly in presidential elections, over a timespan of almost fifty years.

There is then a body of literature that provides grounds for reinterpreting the relationship between economic and political perceptions, at least under certain conditions. It is plausible that a disastrous economy—such as those in some transition societies—would elicit shared and reasonably perceptive responses that are not powerfully affected by political conditioning, but when an economy is relatively stable as is more usually the case in western democracies, partisan "contamination" of voters' understanding of economic performance is much more likely. In such cases yearly changes in economic performance are typically not distinctive enough to produce a shared, accurate assessment of how the economy is doing. To the extent that they are not simply random "nonattitudes" presented to appease interviewers, perceptions of the economy are more likely to reflect other influences. Some of these influences derive from differences in vulnerability to economic events that result from resource differences. For example, income, employment status, and social class are all likely to condition variation in economic perceptions and associated political responses within the electorate (i.e., Duch, Palmer, and Anderson 2000; Weatherford 1978). Moreover, in the absence of very strong and unavoidable cues from the economy itself, political orientation potentially provides a major source of response variation.

The significance of this process for economic models is clear. Although it is arguable that *objective* economic changes (in GDP *per capita* for example) are exogenous—i.e., they are not just constructs in voters' minds, so that the psychological predisposition to support a given party cannot make GDP *per capita* increase—such indicators often fail to predict government popularity in a clearly interpretable way. Not surprisingly, then, many proponents of economic voting tend to focus on subjective assessments of the economy: " . . . the search for the preferred macroeconomic indicators, and their lagged effects pattern, has been largely abandoned. In the second wave of popularity function work, objective economic measures have been replaced with subjective ones. The models now contain aggregate perceptual evaluations of general economic performance instead of hard data on unemployment, inflation, income, or growth" (Lewis-Beck and Stegmaier 2000, 186). If these subjective assessments are influenced by the very phenomena that they are assumed to affect—partisan attitudes—their impact will be overestimated if this reciprocal relationship is not taken into account. It is therefore important to determine the extent to which economic perceptions are influenced by prior partisan attitudes.

Despite these concerns, the influence of political orientations on individuals' economic perceptions has been the focus of surprisingly little research. Using a three-wave panel study over a relatively short one-year period, Conover, Feldman, and Knight (1986, 1987) examined the impact of incumbent partisanship and appraisals of the parties' economic management on voters' perceptions of inflation and unemployment rates in the United States. They found no evidence of partisanship effects and only minor effects of economic management competence. On the other hand, Wlezien, Franklin, and Twiggs' (1997) four-nation study of economic voting in Western Europe found that evaluations of the economy were, at least in part, predicted by vote intention. Their analysis also indicated that retrospective perceptions are more important than prospective ones. That even these effects were overestimated is implied by the fact that several variables measuring government intervention in the economy were assumed to be exogenous even though it is highly likely that they are not. Wilcox and Wlezien (1996) likewise indicate the presence of endogeneity using a survey experiment. Anderson et al. used a short-term, pre-post-election panel to demonstrate that post-election evaluations of the economy's past and future performance are adjusted to make them consistent with vote choice, suggesting that they "cease being exogenous . . . thus calling into question the extent to which the economy truly moves voting behavior" (2004, 684).

A different approach was adopted by Sanders and Price (1995), who used a pooled aggregate and individual-level analysis to argue that economic perceptions have strong effects on vote preference. Macdonald and Heath (1997) disputed these findings, showing that controlling for recalled vote substantially reduces the effects of economic perceptions on party support. In other words, prior partisanship influenced economic perceptions. Price and Sanders' response is that "recalled vote is so seriously contaminated by current vote preference that it is simply not plausible to use it as a predictor of current vote without committing the most blatant act of tautology" (1997, 942).

These inconclusive debates signal the necessity for measures of prior partisanship that are uncontaminated by current political position. They also suggest the need to examine the temporal interconnections between partisanship and economic perceptions, something that is simply not possible without extensive longitudinal data. As Lewis-Beck and Stegmaier argue: "utilizing panel data to explore the temporal dynamic of individual economic voting seems the next frontier in U.S. presidential survey studies" (2000, 195; see also Miller (1999) on the importance of long-term panel data). Nonetheless, to date there has been no panel analysis examining the endogeneity of economic perceptions across an extensive time span. The present article addresses this issue by assessing the interplay between individual economic perceptions and party support during a full electoral cycle using the 1992–1997 British Election Panel Study (BEPS). We start by fitting standard models of Conservative vote and popularity regressed on contemporaneous economic perceptions in 1997. We then present models that include all five usable waves of the BEPS covering the period from 1992 to 1997, allowing us to disentangle the complex temporal relations between economic perceptions and party support.

The 1992–1997 British electoral cycle is an interesting case study for the economic model in that it saw a dramatic reversal in the fortunes of the incumbent Conservative Party during a period in which Britain's economy was performing relatively well. This engendered numerous studies of the aggregate relationship between government popularity, trends in the economy, and various political events during the period. Some commentators attributed Labour's "landslide" victory in 1997 to factors unrelated to the country's macroeconomic performance. These included image problems resulting from perceptions of management incompetence and sleaze—especially the Government's mishandling of the Exchange Rate Mechanism crisis of late 1992 (Evans 1999; Sanders 1999a)— internal divisions within the Conservative Party over European integration (Evans 1998), the emergence of Blair as a charismatic leader, and a public that was simply tired of too many years of Conservative government (Denver 1998). Others, however, attributed a key role to economic perceptions in explaining the outcome of the 1997 election by emphasizing the "new climate of post-Thatcherite economic insecurity" (Sanders 1996, 223; Wickham-Jones 1997). According to this account, despite national aggregate economic growth, many people still *felt* vulnerable: job insecurity, negative property equity, and uncertainty about the future all served to undermine the predictive power of models derived from the generally positive performance of the objective macroeconomy, thus preserving an explanatory role for economic perceptions (Gavin and Sanders 1997). This was consistent with evidence of associations between perceptions of economic well-being (personal and national) and vote choice or government popularity during this period at both the aggregate and individual level (Pattie, Johnston, and Sanders 1999; Sanders 1999a). For Sanders, "(v)oters' economic perceptions continue to be central to the political fortunes of the government" (1996, 223; see also Clarke, Stewart, and Whiteley 1997).

In the present article, we take issue with these conclusions and hypothesize that when the long-term conditioning effects of party support on economic perceptions are taken into account, the estimated effects of economic perceptions on party support are drastically reduced. We further predict that the direction of influence between economic perceptions and political preferences is disproportionately from politics to economics rather than *vice versa*. These hypotheses apply only to perceptions of the macroeconomy, for which they have most obvious implications. We do not predict the same conditioning effects with respect to perceptions of personal economic circumstances. Variations in these are far less likely to be derived from political sources than are those that make reference to the state of the national economy—and by implication, the role of the government—and which are therefore more likely to be conditioned by partisan processes. The sources of information on which judgments are made about personal economic circumstances are likely to be more immediate and more idiosyncratic than are those for perceptions of the national economy. We further predict, therefore, that they are also of less consequence for appraisals of government performance.

Data and Methods

Data

The data for this study are from the 1992–1997 British Election Panel Study (BEPS), which is extended from the 1992 British Election Study. Respondents who took part in the 1992 British Election cross-section survey were followed-up at regular intervals throughout the entire 1992 to 1997 electoral cycle (information on the BEPS is available in Thomson, 2001). The present analysis is restricted to the face-to-face interview waves from 1992, 1994, 1995, 1996, and 1997, which obtained more extensive information from respondents than did the intervening telephone/postal waves. Our primary analyses use only those respondents who participated in all five waves, for an analytical sample size of 1,374. To ensure that sample attrition did not unduly influence the results of the study, we also analyze all available information from all cases for a sample size of 3,534 (see the appendix at the end of this article).

Measurement

Economic Perceptions. Theories of economic voting differ in the importance that they attribute to various types of economic perceptions. One distinction is that between *personal* economic perceptions and perceptions of the state of the *national* economy—so called, "egocentric" (or "pocket-book") and "sociotropic" models of voting. Another concerns the division between *retrospective* and *prospective* models. We restrict our focus to the retrospective perceptions that have formed the basis of influential models of subjective economic voting from Fiorina (1978, 1981) onwards, using standard measures available in the British Election Studies series. Research that examines prospective perceptions (i.e., Sanders 1999a) is not within the remit of this article.

Retrospective sociotropic economic perceptions were measured with the question: "Looking back over the past year or so, would you say that Britain's economy has got stronger, got weaker, or stayed the same?" Got a lot weaker (1); got a little weaker (2); stayed the same (3); got a little stronger (4); got a lot stronger (5).

Retrospective egocentric perceptions were measured with the question: "In the past year, would you say that your household income kept up with prices?" Income was a lot lower than prices (1); income was a little lower than prices (2); income kept up with prices (3); income was a little higher than prices (4); income was much higher than prices (5).

Political Indicators. Our main concern is with party popularity as the dependent variable, but we also fit preliminary models of vote because of the popularity of vote choice as a dependent variable. Nonetheless, vote is likely to be a proxy for, or a consequence of, other factors—in particular, partisanship and related attitudes toward a party. Considering that such partisan attitudes are related to vote choice and may also be correlated with economic perceptions, the relationship between prior political affiliations and current economic evaluations is likely to be best measured using an indicator of party support rather than vote per se. This is especially the case when assessing party support outside of electoral periods when vote intentions are less meaningful. It also removes the contaminating effects of strategic voting, a factor of some significance in both the 1992 and the 1997 elections (Evans 1994; Evans, Curtice, and Norris 1998).

Incumbent Vote. In the 1992 and 1997 surveys respondents were asked: "What party did you vote for in the general election?" This variable was coded so that 1 = a vote for the Conservative Party and 0 = all other responses. We focus on voting for or against the incumbent, so we combine non-Conservative voting respondents into an "other" category. This decision is facilitated by the ideological similarity of Labour and Liberal Democrat positions and supporters (Budge 1999; Sanders 1999b) and by evidence that the overwhelming majority of strategic voting in the 1997 election was between Labour and Liberal Democrat supporters to keep the Conservatives from winning (Evans, Curtice, and Norris 1998). In general terms, then, the 1997 election was one in which the Conservatives were isolated from other political groupings.

Incumbent Popularity. The popularity of the incumbent party was measured with the following question: "Please choose a phrase from this card to say how you feel about the Conservative Party." Strongly against (1); Against (2); Neither in favor nor against (3); In favor (4); Strongly in favor (5). Responses were recoded so that 5 indicates the most positive response ("Strongly in favor") and 1 indicates the most negative response ("Strongly against"). This measure approximates the popularity functions used in many aggregate studies of economic electoral effects.

Control Variables. To limit the possibility of making spurious inferences, we control for a number of factors that affect both political preferences and economic perceptions. Relevant demographic control variables (initially measured in 1992 and updated where changed) included in the models are: social class, age, gender, education, and region as suggested by previous research (Conover, Feldman, and Knight 1987; Curtice and Park 1999; Johnston et al. 2000). *Education* was measured by a six-point interval scale: (0) Other or none; (1) CSE or equivalent; (2) O-level; (3) A-level; (4) Some post-secondary; (5) University degree. *Age* was categorized into four groups: 18–30; 30–45; 46–64; over 65. *Sex:* Female = 1; male = 0. *Region* was divided into five categories: Scotland, Wales, Northern England, the Midlands, and Southern England. *Social class* was measured using the well established and validated schema developed by Goldthorpe and his colleagues (Erikson and Goldthorpe 1992), containing the following categories: Upper service; Lower service; Routine nonmanual; Petty bourgeoisie; Skilled manual workers; Semi- and unskilled manual workers.

We also control for interest in politics and current affairs using questions on attention to politics on TV and in the newspapers. The television news item is as follows: "Leading up to a general election, a lot of time on television news is spent on politics and the election campaign. How much attention do you pay to these items?" Attention to politics in newspapers was included using the following question: "Leading up to a general election, a lot of articles in the newspapers are about politics and the election campaign. How much attention do you generally pay to these articles?" Response options for both items were: none (1); a little (2); some (3); quite a bit (4); a great deal (5). These controls were included both because people with more involvement in politics and current affairs are likely to be better informed about economic performance and also because they are likely to be overrepresented in a panel study with substantial levels of attrition.[1]

Modeling Procedure

The analyses presented in this article are from a set of structural equation models (SEM) fitted using Maximum Likelihood. The first step of the analysis was exploratory, where we uncovered conditional dependencies using graphical chains (Cox and Wermuth 1993, 1996). The basic strategy of the graphical chain modeling is straightforward. Variables are set up in an assumed causal sequence, with each variable being regressed on all variables that come before it in the chain. Paths with P-values greater than .05 are excluded from the final model. Structural equation models were then used to estimate models with identical structures to those uncovered from the graphical chains. SEMs are desirable for panel analysis because they allow specification of correlated errors through time (Bollen 1989; Finkel 1995; Heise 1970). Although our main analysis uses only those respondents for whom we had complete data (i.e., they participated in all waves of the panel), we also consider the potential impact of panel attrition by using Full Information Maximum Likelihood (FIML) to fit models to all observations, including those for which data were missing (see Enders 2001; Enders and Bandalos 2001 for details on the performance of FIML estimators). Since the substantive findings were the same regardless of how the missing cases were handled, we report only the complete case analysis, delegating the FIML models to the appendix. Estimates from the graphical chain analysis are in the web appendix, www.journalofpolitics.org.

We begin by exploring the impact of economic perceptions on Conservative vote and Conservative popularity in standard cross-sectional models using data from 1997 alone. These first models are used to show the kind of models and results typically used when assessing the impact of economic perceptions. We then move to the SEMs, starting with Model A that essentially fits the same Conservative popularity model except that it allows the correlated errors discussed above. We compare the results of this model to those from models using panel data, building the model slowly. We start with Model B, which adds Conservative popularity measured in 1992 but no other information from panels before 1997. Models C and D utilize information on both economic perceptions and Conservative popularity from all waves of the study. Model C specifies economic perceptions to have an immediate impact on Conservative popularity measured at the same time. Economic perceptions, however, are predicted from Conservative popularity measured in the previous year. This model, then, provides a demanding test of our hypotheses in that it makes it more difficult to find effects of Conservative popularity on economic perceptions than the other way around. Model D specifies economic perceptions and Conservative popularity to be on equal causal footing. Rather than fit a nonrecursive model—where there are concurrent reciprocal paths from the economic perceptions and Conservative popularity—we specify covariances between variables measured at the same point in time, assessing only the cross-lagged effects. Both Model C and Model D include all of the control variables as predictors of all endogenous variables. On the basis of the relationships uncovered from the exploratory graphical chain analysis, the errors for the Conservative popularity measures from a particular point in time were correlated with the errors for all previous measures of Conservative popularity, while the errors for each of the economic perceptions models were allowed to correlate only with the same measure in the previous year.

Analysis

The Context: Short-Term Aggregate Changes

Figure 10-1 displays aggregate economic trends in unemployment and the cost of living in Britain from 1992 to 1997. We see that the Retail Price Index dropped between 1992 and 1993, continuing an existing trend, and then remained relatively flat. Unemployment peaked in 1993 and then gradually declined after that point. Both of these economic indicators were slightly more positive in 1997 than they were in 1992. In other words, these measures suggest that the economy had improved slightly from the beginning to the end of the 1992–1997 electoral cycle. Following the economic model of voting, then, this graph provides no reason to expect a decline in Conservative support over the period.

Aggregate trends in government popularity did not parallel the state of the economy. The BEPS data are consistent with what has also been shown in opinion polls for this period in that government popularity dropped from 43% in 1992 to little more than 20% a year later. This precipitous fall leveled out, but by spring

Figure 10-1 Unemployment and Inflation Rate for Great Britain, 1990–1997

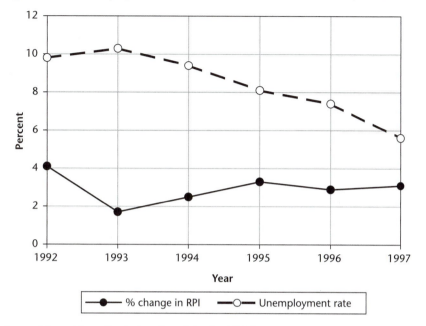

Source: Adapted from Heath, Jowell, and Curtice (2001), 35.

Note: Inflation rate is measured by the Retail Price Index. Unemployment is measured according to the International Labor Office definition.

1995 only about one-fifth of the electorate with a party preference intended to vote Conservative. Similarly, the decline in support for the Conservatives took place relatively soon after the 1992 election—in the 1993 survey only 63% of those who reported voting Conservative in 1992 still intended to do so.

A similar picture is seen in aggregate measures of subjective perceptions of the economy over time. Table 10-1 shows the pattern of mean responses to the two indicators of retrospective economic evaluations in the BEPS, which assess respondents' evaluations of change over the previous twelve months. Comparisons between these figures and aggregate trends are difficult as the BEPS sample is not precisely representative of the population. Nonetheless, even a cursory examination of the patterns in Table 10-1 suggests that subjective economic perceptions cannot account for the dramatically declining levels of aggregate Conservative support in the BEPS sample.

Economic Perceptions and Party Support at the Individual Level

Despite the lack of an observed relationship between the economy and government popularity at the macro level, various commentators have provided

Table 10-1 Descriptive Statistics (Means and Percentages) for Economic
Perceptions and Conservative Vote/Popularity (Standard Deviations
in Parentheses)

	Year					
Variable	1992	1993	1994	1995	1996	1997
Conservative vote	37.5%	24.5%	21.8%	18.4%	20.0%	25.0%
Conservative popularity	3.10	NA	2.41	2.35	2.50	2.52
	(1.31)		(1.21)	(1.19)	(1.17)	(1.20)
Perceptions of household	1.69*	1.44*	2.47	2.48	2.66	2.69
income during last year	(.69)	(.59)	(.99)	(.97)	(.94)	(.90)
Perceptions of British	1.57*	1.54*	2.83	2.78	2.96	3.40
economy during last year	(.69)	(.70)	(1.00)	(.92)	(.89)	(.89)

Notes: In 1992 and 1997 vote for the Conservative Party is reported vote in the General Election; in
all other years it refers to voting intentions.

The popularity of the Conservative Party was not measured in 1993. In all other rounds it was
measured using 5-point scales.

*Economic perceptions were measured on 3-point scales in 1992 and 1993; in 1994–1997 they were
measured on 5-point scales.

evidence for this relationship at the individual level. We also find this relationship
when using cross-sectional data. Table 10-2 shows the effects of retrospective
economic perceptions measured concurrently in 1997 on Conservative vote and
Conservative popularity. We see significant net effects of economic perceptions—
both sociotropic and egocentric—on voting. Those who perceived the macro
economy or their household standard of living to have improved over the previous twelve months were more likely to report voting Conservative. A similar
pattern can be observed for the model predicting Conservative popularity. In
both cases, sociotropic effects are far larger than egocentric effects.

Among the controls, region and gender have significant effects, with Scotland, Northern England, and women less likely to support or vote for the Conservatives. Education effects are present primarily because of the difference
between those with University education and others, with less highly educated
respondents being more negative about the Conservatives, while social class has
significant but limited effect on support and vote—the upper service class and
petty bourgeoisie are more pro-Conservative—which is consistent with previous
cross-sectional analyses which demonstrate that in 1997 the effect of class on vote
was at its lowest point since the British Election Surveys began in 1964 (Andersen
and Heath 2002; Evans, Heath, and Payne 1999).

We now turn to the SEMs, which include measures of both economic perceptions and Conservative popularity. We start with Model A, which includes
only data from the 1997 survey, thus replicating the models of Conservative
popularity presented in Table 10-2 but using SEMs to estimate the coefficients.

Table 10-2 Cross-Sectional Models Predicting Conservative Vote and Conservative Popularity in 1997

Independent Variables	Conservative Vote (Logit Model)		Conservative Popularity (OLS Model)		
	B	S.E.	B	S.E.	Std. B
65+ years old	.300	.276	.180	.116	
46–64 years old	.055	.221	−.034	.091	
30–45 years old	−.273	.218	−.172	.088	
18–30 years old	—	—	—	—	
Men	.457**	.165	.249***	.066	
Upper service	.948***	.287	.281***	.117	
Lower service	.468	.271	.074	.106	
Routine non-manual	.557*	.250	.125	.094	
Petty bourgeoisie	.820*	.319	.328*	.130	
Skilled manual	.453	.283	.115	.105	
Semi & unskilled manual	—	—	—	—	
Other or none	.392	.300	.392**	.127	
CSE or equivalent	.675*	.326	.366**	.142	
O-level	.676*	.280	.373***	.122	
A-level	.418	.293	.351**	.127	
Some post-secondary	.493	.263	.302**	.114	
University degree	—	—	—	—	
Scotland	−.829***	.206	−.303***	.081	
Wales	−.557	.443	−.221	.169	
Northern England	−.653***	.198	−.293***	.082	
Midlands	−.019	.189	.0004	.086	
Southern England	—	—	—	—	
Attention to politics on TV	−.101	.064	.040	.027	
Attention to politics in newspapers	.004	.058	.051	.025	
Egocentric economic perceptions	.392***	.086	.158***	.034	.118
Sociotropic economic perceptions	1.15***	.086	.500***	.036	.370
Intercept	−6.78	.618	−5.69	.220	
Overall Model	LRχ²(22 df) = 316.4***		R^2 = .213		
	N = 1,357		N = 1,374		

$^*p < .05,\ ^{**}p < .01,\ ^{***}p < .001.$

The estimates from this model provide a benchmark against which to compare the magnitude of effects estimated from models that temporally endogenize economic perceptions. As an initial step we include just the 1992 Election wave, then we estimate models with variables measured at five points in time through the electoral cycle.

If we compare Model B with Model A in Figure 10-2 we observe that the inclusion of 1992 support for the Conservatives reduces the coefficient for sociotropic perceptions from .37 to .17. There is also a significant and substantial effect of 1992 party support on 1997 sociotropic perceptions. Egocentric perceptions, in

Figure 10-2 Standardized Coefficient from Structural Equation Models Predicting Conservative Party Popularity

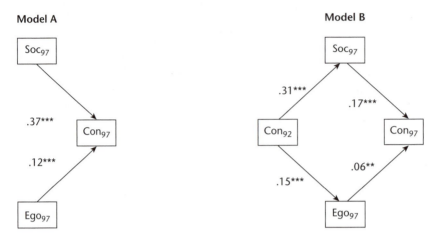

Note: Con = Conservative party popularity; Soc = sociotropic perceptions; Ego = egocentric perceptions. Subscripts are used to indicate year. Controls and error covariances are included in the model but not shown in order to simplify presentation.

contrast, are less strongly conditioned by 1992 party support but their already weaker effect on 1997 support is reduced to only .06 by the inclusion of prior support and economic perceptions.

These results indicate that the relationship between sociotropic economic perceptions in 1997 and Conservative vote and popularity between 1997 are reduced but still significant when previous partisanship measures are included in the model. It is quite possible, however, that during the electoral cycle, economic perceptions followed vote switching rather than preceded or accompanied it. Thus changing economic perceptions over the 1992–1997 period may have followed from the decline in Conservative popularity—much of which occurred early in the electoral cycle—rather than caused it. A fuller specification is needed to test for the pattern of causal influence through time. For this purpose we now fit a SEM that uses measures of both economic perceptions and party popularity measured at five points in time: 1992, 1994, 1995, 1996, and 1997.

We start with Model C, in Figure 10-3, which predicts economic perceptions from lagged Conservative popularity and Conservative popularity from concurrent economic perceptions. The standardized coefficient for the effect of sociotropic economic perceptions on Conservative popularity in the 1997 cross-sectional model is .37. As we see from Figure 10-3, this same coefficient is much smaller, at .11. Model C also provides more evidence that egocentric perceptions are of less importance. We now see that personal household-based appraisals of economic change are effectively "out of the loop" in the temporal relationship between

Figure 10-3 Graphical Depiction of Model C

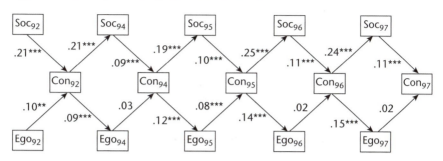

Note: Paths display standardized coefficients. Con = Conservative party popularity; Soc = sociotropic perceptions; Ego = egocentric perceptions. Subscripts are used to indicate year. Controls and error covariances are included in the model but not shown in order to simplify presentation.

sociotropic perceptions and party popularity. Although they appear to be minimally conditioned by prior party support, they are of little or no importance for explaining Conservative popularity.

Most importantly, however, sociotropic economic perceptions are influenced by Conservative party support throughout the electoral cycle and the magnitudes of these lagged effects are much larger than the effects of contemporaneously measured sociotropic perceptions on Conservative party support. For example, in 1997 the coefficient for the effect of current sociotropic perceptions on Conservative popularity is only .11, whereas the lagged effect of Conservative popularity in 1996 on 1997 sociotropic perceptions is .24. The pattern is similar for 1996 (.11 versus .25), 1995 (.10 versus .19), and 1994 (.09 versus .21). In other words, in the year-on-year evolution of party popularity and economic perceptions, it is the former that most strongly drives change.

We now turn to Model D, which specifies the two economic perceptions variables and Conservative popularity to be on equal causal footing. This provides a particularly demanding test of the economic perceptions thesis as their effects on vote are assumed to be lagged by a year. Unsurprisingly, therefore, the results of these models displayed in Figure 10-4 are even more strongly consistent with our hypotheses than are the findings for Model C. In all years the standardized coefficients for the cross-lagged effects of Conservative popularity are at least three times the magnitude of the coefficients for sociotropic economic perceptions. Model D differs somewhat from Model C, however, in that the effects of egocentric perceptions on Conservative popularity are generally statistically significant. Nevertheless, these effects are still relatively small compared to the effects of sociotropic perceptions on Conservative popularity. More importantly, Conservative popularity once again has approximately three times the impact on egocentric economic perceptions as do egocentric perceptions on Conservative popularity.

Figure 10-4 Graphical Depiction of Model D

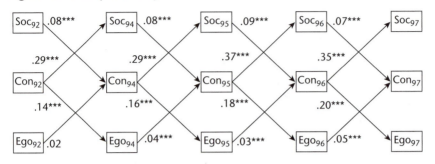

Note: Paths display standardized coefficients. Con = Conservative party popularity; Soc = sociotropic perceptions; Ego = egocentric perceptions. Subscripts are used to indicate year. Controls and error covariances are included in the model but not shown in order to simplify presentation.

The findings from these panel data are clear: individuals' economic perceptions may predict incumbent popularity when measured at the point of outcome, but they have much less direct impact when their relationships with earlier measures of popularity are taken into account. On the other hand, the impact of party popularity on economic perceptions is persistently strong even when previous measures of both variables are considered.

Discussion and Conclusions

Our analysis supports the contention that prior political partisanship, measured as both incumbent (Conservative) popularity and vote, systematically influences economic perceptions. These perceptions should not therefore be assumed to be exogenous variables in models of vote choice or incumbent popularity. In fact, we found that the one-year *lagged* effects of party popularity on economic perceptions are consistently stronger than the reciprocal effects of *concurrent* economic perceptions on incumbent support. This does not unequivocally refute economic interpretations of changes in British electoral behavior during the 1990s, but it does indicate that the role of the economy for individual political preferences has been much overstated. More generally, these findings suggest that the prevailing emphasis on subjective economic explanations of party support and voting should be reconsidered.

It is also important to note that these findings relate specifically to sociotropic measures. Current egocentric retrospective perceptions appear to have little influence on party popularity or *vice versa*. That egocentric perceptions are not generally affected by political preferences further emphasizes the relatively endogenous nature of sociotropic retrospective perceptions. As we would expect, egocentric economic perceptions appear more likely to be conditioned by aspects of voters' own personal experiences and those of their households, than by partisanship.

There are qualifications to these conclusions but we believe the main issues can be dealt with effectively: first, as noted earlier, it can be argued that we have not examined measures of prospective economic perceptions, such as those used by Sanders and his colleagues (i.e., Pattie, Johnston, and Sanders 1999; Sanders 1999a). We have chosen not to do so, however, precisely because evidence from other research indicates that these prospective perceptions are likely to be particularly (and realistically) influenced by whether the party voted for wins the election (Anderson et al. 2004). Our measures of economic perceptions also do not encompass variants of economic perceptions, such as those pertaining to economic management competence (Sanders 1996). Instead our measures link directly to the theoretical literature on retrospective economic voting as it has been more typically conceived and operationalized. Other measures that tap more convincingly into what motivates economic voting in a given economy (such as "interest rates": Sanders and Gavin 2004) might thus prove more robust to these panel-derived endogeneity tests, but these are not the primary variables through which the retrospective economic voting arguments have been validated.

Respondent attrition might likewise be thought an issue for generalizations from panel studies. Yet our FIML estimates (see appendix) are almost identical to those obtained from the more restricted final wave sample, and comparisons of respondents remaining in the final wave with those in the original 1992 sample show evidence of only minor differences in relevant characteristics. Moreover, given that, ceteris paribus, the later waves of any panel study of political attitudes and behavior will tend to contain a greater proportion of politically informed and motivated respondents than are present in the population from which it was sampled—not only through attrition but possibly also because of the conditioning effects of panel responding—attrition serves only to strengthen confidence in our findings. The endogeneity argument derives its persuasiveness from the presence of people in the electorate who take their cues from their party, who are relatively poorly independently informed about economic affairs, and who thus undermine the nonpolitical sources of judgment about the workings of the macroeconomy. In other words, political influences seem to outweigh the reciprocal effects of economic perceptions even among those who are motivated, knowledgeable and interested in politics.

The generalizability of the findings from the British context could also be questioned, but it would seem to be justified in two ways. First, there is no evidence that party loyalties in Britain are more fixed and the British party system more ideologically polarized than in other countries. By the 1997 election British politics was in many ways less polarized and British party supporters less attached, than at any previous time for which measures can be obtained (Budge 1999; Crewe and Thomson 1999; Sanders 1999b; Webb and Farrell 1999). This suggests that short-term influences, such as the economy, might have greater latitude to cause swings in party popularity than in earlier periods (Alvarez, Nagler, and Bowler 2000; Sanders 1999a). Moreover, Sanders and Price present evidence that political events had a substantial influence on economic expectations in Britain even during the 1980s (Sanders and Price 1995). Secondly, it does not appear that this period in British politics is characterized by a muted impact of the economy. The 1992 currency crisis and the decline in negative economic indicators such as unemployment and the retail price index, demonstrate evidence of the variation and salience of economic issues during this period.

In conclusion, our evidence stands as a challenge to the assumptions of retrospective, sociotropic economic voting models and adds more support to the growing body of research examining the pivotal influence of partisan orientations on political perceptions and behavior. Cross-sectional models employing measures of sociotropic economic perceptions as independent variables more than likely overestimate economic effects on voting not only in the samples, time frame, and political context we have analyzed in this article, but also in many other electoral contests. This conclusion produces at least two further implications. Firstly, the need for more panel-based analysis into the individual-level processes that underpin apparent aggregate-level economic voting elsewhere, thus enabling the conditions under which the endogeneity of economic perceptions is more or less pronounced to be identified empirically. This in turn should enable research into the factors that condition the relationship between party support and economic perceptions. A key candidate in this respect is the media, where an increasing number of studies point to its role in linking factors such as individual economic well-being, objective national economic indicators, and perceptions of the national economy (i.e., Funk and García-Monet 1997; Hetherington 1996; Mutz 1998; Mutz and Mondak 1997; Sanders and Gavin 2004).[2]

Secondly, if the intellectual appeal of the economic voting model is that it confirms fundamental notions of democratic accountability—voters respond to objective indicators of government performance and reward or punish as appropriate (Anderson et al. 2004; Mutz 1998)—then evidence questioning the link between the economy and vote brings into question the effectiveness of this accountability. The influence of political attachments on economic evaluations is doubly concerning, as it is the political actors themselves who can weaken the connection between achievement and evaluation. The effect of politicians on economic perceptions may thus help to explain why governments can appear "teflon-coated" despite poor economic performance. Popular incumbent parties carry with them an inbuilt bias among the electorate to perceive their economic performance in a more positive light than might otherwise be the case. The state of the national economy may therefore be a less effective mechanism of democratic accountability than has previously been assumed.

Appendix: FIML Models for Analyses Presented in Figures 10-3 and 10-4

Model C2: Available Case Analysis using FIML (N = 3,524)

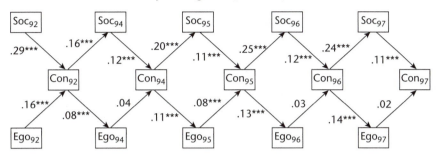

Model D2: Available Case Analysis using FIML (N = 3,534)

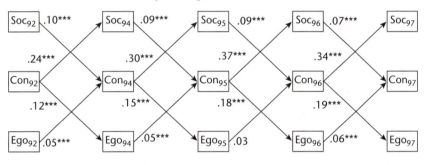

Notes

1. Issues and leader evaluations specific to the 1997 election were also included as controls in preliminary models. Although including these variables produced results that strengthen our argument, diagnostics indicated that the models were overcontrolled, so these variables are not included in the final models reported here. For example, including leader appraisals led to the implausible result that economic perceptions are negatively related to support for the incumbent Conservative Party—i.e., the better the economy was doing, the less popular the Conservatives were. Moreover, since we did not have issue questions for each wave of the study, we exclude them from the analyses reported here. We also exclude left-right values as a predictor in the final model because our analyses indicate that it is not exogenous to political support.

2. There is also evidence that perceptions of the macroeconomy are frequently biased and vary systematically with people's economic self-interest, the information they seek out or receive about the economy, and how they make sense of this information (Duch, Palmer, and Anderson 2000; Haller and Norpoth 1997; Krause 1997).

11. Purple America

Stephen Ansolabehere, Jonathan Rodden, and James M. Snyder Jr.

A merica, we are told, is a nation divided. Maps of the electoral votes cast by the states in recent U.S. presidential elections reveal a striking pattern. The base of the Democratic Party is firmly rooted in the northeast and upper Midwest—a region stretching from Maine to Minnesota—plus the Pacific West, anchored by California. The Republicans are said to own an L-shaped region covering the South, the "breadbasket" states, and Mountain West, extending from the Carolinas to Arizona and up to Montana and Idaho. The cartographers who draw up the maps of U.S. election results have inadvertently branded a new division in American politics: Republican red versus Democratic blue.

What is the source of this division? Most observers point not to the bread-and-butter economic issues of the New Deal alignment but to a "culture war." America, it is argued, is torn by a struggle over issues such as abortion, gay marriage, and school prayer that has transformed the geography of American elections and has eclipsed the traditional political questions of peace and prosperity (for example, Hunter 1991; Wattenberg 1995; Green, Guth, Smidt, and Kellstedt 1996; Williams 1997; Walsh 2000; Brooks 2001; Shogan 2002; Frank 2004; Greenberg 2004).

This view challenges economic theorizing about elections and government policymaking. Most models assume that voters care first and foremost about economic issues: taxation, public goods, regulation, income redistribution, unemployment, and growth (Myerson 1995; Persson and Tabellini 2000; and Mueller 2003 provide surveys and additional references). Many models focus on income redistribution, making the natural assumption that voters with higher incomes favor lower tax rates and less redistribution. This approach leads to a simple understanding of politics in the United States and throughout much of the industrial world since the Great Depression. The Republican Party is viewed as a coalition of business and upper-income voters, who favor lower taxes, less government spending, and minimal economic regulation. The Democratic Party is viewed as the party of labor, favoring economic redistribution via higher taxes, social welfare spending, and regulation.

Students of the culture war contend that the economic models have it wrong, that most Americans now set economic issues aside when thinking about politics. Thomas Frank (2004) offers a biting and ironic critique of the politics of the culture war in his book *What's the Matter with Kansas?* He argues that low-income Americans living in rural areas and small towns vote strongly Republican because

Source: The Journal of Economic Perspectives 20, 2 (Spring 2006): 97–118.

of their moral convictions, even though the Republican Party's economic policies cut strongly against their economic interests.[1] As Shapiro (2005) points out, in many places the flip side of this pattern also holds true—high-income citizens in Cambridge, Massachusetts, and the Upper West Side of New York City vote overwhelmingly Democratic even though the tax policies of the Republican Party treat them much more favorably. Why do they vote this way? Because moral issues, such as abortion and gay marriage, dominate economic self-interest. Citizens' attitudes on moral issues may even shape their beliefs about what policies best serve their economic interests. As a result, the main political cleavage in the United States today cuts across both income and economic liberalism.

The culture war argument, if correct, would have real consequences for public policy. It would lead government to engage in less economic redistribution and provide fewer social services than in a world where citizens merely voted their economic self-interest (Roemer 1998; Lee and Roemer 2005; Hacker and Pierson 2005). If citizens care only about income, then the median voter—whose income will be below average because of skewed distribution of income—will typically demand a large amount of redistribution, and political parties will respond (Romer 1975; Roberts 1977; Meltzer and Richard 1981). But if citizens also care about cross-cutting issues—moral, religious, racial and ethnic—then the equilibrium amount of distribution will shrink as parties compete for votes on these other issues.[2]

In this paper we challenge the culture war argument. This argument makes three claims: First, voters are polarized over moral issues, and this division maps onto important demographic categories like religious affiliation. Second, moral issues have more salience or weight in the minds of voters than economic issues. Third, this division accounts for red and blue cartography—red-state voters are moral conservatives who vote on moral issues without regard for their economic interests or preferences.

Drawing on data from three decades of survey research, we examine how the electorate divides along economic and moral issues. While showing that moral values are not irrelevant, the survey data roundly reject the basic claims of the culture war thesis.

First, like other political scientists who have tackled this issue, we find that most Americans are ideological moderates on both economic and moral issues. Second, our central claim is that economic issues have much more weight in voters' minds than moral issues. Contrary to many claims in this literature, the weight of moral issues does not vary across social groups; even Protestant Evangelicals and rural voters place more emphasis on economic than moral issues. Third, the differences in voting behavior between red states and blue states is driven at least as much by economic as by moral issue preferences. Preferences on economic and moral issues together can account for most of the difference between red- and blue-state voting. Red-state voters are slightly more conservative on economic issues than blue-state voters, and noticeably more conservative on moral issues. However, the relatively large weight that voters place on economic issues means that economic preferences account for much of the difference in voting behavior across states.

We conclude by reaching beyond the era of survey research to put this constellation of issue cleavages and electoral maps into historical perspective. The great divide across the American states is not really much of a divide at all. The difference between "strongly Republican" states like Kansas and "strongly Democratic" states like California is, on average, only 8 percentage points in the vote. That difference pales in comparison with the divisions of a century ago. Over the course of the twentieth century—a period of impressive economic and cultural convergence—we have not seen a great political chasm opening between the states, but rather a noteworthy political convergence.

Issue Preferences of Individual Americans

Is there a deep divide in the American electorate, especially on abortion, gay rights and other moral issues? If so, does the divide map into the political geography of the United States today?

In an exhaustive assessment of survey data, Fiorina, with Abrams and Pope (2005), find scant evidence that there are deep divisions among the American public on a wide variety of issues. To the extent that there are any differences across social groups, they conclude that Protestants, particularly fundamentalists, are somewhat more conservative (see also Page and Shapiro 1992). Here we offer our own assessment of the distribution of public preferences on economic and moral questions. We take a somewhat different approach from Fiorina, Abrams, and Pope (2005). We construct measures of individuals' policy preferences over economic and moral issues. It is difficult to get an overall sense of the distribution of preferences, or to analyze their impact on voting behavior, by sifting through a battery of individual questions. Picking particular survey items leaves too much room for interpretation and manipulation. For example, the wording of questions related to abortion or homosexual rights may have a dramatic impact on the appearance of polarization. Another problem with analyzing individual survey questions is that many items are plagued with measurement error (Achen 1975).

To address these problems, we aggregate as many questions as possible to create two scales to capture economic and moral dimensions of preferences. While the basic idea underlying these scales is straightforward, there are a number of technical details—including the exact questions used—which we describe in online Appendix A. This appendix is available at (http://www.e-jep.org), appended to the online article.

We use two independent surveys, the American National Election Study (ANES) and the General Social Survey (GSS). The GSS has been conducted annually since 1973, and the ANES has been conducted in every national election since 1952. Because of changes in content in the ANES, we focus on the elections from 1992 to 2004. Each of these surveys provides measures of respondents' attitudes on questions concerning economic, moral, social and foreign policy. These studies involve large samples and large numbers of questions, and they are designed to get at exactly the sorts of research questions raised here. We use the two studies in tandem to corroborate each other.[3]

We first classify the questions into two sets according to issue type: economic or moral. Questions on economic issues include topics such as the overall size of government, spending on various social programs, business regulation, environmental protection, Social Security and unemployment insurance. Questions on moral issues include topics such as abortion, school prayer, the rights of homosexuals, the accuracy of the Bible, and women's role in society. We drop questions that are difficult to classify as economic or moral, such as items on crime and civil rights. We then perform factor analyses on each set of questions. In both surveys the factor analysis on each set of questions uncovers a dominant issue dimension. Factor analysis allows us to construct a weighted average of the questions, without having to determine the weights beforehand, or even how many dimensions underlie the data. The results support the idea that there are two dimensions—an Economic Issues Scale and a Moral Issues Scale. These scales are only modestly correlated, indicating that at least two issue dimensions are necessary to account for voters' issue preferences. In the American National Election Study the correlation between the two scales is .28 (for the period 1992–2000), and in the General Social Survey it is .04. We standardize each scale to have a mean of zero and a standard deviation of one, and orient them so that higher scores are associated with more conservative preferences.

What do different positions on these scales mean? Call someone at the 25th percentile a Liberal and someone at the 75th percentile a Conservative. On the economic scale, a respondent who wants to increase government spending on Social Security, food stamps, child care, the poor, the homeless, and education, and has the mean preference on all other items, would be (approximately) a Liberal. A respondent who wants to reduce government spending on welfare and food stamps and hold spending constant on Social Security, child care, the homeless and education,[4] and has the mean preference on all other items, would be (approximately) a Conservative.

On the Moral Issues Scale, a respondent with the following profile would be (approximately) a Liberal: favors laws to protect homosexuals against job discrimination (but not strongly); feels that homosexuals should be allowed to serve in the U.S. Armed Forces (but not strongly); believes that homosexual couples should be legally permitted to adopt children; believes that by law a woman should always be able to obtain an abortion as a matter of personal choice; believes that the law should allow public schools to schedule time when children can pray silently if they wish; and holds the mean preference on all other items. A respondent with the following profile would be (approximately) a Conservative: opposes laws to protect homosexuals against job discrimination (but not strongly); feels that homosexuals should not be allowed to serve in the U.S. Armed Forces (but not strongly); believes that homosexual couples should not be legally permitted to adopt children; believes that the law should permit abortion only in case of rape,

Figure 11-1 Distribution of Voter Preferences on Economic Issues Scale and Moral Issues Scale, 1993–2002

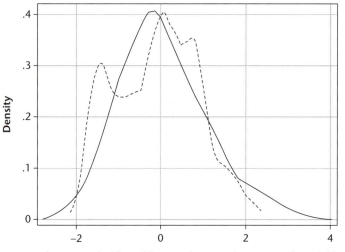

Moral Issues Scale (dotted line) and Economic Issues Scale (solid line)

Note: On the horizontal axis, the Economic Issues Scale and the Moral Issues Scale are normalized to have a mean of zero and a standard deviation of 1. The vertical axis shows the share of responses occurring at each score, such that the total area under the curves represents all responses.

incest, or when the woman's life is in danger; believes that the law should allow public schools to schedule time when children as a group can say a general prayer not tied to a particular religious faith; and holds the mean preference on all other items.

What does the distribution of public preferences look like across these issue dimensions? If Americans are polarized, we should see a distribution of scores with peaks on each side and a valley in the middle. Figure 11-1 graphs the estimated frequency of people at each point on the Economic Issues Scale (solid line) and the Moral Issues Scale (dashed line) for the General Social Survey over the period 1977–2002.

Consistent with Fiorina, with Abrams and Pope (2005), we find that Americans are not polarized on economic issues. The distribution of economic policy preferences follows a bell curve, with a high fraction of respondents expressing moderate opinions. This shape is not due to pooling many years of data, as the distribution looks similar in each year of the General Social Survey. Individual issues, such as whether the respondent favors more government regulation, show similar patterns of moderation. The American National Election Study results produce almost the same picture.

On moral issues, there is apparently more heterogeneity of preferences, though hardly a deep division. In contrast with economic issues, there is a smaller density of voters in the middle, and higher densities closer to the extremes. We hesitate to infer much from this distribution, however, because the analogous histogram for moral issues using the ANES looks more like the economic issues. Moreover, the "polarization" in the GSS Moral Issues Scale is driven by a single issue—abortion.[5]

The "divided America" rhetoric, though, reflects more than polarization in preferences. Different states and regions of the country, it is argued, prefer markedly different moral and economic policies. The high degree of moderation on economic issues might readily be undone if all people in red states hold conservative attitudes and all people in blue states hold liberal views.

Comparing the economic and moral issue preferences of the red- and blue-state voters reveals statistically significant but modest differences across these states. In the General Social Survey, we contrast blue regions (census regions of about five states each) and red regions. In the American National Election Study, which has state identifiers, we contrast blue and red states.[6] Both show significant differences on both economic and moral issues, and the differences are approximately the same in both surveys. On the Economic Issues Scale, respondents who live in blue states are approximately .15 points more liberal than respondents who live in red states. On the Moral Issues Scale, respondents who live in blue states are approximately .32 points more liberal than respondents who live in red states. While statistically significant, the differences between red- and blue-state survey respondents are relatively small (recall that the standard deviation of each scale is 1). Approximately 45 percent of those in red states have economic preferences that are left of the typical blue-state voter, and approximately 40 percent of those in blue states have moral policy preferences that are to the right of the typical red-state voter.

The red/blue division of the American electorate, with its apparent roots in the culture war, is as much about changes over time as it is about current differences. Many observers argue that the rising geographic division in U.S. politics results from an increasing division across the states in the voters' preferences on moral policies.

The General Social Survey (GSS) data suggest otherwise. Figure 11-2 graphs the difference between red-region and blue-region voters in the GSS for the moral issues dimension and the economic dimension for each year from 1977 to 2002.[7] The differences between red-region and blue-region voters were noticeably larger on moral issues than on economic issues in the 1970s and early 1980s. The difference on moral issues was about two-tenths of one standard deviation on the scale, and the difference on economic issues was nil.

There has been change over time, but not of the kind posited in the culture war canon. Red and blue America have converged somewhat on moral issues since the 1970s, and the gap has been relatively stable since then. Even on the polarizing issue of abortion, the differences between the regions have remained steady since

Figure 11-2 Trends in Blue Region vs. Red Region Differences on
Economic Issues Scale and Moral Issues Scale

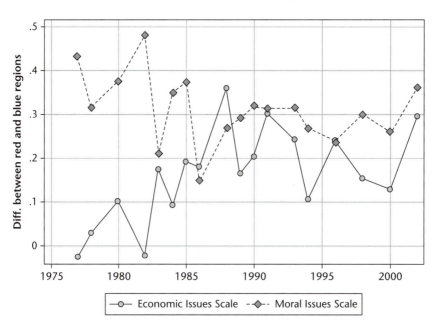

the 1970s. On the other hand, preferences on economic policies have grown further apart. In the late 1970s and early 1980s, preferences on economic policies differed little between the regions that by the 1990s became the red and blue regions. However, by the 1990s, a gap had emerged. Those in blue regions were on average .10 units more liberal on economics than those in red regions. The trends in preferences, then, run wholly counter to the common observation that morals are an increasing division trumping economics in American political geography.

While our focus here is largely on the rhetoric about state-level electoral maps, the expansive literature on the culture war touches on many other possible divisions—especially income and religion—that might help shape those maps. Before proceeding, it is useful to describe some of these divisions, which are displayed graphically in Figure 11-3 along with the red/blue regional division. Consistent with Thomas Frank's (2004) argument, rural voters are more conservative on both moral and economic issues than other voters. Protestants and regular churchgoers are much more conservative on both scales, and especially so on the Moral Issues Scale. In fact, the religious divide in the United States is perhaps the most substantial. Protestants and non-Protestants differ by as much as a full standard deviation on the moral scale and by more than a half of a standard deviation on the economic scale. The difference is even greater when we contrast Evangelical Protestants with the rest of the population.

Figure 11-3 Issue Scale Distributions by Group, GSS, 1977–2002

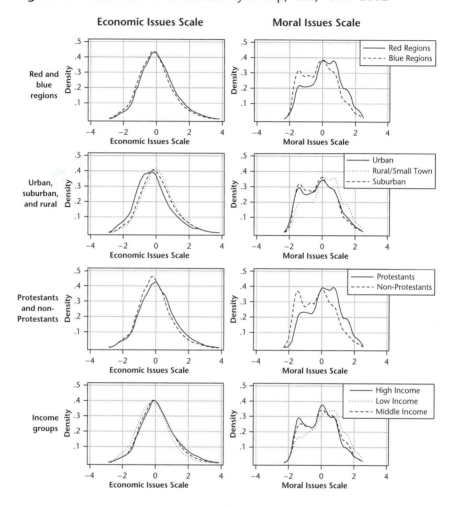

Finally, there is the matter of income, which lies at the center of much economic thinking about policy preferences. Economists commonly assume there is a tight relationship between income and economic preferences. Roemer (1998), Frank (2004), and others argue that moral issues constitute a cross-cutting cleavage—that is, lower-income people, because of their greater propensity to attend church, are morally more conservative. Not surprisingly, income and economic conservatism are positively correlated, but the relationship is not tight. The raw correlation between economic policy preferences and income is only .26 in the American National Election Study and .32 in the General Social Survey. These correlations suggest that wealthier people are more economically conservative, and thus their preferences tend to be "in line" with their self-interest in lower taxes, less redistribution, and so forth. However, the weakness of the relationship suggests that we are not free to equate income or even social class with economic policy preferences. Preferences derive not only from one's status and pecuniary interests, but from beliefs and understanding about what is right or what is in the best interests of the community, the country, or even the world.

The relationship between income and preferences on moral issues is also weak but significant. The correlation between income and moral issue preferences is -.11 in the ANES and -.22 in the GSS. If we divide the electorate into three groups by income—low, middle and high—the lower- and middle-income groups hold slightly more conservative views on moral issues compared to the upper-income group, as shown in the final panel of Figure 11-3. The cross-cutting moral values cleavage is driven as much by the moral liberalism of the wealthy as the moral conservatism of the poor decried by Frank and others. Also, while the degree of polarization on moral issues is not large, it is slightly larger among higher-income individuals than among lower-income individuals.

The Relative Importance of Economic and Moral Issues in Voting

The results in the previous section are notable because they show that statistically significant differences exist across social groups and political geography in the economic and moral policy preferences of American voters. Whether these differences are politically meaningful, though, depends on how much weight voters place on these two dimensions. Issues on which large differences exist may matter little in politics if those issues receive very little weight in voters' thinking. Issues on which only small differences exist will matter greatly if voters weight those issues heavily.

The relative importance of moral and economic questions depends on a variety of factors, including the salience of the issues, the intensities of voters' preferences on the issues, and the policy choices offered by the parties. If an issue is highly salient, such as unemployment in the 1930s, inflation in the 1970s, or crime in the 1980s, then the dimension of which that issue is a component will be more important in voters' minds. If voters have more intense preferences on one dimension than the other, then small policy differences on that dimension will translate into large differences in preferences. If the parties are far apart on an issue, then clear electoral choices on that issue will divide the electorate. We do not attempt to distinguish among these factors. Rather, we estimate the overall importance of issues in voter decisions, leaving open the question of how issues affect voting decisions.

To measure the relative weight of the two issue dimensions we conduct a regression analysis in which the probability of reporting to have voted for the Republican presidential candidate is a function of the voters' economic and moral policy preferences. This approach allows us to determine the relative weight of these two dimensions of political choice and whether they have changed. It does not allow us to determine why the change has occurred.

Also, as noted above, we focus on just these two dimensions because we are following the line of argumentation developed by various writers who have described the polarization of the American electorate in terms of economic and moral issues. Other factors, such as race, foreign policy and candidate traits, matter as well. In this analysis, however, we focus only on the economic and moral dimensions in voting behavior. We do include year-specific fixed effects in our analysis, which may capture much of the voting based on retrospective evaluations of the economy.

Table 11-1 presents the estimated effects of economic preferences and moral policy preferences on partisan attitudes and voting behavior. We measure how well economic and moral policy preferences predict the likelihood of voting for the Republican candidate (rather than the Democrat) in various elections and the effects of these two dimensions of preferences on party identification.[8] Here, we consider the basic findings and their implications.

The numbers in the column labeled "dP/dX" give estimates of the change in the probability of voting for the Republican, or the change in party identification, for a unit change in the voters' preferences along the relevant policy dimension. The numbers in the column marked "Conservative vs. Liberal" correspond to the comparison of a Liberal (someone at the 25th percentile on the relevant scale) and a Conservative (someone at the 75th percentile). The numbers in these columns are the differences in the estimated probabilities that a Conservative and a Liberal on the relevant scale vote for Republican candidates or identify themselves as Republicans, holding all other variables at their mean values.

Table 11-1 shows striking and clear evidence that economic policy preferences are more important than moral policy preferences in accounting for voting behavior and party identification. Compared with the Moral Issues Scale, the Economic Issues Scale is roughly twice as important, even in the most recent elections. Consider the relationship between presidential voting and the two issue dimensions using the General Social Survey for the period 1993–2002. The difference in the rate of Republican voting between an economic Conservative and an economic Liberal is 31 percentage points, while the difference between a moral Conservative and a moral Liberal is only 18 percentage points.

Table 11-1 also shows that the results for presidential voting are not an anomaly. The pattern of coefficients is similar for a variety of other dependent variables, including party identification, voting for U.S. senators and voting for U.S. House representatives. In fact, the relative importance of economic preferences appears to be even larger on these items than it is for presidential voting.

Those who sense a growing culture war in American elections have tapped at least one important trend: Moral issues have become increasingly important over the past 30 years. Such issues have grown from insignificance to a clear second dimension in American elections. As the General Social Survey results in

Table 11-1 Relative Impact of Economic Issues Scale and Moral Issues Scale on Voting and Party Identification

Dependent variable and survey	Economics Issues Scale		Moral Issues Scale	
	dP/dX	Conservative vs. Liberal	dP/dX	Conservative vs. Liberal
Presidential vote, GSS				
All Years	.27*	.29*	.04*	.07*
1977–1980	.22*	.23*	−.01	−.02
1981–1992	.27*	.29*	.02*	.03*
1993–2002	.28*	.31*	.11*	.18*
Presidential vote, ANES				
1992–2000	.31*	.39*	.18*	.24*
2004	.38*	.46*	.18*	.26*
U.S. Senate vote, ANES				
1992–2000	.23*	.30*	.13*	.17*
2004	.27*	.34*	.26*	.24*
U.S. House vote, ANES				
1992–2000	.22*	.28*	.09*	.12*
2004	.28*	.35*	.15*	.22*
	Regression coefficient	Conservative vs. Liberal	Regression coefficient	Conservative vs. Liberal
Party ID, GSS				
All Years	.81*	.91*	.04	.07
1977–1980	.70*	.78*	−.07	−.12
1981–1992	.80*	.90*	−.04	−.06
1993–2002	.86*	.97*	.21*	.34*
Party ID, ANES				
1992–2000	.95*	1.27*	.27*	.36*
2004	1.02*	1.33*	.40*	.60*

Note: * Statistically significant at the .01 level.

Table 11-1 show, voters' positions on the Moral Issues Scale had no discernible impact on partisan voting decisions or party identification in the 1970s, and were of little importance in the 1980s. This pattern could be because the parties were nearly converged on these issues, or it could be because the campaigns chose not to emphasize abortion and other questions. In the 1990s the weight that voters placed on the Moral Issues Scale grew sharply.

However, moral issues have not supplanted economic policy preferences. Instead, Table 11-1 shows that voting decisions depend more on the Economic Issues Scale than in the past. According to the General Social Survey data, the difference in Republican voting between an economic Conservative and an economic Liberal was just over 20 percentage points in the late 1970s. Today, that division has surpassed 30 percentage points.

The growing weight of these two issues does suggest a reorientation of voting behavior. Those who take liberal positions on economics and moral and religious questions are becoming more Democratic, and those who take conservative positions are becoming more Republican. Such a shift may have emerged because politics have become more issue oriented, because voters' preferences have become more intense, or because the parties have become more distinctive. In addition, other factors that are omitted from our analysis—such as the cold war and foreign affairs, racial issues and retrospective voting on the economy—might have become less important.

The data suggest that the American public is being pulled in two directions at once. Both moral and economic issues have grown in importance in American elections. Economic issues pull voters in the direction of voting consistent with their income, because higher-income voters are more conservative economically. At the same time, moral issues can pull voters away from their economic self-interest because higher-income voters tend to be more liberal on moral issues. But to date, the influence of economic policy preferences—on which the vast majority of Americans are moderates—has dominated the more divisive moral issues in explaining vote choice.

Variations on a Theme

On average, economic policy preferences dominate moral policy preferences in accounting for the vote. This pattern may mask important variations in electoral behavior within the American electorate that magnify the importance of moral issues. Such variations may take two forms: First, some demographic or political groups are thought to give very high weight to moral issues and little weight to economics—for example, Evangelical Protestants or rural Americans. Second, politicians and interest groups may be more successful at mobilizing voters on moral issues than on economic issues.

Are Moral Issues More Important to Some Segments of the Electorate?

One line of argument suggests that some social groups, especially those lower on the income scale, place greater weight on moral issues than other social groups. Thomas Frank (2004) suggests that moral issues hold greater sway than economics in determining the votes of low-income Americans, while high-income Americans think more in terms of economic issues, and that moral issues dominate the vote in red states like Kansas, in rural areas, or among evangelical Protestants. Sociologists of religion have suggested that frequent churchgoers are exposed to political messages on moral issues by an increasingly politicized clergy, making them more inclined to vote on moral issues (Hunter 1991; Layman 2001; Layman and Green 2006). Union members might be socialized in the workplace to place more emphasis on economic issues.

To examine these possibilities, we returned to the analysis conducted earlier, but this time we estimated the combined effects of the Moral Issues Scale, the Economic Issues Scale, indicator variables for each of these population subgroups, and their interactions on the likelihood of voting for a Republican presidential candidate. The bottom line of these analyses is clear: whether we use the GSS or

ANES, there is not a single group for which the coefficient on the Moral Issues Scale is nearly as large as the coefficient on the Economic Issues Scale, and the coefficients are strikingly stable across groups.[9]

The results are not at all what one would expect given recent discussions about "moral values" voters. The impact of moral issues on vote choice is actually slightly *smaller* for Protestants (in the GSS), evangelical Protestants (in the ANES) and regular churchgoers (in the ANES) than for the rest of the population. The impact of economic issues on voting is slightly *larger* for these groups than other voters. Even Evangelical Protestants who attend church regularly appear to place more weight on the Economic Issues Scale than on the Moral Issues Scale in voting. Geographic groups also vote the "wrong" way. Moral issues have a slightly *larger* impact on the vote choices of blue-state residents than red-state voters, and a slightly *smaller* impact on the vote choices of rural residents than urban and suburban residents.

The results on income are also interesting. In both data sets, the coefficients for both issue scales are larger among high-income groups than low-income groups. In the General Social Survey, low-income Americans are significantly *less* inclined to vote based on moral values than are high-income groups. In fact, we find that higher-income voters are more inclined to rely on issues (economic and moral) in making their voting decisions.

We should restate our main point, however, so it is not lost. Even for red-state, rural and religious voters, economic policy choices have much greater weight in electoral decisions than moral issues do.

Are Moral Issues Better at Mobilizing Voters?

The possibility of higher or lower voter turnout introduces another possible twist. Political commentators, strategists, and some academics have conjectured that moral conservatives, whether motivated by their convictions or mobilized by their churches, vote more in elections. One conjecture about the 2004 election was that initiatives calling for a ban on gay marriages were placed on the ballot in several states to bring large numbers of moral conservatives to the polls. Ansolabehere and Stewart (2005) compared the returns from the 2000 and 2004 elections and found no evidence that states with gay marriage bans on the ballot had a higher Republican presidential vote than states without such referenda. In every state, the Republican vote share in 2004 was nearly identical to that in 2000, but shifted uniformly toward Bush by approximately 1.5 percentage points.

A closer look at the survey data on voter turnout provides further evidence against the culture war argument. First, the simple correlation between turnout and moral preferences runs counter to popular claims. In both the ANES and the GSS, voters are slightly more Liberal than nonvoters on the Moral Issues Scale— for example, by .05 points in the ANES—not more Conservative. By contrast, voters are noticeably more Conservative than nonvoters on the economic issues scale—by .37 points in the ANES and .27 in the GSS. Thus, differential turnout produces an electorate that is economically Conservative, and (slightly) morally Liberal, relative to the entire population.

Second, the ANES and the GSS reveal that "extremists" on both issue scales are more likely to vote than "moderates"—but economic preferences have at least as large an effect as moral preferences. Controlling for age, education, income and other standard factors that affect the propensity to vote, a moral Conservative or moral Liberal is about 3 percent more likely to vote than a moral moderate (a respondent at 0 on the scale). There is an asymmetry with respect to economic preferences. Economic Conservatives are nearly 6 percent more likely to vote than economic moderates, while economic Liberals are only 1 percent more likely to vote than economic moderates.

Differential turnout may create an electorate that is somewhat more polarized than the overall population. This observation is consistent with a finding from research on political advertising and other communications that campaigns largely reinforce the beliefs and voting behaviors of strong partisans and more ideologically extreme voters (Ansolabehere and Iyengar, 1996). However, we do not want to exaggerate the difference between voters and nonvoters. It reflects a marginal difference compared to the striking degree of centrism exhibited overall by the American electorate. Moreover, this difference only bolsters our central claim that economic preferences are more important than moral values in determining voting behavior.

Accounting for Red States and Blue States

The culture war argument at first blush tastes of an old wine in a new bottle. The old wine is the argument that democratic institutions fail to reflect the economic preferences of voters adequately. The new bottle is the political geography of the United States. Evangelical Protestants in the United States, concentrated in the South, breadbasket states, and the Mountain West as well as in rural counties, reputedly are led by their moral convictions to ignore their economic policy preferences and vote Republican, even though that party does not represent their economic interests.

The evidence presented here suggests this argument is more wrong than right. The divisions among the public, both on policy preferences and voting behavior, are smaller than this view suggests, and voting behavior is shaped primarily by economic rather than moral preferences.

The culture war argument, however, may still be correct as an explanation of the red/blue cartography, but for a subtle reason. The behavior of voters in red and blue states may still be traced to moral issues, but these differences may be attributed not to the way voters think, but to an accident of geography. Even though voters put more weight on economic matters, the distribution of people across areas might imply that moral issues account for most of the divisions across states or counties. In essence, this argument holds that the differences in mean preferences across states is such that more of the difference in predicted vote shares across red and blue states is attributable to moral issues, even though such issues have less salience in voters' minds.

Tacitly, the culture war argument and, indeed, all of the arguments about red and blue America assume that economic- and moral-policy preferences in fact account for geographic differences in voting behavior. Do they? Surprisingly (to us), the answer is yes. However, it is not moral values that matter most.

To examine whether and how geographic differences in voting behavior reflect preferences we conduct two analyses. We begin with a probit regression predicting the probability that respondents voted for the Republican presidential candidate using only the red/blue state indicator. This is analogous to calculating simple differences in means. We then add respondents' economic and moral policy preferences. If preferences explain geographic differences in voting behavior, there should be little or no observable differences in the effects of geography once we control for the individual's economic and moral liberalism.

The results suggest that the differences in voting between red and blue states are largely a function of the distribution of voters' preferences on economic and moral issues. In both the GSS and ANES, respondents from blue states report voting for Democratic presidential candidates in the 1992, 1996 and 2000 elections at a rate 8 to 9 percentage points higher than respondents from red states. When we include the Economic Issues Scale and Moral Issues Scale in the regressions, this difference falls to 1 percentage point in the GSS and 4 percentage points in the ANES, statistically insignificant in both cases. Thus, differences in preferences over economic and moral legislation account for most of the difference in voting behavior between red and blue states.

Which issue dimension does more of the work accounting for regional differences in voting? On one hand, the preferences of red-state and blue-state voters differ more on moral issues than on economic issues. On the other hand, voters put more weight on economic issues in deciding how to vote.

In the General Social Survey, the Economic Issues Scale and the Moral Issues Scale are nearly uncorrelated, so it is straightforward to decompose the vote. In the American National Election Study the scales are somewhat correlated (the correlation is .33 among voters), making it more difficult to decompose the geographic differences according to each of the issues.

Focusing on the recent period in the GSS, we attempt to explain the 8 percent difference between the Republican share of the vote in red and blue regions, and find that while both dimensions matter, the economic dimension appears to matter a bit more. Among voters, the absolute difference between red and blue regions is larger on moral issues (.27) than on economic issues (.14). However, since economic issues have a stronger impact on voting behavior, they can account for a larger share of the voting difference. Multiplying the cross-region preference differences by the appropriate parameters from the vote regressions in Table 11-1 (.28 for economic issues and .11 for moral issues), we discover that preferences over economic issues account for nearly 50 percent of the difference in voting between these two groups of states (.039/.08), while preferences over moral issues only account for about 38 percent of the difference (.03/.08).

If we ignore the correlation between the Economic Issues Scale and the Moral Issues Scale in the ANES, we can perform a similar analysis. We find that in the ANES, moral preferences are slightly more important than economic preferences in accounting for differences between recent red- and blue-state presidential voting, but economic preferences are slightly more important for U.S. Senate and House voting.

Economic and moral policy preferences, then, help us understand most of the variation in the vote across geographic areas. Of the two factors, the economic dimension is at least as important in accounting for this variation. The clearest evidence—from the General Social Survey—suggests that red states are red in part because their voters are morally conservative. But, even more importantly, red states are more reliable supporters of the Republicans because voters in these states are slightly more conservative on economic issues and because those small differences have twice the weight in voters' minds.

Red and Blue America in Historical Perspective

How is it, then, that we can observe that some states are "owned" by Republicans and others by Democrats? The error lies in the popular description of American elections based on a handful of presidential elections. To see the mistake, one must see American elections in historical perspective. From that vantage, red and blue America is a better description of the divisions of the early 1900s, and perhaps the 1950s, than the present. Compared to the past, the political geography of the United States today is purple.

Consider the trends in four indicators of electoral and political competition among the American states: 1) a moving average of the vote margin of the winning candidate for president in each state (Average Winner Vote Margin for President); 2) a moving average of the vote margin for the leading party in each state computed using all statewide offices (Average Winner Vote Margin for Statewide Offices); 3) a moving average of the percentage of races in which one party won more than 55 percent of the vote (Lopsided Races for Statewide Offices); and 4) the average incidence of unified party control of state government (Unified State Government). The first three measures are based on votes, while the last is based on victories.[10]

Figure 11-4 presents all four variables over the past 100 years. The top panel shows 1 and 2, and the bottom panel shows 3 and 4. The data reveal that the partisan division across states has shrunk sharply over time. For example, Average Winner Vote Margin for Statewide Offices averaged .12 during the period 1900–1940, but only .05 over the period 1970–2000. Similarly, the fraction of Unified State Governments fell from an average of .76 during 1900–1940 to .47 during 1970–2000. The practical importance of the compression of the distribution is that since the 1960s, in nearly all states, neither party has held

Figure 11-4 Decline in One-Party Dominance in U.S. States, 1900–2000

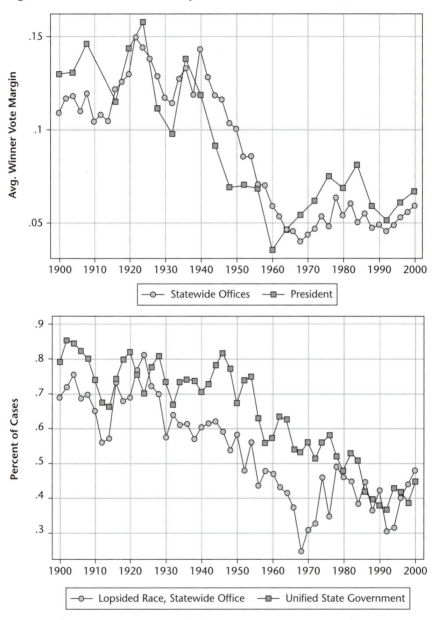

a solid edge in the votes. Nearly everywhere, the party division is smaller than 60 to 40 percent.

Examining the control of state legislatures provides other insights into these divisions. During the period 1900–1928, Republicans held more than 65 percent of the seats in more than half of the legislative chambers in the United States. Democrats had more than 90 percent of the seats in more than 25 percent of the states. There was little middle ground. In only 12 percent of all state legislatures did the two major parties hold between 40 and 60 percent of the seats. Today, the distribution of party divisions of state legislatures follows something more like a normal curve. Typically, neither party holds more than 60 percent of the seats. In no chamber today does one party hold 90 percent of the seats.

The South is particularly interesting in this regard. Casual accounts and current political punditry commonly describes the South as the bastion of Republicanism. This confuses changes with levels. Republican representation in Southern state governments has grown massively since the 1960s, but that increase came from a floor of literally zero. Several Southern states had Democratic governors and *not one* Republican state legislator in the late 1950s. Today, Republicans have wrested control of at least one chamber of the state legislature from the Democrats in almost every Southern state. But the division of seats in the Southern state legislatures is almost exactly even. The South is perhaps the most evenly divided region in terms of state politics.

One may also look within the states. While much has been written about the divisions between urban, rural and suburban voters, there has been a similar century-long decline in the partisan divisions within states. The variation in the vote across counties within states has declined significantly. Many other geographic cleavages have also shrunk, such as the "North-South" division in California and Florida, the "upstate-downstate" differences between Illinois and Indiana, and the "East-West" schism in Tennessee and Massachusetts. What many observers see as an enormous urban-rural difference—Democratic dominance of cities and Republican dominance in many rural areas—is relatively small when viewed in historical perspective. Differences remain today, but they are half of what they were fifty years ago. If these trends continue, geographic differences will become even less meaningful in the American states.

The past century has produced, not a growing political divide, but political convergence among the American states and counties. At least in terms of the distribution of votes and political control of state governments, American states do not sort cleanly into Democratic and Republican camps. The parties can compete almost everywhere. That does not mean that they always do. With scarce resources in a presidential election, for example, the parties may focus on the dozen or so most closely divided states. However, even the governorships of states like California or Kansas or the mayoralty of New York City are not out of reach for either party.

The quest to understand the differences between red and blue states, then, seems to us to be on the wrong track. The question is not why are some states red and some states blue, but why has America become purple? That phenomenon—the political convergence of the American states—is the phenomenon that we believe deserves further exploration and explanation.[11]

Conclusion

The rhetoric of red and blue America emerged from an observation about the geography of American politics. In recent presidential elections, most states appear to be regularly Democratic or regularly Republican. Only a dozen states swing one way or another. Beneath that pattern, it has been conjectured, lies a polarized electorate, especially over hot-button moral issues, and these moral issues allegedly lead low-income Americans to vote against their economic interests.

Little in the survey data squares with that interpretation of the American public. Individuals' policy preferences on moral and economic issues can account for differences in voting between red-state and blue-state voters. However, economic issues, not moral issues, have a much greater impact on voters' decisions. As a result, even though there is a somewhat larger divide between the states on moral issues, if anything economic issues account for more of the difference between "regularly Republican" and "regularly Democratic" states. Moreover, that difference is quite small—only about 8 percentage points.

Economic issues also create a strong centrifugal force in American politics. The great mass of the American electorate holds centrist positions on economic policies. Because the weight of economic issues is so much higher in elections than moral issues, the electoral outcomes are more in line with the distribution of economic preferences than moral preferences. The electorate is indeed pulled in two directions, as suggested by Thomas Frank, John Roemer, and others, but the pull of economic issues is so much stronger that the role of moral issues is clearly of secondary importance.

For economists, it may be tempting to see in this account a ringing endorsement of the economic theory of democracy. The standard model of public finance and political economy has held up reasonably well in one respect: preferences over economic policies appear to dominate in voters' decision making. However, our analysis exposes a deeper problem. The relationship between economic policy preferences and economic self-interest is weaker than commonly supposed by political economists. Those with higher income tend to hold more economically conservative views, but the distribution of economic policy preferences of lower-income and higher-income Americans do not differ much. In Figure 11-3 above, for example, roughly 45 percent of the higher-income Americans have economic policy preferences to the left of the average lower-income American.

Ultimately, individuals' beliefs about what is the right or fair economic policy for the nation are difficult to explain. They are only related weakly to one common indicator of self-interest—income—and they are nearly uncorrected with cultural issues. Since these policy preferences appear to be one of the main forces driving voting behavior, however, explaining them is clearly a key question in American political economy.

Notes

1. Variants of this argument go back at least to Karl Marx and also appear in the writings of Schumpeter (1942), Lipset and Rokkan (1967), and others.
2. The models by Lindbeck and Weibull (1987) and Dixit and Londregan (1995, 1996) also incorporate noneconomic issues and show how these issues affect distributive politics. In particular, these models highlight the importance of "swing" voters.
3. We analyze the 2004 election separately from the other elections for two reasons: First, it is intrinsically interesting because many observers believe that moral issues played an especially prominent role in voter behavior during this election. Second, several of the ANES questions changed or were dropped, so we are a bit uncomfortable combining the 2004 survey with the other surveys.
4. On most spending items, the average response calls for an increase in spending, so holding spending constant is a relatively Conservative position. This is probably due in part to the fact that the questions do not directly mention tradeoffs—such as tax increases spending cuts on other items—that would be required to pay for increases in spending.
5. The General Social Survey has measured attitudes on abortion consistently since the mid-1970s, presenting seven different scenarios and asking the respondent to state when abortion should or should not be allowed (examples include risk to the life of the mother and rape). We scaled these items to extract a single measure of policy preferences on abortion. This measure exhibits a clearly bimodal distribution. At one mode, over 25 percent of the electorate holds the most liberal position on this question, providing for the legality of abortion in all circumstances. The other mode on the scale would allow abortions, but only in the cases of rape, incest, and where the health of the mother is in jeopardy. Few people choose the middle ground on this issue, and few want an outright prohibition. Abortion attitudes were unique; few other items showed any degree of bimodality.
6. Blue states are those in which the average share of the two-party vote cast for the Democratic presidential candidate in 1992, 1996, 2000, and 2004 was .51 or greater. Red states are those for which the average was .47 or less. This leaves nine states— Arkansas, Colorado, Florida, Louisiana, Missouri, New Hampshire, Nevada, Ohio and Tennessee—which we do not classify either as blue or red.
7. We continue to define red and blue states as above, using the elections of 1992, 1996, 2000, and 2004. The vestiges of the southern Democrats and northern Republicans remained in 1976 and 1980. Recall that the General Social Survey does not identify states but regions.
8. More complete details of the analysis are in Appendix B, which is appended to this paper at the website (www.e-jep.org).
9. The interested reader can find more complete results in Tables B2a and B2b of Appendix B, appended to this article at (www.e-jep.org).
10. More precisely, (1) through (4) are constructed as follows. Let d_{jt} be the average Democratic vote share in state j in year t across a chosen set of races. Next, let D_{jt} be the average of d_{jt} in state j over the 9 year interval, $t - 4$ to $t + 4$. Finally, let $M_{jt} = |D_{jt} - .5|$ be the absolute difference of D_{jt} from .5. Let M_t be the average of M_{jt} across states in year t. Also, let $L_{jt} = 1$ if $M_{jt} > .05$ and 0 otherwise, and let L_t be the average

of L_{jt} across states in year t. Then, (1) is M_t where we only use the race for president in computing d_{jt}, (2) is M_t where we use all statewide races in computing d_{jt} (see Ansolabehere and Snyder, 2002, for more details about data and sources), and (3) is L_t where we again use all statewide races in computing d_{jt}. To construct (4), we say that a state has *unified government* in a given year if one party controls the governorship and also controls a majority of the seats in both houses of the state legislature. We define (4) as the fraction of states with unified governments in each year t. Note that we do not take a moving average in constructing this variable. Also, we drop Nebraska and Minnesota during the periods in which these states had nonpartisan state legislatures.

11. In a provocative book, McCarty, Poole, and Rosenthal (1997) argue that the political convergence in the United States reflects the economic growth of the South and the converging income distribution across states. The survey data examined here raise doubts about that explanation. The effect of income on economic preferences, while in the expected direction, is hardly strong, and the effect of income on moral preferences runs in the opposite direction. It is unclear how these two factors balance out, but the effect of income growth on policy preferences and voting is surely complicated.

PART IV
PARTISANSHIP AND
ISSUE PREFERENCES

12. Is the American Electorate Polarized?

That congressional politics has become highly polarized is indisputable. Republicans and Democrats in Congress vote differently from one another, and that difference has been growing for three decades or more. It was common in the 1950s for Southern Democrats to vote with Republicans in a "conservative coalition," but that coalition has faded, and Southern Democrats now usually join their northern copartisans in voting together in opposition to the Republicans. Moderate Republicans, along with moderate Democrats, were then a substantial force in Congress, but their numbers and influence have declined dramatically.[1]

More controversial is the extent to which mass politics has also become polarized. On the face of it, there is extreme partisanship, as evidenced, for example, by intense electoral competition in "battleground states" and by equally intense fights over issues such as abortion and same-sex marriage.[2] In general, there seem to be deep divisions over social/moral/religious issues, with the "culture war" between social liberals and conservatives having now become a partisan conflict. Yet polarization in the electorate may not be as extreme as it seems. The American public is arguably centrist even on cultural issues, and a growing share of the electorate is independent politically (see below). Apparent polarization may largely reflect ideological separation between the major parties' presidential nominees, along with the sometimes hysterical voices of commentators who benefit by stoking the fires of conflict.

Determining the extent of polarization in the general public is rendered difficult by the fact that it can mean any of several things. Perhaps the most obvious definition is that polarization exists when people take opposing positions on a specific issue, or on issues more generally (DiMaggio, Evans, and Bryson 1964; Evans, Bryson, and DiMaggio 2001). If, for example, we were dealing with a liberal-conservative scale, polarization increases as people move to the opposite ideological extremes—what Gelman et al. (2008) call "opinion radicalization" but what we shall refer to simply as "attitudinal polarization." This definition is usually taken to imply that the issue(s) is (are) salient, since the public would not be considered polarized if people had opposite positions on something that no one cared about (Hetherington 2009).

Table 12-1a An Electorate Divided on Issues but Issue Positions Are
Uncorrelated with Party

	Partisanship		
Position on issue(s)	Democrat	Republican	Total
Strongly liberal	50%	50%	50%
In between	0	0	0
Strongly conservative	50	50	50
Total	100%	100%	100%
	(N = 100)	(N = 100)	(N = 200)

Table 12-1b An Electorate Divided on Issues and Issue Positions Coincide
Perfectly with Partisanship

	Partisanship		
Position on issue(s)	Democrat	Republican	Total
Strongly liberal	100%	0	50%
In between	0	0	0
Strongly conservative	0	100%	50
Total	100%	100%	100%
	(N = 100)	(N = 100)	(N = 200)

An alternative definition of polarization refers to the degree that the public is sorted into opposing ideological (or issue) camps in a way that coincides with their party leanings. Theoretically, people could divide into opposing camps on an issue and yet not have this split coincide with partisan tendencies (see Table 12-1a). This might occur, for example, when a new issue arises—say, environmental protection when it first began to be recognized as an important concern. "Partisan sorting," on the other hand, occurs when those on the two sides move to opposing parties, increasing intra-party homogeneity as well as making the parties sharply different from one another (Table 12-1b) (Fiorina and Levendusky 2006). Note, of course, that partisan sorting could occur on an issue without any change in the overall distribution (degree of polarization) in the electorate.[3]

There is also, of course, the question of whether the glass is half-full or half-empty: how great do the differences have to be for there to be polarization or party sorting? If 40 percent of the electorate favors each side of an issue, with only 20 percent in the middle, is this sufficient to call it polarization? Is it party sorting if 55 percent of Democrats favor a policy that only 40 percent of Republicans favor? Similarly, how extreme the differences are depends on how we measure opinions (especially, what the response categories are), so the wording of questions becomes important. Finally, some regard polarization as a process rather than a static notion, suggesting that changes in the extent of disagreement are necessary for polarization to exist.

As this prelude suggests, researchers who debate the matter of polarization and party sorting in the electorate often speak past one another because of how they define the term, as well as how they view partisanship. These definitional matters should be kept in mind as we review the controversy over whether or not the electorate is polarized, and if so, how closely attitudinal differences correspond to party preferences.

A Polarized Electorate

We begin by reviewing how Americans have historically divided themselves between the parties and the extent to which those nominally supportive of each party have voted. Table 12-2 shows the distribution of party identification as measured in the American National Election Studies (ANES) from 1952 through 2008. Several well-studied trends are evident across this lengthy sweep of time. First, the small percentage of "apolitical" respondents dropped almost to zero, largely as a consequence of making politics meaningful for Southern blacks (Converse 1964). Second, there was a lasting increase in the percentage of Independents in the late 1960s and early 1970s, with perhaps another small bump-up in the 2000s. Third, a large Democratic advantage in the 1950s dwindled to a very slight Democratic lead by the early 2000s. In fact, the two parties were of fairly equal strength in terms of partisanship of *voters* in the 2004 presidential election because Democratic identifiers typically turn out to vote at a lower rate than Republican identifiers. However, public dissatisfaction with the George W. Bush administration led to a greater Democratic advantage in identification in 2008 and into 2009 (Weisberg and Devine 2010a). But what is more important here is whether these trends reflect an increase in partisan voting.

Party identification diminished in its effect on the vote from the 1950s through the 1980s (e.g., Nie, Verba, and Petrocik 1979), but even though the number of Independents remained high, the declining effect of partisanship ended and has been reversed. The increased importance of partisanship is vividly displayed in the low rates of partisan defection in the elections of the 1990s and early 2000s (see Table 12-3). In the previous four decades, it was common to have a high proportion of partisans of one party vote for the presidential candidate of the opposite party, as when 41 percent of Democrats voted for President Richard Nixon's reelection in 1972 and 27 percent of Republicans voted for President Lyndon Johnson in 1964. In fact, in each election from 1952 through 1984, at least 18 percent of the partisans of one party voted for the other major party's presidential candidate. Only 8 to 11 percent of either party defected in 2000 and 2004. There was speculation that defection would increase sharply in 2008, as U.S. Senator John McCain's candidacy faltered or as U.S. senator Barack Obama had difficulty appealing to some conservative white Democrats. In the end, some Republicans and some Democrats may have chosen to stay at home rather than

Table 12-2 Party Identification of the American Electorate, by Year

	'52	'56	'60	'64	'68	'72	'76	'80	'84	'88	'92	'96	'00	'04	'08
Strong Democrat	22	21	20	27	20	15	15	18	17	17	18	18	19	17	19
Weak Democrat	25	23	25	25	25	26	25	23	20	18	18	19	15	16	15
Independent Democrat	10	6	6	9	10	11	12	11	11	12	14	14	15	17	17
Pure Independent	6	9	10	8	11	13	15	13	11	11	12	9	12	10	11
Independent Republican	7	8	7	6	9	10	10	10	12	13	12	12	13	12	12
Weak Republican	14	14	14	14	15	13	14	14	15	14	14	15	12	12	13
Strong Republican	14	15	16	11	10	10	9	9	12	14	11	12	12	16	13
Apolitical	3	4	2	1	1	1	1	2	2	2	1	1	1	0	0
Total	101	100	100	101	101	99	101	100	100	101	100	100	99	100	100
N	1,784	1,757	1,911	1,550	1,553	2,694	2,850	1,612	2,236	2,032	2,474	1,710	1,797	1,197	2,083
Democratic presidential vote	44%	42%	50%	61%	43%	38%	50%	42%	41%	46%	43%	49%	48%	48%	53%
Republican presidential vote	55	57	50	38	43	61	48	52	59	54	38	41	48	51	46

Source: American National Election Studies Web site, augmented by 2008 ANES pre-election survey.

Note: This classification is based on the following question series: "Generally speaking, do you usually think of yourself as a Republican, a Democrat, an Independent, or what?" (If partisan:) "Would you call yourself a strong (Republican/Democrat) or a not very strong (Republican/Democrat)?" (If not partisan:) "Do you think of yourself as closer to the Republican or Democratic Party?"

Table 12-3 Defection Rates of Partisans in Voting for President (percentages)

	'52	'56	'60	'64	'68	'72	'76	'80	'84	'88	'92	'96	'00	'04	'08
Democrats voting Republican	30	26	18	11	23	41	19	26	21	15	9	6	11	9	9
Republicans voting Democratic	4	4	8	27	6	8	14	7	5	10	12	16	10	8	10
Total not voting their party identification	18	15	13	15	24	25	16	24	13	12	24	16	12	10	9

Source: American National Election Studies, 1952–2008.

Note: Independent leaners are combined with partisans. The especially high percentages in the bottom row for 1968, 1980, and 1992 reflect the votes for third-party candidates George Wallace, John Anderson, and Ross Perot.

to vote for their party's candidate, but the defection rate among voters was low, with fewer than 10 percent of partisans defecting.

The presentation in Table 12-3 is suggestive, and it is confirmed by Bartels' (2000) sophisticated analysis of the 1952 to 1996 period. Taking into account the full distribution of partisanship among actual voters, he found that the impact of party identification on individual presidential voting declined from when it was first measured in the 1950s to a low in the 1972 election. Its impact on presidential voting increased in every subsequent election, through when he wrote his article, so that it was higher in the 1990s than previously. Straight-ticket voting has also been increasing from a low in 1980 (Hetherington 2001; Stanley and Niemi 2010, 125), which can be regarded as another sign of people polarizing more in their voting.

In describing partisanship as being more important in voting again, one is essentially saying that the public is more polarized *in its voting behavior*. This is also evident in how people react to the two parties. Since the 1960s, the ANES has been asking people to rate the two parties on a "feeling thermometer," where 100 represents very warm feelings, 0 represents very cold feelings, and 50 means neither hot nor cold. The correlation between the ratings of the two parties was negative in the 1960s (-0.28 in 1964 and -0.18 in 1968) but the ratings became independent of each other in the 1970s (0.02 in 1972 and 0.01 in 1976), meaning that liking one party did not lead people to like the other party less. The correlations returned to negative values starting in the 1980s (-0.23 in 1980, -0.40 in 1984, and -0.39 in 1988). The -0.48 correlation between ratings of the Republicans and Democrats in both 2004 and 2008 was the most negative this correlation has been in any presidential election year (Weisberg and Christenson 2007; Weisberg and Devine 2010a). Currently, the more people like one party, the less they like the other, which can be considered to be another sign of polarization.

The more general polarization argument is the popular discussion of a "culture war" between social conservatives and liberals (Hunter 1991). This has become a common argument, especially focused on such hot-button issues as abortion and gay marriage. The parties have polarized on these issues at the elite level, and the result, it is claimed, is that the public is particularly polarized on these social issues. The scholarly literature finds some evidence for this argument, but it is more nuanced than in the popular literature.

One important point, for example, is that some portions of the electorate are more polarized than others. Abramowitz and Saunders, in an article reprinted here, note that the least engaged portion of the electorate is largely centrist, whereas those who are more engaged take more extreme positions on issues. Moreover, polarization has increased over the past twenty years, especially among this portion of the electorate. Religious observance is also correlated with political attitudes, with a considerable gap on cultural issues. Further, they argue that rather than causing the electorate to become politically disengaged, increased polarization has been energizing the electorate, especially as regards increased electoral participation in the 2004 presidential election. This makes polarization all the more significant.

Some scholars have also emphasized polarization on income or social class as much as on social issues. We shall review these arguments below when discussing the dynamics of polarization. Polarization also extends to foreign affairs and military matters, as conflicting views of President George W. Bush and his policies led to sharp disagreements about the Iraq War. These disagreements coincided with partisanship; for example, by early 2006, nearly 80 percent of Republicans still supported the war, compared to only 20 percent of Democrats (Jacobson 2007, 132).

Polarization is also seen when one takes a regional perspective on contemporary politics. For example, Black and Black's (2007) analysis of the 2004 election is that the Southern and Mountain/Plains states are Republican strongholds, while the Northeast and Pacific Rim states are Democratic strongholds. According to their analysis, regional polarization is so extreme that only the Midwest is left as a swing area that can determine election outcomes.

Layman and Carsey (2002) add a theoretical perspective by suggesting that the present polarization is due to the parties becoming increasingly divided on several major policy dimensions at once. They follow Sundquist (1983) in interpreting party change in earlier periods as being a result of "conflict displacement," when the ongoing cleavage between the parties is displaced by a new cleavage. The slavery issue polarized Republicans and Democrats in the 1850s; that division was superseded by agrarian and related currency issues in the 1890s; and then social welfare issues became dominant in the 1930s. In contrast, recent party change has taken the form of "conflict extension." Conflict on social welfare issues remained when civil rights became a basis of party conflict in the 1960s, and the emergence of cultural and moral issue divides has not displaced either of the social welfare or racial equality cleavages. Instead of old divisions being displaced, party conflict is extended to newer issues. The multiple dimensions of partisan conflict, they argue, make party divisions and polarization more intense. Brewer (2005) confirms Layman and Carsey's results, showing how racial and cultural issues have joined economic equality issues in determining or reinforcing partisan identifications.

Hetherington, in an article reprinted and updated in this section, adds another perspective to the notion of partisan polarization. He begins with the familiar observation that party differences in voting in Congress have increased since the 1970s. During the same period (extended in his updated figures through 2004), there has been an increase in people seeing important differences between the parties and in correctly identifying the Democrats as more liberal than the Republicans. He also finds more people being positive toward one party and negative toward the other and people making more comments about the parties. He interprets the increasingly polarized affect and salience of the parties as two aspects of party resurgence.

Furthermore, there is evidence of Democrats becoming more liberal and Republicans becoming more conservative. Abramowitz and Saunders (2006) demonstrate that the correlation between partisanship and ideology increased dramatically over the years, from only 0.35 in the 1972–80 period, to 0.49 in the 1992–2000 period, and up to 0.58 in the 2004 election. They also show that Republican identification increased most among conservatives while decreasing among liberals. A related point is that through 2004, they found fewer states to be competitive in presidential elections, with percent differences on attitudes on current policy issues of 15 percent to 25 percent between "blue" states (that U.S. senator John Kerry won by at least 6 percentage points in 2004) and "red" states (that Bush won by that margin).

Overall, there is evidence of multiple, large fractures in the American electorate, fissures that have grown in the recent past and become more tied to partisanship. The differences are especially evident on cultural issues, though they extend to other issues as well. Not surprisingly, then, they are also visible in voting behavior, such as when comparing blue- and red-state voters as well as secular and religious voters. In short, there are "real divisions within the American electorate" (Abramowitz and Saunders 2008, 54) in both senses noted above. Americans are sharply divided on issues, and those on one side self-identify as Democrats while those on the other side consider themselves Republicans.

The Dynamics of Polarization

Assuming there is increased partisan polarization at the mass level, there is controversy about how it developed. Is it a reflection of increased polarization at the elite level, or a cause of that increased polarization? Is the polarization due to people changing their partisanship or their ideology? And is the polarization due to differences on moral issues, as the cultural wars discussion implies, is it due to personality differences between Liberals and Conservatives, or is it economic in nature, as a form of class warfare?

Hetherington, in the aforementioned reprinted article, focuses on the underlying dynamics of increased partisanship in voting. He employs a "top-down" logic, with the elite setting the terms for the mass public's understanding of politics, suggesting that the public is unlikely to be party-oriented unless politicians provide appropriate cues. As greater partisan voting in Congress began in earnest in the mid-1970s, with further acceleration in the 1990s, a top-down model would imply that the increases in mass awareness and understanding of differences between the parties would occur shortly after elite polarization increased. Multivariate analysis shows that elite polarization is in fact a significant predictor of the public's feelings toward the parties and their salience, with more people being positive toward one party and negative toward the other and people making more comments about the parties subsequent to increased polarization in Congress.

Hetherington's top-down flow of partisan polarization has not gone unchallenged. In particular, Stonecash, Brewer, and Mariani (2003) find elite partisan divisions to be partially explained by divisions at the mass level, with emphasis on a changed constituent base of the two parties. Demographic shifts and realignment have resulted in more northern districts with liberal majorities that elect Democrats to Congress and more Southern districts with conservative majorities that elect Republicans to Congress. Another take is provided by Layman, Carsey, and Horowitz (2006), who suggest that the increased polarization is due not so much to either elected party officials or the electorate but instead to party activists who have more extreme ideological positions than the electorate as a whole and who play important roles in financing and nominating candidates. For example, they show how national nominating convention delegates for the two parties became more polarized through the 1990s, with the mean difference between them increasing on racial, cultural, and social welfare issues. Aldrich (2003, 285) challenges the top-down model in a different way. He doubts the basic assumption that members of Congress would change the behavior that caused their constituents to elect them unless public attitudes had already changed, or at least that the members had reason to believe that the public would react positively to changes in how their representatives would vote. For example, he suggests that the civil rights revolution led to changes in mass beliefs and behavior that preceded the changes in voting by members of Congress.[4]

Jacobson (2000, 26) views the relationship between mass and elites as "inherently interactive," with changes at electoral and congressional levels mutually reinforcing one another. Echoing the same perspective as Aldrich, Jacobson emphasizes that the movement of politicians to take more divergent policy stands is because of the response they expect from voters. Ambitious politicians sense an opening and move accordingly. Thus, he argues that Republicans moved to conservative positions on racial and social issues because they realized they could attract some conservative Democrats; likewise, the Democrats moved to a pro-choice position on abortion since it could help them attract some affluent Republicans. This is very similar to Riker's (1982) notion of "heresthetics," in which politicians will raise new issues as a tactic to try to break apart existing coalitions.

As to the increased relationship between partisanship and ideology, the usual assumption has been that people have been changing their partisanship to agree with their ideology (e.g., Putz 2002),[5] though Miller (1999) shows that party identification has a larger effect on issue positions than vice versa. Stoker and Jennings (2008) show that another important mechanism is the greater party-issue constraint among new cohorts of voters than among the voters they replaced. They argue that greater elite polarization in the 1960s and 1970s led to greater polarization among the mass public thirty to forty years later. Stoker and Jennings suggest a dynamic for increasing partisan polarization that is tied to socialization. They expect that openness to political learning will decrease with age (Converse 1969; Niemi and Jennings 1991; Alwin and Krosnick 1991) and that the constraint between partisanship and issue positions will increase with age. Comparing age cohorts over time in NES surveys, they find increased constraint between political attitudes and party identification over time for each cohort on each of three types of issues (New Deal, race and gender, and cultural issues). They find that the partisanship of people socialized before the 1960s remains tied to New Deal positions. While new issues of race, gender, and culture do not affect that political generation, they do affect the partisanship of later cohorts. Thus, the New Deal partisan alignment is not disappearing, but, in Layman and Carsey's (2002) term, there is "conflict extension" in the electorate with new issues adding to the partisan polarization. As these new issues affect younger generations, the linkages between these issues and partisanship will grow further as those generations age, so that polarization in the electorate is self-reinforcing.[6]

The popular press usually explains the culture wars in terms of social cleavages, such as mainstream religious denominations versus evangelicals. Hetherington and Weiler (2009) instead provide a psychological explanation. They argue that attitudes on cultural issues are structured by the person's degree of authoritarianism, which causes people on opposite sides of the cultural divide to understand the world differently. People differ in their need for order versus their comfort with ambiguity, which Hetherington and Weiler feel explains differences in their authoritarianism. They describe authoritarianism as a worldview that involves a desire to maintain order. By contrast, they associate nonauthoritarians with favoring outgroups (such as supporting aid to blacks because of their experience of past discrimination), seeking balanced information, avoiding ethnocentrism, and favoring personal autonomy over social conformity. They demonstrate that authoritarianism is significantly related to people's views on a host of contemporary issues (including nonsocial issues such as the Iraq War, the use of force in general, and tradeoffs between security and civil liberties). That relationship holds even after controlling for ideology, party identification, moral traditionalism, and standard sociodemographic factors. They find that partisan sorting occurs only on issues that are structured by authoritarianism. Their analysis also shows that perceived threat weakens the effect of authoritarianism—highly authoritarian people already support policies that would impose more order, while those who are low in authoritarianism also support those policies if they perceive a threat from terrorism such as in the aftermath of the terrorist attacks of September 11, 2001.

Other recent work finds an economic basis to polarization, a connection that has grown stronger in recent decades. In particular, McCarty, Poole, and Rosenthal's book (2006), aptly titled *Polarized America,* focuses directly on economic polarization. The authors find an increase among voters in party stratification by income, as measured by the proportion of Republican identifiers in the top income quintile divided by the proportion of Republican identifiers in the bottom income quintile. They demonstrate an increasing rich-poor cleavage between Republican and Democratic identifiers from 1960 through their last data point in 2002, with the polarization being particularly dramatic among Southern whites.[7]

Bartels (2008) confirms the class-based polarization that McCarty, Poole, and Rosenthal find, while pinpointing its sources in more detail. He shows that affluent white voters have decreased in their support for Democratic presidential candidates since the 1950s while poorer white voters have increased in their support. There has been a decline in Democratic identification among both groups, but much sharper among more affluent whites, with the decline among low-income whites being concentrated in the South. He finds that economic issues were important in the voting of all income groups in 2004, while cultural issues were much more important for high-income voters than low-income voters.

Gelman et al.'s (2008) analysis shows that even the class-based polarization considered by Bartels and others is more complex than at first glance. Gelman et al. look at the paradox that the Republican Party gets more of the vote from higher income people, while the Democratic Party gets more of the vote from richer states. Their resolution of this paradox is that the relationship between income and voting varies with the state's income level. In poorer states, like Mississippi, the higher income people are voting more Republican. However, in richer states, like Connecticut, there is very little voting difference between lower income and higher income people. In middle-income states like Ohio, there is a moderate relationship between income and vote, between the extremes found for Mississippi and Connecticut. The Democrats have been winning the votes of poor people in most of the country, except in Texas and some of the Plains and Mountain states, while the Republicans have been winning the votes of upper-income people, except in California, New York, Massachusetts, and Connecticut. In part, this reflects racial differences between the states, in that the income divide in poor Southern states is also a racial divide. It also reflects a rural-urban divide, in that the richer states tend to be more urban than the poorer states. And it reflects a religious divide, since richer people are more likely than poor people to attend church in poor states, while the opposite attendance pattern occurs in rich states. In any case, the McCarty, Poole, and Rosenthal, Bartels, and Gelman et al. work all agree that there is an important economic basis to partisan conflict in the early years of the twenty-first century (see also the discussion of economic factors as vote determinants in chapter 3).

A Moderate Electorate

Given the amount of attention in both the popular press and academic writings to the electorate becoming more polarized, it is important to recognize that a case can be made that polarization at the mass level is not large and has not increased. Even the apparent decrease in party defection rates shown in Table 12-3 can easily be challenged. Partisans may defect less in presidential voting than they once did, but that calculation disregards Independents—and there are more Independents now than in the 1950s. Also, the defection statistics in Table 12-3 only take voters into account—and a sizable proportion of the electorate does not vote. Taking these factors into account, Table 12-4 shows that the decline in partisan defection is less meaningful than it seems at first. Once nonvoters, third-party voters, and pure Independents are taken into account, only half of the public is voting for the presidential candidate of their party.[8]

A leading political scientist has vigorously challenged the claim that the country has become politically polarized. Morris Fiorina (2005) contends that the electorate is moderate, that there is no culture war, and that polarization occurs only at the elite level. He considers the changes at the mass level to be an instance of sorting, rather than polarization. He examines polling data on issue after issue, showing that most Americans have moderate positions, even on social issues like abortion. Comparing public opinion in Republican ("red") states and Democratic ("blue") states, he finds most differences to be fairly small, even on such cultural issues as homosexuality, where he finds only a 10 percent difference in the proportions of partisans strongly agreeing that homosexuality should be accepted by society. Republicans and Democrats have become further apart on twenty-four political and policy attitudes, but the difference increased only mildly: from an average of 12 percent in 1987 to 17 percent in 2003. The gap between the parties on abortion remains small: 10 to 12 percent more Democrats than Republicans

Table 12-4 Percentage of the Total Public Who Voted for Their Party's Candidate for President

'52	'56	'60	'64	'68	'72	'76	'80	'84	'88	'92	'96	'00	'04	'08
47	45	50	49	41	37	40	37	41	43	39	40	43	52	51

Source: Weisberg and Devine (2010).

Note: Those who do not vote for their party's candidate include nonvoters, third-party voters, pure independents, and partisan defectors.

think that abortion should be legal under any circumstances, while 5 to 10 percent more Republicans than Democrats think it should be illegal under all circumstances, with about 50 percent of both Democrats and Republicans saying that it should be legal "only under certain circumstances."

Fiorina also finds that most social characteristics no longer affect voting as much as they used to. Differences between Protestants and Catholics, for example, have diminished.[9] At the same time, he finds that economic cleavages in the electorate have not decayed, with a wide difference in the Democratic vote percentage for president from the lower and upper third of the income spectrum, with about a 24-percentage point difference in 1996, though it fell to only about 8 percent in 2000.

Survey evidence, echoing "inconsistencies" reported as far back as Converse's (1964) analysis of "mass belief systems," also finds that Democrats are not consistently liberal across issues and Republicans are not consistently conservative. Hillygus and Shields (2008, 60) show that, on average, across more than twenty issues, only 54 percent of partisans have views that are congruent with the position of their national party, with 20 percent being neutral and 26 percent having incongruent views. Similarly Gelman et al. (2008) show that 85 percent of Republicans either do not identify themselves as conservative or do not take the conservative position on all three issues that the authors consider basic to ideological disputes between the parties: abortion, affirmative action, and government health insurance. The same is true of Democrats: almost 90 percent of Democrats either do not identify themselves as liberal or do not take the liberal position on all three of those issues. Though they do also find some increased polarization at the mass level, Gelman et al. conclude in the end that Fiorina is correct that Americans are mainly centrists and that it is the two parties that have diverged ideologically.[10]

In a fairly extreme test of congruity, Hillygus and Shields look at ten potential wedge issues (issues such as abortion, gun control, and health care, that parties use to try to divide the other party's supporters), finding that only 33 percent of partisans are congruent with their party on all issues while 67 percent disagreed with their party in 2004 on at least one issue they considered personally important (p. 63). This lack of political polarization allows parties to employ wedge issues, which would work far less successfully if voters were completely polarized. Basinger and Lavine (2005, 173) similarly show that 36 percent of partisans in 2000 were ambivalent in terms of the open-ended comments they made about the political parties versus 18 percent indifferent, while only 46 percent gave responses that were decidedly favorable to one party and negative to the other.

Baldassarri and Gelman (2008) look at how attitudes correlate with each other and with party identification. They find that the correlation between party identification and issue attitudes (which they term "issue partisanship" but more commonly called sorting) has increased much more rapidly in the 1972–2004 period than the correlation among pairs of issues (which they term "issue alignment"). Issue alignment increased, but slowly. The resorting of party labels among voters changed more quickly, especially on moral issues. The parties polarized, according to their perspective, but individuals are only adjusting to the changes at the elite level.[11]

Levendusky (2009a) takes the argument one step further by using 1992–1996 panel data to estimate how much movement actually occurs in issue attitudes and partisanship. He finds that most of the observed change in underlying issue positions cannot be distinguished from measurement error, so the amount of actual change in a two- or four-year period is very limited. As people change their party identification, issue positions should change, but such change is not more than would be expected by chance. Small changes at the individual level over a small number of years could still accumulate to larger changes over a longer time period, but his aggregate analysis shows that most voters did not change their issue positions dramatically over the twelve-year period from 1992 to 2004. Aggregate polarization could occur over a long period of time, but, in fact, the observed levels of issue change, as Fiorina et al. (2008) claim, remain mild.

As to geographical polarization, the 2008 election showed that the regional polarization described by Black and Black (2007) is permeable. Obama was able to make important inroads for the Democrats in both the South and the Mountain/Plains regions. Indeed, Ansolabehere, Rodden, and Snyder (reprinted here in Section III, chapter 11) show that one-party dominance declined in U.S. states over the second half of the twentieth century and, in some respects, over the entire century. The politics of the states has been converging, making geographical polarization an illusion.

The Abramowitz and Saunders work, reprinted as chapter 14 and summarized in the section on "a polarized electorate," was written as a challenge to Fiorina, but Fiorina, Abrams, and Pope (2008), reprinted as chapter 15, rebut that work. They claim that some of the Abramowitz and Saunders results are due to how the two authors coded variables. The General Social Survey and Gallup Poll do not show fewer ideological moderates in the 2000s than in the 1970s. There are fewer people in the middle on some issues, but the growth is toward more liberals on some issues and more conservatives on other issues, not increases at both extremes—and, besides, these shifts are relatively small. They argue that red-state–blue-state polarization is not deep since blue states often elect Republican governors and red states often elect various Democratic candidates; in any event, many states have divided party control of state government. They also disagree with Abramowitz and Saunders as to whether religious divisions in the electorate are now more serious than economic divisions, and they point out again that the greater apparent importance of religion may be due to the nature of the choices the major party nominees offer the electorate today versus a few decades ago. And they remind readers that increases in political participation in 2004 might have been due to greater mobilization efforts by the parties rather than being a reflection of the electorate's higher level of polarization.

But what about the increased importance of partisanship in voting? Fiorina and Abrams (chapter 17) make an important argument: that it is not partisanship as much as it is ideology, which becomes prominent when the parties nominate candidates who are far apart ideologically. When the parties nominate candidates who are similar ideologically, people can easily vote for the candidate of the other party and, as a result, party identification has only a weak correlation with the vote. When the parties nominate candidates who are far apart ideologically, people will vote for the candidate closer to them ideologically and that will be the candidate of their own party, so there is a high correlation between party identification and the vote—but that correlation is really due to the large ideological differences between the candidates.[12] Fiorina (2005) similarly explains the apparent increased importance of moral issues in voting by the candidates that were nominated: moral issues did not affect voting much in the elections of 1980–88 when the candidates were close to the center on the moral dimension but differed on economic matters, but moral issues seem to affect voting more when George W. Bush was seen as a proponent of conventional morality while many Americans saw Bill Clinton as less conventional on such matters. The choice of candidates (or at least how they are perceived by the public), according to Fiorina, is what creates the apparent importance of both party identification and moral issues in affecting the vote.[13]

The Debate Continues

The ongoing nature of this controversy is best testified to by the updates that Abramowitz (chapter 16) and Fiorina and Abrams (chapter 17) have written for this volume. We asked the authors to update their analyses to take into account the 2008 election, and their chapters show that the debate is very much ongoing.

In his update, Abramowitz argues that there is a deepening partisan divide. He provides evidence of geographical, generational, religious, racial, and attitudinal polarization in 2008. For example, the outcomes in more states were decided by a voter landslide; the votes of younger people and older people were more different than in recent elections, as were the votes of whites and blacks; and the voting gap grew between whites who attend religious services regularly and those who do not. While ideological polarization was not extreme, it was greater among high-knowledge voters. His graph of the opinion distribution of Democratic and Republican voters on universal health care shows a high degree of polarization. Obama and McCain both tried appealing to supporters of the opposite party, but Abramowitz seems to show that the electorate was polarized nonetheless.

By contrast, Fiorina and Abrams (chapter 17) argue that the electorate was not polarized in 2008. They show how the electorate was still centrist in liberal-conservative self-placement and policy issues in 2008. Also, attitudes have not become much more liberal or conservative on the ANES seven-point issue scales in the quarter century from 1984 to 2008. They note that voters' choices have become more polarized over the years (i.e., they are faced with a choice between a liberal Democrat and a conservative Republican), but they emphasize that voters themselves have not polarized. At most, partisan sorting has occurred, and even that sorting is incomplete on such issues as abortion. Many Democrats are pro-life and many Republicans are pro-choice, even though the parties' presidential candidates have been taking different stands on abortion over the past several elections. Activists and the media are responsible for the view that there is polarization, but the mass public is not polarized in its issue positions.

In understanding this debate, one should see that Abramowitz and Fiorina have different ideas about what evidence is important. Fiorina focuses on opinion trends over time and sees that the differences between Democrats and Republicans have not grown much, while Abramowitz tends to employ data from individual elections and finds what seem like big differences. Actually, Abramowitz does compare 2004 and 2008, as well as comparing party coalitions in the 1970s versus the 2000s. However, some of his comparisons may not be representative, as in his Table 15-1, in which the victory margins in fewer states were landslides in 1960, 1976, and 2004 than 2008, but those earlier elections were decided by the electoral votes of a single state. Comparisons with more elections would avoid the peculiarities of those elections.

These authors also differ in their descriptions of the distribution of views. Fiorina finds that most people are in the middle, whereas Abramowitz finds that partisans generally take their party's position. Fiorina would respond that focusing on partisans omits Independents and people who are not likely voters, and that looking at the whole electorate gives a different picture. Abramowitz would say that voters and activists are the ones who determine the tone of political discussions.

Note also that Fiorina and Abramowitz generally rely on different survey questions in assessing the degree of polarization. Fiorina analyzes opinions on classical debates, like the tradeoff between government services and spending, aid to minorities, government guarantees of jobs and standard of living, and military spending. Abramowitz instead examines attitudes on current issues like gay marriage, abortion, Iraq, financial regulation, climate change, and offshore drilling. It is not very surprising if there is more polarization on current issues being debated between the parties in an election setting than on classical debates that are less related to current campaign rhetoric. Taking stands on debates that are not central to an election may be too tough a test of polarization, though parroting the issue stands of one's party in an election setting may be a little too easy.

Of course, one also has to pay attention to specific question wordings. Both authors do look at the long-standing matter of abortion. Fiorina relies on a question that allows respondents to choose from among four distinct choices and finds relatively nuanced position-taking. The question in the *Time* poll used by Abramowitz indicates only one extreme ("a woman should be able to get an abortion if she wants one in the first three months of pregnancy, no matter what the reason"). One might strongly oppose this option without taking an unqualified pro-life position, making the high percentage in the extreme categories on this item somewhat misleading.

Another issue that both authors look at is health insurance. Fiorina shows that about 31 percent of respondents who answer the seven-point ANES government insurance question are in positions 1 or 2 and about 17 percent are in positions 6 or 7. Abramowitz reports that 30 percent of likely voters are in positions 0 or 1 on the *Time* eleven-point universal health care question and 20 percent are in positions 9 or 10. It is difficult to compare a seven-point scale on people who answer the question with an eleven-point scale on likely voters, but the results on the proportion taking the two most extreme positions on either side are actually amazingly similar.

Another thing that Fiorina does not take into account is the extent to which partisans internalize at least some of the nasty things that their party's leaders and activists say about the other party. Party leaders calling the other side wrong, dumb, mean, and immoral can lead to partisans feeling very negatively about the other party. Social psychologists would expect that negative attacks on the opposition party and its leaders would affect partisans' views of that party, and this is verified empirically by the negative party thermometer correlations discussed above. Fiorina also cannot measure intensity of preferences. For example, when approximately 20 percent of the electorate takes an extreme position on the aid to minorities scale in Figure 17-3, that is a large enough group that, if members feel strongly, can create a significantly felt gap in preferences. Yet as noted with respect to Abramowitz's results, it is also not entirely clear that strong opposition to an extreme statement correctly captures intensity of feeling.

An interesting question is what to make of geographical polarization. Contrast the situation in which all states are split 50–50 in their voting with an extreme case in which the total vote was split 50–50 but with twenty-five red states all voting 90 percent for the Republican candidate and twenty-five blue states all voting 90 percent for the Democratic candidate. Is there an equal amount of polarization in these two situations, even though the differences in opinion happen to coincide with state lines in the second case? Or should that second case be seen as much more polarized, since there would essentially be two Americas that disagree radically with one another? Fiorina would view them as equally polarized, while Abramowitz would view the latter as geographically polarized. This serves as yet another reminder of how a portion of this controversy is a matter of how polarization is being defined.

Conclusion

While it is incontrovertible that polarization between the parties increased considerably in Congress from the 1950s through the early 2000s, the manifestations of this in the electorate are still open to dispute. There is clearly more partisan voting, but, as Fiorina emphasizes, that could instead be ideological voting. Whether this is polarization or partisan sorting is largely a definitional matter (Hetherington 2009), but the reason for greater partisan voting is a debate that will continue for a long time.

Minimally, we are skeptical of the claim that the country is moving into a "post-partisan" phase. California Governor Arnold Schwarzenegger and New York City Mayor Michael Bloomberg have contended that traditional partisan appeals are no longer relevant. President Obama took up this post-partisan mantle in the 2008 presidential campaign, while John McCain's frequent maverick positions in the Senate also permitted him to run as not fully partisan. However, "post-partisan" is probably just a catchy campaign slogan for candidates who need to appeal to partisans of the opposite party. The Obama campaign recognized the likelihood of losing some votes because of his race, which seems to have occurred (Jackman and Vavreck, 2009; Tesler and Sears, 2009; Weisberg and Devine 2010b), so they wanted to increase his chances of picking up votes from Republicans who were dissatisfied with the George W. Bush presidency. McCain strategists understood that his maverick positions might cause some conservatives to stay at home, so they positioned McCain to appeal to women who were upset when Hillary Clinton did not receive the Democratic nomination. While it might have been to the advantage of these candidates to sound post-partisan, it would be naïve to expect partisanship to vanish from the American political universe.

Note also that the 2008 election did not fit with Fiorina's ideology argument. As Table 12-3 shows, the level of party defection was low, even though the nominees were objectively not ideological extremists. At most, McCain's choice of Sarah Palin as his running mate could have been seen as shifting him more to the right, while Republicans tried but were not very successful in linking Obama to 1960s radical William Ayers. Voting was very partisan in 2008, but that was not a reaction to either candidate being ideologically extreme.

What is interesting is that partisan voting increased during a period when party strength became more evenly balanced. The relative strength of the two parties had become so balanced by 2004 that the outcome of the Bush-Kerry presidential election depended on small differences in defection rates between the two parties as well as the voting decisions made by Independents (Lewis-Beck et al. 2008, chapter 14; Weisberg and Christenson, 2007). If this is a period of partisan polarization, it is truly ironic that presidential election outcomes would depend on the deviations from partisanship. There was enough of a pro-Democratic shift in partisanship by 2008 that Obama could win on the basis of the high degree of partisan loyalty of Democrats. It remains to be seen, however, whether 2008 is the beginning of a new period of Democratic dominance or a temporary deviation from an era of party balance.

Notes

1. The standard reference on partisanship in congressional voting is to the work of Poole and Rosenthal (1997, 2007). Brief explanations of the analysis used to measure polarization in congressional voting, along with graphs of polarization from 1879 to the present, can be found on Poole's website, www.polarizedamerica.com.
2. Since 1998 (through 2009), twenty-nine states have passed ballot propositions banning same-sex marriage, even while public approval of the idea has grown.
3. Gelman et al. (2008) distinguish further between partisan sorting on individual issues and when positions on different issues become more correlated so that liberals (conservatives) take consistently liberal (conservative) positions on a whole spectrum of issues. They refer to this as "issue alignment."
4. This contradicts earlier work by Carmines and Stimson (1989). In their well-known study of "issue evolution," they reported that changes in the position of the parties in Congress on the race issue preceded party polarization on the issue in the mass electorate.
5. For example, Killian and Wilcox (2008) find some movement in party identification associated with abortion attitudes. Their analysis of ANES panel surveys finds that pro-life Democrats were more likely to become Republicans than were other Democrats, and their analysis of longer-term panel data finds that pro-choice Republicans also switched parties.
6. Looking at polarization at the elite and mass levels, Brewer (2005) argues that the greater polarization at one level leads to more polarization at the other level, which in turn increases polarization at the first level, etc., so that polarization is likely to increase until some type of "circuit breaker" stops this progression.
7. A reversal and then a strengthening of the relationship between income and the vote is a major explanation for the Republican realignment in Southern politics in the second half of the twentieth century. See this volume, chapter 18.
8. Bartels (2000, 37) also points out that there has been an erosion of partisanship among nonvoters, with a lesser partisan difference among nonvoters than among voters.
9. He does, though, admit that a "stronger relationship between religiosity and voting . . . has developed recently [and] appears to be genuine and not a spurious reflection of other factors" (p. 68).
10. See also the Ansolabehere et al. article reprinted in chap. 11. Their main point is about the relative influence of moral versus economic issues, but along the way they indicate that voters have relatively moderate issue positions, especially on economic matters.
11. Of course, sorting may be no less effective because it is "only" being done in response to elite changes.
12. In this type of argument, of course, it is important to measure candidate extremity in such a way as to avoid circularity, as in interpreting candidates to be near each other ideologically if there is a great deal of party defection and ideologically distant if there is little party defection. There can be considerable defection from partisanship, quite regardless of the ideological positions of the candidates, when one candidate is very popular personally, as General Dwight Eisenhower was when he ran for president in 1952, or when one candidate is seen as inept.
13. Of course, even if the root cause of party-line voting is that the parties have nominated more extreme candidates, partisans *are* more divided.

Further Readings

Partisanship and Its Underlying Causes and Consequences

Bartels, Larry M., "Partisanship and Voting Behavior, 1952–1996," *American Journal of Political Science* 44 (2000): 35–50. Partisanship has resurged in importance in voting.

Fiorina, Morris P., *Retrospective Voting in American National Elections* (New Haven, Conn.: Yale University Press, 1981). Partisanship as a running tally of political evaluations.

Green, Donald, Bradley Palmquist, and Eric Schickler, *Partisan Hearts and Minds* (New Haven, Conn.: Yale University Press, 2002). A social identity theory approach to partisanship, arguing that aggregate partisanship is very stable.

Keith, Bruce E., et al., *The Myth of the Independent Voter* (Berkeley: University of California Press, 1992). The number of Independents has increased very little, contrary to common beliefs, since leaners are really partisans.

Levendusky, Matthew, *The Partisan Sort* (Chicago: University of Chicago Press, 2009). Thorough discussion of recent alignment of attitudes and partisanship.

MacKuen, Michael B., Robert S. Erikson, and James A. Stimson, "Macropartisanship," *American Political Science Review* 83 (1989): 1125–1142. Aggregate partisanship changes in response to presidential popularity and the economy.

Miller, Warren E., and J. Merrill Shanks, *The New American Voter* (Cambridge, Mass.: Harvard University Press, 1996). Chapter 7 contains a good discussion of generational changes in partisanship in the second half of the twentieth century.

Weisberg, Herbert F., "A Multidimensional Conceptualization of Party Identification," *Political Behavior* 2 (1980): 33–60. Independence can be a separate dimension from partisanship.

Extent of Polarization

Abramowitz, Alan, *The Disappearing Center: Engaged Citizens, Polarization, and American Democracy* (New Haven, Conn.: Yale University Press, 2010). Politically engaged citizens are more polarized than those who are unengaged.

Bartels, Larry M., *Unequal Democracy: The Political Economy of the New Gilded Age* (Princeton, N.J.: Princeton University Press, 2008). The electoral environment has been advantageous for Republican presidential candidates and policies that exacerbate income inequality.

Black, Earl, and Merle Black, *Divided America: The Ferocious Power Struggle in American Politics* (New York: Simon & Schuster, 2007). Americans are sharply divided along regional lines, with the Midwest as the only swing region. Racial and ethnic, religious, and ideological differences within and among the regions help account for the divisions.

Fiorina, Morris P, and Samuel J. Abrams, *Disconnect: The Breakdown of Representation in American Politics* (Norman: University of Oklahoma Press, 2009).

Politicians out of touch with the electorate appeal to narrow interest groups, creating the illusion of a polarized polity.

Fiorina, Morris P., Samuel J. Abrams, and Jeremy C. Pope, *Culture War? The Myth of a Polarized America,* 2nd ed. (New York: Pearson Longman, 2006). There is no polarization along moral issues. The degree of polarization in the American electorate has not grown significantly in recent years.

Gelman, Andrew, David Park, Boris Shor, Joseph Bafumi, and Jeronimo Cortina, *Red State, Blue State, Rich State, Poor State* (Princeton, N.J.: Princeton University Press, 2008). The Republican Party gets more of the vote from higher-income people, yet the Democratic Party gets more of the vote in richer states. The authors explain this paradox by noting that the relationship between income and voting varies with the state's income level.

Hillygus, D. Sunshine, and Todd G. Shields, *The Persuadable Voter: Wedge Issues in Presidential Campaigns.* (Princeton, N.J.: Princeton University Press, 2008). Voters are typically not in complete agreement with their preferred party and are therefore persuadable.

Jacobson, Gary C., *A Divider, Not a Uniter: George W. Bush and the American People,* 2nd ed. (New York: Pearson Longman, 2011). An impressive array of poll data showing the intense polarization surrounding George W. Bush, the Iraq War, and other policies.

Layman, Geoffrey C., and Thomas M. Carsey, "Party Polarization and 'Conflict Extension' in the American Electorate," *American Journal of Political Science* 46 (2002): 786–802. The economic conflict between the parties has been extended into conflict on racial and moral issues.

McCarty, Nolan, Keith T. Poole, and Howard Rosenthal, *Polarized America: The Dance of Ideology and Unequal Riches* (Cambridge, Mass.: MIT Press, 2006). Between 1960 and 2002, voters became increasingly stratified by income (wealthy-voting Republican, poor-voting Democratic), especially in the South.

Causes and Processes of Polarization

Aldrich, John, "Electoral Politics during Politics as Usual—and Unusual." In *Electoral Democracy,* ed. Michael B. MacKuen and George Rabinowitz (Ann Arbor: University of Michigan Press, 2003). Mass belief changes underlie increased polarization of elites, as members of Congress react to constituent attitudes or lead in ways constituents will follow.

Hetherington, Marc J., and Jonathan Weiler, *Authoritarianism and Polarization in American Politics* (New York: Cambridge University Press, 2009). Political polarization is due to personality differences.

Layman, Geoffrey C., Thomas M. Carsey, and Juliana Menasce Horowitz, "Party Polarization in American Politics," *Annual Review of Political Science* 9 (2006): 83–110. Increased polarization is due to party activists who have extreme ideological positions and who play important roles in financing and nominating candidates.

Stoker, Laura, and M. Kent Jennings, "Of Time and the Development of Partisan Polarization," *American Journal of Political Science* 52 (2008): 619–635. A generational/socialization perspective on polarization; constraint between issue positions and partisanship has grown over time within cohorts, and partisanship is tied to issues that are especially relevant to each cohort.

Stonecash, Jeffrey M., Mark D. Brewer, and Mack D. Mariani, *Diverging Parties: Social Change, Realignment, and Party Polarization* (Boulder, Colo: Westview, 2003). Demographic changes and realignment have changed the constituency base of the parties, leading to the election of more polarized elites (liberal Democrats and conservative Republicans).

13. Resurgent Mass Partisanship: The Role of Elite Polarization (Updated)

Marc J. Hetherington

With few exceptions (see Keith et al. 1992), research on American political parties in the electorate centers on its weakness. Although scholars disagree about its sources—whether people are more negative (Nie, Verba, and Petrocik 1979) or neutral (Wattenberg 1984)—and its abruptness—whether precipitous (Wattenberg 1984) or less steep but still meaningful (Konda and Sigelman 1987)—the conventional wisdom is that parties are irrelevant to many. Indeed, Bartels (2000) cites a litany of scholarly work suggesting party decline in the electorate persists into the twenty-first century,[1] a trend, according to some, that is potentially irreversible given the antiparty electoral changes implemented in the 1960s and 1970s (e.g. Aldrich 1995, 245–253; Beck 1997, 385).

That party decline remains so central to the thinking of public opinion scholars is curious, especially because Congress scholars discovered years ago that parties are resurgent on the elite level (e.g. Poole and Rosenthal 1997; Rohde 1991). Since most theories of public opinion change center on the behavior of elites (Brody 1991; Carmines and Stimson 1989; Page and Shapiro 1992; Zaller 1992), party resurgence in Congress should be consequential in understanding mass attitudes toward parties. Mass behavior should come to reflect, at least to some degree, elite behavior. Hence mass party strength should have increased as a result of this greater elite level partisanship.

In fact, it has. I demonstrate that the measures scholars have used as evidence of mass party decline now point to party resurgence. In most cases, the movement has been extraordinary, especially given the glacial pace characteristic of most public opinion change. This increase, moreover, can best be explained by the increase in ideological polarization along congressional party lines.

This chapter originally appeared in the September 2001 issue of the *American Political Science Review*. This version includes several changes. First, the original data analysis ran through 1996, and I have updated it here to run through 2004. Second, my continued interest in partisanship after the article's original publication allowed me to identify another dependent variable (caring who wins the presidential election) that followed the same pattern as the other measures of party strength analyzed previously. Third, I have made a minor change to the models that appear in Table 13-1, which allows me to extend the data analysis for several of the dependent variables back to 1972 rather than 1984; adding these additional data points makes the statistical results more convincing. Finally, it is worth noting that Figure 13-4 in this version differs slightly from the one that appeared in the original article due to a minor computational error, which has been corrected here.

I show that elite polarization has clarified people's perceptions of the parties' ideological differences, which, in turn, has led to a resurgence of parties in the electorate.

Individual-Level Evidence for Party Decline

While scholars have detailed party decline using both aggregate- and individual-level data, I confine my analysis to the latter, using data collected by the American National Election Studies (ANES). To public opinion scholars, the most familiar evidence of party decline is the rapid increase in political independence and the accompanying decrease in strong partisanship after the 1950s. While the percentage of independent leaners nearly doubled between 1960 and 1980, the percentage of strong partisans dipped by more than one-third (Wattenberg 1984).[2] One prominent explanation for party decline is that, in a candidate-centered era, parties have become irrelevant to many citizens. As evidence, Wattenberg (1984) found a rapid increase in the percentage of Americans who were neutral toward both parties, as tapped by the ANES' likes/dislikes questions.

Although they expressed concerns about Wattenberg's measures, Konda and Sigelman (1987) found further support, albeit muted, for the neutrality thesis. Measuring party engagement as the total number of party likes and dislikes provided by respondents, they discovered that engagement declined substantially between 1952 and 1984. In later editions, Wattenberg (1994, 1996, 1998) focused on the candidacies of independent H. Ross Perot in arguing that the parties were still in decline. Seemingly indicative of major party failure, Perot received more votes in 1992 than any third-party candidate since Theodore Roosevelt eighty years earlier. In addition, split-ticket voting reached a survey-era apex. Of course, Perot's historically strong showing absent congressional Reform Party candidates potentially explains the increase in split ticket voting, though this phenomenon is often considered a symptom of party decline (e.g. Beck 1997; Keefe 1998).

Individual-Level Evidence of Party Resurgence

Given the strong hold of this conventional wisdom, I must first demonstrate that a mass-level resurgence of party has occurred. I do so by relying on many of the measures employed originally in the 1980s to show party decline. Key to Wattenberg's (1984) argument was an increase in the percentage of people with neutral feelings toward both parties, as measured by the net number of likes and dislikes offered by respondents. If people offer more reasons for liking a party than disliking it, they are considered positive toward that party. If they provide more dislikes than likes, they are considered negative. And, if they provide an equal number of likes and dislikes or if they provide no responses at all, they are considered neutral.

Figure 13-1 Feelings about the Parties, Likes-Dislikes and Feeling
Thermometers, 1952–2004

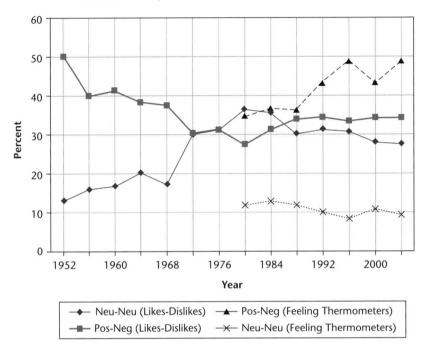

The solid lines in Figure 13-1 track changes in the most partisan and most
neutral categories. The percentage of those neutral toward both parties declined
by nine points between 1980 and 2004, while the percentage of those positive
toward one party and negative toward the other increased by seven points. In fact,
positive-negative replaced neutral-neutral as the modal category in 1988, continuing as the mode through the rest of the time series. Although the proportion
of positive-negatives in 2004 does not approach that of 1952, a movement toward
a more partisan environment is still evident.

Using the likes-dislikes measures in this manner has several problems. In
addition to obscuring differences between categories and overstating neutrality
(see Konda and Sigelman 1987; Stanga and Sheffield 1987; DeSart 1995), the
measure lacks a stated neutral point. People are classified as neutral if they unwit-
tingly balance the number of likes and dislikes, or, perhaps more problematically,
if they provide no answers at all. Feeling thermometers are more attractive because
they have an explicit neutral point, 50 degrees, and almost all respondents provide
valid answers (Craig 1985).[3]

Using the party thermometers, I can construct a measure of affect similar to
Wattenberg's, classifying those who answer 50 degrees to both thermometers as

Figure 13-2 Mean Total Number of Likes and Dislikes about the Parties, 1952–2004

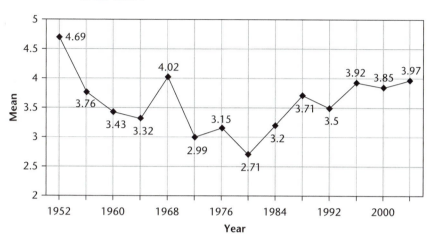

neutral-neutral, those who answer above 50 degrees to one party and below 50 degrees to the other as positive-negative, and so forth. The results of this analysis appear as the broken lines in Figure 13-1. The most noteworthy finding is the upsurge in positive-negatives. Whereas only about 35 percent fell into this most partisan category in 1980, nearly half did in 2004, which represents a 40 percent increase.

Konda and Sigelman (1987) measure party engagement as the total number of likes and dislikes that respondents provide about the parties. Figure 13-2 demonstrates that parties are far more salient in the 2000s than in the 1970s and 1980s, with the mean number of responses in 2004 higher than any year except 1952 and 1968. By this measure, the salience of party has increased by more than 45 percent since 1980.

Lastly, consistent with more party-centric attitudes, straight-ticket voting has become more common. Although Wattenberg (1994) notes that voting for a presidential candidate and House member of different parties reached a survey-era high in 1992, the results in Figure 13-3 suggest that 1992 was an anomaly and mostly a function of voters having three choices rather than the usual two. Even when accounting for third-party voters, there has been a trend toward straight-ticket voting since 1972. In fact, a higher percentage of Americans reported voting for a presidential and House candidate of the same party in 2004 than in any year since 1964. The trend is even starker among major-party presidential voters. Straight-ticket voting for president and House among this group increased almost without exception since 1980. Even in 1992, those who voted for George H. W. Bush and Bill Clinton were more inclined to vote for the same party in their House election than those who voted for Bush and Michael Dukakis or Ronald Reagan and Walter Mondale.[4]

Figure 13-3 Percentage of Voters Casting a Straight Ticket for President and House, 1952–2004

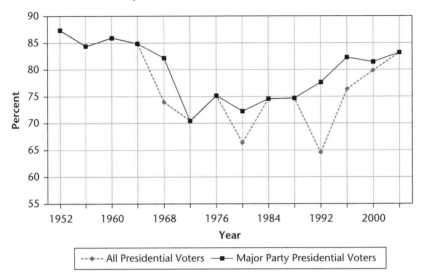

Though these data suggest a dramatic resurgence in party, Perot's historically large vote share still seemingly suggests the opposite. Scholars have shown, however, that factors such as the third-party candidate's personal characteristics (Rosenstone, Behr, and Lazarus 1996) and respondents' trust in government (Hetherington 1999) better explain third-party voting than strength of partisanship. Moreover, Perot's personal fortune allowed him to overcome many of the handicaps, such as ballot-access laws, small advertising budgets, and dismissive news reporting, faced by most third-party candidacies (Rosenstone, Behr, and Lazarus 1996). Perot's showing, then, resulted primarily from factors other than party decline.

What Causes Mass Opinion to Change?

Mass opinion in the aggregate tends to move glacially if at all (Page and Shapiro 1992). When it does move, however, it usually responds to changes in the information environment provided by elites. Although the authors of *The American Voter* partially blamed cognitive limitations for Americans' lack of ideological sophistication, they also recognized the importance of elite-level cues. "[T]here are periods in which the heat of partisan debate slackens and becomes almost perfunctory, and the positions of the parties become relatively indistinct on basic issues. In times such as these, even the person sensitive to a range of political philosophies may not feel this knowledge to be helpful in an evaluation of current politics" (Campbell et al. 1960, 256). V.O. Key's (1966) echo-chamber analogy further suggests that elite behavior will set the terms by which the masses think about politics (see also Nie, Verba, and Petrocik 1979; Page 1978). If politicians provide party-oriented or issue-oriented cues, then the public will respond in a party-centric or issue-centric manner. They are unlikely to do so otherwise.

Indeed, the most sophisticated recent theories of public opinion place elite level behavior at the center of individual opinion change (Brody 1991; Carmines and Stimson 1989; Zaller 1992). For example, Carmines and Stimson (1989) identify changes in the behavior of Republican and Democratic elites as the engine for an issue evolution on race in the 1960s. Similarly, Brody (1991) argues that we can best understand presidential approval by observing elite behavior. Elite consensus generally predicts higher approval ratings while division usually means lower approval (see also Mermin 1999).

Zaller (1992) develops the connection between elite behavior and mass opinion most completely, concluding that even those most attentive to politics "respond to new issues mainly on the basis of the partisanship and ideology of the elite sources in the messages" (311). If people are exposed to a heavily partisan stream of information, which will be more likely if elites are behaving in a partisan manner, it follows that respondents will express opinions reflective of that heavily partisan stream. Since greater ideological differences between the parties on the elite level should produce a more partisan information stream, polarization should produce a more partisan mass response.

Party Resurgence on the Elite Level

One measure that taps changing elite behavior is Poole and Rosenthal's DW-NOMINATE scores for members of Congress.[5] These scores allow for both between-member and between-year comparisons. An increasing ideological distance between Democratic and Republican elites should produce a more partisan information environment for ordinary Americans, particularly given the media's well-known bias toward framing politics in terms of conflict (Graber 1997, chapter 4).

I measure party polarization in the House by dividing members by party, calculating the mean DW-NOMINATE score on each dimension for each caucus, and calculating the weighted Euclidean distance between them.[6] Figure 13-4 tracks the distance between the House Republican and Democratic caucuses from the 81st Congress, which began a few days into 1949, to the 107th Congress, which ended a few days into 2003. Polarization declined steadily from the late 1950s into the late 1960s and remained relatively constant until the late 1970s, a trough that coincides with the decline of party in the electorate. Congressional behavior then changed in the late 1970s. With the 96th Congress, ideological polarization between the parties began a steady increase.[7]

These changes in congressional behavior correspond closely with, but slightly precede, the increases in measures of mass partisanship described above. For example, a significant chunk of the increase in elite polarization occurred between

Figure 13-4 Mean Euclidean Distance between Republican and Democratic Party DW-NOMINATE Scores, House of Representatives, 1949–2003

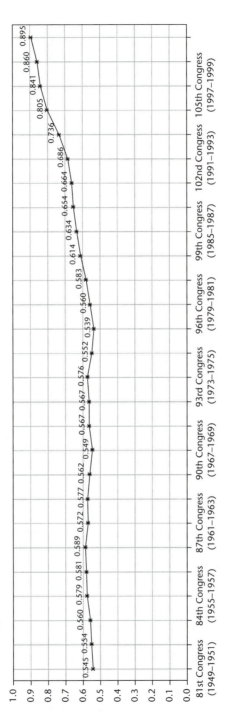

the last Congress in the Jimmy Carter administration and the first Congress in the second Ronald Reagan administration. The start of the substantial increases in the total number of likes and dislikes and the trend toward straight-ticket voting took hold in the election cycles that followed. On the heels of the second spike in elite polarization, which started during the second Congress of the George H.W. Bush administration, all measures of party strength responded in kind. Elite polarization, therefore, appears to be a potential engine for mass-level change.

Increased Clarity of Party Images as an Intermediate Step

Having placed elite polarization at the heart of the explanation for party resurgence, I hypothesize a set of causal dynamics between elites and ordinary Americans similar to those posited and demonstrated by Carmines and Stimson (1989, 160) regarding racial issue positions. More partisan elite behavior caused by party polarization should first lead to greater mass level clarity about the parties' positions, which should, in turn, influence the importance and salience of parties.[8]

One way to test whether clarity has increased is simply to ask people if they see important differences between what the parties stand for. The ANES does so, and the solid line in Figure 13-5 tracks this trend. From 1960 to 1976, the percentage seeing important differences ranged from the high 40s to the mid-50s. A marked upturn began in 1980, with 58 percent or more seeing important differences every year since. In fact, the percentage had grown to 76 percent by 2004, by far the highest level in the series.[9]

While the "important differences" question suggests greater clarity, it does not suggest its nature. Since the polarization in Congress has been ideological, ideological differences are a good bet. One measure of this is whether or not the public can array the parties correctly on a liberal-conservative scale. If ideological clarity has increased, people should be both better able to place the Democrats to the left of the Republicans and more likely to perceive larger distances between them.

The lower broken line in Figure 13-5 demonstrates that Americans are increasingly better able to array the parties ideologically. From 1984 until 1990, only about 50 percent of the public did so correctly, but this percentage has increased substantially since, with 67 percent correct in 2004.[10] Again this is by far the highest entry in the time series. In addition to arraying the parties correctly, respondents perceive a widening ideological gulf between them. According to data taken from the ANES Cumulative File (Sapiro, Rosenstone, Miller, and the ANES 1997), the mean signed ideological distance between the parties increased from 1.52 points in 1984 to 2.10 points in 2004, an increase of 38 percent. Finally, this increased ideological clarity has increased people's investment in the presidential candidates. The upper broken line tracks the percentage of Americans who say they care who wins the presidential election. When Jimmy Carter twice contested the presidency in 1976 and 1980, barely half of Americans said they cared. In 2004, fully 85 percent did, more than a 50-percent increase.

Figure 13-5 Percentage of Respondents Who See Important Differences between the Parties, Care Who Wins the Presidential Election, and Correctly Place the Parties Ideologically, 1960–2004

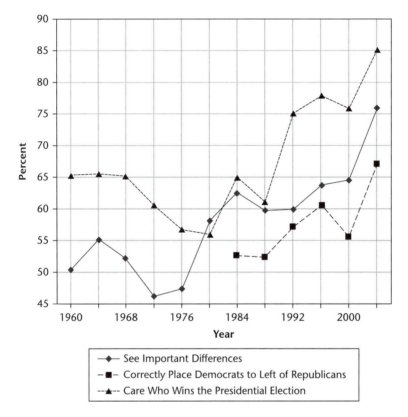

Similar to the indicators of party resurgence, these increases in party clarity occurred soon after increases in elite polarization. It seems that, as party elites began to provide increasingly clear ideological cues, citizens became less inclined to see the parties as Tweedledee and Tweedledum. As people correctly perceive that who wins and loses will lead to increasingly distinct futures, they should develop more partisan feelings and become more inclined to organize politics in partisan terms.

Data and Methods

To assess the impact of increasing elite polarization on these measures of mass party clarity, affect, and salience, I employ a pooled cross-sectional design, using data gathered by the ANES in both presidential and off-year elections between 1960 and 2004. This design allows me to merge over-time contextual information, namely the aggregate measures of ideological polarization in the House, with the survey data. Due to data limitations, I am sometimes confined to the surveys taken between 1972 and 2004.

Explaining Increased Party Clarity

As parties in Congress have become more polarized along party lines, people have become more inclined to see important differences between what the parties stand for, place them correctly in an ideological space, perceive larger ideological distances between them, and care who wins elections. I next test whether there is a causal connection between elite polarization and these mass responses.

The first dependent variable is whether or not a respondent *Sees important differences* between what the parties stand for. It is coded 1 if the respondent claims to see important differences and 0 otherwise. The second dependent variable is *Correct ideological view of the parties*, which is coded 1 if the respondent places the Democratic Party to the left of the Republican Party and 0 otherwise.[11] The third dependent variable is *Perceived ideological distance between the parties.* This variable is measured as the signed difference between where respondents place the Republican and Democratic parties on the ANES's seven-point liberal-conservative scale. I use the signed rather than absolute ideological distance because elite polarization should also help people to array the parties correctly. Using the absolute distance would make equivalent placing the Democrats one unit to the left or right of the Republicans, obscuring the increasing proportion of correct placements. The fourth dependent variable is whether people say they *Care who wins the presidential election,* which is coded 1 if people report that they "care a good deal" and 0 otherwise.

These four measures should be a function of a number of different attitudinal and contextual variables. Most important for my purposes is *Elite polarization.* I tap elite polarization as the mean Euclidean distance in the DW-NOMINATE scores between the Democratic and Republican House caucuses, which I lag by one Congress for two reasons. First, since a Congress officially ends after even most post-election surveys have been completed, using a contemporaneous term would suggest that, for example, congressional behavior in 1993 affects 1992 attitudes, which makes no temporal sense. Second, the public requires time to perceive changes in elite behavior. Public opinion on race, for instance, did not react immediately to the parties' changing positions, but rather operated at a lag (Carmines and Stimson 1989). In merging the contextual with the individual level data, each 2004 respondent receives the mean Euclidean distance from the 2001–2003 session of Congress, each 2002 respondent receives the mean Euclidean distance from the 1999–2001 session, and so forth.[12]

A number of attitudinal measures should also affect these dependent variables, so they are added as controls. *Strength of ideology* and *Strength of partisanship* should play important roles. Those who place themselves near the poles of these seven-point scales demonstrate an understanding of ideology and partisanship and hence should be more inclined to see differences than those who place themselves at mid-scale. In addition, several social characteristics are relevant. Those with more *Education* will be less inclined to provide mid-scale responses than those with less (Delli Carpini and Keeter 1996), which will increase both the probability that they will see differences between the parties and the potential distance they see between them. *Age* should have a similar effect, with older respondents, who have more political experience than younger ones, more inclined to see important differences, array the parties correctly, and see a wider gulf between them. In contrast, *Women* and *African Americans* exhibit less political expertise (see e.g. Mondak 1999), so they should be less likely to see such differences.[13]

I must also account for contextual factors. People pay less attention and vote less in *Off-year elections,* so they should tend to see the parties as less distinct in nonpresidential years. In addition, years characterized by *Divided government* might make a difference. On the one hand, divided government provides both parties with a prominent voice in government, which might increase people's ability to identify the parties ideologically. On the other hand, people might have a harder time deciding whether a president of one party or a Congress of the other is driving the ideological direction of the country. Indeed, in 1990, fewer than half of Americans could even identify which party controlled the House, despite the fact that the Democrats had done so for nearly forty years, so two voices may only serve to confuse citizens. Finally, for the two models that make use of questions involving placing the parties in an ideological space, I include a dummy variable for *Pre-1984* cases. Before 1984, respondents who refused to place themselves on a seven-point ideology scale or said they did not know where they fit on it were not asked to place the parties on the scale. Beginning in 1984, such respondents were asked a follow-up question, asking them "if they had to choose" what would they consider themselves. Only those who refused the follow-up as well were not asked to place the parties, which reduced missing data substantially. To account for this difference while adding several years to the time series, the dummy variable is important.

In sum, I estimate the following models to analyze the importance of elite polarization on these three measures of mass level clarity about the parties.

Pr(Sees Important Differences) = f(elite polarization, strength
of partisanship, education, age, black, female, off-year election,
divided government)[14]   (1)

Pr(Correctly places the parties ideologically) = f(elite polarization,
strength of ideology, strength of partisanship, education, age,
black, female, off-year election, divided government, pre-1984)   (2)

Perceived Ideological Distance = f(elite polarization, strength of
ideology, strength of partisanship, education, age, black, female,
off-year election, divided government, pre-1984)   (3)

Pr(Cares who wins Presidential Election) = f(elite polarization,
strength of ideology, strength of partisanship, education, age,
black, female, divided government)   (4)

Since three of the dependent variables are binary, ordinary least squares
(OLS) estimates will be biased. Hence I use logistic regression to estimate these
models and use OLS to estimate the fourth.

Results for Ideological Clarity

The results in the first column of Table 13-1 suggest that elite polarization
has a significant effect on whether or not people see important differences
between the parties.[15] In fact, all variables perform as expected, except for age,
which is insignificant, and the sign on the dummy variable for African Americans, which is positive. That the Democrats have been much friendlier to the
interests of African Americans appears to be of great import to this group in
identifying important differences.

Achieving statistical significance in a twenty-three-thousand-person
sample is no great feat. More importantly, the effect of elite polarization is substantively important as well. If I account for the 1960 context of divided government in a presidential year and set the other variables to their 1960 mean values,
the predicted probability of seeing a difference between the parties is .505, which
is almost identical to the 50.3 percent of respondents who reported seeing a difference in 1960. If I hold all variables constant at their 1960 means, again account
for divided government and election context, but increase elite polarization to its
2004 level, the predicted probability of seeing important differences increases to
.656, an increase of .151, or about 15 percentage points.

Between 1960 and 2004, only education among the other independent variables changed such that it would increase the probability of seeing important
differences between the parties. If I carry out a simulation similar to the one
above, holding elite polarization and all other variables at their 1960 means, and
accounting only for the increase in education, the predicted probability of seeing
important differences increases by .092. Although both factors are important,
increased elite polarization is more important than increased education in explaining change over time.

The results in the second column in Table 13-1 suggest that elite polarization has clarified mass perceptions of the parties' ideological differences, specifically. Between the 97th and 107th Congresses, the mean Euclidean distance
between party members' DW-NOMINATE scores in the House increased
from .583 to .895. Increasing elite polarization by this amount, while setting
divided government to one, setting off-year election to 0, setting post-1984
cases to 1, and holding all other variables constant at their 1984 means, increases
the predicted probability that a respondent correctly places the Democratic
Party's ideology to the left of the Republican Party's by a little more than four

Table 13-1 Perceptions of Ideological Clarity and Measures of Party Strength as a Function of Elite Polarization, Political Attitudes, Social Characteristics, and Contextual Factors

Variable	(I) Sees Important Differences 1960–2004 Param. Est. (Std. Err.)	(II) Places Dems. to Left of Reps. 1972–2004 Param. Est. (Std. Err.)	(III) Perceived Ideological Dist. 1972–2004 Param. Est. (Std. Err.)	(IV) Cares Who Wins Pres. Election 1960–2004 Param. Est. (Std. Err.)	(V) Respondent is a Positive–Negative 1980–2004 Param. Est. (Std. Err.)	(VI) Total Party Likes and Dislikes 1972–2004 Param. Est. (Std. Err.)
Elite Polarization	1.997*** (0.152)	0.756** (0.239)	1.111*** (0.224)	3.463*** (0.170)	1.939*** (0.228)	1.788*** (0.377)
Perceived Ideological Distance	—	—	—	—	0.122*** (0.008)	0.287*** (0.013)
Education	0.509*** (0.016)	0.758*** (0.021)	0.585*** (0.018)	0.310*** (0.018)	0.254*** (0.020)	0.959*** (0.029)
Strength of Partisanship	0.526*** (0.015)	0.186*** (0.017)	0.136*** (0.017)	0.650*** (0.016)	0.636*** (0.020)	0.488*** (0.027)
Strength of Ideology	—	0.381*** (0.019)	0.406*** (0.017)	—	0.319*** (0.019)	0.382*** (0.028)
Race (African-American)	0.141** (0.044)	-0.400*** (0.049)	-0.473*** (0.051)	0.157** (0.049)	-0.112* (0.055)	-0.154* (0.083)
Age	0.000 (0.001)	0.013*** (0.001)	0.012*** (0.001)	0.005 (0.001)	-0.003** (0.001)	0.020*** (0.002)
Sex (Female)	-0.315*** (0.028)	-0.117*** (0.032)	-0.047 (0.031)	-0.113*** (0.030)	-0.009 (0.034)	-0.715*** (0.050)
Divided Government	-0.140*** (0.030)	0.047 (0.042)	-0.051 (0.050)	-0.065 (0.035)	0.108* (0.047)	0.497*** (0.066)
Off-Year Election	-0.510*** (0.033)	-0.233*** (0.033)	-0.256*** (0.032)	—	-0.116*** (0.035)	-0.052 (0.060)

Table 13-1 *(continued)*

Variable	(I) Sees Important Differences 1960–2004 Param. Est. (Std. Err.)	(II) Places Dems. to Left of Reps. 1972–2004 Param. Est. (Std. Err.)	(III) Perceived Ideological Dist. 1972–2004 Param. Est. (Std. Err.)	(IV) Cares Who Wins Pres. Election 1960–2004 Param. Est. (Std. Err.)	(V) Respondent is a Positive–Negative 1980–2004 Param. Est. (Std. Err.)	(VI) Total Party Likes and Dislikes 1972–2004 Param. Est. (Std. Err.)
Pre-1984	—	0.345*** (0.046)	0.213*** (0.044)	—	-0.016 (0.078)	0.026 (0.083)
Perceived Ideological Difference × Pre-1984	—	—	—	—	0.050** (0.021)	-0.053* (0.023)
Intercept	-3.437*** (0.294)	-3.240*** (0.199)	-2.109*** (0.185)	-4.127*** (0.128)	-4.884*** (0.201)	-3.182*** (0.314)
χ^2	3148.00***	2790.614***	—	2953.618***	2770.679***	—
Adjusted R^2	—	—	.33	—	—	.20
SEE	—	—	2.245	—	—	3.121
Number of Cases	23,044	20,753	21,540	21,792	16,860	15,935

Source: American National Election Studies, Cumulative File, 1948–2004.

*$p < .05$, **$p < .01$, ***$p < .001$ - one-tailed tests

percentage points, which accounts for a sizable chunk of the change that actually occurred.

Although variables such as education, strength of ideology, and strength of partisanship all have larger effects across their entire ranges than does elite polarization, none increased by as much as 5 percent between these two points in time. Indeed, only the increases in education and strength of ideology were statistically significant. Performing parallel simulations for these two variables, I find that the predicted probability of arraying the parties correctly increases by .038 and .009 points, respectively.

The same pattern of results emerges in explaining perceived ideological distance between the parties, with the effect of elite polarization again substantively important. These results appear in the third column of Table 13-1. Multiplying its parameter estimate by the .312 points it increased between 1984 and 2000 produces a .346 point increase in perceived ideological distance. Given that the dependent variable increased by about .6 points between 1984 and 2004, the increase in elite polarization accounts for better than 50 percent of the change, other things being equal.

For this third equation, the attitudinal variables and the social characteristics perform as expected. It is again important to note, however, that only education and strength of ideology increased significantly between 1984 and 2004. Multiplying their respective parameter estimates by their differences in means provides their contribution to the roughly .6 point increase. These calculations yield .140, and .045 increases, respectively. Both effects pale in comparison to that of elite polarization.

The effects of elite polarization are also strong in explaining whether respondents care about who wins the presidential election. Between the 1960 and 2004 presidential elections, the mean Euclidean distance between party members' DW-NOMINATE scores in the House increased from .314 points. Increasing elite polarization by this amount, while accounting for the political context, and holding all other variables constant at their 1960 means, increases the predicted probability that a respondent cares who wins the presidential election from .631 in 1960 to .840 in 2004. Again, the dynamic effect of elite polarization is much greater than that of education.

Explaining Party Resurgence

As Carmines and Stimson (1989) would predict, the results thus far suggest that elite polarization has clarified people's perceptions of the parties' ideological positions. But, what difference does greater clarity make? While some have suggested that perceptions of polarized parties might cause dissatisfaction (e.g. Dionne 1991; Fiorina 1996; Hibbing and Theiss-Morse 1995; King 1997), I contend that greater ideological clarity should invigorate partisan attitudes. When people perceive that parties provide choices, not echoes (Key 1966; Nie, Verba, and Petrocik 1979; Page 1978), the party that dictates public policy ought to matter more. As people come to realize that Democrats and Republicans will pursue substantially different courses, attachment to one side or the other becomes more consequential and party images become more salient (see also Carmines and Stimson 1989).

To test the influence of elite polarization on party affect and salience, I estimate models for two measures of party resurgence: first, whether or not someone is a *Positive-negative* using the party feeling thermometers and, second, the *Total number of party likes and dislikes* provided by a respondent. I use the same right-hand side variables as above for the same reasons, but I add the third measure of party clarity, *Perceived ideological distance*, to the right-hand side as well. If people see sharper distinctions between the parties, parties should be more important and salient to them. Because of the differences between who was asked to place the parties ideologically pre- and post-1984, I also include an interaction between *Perceived Ideological Distance* and *Pre-1984* cases. This specification allows elite polarization to have both a direct effect on party affect and an indirect effect through perceived ideological distance.

In functional form, the models are the following:

Pr(Respondent is a Positive-Negative) = f(elite polarization, strength of ideology, strength of partisanship, education, age, black, female, off-year election, divided government, perceived ideological distance, pre-1984, pre-1984 x perceived ideological distance)   (5)

Total Number of Party Likes and Dislikes = f(elite polarization, strength of ideology, strength of partisanship, education, age, black, female, off-year election, divided government, perceived ideological distance, pre-1984, pre-1984 x perceived ideological distance)   (6)

Again the first dependent variable is binary, prompting the use of logistic regression, while the second dependent variable is interval scale, allowing the use of OLS.

Results for Party Resurgence

The results from these models appear in the fifth and sixth columns of Table 13-1. Elite polarization is again positively signed and statistically significant for both dependent variables. Its effect, moreover, is substantial. Increasing elite polarization from its 1984 to its 2004 level, while accounting for divided government, a presidential election year, and holding all other variables constant at their 1984 mean values increases the predicted probability that a respondent will be a positive-negative from .344 to .490. In addition, elite polarization has an indirect effect through perceived ideological distance. Recall that elite polarization increased perceived ideological distance between the parties by .346 points. If one increases perceived ideological distance by this amount above its 1984 mean, the probability of identifying as a positive-negative increases by another .011, bringing the total effect of elite polarization to .157, *ceteris paribus*. Again, neither the effect of increasing education nor increasing strength of ideology approaches that of increasing elite polarization.

The same pattern of results emerges for the total number of likes and dislikes mentioned about the parties. These results appear in the last column of Table 13-1. The parameter estimate of 1.788 for elite polarization suggests that its .314 point increase between 1984 and 2004 caused an estimated .561 point increase in the number of likes and dislikes mentioned. Accounting for the .346 point increase in perceived ideological distance caused by elite polarization adds an additional .099 point increase in the dependent variable. Thus, the total effect of elite polarization is .660, which is better than 85 percent of the .77 point increase in the dependent variable over this time period. In comparison, the total effects caused by increases in education and strength of ideology between 1984 and 2004 are each less than a quarter of that of elite polarization. Taken together, these results suggest that increasingly strong partisan orientations on the mass level are a function of increasing ideological polarization on the elite level.

Reception of Elite Polarization

Although the results thus far provide strong evidence that elite ideological polarization has produced a more partisan electorate, an even sterner test is to account for people's differing ability to absorb this information. A more ideologically polarized House should produce a more ideologically polarized issue environment, but those with more political expertise should reflect it better than those with less.

Many suggest that a measure of objective political knowledge is the best indicator of political expertise (e.g. Zaller 1992; Price and Zaller 1993; Delli Carpini and Keeter 1996). Unfortunately, the ANES only began asking a detailed battery of factual questions in 1988. Although using education as a proxy for knowledge is not ideal (see Luskin 1987), many have done so previously (see, e.g., Sniderman, Brody, and Tetlock 1991; Popkin 1994). Indeed, those with more education should, on average, have better developed cognitive tools, which should allow them to absorb more political information. If a knowledge battery was available over a sufficiently long period, I would expect the results to be even stronger than those presented below.[16]

I replicate each of the full models from Table 13-1, introducing an interaction between elite polarization and education. Education is coded 1 for those with a grade school education, 2 for those who attended or graduated from high school, 3 for those who attended some college, and 4 for college graduates and those with graduate degrees. The interaction should carry a positive sign, indicating that those who can best use the more polarized information environment are the most inclined to see differences between the parties and provide more partisan opinions.

Since the effects of each of the variables not included in the interactions are almost identical to those presented in Table 13-1, I include only the estimates for the interaction and its component parts in Table 13-2. In five of the six cases, the interaction is properly signed and statistically significant. To interpret the interaction, I calculate the total effect of elite polarization for the perceived ideological distance and the total number of likes and dislikes. Although the pattern is the same for three of the four logit models, interpreting nonadditive OLS models is more straightforward. The total effect of elite polarization is derived as follows:

$$E_{\text{Elite Polarization}} = \beta_1 + \beta_3(\text{Education}_i) \qquad (6)$$

where $E_{\text{Elite Polarization}}$ is the total effect of elite polarization and Education_i is the "ith" respondent's level of education. In the perceived ideological distance equation, the estimate for β_1 is -2.302 and β_3 is 1.221, and, in the total number of likes and dislikes equation, β_1 is -1.312 and β_3 is 1.106.

Given these estimated effects for the total number of likes and dislikes, elite polarization has no effect (E= -0.206) for those with a grade school education (education = 1), and its effect for those with a high school education (education = 2) is a relatively small 0.900. But, for those who attended at least some college (education = 3) and those who graduated from college (education = 4), the effect of elite polarization is substantial, 2.006 and 3.122, respectively. The results for perceived ideological distance are similar. Elite polarization has no effect on people with less cognitive training. However, among those who attended some college and those who graduated from college, the effect of elite polarization is a substantial 1.361 and 2.582, respectively.

In sum, these results should increase confidence that elite polarization is driving the impressive increase in party-centric thinking on the mass level. People with the greatest ability to assimilate new information—those with more formal education—are most affected by elite polarization. This set of findings is all the more impressive given that education is not an optimal proxy for political knowledge.

Conclusion

The results presented here suggest that parties in the electorate have rebounded significantly since 1980, further suggesting that the party decline thesis is in need of revision (see also Bartels 2000). Although the results do not suggest an environment mirroring the 1950s, Americans in the 2000s are more likely to think about one party positively and one negatively, less likely to feel neutral toward either party, and better able to list reasons why they like and dislike the parties than they were decades ago.[17] Consistent with most theories of public opinion, these mass level changes resulted from changes in elite behavior. Greater ideological polarization in Congress clarified people's perceptions of the parties' ideologies, producing a more partisan electorate.

Table 13-2 Replication of Models in Table 13-1 Adding an Interaction between Elite Polarization and Education

Variable	Sees Important Differences		Places Democrats to Left of Republicans		Perceived Ideological Distance		Cares Who Wins Presidential Election		Respondent is a Positive – Negative		Total Party Likes and Dislikes	
	Parameter Estimate	(Standard Error)	Parameter Estimate	(Standard Error)	Parameter Estimate	(Standard Error)	Parameter Estimate	(Standard Error)	Parameter Estimate	(Standard Error)	Parameter Estimate	(Standard Error)
Elite Polarization	-0.910*	(0.408)	-1.560*	(0.618)	-2.302***	(0.565)	1.791***	(0.517)	2.441***	(0.612)	-1.312	(0.930)
Education	-0.236**	(0.086)	0.165	(0.148)	-0.197	(0.120)	-0.107	(0.124)	0.373**	(0.136)	0.256	(0.195)
Elite Polarization × Education	1.172***	(0.174)	0.928***	(0.230)	1.221***	(0.185)	0.675***	(0.199)	-0.180	(0.204)	1.106***	(0.303)

Source: American National Election Studies, Cumulative File, 1948–2004.

*p < .05, **p < .01, ***p < .001 - one-tailed tests

Although I have focused on strength, as opposed to direction, of partisanship, my results may have implications for the latter as well. In discussing macropartisanship, some suggest that short-term influences such as changes in economic conditions and presidential approval have profound effects on the distribution of Republicans and Democrats (e.g. MacKuen, Erikson, and Stimson 1989; Erikson, MacKuen, and Stimson 1998), while others argue that their effects are minimal (e.g. Green, Palmquist, and Schickler 1998). Given that strength of partisanship in the aggregate has fluctuated markedly over the last fifty years, heterogeneity in the time series is likely. When people hold their partisan ties more intensely, it reduces the probability of party identification change. Hence the effect of short-term forces on macropartisanship should be smaller when strength of partisanship is relatively high and larger when it is relatively low.[18]

The resurgence of party is, of course, good news for those who trumpet the unique role that parties have traditionally played in organizing political conflict (e.g. Schattschneider 1975). Voting theories work best when people perceive that the parties are offering distinct ideologies, allowing voters to make rational calculations about alternative futures (e.g. Downs 1957; Hinich and Munger 1994). My results suggest that voters are now much better able to make such ideological distinctions. Since party voting will, on average, allow less sophisticated Americans to connect their values and interests with vote choice (Delli Carpini and Keeter 1996), voters should be able to participate more effectively as a result.

The election of 2008 provides further empirical evidence of mass party resurgence. Exit poll data suggests that better than 90 percent of both Democratic and Republican identifiers voted for their party's presidential candidate, a particularly remarkable result for Republicans given than John McCain lost by seven percentage points. According to the 2008 ANES, straight-ticket voting for president and House remained above 80 percent among major party presidential voters. Indeed straight-ticket voting in the last four elections bears a striking resemblance to that of the 1956 to 1964 period. Moreover, the ANES data reveal that more Americans cared who won the presidential election and saw important differences between the parties than at any other point in the survey era.

It is easy to overlook a party resurgence when symptoms often associated with weak parties, such as third-party candidacies and divided government, remained, for a time, regular features of the political environment. Such phenomena, however, result from other factors, in addition to weak partisanship. Although Ross Perot certainly benefited from party independence, his success was mostly a function of his personal style and fortune (Rosenstone, Behr, and Lazarus 1996). To the extent that weak parties do help third-party efforts, moreover, it is noteworthy that third parties drew fewer votes between 1996 and 2004 as partisan resurgence continued to gain momentum. In addition, strong parties do not automatically produce unified government (Fiorina 1992). Although the late nineteenth century was perhaps America's most partisan era, divided governments were the norm. Today, candidate quality and fundraising play a dominant role in understanding which voters split their tickets (Burden and Kimball 1999). Moreover, the first decade of the twenty-first century has mostly featured unified governments, which is consistent with the resurgence of partisanship traced throughout this article.

APPENDIX A

Question Wording

Partisanship

Generally speaking, do you usually think of yourself as a Republican, a Democrat, an Independent, or what? (If Republican or Democrat). Would you call yourself a strong (Republican/Democrat) or a not very strong (Republican/Democrat)? (If Independent, other, or no preference]:) Do you think of yourself as closer to the Republican or Democratic Party?

Ideology Questions

We hear a lot of talk these days about liberals and conservatives. I'm going to show you (in 1996: "Here is") a seven-point scale on which the political views that people might hold are arranged from extremely liberal to extremely conservative. Where would you place yourself on this scale, or haven't you thought much about this?

Where would you place the Democratic Party?

Where would you place the Republican Party?

Sees Important Differences

Do you think there are any important differences in what the Republicans and Democrats stand for?

Party Feeling Thermometers

I'd like to get your feelings toward some of our political leaders and other people who are in the news these days (in 1990: "who have been in the news"). I'll read the name of a person and I'd like you to rate that person using the feeling thermometer. Ratings between 50 and 100 degrees mean that you feel favorably and warm toward the person; ratings between 0 and 50 degrees mean that you don't feel favorably toward the person and that you don't care too much for that person. You would rate the person at the 50-degree mark if you don't feel particularly warm or cold toward the person. If we come to a person whose name you don't recognize, you don't need to rate that person. Just tell me and we'll move on to the next one.

The Democratic Party
The Republican Party

Likes/Dislikes

Is there anything in particular that you like about the Democratic party? What is that? Anything else [you like about the Democratic Party]? UP TO FIVE MENTIONS

Is there anything in particular that you dislike about the Democratic party? What is that? Anything else [you dislike about the Democratic Party]? UP TO FIVE MENTIONS

Is there anything in particular that you like about the Republican party? What is that? Anything else [you like about the Republican Party]? UP TO FIVE MENTIONS

Is there anything in particular that you dislike about the Republican party? What is that? Anything else [you dislike about the Republican Party]? UP TO FIVE MENTIONS

Notes

1. The data used in this study were obtained from the Interuniversity Consortium for Political and Social Research. The Consortium bears no responsibility for their use.

   In demonstrating that party identification has an increasingly large effect on presidential and congressional vote choice, Bartels (2000) is largely alone in challenging the party decline thesis, although other public opinion scholars do note the resurgence on the elite level (see e.g. Aldrich 1995; Beck 1997).
2. Bartels (2000) demonstrates that these trends have reversed recently, especially among the politically active. Among voters, the proportion of party identifiers was higher in 1996 than in any election since 1964.
3. The ANES changed the object of its party thermometer questions in 1978. Before 1978, respondents were asked how they felt about "Republicans" and "Democrats." Since then, they have been asked about the "Republican Party" and the "Democratic Party." In 1980, the ANES asked both versions, and the difference in means is quite large. Hence I cannot extend the analysis back any further.
4. Some might argue that third-party presidential voters are the least partisan and hence least likely to vote a straight ticket. By focusing only on major-party presidential voters, therefore, I may overstate increasing party loyalty. If this were true, however, the higher level of straight-ticket voting should have occurred in 1992, since Perot received 19 percent of the vote compared with just 9 percent in 1996. Instead, of the 81 percent of major-party presidential voters in 1992, 78 percent voted for a House candidate of the same party. Of the 91 percent of voters who cast ballots for either Clinton or Bob Dole in 1996, fully 82 percent voted for a House candidate of the same party.
5. DW-NOMINATE scores are the most commonly used estimate of the ideological positions of members of Congress. Members' ideal points are derived using a dynamic, weighted, nominal three-step estimation procedure based on all non-unanimous roll call votes taken in each Congress (see Poole and Rosenthal 1997 for details).

6. Since Poole and Rosenthal computed the coordinates using a weighted utility model, any use of the DW-NOMINATE scores to calculate a distance requires that the second dimension be weighted by .3 (see Poole and Rosenthal 1997). Scores for the Senate, while less polarized, follow much the same pattern as those for the House (Poole 1998).

7. Scholars have suggested several alternatives to the measure of polarization used here. For example, Aldrich, Berger, and Rohde (1999) employ a number of measures of both polarization and homogeneity, including the median distance between the parties, the intraparty homogeneity along the NOMINATE score's first dimension, and the proportion of members of one party that ideologically overlap the other party on the first dimension. It is worth noting that the mean Euclidean distance measure that I employ here is correlated with these three measures at .99, .99, and .97, respectively, when I use data from the 85th to the 103rd Congresses.

8. I should note that, in exploring the influence of party activists on party ideologies, Aldrich (1995, chapter 6) explores variations on several of these measures of clarity, finding results consistent with mine. He does not, however, suggest that greater clarity reinvigorated mass-level partisanship.

9. Wattenberg (1990) also identifies but dismisses this trend, noting that people are not also more likely to think one of the parties is better able to solve their important problems. A potential explanation for this contradiction is that, while people do perceive increasing party polarization, they are not necessarily enthusiastic about it (Dionne 1991; Hibbing and Theiss-Morse 1995). In that sense, people may not think the parties will do an ideal job, but they think they will do a different job.

10. I can only safely compare respondents in 1984 and after because of changes in question administration, which I deal with in more detail in the model section below.

11. To conserve cases, I include in the analysis both those who placed themselves ideologically and those who did not. This means that all those who failed to place themselves and were thus not asked to place the parties are coded as having failed to array the parties correctly.

12. While I specify a model where causation runs from the elite to mass level, Rohde (1991) suggests the reverse causation. Our goals, however, differ. Rohde's work explores changes in the *direction* of white Southerners' party identification, whereas my concern is the *strength* of partisan attitudes. It is more likely that mass-level strength intensified over time in response to a more partisan elite-level environment than a sudden, unexplained influx of stronger partisans in the electorate paved the way for the likes of Newt Gingrich and Jim Wright. Moreover, even the directional changes in Southern partisanship described by Rohde had at their root changes in elite behavior on civil rights issues (Carmines and Stimson 1989).

13. Although I would like to include an objective measure of political knowledge, the ANES does not provide a consistent battery of knowledge items until 1988. Scholars often use formal education, which I do include in the model, as a proxy for political knowledge (e.g. Sniderman, Brody, and Tetlock 1991).

14. Since the ANES only started to ask people to place themselves ideologically in 1972, I drop strength of ideology from the important differences equation, so I can include data from 1960, 1964, and 1968. Dropping strength of ideology should not affect the results unduly, given that the partial correlation between elite polarization and the percentage seeing important differences between the parties is an extremely robust .87, controlling for off-year election years.

15. Since my measure of elite polarization is not independent from year to year, some might be concerned about autocorrelation. Regression diagnostics suggest no such problems. For instance, the Durbin-Watson statistics for the OLS models presented below are 1.75 and 1.92, respectively, which indicate that this is not an issue.

16. The ANES has asked one factual item in almost every survey since 1960: whether the respondent knows which party controlled the House of Representatives prior to the election. If I specify an interaction between whether or not the respondent answered this question correctly and elite polarization, the same basic pattern of results emerges. Since this is a single item and one that many likely get right by guessing (Luskin 2000), I opted to use education instead.

17. Although the results are not presented here due to space considerations, elite polarization has also increased the tendency of respondents to vote for presidential and House candidates of the same party, controlling for strength of partisanship, strength of ideology, race, age, sex, whether a House seat is open, whether a House seat is contested, whether a third-party presidential candidate is running, and whether the House incumbent is of the party opposite the respondent's party identification.

18. In noting that the proportion of Democratic identifiers has not increased substantially in the 1990s despite extraordinary increases in consumer confidence and consistently high presidential approval ratings, Green, Palmquist, and Schickler (2000) persuasively cast further doubt on the import of short-term forces. Although, as they argue, this might be the result of questionable estimation decisions made by MacKuen, Erikson, and Stimson, it also might result from the fact that it has become harder to move macropartisanship in the 1990s because strength of partisanship has increased.

14. Is Polarization a Myth?

Alan I. Abramowitz and Kyle L. Saunders

Americans are closely divided, but we are not deeply divided, and we are
closely divided because many of us are ambivalent and uncertain, and consequently reluctant to make firm commitments to parties, politicians, or
policies. We divide evenly in elections or sit them out entirely because we
instinctively seek the center while the parties and candidates hang out on
the extremes. (Fiorina 2006, xiii)

The extent of ideological thinking in the American electorate has been a
subject of great interest to students of public opinion and voting behavior since
the publication of Converse's seminal paper on "The Nature of Belief Systems in
Mass Publics" (1964). Based on his analysis of data from the 1956 and 1960
American National Election Studies, Converse concluded that the sort of ideological thinking common among political elites was confined to a small minority
of the American public. The vast majority of ordinary voters showed little evidence of using an ideological framework to evaluate political parties or presidential candidates and very limited understanding of basic ideological concepts such
as liberalism and conservatism.

American politics and the American electorate have changed dramatically
since the 1950s in ways that might lead one to expect an increase in the prevalence of ideological thinking in the public, as Converse himself has acknowledged
(2006). One important change has been a very substantial increase in the educational attainment of the electorate. In his original study, Converse found that
education was a strong predictor of ideological sophistication: college-educated
voters displayed much higher levels of ideological sophistication than grade
school- or high school-educated voters. Between 1956 and 2004, the proportion
of ANES respondents with only a grade-school education fell from 37% to 3%
while the proportion with at least some college education rose from 19% to 61%.
Based on this trend alone, one would expect a much larger proportion of today's
voters to be capable of understanding and using ideological concepts.

Another development that might be expected to raise the level of ideological
awareness among the public has been the growing intensity of ideological conflict
among political elites in the United States. For several decades, Democratic
officeholders, candidates, and activists have been moving to the left while Republican officeholders, candidates, and activists have been moving to the right. Conservative Democrats and liberal Republicans, who were common in American

Source: The Journal of Politics 70, 2 (April 2008): 542–555.

politics during the 1950s and 1960s, are now extremely rare. At the elite level, ideological differences between the parties are probably greater now than at any time in the past half century (Poole and Rosenthal 1997; 2001; Stonecash, Brewer, and Mariani 2003).

There is widespread agreement among scholars concerning the growing importance of ideological divisions at the elite level in American politics. There is much less agreement, however, about the significance of these divisions at the mass level. Some studies have found evidence that growing elite polarization has led to an increase in ideological awareness and polarization among the public (Abramowitz and Saunders 1998; Hetherington, 2001; Layman and Carsey 2002). However, other scholars, most notably Morris Fiorina and his collaborators, have argued that when it comes to the political beliefs of the mass public, very little has changed since the 1950s.

In his popular and influential book *Culture War? The Myth of a Polarized America,* Fiorina claims that Converse's portrait of the American electorate "still holds up pretty well." According to Fiorina, the ideological disputes that engage political elites and activists have little resonance among the American mass public: like their mid-twentieth-century counterparts, ordinary twenty-first-century Americans "are not very well-informed about politics, do not hold many of their views very strongly, and are not ideological" (2006, 19).

The argument that polarization in America is almost entirely an elite phenomenon appears to be contradicted by a large body of research by political scientists on recent trends in American public opinion. While there have been relatively few studies directly addressing Fiorina's evidence and conclusions (Abramowitz and Saunders 2005; Demerath 2005; Evans and Nunn 2005; Klinkner 2004; Klinkner and Hapanowicz 2005; Rosenthal 2005), a growing body of research indicates that political and cultural divisions within the American public have deepened considerably since the 1970s. These studies have found that the political beliefs of Democratic and Republican voters have become much more distinctive over the past thirty years (Abramowitz and Saunders 1998; Hetherington 2001; Jacobson 2004, 2005; Jelen and Wilcox 2003; Layman and Carsey 2002; Lindaman and Haider-Markel 2002; Stonecash, Brewer, and Mariani 2003; White 2003), that political divisions within the public increasingly reflect differences in religious beliefs and practices (Layman 1997, 2001; Layman and Carmines 1997) as well as deep-seated psychological orientations (Jost 2006), and that ideological polarization among party elites is explained in part by ideological polarization among party supporters in the electorate (Jacobson 2000).

This article uses data from the American National Election Studies and national exit polls to test five major claims made by Fiorina and his collaborators about polarization in the United States. This evidence indicates that while some claims by culture war proponents about deep political divisions among the public have been overstated, Fiorina systematically understates the significance of these divisions. Americans may not be heading to the barricades to do battle over abortion, gay marriage, and other emotionally charged issues as some have alleged

(Hunter 1995), but there are large differences in outlook between Democrats and Republicans, between red state voters and blue state voters, and between religious voters and secular voters. These divisions are not confined to a small minority of elected officials and activists—they involve a large segment of the public and the deepest divisions are found among the most interested, informed, and active members of the public. Moreover, contrary to Fiorina's claim that polarization turns off voters and depresses turnout, we find that the intense polarization of the electorate over George W. Bush and his policies energized the electorate and contributed to a dramatic increase in voting and other forms of political participation in 2004.

Fiorina's Five Claims

1. Moderation. The broadest claim made by Fiorina and the one that underlies all of the others is that the American public is basically moderate—the public is closely divided but not deeply divided. Today as in the past, most Americans are ideological moderates, holding a mixture of liberal and conservative views on different issues. There has been no increase in ideological polarization among the public.

2. Partisan Polarization. While differences between Democratic and Republican identifiers on issues have increased, they are only slightly greater than in the past. Partisan polarization is largely an elite phenomenon—only a thin layer of elected officials and activists are truly polarized in their views.

3. Geographical Polarization. Cultural and political differences between red states and blue states are actually fairly small. The similarities between voters in these two sets of states are much more striking than the differences.

4. Social Cleavages. Divisions within the public based on social characteristics such as age, race, gender, and religious affiliation have been diminishing. While divisions based on religious beliefs and practices have increased, they remain modest and have not supplanted traditional economic divisions as determinants of party identification or voting behavior.

5. Voter Engagement and Participation. Growing polarization of party elites and activists turns off large numbers of voters and depresses turnout in elections.

The Evidence: Moderation

Fiorina's central claim is that there has been no increase in ideological polarization among the American public in recent years. It is difficult to compare the ideological views of Americans today with the ideological views of Americans during the 1950s, 1960s, or 1970s because very few issue questions have been included in public opinion surveys throughout this time span. However, since 1982 seven issue questions have been included in almost every ANES survey: liberal-conservative identification, aid to blacks, defense spending, jobs and living standards, health insurance, government services and spending, and abortion.[1]

We used these questions to construct a measure of ideological polarization ranging from 0 to 7 by computing the absolute value of the difference between the
number of liberal positions and the number of conservative positions. We then
recoded the polarization scale so that those with a score of 0 or 1 were coded as
low, those with a score of 2 or 3 were coded as moderate, and those with a score
of 4 or greater were coded as high.[2]

Table 14-1 displays the trend in ideological polarization from the 1980s
through the first decade of the twenty-first century based on the recoded 7-issue
scale. Contrary to Fiorina's claim that polarization has not increased among the
American public, the results displayed in Table 14-1 show that there has been an
increase in ideological polarization since the 1980s: the percentage of respondents
at the low end of the polarization scale fell from 39% during the 1980s to 32% in
2002–2004 while the percentage at the high end rose from 24% to 33%. These
results indicate that ideological thinking is more prevalent among the American
public today than in the past.

This trend can also be seen by examining the correlations among the items
included in the ideological polarization scale. As Knight (2006) has argued,
coherence of opinions across issues is generally regarded as one of the key indicators of ideological thinking. It is also closely related to another indicator of ideological thinking—contrast between the beliefs of those in opposing ideological
camps. The higher the correlations among respondents' issue positions, the larger
the proportion of respondents holding consistently liberal and consistently conservative positions. Thus, the fact that the average correlation among these seven
items increased from .20 during the 1980s to .26 during the 1990s and .32 in
2002–2004 indicates that there was a significant increase in ideological thinking
among the American public during this time period.

Fiorina's claim that Americans "instinctively seek the center" also ignores
important differences in ideological thinking within the public. Some Americans
have little or no interest in politics while others care deeply about political issues.
Some know very little about politics while others are quite knowledgeable. And,
of course, some seldom or never participate in the political process while others
participate regularly. Based on past research, we would expect ideological thinking
to be more prevalent among the well informed and politically engaged than among
the poorly informed and politically disengaged (Converse 1964; Jennings 1992;
Saunders and Abramowitz 2004; Stimson 1975), and it is the well informed and
politically engaged whose opinions matter most to candidates and officeholders.

The results in Table 14-1 strongly support this hypothesis: ideological polarization is consistently greater among the well educated and politically engaged
segment of the American public than among the poorly educated and politically
disengaged segment. Moreover, the increase in ideological polarization since the
1980s has been concentrated among the more educated and politically engaged
segment of the public.

In order to measure ideological polarization among the American public in
2004, we created a scale based on responses to sixteen issues included in the

Table 14-1 Ideological Polarization in the American Electorate by Decade

Group	1982–1990	1992–2000	2002–2004
All Respondents	24	29	33
Nonvoters	18	19	19
Voters	27	34	37
Low Knowledge	16	17	19
High Knowledge	38	43	48
Low Interest	19	18	21
High Interest	34	39	45
No College	19	20	21
Some College	29	32	32
College Grads	36	43	49

Source: ANES Cumulative File

Note: Entries represent percentage of respondents with consistently liberal or conservative views across seven issue questions.

American National Election Study survey. The issues ranged from government responsibility for jobs and living standards to gay marriage, health insurance, abortion, defense spending, and gun control, and the scale has a reliability coefficient (Cronbach's alpha) of .80. Scores on the original scale ranged from -16 for respondents who gave liberal responses to all 16 issues to +16 for respondents who gave conservative responses to all 16 issues. We then recoded the original 33-point scale into an 11-point scale for clarity in presentation.[3]

Table 14-2 displays the relationship between ideological consistency and three measures of political engagement: interest, knowledge, and participation.[4] The results strongly support the political engagement hypothesis. It was primarily the least interested, least informed, and least politically active Americans who were clustered around the center of the liberal-conservative spectrum. The more interested, informed, and politically active Americans were, the more likely they were to take consistently liberal or consistently conservative positions.

The implication of the findings in Table 14-2 is that the most politically engaged citizens are also the most polarized in their political views. In order to directly test this hypothesis, we combined the political interest, knowledge, and participation scales to create an overall index of political engagement. We then divided the respondents in the 2004 ANES sample into three groups of approximately equal size: the least politically engaged, a middle group, and the most politically engaged. The politically engaged group included 37% of all respondents in the survey and close to half of the voters.

Figure 14-1 compares the ideological orientations of the least politically engaged group with the ideological orientations of the most politically engaged group. These results strongly support the political engagement hypothesis. The high-engagement group was much more polarized in its policy preferences than the low-engagement group. Although the means of the two distributions are

Table 14-2 Political Engagement and Ideological Polarization in 2004

	Ideological Polarization			
	Low	Moderate	High	Total
Campaign Interest				
Moderate to Low	40%	33	27	100%
High	24%	27	49	100%
Political Knowledge				
Low (0–4)	44%	38	18	100%
Moderate (5–7)	30%	29	41	100%
High (8–10)	15%	19	66	100%
Participation				
Low (0–1)	39%	35	26	100%
Moderate (2)	30%	30	40	100%
High (3+)	17%	18	65	100%

Source: 2004 American National Election Study

almost identical (6.1 vs. 6.2), the standard deviation of the high-engagement group (2.8) is almost twice as large as the standard deviation of the low-engagement group (1.5). Very few individuals in the low-engagement group had consistent policy preferences: 13% were consistent liberals (1–4) while 19% were consistent conservatives (8–11). In contrast, a large proportion of individuals in the high-engagement group had fairly consistent policy preferences: 32% were consistent liberals while 39% were consistent conservatives (see Figure 14-1).

These results indicate that the politically engaged segment of the American electorate is in fact quite polarized in its political attitudes. We would expect political elites to be much more concerned about the views of the politically engaged than about the views of the politically disengaged. It is the politically engaged who pay attention to the positions taken by candidates and officeholders and who consistently turn out to vote in primaries as well as general elections. However, the existence of polarization in a society does not just depend on the overall distribution of political attitudes among the public. It also depends on whether there are differences between the views of important subgroups and perhaps the most politically significant subgroups in a democracy are political parties.

The Evidence: Partisan Polarization

Fiorina argues that partisan polarization is largely an elite phenomenon and that there has been only a slight increase in partisan polarization within the American electorate over the past several decades. Our evidence does not support either of these claims. The evidence from the 2004 ANES survey displayed in Figure 14-2 shows that partisan polarization is not confined to a small group of leaders and activists. The ideological preferences of Democratic and Republican identifiers (including leaning independents) actually differed rather sharply.

Figure 14-1 Ideological Polarization of U.S. Electorate in 2004 by Level of Political Engagement

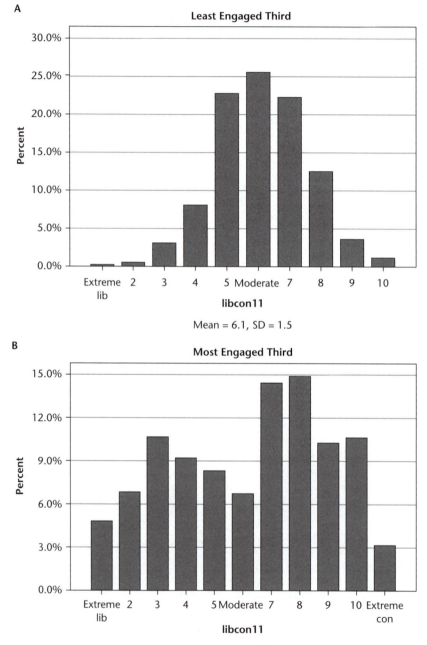

A

Least Engaged Third

Mean = 6.1, SD = 1.5

B

Most Engaged Third

Mean = 6.2, SD = 2.8

Source: 2004 American National Election Study

Figure 14-2 Liberal-Conservative Policy Preferences of Democratic and
Republican Identifiers in 2004

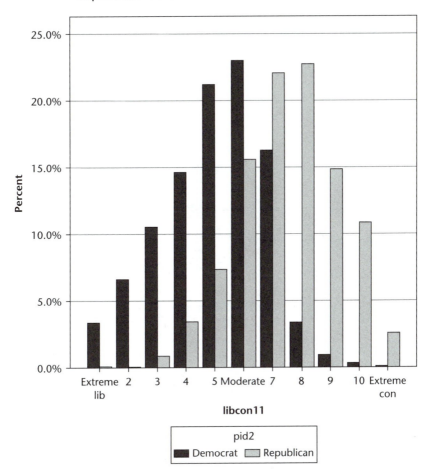

Source: 2004 American National Election Study

Democratic identifiers tended to be fairly liberal while Republican identifiers tend to be fairly conservative. The mean scores on the 11-point ideology scale were 5.0 for Democrats compared with 7.5 for Republicans. This difference is highly statistically significant (p < .001). It is also substantively significant. Fifty-six percent of Democrats were on the liberal side of the scale (1–5) compared with only 12% of Republicans; 73% of Republicans were on the conservative side of the scale (7–11) compared with only 21% of Democrats.

Evidence from the American National Election Studies indicates that partisan polarization has increased considerably over the past several decades.

Figure 14-3 Correlation of Party Identification with Liberal-Conservative
Identification, 1972–2004

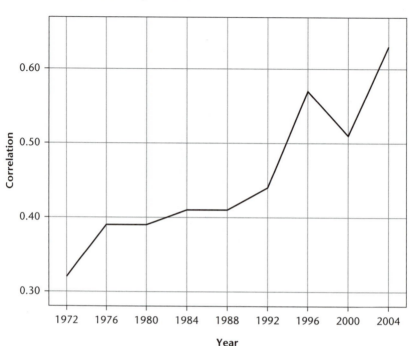

Source: American National Election Studies

Note: Correlation coefficient is Pearson's *r* based on 7-point party Identification scale and
7-point liberal-conservative identification scale.

Figure 14-3 displays the trend in the correlation between liberal-conservative
identification and party identification between 1972, when the ideology question
was first included in the ANES survey, and 2004. This graph shows that contrary
to the claim that partisan polarization has increased only slightly, there has actually been a dramatic increase in the correlation between party identification and
ideological identification since 1972 and especially since 1992. In 1972, the correlation between ideology and party identification was .32. In 1992, it was .44.
In 2004, it was .63. Nor was this trend due simply to party realignment in the
southern states. In the South, the correlation between ideology and party identification increased from .24 in 1972 to .56 in 2004; outside of the South, the
correlation increased from .37 in 1972 to .66 in 2004.

The result of the growing relationship between ideological identification
and party identification has been a marked increase in ideological polarization
between Democratic and Republican identifiers. Between 1972 and 2004, the

Table 14-3 Trends in Partisan Polarization on Issues, 1972–2004

Issue	1972–1980	1984–1992	1996–2004
Aid to Blacks	.20	.27	.35
Abortion	−.03	.08	.18
Jobs/Living Standards	.28	.34	.40
Health Insurance	.25	.31	.39
Lib/Con Id	.42	.49	.62
Presidential Approval	.42	.56	.61
Average	.26	.34	.43

Source: American National Election Studies

Note: Entries shown are average correlations (Kendall's tau) between issues and party identification (strong, weak, and independent Democrats vs. strong, weak, and independent Republicans).

difference between the mean score of Democratic identifiers and the mean score of Republican identifiers on the 7-point liberal conservative identification scale doubled from 0.9 units to 1.8 units. Given the limited range of this scale—the standard deviation was 1.46 in 2004—this is a substantial increase in polarization.

Differences between Democratic and Republican identifiers have also increased over the past three decades on a wide range of issues. Table 14-3 displays the correlations between party identification and positions on six different issues during 1972–1980, 1984–1992, and 1996–2004: the larger the correlation coefficient, the greater the degree of partisan polarization on an issue. On every one of these issues, ranging from jobs and living standards to health insurance to presidential approval, partisan polarization increased substantially.

Evaluations of presidential performance have become increasingly divided along party lines since the 1970s and evaluations of George W. Bush in 2004 were sharply divided along party lines. According to data from the 2004 ANES survey, 90% of Republican identifiers approved of Bush's performance and 66% approved strongly; in contrast, 81% of Democratic identifiers disapproved of Bush's performance and 64% disapproved strongly. Evaluations of George W. Bush were more divided along party lines than those of any president since the ANES began asking the presidential approval question in 1972. However, the highly polarized evaluations of George Bush in 2004 were not unique—they represented a continuation of a trend that goes back several decades: the difference between the percentage of Democratic identifiers approving of the president's performance and the percentage of Republican identifiers approving of the president's performance was 36 points for Richard Nixon in 1972, 42 points for Jimmy Carter in 1980, 52 points for Ronald Reagan in 1988, 55 points for Bill Clinton in 1996, and 71 points for George W. Bush in 2004.

Figure 14-4 Liberal-Conservative Policy Preferences of Politically Engaged
Democratic and Republican Identifiers

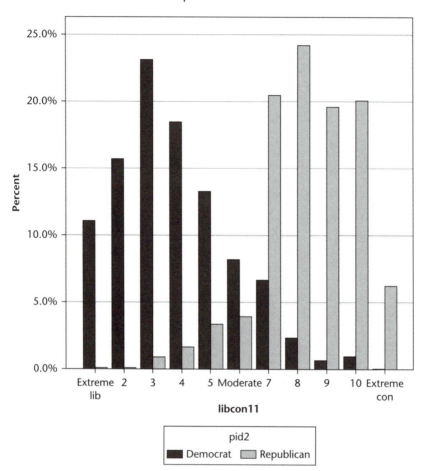

Source: 2004 American National Election Study

Figure 14-4 shows that partisan polarization was considerably greater among politically engaged Americans in 2004 than among the general public. The mean scores on the 11-point liberal-conservative policy scale were 3.8 for politically engaged Democrats compared with 8.3 for politically engaged Republicans. This difference is both substantively and statistically significant ($p < .001$). Eighty-two percent of politically engaged Democrats were on the liberal side of the scale (1–5) compared with only 7% of politically engaged Republicans; 91% of politically engaged Republicans were on the conservative side of the scale (7–11) compared with only 12% of politically engaged Democrats.

Table 14-4 Policy Liberalism among Politically Engaged Partisans in 2004

Issue	Democrats	Republicans
Abortion	67%	25%
Death Penalty	52%	10%
Diplomacy vs. Force	74%	15%
Environment vs. Jobs	74%	27%
Gay Marriage	69%	18%
Jobs/Living Standards	52%	9%
Health Insurance	66%	16%
Spending/Services	65%	18%

Source: 2004 American National Election Study

There were dramatic differences between the positions of politically engaged Democrats and Republicans on a wide range of specific issues in 2004. Some of these issue differences are displayed in Table 14-4. On every one of the eight issues included in Table 14-4, politically engaged Democrats were much more liberal than politically engaged Republicans. This was true on social issues, economic issues, and foreign policy issues. The smallest differences, 42 percentage points, were on the issues of abortion and the death penalty. The largest difference, 59 percentage points, was on the use of military force versus diplomacy in the conduct of foreign policy. Across these eight issues, an average of 65% of politically engaged Democrats took the liberal position compared with an average of 17% of politically engaged Republicans.

Politically engaged partisans have always been more polarized along ideological lines than ordinary party identifiers. However, like ordinary party identifiers, politically engaged partisans have become increasingly polarized over time.[5] Between 1972 and 2004, the correlation (Pearson's *r*) between party identification and ideological identification among the most politically engaged citizens increased from .47 to .77. As a result, the difference between the average score of politically engaged Democrats and the average score of politically engaged Republicans on the 7-point liberal-conservative scale increased from 1.4 units in 1972 to 2.7 units in 2008. The level of polarization among politically engaged partisans in 2004 was the highest in the history of the ANES even though the proportion of citizens classified as politically engaged was also the highest in the history of the ANES.

The Evidence: Geographical Polarization

Fiorina claims there has been little increase in geographical polarization in recent decades and that the differences between red states and blue states have been greatly exaggerated. However, the evidence displayed in Table 14-5 shows

Table 14-5 The Shrinking Battlefield: A Comparison of the 1960, 1976, 2000, and 2004 Presidential Elections

	1960	1976	2000	2004
National vote margin	0.2%	2.1%	0.5%	2.5%
Average state margin	8.0%	8.9%	13.8%	14.8%
Number of states that were:				
Uncompetitive (10% +)	18	19	29	31
Battlegrounds(0–5%)	24	24	15	12
Electoral votes of:				
Uncompetitive states	124	131	314	332
Competitive states	327	337	167	141

Source: Congressional Quarterly's Guide to U.S. Elections, 4th ed. For 2004 election: www.uselectionatlas.org.

that states have become much more sharply divided along party lines since the 1960s: red states have been getting redder while blue states have been getting bluer. While the 2000 and 2004 presidential elections were highly competitive at the national level, the large majority of states were not competitive. Compared with the presidential elections of 1960 and 1976, which were also closely contested at the national level, there were far fewer battleground states in 2000 and 2004 and the percentage of electoral votes in these battleground states was much smaller. The average margin of victory at the state level has increased dramatically over time and far more states with far more electoral votes are now either solidly Democratic or solidly Republican.

In the 2004 presidential election, 38 of 50 states were carried by George Bush or John Kerry by a margin of more than 5 percentage points.[6] These states included more than two-thirds of the nation's voters. And contrary to Fiorina's claim that there are few major differences between red state voters and blue state voters, the evidence from the 2004 National Exit Poll displayed in Table 14-6 shows that when we compare voters in states that supported Bush or Kerry by a margin of more than 5 points, there were large differences between the social characteristics and political attitudes of red state voters and blue state voters. Compared with blue state voters, red state voters were much more likely to be Protestants, to consider themselves born-again or evangelical Christians, and to attend religious services at least once per week. They were also much more likely to have a gun owner in their household and much less likely to have a union member in their household. Red state voters were much more likely to take a pro-life position on abortion, to oppose marriage or civil unions for gay couples, to support the war in Iraq, to approve of George Bush's job performance, to describe themselves as conservative, to identify with the Republican Party and, of course, to vote for George Bush for president.

Table 14-6 A Comparison of Red State Voters and Blue State Voters in 2004

	Red State Voters	Blue State Voters	Difference
Religion:			
Protestant	69%	41%	+28%
Catholic	16%	35%	−19%
Jewish, other, none	15%	24%	−9%
Church Attendance:			
Weekly or more	54%	34%	+20%
Seldom, never	32%	53%	−21%
Evangelical, born-again	51%	22%	+29%
Gun owning household	53%	28%	+25%
Union household	16%	31%	−15%
Pro-choice on abortion	46%	69%	−23%
Oppose gay marriage or civil unions	51%	26%	+25%
Approve of Bush's job performance	63%	45%	+18%
Approve of Iraq war	60%	45%	+15%
Conservative identification	41%	27%	+14%
Republican identification	44%	30%	+14%
Voted for Bush	60%	44%	+16%

Source: 2004 National Exit Poll

Note: Red states were carried by George Bush by a margin of at least 6 percentage points; blue states were carried by John Kerry by a margin of at least 6 percentage points.

The Evidence: Religious Polarization

It is no coincidence that the largest differences between red state voters and blue state voters involved religious beliefs and practices. Religion has long been an important dividing line in American politics. During most of the nineteenth and twentieth centuries, Catholic voters generally supported the Democratic Party while Protestant voters outside of the South generally supported the Republican Party. However, the most important religious divide in American politics today is not between Protestants and Catholics but between religious voters and secular voters (Layman 1997, 2001).

Americans are much more religiously observant than citizens of other Western democracies (Dalton 2002, 113–114). However, evidence from the 2004 National Exit Poll (NEP) shows that there is a clear divide within the American electorate based on frequency of religious observance. The large majority of voters were either highly observant or nonobservant. Forty-three percent of voters reported that they attended religious services at least once per week; another 43% reported that they seldom or never attended religious services. Only 14% of voters reported that they attended religious services a few times a month.

Among white voters in the United States, religious observance is now highly correlated with political attitudes and behavior. The evidence displayed in

Table 14-7 Political Attitudes of Religious and Nonreligious Whites in 2004

	Attend Religious Services	
Issue	Weekly or More	Seldom or Never
Oppose legal abortion	69%	22%
Oppose marriage or civil unions for gays	54%	21%
Approve of Iraq war	68%	49%
Approve of Bush job	72%	48%
Conservative identification	49%	24%
Republican identification	55%	32%
Voted for Bush	71%	46%

Source: 2004 National Exit Poll

Table 14-7 from the 2004 NEP shows that there was a very wide gulf in political attitudes and behavior between white voters who regularly attended religious services and those who seldom or never attended religious services. Not surprisingly, the gap was greatest on cultural issues: there was a 47-point difference on the issue of abortion and a 33-point difference on the issue of gay marriage. However, the gap was very large on other issues as well: 19 points on the war in Iraq, 24 points on President Bush's job performance, 25 points on ideological identification, 23 points on party identification, and 25 points on presidential candidate preference.

Contrary to Fiorina's claim that economic cleavages remain as important or more important than religious cleavages, the evidence from the 2004 NEP displayed in Table 14-8 shows that among white voters, two variables measuring religious beliefs and practices, church attendance and born-again or evangelical identification were more strongly correlated with party identification and presidential candidate choice than other social characteristics including income, education, sex, marital status, and union membership.

In order to directly compare the influence of religiosity with other social characteristics, we conducted a logistic regression analysis of presidential vote choice among whites in 2004. The independent variables in this analysis were age, sex, marital status, income, education, household union membership, and a religiosity scale based on frequency of church attendance and born-again/evangelical identification. The results displayed in Table 14-9 confirm the findings of the bivariate analysis. Among white voters, religiosity had a stronger influence on candidate choice than any other social characteristic. According to these results, with all other independent variables set at their medians, the probability of a Bush vote was .34 for the least religious white voters compared with .81 for the most religious white voters.

These findings indicate that among white voters in the United States, the religious divide is now much deeper than the class divide. Thus, in the 2004 presidential election, 69% of highly observant whites with family incomes below

Table 14-8 Correlates of Partisanship and Presidential Vote among Whites in 2004

	Correlation with	
Characteristic	Party Identification	Presidential Vote
Family Income	.094	.107
Education	−.020	−.077
Marital Status/Married	.136	.151
Age	−.058	−.021
Gender/Female	−.077	−.069
Union Household	−.139	−.130
Church Attendance	.205	.287
Born Again or Evangelical	.219	.280

Source: 2004 National Exit Poll

Note: Correlations are Kendall's tau. Party identification and presidential vote coded in Republican direction.

Table 14-9 Results of Logistic Regression Analysis of Presidential Vote among Whites in 2004

Variable	B	(S.E.)	Z-score	Change in Probability	Sig.
Age	−.086	(.015)	−5.69	−.166	.001
Education	−.291	(.033)	−8.81	−.277	.001
Income	.140	(.022)	6.37	.232	.001
Married	.411	(.073)	−5.60	.102	.001
Female	−.515	(.066)	−7.79	−.119	.001
Nonunion	.765	(.078)	9.79	.189	.001
Religiosity	.435	(.023)	19.24	.469	.001
Constant	−.331	(.261)	−1.27		N.S.

Source: 2004 National Exit Poll

Note: Presidential vote coded in Republican direction. Change in probability is estimated change in the probability of Republican vote between minimum and maximum value of each independent variable with all other independent variables set at their medians.

thirty thousand dollars voted for George Bush while 56% of nonobservant whites with family incomes above two-hundred thousand dollars voted for John Kerry. Moreover, the religious divide is likely to deepen in the future because secular voters constitute a growing proportion of the electorate and because religious commitment is increasingly correlated with political attitudes and behavior. According to ANES data, the proportion of Americans giving their religious affiliation as "other" or "none" increased from 3% during the 1950s to 5% during the 1960s, 8% during the 1970s, 11% during the 1980s, and 15% during the 1990s. The same data show that the correlation between frequency of church

Figure 14-5 Mean Party Identification Score of Observant and
Nonobservant Whites in National Election Study Surveys
by Decade

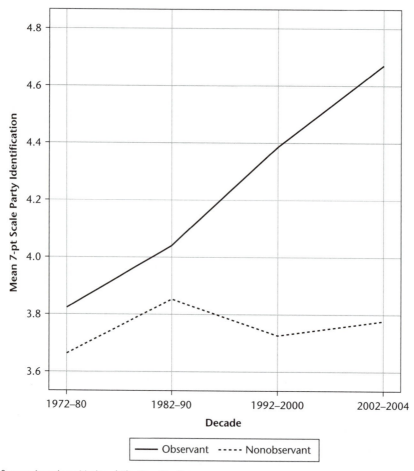

Source: American National Election Studies

attendance and presidential candidate choice among whites increased from .02
during the 1950s and .03 during the 1960s to .10 during the 1970s, .08 during
the 1980s and .29 during the 1990s.

Data from the American National Election Studies show that religiosity has
become increasingly correlated with party identification as well as presidential
candidate choice among white voters. Figure 14-5 displays the trend in the mean
score of observant and nonobservant whites on the 7-point party identification
scale since the 1970s. Before 1980 there was almost no difference in party identification between religious and nonreligious whites. In 1956, for example, 52%

of whites who were regular churchgoers identified with the Democratic Party as did 50% of whites who seldom or never attended church. As recently as 1976, 46% of whites who were regular churchgoers identified with the Democratic Party as did 46% of whites who seldom or never attended church. By 1992, however, there was a large gap in party identification between religious and nonreligious whites: only 38% of whites who were regular churchgoers identified with the Democratic Party compared with 51% of whites who seldom or never attended church. The results in 2004 were very similar: only 35% of whites who were regular churchgoers identified with the Democratic Party compared with 51% of whites who seldom or never attended church.

The Evidence: Polarization and Participation

In the 2004 presidential election, Americans were closely divided, but they were not ambivalent or uncertain about George W. Bush. Americans were in fact deeply divided about George Bush, and that division drove a record number of them to the polls. Over 122 million Americans voted in 2004, an increase of 17 million over the 2000 presidential election. Turnout jumped from 54% of eligible voters in 2000 to 61% in 2004—close to the levels seen during the 1950s and 1960s before the voting age was lowered from 21 to 18 (McDonald 2004).

It was not only voting that was way up in 2004. According to data from the American National Election Studies, participation in other campaign activities also increased dramatically between 2000 and 2004. Twenty-one percent of Americans displayed a button, bumper sticker, or yard sign during the campaign, matching the all-time high set in 1960. In 2000, despite the closeness of the presidential race, only 10% of Americans displayed a button, bumper sticker, or yard sign. Even more impressively, 48% of Americans reported that they talked to someone during the 2004 campaign to try to influence their vote. This was by far the highest proportion in the history of the ANES and a dramatic increase from the 32% who reported engaging in personal persuasion during the 2000 campaign.

The intense polarization of the American electorate about George W. Bush contributed to the high level of public engagement in the 2004 presidential election. Students of voting behavior have long recognized that there is a relationship between polarization and voter engagement (e.g., Downs 1957). The greater the difference voters perceive between the candidates and parties, the greater their stake in the outcome and the more engaged they are likely to be.

Figure 14-6 displays the trend between 1952 and 2004 in the percentage of Americans who perceived important differences between the Democratic and Republican parties and the percentage who said they cared "a good deal" about the outcome of the presidential election. In 2004, about 75% of Americans felt that there were important differences between the parties and about 85% cared about who won the presidential election. Both of these figures were all-time

Figure 14-6 Percentage Perceiving Important Differences and Caring
Who Wins Presidential Election, 1952–2004

Source: American National Election Studies

records, breaking the previous records set during the 2000 campaign. By way of
contrast, during the 1950s and 1960s, only about 50% of Americans perceived
important differences between the parties and only about 65% cared about who
won the presidential election.

Americans were more engaged in the 2004 presidential election than in any
presidential contest in the past fifty years. However, the high level of public
engagement in the 2004 election represented a continuation of a trend that began

Figure 14-7 Percentage Perceiving Important Differences and Caring
Who Wins by 2004 Bush Feeling Thermometer

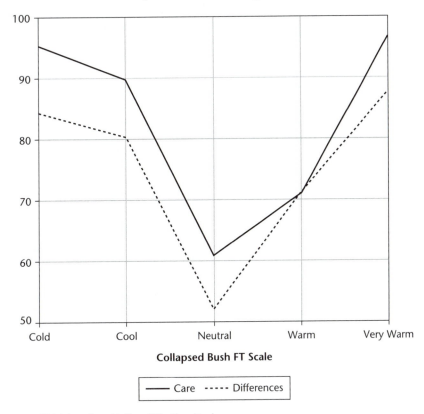

Source: 2004 American National Election Study

during the 1980s and 1990s. As the Democratic and Republican parties have
become more polarized and party identification in the electorate has become
more consistent with ideological identification and issue positions (Abramowitz
and Saunders 1998), voters have come to perceive a greater stake in the outcomes
of elections.

The extraordinary level of public engagement in the 2004 presidential election reflected the intense polarization of the electorate about George W. Bush.
Figure 14-7 displays the relationship between two measures of engagement—
perceptions of important party differences and concern about the outcome of the
election—and ratings of George W. Bush on the feeling thermometer scale. The
pattern is consistent with the polarization hypothesis: the more voters liked Bush
or disliked Bush, the more likely they were to perceive important differences and
care about the outcome of the election. The most engaged voters were those who
rated Bush either below 30 degrees (cold) or above 80 degrees (very warm) on

the feeling thermometer. These two groups made up over half of the electorate. The least engaged voters were those who were neutral toward Bush (50 degrees). However, this group made up less than 10% of the electorate.

Rather than turning off voters, these data suggest that the intense polarization of the American electorate over George W. Bush increased public engagement and stimulated participation in the 2004 election. As a further test of this hypothesis, we conducted logistic regression analyses of turnout and activism in the 2004 election. The dependent variable in the turnout analysis was simply whether a respondent reported voting in the presidential election. The dependent variable in the activism analysis was whether a respondent reported engaging in two or more campaign activities beyond voting. The independent variables in both analyses were age, education, family income, partisan intensity, ideological extremism, and intensity of feeling toward George W. Bush. Ideological extremism was measured by the absolute value of the difference between self-placement on the liberal-conservative scale and the centrist position of 4, with respondents who declined to place themselves on the scale assigned to the centrist position. Intensity of feeling toward Bush was measured by the absolute value of the difference between the Bush feeling thermometer score and 50, which is the neutral point on the feeling thermometer scale. The results of the logistic regression analyses are displayed in Table 14-10.

The results in Table 14-10 strongly support the polarization hypothesis. After controlling for age, education, family income, and partisanship, intensity of positive or negative feeling toward George Bush had a significant influence on turnout in the 2004 presidential election. According to these results, after controlling for all of the other independent variables in the model, an increase from

Table 14-10 Results of Logistic Regression Analyses of Turnout and Activism in 2004 Presidential Election

Independent Variable	Turnout Model			Activism Model		
	B (S.E.)	Change in Prob.	Sig.	B (S.E.)	Change in Prob.	Sig.
Age	.019 (.005)	.075	.001	.003 (.005)	.014	N.S.
Education	.377 (.070)	.148	.001	.161 (.056)	.086	.01
Income	.060 (.016)	.073	.001	.020 (.015)	.028	N.S.
Partisanship	.833 (.162)	.092	.001	.518 (.152)	.100	.001
Ideology	.112 (.102)	.033	N.S.	.364 (.085)	.124	.001
Bush FT	.014 (.006)	.061	.02	.029 (.006)	.146	.001

Source: 2004 American National Election Study

Note: Constant omitted. Ideology measured by extremism on 7-point ideological identification scale. Bush FT measured by absolute value of difference between Bush feeling thermometer score and 50. Change in probability is estimated change in probability of turnout or activism based on an increase from the 25th percentile to the 75th percentile on an independent variable with all other independent variables set at their medians.

the 25th to the 75th percentile on the Bush intensity scale was associated with an increase of 6.1% in the probability of voting. Both ideological extremism and intensity of positive or negative feeling toward Bush had significant effects on campaign activism in 2004 and the influence of Bush intensity on activism was much stronger than its influence on turnout. After controlling for all of the other independent variables in the model, an increase from the 25th to the 75th percentile on the Bush intensity scale was associated with an increase of 14.6% in the probability of engaging in campaign activism. This was the largest effect of any of the independent variables in the activism model.

Conclusions

The evidence presented in this article does not support Fiorina's assertion that polarization in America is largely a myth concocted by social scientists and media commentators. Fiorina argues that "we [ordinary Americans] instinctively seek the center while the parties and candidates hang out on the extremes" (2006, xiii). But it is mainly the least interested, least informed and least politically active members of the public who are clustered near the center of the ideological spectrum. The most interested, informed, and active citizens are much more polarized in their political views. Moreover, there are large differences in outlook between Democrats and Republicans, between red state voters and blue state voters, and between religious voters and secular voters. The high level of ideological polarization evident among political elites in the United States reflects real divisions within the American electorate.

Increasing polarization has not caused Americans to become disengaged from the political process. In 2004, according to data from the American National Election Studies, more Americans than ever perceived important differences between the political parties and cared about the outcome of the presidential election. As a result, voter turnout increased dramatically between 2000 and 2004, and record numbers of Americans engaged in campaign activities such as trying to influence their friends and neighbors, displaying bumper stickers and yard signs, and contributing money to the parties and candidates. The evidence indicates that rather than turning off the public and depressing turnout, polarization energizes the electorate and stimulates political participation.

Fiorina's claim that polarization is almost entirely an elite phenomenon has been warmly received by the mass media because it strongly appeals to the populist ethos of the nation. According to his argument, ordinary Americans are not to blame for the political divisiveness that the country has been experiencing. The American people are fundamentally moderate and sensible. It is only the elites and a "thin sliver" of activists who are at fault. Fiorina reinforces this point by using the rhetorical "we" throughout the book to refer to the American mass public. By using this device, he clearly means to identify himself with ordinary Americans who have been the innocent victims of extremist elites and activists.

Fiorina's theme of good people versus bad elites is as old as the nation itself. However, as the evidence presented in this paper shows, it is simplistic and misleading. Polarization in America is not just an elite phenomenon. The American people, especially those who care about politics, have also become much more polarized in recent years. To a considerable extent, the divisions that exist among policymakers in Washington reflect real divisions among the American people. When it comes to polarization, in the immortal words of Pogo, "we have met the enemy and he is us."

Appendix: Red, Purple, and Blue States in 2004 National Exit Poll

Red States (21)	Purple States (12)	Blue States (12)
Alabama	Colorado	California
Alaska	Florida	Connecticut
Arizona	Iowa	Delaware
Arkansas	Michigan	Illinois
Georgia	Minnesota	Maine
Idaho	Nevada	Maryland
Indiana	New Hampshire	Massachusetts
Kansas	New Mexico	New Jersey
Kentucky	Ohio	New York
Louisiana	Oregon	Rhode Island
Mississippi	Pennsylvania	Vermont
Missouri	Wisconsin	Washington
Montana		
Nebraska		
North Carolina		
Oklahoma		
South Carolina		
Tennessee		
Texas		
Utah		
Virginia		

Note: District of Columbia, Hawaii, North Dakota, South Dakota, West Virginia, and Wyoming not included in 2004 NEP sample.

Notes

1. None of the issue items except liberal-conservative identification are available for 2002. Therefore, all of the issue scales for the 2002–2004 decade are based exclusively on 2004 data. In constructing the polarization measure, 7-point scales were collapsed into three categories: 1–3, 4, and 5–7; respondents who declined to place themselves on a 7-point scale were assigned to the middle position on the scale; the 4-point abortion scale was recoded into three categories: 1–2 (conservative), 3 (moderate), and 4 (liberal).

2. The procedure followed here for collapsing the individual items has no effect on our comparison over time since we used the same procedure in every year. Moreover, using a simple additive index consisting of the same items produces nearly identical results concerning the trend in polarization between 1984 and 2004.

3. All of the issue questions except the death penalty question were collapsed into 3 categories (liberal, moderate, and conservative) before they were combined. On all of the 7-point scales, categories 1–3 and 5–7 were combined. On the 4-category abortion scale, categories 1–2 were combined. On the 4-category death penalty question, categories 1–2 and 3–4 were combined. All questions were coded in a conservative direction. We then computed a simple additive scale ranging from −16 to +16. This 33-point scale was collapsed into an 11-point scale by combining categories 1–3, 4–6, 7–9, 10–12, 13–15, 16–18, 19–21, 22–24, 25–27, 28–30, and 31–33.

4. Interest is measured by a single question asking about interest in the presidential campaign. Knowledge is measured by ten items, including questions about party control of the House and Senate, the jobs held by various political leaders, and ability to accurately place the presidential candidates on a liberal-conservative ideology scale and an abortion policy scale.

5. In order to measure political engagement over the entire time period between 1972 and 2004, we created an additive scale based on one question asking about interest in the campaign, one question asking how much respondents cared about the outcome of the presidential election, and an index of campaign activities. We coded those who scored at the upper end of this scale as politically engaged. The proportion of respondents classified as politically engaged ranged from 12% in 1956 to 26% in 2004.

6. A list of red states (those carried by Bush by more than 5 points), blue states (those carried by Kerry by more than 5 points), and purple states (those decided by 5 points or less) is provided in the appendix.

15. Polarization in the American Public: Misconceptions and Misreadings

Morris P. Fiorina, Samuel J. Abrams, and Jeremy C. Pope

Although we are surprised that Abramowitz and Saunders continue to advance arguments that we have rebutted in other publications, we are grateful to the *Journal* for providing another opportunity to address some misconceptions in the study of popular polarization. We will reply point by-point to the Abramowitz and Saunders critique, but given that our responses have been elaborated at length elsewhere, we refer interested readers to these sources for more detailed discussions (Fiorina and Abrams 2008; Fiorina, Abrams, and Pope 2006; Fiorina and Levendusky 2006).

Before proceeding, we emphasize one observation that partially vitiates several of the Abramowitz and Saunders criticisms. Much of the data they view as contradicting our conclusions consists of vote reports, election returns, and approval ratings. These variables obviously are of paramount political concern, but they cannot be used as evidence of polarization—for or against. As explained in *Culture War?* centrist voters can register polarized choices, and even if the beliefs and positions of voters remain constant, their voting decisions and political evaluations will appear more polarized when the positions candidates adopt and the actions elected officials take become more extreme.[1] When statistical relationships change, students of voting behavior have a tendency to locate the source of the change in voter attitudes, but unchanging voters may simply be responding to changes in candidate strategy and behavior. Abramowitz and Saunders exemplify this tendency and much of their critique goes astray as a result.

Abramowitz and Saunders Criticism 1: The American public is less moderate than we argue and has become even less so in recent years.

Fiorina and Levendusky (2006) have explained how the coding and aggregating procedures in Abramowitz and Saunders exaggerate attitudinal polarization. For present purposes, consider two types of raw data. First, the distribution of liberal conservative self-identification shows little change between the 1970s and the present. The ANES 7-point measure shows a slight drop in "don't knows" who are usually classified as moderates.[2] On the other hand, the GSS 7-point measure (which does not offer "or haven't you thought much about it?" as a response option) shows no change at all. A Gallup 5-point measure shows *more* moderates in the 2000s than in the 1970s.[3] While to some extent polarization is

Source: The Journal of Politics 70, 2 (April 2008): 556–560.

Table 15-1 No Polarization of Policy Views: 1984–2004

(Percentage Point Changes in Seven-Point Scale Position, 1984 to 2004)

Extremely Liberal ─────────────────────────────→ Extremely Conservative						
Left Shift						
Health Insurance	6%	2	3	0(–9)*	0	–2	–2
Spending/Services	5	4	5	–3(–5)	–3	–3	–2
Right Shift						
Aid to Blacks	0	–2	–5	–5(–7)	–1	6	8
Defense Spending	–5	–4	–3	–5(–4)	8	4	2
Polarization						
Jobs/Standard of Living	2	1	0	–2(–7)	0	1	3
No Change						
Abortion	1		–1			3	–1

*numbers in ( ) are changes when "don't knows" are treated as moderates

in the eye of the beholder, either the American population is not more ideologically polarized today than a generation ago, or it was already polarized a generation ago but no one noticed.

Second, consider the same ANES issue measures used by Abramowitz and Saunders. Table 15-1 lists the percentage point decline in each response category between 1984 and 2004—the end-point years for their measures of change.[4] Five scales offer seven positions running from the most liberal to the most conservative stance on the issue:

- More government services/higher spending—fewer services/less spending
- Government health insurance—private health insurance
- More government aid for blacks—blacks should help themselves
- Greatly decrease military spending—greatly increase spending
- Government guaranteed job and standard of living—get ahead on your own

A sixth item asks respondents to choose between four positions on abortion ranging from most to least restricted.

How much have the distributions changed? Not much. And what little change there is hardly suggests polarization. The standard deviations of the distributions tend to diminish slightly over time, and adopting the common-sense notion of polarization as a movement from the center toward the extremes, one searches in vain for evidence of increasing bimodality. On only one scale—government responsibility for jobs and standard of living—is there any evidence of polarization. Between 1984 and 2004 there is a small decline (two percentage points) in the number of people placing themselves in the exact center of the scale and a marginal increase in the number placing themselves on the left (three percentage points) and the right (four percentage points).

The other five issues do not show even this insignificant degree of rising polarization. On three of the scales there is a single-digit decline in the number of respondents who choose the exact middle of the scale, but on none of the scales does the middle lose to *both* extremes. Rather, on two scales the population shifted leftward. In 2004 11% more Americans favored government health insurance and 4% fewer favored private insurance than in 1984. A similar pattern holds for the choice between more public services versus lower public spending. In 2004 14% more Americans placed themselves on the liberal slide of the scale than in 1984 compared to 8% fewer on the conservative side.

On two other scales the population shifted rightward. On aid to minorities the right gained from the left and the middle—14% more Americans favor the two rightmost scale positions (individual initiative and self-help) in 2004 than in 1984. Military spending shows an even more notable shift. The doves lost 12% and the hawks gained 14%. Finally, the 4-position abortion scale shows virtually no change in popular opinion over the 20-year period. When Abramowitz and Saunders recode this raw data, aggregate it into an index, and recode again, they report a great deal of polarization, but the results clearly have little or no basis in the raw data.

Abramowitz and Saunders Criticism 2. Partisan polarization is greater and extends more deeply into the general public than we claim.

In recent decades some party polarization (or party sorting as we prefer to term it) certainly has occurred. That is, while population opinion distributions have changed little, party subpopulations have become more distinct as conservative identification declined among Democrats and liberal identification declined among Republicans (Abramowitz and Saunders 1998). Current discussion in the literature centers around the breadth (across issue domains) and depth (how deeply it extends into the population) of the sorting. There is general agreement that party elites have become significantly more distinct over the course of the past several decades—Democrats and Republicans in Congress show little or no overlap, for example. The picture for the general public is less clear. At one pole Abramowitz and Saunders construct an index that shows very highly differentiated parties. At another pole the Pew Center reports that between 1987 and 2007 the average difference between Republican and Democratic identifiers on 40 political and social issues increased from 10% to 14%, a surprisingly small difference (Figure 15-1).

We think the truth lies somewhere in between. The most detailed work is by Levendusky (2006) who analyzes party sorting on an issue-by-issue basis, finding a considerable amount of variability. Party sorting has proceeded far on some issues, less on others, and on some issues one party has become more homogeneous, while the other has not changed. Moreover, party sorting has proceeded much less in the general public than among party elites. The abortion issue is a striking example of the limits of party sorting. For two decades the

Figure 15-1 Mass Party Differences Have Increased Slightly

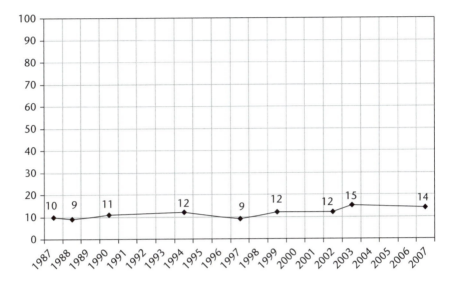

issue has served as an unofficial litmus test for presidential nominees. And sort-ing has clearly occurred among party identifiers (Adams 1997), although it took two decades after Roe for partisan majorities to get on their party's side of the issue. But consider the responses of *strong* Democrats and *strong* Republicans to the ANES abortion question in 2004: 10% of strong Democrats believe abor-tion should never be legal and another 23% only in cases of rape, incest, or threats to the mother's life—one-third of strong Democrats are seriously out of step with their party's platform. The picture is even more striking for strong Republicans: 23% believe abortion should *always* be legal and another 18% legal anytime there is a clear need. More than two-fifths of strong Republicans are pro-choice in the ordinary meaning of the term. Democratic elites may dance to the tune called by NARAL and Republican elites to the tune called by Focus on the Family, but one-third to two-fifths of their strongest adherents appear to be tone-deaf.

> *Abramowitz and Saunders Criticism 3. "Fiorina claims that there has been little increase in geographical polarization in recent decades and the differences between red states and blue states have been greatly exaggerated."*

Of the second assertion there can be no doubt: when the red-blue map first appeared in 2000 the media grossly exaggerated the differences between red and blue states. Contrary to claims of a country split down the middle, in 2004 on only one of the many policy issues included in the ANES did majorities in red and blue states disagree—on the newer and somewhat esoteric issue of homosexual adoption (Fiorina, Abrams, and Pope 2006, 49). We stand by our demonstration that red-blue differences were and continue to be exaggerations.

In their objection, Abramowitz and Saunders adopt a scattershot approach, throwing out numerous variables and hoping that readers will find something convincing (see their Table 14-6). The usual sociological factoids appear—gun ownership, union membership, Evangelical self-classification, and so on. But the correlations between most such measures and political positions are weaker than usually presumed. For example, in 2004 more than one-third of gun owners voted for John Kerry, as did slightly less than one-third of white evangelicals. Political differences are generally much smaller than sociological differences might suggest. Other evidence Abramowitz and Saunders present consists of election returns and performance ratings, which, as we have indicated, cannot be used to measure polarization.

In *Culture War?*, we did not take a position on the argument that Americans have become increasingly geographically sorted, although we took brief note of that argument and its critics (Bishop 2004; cf. Klinkner 2004). Several more recent studies report little or no evidence of increasing geographic polarization (Glaeser and Ward 2006; Klinkner and Hapanowicz 2005; Evans and Nunn 2006). We still have no position in this debate although it does seem to us unlikely that Massachusetts and Mississippi voters differed less before the jet plane, broadcast TV, and the internet than they do today.

Finally, if red-blue polarization was as deep as Abramowitz and Saunders believe it to be, why would voting patterns for other offices not produce exactly the same red-blue map that presidential voting does? But blue states elect Republican governors and red states elect Democratic governors. And half the states have divided party control of state government. Such differing voting patterns indicate that when the parties offer different candidates who emphasize different issues and take different positions, the same voters vote differently (Fiorina and Abrams 2008).

Abramowitz and Saunders Criticism 4: Fiorina claims "that economic cleavages remain as important or more important than religious cleavages . . . Among white voters in the United States, the religious divide is now much deeper than the class divide."

On the contrary, what we actually wrote was "We do not wish to draw any firm conclusions about the relative importance of income and religious differences in contemporary elections. Such an estimate of relative importance would require a far more elaborate analysis than we have carried out . . . " (Fiorina, Abrams, and Pope 2006, 137). Abramowitz and Saunders do not provide such an analysis. Their logistic regression analysis completely ignores our demonstration

(2006, 177–179) that the coefficients in such an analysis can reflect the positions of the candidates, not any change in the relative importance the voters attach to the issues.

As for more elaborate analyses than we carried out, some have since been reported (Ansolabehere, Rodden, and Snyder 2006; Bartels 2006), the findings of which contradict Abramowitz and Saunders on the relative importance of economics and religion.[5] The more general point to keep in mind is that the importance of an issue depends both on a voter's concern about that issue and the choice that the candidates offer her. As we asked in *Culture War?* (2006, 179–181), in 1992 did tens of millions of voters suddenly decide that religion was more important to them than they had previously realized, or did the increasing secularization of the Democratic Party and the capture of the Republican Party by social conservatives lead voters to see religion and morality as more relevant than when Michael Dukakis, Walter Mondale, and Jimmy Carter were Democratic nominees and Bush 41, Reagan, and Ford were their Republican opponents?

Abramowitz and Saunders Criticism 5: "Americans were more engaged in the 2004 presidential election than in any presidential contest in the past 50 years."

Let's not get carried away here. Yes, turnout in 2004 surged to levels not seen since the 1960s. Perceptions of party differences and concern over the outcome both increased—a natural consequence of more polarized candidate choices. There was an increase in low-cost activity such as talking about the election and wearing a button or displaying a bumper sticker. But by other ANES measures 2004 looks little different from other presidential elections of the past generation. Time-intensive activities like working for a party or candidate and attending a meeting or rally were at perfectly normal single digit levels, and the financial sacrifice entailed by writing a check increased only a little (Fiorina and Levendusky 2006).

Moreover, in arguing for a record level of engagement Abramowitz and Saunders completely ignore an obvious alternative hypothesis: mobilization. In recent presidential elections the parties have implemented a much more intensive "ground game." Their activities are reflected in ANES reports about party contacts which jumped in the past two elections—eight percentage points between 2000 and 2004. Note that interest in the campaign was well within normal levels. Increases in undemanding campaign activities without corresponding increases in campaign interest are consistent with a mobilization hypothesis. Rather than a record number of newly engaged Americans jumping into the 2004 campaign, more of them than usual may have been pushed.

We are perfectly willing—indeed happy—to recognize that our fear that polarized politics will demobilize the more reasonable portions of the electorate, does not seem to be occurring, a salutary development should it continue. But to confidently assert the opposite, as Abramowitz and Saunders do, is at the very least, highly premature.

Summary

Abramowitz and Saunders contend that the electorate as a whole is less moderate than we believe and that partisans are far more deeply polarized than we believe. If one examines the data without resort to multiple recodings and aggregations, their case disappears. Regarding geographic polarization, Abramowitz and Saunders argue that we have understated its extent and that such polarization is increasing. We continue to believe that the red-blue divide is a misleading exaggeration, and we note that recent research on changes in geographic polarization indicates that they are wrong. Regarding religious polarization, Abramowitz and Saunders claim that our claim that economic differences are deeper than religious differences is wrong. We made no such claim, and again, recent research indicates that their claim is wrong. Finally, Abramowitz and Saunders argue that polarization enhances citizen engagement. Their evidence is based on one election, and it neglects to consider an obvious alternative hypothesis. All in all, their critique provides no reason to revise the conclusions of *Culture War?*

Notes

1 See especially (2006, 25–32, 170–182). The opposite is true as well, of course, voter beliefs and positions could change but their votes and evaluations might not change if the parties and candidates acted in such a way as to offset the voter changes. The general point is that the interpretation of votes and evaluations requires information on both the voters and the candidates/parties.

2 As Converse (2006) notes, declining response rates may result in somewhat more informed samples today compared to earlier decades.

3 For graphs of the data see Fiorina and Abrams (2008).

4 As pointed out by Fiorina and Levendusky (2006), most of the change between 1984 and 2004 comes between 2000 and 2004. While journalists often take the results of one election as indicative of the arrival of a new political world, political scientists should be more cautious.

5 Indeed, McCarty, Poole, and Rosenthal report that "born again and evangelical Christians are particularly sensitive to income effects on political preferences" (2006, 107–108).

16. The 2008 Election: Polarization Continues

Alan I. Abramowitz

On November 4, 2008, in one of the most remarkable elections in American history, Barack Obama, the son of a white mother from Kansas and a black father from Kenya, was chosen to be the forty-fourth president of the United States. On his way to becoming the nation's first African-American president, the junior senator from Illinois had to overcome not just racial prejudice but persistent rumors that he was a Muslim and widespread doubts about his readiness for national office. Despite these concerns, a nation in the throes of a severe economic crisis and fighting two prolonged and costly wars voted decisively for a candidate who promised major changes in both domestic and foreign policy. Barack Obama would become not just the first African-American president, but the first non-Southern Democratic president in almost half a century. The election results reflected the dire condition of the U.S. economy and widespread discontent with the incumbent Republican president but also deep divisions in American society—divisions based on geography, age, race, and above all, partisanship.

A Deepening Red-Blue Divide

At precisely 11 p.m. Eastern Standard Time on November 4, just as the polls closed in California, Oregon, and Washington, all of the major television networks and news services declared Barack Obama to be the winner of the 2008 presidential election. After more than a year of campaigning, it took only a few hours of vote-counting to determine that Obama would have the 270 electoral votes that he needed to become the forty-fourth president of the United States. In fact, he would eventually receive 365 electoral votes, the largest total since Bill Clinton in 1996. It was an impressive victory, but a close examination of the 2008 electoral map reveals that the Democratic tide was far from uniform.

In *Culture War? The Myth of a Polarized America,* Morris Fiorina and his collaborators (Fiorina, Abrams, and Pope 2006, chapter 3) argue that political differences between the red and blue states are often exaggerated by pundits and academics. But the evidence from the 2008 election shows that with regard to presidential candidate preference, the red-blue divide was larger than at any time in the past half-century. The Obama-Biden ticket carried many states by landslide or near-landslide margins, including several of the most populous states. The Democrats carried California by 24 points, New York by 27 points, Illinois

Source: This piece is an original essay commissioned for this volume.

by 25 points, Michigan by 16 points, and New Jersey by 16 points. Of the twenty-eight states carried by the Democrats, the margin of victory was greater than 10 points in twenty-two states and less than 5 points in only four states. Yet despite the decisive Democratic victory in the election, many states voted for the Republican ticket by landslide or near-landslide margins. Of the twenty-two states carried by John McCain, the margin of victory was greater than 10 points in fifteen states and less than 5 points in only two states. And while the nation as a whole was moving in a Democratic direction between 2004 and 2008, Republicans managed to increase their margin of victory in Oklahoma, Arkansas, Louisiana, and Tennessee.

The overall picture that emerges from an examination of the 2008 electoral map is one of a country that had moved decisively in a Democratic direction since 2004 but that remained deeply divided. There were more blue states and fewer red states, but the divide between the two was even deeper than in 2004. Across all fifty states, the average margin of victory for the winning presidential candidate increased from 13.9 points in 2004 to 16.2 points in 2008: the average margin of victory for Obama was 16.8 points, while the average margin of victory for McCain was 15.4 points. There were more landslide and near-landslide states and fewer closely contested states: the number of states in which the winning candidate's margin of victory was greater than 15 points increased from twenty-one to twenty-six, while the number in which the winning candidate's margin of victory was less than 5 points decreased from eleven to six. Of the seven most populous states, only Florida and Ohio were decided by less than 5 points while New York, California, and Illinois were decided by more than 20 points.

There was wide divergence in support for the presidential candidates across states and regions of the country. Although Obama made inroads into the Republican Party's Southern base by carrying Virginia, North Carolina, and Florida, McCain carried the other eight states of the old Confederacy along with the border states of Kentucky, West Virginia, and Oklahoma, winning most of them by double-digit margins. Altogether, McCain won 54 percent of the vote in the South while Obama won 57 percent of the vote in the rest of the country. The election was a landslide for Obama outside of the South and a near-landslide for McCain in the South.

The high degree of geographic polarization in 2008 is consistent with the pattern evident in other recent presidential elections, including the 2004 election, but it represents a dramatic change from the voting patterns of the 1960s and 1970s as the evidence in Table 16-1 demonstrates. In the competitive 1960 and 1976 elections, for example, there were far more closely contested states and far fewer landslide states than in recent presidential elections. In 1960, twenty states were decided by less than 5 points and only nine by more than 15 points; in 1976, twenty states were decided by less than 5 points and only ten by more than 15 points. And in both of those elections, all of the most populous states were closely contested, including California, New York, Illinois, and Texas. The divisions between red states and blue states are far deeper today than they were

Table 16-1 Geographic Polarization in 1960, 1976, 2004, and 2008 Presidential
Elections

State Margin	1960	1976	2004	2008
0–4.99%	20	20	11	6
5–9.99%	14	11	10	9
10–14.99%	7	9	8	9
15% +	9	10	21	26
Total	50	50	50	50
Swing-State Electoral Votes	256	298	114	87
Landslide-State Electoral Votes	71	63	183	274

Source: http://uselectionatlas.org.

thirty or forty years ago.[1] As a result, far fewer states and far fewer electoral votes are actually in play in presidential elections.

Growing Generational and Racial Divides and a Continuing Religious Divide

Geography was not the only major divide in the 2008 election. The choice between Obama and McCain also divided Americans along generational, racial, and religious lines. Contrary to the claim made by Fiorina and his collaborators that demographic divisions have been diminishing over time (Fiorina, Abrams, and Pope 2006, 58–61), the generational and racial divides in candidate preference were both the largest in recent history and the religious divide among white voters was at least as large as in 2004 despite a Republican nominee who generated little enthusiasm among evangelical voters.

Data from national exit polls indicate that Obama did better than the Democrats' 2004 nominee, John Kerry, among many voting groups, including men and women, college graduates and nongraduates, and lower- and upper-income voters. However, Obama's gains were much greater among some groups than others. While nonwhites and younger voters of all races flocked to Obama's banner, older whites found Obama's message much less compelling. Obama carried voters under the age of thirty by a margin of 34 points versus only 9 points for Kerry. However, he did slightly worse than Kerry among voters over the age of sixty-five, losing that group by 8 points versus 6 points for Kerry. As a result, the generation gap in candidate preference was much larger in 2008 than in 2004. In fact, the difference between the youngest and oldest age groups was by far the largest in the history of national exit polls going back to 1972. The youth vote was a major factor in Obama's decisive victory: based on the national exit poll results, we can estimate that voters under the age of thirty provided Obama with a plurality of almost 8 million votes which was more than 80 percent of his overall popular vote margin.

Obama also made much larger gains among African-American and Hispanic voters than among white voters. In addition to increasing African-American turnout, Obama won a substantially larger share of the African-American vote than did Kerry—95 percent versus 88 percent. However, the most dramatic improvement in Democratic performance between 2004 and 2008 occurred among Hispanic voters. According to the exit poll data, Obama won 66 percent of the Hispanic vote versus Kerry's 54 percent. In contrast, the improvement in Democratic performance among white voters was much smaller. Obama received 43 percent of the white vote versus Kerry's 41 percent. The-52 point difference in candidate preference between whites and blacks in 2008 was the largest since 1984.

No Democratic presidential candidate since Lyndon Johnson has won a majority of the white vote, so the fact that Obama lost the white vote was hardly surprising. Obama's 12-point deficit among white voters was identical to that of Al Gore in 2000. However, the fact that white voters favored the Republican presidential candidate by a double-digit margin in 2008 despite the poor condition of the economy and the extraordinary unpopularity of the incumbent Republican president suggests that racial attitudes had an impact on the level of white support for the Democratic candidate.

White support for Obama varied dramatically across regions and states, ranging from a low of around 10 percent in the Deep South to close to 60 percent in parts of the Northeast and West. In many states outside the South, Obama did substantially better than Kerry among white voters. Between 2004 and 2008, the Democratic share of the white vote increased by 5 points in California and Washington, 7 points in Michigan and Wisconsin, 8 points in Colorado, 9 points in Oregon, and 11 points in Indiana. In many Southern and border South states, however, Obama did no better or worse than Kerry among white voters. Between 2004 and 2008, the Democratic share of the white vote fell by 4 points in Mississippi, 6 points in Arkansas, 9 points in Alabama, and 10 points in Louisiana. More than forty years after the passage of the Voting Rights Act, the racial divide in much of the South remained enormous, with blacks overwhelmingly Democratic and whites overwhelmingly Republican.

There is little doubt that discomfort with the idea of an African-American president played a role in limiting white support for Obama, especially in the Deep South and in some of the Border South states. Otherwise it is difficult to understand why Obama did worse than Kerry among white voters in these states. But Obama's losses among whites in the South and Border South were offset by gains among white voters in other parts of the country and by extraordinary turnout and support for Obama among nonwhites. Based on the National Exit Poll results, we can estimate that white voters gave McCain a plurality of close to twelve million votes in 2008. While this was somewhat smaller than George W. Bush's plurality among white voters in 2004, it was more than a million votes larger than Bush's plurality among white voters in 2000. Yet Obama won the national popular vote by more than 9.5 million votes while Gore only won the national popular vote by about half a million votes in 2000. The difference between 2000 and 2008 was that Obama's margin among nonwhites was more than ten million votes larger than Gore's margin among nonwhites.

The 2008 results also revealed a continuing religious divide among white voters. According to data from the American National Election Studies (ANES), Obama won 56 percent of the vote among whites who reported that they seldom or never attended religious services, a slight improvement over the 52 percent that Kerry received from this group. But Obama won only 27 percent of the vote among whites who reported attending religious services every week or almost every week, a 5-point decline from the 32 percent that Kerry received from this group. As a result, the gap in candidate preference between these two groups grew from 20 points in 2004 to 29 points in 2008. And this occurred despite widespread dissatisfaction with McCain among conservative evangelicals and a high-profile effort by Obama to reach out to the evangelical community.

Evolving Party Coalitions and Deepening Partisan Divisions

Ideological realignment and the growth of the nonwhite electorate have dramatically altered the composition of the Democratic and Republican electoral coalitions over the past three decades. A comparison of exit poll data from the 1976, 1992, and 2008 elections shows that the coalition that elected Obama was very different from the coalition that elected Clinton and even more different from the coalition that elected Jimmy Carter. And while the changes in the composition of the Republican electoral coalition have not been as great, it is also clear that the coalition that supported McCain was quite different from the coalitions that supported George H. W. Bush and Gerald Ford.

The racial and ideological divisions between the parties in the electorate are far deeper today than they were in the 1970s or even the 1990s. On the Democratic side, the proportion of moderate-to-conservative whites has decreased considerably while the contributions of liberal whites and especially nonwhites have increased. While moderate-to-conservative whites made up a majority of those who voted for Carter, they comprised barely a quarter of those who voted for Obama. Nonwhites, who made up less than a fifth of Carter's voters, comprised more than a third of Obama's voters. On the Republican side, the proportion of conservative whites has risen from 58 percent in 1976 to 70 percent in 2008 while the proportion of moderate-to-liberal whites has fallen from 38 percent in 1976 to 25 percent in 2008. And despite the dramatic growth of the nonwhite electorate over the past three decades, the nonwhite share of the Republican vote has been stagnant, going from 4 percent in 1976 and 9 percent in 1992 to 6 percent in 2008.

As a result of these trends, the electoral base of the Democratic Party is now dominated by white liberals and nonwhites. In 2008, these two groups made up 73 percent of Democratic voters but only 11 percent of Republican voters. On the other hand, the electoral base of the Republican Party is now dominated by white conservatives. In 2008 this group made up 70 percent of Republican voters but only 9 percent of Democratic voters. Fiorina and his collaborators refer to the transformation of the party coalitions over the past several decades as "sorting" and claim that it is different from polarization, but this transformation has been one of the most important drivers of polarization in the public. In fact, the partisan divide underlies almost all of the other divisions within the public including the gender gap, the marriage gap, the generation gap, and the religious gap.

Explaining the Deep Partisan Divide:
Polarized Choices or Polarized Preferences?

According to Fiorina and his collaborators, the intense partisanship that has characterized the American electorate in recent years was not caused by deep ideological divisions within the public but by Democratic and Republican politicians presenting the electorate with polarized choices that made it appear that the electorate was deeply divided (Fiorina et al., 2006, chapter 9). The politicians and their activist supporters were polarized, not the voters. So when the 2008 Democratic and Republican presidential candidates both promised to campaign in red states and blue states and to seek support from Democrats, Republicans, and independents, one might have expected these partisan divisions to diminish.

An examination of voting patterns in 2008 indicates that this did not occur, however. Even without George W. Bush on the ballot, the partisan divide within the electorate was as large in 2008 as in 2004. According to the 2008 ANES, 91 percent of Democratic identifiers and leaners voted for Obama while 90 percent of Republican identifiers and leaners voted for McCain. Moreover, evidence from other national surveys shows that the partisan divide within the electorate was not just a result of polarized choices. This evidence shows that the voters themselves were sharply divided on major issues in the election including the war in Iraq, health care, abortion, and gay marriage.

In a *Time* magazine poll conducted October 3–6, 2008, approximately one thousand likely voters were asked for their opinions on ten policy issues including abortion, gay marriage, the war in Iraq, climate change, and health care.[2] On each issue, respondents were asked to place themselves on a 0–10 scale with 0 indicating strong opposition and 10 indicating strong support for a specific position. Table 16-2 displays the distribution of opinion on nine issues on which the liberal and conservative positions could be identified.[3] The results indicate that on some of the most important issues in the election, public opinion was highly polarized, with far more likely voters placing themselves near the extremes (0–1 or 9–10) than near the center (4–6). Those with extreme views outnumbered those with centrist views by 41 percent to 28 percent on the issue of climate change, 50 percent to 22 percent on the issue of health care, 52 percent to 19 percent on the issue of Iraq, 70 percent to 16 percent on the issue of abortion, and 72 percent to 14 percent on the issue of gay marriage. There were only two issues—business tax

Table 16-2 Distribution of Public Opinion on Nine Policy Issues

Issue	Strongly Liberal (0–1)	Liberal (2–3)	Centrist (4–6)	Conservative (7–8)	Strongly Conservative (9–10)
Gay Marriage	31%	7	14	6	41
Abortion	43%	9	16	4	27
Iraq War	30%	14	19	15	22
Offshore Drilling	10%	7	19	17	47
Health Care	30%	18	22	10	20
Financial Regulation	36%	21	25	6	11
Climate Change	30%	23	28	7	12
Business Tax Cuts	12%	9	37	20	22
Mortgage Assistance	18%	18	38	10	16
Average of 9 Issues	27%	14	24	11	24

Source: Time Magazine poll, Oct. 3–6, 2008.

Note: Likely voters only.

cuts and home mortgage assistance—on which more likely voters placed themselves close to the center of the scale than close to the extremes. Across all nine issues, an average of 51 percent of likely voters placed themselves close to one extreme or the other, while only 24 percent placed themselves close to the center.

The high degree of polarization of public opinion on some of the major issues in the 2008 election reflected the existence of deep divisions between supporters of the two parties. For example, only 12 percent of Obama supporters favored keeping U.S. troops in Iraq without a withdrawal timetable versus 77 percent of McCain supporters. Similarly, 84 percent of Obama supporters favored a government guarantee of health insurance for all Americans versus only 19 percent of McCain supporters, 76 percent of Obama supporters favored a woman's unrestricted right to choose an abortion during the first three months of pregnancy versus only 29 percent of McCain voters, 84 percent of Obama supporters favored stronger policies to reduce the threat of climate change even if the economic costs were high versus 36 percent of McCain voters, and 64 percent of Obama supporters favored legalizing same-sex marriage versus only 14 percent of McCain voters.

Moreover, opinions on many of these issues were closely connected. For example, opinions on climate change were strongly related to opinions on health care: the correlation between opinions on these two issues was a robust .59. Seventy-one percent of those who took a liberal position on climate change also took a liberal position on health care, while 72 percent of those who took a conservative position on climate change also took a conservative position on health care. As a result, these opinions tended to reinforce each other, pushing voters in the same partisan direction.

As Philip Converse (1964) first noted in his seminal article, "The Nature of Belief Systems in Mass Publics," the degree of consistency or constraint in opinions across issues is an important indicator of ideological thinking in the electorate. Converse found little evidence of such ideological thinking in the electorate of the 1950s, and according to Fiorina and his collaborators not much has changed in the decades since then: despite rising education levels and a growing ideological divide at the elite level, they claim that Americans today "are not very well-informed about politics, do not hold many of their views very strongly, and are not ideological" (Fiorina et al., 2006, 19). However, the evidence from the *Time* poll does not support this conclusion. This evidence shows that there was actually a high degree of constraint in opinions across many of the key issues in the 2008 election, indicating that a large proportion of voters were responding to these issues on the basis of an underlying liberal or conservative ideology.

Opinions on seven policy issues in the *Time* poll were correlated strongly enough to create a coherent liberal-conservative issues scale. The seven issues included in the scale were abortion, gay marriage, health insurance, offshore oil drilling, global warming, the war in Iraq, and regulation of financial institutions. The average correlation among these seven issues is an impressive .43 and the scale has a reliability coefficient (Cronbach's alpha) of .84, which is well above the generally accepted minimum of .70. Scores on the scale ranged from 0 for those who took the most conservative position on all seven issues to 70 for those who took the most liberal position on all seven issues. I then collapsed the scale by combining scores of 0–10, 11–20, 21–30, 31–40, 41–50, 51–60, and 61–70 to form a seven-point scale with 1 the most conservative score and 7 the most liberal score. Nine percent of likely voters were classified as extremely conservative (1), 16 percent as very conservative (2), 12 percent as slightly conservative (3), 16 percent as moderate (4), 17 percent as slightly liberal (5), 19 percent as strongly liberal (6), and 10 percent as extremely liberal (7).

The validity of this seven-point liberal-conservative issues scale is demonstrated by the fact that it strongly predicted presidential candidate preference: 93 percent of those on the liberal side of the scale (5–7) supported Obama, while 92 percent of those on the conservative side of the scale (1–3) supported McCain. The relatively small group of moderates split their support almost evenly between the two candidates with 53 percent favoring McCain and 47 percent favoring Obama. Moreover, the ideological divide between supporters of the two candidates was deepest among the most politically engaged members of the electorate—those whose opinions would be of the greatest concern to candidates and elected officials.

Figure 16-1 shows the distribution of Obama and McCain supporters on the seven-point issues scale for two sets of voters: those with low and high scores on a five-item political knowledge test. Altogether, 36 percent of likely voters in the *Time* poll received low scores (0–2) on this political knowledge test while 64 percent received high scores (3–5). The results in Figure 16-1 show that

Figure 16-1 Ideological Orientations of Obama and McCain Voters by Political Knowledge

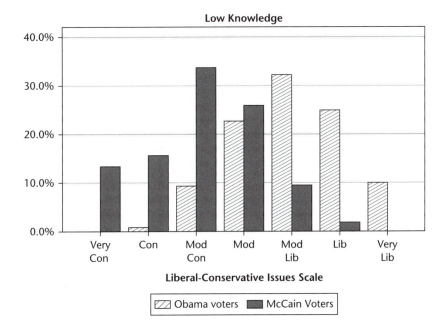

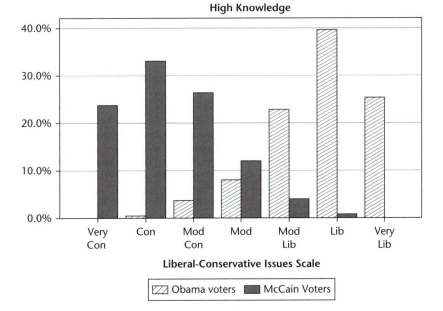

Source: Time Magazine poll, Oct. 3–6, 2008

the better-informed voters were far more polarized along ideological lines than the minority less-informed voters. In the low-information group, there was considerable overlap between supporters of the two candidates. In the high-information group, there was almost no overlap: 88 percent of informed Obama supporters were on the liberal side of the scale compared with only 5 percent of informed McCain supporters; 83 percent of informed McCain supporters were on the conservative side of the scale compared with only 4 percent of informed Obama supporters.

Constraint, Ideological Thinking, and the Rise of Polarization

Fiorina and Abrams (this volume) argue that the fact that there has been little change in the distribution of responses on individual issues in ANES surveys over the past three decades shows that there has been no increase in ideological thinking or polarization in the American public. But this claim ignores one of the most important changes in American public opinion during this time period—the growing consistency of Americans' opinions across different issues as well as between their issue positions and their party identification. We have already seen striking evidence of constraint in voters' opinions across a wide range of issues in the 2008 *Time Magazine* poll. Data from ANES surveys also show clear evidence of growing constraint in voters' issue positions over time. For example, between 1980 and 2008 the correlation between voters' opinions on the issues of health insurance and defense spending increased from .10 to .36, the correlation between their opinions on government guaranteed jobs and health insurance increased from .33 to .52, and the correlation between their opinions on abortion and health insurance increased from .04 to .21. Not only are Americans much better "sorted" by party today, but their opinions on different issues are much more consistent today, and greater consistency across issues means greater polarization in the public just as it does in the Congress.

No Disconnect between the Political Elite and the Public: The Case of Health Care Reform

Since January of 2009 a number of political commentators have expressed disappointment at the continued bickering and lack of cooperation between Democratic and Republican leaders in Washington. But calls for bipartisanship ignore the deep ideological divide between the two parties today. And based on the opinions expressed by Democratic and Republican voters in 2008, Democratic and Republican leaders are accurately representing the views of their parties' supporters—especially their parties' politically engaged supporters. Nowhere is this more evident than on what has emerged as the most important and contentious policy issue facing the country in 2009 and beyond: health care reform.

Figure 16-2 Opinions of Democratic and Republican Voters on Health Care Reform

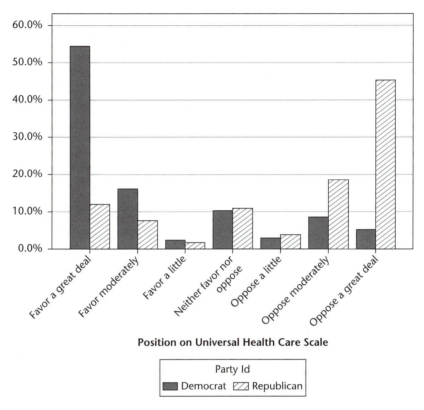

Position on Universal Health Care Scale

| Party Id |
| Democrat ▨ Republican |

Source: 2008 Amercian National Election Study

Figure 16-2 displays the opinions of Democratic and Republican voters on the ANES health care policy scale. The ANES question asked respondents to place themselves on a seven-point scale indicating support or opposition to a plan to have the federal government pay for all of the cost of medical care for Americans. The results demonstrate that even before the debate over health care reform began in earnest in Washington, the American public was deeply divided over this issue with Democratic identifiers and leaners overwhelmingly supporting a universal health care plan and Republican identifiers and leaners overwhelmingly opposing such a plan: almost three-fourths of Democrats placed themselves at 1 or 2 on the scale while almost two-thirds of Republicans placed themselves at 6 or 7. Contrary to the argument of Fiorina and his collaborators, there is no disconnect between the political elite and the public on this issue. The deep partisan divide in Washington reflects a real and deep partisan divide within the American electorate.

Notes

1. For an in-depth analysis of the new regional divisions in American politics, see Black and Black (2007).
2. For this survey, interviews were conducted by landline and cellular telephone with 1,053 registered likely voters. The data and documentation are available at the Roper Center Website: www.ropercenter.uconn.edu, Study USSRBI2008–4567.
3. It was not clear what the liberal and conservative positions were on the issue of government bailouts of major financial institutions as positions on this issue were uncorrelated with either ideological identification or party identification.

17. Where's the Polarization?

Morris P. Fiorina and Samuel J. Abrams

During the past decade, political commentators repeatedly claimed that the United States had become a polarized nation. More often than not, such claims failed to specify their terms. Polarized relative to what? To other countries? To our own past? What is polarized? American lifestyles? Ideologies? Positions on the issues? Approval ratings and vote choices? And most fundamentally, what, exactly, does polarization mean? In this brief article we seek to clarify the debate, addressing the preceding questions in reverse order.

What Is Polarization?

Polarization is not a synonym for disagreement. The raw material of politics is disagreement; if there were no disagreement about what government should do and how it should do it, politics would be unnecessary. For public opinion to be polarized, two conditions must be met. First, the substance of the disagreement must be major. Second, the public must be closely divided. For example, if 90 percent of the electorate strongly supports Social Security in its present form and the remaining 10 percent wish to abolish the program, that is not polarization: although the substantive disagreement is major, only a small minority holds one of the positions. Or if 50 percent of the electorate thinks that the Social Security retirement age should be 66 and the other 50 percent thinks it should be raised to 67, that is not polarization: although the public is evenly split, the substance of the disagreement is minor.

Figure 17-1 contrasts two hypothetical public opinion distributions that capture the preceding notions. In both panels, the electorate is split down the middle—half left of center, half right of center. But while most people would judge the top panel to be an instance of polarization, few would judge the bottom panel to be an example. In the top panel most of the electorate is clustered at the extremes of the opinion scale, whereas in the bottom panel most of the electorate is clustered in the center.

Does the distribution of American public opinion look like the hypothetical distribution in the top panel of Figure 17-1, as numerous commentators claim? No. Most public opinion distributions look more like the bottom panel than the top panel, including those in the purportedly polarized 2004 and 2008 elections. Consider the familiar seven-point liberal-conservative scale included in the American National Election Studies (ANES) and the General Social Survey

Source: This piece is an original essay commissioned for this volume.

Figure 17-1 Polarized and Nonpolarized Distributions

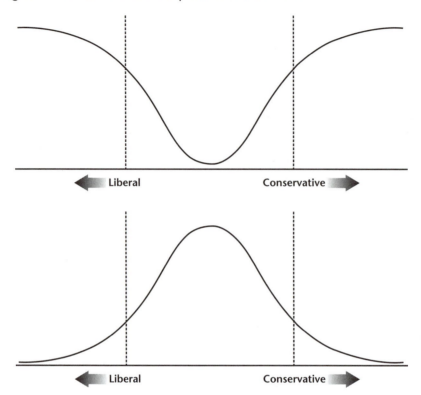

(GSS). The allowable responses run from extremely conservative to extremely liberal with moderate or middle of the road in between. Political scientists customarily recode "don't know" responses as moderate. If that convention is followed, Figure 17-2a shows that in 2008, the American public was overwhelmingly centrist according to either survey.[1] If the "don't know" responses are kept separate, Figure 17-2b shows more variation in ideological responses, but moderate and don't know are the two largest categories in the ANES and the diagrams clearly resemble the bottom panel in Figure 17-1 more than the top panel.

Of course, political scientists have known for nearly half a century that the American public is not very ideological (Converse 1964) and, as shown in the ANES "haven't thought much about it" response category, the labels mean little or nothing to a significant fraction of the public. So, alternatively, consider the electorate's views on specific issues that were included in the 2008 ANES. As shown in Figure 17-3, on a series of important contemporary issues the shape of public opinion looks much closer to the bottom panel in Figure 17-1 than to the top panel, with Americans bunching up near the center rather than clustering at

Figure 17-2a No Ideological Polarization in 2008

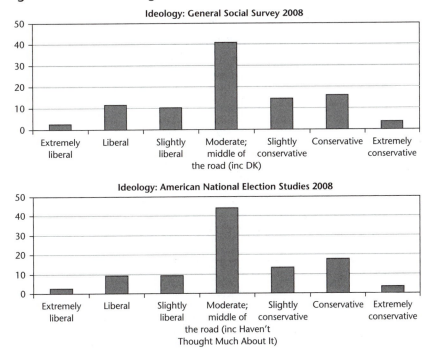

Figure 17-2b No Ideological Polarization in 2008

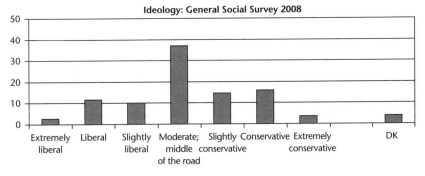

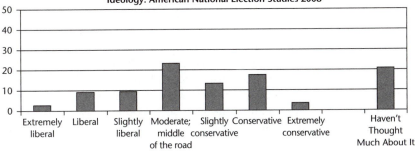

Figure 17-3a No Polarization on Policy Issues in 2008*

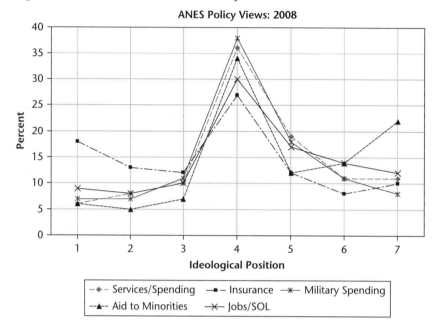

Source: 2008 ANES.

*"Haven't thought much about it" responses recoded as moderates.

opposite extremes. The picture of a centrist electorate is overwhelmingly evident when the convention of coding "don't knows" as "middle of the roaders" is followed (Figure 17-3a), but it is also clear when these responses are treated separately (Figure 17-3b).

All in all, the available evidence suggests an unambiguous conclusion. Considering their general ideological self-locations, as well as their attitudes on specific public policy issues, the American electorate in 2008 is much better described as centrist than as polarized.

Has Polarization Increased?

Even if public opinion has not yet reached a stage that merits description as polarized, perhaps the claims of journalist and politicos reflect movement of public opinion in that direction. This claim requires that we look at trends over time rather than a snapshot of 2008. Referring back to Figure 17-1, if public opinion is changing away from the shape in the bottom panel toward the shape in the top panel, it would be appropriate to characterize such movement as polarizing even if it still more closely resembled the shape of the bottom panel. Is there evidence of such movement? No.

Figure 17-3b No Polarization on Policy Issues in 2008*

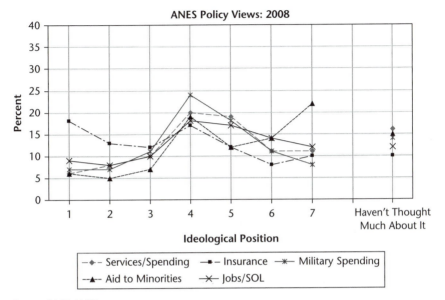

Source: 2008 ANES.
*"Haven't thought much about it" responses indicated separately.

Consider Figure 17-4, which plots the percentage of respondents choosing "moderate" or "middle-of-the-road" positions on the ideological self-placement items in the ANES and GSS surveys, as well as analogous items in two well-known commercial surveys—Gallup and Harris. Since the 1970s the ANES shows a slight decline in moderates (which mainly reflects a decline in the "haven't thought much about it" category), Gallup shows a slight increase in moderates, and GSS and Harris show little change. It seems safe to say that there is no evidence that the ideological orientations of Americans have polarized over the course of the past generation.

The same is true for their views on specific issues. Table 17-1 reports the percentage-point changes in each of the seven categories of the ANES policy issue scales from Figure 17-3. These were first asked in the 1984 survey, twenty-four years and seven presidential elections ago. The changes are small for the most part and do not show the kind of consistency one might expect from the 2008 election outcome. On two issues, health care and the trade-off between government spending and government services, we see a shift to the left. On health care the public shows a 17-percentage point net leftward movement between 1984 and 2008, with 12 percent more respondents on the left side of the scale (government insurance plan) and 5 percent fewer respondents on the right side of the scale.[2] On government spending the net shift is 16 percent in favor of

Figure 17-4 No Increasing Ideological Polarization: 1968–2008

Percentage of Americans who classify themselves as moderates (or answered "don't know/haven't thought much about it")

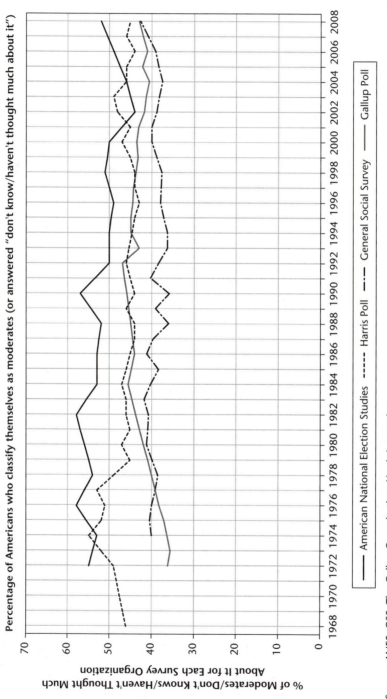

Sources: ANES, GSS, The Gallup Organization, Harris Interactive.

Table 17-1 No Increased Policy Polarization, 1984–2008

| | Extremely Liberal ----------------------- Extremely Conservative | | | | | | |
	1	2	3	4	5	6	7
Health Insurance	5*	4	3	0 (−8)**	−1	−4	0
Spending/Services	4	3	5	−6 (−6)	−3	−1	0
Aid to minorities	−2	−2	−6	−8 (−6)	−4	5	14
Military spending	−1	−2	0	−4 (−3)	2	2	1
Jobs/SOL	−1	1	−1	−2 (−4)	1	1	3

Abortion	Never Permitted	Rape, Incest, Danger	Clear Need	Always as Personal Choice	Don't Know, Other
	2	−2	−1	4	−2

Source: 1984 and 2008 ANES

*Each number is the difference between the percentage of 2008 respondents who placed themselves in the scale category compared to the percentage of 1984 respondents who placed themselves in the same scale category. Positive numbers indicate a higher proportion in the category in 2008, negative numbers indicate a higher proportion in 1984.

**Figures in parentheses represent changes when "haven't thought much about it" responses are recoded as moderates.

more government spending for more services. Perhaps surprisingly, on three issues the public shifted *rightward* between 1984 and 2008, significantly so in the case of government aid to minorities. On defense spending an insignificant move to the right (higher spending) is apparent, and support for a government-guaranteed job and standard of living (*not* the government's responsibility) shows a similar insignificant shift. Finally, on a four-position abortion scale, there is no significant change between 1984 and 2008. In sum, between the overwhelming reelection of Ronald Reagan and the election of Barack Obama, the positions of the electorate on major national issues changed relatively little, and on no issue did the middle lose to both extremes, the definition of polarization.[3]

So, in terms of their ideological orientations the American electorate today looks about the same as it did when Democrat Jimmy Carter defeated Republican Gerald Ford in the not-very-polarized 1976 election. And while data on specific issues only goes back to the mid-1980s, the movements in the past quarter-century are not large and do not put one in mind of polarization so much as an electorate slightly adjusting its views as conditions in the world change.

So, Where's the Polarization?

How do we reconcile the lack of evidence for polarization in a systematic examination of public opinion with the frequent claims that the mass electorate has become more polarized? A close look at such claims reveals that they are often advanced without systematic evidence like that presented in Figures 17-2 and

17-3, or with evidence that lacks any temporal dimension like that presented in Figure 17-4 and Table 17-1. Polarization is a relational concept and all too often no baseline or comparison point is presented.

As we have discussed at length elsewhere (Fiorina and Abrams 2009), there are several other sources of confusion as well. One is a tendency to regard sociocultural differences such as gun ownership, church attendance, and NASCAR interest as perfect reflections of political views, when they are not. For example, according to the national exit poll, nearly 40 percent of gun owners voted for Obama in 2008, as did more than one-quarter of white evangelical Protestants.

Another contributor to the inaccurate perception of polarization is a widespread confusion between polarization and sorting (see, for example, Abramowitz, in this volume). As the data presented above show, there are about the same proportions of liberals, moderates, and conservatives on most issues as a generation ago. But they are more neatly sorted into the parties now—liberals in the Democratic Party, conservatives in the Republican Party—than a generation ago. Thus, partisan differences among voters have increased, but that development obscures the fact that the center in American politics has not diminished; only its representation has. For example, consider the abortion issue, which for a generation has been a litmus test in presidential politics—Democratic candidates must be strongly pro-choice to have any chance to win the nomination and Republican candidates must be strongly pro-life. But consider the views of self-identified Democrats and Republicans in the population in 2008 (Table 17-2). While Democrats and Republicans certainly differ, many political observers would be surprised to learn that one-third of Democratic identifiers are arguably pro-life; certainly they are closer to the announced position of the Republican Party (never, or only in cases of rape, incest, or a threat to the woman's life) than to that of their own. Probably even more surprisingly, one-quarter of Republican identifiers are clearly pro-choice (always available), and arguably nearly half are closer to the announced position of the Democratic Party (always, for a clear need) than to their own. Party sorting has occurred in recent decades, but there is still far more heterogeneity of opinion in the mass bases of the two parties than there is among the party activists and officials.[4]

Table 17-2 Imperfect Party Sorting on Abortion, 2008

Circumstances in which abortion should be legal	Democrats	Republicans
Never	11	19
Only in case of rape, incest, or when the woman's life is in danger	23	33
For a clear need	16	21
Always a personal choice	50	26

Source: 2008 ANES.

Still another source of confusion is the fact that voters' choices have become more polarized even while their views on political issues have not. That is, in recent presidential elections, close to 90 percent of partisans have voted for the candidate of their own party. Republicans have always been that loyal (Fiorina, Abrams, and Pope 2006, 26–27), but Democrats have become much more consistent. In part that reflects the sorting noted above—there are not as many conservative Democrats as there used to be, many of whom regularly defected to vote for Republican presidential candidates. But in addition, partisan solidarity in voting reflects the candidates between whom voters choose. In recent decades, moderate Democrats and Republicans increasingly have faced a choice between a liberal Democrat and a conservative Republican; naturally they tend to vote for the candidate on their side of the spectrum, although they might well have preferred more moderate choices.

In our view, the words and actions of a polarized political class—the candidates and elected officials, issue activists, interest group leaders, and infotainment media—give rise to a greatly exaggerated picture of a polarized America. Thus, in primary elections only a small proportion of voters disproportionately representing the extremes of the parties turn out, resulting in immoderate candidates defeating more moderate ones. And the media portray the harsh rhetoric and noisy actions of activists as representative of the broader public when they are not. In August 2009, cable television and the Internet deluged Americans with pictures of angry and aggressive demonstrators at congressional town hall meetings called to discuss the health care legislation then pending in Congress. While it is certainly true that tens of millions of America had concerns and doubts about the legislation, it is not true that tens of millions of Americans attended the meetings and behaved like tantrum-throwing children, which is the impression a visitor from another country might get from watching American TV.

In 1992 Bill Clinton ran as a "new Democrat" who would pull the party away from its "tax-and-spend" past and reposition it nearer the center of the American political landscape, but once elected, he deferred to the "permanent" Democratic majorities in Congress, whose leadership saw no reason to change. The result was the Republican Revolution of 1994, which by the end of the decade had gone too far in the view of a majority. In the 2000 campaign, George W. Bush ran as a compassionate conservative and promised to govern as a uniter not a divider, but in office he governed as the greatest divider since the availability of modern survey data (Jacobson 2007). Most recently Barack Obama seemingly adopted a more centrist stance and promised to overcome the polarized politics of recent decades. But, despite the rhetoric, the electorate viewed him as virtually identical to John Kerry in 2004 and slightly left of Al Gore in 2000 (Table 17-3).[5] Evidently his moderate stance was not communicated or not believed. Perhaps the image of the Democratic Party was too well established for Obama to change in the short run. Or perhaps well-publicized associations like that with the controversial Reverend Jeremiah Wright offset his centrist rhetoric. Or perhaps the electorate was correct in its collective perception. In his first year, Obama, like

Table 17-3 Perceived Locations of Presidential Candidates on Seven-Point
Liberal-Conservative Scale*

	Democrat		Republican	
2000	3.2**	3.3	5.1**	4.9
2004	3.0	3.1	5.2	5.1
2008	3.0	3.1	5.0	4.9

Source: 2000, 2004, 2008 ANES.

*1 = extremely liberal, 7 = extremely conservative

**First column under a party label is with "Haven't thought much about it" responses recoded as moderates, second number with such responses omitted.

Clinton in 1992, deferred to Democratic congressional majorities that are arguably more liberal than the country as a whole. And at the time of this writing in late summer, his approval numbers have tumbled.

The bottom line is that those who decry the current polarization of American politics should place the blame on public officials, candidates, and the thin stratum of active citizens who constitute the political class. The electorate is not to blame.

Notes

1. The ANES allows respondents to opt out by choosing "haven't thought much about it" whereas the GSS codes responses as "don't know" only if they are volunteered. The result is a much higher proportion of "don't knows" in the ANES. There are correspondingly more moderates in the GSS, suggesting that respondents who really do not know what they are place themselves in the middle, providing some justification for the common practice of combining the two categories.
2. Surveys showed the public shifting back toward the right by late summer of 2009. See, for example, Langer (2009).
3. In a recent paper Mayer (2009) examines trends in fifteen NES seven-point and thermometer scales. He finds increased polarization in one, decreased polarization in three, and no change in eleven. He concludes that "issues and groups that are divisive today were just as divisive in the 1970s and 1980s."
4. For an extensive treatment of party sorting, see Levendusky (2009b).
5. As shown in the table, McCain was perceived as about the same as Bush in 2000.

PART V
PARTY SYSTEM CHANGE

18. What Are the Sources of the Republican
Realignment in the South?

To make sense of the 200+ years of American electoral history, political scientists have adopted the concept of "realignment," an idea that is at once theoretically and empirically rich and at the same time ill-defined, overused, and highly criticized. The realignment concept has been used to divide our past into major electoral "periods" or "party systems" in a way that gives meaning to changes in party control, voter turnout, and voting behavior itself.[1] It has proved impossible, however, to pinpoint realignments in a convincing manner. Yet regardless of how one interprets the whole sweep of our election history, observers of electoral developments in the American South since the middle of the twentieth century are likely to agree that these changes indeed constitute a realignment.

In broad terms, realignment is most often conceived of as an enduring change in the majority coalition and in party control of government. However, even when V. O. Key Jr. (1955; 1959) introduced the term to the political science literature, he gave us two different versions. Initially, most scholarly attention was devoted to "critical" realignments, in which a single election produces a dramatic and lasting break in party fortunes. For example, the elections of 1896 (the start of Republican Party control of government for many years) and 1932 (ushering in the New Deal dominance of the Democratic Party) are often seen as realigning elections in the United States. Commonly, the mechanism producing a partisan realignment is a newly salient issue that creates fresh divisions between political parties.

The critical realignment concept has been a common source of controversy. One controversy is whether there is a periodicity to critical realignments. The theory generally posits that critical realignments occur once a generation, lasting roughly thirty-two to thirty-six years. However, according to this reasoning, a realignment should have occurred in the 1960s, yet none was observed.[2] More generally, Mayhew (2002) offers a forceful critique of the realignment concept itself by casting doubt on the cyclical appearance of critical realignments. The concept has its defenders, however. Meffert and his colleagues (2001) defend the realignment concept and argue that the 1980 election was a realigning one that produced significant growth in Republican Party identification. More recently, Merrill, Grofman, and Brunell (2008) argue that political realignments occur quite regularly but relatively frequently in response to changes in public mood and the ideological extremism of the governing majority. They find evidence of realignments occurring in roughly twelve-year increments, similar to cyclical patterns in other areas of politics, such as foreign policy attitudes (Klingberg 1952).

The second important realignment concept from Key (1959) is that of a "secular" realignment, one that reflects gradual shifts in party coalitions and party success. Growth in one party's coalition may take years or even decades to develop. Since secular realignments do not necessarily occur in periodic intervals, there is less controversy over this interpretation. And with a wealth of polling data for the last sixty years, it has become easier to document slowly developing changes in party coalitions. Rather, controversies tend to focus on competing explanations for the observed changes in party coalitions, as is the case with party change in the American South in the last sixty years.

Party Realignment in the South

There is no dispute that significant political change has occurred in the South since the end of World War II. Once the base of the Democratic Party's New Deal coalition, the South has become a Republican Party stronghold in recent elections. More specifically, white voters (the majority race in each state of the former Confederacy) have shifted their allegiance away from the Democratic Party over a long period of time (Stanley and Niemi 2006). Figure 18-1 indicates a steady change in Southern white partisanship by decade over the last sixty years. While Democrats dramatically outnumbered Republicans in the 1950s, by the first decade of the twenty-first century the GOP has developed a clear party identification advantage. Each decade brought further erosion in Democratic Party identification and similar growth in Republican Party identification. This almost linear pattern is a textbook example of secular realignment. The Republican Party now enjoys a significant advantage in party identification among white Southern voters, and the South is the most Republican region of the country among white voters (Black and Black 2007, 46). By comparison, party identification has not changed as significantly among non-Southern whites during the same period. As Figure 18-2 indicates, identification with each party among non-Southern whites has hovered between 40 and 50 percent over the last six decades. Thus, the South is the main source of significant gains made by the GOP in recent decades.

Party identification is something of a lagging indicator of partisan change. Changes in voting behavior are sometimes more evident before changes in party identification during realignments (Gamm 1989). The changing fortunes of the two major political parties in the South can also be seen in election outcomes. While Democratic candidates for president carried a majority of Southern states in the 1940s and 1950s, the results are quite different now. Neither Tennessee native Al Gore in 2000 nor John Kerry in 2004 carried a single Southern state in their campaigns as Democratic candidates for president. In the 2008 presidential

Figure 18-1 Party Identification of Southern Whites by Decade

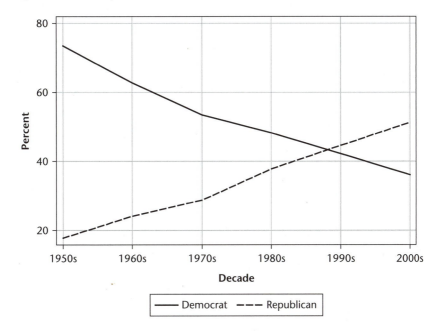

Source: ANES Cumulative File, 1948–2004, and ANES 2008 Time Series Study

Note: Leaners are coded as party identifiers.

election, Barack Obama, a black Democratic candidate, reversed the tide some-what by carrying three Southern states (Florida, North Carolina, and Virginia). However, according to data from the ANES surveys and the national exit polls, Obama's share of the Southern white vote in 2008 was not significantly better than what Gore and Kerry earned in the two previous elections. In fact, Obama did worse than Kerry among white voters in some Southern states (Persily, Ansol-abehere, and Stewart, 2010). Obama did improve on the Democratic vote share among nonwhites throughout the nation and among whites outside of the South, and Democrats succeeded in turning out racial minorities and young voters at higher rates in 2008 (Ansolabehere and Stewart 2009). The boost in turnout among key elements of the Democratic coalition, rather than improved support among Southern whites, is what helped elect President Obama in 2008.

In addition, Republicans now hold a majority of Southern seats in the U.S. Senate and the House of Representatives, and the GOP is nearly even with Dem-ocrats in holding state legislative seats in the South (Bullock 2009, 10). As a result, the South has assumed a prominent role in the organizational base and leadership of the Republican Party. In recent years, Southern politicians have held top leadership positions for the Republican Party in the House and Senate. In the

Figure 18-2 Party Identification of Non-Southern Whites by Decade

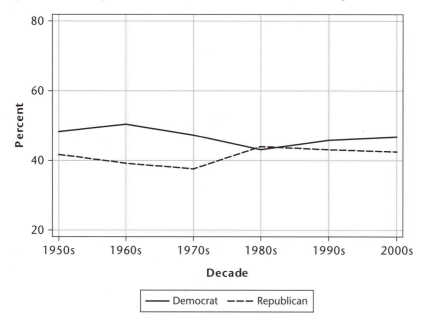

Source: ANES Cumulative File, 1948–2004, and ANES 2008 Time Series Study

Note: Leaners are coded as party identifiers.

contest to elect a new chairman of the Republican National Committee in 2009, two of the six final candidates were from the South and another two candidates were from states bordering the old Confederacy.[3]

Given the meager performance of the Republican Party fifty years ago in the South, the South's critical place in the GOP today is remarkable. However, explaining the Republican Party ascendance in the South has generated significant scholarly debate. Studies by Abramowitz and colleagues (Abramowitz and Saunders 1998; Abramowitz and Knotts 2006) note a growing correspondence between ideology and partisanship, particularly in the South. Over time, conservatives have increasingly identified with the Republican Party. The scholarly debate in some degree involves whether conservative ideology is defined primarily by race, economics, or moral values.

Race and the GOP Realignment in the South

Many researchers have examined voting patterns and public opinion in the South, generating a lively debate over the sources of this secular realignment. To be fair, none of the scholars in this debate insist on a single explanation for Republican gains. All seem to acknowledge multiple sources of party change.

However, they disagree in terms of which factor to emphasize the most. The most common explanations have emphasized the central role of race and the politics of civil rights. Key's (1949) influential study of Southern politics in the 1930s and 1940s focuses partly on racial group conflict, in what has come to be known as a theory of "racial threat." Key observed that in Democratic Party primaries, race-baiting segregationist candidates tended to receive the strongest electoral support from white voters in counties with large concentrations of black residents. An interest in thwarting black political power seemed to be strongly held among whites living in closer proximity to blacks. When the leadership of the national Democratic Party shifted more in favor of civil rights in the 1960s, a white back-lash ensued, particularly in the South. This provided an opportunity for the Republican Party to appeal to Southern whites.

President Lyndon Johnson, after signing the Civil Rights Act of 1964, is often quoted as saying he had just delivered the South to the Republican Party (Hillygus and Shields 2008, 118). In an influential book, Carmines and Stimson's (1989) study of "issue evolution" emphasizes race as a key source of opinion changes in the United States after passage of the Civil Rights and Voting Rights Acts, laws aimed at ending legalized segregation and voter discrimination, primarily in the South. They argue that the ideological terms "liberal" and "conservative" came to be defined in terms of race when debate focused on the federal government's role in promoting civil rights. As a result, desegregation attitudes of party identifiers polarized sharply after the 1963–1965 civil rights era—the "critical moment" in their dynamic model of issue evolution. Their evidence indicates that political elites first polarized over civil rights, with Democratic politicians adopting a more liberal posture and Republicans a conservative position. Then, as party positions on civil rights issues became clearer to voters, whites with conservative racial attitudes shifted toward the Republican Party (see chapter 12 on partisan polarization for further discussion of elite influences on public opinion).

According to standard explanations of Southern politics, the centrality of race in the region's political conflicts fueled the GOP's "Southern strategy" for winning presidential elections and building party support among white voters (Aistrup 1996; Black and Black 1992; 2002). These explanations continue to employ the racial threat hypothesis. For example, Giles and Hertz (1994), in a study of party registration in Louisiana parishes from 1975 to 1990, find that Republican Party registration among whites increased the most in parishes (counties) with the largest concentration of black voters. Glaser (1994, 1996) provides evidence that the racial attitudes of Southern whites are partly a function of racial context. White Democrats in counties with large black populations had more conservative racial attitudes and held less favorable evaluations of Jesse Jackson's candidacy for president in the 1980s. Recent historical studies of politics in the 1960s and 1970s also emphasize the primary role of race and a white back-lash against civil rights in explaining the mass movement of white voters to the Republican Party, particularly in the South (Perlstein 2001; Kruse 2005; Lassiter 2006; Lowndes 2008).

A compelling analysis by Hillygus and Shields (2008, chapter 5) documents the racial element of the "Southern strategy" in the presidential campaigns of Richard Nixon. In addition, they find that Republican campaigns succeeded in persuading Southern white Democrats with conservative racial attitudes to vote for GOP candidates in the 1970s and 1980s. A portion of their analysis is reprinted here as chapter 21. In this excerpt, Hillygus and Shields note the extensive emphasis on racial content in news coverage and of cross-pressures on voters throughout the 1960s and 1970s and into the 1980s.

Green, Palmquist, and Schickler's (2002, chapter 6) study of partisanship also places race at the center of its explanation of realignment in the South. Two studies by Hood, Kidd, and Morris (2004; 2008) examine race in Southern politics in terms of group control of political party organizations. Rather than simple proximity to blacks, they hypothesize that the mobilization of blacks into the Democratic Party fueled the movement of Southern whites to the GOP. According to their theory of relative party advantage, the enfranchisement and mobilization of Southern African-American voters made it harder for conservative whites to remain in control of local Democratic Party organizations. In addition, the Republican Party was beginning to build more viable organizations and field candidates to challenge Democrats in many parts of the South after the 1960s. The combination of these two developments gave the Republican Party an advantage in appealing to Southern whites with conservative views on racial issues.

In an article reprinted and updated here, with a new epilogue from the authors, Hood and colleagues (2004) examine GOP performance in gubernatorial and congressional elections in Southern states from 1960 to 2000. They find that electoral support for the Republican Party increased the most in states with the greatest mobilization of black voters. Thus, they argue that it was the movement of blacks into the electorate, rather than the concentration of blacks in a state's population, that is associated with growing white support for the Republican Party. In addition, they find little correlation between GOP electoral strength and economic development, migration, or the growth of evangelical Protestants in Southern states, as hypothesized by alternative perspectives discussed below. In a more recent study, Hood and colleagues (2008) extend their data to 2004 and find a reciprocal relationship between Republican Party performance and black voter mobilization in Southern states with the largest black populations (mainly in the Deep South). Growing mobilization of black voters fueled increasing support of the Republican Party by white voters. At the same time, the movement of white voters to the Republican Party opened up more opportunities for blacks to shape the Democratic Party, leading to further mobilization of black voters.

A study by Valentino and Sears (2005) links the GOP realignment in the South to the racial attitudes of Southern white voters. They make a distinction between older "Jim Crow racism" (based on beliefs about legalized racial discrimination and inferiority of blacks) and "symbolic racism" (which combines racial resentment and beliefs that blacks do not uphold traditional American values). Valentino and Sears find that Jim Crow racism has declined significantly, including in the South, and does not account for the movement of white voters to the Republican Party. In contrast, symbolic racism has not declined and is more prevalent in the South. Furthermore, they find that the impact of symbolic racism on the partisan identification and presidential voting of Southern white voters has increased over time. Knuckey (2005; 2006) reaches similar conclusions about the impact of symbolic racism on GOP identification among Southern whites in the 1990s. The symbolic racism concept has been debated for some time (Sniderman and Tetlock 1986; Sniderman et al. 1991; Tarman and Sears 2005), and some may question whether the Valentino and Sears study adequately controls for some of the other hypothesized sources of Republican growth in the South discussed below.[4]

Nevertheless, race remains the most common factor in explaining partisan realignment in the South. In particular, explanations emphasizing racial politics suggest that the movement of Southern whites toward the Republican Party accelerated after the passage of the Voting Rights Act in 1965 and subsequent GOP campaigns using race policies to target Southern white voters.

Economics and the GOP Realignment in the South

A growing revisionist literature emphasizes the importance of income and economic attitudes as critical sources of growth in Republican identification and voting in the South. The revisionists suggest that economic development and conventional class cleavages, rather than race, are the most important source of Republican political gains in the South. The most forceful argument comes from Shafer and Johnston (2006, 2001), part of which is reproduced in this volume.

Several scholars note the rapid economic growth, as well as a dramatic decline in the farm population, in the South after World War II (Scher 1997; Polsby 2004; Shafer and Johnston 2006). In a chapter reprinted here, Shafer and Johnston argue that this economic growth cultivated a new class-based political cleavage in the South as high-income and middle-income whites came to see their economic interests aligned with GOP policies. They note that movement to the GOP began in the 1950s, before the civil rights politics of the 1960s. In addition, this perspective notes that the addition of many Southern blacks (mostly low-income) to the Democratic Party increased interparty class differences and made the economic cleavage between the parties more evident to white voters (Shafer and Johnston 2006, chapter 3). Voting differences between high-income and low-income Southern whites in presidential and congressional elections became much more pronounced. In the 1950s, income differences in voting behavior were rather small in the South, with high-income whites favoring the Democrats more than low-income whites in some areas. By the 1990s, high-income whites had moved to a position of strongly supporting Republican candidates. At the same time, a growing voting cleavage defined by social welfare attitudes emerged in the South.[5]

Other recent studies also observe the emergence of class divisions among Southern voters. Nadeau and his colleagues (1993, 2004), like Shafer and Johnston, note that the relationship between class and partisanship among Southern whites reversed and strengthened from the 1950s to the 1990s. At the height of the New Deal, white-collar Southern whites identified more as Democrats than blue-collar whites. Over time, what we often consider the "normal" relationship between income and partisanship emerged. McCarty, Poole, and Rosenthal (2006) find a similar pattern using a more sophisticated statistical analysis. Stonecash (2000), Lublin (2004), and Bartels (2008), likewise note a growing class cleavage in the United States, and especially the South.

The result is that geographic political divisions in the South have come to resemble those outside the region: high-income Republican areas pitted against low-income Democratic areas (Shafer and Johnston 2006). For example, McCarty, Poole, and Rosenthal (2006) note that the difference in median family income between House districts held by Republicans and districts represented by Democrats increased substantially in the South from the 1960s to the 2000s. As a result, upper-income counties in the South have provided the largest voter support for Republican presidential candidates in recent elections (Gelman 2008).

Some note the in-migration of Republican voters to the South and the out-migration of blacks to the North as another contributing factor to the growing class cleavage and the rising GOP fortunes in the South (Scher 1997; Polsby 2004). The migration of Republican whites to Southern states helped form a critical mass that encouraged native-born white conservatives to shift their party registration and voting behavior from the Democrats to the Republicans. Polsby emphasizes the development of residential air-conditioning in the 1950s, which made the South a more appealing destination for those raised in the North. The transplanted Northerners tended to be well-off financially and brought a Republican Party identification with them, thus boosting the GOP. However, engaging as the explanation is, the evidence in support of the causal impact of air-conditioning is somewhat slim. In addition, in some other studies the movement of Republicans to the South is not seen as a major factor in the regional realignment (Miller and Shanks 1996; Black and Black 1992).

Shafer and Johnston (2006) go further and argue that the impact of race on Southern voters has been exaggerated. They find little evidence of racial threat in the movement of Southern whites to the Republican Party. Southern whites in congressional districts where the population is more than 20 percent black were in fact less likely to vote for Republican House and Senate candidates than whites in districts where blacks comprise less than 20 percent of the population. Only in voting for president did Shafer and Johnston find results consistent with the racial threat hypothesis, and even then the impact of racial context was still substantially smaller than the impact of economic development on voting. These results contrast with other studies measuring racial context in the South at the county level (Glaser 1994; Giles and Hertz 1994). Aside from the analysis of states by Hood and colleagues, scholars testing the racial-threat hypothesis have generally examined smaller geographic units, such as counties or voting precincts. It is unlikely that large congressional districts offer a comparable racial context. In fact, the impact of racial context on voting and public opinion is heavily conditioned by the size of the geographic units used as the basis for comparison (Voss 1996; Baybeck 2006).

Shafer and Johnston (2006), despite their overall support for an economic explanation, do find that racial attitudes increasingly contributed to Republican voting support in the South, but the effect varied for different political institutions. In voting for president, economic attitudes outweighed racial attitudes until the 1990s. In voting for House and Senate in the 1950s, economic attitudes were inconsequential but racial conservatives favored the Democratic Party. It was not until the 1990s that the impacts of economic and racial attitudes on Southern voters were similar in both congressional and presidential elections. The advantages of incumbency and the conservative views of Southern Democrats in Congress helped legislators repel the growing power of economic conservatism. The authors also note an important difference between "local" Democratic incumbents (born and educated in their home state) and "cosmopolitan" Democrats (incumbents raised or educated outside the state). In districts represented by cosmopolitan Democrats, voting was influenced more by attitudes (both racial and economic) in ways that favored GOP challengers (see also Fenno 2000; Black and Black 2002, 138–204). By contrast, in districts represented by local Democrats, voting was determined more by demographics (income and racial context) and Democrats were largely successful in defeating Republican challengers. That permitted some Democratic incumbents to stall the Republican realignment for a few decades.

Economic attitudes and income differences have become more common components of explanations of political change in the South.[6] In the ongoing debate about the growing ideological differences between Democrats and Republicans in the United States (see Part IV), party differences are sometimes defined or observed in terms of economic issues (e.g., McCarty, Poole, and Rosenthal 2006; Bartels 2008). The movement of conservative Southern whites to the Republican Party thus coincides with and contributes to growing party polarization in the nation. Importantly, however, the economic explanation of political change suggests that the Republican realignment in the South began before the 1960s, prior to recent "sorting" of partisanship and ideology (Fiorina 2005; Levendusky 2009b).

Moral/Cultural Issues and the GOP Realignment in the South

A more recent portion of the voting behavior literature emphasizes cultural issues and religious conservatism as important factors in American politics. The debate about polarization in the American mass public is partially a debate about growing differences over cultural issues (see Part IV). A smaller literature on Southern politics examines religion and cultural issues as sources of Republican

Party gains in the South. In response to growing policy differences between the parties on moral issues, the mass public has become more polarized (or sorted, to use Fiorina's language) along party lines in terms of religious adherence and opinions on cultural issues, such as abortion (Adams 1997; Carmines and Woods 2002: Carsey and Layman 2006; Brewer and Stonecash 2007; Brewer 2009). Given the relative importance of religious institutions in the South, it is remarkable that some accounts of partisan change in the South have neglected these factors.

Kellstedt, Guth, Green, and Smidt (2007) define two important concepts for understanding the role of religion in Southern voting behavior. First, religious traditions refer to major faith communities or denominations. Evangelical Protestants, who tend to view the Bible as the sole religious authority and hold orthodox religious beliefs, are a key constituency (Jelen 2006). Second, religious commitment denotes the importance of one's religious beliefs and how often one attends worship services. "High commitment" religious citizens also tend to be more open to GOP appeals on social issues. As Kellstedt and colleagues note, the share of high commitment evangelicals among Southern white voters has increased, particularly since the 1990s. The South now has the largest share of evangelical Protestants of any region in the country (Black and Black 2007, 54). Furthermore, since the 1960s high commitment evangelicals in the South have shifted toward the GOP in voting and party identification (Kellstedt et al. 2007). The 2008 presidential election continued the trend, when one estimate indicates that 86 percent of Southern white evangelicals voted for John McCain (Green et al. 2009).

Some accounts of political change in the South note the prominence of the Southern Baptist Convention (SBC). SBC ministers serve as important leaders of public opinion among whites. For example, Guth (2005) examines the increasing GOP activism of SBC ministers after 1980. In "issue evolution" fashion, SBC lay members (particularly those with high levels of religious commitment) moved toward the Republican Party after the SBC clergy (Kellstedt et al. 2007; Green et al. 2009). Thus, religious leaders may be partly responsible for party change in the South.

Lublin (2004) assesses the relative contributions of economic, racial, and cultural issue attitudes on the partisanship and voting behavior of Southern whites. He observes increasing partisan polarization in all three issue domains. Lublin's analysis indicates that economic attitudes were the strongest predictor of partisanship and voting among white Southerners through the mid-1980s. However, abortion and racial attitudes gained strength and almost equaled the impact of economic attitudes on partisanship and voting by the 1990s and into 2000. A similar study by Knuckey (2006) finds that Republican Party identification among Southern whites in the 1990s is predicted by a combination of moral beliefs, racial attitudes, economic issues, and general conservatism. Black and Black (1992, 141–175) also note the growing importance of religious conservatism to help explain the movement of Southern white voters to the Republican Party. Finally,

Hillygus and Shields, in the material reprinted here (chapter 21), argue that the GOP Southern strategy shifted from racial issues to moral issues after the 1980s as a way to appeal to conflicted Democratic voters (see also Miller and Schofield 2003).

Researchers are paying closer attention to religious faith traditions and cultural beliefs as sources of voting behavior in the United States (Leege et al. 2002; Layman and Green 2006; Campbell 2002; Barker and Tinnick 2006). Cultural and religious explanations of voting behavior suggest that the movement of Southern whites to the GOP accelerated since the 1970s, when social issues such as abortion and gay rights became more salient in American politics.

Electoral Institutions and the GOP Realignment in the South

A final and narrower debate exists about the role of electoral institutions in supporting GOP gains in the South. Specifically, some argue that congressional redistricting after the 1990 census helped Republicans win more House seats in the South, particularly in the 1994 GOP landslide. Racial redistricting in the 1990s created a number of majority-black districts in the South. This move packed many Democrats into majority-black districts, leaving the surrounding districts more hospitable to Republican candidates. According to some observers, the net result of redistricting helped Republican candidates win more seats in the South (Lublin and Voss 2000; Lublin 2004; McKee 2009). However, there is disagreement about the extent to which racial redistricting favors one political party (Shotts 2003; Lublin and Voss 2003; Petrocik and Desposato 1998; Epstein and O'Halloran 1999). In addition, the same 1994 election that produced a Republican majority in the House also shifted the Senate (where redistricting is not a factor) to GOP control. Thus, the Republican gains in the South are largely the result of race, economics, and cultural factors, rather than electoral institutions.

Conclusion

The steady movement of Southern white voters toward the Republican Party is undeniable and has been occurring now for several decades. Nevertheless, the contribution of various factors to realignment remains controversial. Competing theories point to explanations for the movement of Southern whites to the Republican Party based on racial attitudes, economic changes, and religious and moral beliefs. In trying to evaluate the evidence supporting these theories, a problem is that different bodies of evidence are difficult to square with one another. Aggregate data on voter registration and electoral performance of the parties indicates the continuing importance of race in Southern politics. On the other hand, individual-level data indicates that party identification and voting choices among Southern whites are closely associated with general ideological positions and economic attitudes, in addition to (sometimes instead of) racial attitudes.

Perhaps this reflects the difficulty of measuring the impact of individual attitudes on sensitive topics such as race.

Given the extended length of this secular realignment in party identification and voting, it may reflect the combined effects of all of the contributing factors noted in this chapter. Each explanation hints at a different starting point for partisan realignment in the South. Class-based explanations identify the start in the 1950s. Race-based explanations tend to identify the 1960s as the starting point. Religious and cultural explanations for party change suggest movement after the 1970s. It may be that all three factors have played an important role at different points in sustaining a partisan change that has continued for some fifty to sixty years. In addition, it is likely that all three factors continue to shape Southern politics today. A recent set of case studies of congressional campaigns in the South finds that race is still an important part of the region's electoral politics, along with frequent debates over economic and cultural issues (Glaser 2005).

There are reasons to expect continued growth for the Republican Party in the South. Black (2004) discusses the difficulties facing the Democratic Party in that region, while Hayes and McKee (2008) provide an optimistic outlook for the GOP. Southern whites tend to be the most conservative voters in the United States, whether one focuses on economic, racial, or cultural attitudes. In addition, they are among the most religious voters in the United States. If the political parties remain polarized on all three dimensions, there may be room for the GOP to continue to add to its recent success in the area. The Republican Party has grown so strong now that some analysts argue that Democratic candidates for president should bypass the South altogether (Schaller 2006).

On the other hand, Republican losses in recent elections may indicate the limits of race as a GOP campaign tool and Republican growth in the South. Barack Obama, a black Democrat, carried three Southern states in the 2008 election after white Democrats failed to carry any in the two previous elections. In addition, Democrats won back some Southern House and Senate seats in the last two election cycles. Those congressional victories were largely concentrated in the same three states that Obama won in 2008 (Florida, North Carolina, and Virginia). Future studies may examine whether there are features that make these Southern states more resistant to Republican control.

Notes

1. See Niemi and Weisberg (1993, Part VI) for an interpretation and abridgement of some of the classic material from the early realignment literature.
2. While agreeing that a *realignment* (a major, long-term shifting of power from one party to the other) did not occur "on time," Aldrich and Niemi (1995) argue that the significant changes in partisanship, political trust, split-ticket voting, and so on that occurred in the mid- to late 1960s triggered the onset of a sixth American party system, commonly referred to as a "candidate-centered" party system. One could

argue that this period ended when partisanship reasserted itself later in the twentieth century and gave way to the intense partisan polarization observed currently.

3. Generally regarded as finalists for the position were Saul Anuzis (MI), Kenneth Blackwell (OH), Katon Dawson (SC), Mike Duncan (KY), Chip Saltsman (TN), and Michael Steele (MD).

4. Recently, symbolic racism has also been used to explain voting in the 2008 Democratic primary. See Jackman and Vavreck (2010).

5. However, Gilens (1999) argues that poverty and other social welfare issues were often framed in racial terms during this period.

6. Abramowitz (1994) made a related but slightly different argument in an early rebuttal of Carmines and Stimson's (1989) theory of "issue evolution" on civil rights issues. Abramowitz argued that social welfare and national security attitudes, rather than racial attitudes, explained the movement of white voters away from the Democratic Party in the 1980s.

Further Readings

Race and Partisan Realignment

Carmines, Edward G., and James A. Stimson, *Issue Evolution* (Princeton, N.J.: Princeton University Press, 1989). Classic study develops a theory of issue evolution and applies it to racial politics in the United States. Argues that a secular realignment occurred on race in the 1960s, with elite polarization preceding movement in the partisanship of the mass public.

Hillygus, D. Sunshine, and Todd G. Shields, *The Persuadable Voter: Wedge Issues in Presidential Campaigns* (Princeton, N.J.: Princeton University Press, 2008). Chapter 5 is an in-depth case study of the Nixon campaign's Southern strategy and the impact of racial and moral issues on white swing voters in the South.

Valentino, Nicholas A., and David O. Sears, "Old Times There Are Not Forgotten: Race and Partisan Realignment in the Contemporary South," *American Journal of Political Science* 49 (2005): 672–688. Racial resentment is an important predictor of Republican gains among Southern whites.

Economics and Partisan Realignment

Nadeau, Richard, Richard G. Niemi, Harold W. Stanley, and Jean-François Godbout, "Class, Party, and South/Non-South Differences: An Update," *American Politics Research* 32 (2004): 52–67. Reports that income differences have become a more potent voting cleavage among white Southern voters.

Polsby, Nelson W., *How Congress Evolves* (New York: Oxford University Press, 2004). Argues that economic growth brought dramatic political change to the South.

Religion, Moral Issues, and Realignment

Adams, Greg D., "Abortion: Evidence of an Issue Evolution," *American Journal of Political Science* 41 (1997): 718-737. Finds evidence of issue evolution on the abortion issue in the 1980s, although not of the same magnitude as race.

Green, John C., Lyman A. Kellstedt, Corwin E. Smidt, and James L. Guth, "The Soul of the South: Religion and Southern Politics in the New Millennium." In *The New Politics of the Old South*, 4th ed., ed. Charles S. Bullock III and Mark J. Rozell (Lanham, Md.: Rowman & Littlefield, 2009). Argues that religion is an important factor in the growth of Republican support among white Southern voters.

Miller, Gary, and Norman Schofield, "Activists and Partisan Realignment in the United States," *American Political Science Review* 97 (2003): 245–260. While not focused solely on the South, this article contends that party activists have created new party cleavages based on race and social issues.

The Timing of National Realignments

Mayhew, David R., *Electoral Realignments: A Critique of an American Genre* (New Haven, Conn.: Yale University Press, 2002). Strong, unfavorable assessment of the critical realignment paradigm.

Meffert, Michael F., Helmut Norpoth, and Anirudh V. S. Ruhil, "Realignment and Macropartisanship." *American Political Science Review* 95 (2001): 953–962. Argues that the 1980 election precipitated a national realignment toward the Republican Party.

Merrill, Samuel III, Bernard Grofman, and Thomas L. Brunell, "Cycles in American National Electoral Politics, 1854–2006: Statistical Evidence and an Explanatory Model," *American Political Science Review* 102 (2008): 1–17. Makes the case that partisan realignments in the United States occur in twelve-year cycles.

Niemi, Richard G., and Herbert F. Weisberg, *Classics in Voting Behavior* (Washington, D.C.: CQ Press, 1993). Interprets and reprints some of the classic literature on party systems and realignments and their causes and on nineteenth-century voting behavior.

19. Economic Development and a Politics of Class

Byron E. Shafer and Richard Johnston

Economic development was destined to come to the postwar South, and the politics of social class that might be expected to come with economic change did inexorably follow. Both would prove central to the rise of a Southern Republican Party. By the time they arrived, a politics of class would long since have become established—old news—in the non-South, where it had served for more than a generation as a diagnostic characteristic of the New Deal party system. Nevertheless, even if all that were not true, it makes sense to begin the story of postwar partisan change in the South by way of economic development and class politics for another, obvious reason.

Economic development and legal desegregation, and with them a politics both of class and of race, would remain intertwined during the postwar years in the American South. Yet if the racial reorganization of Southern society was to be the more dramatic and emotive of these two impacts, the economic reorganization of Southern society was effectively under way first. Or at least, and critically for our purposes, its impacts are present earlier in the data. A one-party South had, by definition, repressed the main cleavage, social class, which had defined the non-Southern—the New Deal—party system elsewhere, with a blue-collar Democracy facing a white-collar GOP. Its restoration, bringing the South back into the partisan union at long last, would finally make that party system fully national.

Beginning with the politics of class does, in turn, imply beginning with a focus on the white South. During the 1950s, there was some natural increase in the share of the Southern electorate contributed by black Southerners, the key trigger for a reorganization in the politics of race. Yet into the 1960s, this was still an inconsequential number of black voters: a region that was 20+ percent black had a black electorate in the 1950s, after it had begun to grow, of about 4 percent. That fact alone almost mandates an opening focus on the white South and its divisions, first incipient and then very real, on lines of economic interest. Nevertheless, it is worth remembering that even in this most-black section of the United States, the Southern electorate was and would remain overwhelmingly white, so that any major divisions among white Southerners would perforce be a crucial part of the postwar Southern story.

Curiously, much existing analysis of this fundamental structural shift, from economic development to class politics to resurgent Southern Republicanism, has remained rooted in descriptions of the Southern political world *pre-change*. It is

Source: Byron E. Shafer and Richard Johnston, *The End of Southern Exceptionalism,* Cambridge, Mass.: Harvard University Press, 2006, chap. 2, pp. 22–50.

as if an analysis appropriate to the 1920s, even the 1890s, has merely been brought forward with the dials adjusted. A major secondary purpose of this chapter, accordingly, is to help shift the overall frame of reference for the analysis of Southern politics, away from one more appropriate to the old order. A major secondary benefit of beginning with class politics is that it does precisely that.

The reconstitution and then invigoration of a basic class cleavage in the American South is thus the essential opening part of the story. And the critical body of data for such an analysis, of economic growth, class division, and Republican prospects, is the series of opinion surveys that was to become the American National Election Studies (NES). Serendipitously, their creation was to coincide with the rise of Southern Republicanism. That series received a kind of unofficial "pre-test" in 1948, with a small sample and very limited questions.[1] But the real start of what was to become the central tool for the study of voting behavior in the United States came in 1952. Accordingly, this analysis needs to begin there as well.

Fortunately, the pattern of politics that V. O. Key set out for the old South can still be discerned easily with 1950s data in the case of Congress, and can be teased out of that data in the case of the presidency. On the other hand, while it would have been ideal to have some composite measure of social class when addressing the impact of economic change on the white electorate, the NES presents obvious problems in this regard. Shifting occupational categories, coupled with shifting means for their assessment, along with different ways of treating spouses and/or breadwinners, make direct analyses in terms of "social class" as a comprehensive concept highly problematic, especially in the earlier years which are critical to this particular story.

Nevertheless, the NES does categorize by *family income* across the whole period from 1952 to 2000. While these are still income bands rather than precise figures, they do allow an easy division into terciles for the nation as a whole: bottom, middle, and top thirds by income. Moreover, such a division has a special advantage for an examination of the South. If income terciles are calculated for the nation as a whole, then the South can begin poor (with a disproportionate bottom third) and grow richer (with a top third growing disproportionately), as in fact it did.

Social Class and Southern Republicanism: The House

For two main reasons, it makes additional sense to begin searching for the institutional impacts of economic change on partisan outcomes by way of the U.S. House of Representatives (Rohde 1991; Polsby 1997; Fenno 2000). From one side, as we have seen in Chapter 1 [of Shafer and Johnston 2006], House votes and aggregate House outcomes were much less volatile than presidential votes and Electoral College outcomes. The main storyline is thus easier to recognize through the House. From the other side, the presidential candidacy of Dwight Eisenhower was such an important individualized phenomenon in the 1950s that, without some further analytic background, his candidacy risks opening the story through a potentially idiosyncratic focus. It is not immediately obvious how the analyst should separate the man from the moment.

Yet Eisenhower is ultimately a specific instance of a more generic problem. For the presidency as an institutional lens is always open to precisely the sort of analysis we hope to avoid, one focused on individuals and idiosyncrasies—a different kind of "local knowledge"—rather than on social forces, institutional structures, and regularized behavior by the mass public. Moreover, because the presidency provides a single contest every four years, major idiosyncratic elements will intermittently present a second set of continuing problems, involving the proper basis for aggregation. We address these initially in Tables 19-3 and 19-5 below. By contrast, the House offers more than a hundred contests every two years, so that its analytic charm is the opposite. The wiping away of specific individuals encourages a focus on larger trends shaping aggregated cohorts.

All three nationally elective institutions of American government—the presidency, Senate, and House—need ultimately to enter the analysis, since all three were available to register social change and its partisan impact, and especially since both their common stories and their institutional differences are important. Yet the advantage of beginning with House elections is not just that there are sufficient House districts to allow an analysis that is not specific to personalities. It is also that, whereas the presidency often led in the registration of electoral trends, the House was the body that most obviously consolidated them into stable and ongoing patterns of politics. For interpretive purposes, then, the common insistence on the primacy of the presidency, a priori, can be actively distortive.

In any case, Table 19-1 starts the analysis of the change underlying this postwar trajectory by looking at House elections by decade from the 1950s onward.[2] At the beginning of this period, Southern Republican congressmen were confined to a handful of Appalachian districts, which were among the poorest in the entire nation. For our purposes, their confinement meant that any class relationship was automatically attenuated. Nevertheless, in the old world of Southern politics, the relationship that did appear was inverse to the pattern outside the South. Which is to say: the poor were modestly more likely to vote Republican (Table 19-1A).

This situation changed, and the engine for a shift toward Southern Republicanism stood abruptly revealed, in the 1960s. Indeed, from one decade to the next, the overall relationship actually reversed. A politics of economic interest had evidently arrived. The wealthiest tercile was now most likely to vote Republican, the poorest tercile least likely—in a turn that was never in any way threatened thereafter. And while the move from the 1950s to the 1960s was the strongest overall shift, all subsequent decadal changes were to move further in the same direction.

Table 19-1A does contain what will prove to be the overall story of partisan change among Southern whites during all the postwar years. Yet its aggregation still very much masks the extent of the change, even in just this one institution,

Table 19-1 Social Class and the Coming of Southern Republicanism:
The House

Decade	Income Terciles			Total	Range (High-Low)
	Low	Mid	High		
A. Republican Percentage among All Whites					
1950s	18	15	15	16	−3
(N)	(200)	(140)	(220)	(560)	
1960s	25	28	35	29	+10
(N)	(223)	(208)	(225)	(656)	
1970s	24	33	38	32	+14
(N)	(271)	(317)	(296)	(884)	
1980s	26	37	48	38	+22
(N)	(232)	(305)	(313)	(850)	
1990s	41	60	70	60	+29
(N)	(254)	(329)	(423)	(1006)	
B. Republican Percentage among All Whites in Contested Districts					
1950s	40	32	25	31	−15
(N)	(80)	(59)	(100)	(239)	
1960s	31	37	44	37	+13
(N)	(137)	(113)	(122)	(372)	
1970s	34	44	50	43	+16
(N)	(184)	(217)	(201)	(602)	
1980s	34	49	53	47	+19
(N)	(131)	(202)	(230)	(563)	
1990s	40	58	64	56	+24
(N)	(225)	(270)	(338)	(833)	

because it still includes many who *could not* vote Republican for the House of Representatives because they had no Republican candidate. Accordingly, the analysis should really be restricted to white Southerners who possessed both a Democratic and a Republican congressional alternative. When this restriction is imposed, the same patterns recur, writ larger still.

The column marked "Total" still shows relentless Republican progress across all these years, decade by decade (Table 19-1B). In the 1950s, even when the analysis is limited only to those districts that did indeed have Republican candidates, the party could attract less than a third of the total vote. By the 1990s, the Republican Party had reached majority status, at least among white voters, and it had done so on a far broader base of competition. Rather than drawing a third of the vote within the minority of seats that it could manage to contest, it drew a majority in a world where remarkably few seats lay beyond its aspirations.

More to the point of explaining this growth, however, is the class shift that accompanied and underpinned it. The 1950s, as captured by these individual-level data in tabular form, stand out as the decade of the old South, a piece of the same world that V. O. Key had captured with ecological data graphed onto maps. As such, the Republican vote that did exist still featured a clear class inversion: the wealthy were least likely to vote Republican, the poor most likely to do so.

The 1960s then reversed these old class patterns and laid the groundwork for Republican gains, forging a new link between partisan choice and social class, a link that had characterized the North at least since the New Deal. From the 1960s and ever onward, at least as this is being written, the wealthy became most likely to vote Republican, in the South and not just in the North. In our terms, the top tercile became most likely to vote Republican, the bottom tercile least likely to do so.

But in fact, there was more. At the beginning of this switch, it was the top income tercile that really contributed the great change, detaching itself from the Democrats and moving to support the Republicans. This proved to be a fearsome shift: the top tercile went on to reach majority status for a Republican House by the 1970s. The middle tercile followed at a distance, getting to that same point only in the 1990s, when it brought the party as a whole to (white) majority status. By then, the top tercile was approaching the two-thirds mark in Republican support.

At the same time, the bottom tercile, creeping upward with overall Republican successes, had only just achieved the level of support it possessed even in the 1950s. Low-income Southerners participated in the new class politics of the 1960s by actually moving away from a newly energized Republican Party. In a new class politics, that party apparently lacked attraction for the low-income South, at least when examined by way of the House of Representatives, our benchmark for a stable and recurring partisan vote. In fact, low-income (white) Southerners were no more Republican in the 1990s than they had been in the 1950s.

A politics newly built around social class should also have been a politics newly built around social welfare as a policy concern, as it turned out to be. This was not just because societal divisions and issue cleavages cohere naturally and logically: no social basis, no policy difference. Nor was it just because when politics in the North had shifted from an essentially geographic to an essentially economic division, social welfare issues had been part and parcel of that change. Nor was it only because the essence of the dominant policy agenda of the immediate postwar era, the New Deal agenda of Presidents Franklin Roosevelt and Harry Truman, was economics and social welfare. Rather, all three preconditions were present. On the other hand, they had been present in the North for a generation without infusing Southern politics to nearly the same degree (Ladd and Hadley 1975; Geer 1992).

Fortunately, the National Election Studies asked one or more social welfare questions from the very first survey in 1948 onward. Even more fortunately, the longest-running single focus in the entire series is built around a welfare item first asked in 1952, so that its progeny can be used for a simple check on the policy implications of this Southern class shift. Tapping governmental interventions on behalf of employment opportunities and economic well-being, this became the effective "marker item" whose surface content addressed welfare policy:

> Some people feel that the government in Washington should see to it that every person has a job and a good standard of living. Others think that the government should just let each person get ahead on their own.

In 1952, what was to become "a job and a good standard of living" was instead the many-headed mandate "unemployment, education, housing, and so on"; for 1956 and 1960, it was just "a job"; for 1964, just "a good standard of living"; and at that point, it became "a job and a good standard of living" in every year thereafter. For the 1950s, there was only a two-part answer: agree/disagree. For the 1960s, there was a four-part answer, from strongly agreeing with the first premise through strongly agreeing with the second. And for the 1970s onward, there was a seven-point range of agreement. At a minimum, then, it is possible to have a consistent liberal versus conservative dichotomy for the entire postwar period, with "0" the liberal point and "1" the conservative point. Table 19-2 reflects this dichotomy.

Arrayed this way, the pattern of issue preferences and their relationship to partisan politics parallels the pattern of class memberships and their partisan relationship, with an opening twist. In the 1950s, preferences on welfare policy were not so much inverted as simply unrelated to a Republican or Democratic vote. This is, of course, the time when lower-income individuals were more likely to be voting Republican in the South. Yet the national parties had largely aligned themselves the other way around, and welfare policy was central to this alignment:

Table 19-2 Welfare Attitudes and the Coming of Southern Republicanism: The House

	Republican Percentage among All Whites in Contested Districts		
	Welfare Attitudes		
	Liberal	Conservative	Range (High-Low)
1950s	31	31	0
(N)	(137)	(64)	
1960s	24	38	+14
(N)	(59)	(125)	
1970s	36	48	+12
(N)	(112)	(224)	
1980s	27	58	+31
(N)	(99)	(213)	
1990s	32	68	+36
(N)	(171)	(462)	

national Democrats supported the welfare programs of the New Deal, while national Republicans opposed them. Moreover, just to confuse matters further in the South, national Republicans from poorer constituencies could be quite moderate on welfare issues, while *Southern* Democrats could stand almost anywhere in this policy realm.

The result among white Southerners was a lack of any policy alignment. This is presumably another reflection of the old South, where most individuals had acquired their partisan attachments in a direct line to the Civil War and Reconstruction, events with no obvious relevance to modern welfare preferences. Yet the moment a change in class attachments to the two political parties arrived, in the 1960s, it brought with it a change, and a lasting one, in policy attachments. Conservatives on social welfare were now more likely to pull the Republican lever, liberals on social welfare to vote Democratic. And this relationship only got stronger as the postwar era aged.

Moreover, the main secondary effect from a class inversion—the distinctive paths of low-income versus high-income Southerners within the overall picture— was likewise recapitulated with welfare preferences. With social class, the top tercile led the move to a new congressional Republicanism. This was the stratum of society that made the original break, while the bottom tercile remained impervious to Republican attractions. In an echo of the same phenomenon, Republican progress over time occurred almost entirely among those with conservative preferences on social welfare, while the congressional Republican Party scored hardly any gains at all among those with liberal preferences (Table 19-2). Remarkably, they still stood in the 1990s where they had stood in the 1950s, despite massive partisan change around them.[3]

Social Class and Southern Republicanism: The Presidency

In the immediate postwar years, however, all this change was still to come, and congressional politicking in the old South looked as sleepy as ever. The same could not be said of presidential politicking. If Congress was to begin (at least superficially) as an indicator of stasis in Southern politics, an implicit argument that the old order adapted and endured, the presidency was to elicit an immediate stream of predictions that something major had changed, was changing, or would inevitably change. Most of these predictions were not otherwise consistent with each other. Moreover, the volatility of postwar presidential outcomes, now in the American South as well, meant that each seemed temporarily to disconfirm its predecessor.

Nevertheless, the same underlying structural factors that were transforming the South, and that were to change congressional politics so dramatically, were in fact transforming presidential politics as well. Such an outcome was not an absolute necessity. In theory, presidential politicking might have been so different from congressional politicking, through either differing policy substance or differing electoral strategy, that grand factors shaping the one would still largely bypass the other. In practice, they did not, and with structural shifts as large as these—with economic development and racial desegregation on this scale—it is hard in retrospect to see how they really could have.

For seventy-five years, Republican candidates for President had been awaiting a serious and recurrent Republican vote from the American South. With the House, the harvesting of any such vote, the partisan product of social change, was partially dependent on the recruiting of candidates to capitalize upon it: no congressional challenger, no Republican vote. With the presidency, this secondary problem did not exist—there had been Republican presidential nominees across the South since the end of the Civil War. It was just that there had been no rising Republican vote to harvest.

In 1952, that vote arrived. Moreover, it arrived in its modern form—the new South and not the old—with a new class connection, that is, with the class connection that it would have offered in the North for a generation before (Eulau 1962). Dwight Eisenhower not only drew a vastly expanded Southern vote for President, by comparison with Thomas Dewey in 1948 or Wendell Willkie in 1944, he also opened the era in which Republican candidates attracted that vote most heavily within the top income tercile, least heavily within the bottom (Table 19-3A).

John Kennedy was to wrest the presidency back for the Democrats eight years later. What he did not do was to restore the old class order. The sharpness of this class cut in the Republican vote for president then jumped up again in the 1960s. At one end of the income spectrum, the Republican vote among low-income Southerners actually managed to fall, to its lowest level of the postwar era. But at the other end of the spectrum, the Republican vote among low-income Southerners continued upward, so that the gap between high- and low-income terciles essentially doubled. In the process, the modern pattern—had anyone known—was effectively established.

It is possible to make this change look additionally like the story for the House of Representatives, thereby emphasizing its common roots, by focusing on the Republican share of the two-party vote, since a major independent candidacy by George Wallace in the 1960s, along with a lesser independent effort from Ross Perot in the 1990s, does color all the numbers in Table 19-3A. Again, a class reversal in the old Southern pattern of the vote was already present in the 1950s (Table 19-3B). Again, it jumped up sharply in the 1960s. But seen this way, the line of Republican progress did not vacillate thereafter. Seen this way, in other words, the class escalator remained relentless for the presidency too.

All of this helps to remove any individual peculiarity—any potential Eisenhower idiosyncrasy—from the coming of a Republican vote for President in 1952. In principle, it would have been possible for Eisenhower, the great American hero of his time, to expand the Southern Republican vote across the board, and for an expanded vote to acquire a class differentiation *after* he had left the political scene. This clearly was not the story. Instead, sharply rising Republican prospects in the South were tied to the arrival of a partisan attachment to income differences. In

Table 19-3 Social Class and the Coming of Southern Republicanism: The Presidency

Decade	Low	Mid	High	Total	Range (High-Low)
	Income Terciles				
A. Republican Percentage among All Whites					
1950s	43	47	53	48	+10
(N)	(200)	(134)	(201)	(535)	
1960s	37	38.	56	43	+19
(N)	(143)	(103)	(106)	(352)	
1970s	56	64	72	64	+16
(N)	(223)	(256)	(238)	(717)	
1980s	51	63	77	65	+26
(N)	(125)	(194)	(167)	(486)	
1990s	38	54	57	51	+19
(N)	(228)	(289)	(323)	(840)	
B. Republican Percentage of the White Two-Party Vote					
1950s	43	47	53	48	+10
(N)	(200)	(134)	(201)	(535)	
1960s	44	47	62	51	+18
(N)	(121)	(83)	(95)	(299)	
1970s	56	66	73	65	+17
(N)	(222)	(251)	(235)	(708)	
1980s	51	63	77	65	+23
(N)	(125)	(194)	(167)	(486)	
1990s	41	58	65	56	+24
(N)	(211)	(271)	(285)	(767)	

the process, Eisenhower served as the vehicle to register a pattern of class voting opposite to what had existed before, not as a transition to that outcome, much less as a brake upon it.

The candidate himself would probably have been horrified at this contribution—no class warrior, he. Nevertheless, he was to serve as the crystallizing vehicle for a new and different attachment between social class and Republican voting for president in the South. Moreover, this attachment did not go on thereafter to drag all income levels up in roughly proportional fashion, as economic growth progressed and the postwar period aged. As with the House, the top income tercile led the charge to a new Republicanism. And as with the House, despite unprecedented general Republican growth, the bottom tercile, the poorest third of the white South, remained disproportionately immune to Republican attractions.

The presence of a serious Republican vote for President in the first postwar election for which we have individual-level data does deny to the presidential tables one element of drama that the congressional tables possessed. With the Republican vote for Congress, one can see the Republican vote arrive *and* see that it represents a class reversal when it does (Table 19-1). That is, we possess the necessary "before" and "after" elections, before and after that reversal of the voting relationship to social class. With the Republican vote for President, one can see this arrival but not the change in class connection that came with it, at least not directly. Strictly speaking, there is no "before."

This missing data point is really a small matter, given the background situation. There was, after all, a remarkable absence of economic growth in the South before the 1940s. A poor agricultural economy had been only further devastated by the Great Depression. There was likewise a remarkable absence of a Republican presidential vote, in a line of electoral votes still running effectively at zero (Figure 1.2 [in Shafer and Johnston 2006]). When this Republican vote did appear, on the other hand, it arrived in the company of a clear income differentiation (Table 19-3). And this contextual before-and-after logic could be directly confirmed with individual-level data in Congress (Table 19-1).

There is, however, one further means of looking for this temporal comparison in the case of the presidency, and if it is hardly ideal in terms of its measurement, it does coincide powerfully with the old South argument of V. O. Key and the new South patterns revealed in the House. What this also affirms, once more, is that the Republican surge around the Eisenhower candidacy, for all the attractions of its hero-candidate, was essentially a vehicle for tapping Southern economic development, with its new politics of economic interest.

The way to do this additional investigation is to classify congressional districts according to whether they actually possessed a Republican candidate for Congress in 1952, before Eisenhower was nominated and then went on to expand the presidential vote. Districts that possessed Republican House candidates before Eisenhower thus become "old Republican"; all others are classified as "new." Even then, the National Election Study did not code survey respondents in 1952 according to their congressional district. But the NES did code respondents that way in 1956 and thereafter, so that it is possible to look for structural resonances from the old South, and for contemporary differences between the old and the new.

Looked at this way, these differences—the geological strata of Southern politics—stand out strongly (Table 19-4). For the 1950s, in fact, four things stand out:

- First, despite the superficially seismic impact of Dwight Eisenhower, old Republican areas were still considerably more sympathetic to the Republican candidate for president. That did not change.
- Second, old Republican areas simultaneously demonstrated the class inversion characteristic of the old South: the poor were most likely to vote Republican, the wealthy least likely to do so. By contrast, new Republican areas had this class tilt reversed—"righted."

- As a result, the difference in the class-based range of Republican support in old versus new Republican areas was huge: −12 percent in old areas to +19 percent in new ones, a massive reverse alignment.
- And just to emphasize the nature of the change, this difference was at its most extreme among low-income whites: Eisenhower was hugely attractive to them in old Republican areas, garnering 60 percent of their votes, but notably unattractive in newer areas, at just 31 percent.

The 1960s then began an evolution, showing the gradual but insistent dominance of the new order, infusing but not yet obliterating the old (Table 19-4B). The gap in Republican presidential prospects between old and new Republican areas remained alive, with a real but rapidly declining advantage to old Republican areas. Yet by the 1960s, both areas showed the impact of the new (not the old) class-based voting patterns. These were strongly present (and strongly positive) in the new Republican areas, more shakily present—apparently still in transition—in the old.

By the 1970s, the old South had disappeared (Table 19-4C). Old and new Republican areas were making an essentially equal contribution to the national Republican vote. Moreover, both now gave Republican presidential candidates a healthy majority. Old and new Republican areas could no longer be distinguished by the relationship between presidential voting and social class either; both now offered roughly the same percentage of support from lower-, middle-, and upper-income voters. This also meant that old and new Republican areas could no longer be distinguished by the behavior of their low-income denizens.

Policy implications, at least in the social welfare realm, followed logically from these class impacts (Table 19-5A). Unlike the situation in voting for the

Table 19-4 The Timing of a Class Reversal: The Presidency

| | Republican Percentage among All Whites | | | | | |
| | Income Terciles | | | | | |
	Low	Mid	High	Range (High-Low)	Total	[N]
A. The 1950s						
Old Republican Areas	60	58	48	−12	56	[124]
New Republican Areas	31	44	50	+19	42	[250]
B. The 1960s						
Old Republican Areas	44	32	57	+13	46	[112]
New Republican Areas	35	41	55	+20	42	[240]
C. The 1970s						
Old Republican Areas	58	67	71	+13	65	[268]
New Republican Areas	55	63	73	+18	64	[449]

Table 19-5 Welfare Attitudes and the Coming of Southern Republicanism: The Presidency

	Welfare Attitudes		
	Liberal	Conservative	Range (High-Low)
A. Republican Percentage among All Whites by Decade			
1950s	43	53	+10
(N)	(207)	(93)	
1960s	37	56	+19
(N)	(84)	(198)	
1970s	56	72	+16
(N)	(145)	(368)	
1980s	51	77	+26
(N)	(103)	(273)	
1990s	38	57	+19
(N)	(161)	(427)	
B. Republican Percentage among All Whites by Grouped Presidencies			
Eisenhower-Kennedy	43	53	+10
(N)	(207)	(93)	
Johnson-Nixon	46	66	+20
(N)	(136)	(345)	
Carter-Reagan	44	69	+25
(N)	(151)	(355)	
Bush-Clinton	27	63	+36
(N)	(189)	(470)	

House, the modern class pattern was already present in overall voting for the presidency by the 1950s, with the rich more Republican and the poor more Democratic. Not surprisingly, the modern pattern of welfare preferences was likewise present, with conservatives voting Republican and liberals voting Democratic. This relationship was then confirmed and enlarged in the 1960s. Again unsurprisingly, the relationship between welfare preferences and the vote, having taken root a decade before the same relationship surfaced for the House, remained substantially stronger for the presidency (compare with Table 19-2).

It would be possible to disaggregate the 1950s of Table 19-5A into old and new Republican areas, in the same manner as shown in Table 19-4. But in the case of welfare attitudes, there would be little point. Both new and established Republican areas showed the modern relationship to welfare attitudes by the 1950s, with liberals being Democratic and conservatives Republican. Established areas were still more Republican overall, as they would have to be. But within both older and newer areas, welfare ideology conduced toward Republican support in the modern fashion (table not shown).

One should not, however, miss the element of distinctiveness in this. With social class, older areas had shown an inverse relationship to the modern pattern; only the newer areas came with the modern relationship fully formed. With welfare ideology, on the other hand, the modern relationship arrived fully formed everywhere. In other words, in the old world of Southern politics, class attachments (dating to the Civil War) were inverse, but ideological attachments had come to reflect the policy positions of the national parties. In the newly emergent Southern world, by contrast, both class attachments and ideological positions were consistent with the modern world when they arrived, for they simply had no "old world" from which they needed to become disentangled.

Table 19-5A, however, is one of those tables where the process of aggregating presidencies by decade rather than in equal groupings, putting two elections in some decades and three in others, suggests that subsequent developments were less linear—more wobbly—than was probably the case. Accordingly, Table 19-5B takes the same relationship between welfare preferences and the vote and presents it in three-election aggregates. The positive relationship between welfare conservatism or liberalism and voting Republican or Democratic is unchanged for the earliest period, the Eisenhower-Kennedy elections. That relationship is still confirmed and enhanced in the next period, the Johnson-Nixon elections. But it then moves up in an essentially straightforward fashion through the next two periods as well, that is, through the Carter-Reagan and then the Bush-Clinton elections too.

Social Class and Southern Republicanism: The Senate

The other branch of Congress, the Senate, requires several short digressions on institutional structure and its impact on data-handling before we can proceed to analysis of the link between economic development and partisan change. Part of this is statistical in an elementary way. With the presidency, while there was a presidential contest only every four years, that contest did feature a Republican candidate in every voting district. With the Senate, especially in the early years, it did not. For the House, although the provision of Republican candidates was also a major challenge, there were over a hundred contests every two years, over five hundred every decade. But for the Senate, that is, for the eleven states of the Old Confederacy with their twenty-two Senators serving six-year terms, there were on average *seven* contests every other year, and thus only about thirty-five per decade.

As a result, some of the statistical manipulations that are possible for the House and the presidency are just impossible with the Senate, and many others present a "choppier" picture. The situation is made worse by the fact that the NES is a national—not necessarily a regional—random sample, so that a year with few Senate elections on the calendar, and fewer contested elections within them, can also find them seriously under-sampled. This problem is at its worst for the 1950s and early 1960s, when NES samples tended to be more tightly clustered in geographic terms. The best we can do is to raise these cautions when the particular analysis appears to make them especially pertinent.

Otherwise, when the focus is institutional arrangements with the potential to shape a relationship between social change and partisan shifts, there are some respects in which the Senate looks more like the presidency than the House. For example, the Senate and the presidency have effectively the same electoral districts, so that both allocate the spoils of victory, either a full term in office or a full complement of electoral votes, to the plurality winner statewide. In most regards, however, the Senate is institutionally closer to the House than to the presidency, starting with the fundamental facts that both are collective (rather than individual) and legislative (rather than executive) institutions.

House and Senate districts did differ in potentially important ways. To begin with, the individual Southern states comprised as few as 6 and as many as 22 congressional districts in the 1950s, as few as 4 and as many as 30 by the 1990s. This meant that House districts were inevitably more homogeneous than any single state could be. Seen the other way around, however, the more important consequence is that Senate districts, being a blend of their House components, varied less among themselves—among the states—than did these component parts. There was just inherently less variation among the 11 states of the Old Confederacy than among the 106 congressional districts of the 1950s or the 123 of the 1990s.

As a result, when partisan change began, the social changes that were contributing to it had the potential to register earlier in some minority of House seats, where they were always more concentrated. In the crucial example, there were congressional districts with white-collar majorities well before there were any Senate districts (that is, states) that could make this claim. Thereafter, this differential variance between House and Senate districts meant that relationships between changing social characteristics and changing partisan behavior were likely to be stronger across House as opposed to Senate districts. In the crucial example here, there would always be a minority of House districts that were disproportionately white, along with a minority of House districts that were disproportionately black—disproportionate in both cases to any Senate seat—so that when racial context mattered, it ought to have mattered more in the House.

Yet despite clear differences in their electoral districting, the Senate and the House often behaved in highly parallel ways, and this fact will sometimes prove to be a route around the statistical problems that the small number of Senate seats can introduce. Two House-Senate comparisons underline this parallelism. The first involves voting behavior and can be presented year by year. If we compare the mean Republican vote in contested districts across the postwar years, the two bodies are effectively indistinguishable (Figure 19-1A). Because there can be as few as two or three contested Senate elections from the South in any given year, we cannot reasonably compare outcomes—wins and losses—by year, but we can aggregate these by decade (Figure 19-1B). Once more, the resulting differences are inconsequential.

Moreover, it may be surprising to discover how closely the Senate hewed to both the House and the presidency stories. That is, it is possible to see the same class reversal arrive with the Senate as it did with the House and the presidency, and it is even possible to isolate the apparent timing of the change. At first glance, aggregated by decade, both the 1950s and the 1960s show only unsystematic flux in the relationship between income terciles and a Republican vote for the U.S.

Figure 19-1 The Congressional Story Revisited

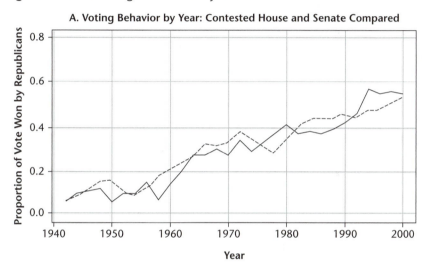

A. Voting Behavior by Year: Contested House and Senate Compared

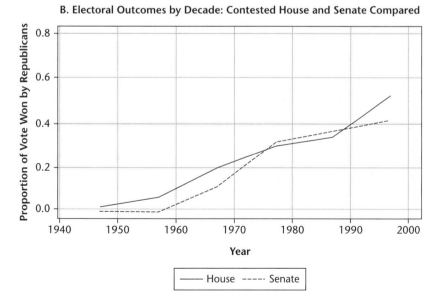

B. Electoral Outcomes by Decade: Contested House and Senate Compared

Table 19-6 The Timing of a Class Reversal: The Senate

	Republican Percentage among All Whites in Contested States					
	Income Terciles					
Decade	Low	Mid	High		Range (High–Low)	Decadal Change
1952–1966	26	20	27	25	+1	—
(N)	(139)	(95)	(122)	(356)		
1968–1980	42	44	53	47	+11	+10
(N)	(227)	(259)	(257)	(743)		
1982–1990	35	38	46	40	+11	0
(N)	(162)	(208)	(222)	(592)		
1992–2000	43	56	64	56	+21	+10
(N)	(165)	(226)	(288)	(679)		

Senate, so that the overall effect of a class reversal cannot be elicited until after 1970 (table not shown). By then, the story had become the same.

In fact, however, this appears to be one of those cases where imposition of a temporal cut appropriate to the House and the presidency is modestly misleading with the Senate data. For even with a serious shortage of open seats and a chronic dearth of Republican candidates, it is possible, by examining Senate results year by year, to let the data themselves aggregate the early years a bit differently. If the point is to isolate the sharpest available shift from the old world (with its class inversion) to the new, then alternative ways of dividing the 1960s should be permitted. If they are, then Table 19-6 is the result.

Seen this way, for the period from the beginning of the National Election Studies through 1966, there was no evident patterning to the relationship between income terciles and Republican voting for the U.S. Senate in the American South. There was then a sharp jump toward the modern pattern from 1968 onward. That pattern was sustained in the 1980s. And it jumped again in the 1990s, as Republicans moved to majority status. Cut this way, the Senate looks powerfully like the House, and the apparent time lag in its responsiveness shrinks substantially. The Republican breakthrough occurred perhaps four years earlier in the House than in the Senate, but that was all.

A direct link to policy conflicts from this class shift, however, did lag the most for the Senate. Direct links to public preferences on social welfare were already there with the presidency in the 1950s, and they were destined to grow only stronger (Table 19-5). These same links arrived for the House in the 1960s, the point at which the old class inversion righted itself in this institution too, and they grew thereafter for the House as well (Table 19-2). Yet they did not really arrive for the Senate until the 1980s, at least a decade after the old class inversion had disappeared (Table 19-7). If the class inversion characterizing postwar politics arrived a bit later with the Senate, then, its social welfare link arrived later still.

Table 19-7 Welfare Attitudes and the Coming of Southern Republicanism: The Senate

| | Republican Percentage among All Whites in Contested States | | |
| | Welfare Attitudes | | |
Decade	Liberal	Conservative	Range (High-Low)
1950s	22	25	+3
(N)	(109)	(56)	
1960s	37	41	+4
(N)	(41)	(110)	
1970s	50	53	+3
(N)	(104)	(301)	
1980s	26	49	+23
(N)	(119)	(299)	
1990s	30	68	+38
(N)	(141)	(359)	

On the other hand, what came to characterize both the House and the presidency with regard to the place of public preferences on welfare policy could not be delayed indefinitely, and indeed it was not. The world of the old South for the Senate, like that same world when examined through the House, featured nearly no relationship between welfare attitudes and Republican voting. By the 1980s, that relationship was instead strongly present. By the 1990s, it was surging, becoming every bit as strong as the link to welfare attitudes for the other two nationally elective institutions, almost as if to make up for the delay. In other words, some mix of institutional and candidate characteristics kept the Senate from looking like the new South for a little longer, though not by much.

Economic Development as Partisan Engine

Economic development came to the American South in the years following World War II, in a manner that it had not experienced since well before the Civil War. And economic development proved to be directly associated with partisan change, most especially by way of the prospects, at long last, for a Southern Republican Party. The specific events of postwar politics still shaped these prospects in measurable ways: war and peace, boom and recession, achievement and scandal. So did the identities and abilities of individual candidates—for the presidency, for the Senate, and for the House. Yet what is more impressive, in the face of all these implicit sources of variation, is not just the relentlessness by which economic development remade Southern politics, but the essential *homogeneity* of its impact.

When the focus was the share of actual wins and losses for public office, as it was in Figure 1.2 [in Shafer and Johnston 2006], then the picture of relentless

Figure 19-2 Class Effects by Institution

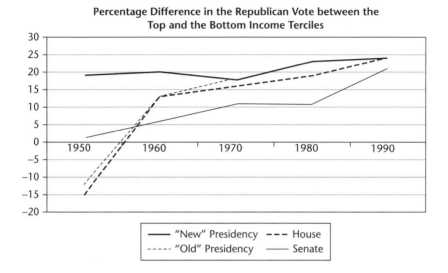

Percentage Difference in the Republican Vote between the Top and the Bottom Income Terciles

Legend:
——— "New" Presidency – – – House
----- "Old" Presidency ——— Senate

Republican progress did show some differential volatility, institution by institution. But when the focus is instead the relationship between social class and partisan choice, as it has been throughout this chapter, then volatility was only initial for all three institutions. Within an impressively short time, each came into line with the class patterns of the new and not the old South. Thereafter, what was striking was the extent to which the three separate institutions did not differ. Figure 19-2 plots the percentage difference in the Republican vote between the top and bottom income terciles by decade for the three governmental institutions, with the presidency divided into old and new areas for the early years.

At one extreme, the areas for a new Republican vote, those areas that had never previously provided a serious vote for Republican presidential candidates, arrived with the modern class relationship fully formed. This is the line for the "New" Presidency in Figure 19-2. Thereafter, these areas differed very little from decade to decade in the range of their success among upper-income as opposed to lower-income sectors of society. The aggregate total for the Republican candidate could still vary enormously, from 42 percent in the 1950s to 65 percent in the 1980s. But the class relationship within that aggregate varied almost not at all. It should also be noted that this was not the presidency "dragging up" the Republican vote. If institutional dynamics were the story, they should have appeared earlier and continued later. Rather, social forces were "welling up" from the bottom and being reflected in newly Republican areas.

It took a further decade for the older areas of Republican support, those that had always offered a serious vote to the Republican presidential candidate, to come into line with these new areas. Seen the other way around, however, it took *only* another decade: this is the line for the "Old" Presidency in Figure 19-2. The class relationships of the old South, where the lower-income sector was more likely to vote Republican rather than Democratic, naturally provided some resistance to the class relationships emerging in the new South. People had presumably been voting opposite to these new patterns—inversely—for generations. Yet it took only another decade before the difference between old and new Republican areas was close to elimination, not by splitting the difference but by settling on the new Republican pattern.

As the postwar era began, the House of Representatives actually looked most like the old presidency in terms of its voting relationships (Figure 19-2). This is the world sketched so richly by V. O. Key in *Southern Politics in State and Nation*, and it began with the strongest negative relationship between class and Republican support among the three nationally elective governmental institutions. Yet within a single decade, this pattern had reversed. Now, upper-income Southerners were voting Republican, lower-income Southerners Democratic, as they had in the North for a generation and a half, and as they would in the South forever after. By the 1960s, the House relationship was well on its way to convergence with the presidency. By the 1970s, it was effectively indistinguishable.

The Senate, finally, fell in between. At the start of the postwar era, voting relationships to social class were neither as inverted as they were for the House nor as contemporary as they were for newly Republican areas of the presidency (Figure 19-2). This initial ambiguity, coupled with the much smaller number of Senate contests, the presence of many long-lived incumbents, and some personal idiosyncrasies, appeared to delay the aligning impact of economic development on partisan politics. Yet by the 1970s, the Senate too had begun its move toward class convergence with the presidency and the House. By the 1990s, it had experienced a second sharp correction, essentially converging on the presidency/House pattern.

A tabular way to see the same thing is just to recast the postwar presidential vote in a fashion precisely parallel to the postwar vote for the House of Representatives (Table 19-8). In the real world of practical politics, it makes no sense to do this: the two parties had presidential candidates everywhere, after all, and the degree to which they attracted votes is the appropriate measure of presidential Republican strength (Table 19-3). Moreover, if our concern is with the transition from an old Republican vote to a new, then the proper calculation is the Republican vote in areas with an established Republican Party by the time of Dwight Eisenhower, versus the Republican vote in areas that were not previously characterized by an organized Republican presence (Table 19-4).

Yet there is no problem mechanically in looking at the effect of social class on Republican voting for the presidency in only those congressional districts that also possessed both Republican and Democratic House candidates, and comparing it with the effect of social class on Republican voting for the House in presidential years only, thereby creating a precisely parallel calculation. When this is done, the story the two institutions tell is remarkably parallel:

Table 19-8 Social Class and the Coming of Southern Republicanism: The Presidency in Contested House Districts

| Decade | Republican Percentage among All Whites | | | | |
| | Income Terciles | | | | |
	Low	Mid	High	Presidential Range	House Range
1950s	55	52	46	−9	−13
(N)	(71)	(60)	(93)	(224)	(201)
1960s	34	39	57	+23	+25
(N)	(106)	(75)	(74)	(255)	(234)
1970s	53	58	69	+16	+20
(N)	(141)	(156)	(169)	(466)	(418)
1980s	52	68	80	+28	+14
(N)	(62)	(127)	(117)	(306)	(285)
1990s	36	53	56	+20	+25
(N)	(204)	(234)	(275)	(713)	(609)

- Now, both the presidency and the House showed the old Southern class inversion for the 1950s.
- Now, that inversion was righted dramatically in the 1960s, with almost precisely the same amount of change.
- For both—compare Table 19-8 with Table 19-1—it was the upper-income tercile that shifted its loyalties to start this change.
- For both—same comparison—the lower-income tercile effectively sat in the 1990s where it had in the 1950s.
- By the 1970s, the presidency and the House, calculated in this way, had converged on the same point.
- By the 1990s, they had moved on, to a point of Republican progress that was nevertheless essentially the same.

In any event, a new Southern politics had clearly emerged by the 1960s. Implicitly present by the 1950s, it was to acquire its fully modern form by the 1970s. And it would move relentlessly in the same direction thereafter. What was this politics about, the new politics that came with a changed economic universe and its new social alignments? The obvious answer is "social welfare," and it is obvious in two senses. First, a politics of social class was likely to be most centrally about social insurance and material (re)distribution. And second, the politics of the New Deal order—the Northern, class-based politics of the time—was profoundly about just that.

It came as no surprise, then, when the main events of a great class reversal were reflected in economic ideology. To see this, Table 19-9 takes the contents of

Table 19-9 Welfare Attitudes of Partisan Voters: The Presidency, the House, and the Senate

| | Mean Welfare Scores for Party Voters by Decade | | | | | | | | |
| | The Presidency | | | Contested House | | | Contested Senate | | |
Decade	Dems	Reps	Margin	Dems	Reps	Margin	Dems	Reps	Margin
1950s	.27	.36	+.09	.33	.36	+.03	.33	.32	−.01
1960s	.60	.81	+.21	.67	.78	+.11	.72	.75	+.03
1970s	.64	.76	+.12	.71	.78	+.07	.73	.72	+.02
1980s	.50	.84	+.34	.64	.86	+.22	.64	.83	+.19
1990s	.54	.87	+.33	.56	.84	+.28	.54	.85	+.31

Tables 19-2, 19-5, and 19-7, showing the relationship of welfare attitudes to the coming of Southern Republicanism, and calculates them "the other way around": the mean economic liberalism/conservatism of those who voted Republican or Democratic for each of these three national offices in all of the five postwar decades, where higher numbers are more conservative. What results is another variant of a familiar picture:

• There was little or no difference in the welfare preferences of Democratic and Republican voters for the House or the Senate in the old world of the 1950s. Partisan attachments had not been formed through welfare attitudes, and they did not reflect them. There were, however, clear and strong beginnings of a difference—to go with an evident class reversal—in the case of the presidency.

• Partisan voting for President moved forward to an even stronger link with public preferences on welfare policy in the 1960s, and partisan voting for the House now assumed the same alignment. Only the Senate continued its lack of alignment with welfare policy conflict—not reverse alignment, just non-alignment.

• Both the presidency and the House actually fell back a bit in the 1970s, before moving forward strongly in the 1980s. At this point the Senate moved, belatedly but strongly, to join them. Welfare policy differences between partisan voters were still greatest with the presidency, least with the Senate, but even for the latter, the relationship no longer looked problematic.

• And that led to the strong policy differences of the modern era, in which Democratic voters were sharply more liberal and Republican voters sharply more conservative on welfare issues across all three national institutions. Not only had all three relationships strengthened over time, they were also at their most congruent across the three great institutions by the 1990s.

Class Politics and the New South

Huge social forces reconfigured postwar society in the American South. Partisan shifts followed more or less ineluctably. Economic development, in particular, began its take-off as the Second World War ended. In truth, wartime industry had already helped in this transition, and the overall boom in the postwar economy then took over. This postwar American boom would be remarkable nearly everywhere, but the South actually caught up with the rest of the nation during its occurrence. Out-migration in search of a better life was a continuing motif of the old South, though the loss of the economically ambitious could only exacerbate the problems they left behind. Remarkably, in-migration in search of a better life would be a counter-motif in the new South—the famous Michigan-to-Texas, rust-belt-to-sun-belt stories of the 1980s being only a dramatic vignette (Gober 1993).

In turn, the coming of economic development, and with it a new class structure, led to a crucial class reversal in partisan politics. Once—and presumably for generations before we have individual-level data to confirm the relationship—class attachments to the political parties were inverse. Inverse, that is, with regard to the situation in the North and to the overall New Deal order. The better-off in the South leaned Democratic, the worse-off Republican. This was not so much a class alignment directly as it was an indirect reflection of the social base of partisan identifications at the time of the Civil War, but it nevertheless contributed an inverse class relationship.

Regardless, in the immediate postwar years, that relationship began to change. At long last, it came into alignment with the situation in the North, and the Republicans, not the Democrats, thereby became the party of the better-off. This also meant, portentously, that the Republicans were now aligned with the growth segments of Southern society (Figure 19-3). As its economic prospects grew, so did their political prospects: economic development proved a relentless partisan escalator for a new Southern Republican Party. One of the two great engines for partisan change in the American South was finally on the scene, pumping away. Figure 19-3 just retells that story in one more way.

Following on from this class reversal—part and parcel of it, but with a partially autonomous relationship to the partisan outcome—was a shift in policy conflict for the postwar South. As in the North, so in the South: a political order built upon social class was also a political order themed around social welfare. Class politics could, in principle, support any policy conflicts that were capable of being aligned with class differences. But in the late New Deal era, these were first and foremost conflicts over social welfare, and while these might be joined by other concerns as the postwar era aged, they would actually never recede. Indeed, they would only advance.

The simplest way, to bring all of this together in a single exhibit, thus providing a final summary device, is by means of elementary cross-tabulations between welfare preferences and income terciles (Table 19-10). Welfare preferences are

Figure 19-3 The Class Escalator: White–Collar Shares by Congressional
District

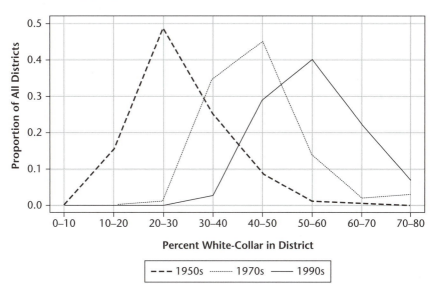

presented as a liberal-conservative dichotomy, since that allows a consistent scale
over fifty years. Social class is captured by comparing top and bottom income
terciles. The postwar years are divided into the old order of the 1950s, the transitional period of the 1960s through the 1980s, and the new world of the 1990s.[4]
And the presidency, the Senate, and the House are analyzed separately, to capture
any institutional differences along the way.

Cell entries are then just the percentage voting Republican.[5] Even in this
simplified format, the evidence from the 1950s is fragile, with small sample sizes
and item formats that saw respondents opting more for the "Don't Know" category than they would in subsequent years. We think that the bivariate format of
earlier tables in this chapter is a better representation of relationships at this
period in many regards. Nevertheless, the picture that emerges here of the opening years of the postwar era is easily recognizable from what has gone before.

The House remained the world of the old South. There was no policy relationship to the vote, and the class relationship, which clearly did exist, was
inverse. That is to say: liberals or conservatives on social welfare did not differ in
their partisan choices, but the *poor* were more likely to vote Republican and the
rich Democratic. By contrast, social change was already beginning to reach into
voting for the presidency, so that it offered a more complex picture of the impact
of social class and welfare preferences. Welfare ideology had arrived as an influence, with conservatives more likely to vote Republican for President than liberals, though this was especially true among low-income voters. And the wealthy

Table 19-10 Social Class, Welfare Preference, and Partisan Change, 1952–2000

	Republican Percentage among All Whites								
	A. Presidency Income			B. Senate Income			C. House Income		
	Low	High		Low	High		Low	High	
Welfare Attitude	1950s			1950s			1950s		
Lib	38	44	+6	23	30	+7	39	30	−9
	(90)	(54)		(64)	(30)		(57)	(44)	
Con	72	48	−24	50	31	−19	38	30	−8
	(18)	(48)		(26)	(54)		(13)	(37)	
	+34	+4		+27	+1		−1	0	
	1960s–1980s			1960s–1980s			1960s–1980s		
Lib	37	56	+19	33	38	+5	29	33	+4
	(131)	(59)		(85)	(53)		(98)	(57)	
Con	59	75	+26	45	53	+8	36	54	+18
	(185)	(329)		(137)	(274)		(151)	(309)	
	+22	+19		+12	+15		+7	+21	
	1990s			1990s			1990s		
Lib	25	25	0	23	30	+7	29	34	+5
	(55)	(44)		(40)	(44)		(52)	(50)	
Con	49	69	+20	55	73	+18	55	74	+19
	(78)	(169)		(62)	(149)		(91)	(190)	
	+24	+34		+32	+43		+26	+40	

had become more likely overall to vote Republican, the poor to vote Democratic, though this effect was concentrated among welfare liberals and did not apply to welfare conservatives.

On the other hand, there were so few low-income conservatives on social welfare that they should probably be disregarded. If they are, the story of the presidency in this period is that both class and race had become aligned, in what would come to be recognized as the modern pattern. The wealthy were more Republican than the poor, and welfare conservatives more Republican than welfare liberals, within each tercile. This was in striking contrast to the House, where the poor were more Republican than the wealthy, and where welfare preferences remained irrelevant within both groups. The Senate then approximated the presidency more than the House, again showing the beginnings of modern impacts from both social class and welfare preference, though in a weaker fashion than with the presidency.

The transitional decades, from the 1960s through the 1980s, bring more robust data and tell a very different story:

- For all three institutions, social class had become aligned with partisan choice. The upper tercile was going Republican, the lower tercile Democratic, and policy preferences were no longer a confusing factor in this relationship. This effect was strongest for the presidency and weakest for the Senate, though the greatest change came in the House, where an actual negative relationship had been reversed.

- For all three institutions, policy preference too was now aligned with partisan choice. Conservatives were voting Republican, liberals Democratic, and social class was no longer a confusing factor in this relationship. Again, the effect was strongest for the presidency. And again, it was the House that had made the largest overall shift, though low-income voters still lagged; it was upper-income voters who had most fully come into alignment with the other two institutions.

- That said, the main point was a powerful symmetry emerging among all three institutions. High-income conservatives were uniformly most Republican. Low-income liberals were uniformly least Republican. And there was little to choose between high-income liberals or low-income conservatives in terms of their Republican proclivities.

The modern era, the 1990s, is then easily recognizable as a further evolution of this transition period. The overall class effect remained, and remained unconfused by the impact of policy preferences. The overall attitudinal effect remained as well, though by the 1990s, it was clearly the stronger of the two: differences between liberals and conservatives were larger than differences between the poor and the rich for every institution. As a result, the overall symmetry was additionally neat. Now, upper-income conservatives were the most Republican; lower-income conservatives came next; upper-income liberals followed them; and lower-income liberals were the least Republican. On the one hand, welfare liberals, rich or poor, were pretty uniformly resistant to Republican attractions. On the other, this was not much of a firewall against Republican gains: the vast majority of white Southerners were welfare conservatives.

In the end, then, what emerges most strikingly is the consistent pattern of a new Southern politics, one built upon—indeed, generated by—economic growth, social class, and an underlying class reversion. The basic class change, away from the pattern of the old South but still visible in the 1950s, was a hugely powerful phenomenon. Yet the impact of policy preferences on social welfare also became

a powerful relationship as the new South consolidated, culminating in a remarkably powerful effect of its own by the 1990s. Thus in the end, there was a composite political world strikingly different from the one that had gone before, and
had lasted for so long.

Notes

1. And, fatally for us, with no way to distinguish South from non-South among the
   respondents.
2. In our analysis, decades are grouped from the year "2" through the year "0," to keep
   them in line with the decennial census, and, especially, with the congressional districting that followed from it. Thus the 1950s run from 1952–1960, the 1960s from
   1962–1970, and so on. This has the added advantage of not pooling on the basis of
   particular partisan outcomes; partisan change must register within analytically neutral
   time-periods if it is to register at all. On those occasions where a division into census
   decades threatens to introduce a substantive distortion, as in Table 19-6, we address
   the problem in context.
3. It might seem that a further shift of substantive consequence occurred between the
   1950s and 1960s, as the marginals became more conservative overall. We believe that
   this is an artifactual shift, rooted in measurement reform rather than social change.
   Part of it must be traced to available item responses: these were broadened substantially after the 1950s, removing a kind of forced choice of the extremes. More of it,
   we think, is due to the way in which question referents in the 1950s involve aspects
   of social insurance ("a job," etc.), whereas referents after 1960 all feature economic
   redistribution ("a good standard of living"). Majorities of Americans have always been
   more supportive of the former than the latter (Jaffe 1978; Shapiro and Young 1990;
   Cook and Barrett 1992). This interpretation is reinforced by the fact that the same
   shift in the marginals occurred at the same time in the non-South, thereby guarantee-
   ing that the relevant influences are not Southern.
4. As in Tables 19-6 and 19-7, "the 1950s" for the Senate encompass the years 1952–
   1966, while "the 1960s–1980s" are actually 1968–1990.
5. Because Table 19-10 is a cross-tabulation of two bivariate relations for each institution, drawn from Tables 19-1 and 19-2, 19-3 and 19-5, plus 19-6 and 19-7, there is
   some inevitable attrition of the sample in demanding both income tercile and welfare
   attitude. It is a simple matter, however, to take those who appear in Table 19-10 and
   rerun the previous tables with this particular, slightly smaller sample. When this is
   done, none of the previous class or attitude marginals change in substantial ways, and
   no overall relations change at all.

20. The Reintroduction of the *Elephas Maximus*[1] to the Southern United States

The Rise of Republican State Parties, 1960 to 2000 (Updated)

M. V. Hood III, Quentin Kidd, and Irwin L. Morris

The American South provides a unique laboratory for the examination of representation in a late twentieth century democracy. Since the late 1960s, no region has witnessed a more thorough political transformation than the South. In 1960, Democrat John F. Kennedy captured a popular vote margin in seven (a majority) of the former states of the Confederacy. Forty years later, Vice President Al Gore, Democratic presidential nominee, failed to win a single Southern state—including his home state of Tennessee. The years of single party politics in the *solid South* have been replaced by an intensely competitive two-party system. Where Democrats once reigned supreme, Republicans are quickly becoming the dominant party.

Although Southern Republicans had few realistic political aspirations during the first half of the twentieth century and party stalwarts were few in number, pockets of Southern Republicanism have existed since the end of Reconstruction. Key (1949) described these partisans in various colorful ways—mountain Republicans, for example. Although Key's characterization of Southern Republicans at midcentury captured the party's electoral destitution, he also presciently catalogued the social forces that would grow a political force capable of eclipsing the seemingly eternal solid South.

Although the roots of this political transformation extend far deeper, the passage of the Voting Rights Act (VRA) in 1965 clearly marked the end of an era in Southern politics. The VRA was one of the most important suffrage documents in American history, because it provided the opportunity for disenfranchised Black Southerners to return to the political fold from which they were banished at the end of Reconstruction. As Black and Black (1987) argued, "The Voting Rights Act was the grand turning point in modern times for the reentry of Blacks into Southern politics" (p. 136). Likewise, the VRA was a milestone in the development of the Republican Party in the South. Prior to the passage of the VRA, the South had one post-Reconstruction Republican senator (John Tower—Texas); however, at this writing, 13 of 22 Senate seats, 76 of 131 House seats, and 7 of 11 governors are Republican. According to the *American National Election Studies*, Southern Democrats outnumbered their Republican counterparts by a margin of 6 to 1 in 1952. By the late 1990s, that advantage had all but disappeared.

Source: American Politics Research 32, 1 (January 2004): 68–101. The authors updated the analysis shown in Figure 20-1 and Table 20-1 and added an epilogue.

Theoretical Background: The Study of
Southern Party Transformation

The transformation of the party system in the South, the mobilization of an entirely new voting population, and the rise of the Republican Party that Key, at least in part, foresaw have been the subject of numerous books and articles. Given the sheer weight of the printed volumes of research on this topic, our understanding of this dramatic political transformation is surprisingly limited. As Stanley and Castle (1988) realized,

> One hallmark of scientific research, cumulative knowledge, has not characterized the study of Southern partisan change. Indeed, scholars disagree not only about the overall trends but also about the impact of the . . . processes capable of producing shifts in Southern partisanship. (p. 240)

In the most basic terms, a number of significant empirical questions remain unanswered. For example, to what extent did the mobilization of the Black electorate in the South (as Democrats)—and not just the presence of large concentrations of Blacks in the Black-belt region (see Giles and Hertz 1994)—foster an increase in Republican voting behavior (almost completely among Whites)? We know Black mobilization did influence roll-call voting patterns of both House and Senate members from the region (e.g., see Hood, Kidd, and Morris 1999). Did this mobilization indirectly bolster Republican ranks? What portion, if any, of the growth of Republicanism can be attributed to in-migration from other regions of the United States? How has the South's economic transformation (as manifested in a decreasing dependence on an agriculturally based economy) affected Southern partisanship? Finally, to what extent did organizational factors such as party competitiveness promote the growth of Southern Republicanism?

Although scholars of Southern politics have made significant headway in providing explanations for two-party growth, we argue that this body of literature is still somewhat disjointed and that the wide array of methodological approaches, units of analysis, explanatory variables, and timeframes characteristic of this literature have hindered the development of a coherent explanation of Republican growth. The stated goal of this manuscript is to employ a methodology in which competing explanations for two-party growth in the South—political, economic, and demographic—can be simultaneously analyzed across comparable geographic units over a long time horizon. Although definitive answers are always beyond the reach of social science research, we hope such a strategy will produce a clearer picture of the exact mechanisms that most directly led to the advent of a viable Republican Party in the South over the last half of the twentieth century.

Besides Key (1949), one of the earliest works to deal with the growth of Southern Republicanism was Heard's *A Two Party South* (1952). Not long thereafter, Strong addressed the potential for Republican growth in a *Journal of Politics* article, entitled "The Presidential Election in the South, 1952" (1955), and in the related work, *Urban Republicanism in the South* (1960). Since Strom Thurmond's Dixiecrat presidential campaign in 1948, Southern Democrats faced a serious and continuing threat from the Republican Party. In the early 1970s, Tindall (1972) concluded,

> 1948, unlike 1928, was the start of an ongoing rebellion. Since that time the South has split its electoral vote in five presidential elections, and in two of these it has divided three ways. It has experienced a sizeable growth of presidential Republicanism; and in the 1960s a breakthrough in congressional, state, and local Republicanism. (p. 37)

The increasingly liberal orientation of the national Democratic Party on the issue of civil rights clearly engendered the dissatisfaction of White Southern Democrats with their own party. Southern delegations to the 1948 Democratic convention took a dim view of Truman's support for a liberal civil rights plank in the party platform, and his candidacy—even as an incumbent president—was vehemently opposed by several Southern delegations.[2] Although wholesale party system transformation was years away, the 1948 Dixiecrat convention in Birmingham presaged the subsequent growth of Southern Republicanism.

Although national party dynamics may have provided the initial impetus for the region-wide growth of Republican voting behavior (see Black and Black 1987, 2002; Carmines and Stimson 1989), it is also obvious that the rate of growth varied considerably among the states, and such variance cannot be explained by national party politics alone. To explain subregional differences in Republican growth, scholars have focused on a variety of disparate demographic and economic factors such as in-migration, economic growth and transformation, the waning significance of agriculture, religious conservatism, and racial context among others.[3] Although it is often necessary in social science research to employ demographic variables as proxies for political phenomena, we would argue that a greater effort needs to be undertaken in Southern politics to incorporate more precise measures of theoretically salient political correlates. Continuing along this train of thought, we seek to develop a model to more directly test the supposition that the variation in state-level Republican growth in the South is fundamentally itself a byproduct of political change.

The Theory of Relative Advantage

We argue that the size of the Republican Party in the South grew, over the time period of our analysis, because the benefits of voting and identification with the Republican Party for conservative Whites, compared to the benefits of Democratic affiliation, increased.[4] So, from a political standpoint, the *relative advantage* of the Republican Party increased over this time period, but the extent of this relative advantage for the GOP varied considerably across the Southern states.

Political sociology has long recognized that certain societal cleavages can coalesce into specific party systems. In their work *Party Systems and Voter Alignments,* Lipset and Rokkan (1967) provided a useful framework for discussing social cleavages that is related to relative advantage theory. Especially relevant for the present study is the idea that various cleavage structures can lead to certain advantages for a specific party relative to another party or parties. This supposition has long been recognized by scholars studying realignments in the American party system (e.g., see Sundquist,1983). Although not all cleavages may relate to the concept of relative advantage, the racial dichotomy in the South certainly produced a context in which a defunct Republican Party once again became a viable party alternative in the wake of the political disturbance brought about by the enfranchisement of Blacks in the region (Katz 2001).

Although related to the formation of societal cleavages, the idea of relative advantage encompasses more than the demographic foundations of partisan change. Some catalyst must also present itself, this spark often taking the form of policy orientations and/or ideological positions held by existing political structures. Citizens identify with and vote for candidates of political parties for a variety of reasons.

Among the factors that influence peoples' decisions to support one party or the other are (a) the relative competitiveness of the party in a wide variety of political arenas and (b) the relative consistency of each party's political objectives with a citizen's own political objectives. In the Southern context, Republican Party support (relative to Democratic Party support) became more valuable because:

1. Republicans were fielding increasing numbers of candidates for political office at all levels thereby causing the traditional Democratic Party monopoly over party nominations to dissipate.
2. The mobilization of the Black population—an almost uniformly Democratic electorate—made it increasingly difficult for Southern conservative Whites to maintain control of the local Democratic Party machinery. As the local Democratic Party became more difficult to control, the party apparatus became less valuable.

Two-Party Emergence

There is no doubt that the Republican Party, as a viable electoral organization, is a relatively new aspect of Southern politics. One of Key's (1949) primary criticisms of the Southern party system of his time was the absence of active and significant party competition in the region. Key hypothesized that it was this decided lack of interparty competition that, in turn, stunted the development of viable party organizations in the region.[5] During the last three decades, however, the Southern GOP has become an organizational equal of, and sometimes superior to, the Democratic Party in the region (e.g., see Maggiotto and Wekkin 2000). In reference to this point, Aldrich (2000) noted,

The development of southern parties in the twentieth century follows rather closely the lines Key's analysis suggested. The emergence of serious and sustained opposition at all levels of office to Democratic candidates by Republicans is closely associated in time with the development of perhaps the strongest and most effectively organized dual party system in Southern history and at least at levels currently found outside the South, if not even higher. (p. 661)

Students of Southern politics have been preoccupied with the pattern of two-party emergence in the South for at least three decades. One prominent theory posits that two-party competition in the region began as a product of support for Republican presidential candidates (for support of this theory of party change, see Aistrup 1996; Lamis 1988). Success at the presidential level then filtered down to statewide offices (i.e., governor, U.S. senator), which, in turn, led to increased levels of voting for GOP congressional candidates. Finally, this top-down process culminated in GOP viability at the substate level (i.e., state legislative seats). In *The Rise of Southern Republicans,* Black and Black (2002) highlighted the importance of presidential campaigns, especially Ronald Reagan's, in producing a realignment at the congressional level in the region. Likewise, other research has uncovered a linkage between GOP state party election strategies and recruiting candidates to run in legislative districts with a tendency to vote for Republican presidential candidates (Bullock and Shafer 1997).

Recently, however, Aldrich (2000) and Aldrich and Griffin (2000) have challenged the top-down theory of party change in the region. Using a series of Granger causality tests, these studies demonstrated that GOP electoral successes at the national level is a direct product of, or is caused by, prior victories at the state level. Likewise, success in state legislative races was a precursor to winning U.S. House elections. At least some evidence exists, therefore, to assert that state GOP party-building efforts were the result of a highly complex process operating at multiple levels.

As theorized, Republican Party strength at the state-level relative to that of the Democratic Party is in part associated with the ability of the GOP to offer an alternative platform for nomination and election of candidates to pursue policy objectives. The mechanisms that produce interparty competition, therefore, are paramount to explaining the rise of the GOP in the South. Given the prior emphasis on, and disagreement about, Republican Party formation in the postwar South, it is imperative that we properly model this political dynamic. In an effort to examine the device(s) that induced two-party competition and, as a result, viable Republican Parties at the state-level, we include measures designed to test the import of party competition at various office-holding levels.

African American Mobilization

We cannot expect to understand partisan politics in the South without an appreciation for the role that race has played and continues to play in the region.

Key (1949) realized this a half-century ago, and as one student of Southern politics admitted,

> Running through the entire period of [partisan] change is the constant and ever visible thread of race. Nothing affected the party struggle in the South, and the political battle for control of the South, more than this central theme of Southern politics. (Spencer B. King, as printed in the forward to Tindall 1972)

More than 50 years later, race remains the centerpiece of research on the South and its politics (see Black and Black 1987, 1992; Glaser 1994).

For many years, White conservatism was directly related to the size of the Black population. As proximity to Blacks increased, the racial threat perceived by Whites increased. This dynamic, what Key (1949) called the Black-belt hypothesis, resulted in greater support for conservative candidates in areas with proportionately more Blacks. A number of subsequent analyses uncovered evidence that supports this hypothesis (see Aistrup, 1996; E. Black 1976; M. Black 1978; Giles 1977; Giles and Buckner 1993, 1996; Giles and Evans 1986; Giles and Hertz 1994; Glaser 1994; Matthews and Prothro 1966; Wright 1977). To the extent that the Republican Party was increasingly seen as the party of conservatism—again, especially racial conservatism—it became an increasingly desirable alternative to the Democratic Party. Some limited evidence indicates that Black context is directly related to growth in Republican partisanship (e.g., see Giles and Hertz 1994).

Although support for the Key (1949) hypothesis is strong, it is not unequivocal (see Bullock 1985; Combs, Hibbing, and Welch 1984; Voss 1996; Whitby 1985). A number of practical issues makes the attribution of Republican growth to Black racial context problematic. First, although conservative White voters may have changed their allegiance to the Republican Party, Blacks were overwhelmingly supportive of Democrats. So, in those areas where White flight is most likely, the Black Democratic base will be most numerous. Thus, in areas with large Black populations, there is both a very real ceiling placed on potential Republican support and a very real floor placed on the loss of Democratic support. Also, the striking growth in Republican voting behavior has come during a time when the relative size of the Black population in the South has actually decreased. The question thus becomes, how is it possible to attribute substantial Republican growth to Black context when the relative size of the Black population has not grown at all and, in some areas, has experienced a relative decline?

One possibility is that White voters have reacted not to Black context, as Key (1949) argued, but, instead, to Black mobilization. Since the passage of the VRA, the mobilization of Southern Blacks has been extensive (Grofman, Griffin, and Glazer 1992), and there is evidence that the mobilization of Southern Blacks has had systemic political implications (Hood et al. 1999). Initially, Southern conservatives opposed the development of the Republican Party. However, once disenfranchised Black voters returned to the political arena, Southern conservatives shifted strategies and began to build a local Republican Party that would serve as an organized political alternative to the Democratic Party, which was increasingly the party of choice for Black Americans (see Aistrup 1996; Aldrich and Griffin 2000; Maggiotto and Wekkin 2000; Rhodes 2000). As Blacks moved into the Democratic Party in significant numbers, conservative White Southerners were forced to seek an alternative vehicle for their political ambitions and objectives. Similarly, to the extent Blacks were perceived as a threat, we would expect to see the conservative White reaction to this perceived threat to be greatest in those areas in which Blacks actually became a major force in local and state politics. We test this hypothesis as well as the more traditional and competing Black-belt hypothesis.

In-Migration and Out-Migration: Coming, Going, and Southern Republicanism

Several studies have suggested that a driving force in the growth of the Republican Party in the South has been the influx of Republican-minded migrants from other regions of the country and the exit of Southern Blacks—a consistently Democratic constituency (see Bass and De Vries 1976). The out-migration of Blacks—particularly during the decades of the 50s, 60s, and 70s—prevented the relative growth of the Southern Black population and, thus, the growth of this component of the Democratic Party in the region. To the extent that this out-migration enabled Republican growth, it will be captured by the variables tapping Black context and Black mobilization. However, the in-migration of Whites from other regions—and most in-migrants have been White (see Scher 1997; Stanley and Castle 1988)—requires further elaboration.

An increasingly large body of research indicates that the bulk of Southern in-migrants during the past fifty years were White and middle class and that these migrants have become integral components of the Southern GOP. According to Scher (1997),

> One of the most important factors contributing to the growth of Republican success in the South has been in-migration since World War II . . . In-migration to the South since World War II has been heavily White and middle-class. That this group has formed the core of modern Republicanism in the region has been noted for some time. (pp. 143–144; also see Black and Black 1987; Lamis 1988)

Although it is difficult to argue with the contention that in-migration has had some impact on the relative strength of the two major political parties in the South, the magnitude and extent of this effect remains unclear. For example, some suggest that the impact of in-migration on Southern partisanship has ebbed in the last two decades—a time period in which the party loyalties of Southerners differed little (and were actually somewhat more Republican) than the party loyalties of Americans in other regions of the country (Stanley and Castle 1988).

Still others argue that cohort replacement and conversion of existing voters, as opposed to in-migration, explain the growing tendency among Southerners to identify as Republicans (Petrocik 1987). In light of these alternative points of view, we seek to reexamine the role of in-migration and its effect on the growth of the Republican Party in the South.

Economic Transformation and the GOP

Historians have long pointed to the transformation of the South's economy following the Second World War as a watershed event for the region (for a discussion of this event, see Cobb 1999; Sosna 1987). In a matter of decades, the region's economy was completely reoriented. The single-commodity agricultural economy gave way to one based on manufacturing and, later, to one characterized as information or service oriented.

The unfolding of this transformation was not lost on political scientists who noted the potential political consequences that economic change could produce in the region. As far back as 1949, Key mentioned the possible political ramifications associated with what he termed the *dilution* of the region's agricultural economy. Key stated that a natural outgrowth of this economic transformation would include "industrial and financial interests that have a fellow feeling with northern Republicanism" (p. 674) to thereby create a stronger, and in some ways, more natural linkage between Southerners and the GOP. More recently, Shafer and Johnston (2001) credited economic development as the driving engine behind partisan change in the Southern U.S. House delegation.

To examine the effect of economic transformation on the growth of Southern Republicanism, we incorporate measures tapping employment in the agricultural sector and per capita income into our analysis. We would expect to find a negative relationship between Republican growth and the relative importance of agriculture in a state's economy. In relation to relative income growth and the size of the GOP, we expect the conventional relationship to hold true for our sample: Gains in income should be accompanied by increases in Republican partisanship.

Evangelicals and Southern Republicanism

Finally, scholars studying the intersection of religion and politics note that White, evangelical Protestants have become increasingly more likely to identify with and vote for the Republican Party (see Green, Guth, Smidt, and Kellstedt 1996; Green, Kellstedt, Smidt, and Guth 1998; Kellstedt 1989). The individual-level survey data indicate that White evangelicals are more likely than those of other religious traditions to hold conservative views, especially in regard to social issues (Wilcox 2000). Over the last several decades, evangelicals have become increasingly drawn to a Republican Party identified as the standard bearer for social conservatism. Specific evidence of this trend is plentiful. For example, White evangelicals made up half (50%) of the combined Republican vote for presidential contests in the 1990s (Green et al. 1998). In the pivotal 1994 congressional elections, three quarters of this group (75%) voted Republican. In the same year, White evangelicals comprised the plurality of the GOP to make up 30% of Republican Party identifiers nationwide (Green et al. 1996).

This effect, however, is especially pronounced in the South, which, as a region, has more than an ample supply of evangelical Protestants. In the 1990s, more than one third (37%) of Southerners identified as evangelical Protestants. In addition, there is also sufficient evidence to indicate that White, evangelical Protestants in the region are altering their behavior politically by voting and identifying at increasingly higher rates for the GOP (see Green et al. 1998). It should also be noted that the number of White, evangelical Protestants in the South varies greatly from state to state. Thirty-three percent of Alabamans could be classified as evangelical Protestants in 1998 compared to only 11% of Floridians. As an apparently ready-made source of converts to the Republican Party, one would expect states in the region with a sizable percentage of evangelical Protestant adherents to display greater GOP growth over the time period under study.

Data and Method

We are interested in understanding both the cross-sectional and the temporal variation in Southern Republicanism. To accomplish our objective, we utilize a pooled time series methodology that provides us with the leverage to distinguish between the various temporal and cross-sectional forces that might have shaped the growth of the GOP in the South. Analyses of the entire region preclude the examination of subregional demographic, economic, and political dynamics that might influence Republican growth. Likewise, analyses based on individual states, even when grouped with other one-state studies, tend to ignore regionwide trends that played important roles in partisan development. Our research effort takes a middle-of-the-road approach to avoid the shortcomings of these two more limited methods.[6]

Parameter estimates of state-level Republican strength are generated using ordinary least squares (OLS), and we control for autocorrelation via the inclusion of a lagged dependent variable in the model. Even in the presence of this control, some residual autocorrelation remains. For this reason, we also estimate an instrumental variables (IV) model, as Beck and Katz (1996) and Greene (2000) suggest.[7] We present both sets of findings and note that the substantive results are identical.[8] The issue of heteroskedasticity is addressed by the use of panel-corrected standard errors (see Beck and Katz,1995, 1996). Multicollinearity is not a problem in either the original OLS models or IV models.[9]

For this study, the Southern state serves as our unit of analysis to produce a total of 11 cross-sections over a 38-year period—from 1962 to 2000.[10] The dependent variable, Republican strength, is measured at the state level utilizing a method developed by David (1972).[11] General election vote percentages for Republican candidates in gubernatorial, Senate, and congressional elections were utilized to create a composite state-level index of GOP strength.[12] Following the construction of each GOP state index, a 10-year (5 time point) moving average was applied to smooth any sharp variations present in each series.[13] The David Index of Party Strength was the method of choice for Lamis (1988) in his detailed study of party change in the South.

Independent variables representing possible explanations for Republican Party growth in the South can be classified into three groups: political, economic, and demographic. Variables designed to tap political concerns include Black electoral strength, % Black, substate party competition, and two sets of variables designed to represent the effects of presidential campaigns. The first of these variables taps into the potential influence that the political mobilization of Blacks had on Republican growth. Black electoral strength is calculated at the state level as the number of Black registered voters divided by the total number of registered voters. Operationalized as it is, our measure of Black electoral strength places Blacks within the context of the existing electorate—a much more precise method for estimating the potential influence of Blacks as an electoral presence than alternative indicators (i.e., the percentage of Blacks registered to vote).

To control for the size of the overall Black population in each state, we include a variable tapping the number of Blacks in the population divided by the total state population in the model (% Black). Although Blacks are a ubiquitous presence in the Southern political scene, their numbers are not uniform throughout the region. Most studies of Southern politics, therefore, include some control for the relative size of the Black population (e.g., see Nye and Bullock 1993).

To examine claims that the emergence of two-party competition in the region was a product of national political dynamics, we include a number of specific indicators in an effort to differentiate between the effects of party competition at the national level with those at a more localized, grassroots level. Given the important emphasis on presidential campaigns and state-level party growth in the South, we include two distinct sets of variables in an effort to capture this dynamic. The first indicator was based on the actual percentage of a state's vote captured by the Republican presidential candidate.[14] A second set of models was also estimated using a set of $n - 1$ dummy variables designed to measure the effects of specific presidential campaigns. These variables were coded 1 during the presidential election year (i.e., Goldwater in 1964) as well as for the subsequent off-year election (i.e., Goldwater in 1966).

To directly test the effects of substate party competition on state-level GOP growth, we include a measure designed to capture this process in both of the models presented in Table 20-1. The viability of the Republican Party at the substate level in the South varied greatly both over time and among states. For our model to account for this fact, an index was created to measure the relative level of competitive strength for the GOP among the eleven states in our sample.[15] In creating such a measure, we draw directly from the work of Aistrup (1996) and Anderson (1997), making some modest alterations to their measures of GOP competitiveness.[16]

In a given election cycle, substate party competition is calculated by summing the percentage of seats contested by the GOP in both the upper and lower houses in a state's legislative body along with the percentage of seats won by GOP candidates, again, in both houses. This figure is then divided by 4 to yield an index ranging from 0 to 1 with the former an indicator of essentially no two-party competition and the latter a sign of complete Republican dominance. In the models presented in Table 20-1, substate party competition is lagged behind the dependent variable by one election cycle with the idea that competitive gains made by the GOP at the subnational level will not translate into concomitant Republican Party gains at the state level until the following election cycle.

A competing explanation for growth of the Republican Party focuses on the extensive economic changes that forever altered the region. To examine the Southern transformation from an economy based intensively in agricultural production to one increasingly dominated by manufacturing and, today, information, we include a measure tapping the percentage of the workforce employed in the agricultural sector. Agricultural employment is measured as the number of state workers employed in the farming and agricultural sector of the economy divided by the total workforce of the state. According to the economic transformation theory, one should expect to see increases in GOP strength in states where the percentage of workers employed in agricultural pursuits is declining. A second variable designed to model economic change is also included in the analysis. Per capita income measures the changes in a state's income level over time. Operationalized as the nominal income of a state in relation to the size of its population, this measure of wealth is a direct correlate with the growth of the Southern economy. Rapidly expanding income levels should translate into ever increasing numbers of Republican Party loyalists.

As indicated, our model also includes a set of noneconomic demographic factors thought to be associated with GOP growth in the South. In-migration is measured as the proportion of a state's population that is composed of White residents born outside the Southern region. To the extent that Republican growth is at least partially driven by the in-migration of White Republican sympathizers, it should be captured by this variable. A final demographic variable is designed to represent the proportion of a state's population that are members of an evangelical Protestant denomination.[17] Specifically linked to GOP growth, evangelical Protestantism is hypothesized to be positively related to the Republican strength at the state level (see Appendix A for more detailed information concerning variable construction and see Appendix B for data sources).

Table 20-1 Explaining State-Level GOP Party Growth in the South, 1962–2006

	1962–2000				1962–2006			
	Model 1		Model 2		Model 1		Model 2	
	OLS	IV	OLS	IV	OLS	IV	OLS	IV
Constant	.0028 (.0121)	.0061 (.0116)	.0103 (.0101)	.0201* (.0092)	.0086 (.0119)	.0155 (.0083)	.0193 (.0102)	.0250** (.0080)
Political:								
Republican Strength$_{t-1}$	.8845** (.0231)	.8715** (.0254)	.9273** (.0253)	.8946** (.0313)	.8871** (.0223)	.8163** (.0341)	.9266** (.0235)	.8533** (.0350)
Sub-State Party Competition$_{t-1}$	.0730** (.0153)	.0749** (.0156)	.0346* (.0148)	.0447** (.0152)	.0634** (.0144)	.0760** (.0153)	.0285* (.0133)	.0500** (.0146)
Presidential Vote	.00018 (.00013)	.00015 (.00014)	—	—	.0002 (.0001)	.0001 (.0001)	—	—
Black Electoral Strength	.1630** (.0383)	.1382** (.0460)	.1305** (.0353)	.1206** (.0372)	.1533** (.0362)	.0831** (.0415)	.1272** (.0345)	.1057** (.0360)
% Black	-.0812* (.0343)	-.0681 (.0429)	-.0565 (.0325)	-.0631 (.0416)	-.0839* (.0339)	-.0444 (.0521)	-.0677* (.0331)	-.0707 (.0488)
Goldwater 1964	—	—	.0094** (.0042)	—a	—	—	.0099* (.0046)	—a
Nixon 1968	—	—	.0155** (.0053)	.0039 (.0040)	—	—	.0167** (.0056)	-.0028 (.0046)
Nixon 1972	—	—	.0086 (.0057)	-.0016 (.0053)	—	—	.0096 (.0058)	-.0016 (.0062)
Ford 1976	—	—	-.0180** (.0062)	-.0255** (.0062)	—	—	-.0171** (.0063)	-.0233** (.0073)
Reagan 1980	—	—	-.0050 (.0064)	-.0117 (.0063)	—	—	-.0038 (.0066)	-.0093 (.0075)
Reagan 1984	—	—	-.0028 (.0067)	-.0114 (.0067)	—	—	-.0015 (.0068)	-.0096 (.0080)

Table 20-1 (continued)

	1962–2000				1962–2006			
	Model 1		Model 2		Model 1		Model 2	
	OLS	IV	OLS	IV	OLS	IV	OLS	IV
Bush 1988	—	—	-.0021 (.0074)	-.0095 (.0074)	—	—	-.0004 (.0075)	-.0062 (.0087)
Bush 1992	—	—	-.0097 (.0081)	-.0153 (.0080)	—	—	-.0076 (.0081)	-.0105 (.0092)
Dole 1996	—	—	.0004 (.0087)	-.0065 (.0087)	—	—	.0030 (.0087)	-.0017 (.0100)
Bush 2000	—	—	-.0017 (.0102)	-.0065 (.0100)	—	—	.0044 (.0098)	-.0018 (.0112)
Bush 2004	—	—	—	—	—	—	-.0036 (.0103)	-.0026 (.0121)
Demographic:								
In-Migration	.0519 (.0330)	.0468 (.0374)	.0405 (.0328)	.0283 (.0437)	.0255 (.0276)	.0158 (.0400)	.0093 (.0264)	-.0070 (.0430)
Evangelical Protestants	.0230 (.0240)	.0320 (.0271)	.0229 (.0228)	.0303 (.0295)	.0239 (.0216)	.0511 (.0383)	.0180 (.0202)	.0292 (.0349)
Economic:								
Per Capita Income ($1,000)	-.0005 (.0003)	-.0004 (.0004)	—b	—b	-.0003 (.0003)	.00007 (.0004)	—b	—b
Agricultural Sector Employment	.0766 (.0565)	.0657 (.0652)	.0009 (.0513)	-.0071 (.0568)	.0645 (.0557)	-.0327 (.0816)	-.0100 (.0513)	-.0344 (.0614)
R^2	.978	.960	.981	.962	.980	.929	.983	.941
N	220	209	220	209	253	242	253	242

Notes: OLS = ordinary least squares; IV = instrumental variables. OLS coefficients with panel corrected standard errors in parentheses.

*p < .05 (two-tailed test) **p < .01 (two-tailed test)

aGoldwater 1964 was dropped from Model 2 (IV) because of the necessary incorporation of an additional lag that truncated the time series at 1964.

bPer Capita Income was eliminated from Model 2 due to extreme multicollinearity.

Findings and Discussion

The series of box plots presented in Figure 20-1 charts Republican Party growth in the South over the past forty years using the state-level index of GOP strength. The pattern clearly indicates a consistent increase in GOP strength during the time period under study. In 1960, the median GOP strength level in the South was a miniscule 11%. By 2000, this figure had more than quadrupled rising to 51%.[18]

Although the median level of Republican Party strength in the region has steadily increased since the early 1960s, the rate of growth among states has been anything but uniform (note the relatively large span of the boxes and corresponding whiskers over most of the time period). The wide degree of dispersion between states is evident when one notes that, in 1960, the Republican strength level ranged from a low of 0.9% in Mississippi to a high of 31% in North Carolina—a 30-point gap. Although the gap has considerably narrowed over the last forty years, 13 percentage points still separated Arkansas (43%) and Mississippi (56%) in 2000.

What factors—economic, political, or demographic—led to the observed growth of the Republican Party in the region over the second half of the twentieth century? The results of our multivariate models presented in Table 20-1 indicate the expansion of the GOP in the region was primarily the product of political factors as opposed to economic or demographic determinants.

First, relative increases in Black voting strength produced an increase in GOP strength. The racial composition of a state's electorate is directly and positively associated with the rate of growth in the Republican Party. For each percentage point increase in the number of Blacks comprising the Southern electorate, there is a corresponding increase in the GOP index of more than a one tenth of a percentage point (Model 1, IV). So even with the vast majority of mobilized Blacks moving into the Democratic Party, the White reaction was sufficiently large to result in a relative increase in Republican tendencies. The perception of an active threat to White dominance within the Democratic Party (and in Southern politics more generally) both galvanized and sustained the observed growth in Southern Republicanism. In fact, once we control for Black mobilization, we find little evidence of a relationship between Black concentration and Republican growth.[19]

Obviously, this finding provides a striking contrast to a considerable body of literature (for a bibliography, see Giles and Hertz 1994) that draws a simple connection between the size of the Black population and the strength of the Republican Party. The distinction between the politically mobilized Black population—which for many years was artificially constrained by poll taxes, literacy tests, and outright violence—and the general Black population is clearly important. Previous literature has failed to account for this distinction, and it is a distinction that merits further attention.

Our own previous work indicates that the liberalization of the Democratic Party in the South was a result of the joint growth in the number of Republican

Figure 20-1 Republican Growth in the South—State Boxplots, 1960–2000 (and Extension to 2006)*

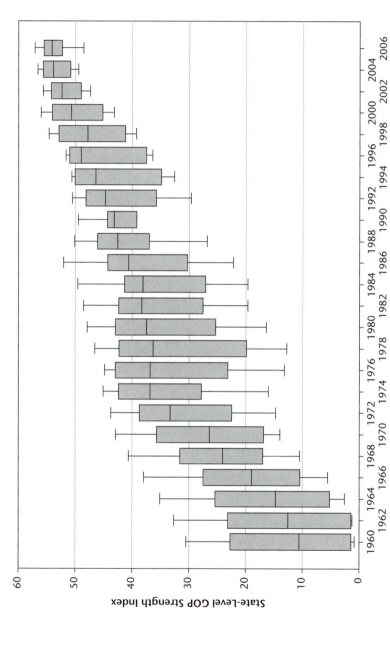

*Figure 1 from the original article is reproduced but has been extended to include data for 2002, 2004, and 2006. The extension is discussed in the Epilogue.

Party adherents and the relative size of the Black electorate (e.g., see Hood et al. 1999). From these findings, along with the results from this study, we conjecture that much of the enormous political change witnessed in the South during the second half of the twentieth century was triggered by a single historical event, namely the 1965 VRA. Although few question the tremendous impact that this legislation has produced in American history, we are only now beginning to piece together the specific causal mechanisms through which such change occurred. These findings take us a step closer to a more precise understanding of how the civil rights movement forever altered the American landscape and, more specifically, the South as a political entity.

Second, as many participants in the political process will attest to, substate party competition is also a necessary precursor of state-level Republican growth. Clearly, the ability of Republicans to develop party organizations that were capable of contesting and winning lower-level elections in the South produced a subsequent increase in party viability at the state level. From this perspective, the Democratic monopoly on local and state offices seriously constrained Republican growth, because the Republican Party was not viewed as an effective vehicle for those interested in taking an active role in state or local politics. In their research on the behavior of state party activists in the South, Clark and Lockerbie (1998) found evidence of this dynamic. More specifically, they reported, "The problem for the state Republican Parties is that many party activists appear to believe that the state party is inconsequential" (pp. 123–124). This problem, however, appears to be ameliorated by the election of Republicans to state and substate offices (Clark and Lockerbie 1998).

During the time period of our analysis, the number of Republican candidates vying for subnational office increased exponentially. Not surprisingly, this increase in contested races eventually produced larger numbers of Republicans elected to office. As the number of local Republican officeholders rose and as the size of GOP majorities in state legislative bodies grew, so did the relative advantage for individuals to vote and/or identify as Republicans. On the other hand, there appears to be only limited empirical evidence to support the contention that state-level party building was the result of party forces at the national level. Model 1 utilizes the Republican presidential vote by state as a surrogate for the effect of national-level campaigns. The results of both the OLS and IV models using this operationalization indicate that presidential campaigns had no significant empirical effect on the growth of the GOP at the state level.

The campaign dummy variable formulation in Model 2 indicates that GOP presidential campaigns early in the time series apparently acted as a catalyst for growth during the 1960s.[20] Given the fact that local GOP party structures were either nonexistent or present only in embryonic form during this time period, it comes as little surprise that the Goldwater campaign of 1964 as well as the 1968 Nixon candidacy had a substantial effect on Republican growth at the state level. Certainly, this observation underscores the fact that a lack of party infrastructure at the substate level could have actually slowed initial Republican growth, and later dominance, in the region. Whereas the GOP experienced relative advantage gains among White Southerners beginning in the 1960s, it took Republican state parties decades to fully exploit this disparity.

The 1976 Ford campaign, or perhaps more aptly stated as the Carter campaign, exerted a negative effect on the rate of GOP growth in the South. In both the OLS and IV models presented, the sign and significance of this variable represents a short-lived resurgence on the part of the Democratic Party in the region led by the election of popular native son Jimmy Carter from Georgia and the continued aversion to a scandal-ridden Nixon administration. As a result of these electoral dynamics, losses across all office-holding levels—from local to federal levels—were concomitantly experienced by the GOP during this period of time.

Finally, although the lag of the Republican strength variable in the models acts as a methodological control, it is also important to note that the coefficient, at .87, is close to 1. Such a finding closely mirrors the almost monotonic growth in Republican state parties in the South over the time period under study (see Figure 20-1). The rate of conversion and replacement on the part of individuals to the GOP in this light appears highly stable with additions forming an ever-growing base for the party during subsequent election cycles. When or where the momentum of this positive growth rate will be slowed or reversed remains a question for the future.

Surprisingly, several prominent explanations of GOP growth receive no support in our analysis. For example, we find no evidence that factors such as White in-migration or the number of evangelical Protestants had any direct influence on GOP growth. In reference to the latter, our results suggest that, rather than owing its current successes to the religious right, the Republican Party in the South may, in fact, have only provided a platform for their message. Conversely, the religious right may owe the Republican Party for its recent successes.

These are important null findings, because they are inconsistent with the existing literature on the evolution of a viable two-party system in the South. Once we account for the political dynamics that drove Republican growth, demographic factors appear to have made little difference. In addition, economic factors such as per capita income and agricultural sector employment, which have long been one of a number of reliable explanations for the rise of the Republican Party in the South, are shown to play no significant role when compared to political explanations.

The modeling strategy chosen is a powerful method for succinctly summarizing change over time and across units of analysis—excellent for creating a composite snapshot. In our case, the pooled time series model indicates that specific political factors (i.e., Black electoral strength and substate party competition) are apt indicators of processes at work that did exert a direct and consistently positive effect on state-level GOP growth during the entire 40-year time range under study. This fact should not diminish the possibility that other indicators may have exerted positive influences at various points in the time period under study, either directly or indirectly.

For example, in-migration does appear to affect state-level Republican growth during the 1960s and 1970s but, apparently, not later.[21] Certainly, it is possible to envision model formulations in which economic variables or religious affiliation *may* exert significant effects on GOP growth. But much more detailed theoretical rationales would have to be sought to justify the presence of unit or time-specific effects. Unfortunately, such constructions would defeat the simplicity and directness of the models presented in Table 20-1 and, we would argue, are beyond the scope of the present endeavor, which is foremost predicated on establishing a set of baseline effects for two-party formation.

Conclusion

Our study is the first to systematically analyze the demographic, political, and economic determinants of GOP growth in all eleven Southern states across time. We find, contrary to other studies focusing on political change in the region, that alterations to the political system produced the observed development of a viable two-party system in the South. Stated succinctly, political factors begat political change. Although there is no doubt that regional in-migration and economic transformation were ongoing phenomena during the period of time under study, these factors, along with other demographic variables such as Black context and Evangelicalism, do not appear to have had a consistent impact on the growth of Southern Republicanism. We find no reason to believe, then, that economic or demographic change alone, however profound, would have broken the long-held constant in Southern politics of one-party Democratic dominance absent political changes. Our findings and conclusions contrast sharply with the body of existing literature on the growth of the Republican Party in the South.

Even with a basic understanding of the political dynamics of the growth of Southern Republicanism, a number of important questions remain. First, what factors fostered (or constrained) the mobilization of the Black electorate? To what extent did political organizations such as the NAACP boost mobilization, and did the efforts of extremist Whites (e.g., civil rights violations) restrict Black political mobilization? And how can we explain the wide variance in substate Republican competitiveness? Did a variety of local factors boost competitiveness in specific regions, or did national party efforts in particular locales boost competitiveness? Or is it some mixture of the two? In addition, an exhaustive effort should be undertaken to understand the linkage between the effect of economic and demographic change in the region and the corresponding political alterations that led to the formation of a two-party system. To fully understand the transformation of the Southern party system, and party systems more generally, we must find answers to these important questions.

Epilogue

A region once characterized as the "Solid South" because of its consistent and overwhelming support for Democrats at all levels of government has now become the epicenter of twenty-first-century Republicanism. In the article reprinted here, we highlighted this transformation and the racial and political dynamics that produced it. The full realization of the theory and analysis presented in that work has since manifested itself in twenty-first-century Southern politics: Regardless of the variety of demographic, economic, and social changes which the South has undergone in the past half-century, the growth of Southern Republicanism is primarily a function of racial and political dynamics. That was the story from 1960–2000, and that is still the story today. In this epilogue we update the analysis, discuss the significance of the new findings, sketch the likely trajectory (or potential trajectories) of Southern Republicanism, and highlight the most interesting open questions related to the future of partisanship and partisan politics in the modern South.

Updated Analysis

We returned to the data from our 1960–2000 analysis and updated each variable to the extent possible. Full data were not yet available for the 2008 election year, so the update is through 2006. Using the estimation procedures implemented in the original analysis, we generated the updated results presented above in Table 20-1.

Though the last decade has witnessed a significant transformation in racial and ethnic politics, the results are strikingly similar across the two sets of analyses. The one subtle difference between the analyses is the increased significance of the Black context variable; the variable is now significant in an additional model (see Table 20-1, Models 1 and 2). Given the increase in the sample size, even this change is not especially unexpected. Yet the increased evidence of a negative effect of Black context on Republicanism—after fully accounting for the positive effect of Black mobilization—enhances the plausibility of the original perspective. We now have greater evidence that Black context limits the upper bound of Republican growth—an intuitive result and one that is now more fully corroborated by the empirical analysis.

More generally, we again find little evidence that factors such as presidential elections, income growth, evangelicalism, in-migration, or size of the agricultural sector significantly influenced the state-level variation in the growth of Southern Republicanism. We would not conclude that these factors played no role in the broad partisan transformation of the South, but we certainly see no evidence that they acted as an engine directly driving Republican growth in the region. The state-level growth of the Southern Republican Party was a function of two primary factors: sub-state party competition—the increasing development of competitive Republican candidates at the sub-state level—and Black mobilization. Again, the evidence strongly supports the contention that Black electoral mobilization led directly to Republican growth in the South. The results of our extended models also provide strong empirical support for the bottom-up theory of two-party development in the South over that of the top-down school. We can conclude the state-level GOP growth was, in part, propelled by Republican success at lower office-holding levels.

In subsequent research on the relationship between Black mobilization and Republican growth (Hood, Kidd, and Morris 2008), we assessed the robustness of the time series–cross section (TSCS) results presented in our original article. Employing a Granger causality test especially tailored for TSCS data, we evaluated the extent that Black mobilization *causes* Republican growth for both the deep South and the rim South and, subsequently, each of the eleven Southern states.[22] We found strong evidence of a direct causal relationship where Black mobilization leads to Republican growth across both subregions and within all states in the region. We also found evidence of a feedback loop in the deep South where Republican growth produces further black mobilization. This reciprocal relationship is not present, however, in the peripheral South.[23]

The results of our Granger analysis in the *Political Analysis* article and the subsequent results for an extended time frame suggest a partisan political dynamic leading to state-level Republican parties that are significantly larger than their mid-twentieth century Southern counterparts. Black mobilization and increasing substate party competition have provided the catalyst for Republican growth over this time period.

As there is evidence of a feedback loop in the deep South [*Black Mobilization$_{t-1}$ → Republican Growth$_t$ → Black Mobilization$_{t+1}$ → Republican Growth$_{t+2}$*], we would expect to see an explosion of Republican growth in this subregion. To some extent this has been the case—certainly enough to move this set of states ahead of those in the rim South in terms of the relative extent of Republicanism (see Figure 20-2). However, because the relative size of the black population has a dampening effect on the growth of Republicanism—historically providing a ceiling for the growth of the Republican Party in each state because of the overwhelming support of African Americans for the Democratic Party—our model suggests that the maximum size of the Republican Party in any Southern state is something less than 60 percent of the *entire* voting population. In the rim South, where the ceiling set by the relative size of the Black population is relatively higher than it is in the deep South, the extent of Black mobilization is also significantly less, producing, in turn, less pressure for Republican growth. Empirically, these dynamics have resulted in a significant growth in the Republican Party in every Southern state (since the 1960s) and a dramatic decrease in the variation of state-level Republicanism over the same time period.

Figure 20-1 depicts the range and distribution of the growth of state-level Republicanism over the period extending to 2006. What we see is a relatively low maximum (slightly more than 30 percent of voters) and significant variation (nearly 30 points between the maximum and minimum values) for the Republican Party early in the time period. As we move forward in time, we see an

Figure 20-2 GOP Growth by Subregion, 1952–2008

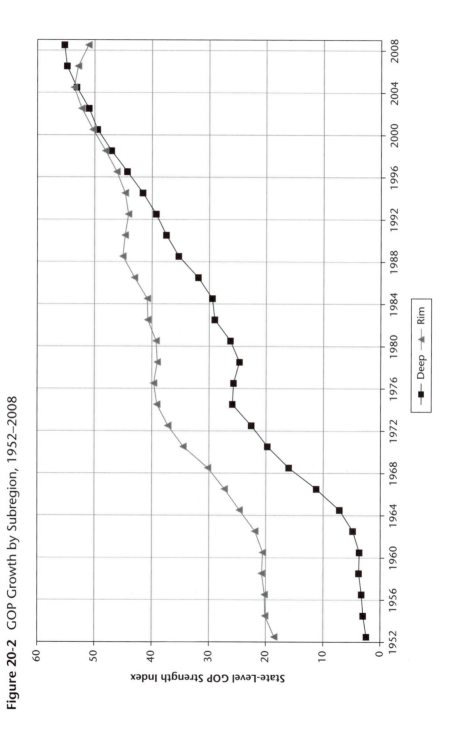

increase in the maximum level for state-level Republicanism and an even larger increase in the smallest state-level Republican Party. By the end of our time period, the largest state-level Republican Party is nearly twice the size of the largest Republican Party in the early 1960s, and the smallest Republican Party is nearly *twenty* times the size of the smallest such party. The data plainly illustrate the dramatic growth and the significant drop in state-level variation that we should expect to see.

Though the data reflect the dynamics predicted by the theory of relative advantage introduced in our 2004 article, we still lack a full understanding of the relationship between Black mobilization and Republican growth. Data limitations make it difficult (but not impossible) to examine this dynamic at the sub-state level, so further work remains to be done on this issue. And we still lack a full characterization of the individual-level dynamics that produce the aggregate-level results we find. Just what is at work at the individual level that ties Black mobilization and Republican growth—and, in some states, Republican growth and Black mobilization—in the South? We are simply not sure at this point.

The Future of the Republican Party in the South

It is hazardous to make predictions in politics. That said, we can look at some current trends and project where these may lead in the near future. First, again looking at Figure 20-2 we can make some projections concerning GOP growth in the near future. First, it is notable that in 2006 the GOP strength index for the deep South overtook the same measure for the rim South for the first time. From 2004 to 2008 GOP party strength managed about 2.1 points of positive growth, while the rim South experienced a decline on the order of about 2.5 points. These trends are notable because both in the deep and rim South GOP growth has essentially been monotonic since approximately 1960.

The deep South that was fifty years ago the bastion of the solid Democratic South is now more Republican than its subregional counterpart. There are still gains that can be realized for the Republican Party in these states; however, these are also the five states in the region that contain the highest numbers of Black citizens as well. These overwhelmingly Democratic demographics place a real ceiling on the degree to which the Republican Party can expand in this part of the region.

The impact of the election of the nation's first Black president in 2008 on Southern politics deserves some degree of attention. While Black Southerners have traditionally voted Democratic in presidential elections at overwhelming rates, the Barack Obama candidacy is a story more about mobilization and turn-out. There is little doubt that Obama's candidacy helped to bring huge numbers of Black registrants into the electorate in the South while, at the same time, reinvigorating the existing Black electorate. Black turnout in the 2008 general election was not conditioned on the state-level competitiveness of the presidential contest. The additional degree of Black mobilization beyond that which can be explained by electoral competitiveness and standard sociodemographic factors has been labeled the *Obama Effect* and is related to the draw for Black Americans specific to Obama's historic candidacy (McKee and Hill 2009). Obama's victories in Florida, North Carolina, and Virginia are, in part, explained by this additional mobilization. Virginia last went to the Democratic presidential column in 1960 and North Carolina in 1976, both considerable periods of time.

It is informative to compare White (non-Hispanic) and Black registration and turnout from the 2004 and 2008 general elections in Georgia, which tabulate registration and turnout data by race. These two groups account for over 90 percent of registrants in the state. From 2004 to 2008 the share of White registrants as a proportion of the electorate dropped by about 6 percentage points, from 69 percent down to 63 percent. Conversely, the share of Black registration over the same period rose by 2.8 percent points from 27 percent to 30 percent. At the same time, among Blacks, voter turnout rates across these two elections increased approximately 4 percentage points compared to a drop of almost 3 percentage points for whites. These effects are even more pronounced when one looks at voters in the 18 to 29 range. Voter turnout among younger Whites dropped 6.5 points from 2004 to 2008, compared with a 5-point increase among Black voters in the same age category.[24]

In the deep South we have demonstrated that increases in the size of the Black electorate are related to future gains in state-level Republican strength. If this relationship is still valid, it is quite possible that recent gains in Black registration, which obviously benefit the Democratic Party, may also lead to a concomitant expansion in Republican identifiers. The jury is also out, however, on whether these mobilized Black voters, especially younger first-time registrants, will continue to participate at similar rates in the future in the absence of a Black Democratic candidate at the top of the ticket.

Conversely, one might also ask what fortunes lie on the horizon for the GOP in the peripheral South. Is the downturn evident over the most recent election cycles likely to continue? What is the chance that the trend line might level off or even increase? Two long-term demographic shifts make continued Republican growth somewhat problematic in the rim South. These are the growing Hispanic population in the region, especially in Texas and Florida, and the changing nature of immigration to these areas.

First, let us turn our attention to the Hispanic question. Texas is currently one of only four states where Anglos (non-Hispanic Whites) do not represent the majority racial/ethnic group. By 2015 it is predicted that Hispanics will become a majority in Texas (Lone Star Rising 2009). Though Hispanics are not monolithic, in political or other terms, Hispanics outside of those of Cuban origin in south Florida tend to identify and vote Democratic more than a majority of the time.[25] Given the growth in this segment of the population this trend should be troubling to the Republican Party in the region.

Many Hispanics are conservative on social issues but fairly liberal on economic matters. The former should tend to benefit Republicans and the latter

Democrats. So, unlike the Black electorate, there does appear to be some maneuvering room for Republicans with this particular group. However, the party's current stance on the immigration issue has proven to be a stumbling block for the GOP's effort to court Hispanics. For a population segment with comparatively higher degrees of poverty and lower levels of educational attainment, the draw from economic issues would also seem to benefit the Democratic Party. Party registration figures from North Carolina indicate that approximately 40 percent of Hispanics identify as Democrats, compared to 28 percent for the Republican Party, and 32 percent who chose no party affiliation (Bullock and Hood 2006). In short, the jury is still out on which camp a majority of Hispanics may choose in terms of partisan affiliation.

A number of factors will work to mute the influence of Hispanics in the region for several decades into the future, even in Texas and Florida. Figure 20-3 presents the Hispanic share of the population for each Southern state along with the Hispanic voting age population using data from the 2000 Census (which most certainly underestimates the size of this group at the end of the decade). For every state except Texas, Florida, and Georgia, Hispanics comprised less than 5 percent of the total population in 2000. It should be noted that even these small percentages represent substantial growth in a region where Hispanics were a negligible presence in many states before 1990. Total population estimates for 2008 show an increase in the number of states with a Hispanic population over 5 percent increasing to six, all of which are located in the rim South with the exception of Georgia. These 2008 estimates place the Hispanic population in Florida and Texas at 21 percent and 36.5 percent respectively.

Despite a growing presence throughout the region, recent research indicates Hispanics will be slow to reshape the politics of the South. One recent study estimates that it could be the 2030s before growth in the Hispanic population alone would help Democrats to reach parity with the GOP in Texas (Stanley 2008). A number of factors currently work to constrain the political influence of Hispanics in the region. One of these is the fact that the Hispanic population is, on average, currently younger than the non-Hispanic population. In Texas where Hispanics make up more than a third of the state's total population, this group comprises only about a fifth of the voting age population. A second limiting factor relates to the issue of citizenship. A large percentage of Hispanics who have migrated to the South (with the exception of Florida and Texas) are non-citizens and, therefore, cannot vote. Census estimates from the 2008 election cycle indicate that Hispanics comprised only 16.0 percent of the citizen voting age population in Florida, compared to a 20.7 percent share of the VAP.

The potential for Hispanic political influence is also limited by the fact that Hispanic citizens in the South register and vote at lower levels than Blacks or Whites. For the 2008 election, the Census Bureau put Hispanic registration among citizens to be to be 54.3 percent in Texas, compared to 73.7 percent for Blacks and 73.6 percent for Whites. The same source indicates that 37.8 percent of Hispanic citizens voted in the 2008 general, far below 64.9 percent and

Figure 20-3 Hispanic Population by State

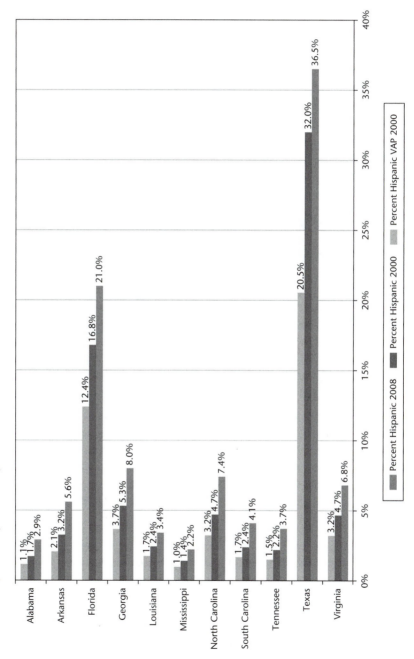

Percent Hispanic 2008   Percent Hispanic 2000   Percent Hispanic VAP 2000

Alabama: 1.1%, 1.7%, 2.9%
Arkansas: 2.1%, 3.2%, 5.6%
Florida: 12.4%, 16.8%, 21.0%
Georgia: 3.7%, 5.3%, 8.0%
Louisiana: 1.7%, 2.4%, 3.4%
Mississippi: 1.0%, 1.4%, 2.2%
North Carolina: 3.2%, 4.7%, 7.4%
South Carolina: 1.7%, 2.4%, 4.1%
Tennessee: 1.5%, 2.2%, 3.7%
Texas: 20.5%, 32.0%, 36.5%
Virginia: 3.2%, 4.7%, 6.8%

64.7 percent for Blacks and Whites, respectively. In Georgia, where we do not have to rely on estimates, Hispanic turnout in the 2008 general was 59.6 percent. Again, this figure is far below turnout rates for Blacks at 75.8 percent and Whites at 77.4 percent. The bottom line is that until such disparities dissipate, Hispanics will not reach their full political potential in any Southern state, despite their growing population base.

Another disconcerting demographic pattern for Republicans involves recent in-migration patterns, especially in the peripheral South. While in-migration at one time boosted GOP fortunes with an influx of non-Southern Republican identifiers, the latest trends are not nearly so advantageous. The 2000 Census reports that less than half of Floridians (45.7 percent) are native Southerners, with a fifth of the Sunshine State's population having been born in the Northeast. Recent scholarship points to in-migration patterns as one of the chief culprits for declining success of Republican congressional candidates in the rim South compared to those running in the deep South (see McKee 2009).

Other research demonstrates that Obama's narrow win in the Tar Heel State can be, in part, explained by an ever-increasing stream of non-Southern migrants from the rust belt and Northeastern states. One analysis found that the most recent growth in voter registration is among those not claiming a specific party affiliation, and it is among this category where non-Southern in-migrants dominate. These in-migrants were also linked to higher rates of voting for Obama (Hood and McKee 2010). In a state won by the Democrats by only about a third of a percentage point, the message is clear that this new breed of in-migrant contributed to that razor-thin margin. The influx of non-Southerners into the region, especially the rim South, may be indicative of a long-term pattern benefiting the Democratic Party.

As of this writing many have lamented the downfall of the national GOP beginning with the Democratic takeover of Congress in 2006. For the first time since 1996 the Democratic Party made major gains outside the region propelled by an unpopular Republican president presiding over an unpopular war and later an economic recession. Many also call attention to the Republican congressional caucus, which was dominated by a very conservative Southern delegation as being yet another culprit for this downfall. Ironically, the growing Southern Republican majority that allowed the GOP to take control of Congress in 1996 may have inadvertently also led to its rather quick demise by pulling the party ideologically too far to the right for mainstream America.

In the more immediate future, the effects linked to the election and subsequent presidential administration of Barack Obama on the Southern political landscape remain to be seen. Obama's victories in Florida, North Carolina, and Virginia signaled potential new inroads for the Democratic Party in the region. It is no surprise that the states that Obama won were rim South states, but whether or not the Democratic Party can build on these results from a single election is still an open question. As McKee (2009) notes, President Obama may be a president of "reconstruction" along the lines of Lincoln, Franklin Roosevelt, and

Reagan (see Skowronek 1993 and 2008), and if that is the case, then his presidency might result in a new partisan transformation of Southern politics. However, if our current economic difficulties are more serious than we realize (or more difficult for the Obama administration to address), then the Obama presidency may be a presidency of preemption, in which case its lasting impact on Southern politics (and American politics more generally) will be far more limited.

So, what might be the GOP's future in the South? With a strong cadre of White social and economic conservatives, short-term trends continue to favor the GOP. For this group the Republican Party will likely remain the party of choice for some time to come. Short-term growth may even continue at the substate level in the deep South. Longer-term trends, as mentioned, are much more difficult to pin down. Secular patterns, especially a growing Hispanic citizenry and in-migration from traditional Democratic areas, are not likely to help the GOP imperative that the GOP reach out to the fastest growing racial/ethnic group (Hispanics) in the region in order to remain competitive in the future.

Appendix A

Variable Construction

State-level Republican strength (dependent variable)
For a given year, this index was calculated as follows:

[% Republican vote (Senate election) + % Republican vote (gubernatorial election) + % Republican vote (average Republican congressional vote)]/3[26]

Presidential vote
By state, this is the percentage of the vote won by the Republican presidential candidate. These figures were carried over for off-election years in the dataset.

Presidential campaign dummies
A set of $n - 1$ dummy variables were created to represent each presidential election beginning with the 1964 Goldwater campaign and continuing through the Bush campaign of 2000. Each dummy variable took on a value of 1 during the presidential election year and the subsequent off-election year (e.g., Goldwater campaign: 1964 and 1966 = 1; else = 0). The 1960 Nixon campaign served as the excluded category.

% Black
For each state in the analysis, % Black was calculated as follows: (Black population)/(total population)

It was necessary to interpolate estimates of Black populations using the two actual sets of figures available. Using a technique very similar in manner to one developed by Combs et al. (1984), we took the percent of the state population labeled as Black for each decade, subtracted the figure for the preceding decade, and then divided by 10 (years). The aforementioned calculation allowed us to fill in the gaps (1960 to 1970, 1970 to 1980, 1980 to 1990, 1990 to 2000) using a linear growth pattern.[27]

Black electoral strength

For each state in the analysis, this variable was calculated as follows:[28] (number of Blacks registered to vote)/(total number of registered voters)

In-migration

In-migration is calculated for each state in our analysis as follows:

(number of White residents born outside the Southern region[29])/(total state population)

A straight-line linear interpolation/extrapolation method was used to create annual estimates.

Agricultural employment

This economic transformation variable was calculated using the following formula:

(number of workers employed in the farming and agricultural sector of the economy)/(total employed persons 16 and older)

Per capita income

Per capita income was calculated as follows:

(total personal income [in nominal $] by state)/(total state population)

Evangelical Protestant

This variable was calculated using the following formula:

(number of evangelical Protestant adherents)/(total state population)

The scheme used to classify Protestant denominations as *evangelical* is found in Green et al. (1996, 188–189). The number of evangelical Protestant adherents in a state was calculated using Southern Baptist membership figures as a base. Southern Baptists constitute greater than a majority of Evangelical Protestant membership in all of the states in our analysis and membership information for this denomination is available on an annual basis. Membership figures for the remaining evangelical denominations were gathered from national surveys conducted by the Glenmary Research Center. Because these surveys were not conducted annually, we used a linear interpolation technique (described above) to create annual estimates of non–Southern Baptist evangelical Protestant membership.

Substate party competition

This variable is a four-part index calculated every other year as follows:

[(percentage of state legislative seats contested by GOP in the lower house) + (percentage of state legislative seats contested by GOP in the upper house) + (percentage of state legislative seats won by GOP in the lower house) + (percentage of state legislative seats won by GOP in the lower house)]/4

NOTE: The data used to construct the variables described above come from a variety of both primary and secondary sources. Secondary sources include a large number of Census documents, newspaper articles, and archived datasets. Primary sources include church membership records, state elections records (in both paper and electronic formats), and organization newsletters. Additional questions concerning sources and/or variable construction can be directed to Trey Hood at th@uga.edu.

Appendix B

Data Sources

State-level Republican strength (dependent variable)/Presidential vote:

Congressional Quarterly Press. (1994). *Guide to U.S. elections* (3rd ed.). Washington, DC: Author.

Congressional Quarterly Press. (1996, 1998, 2000, 2002). *America votes*. Washington, DC: Author.

David, P.T. (1972). *Party strength in the United States, 1872–1970.* Charlottesville: University Press of Virginia.

% Black:

U.S. Department of Commerce, Bureau of the Census. (1960, Table 96; 1970, Table 20; 1980, Table 19; 1990, Table 19; 2000, Table QT-PL [American FactFinder]). General population characteristics. Washington, DC: U.S. Government Printing Office.

Black electoral strength:

Southern Regional Council. (1968, 2[4]; 1969, 5[12]; 1970,4[1–2]). *VEP (Voter Education Project) news.* Atlanta, GA: Author.

U.S. Bureau of the Census. (1976, Table 747; 1979, Table 840; 1980, Table 849). *Statistical abstract of the U.S.* Washington, DC: U.S. Government Printing Office.

U.S. Department of Commerce, Bureau of the Census. (1980, Table 5; 1982, Table 16; 1984, Table 2; 1986, Table 4; 1988, Table 2; 1990, Table 4; 1992, Table 4; 1994, Table 4a [electronic version (e.v.)]; 1996, Table 4 [e.v.]; 1998, Table 4 [e.v.]; 2000, Table 4a [e.v.]). *Current population reports: P-20 series on voting and registration.* Washington, DC: Government Printing Office.

In-migration:

U.S. Department of Commerce, Bureau of the Census. (1960, Tables 39 and 98; 1970, Table 50; 1980, Tables 75 and 85; 1990, Table P042 [American FactFinder]; 2000, Table PCT63A [American FactFinder]). *Census of population, place of birth.* Washington, DC: U.S. Government Printing Office.[30]

Agricultural sector employment:

U.S. Department of Commerce, Bureau of the Census. (1960, Table 128; 1970, Table 167; 1980, Table 242; 1990, Table 151; 2000, DP-3 [American FactFinder]). *General population characteristics.* Washington, DC: U.S. Government Printing Office.

Per capita income:

U.S. Department of Commerce, Bureau of Economic Analysis. (1989). *State personal income: 1929–1987.* Washington, DC: Government Printing Office.

U.S. Department of Commerce, Bureau of Economic Analysis, Regional Accounts Data, Local Area Personal Income. (2003). *CA1–3. Personal income and summary estimates, 1969–2003.* Retrieved 2003 from www.bea.doc.gov/bea/regional/reis/

Substate party competition:
Electronic data:

Inter-University Consortium for Political and Social Research. (1992). *State legislative election returns in The United States, 1968–1989* (5th ICPSR ed.) [Computer file]. Ann Arbor, MI: Inter-university Consortium for Political and Social Research.

Books:

Aistrup, J.A. (1996). *The Southern strategy revisited: Republican top-down advancement in the South.* Lexington: University of Kentucky Press. [Tables 4.1, 4.2, 4.3]

Council of State Governments. (1960/1961–2000/2001). *The book of the states.* Lexington, KY: Author.

Jewell, M.E. (1967). *Legislative representation in the contemporary South.* Durham, NC: Duke University Press. [Table 4.1]

Jewell, M.E., and Olson, D.M. (1982). *American state political parties and elections* (2nd ed.). Homewood, IL: Dorsey Press. [Table 3.5]

State Publications:

Tennessee Blue Book [electronic version]: 1996, 1998.

Mississippi Blue Book: 1995, 1997, 1999.

Georgia Official and Statistical Register: 1966, 1968.

Arkansas Votes: 1968.

Newspapers:

The Washington Post (VA): 1959, 1961, 1963, 1965, 1967.

The Commercial Appeal (MS): 1959, 1961.

Arkansas Gazette (AR): 1960–1966.

The Clarion Ledger (MS): 1959.

Original voting records/reports from government entities for the following states:

Mississippi: 1963, 1967.

North Carolina: 1968, 1986, 1988.

Virginia: 1959.

Georgia: 1960, 1962, 1964.

Secretary of state/state board of elections electronic returns for the following:

Alabama: 1998.

Arkansas: 1996, 1998, 2000.

Florida: 1994, 1996, 1998, 2000.

Georgia: 1994, 1996, 1998, 2000.

Louisiana: 1991, 1995, 1999.

Mississippi: 1999.

North Carolina: 1996, 1998.

South Carolina: 1994, 1996, 1998, 2000.

Texas: 1994, 1996, 1998, 2000.

Virginia: 1995, 1999.

Evangelical Protestants:
Sources for evangelical Protestant membership:

Bradley, M.B., Green, N.M., Jr., Jones, D.E., Lynn, M., and McNeil, L. (1992). *Churches and church membership in the United States, 1990.* Atlanta, GA: Glenmary Research Center.

Johnson, D.W., Picard, P.R., and Quinn, B. (1974). *Churches and church membership in the United States, 1971.* Washington, DC: Glenmary Research Center.

Jones, D.E. (2002). *Religious congregations and membership in the United States: 2000* [electronic version]. Nashville, TN: Glenmary Research Center.

National Council of the Churches of Christ in the United States of America. (1956). *Churches and church membership in the United States.* New York: Author.

Quinn, B., Anderson, H., Bradley, M., Goetting, P., and Shriver, P. (1982). *Churches and church membership in the United States, 1980.* Atlanta, GA: Glenmary Research Center.

Summary of Churches by State Convention. (1993–2000). Alpharetta, GA: North American Mission Board, Southern Baptist Convention. Available from www.namb.net.

Sunday School Board of the Southern Baptist Convention. (1960–1992). *Southern Baptist handbook.* Nashville, TN: Author.

Sources for state population estimates:

U.S. Department of Commerce, Bureau of the Census. *Historical annual time series of state population estimates and demographic components of change, 1900 to 1990. Total population estimates.* Available from www.census.gov/population/www/estimates/st_stts.html.

U.S. Department of Commerce, Bureau of the Census. *State population estimates: Annual time series, July 1, 1990 to July 1, 1999.* Available from www.census.gov/population/estimates/state/st-99–3.txt.

Notes

1. Common name: Asiatic elephant.
2. Mississippi's delegation left the convention, and Truman only received the support of thirteen Southern delegates (all from North Carolina; see Scher, 1997).
3. See Nadeau and Stanley (1993), Shafer and Johnston (2001), and Rhodes (2000) for general overviews of this literature.
4. Although we recognize the difference between partisan identification and voting behavior, the two are very closely related in the South during this period of time (see note 13 for a more detailed empirical comparison between our composite measure of state-level Republican strength and party registration figures).
5. Lipset and Rokkan (1967) also highlighted the significance of the development of competitive local party organizations for long-term partisan growth.
6. The time-series–cross-sectional framework, although relatively uncommon in studies of Southern politics, is becoming an increasingly important and prominent analytical tool within the literature (e.g., see Hood et al., 1999).
7. Although the use of instrumental variables (IV) to address potentially problematic serial correlation is a common practice in conventional time series analysis, its use in panel data is somewhat less common. The rationale for the use of IV, however, is the same in both cases. The IV approach is employed when serial correlation remains even after the inclusion of a lagged dependent variable. A detailed description of the procedure we used to generate IV estimates in the panel data context is presented in Greene (2000, pp. 550–551). Both Ostrom (1978) and Gujarati (1988) provide a somewhat less mathematically complex discussion of the intuition behind the IV method and the procedure for its implementation in the single time series framework.
8. The similarity of the results is likely because of the low level of autocorrelation in the model with the lagged dependent variable. Although we could not reject, from a statistical standpoint, the hypothesis that no autocorrelation remained (using a conventional Lagrange multiplier test), the substantive impact of the remaining autocorrelation was clearly minimal.

9. All variance inflation factors were below 4.
10. Only even years are included in the analysis (i.e., 1962, 1964, . . . 2000).
11. We examined the possibility that the dependent variable, Republican strength, is non-stationary. Using the Levin-Lin-Chu (2001) unit root test specifically designed for panel data, we were able to reject the null hypothesis of non-stationarity (t star statistic = -6.88, $p < .001$).
12. Estimates from 1960 through 1970 are obtained from David's (1972) work, and estimates for the remaining years are calculated by the authors.
13. Comparisons between our measure of Republican Party strength and actual party registration data from Louisiana and Florida from 1950 to 2000 (the only two Southern states that did track party registration during the time of our study) indicate a high level of congruity ($r = .94$ for Louisiana and .94 for Florida). (Data available from the authors upon request.)
14. These presidential vote percentages were duplicated for time points containing off-year elections (i.e., 1962, 1966).
15. It should be noted that, although we can gauge interparty competition directly, there is no equivalent way to measure the relative strength of party organizations in the region during the time period under study. The most comprehensive study of party organization to date is the Cotter, Gibson, Bibby, and Huckshorn (1984) party transformation study. This study measures party organizational strength (POS) by administering a detailed questionnaire to a multipart sample of party officials at both the state and county level. In this manner, Cotter et al. were able to create a composite measure of POS using responses from a variety of items dealing with such issues as budget, staff, and candidate recruitment activities. Although the Cotter et al. measure is a proven and highly reliable indicator of party organization strength at the subnational level, a number of issues prevent its use in this analysis. To begin, the POS measures were only calculated at the state-level from 1960 through 1984 and, within this time frame, only every five years. In addition, some state parties are missing from their analysis. In conducting a model over time with panel data, the use of the Cotter et al. POS measure would produce unacceptable gaps both over time and across states.
16. Given that our dependent variable is a composite index derived from vote percentages, we do not include a legislative vote component, in contrast to Aistrup (1996), in our index of substate party competition.
17. Although, undoubtedly, some Blacks are included in this measure, most of the denominations that collectively yield the total number of evangelical Protestants have very few Black adherents.
18. State observations constituting outliers are plotted in Figure 20-1 using circles. Surprisingly only Louisiana (1988, 1990) and Georgia (1990) are more than 1.5 times the interquartile range for those time periods. Upon further examination, these cases do not appear to be a function of any previously unrecognized substantive factors.
19. Black context (% Black) is only significant in the Model 1 specification unadjusted for residual autocorrelation thereby leaving the overall impact of this variable in some question. The negatively signed coefficient is not unexpected and has been observed often in previous research. Large, but politically immobilized, Black populations have been associated with White conservatism in a one-party setting and, as such, as a hindrance to Republican growth (for a discussion of his Black-belt hypothesis, see Key, 1949).

20. Interpretation of the presidential campaign dummies presented in Model 2 should be tempered with a note of caution as only the Ford campaign is found to have a significant (and negative) effect in the IV model formulation.

21. In another model formulation, we added a variable to represent the period of time ranging from 1962 to 1980 and created an interactive variable using this dummy and in-migration. The results of this model indicate that in-migration had a positive and significant effect on GOP growth during the earlier time period. The other model findings remained substantively unchanged.

22. The deep South is composed of Louisiana, Mississippi, Alabama, Georgia and South Carolina and the rim or peripheral South is comprised of Texas, Arkansas, Tennessee, North Carolina, Florida, and Virginia.

23. The single exception to this pattern is North Carolina, the rim South state with the highest proportion of African Americans.

24. Data Source: Georgia Secretary of State. Retrieved from http://sos.georgia.gov/elections.

25. Data Source: *America Votes* 2004.

26. Special transformations had to be made for Louisiana for each election following the 1978 institution of an open primary system. We used the following method to calculate our index of GOP party strength for 1978 through 1994:

    1. If there was only one election (open primary), GOP = % of total Republican vote (including votes won by other Republican candidates in the primary).
    2. If there was both a primary and a general election and:
       a. The general election contained both a Republican and a Democrat, GOP = % of total vote won by a Republican candidate.
       b. The general election contained two Democratic candidates, GOP = 0%.
       c. The general election contained two Republican candidates, GOP = 100%.

27. For example, in 1960, the Black population in Georgia was 28.4%. In 1970, Blacks composed 25.8% of the state's population. The growth rate for Blacks in Georgia during this time period was, therefore, $(25.8 - 28.4)/10 = -.26$.

28. Interpolation was used to fill in the gaps between missing years for both the number of Blacks who were registered to vote and for the total number of registered voters in each Southern state.

29. The Census Bureau defines the Southern region as the eleven original states of the Confederacy plus five border states: Delaware, Kentucky, Maryland, Oklahoma, and West Virginia.

30. For more information on this variable, see Jewett (1997).

21. Racial and Moral Issues in the Evolution of the "Southern Strategy"

D. Sunshine Hillygus and Todd G. Shields

[N ow] we turn to a broader longitudinal analysis that considers the evolution of the original GOP "Southern strategy," as it moved to incorporate cultural or moral issues. Using the closed-ended questions from the NES cumulative file, we estimate the relative effects of racial and moral cross-pressures across election years.

Why would the original Southern strategy need to change? Perhaps because of its success. The GOP's emphasis on racial conservatism appealed to many white Democrats, but gradually some of those racially conservative Democrats realigned to the Republican Party.[1] While scholars disagree over the exact causes of the transformation of the once solidly Democratic South to the current stronghold of the GOP, the result was that by the end of the 1980s, Republican presidential candidates could reliably count on substantial support among Southern voters.[2] As the party coalitions changed, so too did the potential cleavages available to Republican candidates.

Explicitly emphasizing racial issues during campaigns also increasingly risked violating the American norm of equality, and was earning the Republican Party the reputation of racial insensitivity. Many scholars and journalists have argued that Ronald Reagan strategically moved away from explicit racial appeals and instead implicitly primed negative racial predispositions among white voters by emphasizing issues like welfare and crime (Mendelberg 2001, chap. 3; Black and Black 2002; Aistrup 1996; Glaser 1996, 69–70). In *The Race Card*, Tali Mendelberg (2001, 67) argues that "racial appeals did not disappear; they were transformed, often consciously and strategically." In a much-quoted interview about the use of racial campaign appeals, Reagan's political advisor Lee Atwater, explained the evolution of the Republican Southern strategy,

> As to the whole Southern strategy that Harry Dent and others put together in 1968, opposition to the Voting Rights Act would have been a central part of keeping the South. Now [a candidate] doesn't have to do that. All you have to do to keep the South is for Reagan to run in place on the issues he's campaigned on since 1964 . . . and that's fiscal conservatism, balancing the budget, cut taxes, you know, the whole cluster. . . . You start out in 1954 by saying "nigger, nigger, nigger." By 1968 you can't say "nigger"—that

Source: D. Sunshine Hillygus and Todd G. Shields, *The Persuadable Voter: Wedge Issues in Presidential Campaigns,* Princeton, N.J.: Princeton University Press, 2008, pp. 136–143.

hurts you. Backfires. So you say stuff like forced busing, states' rights and all that stuff. You're getting so abstract now [that] you're talking about cutting taxes, and all these things you're talking about are totally economic things and a byproduct of them is [that] blacks get hurt worse than whites. And subconsciously maybe that is part of it. I'm not saying that. But I'm saying that if it is getting that abstract, and that coded, that we are doing away with the racial problem one way or the other. You follow me—because obviously sitting around saying, "we want to cut this," is much more abstract than even the busing thing, and a hell of a lot more abstract than "nigger, nigger." (Lamis 1988, 8)

Certainly by the 1990s, following reactions to the infamous "Willie Horton" ad during the 1988 presidential election, many Republicans worried about a backlash among new groups of swing voters they were hoping to court, especially women (Hutchings et al. 2004). The national Republican Party, for instance, quickly distanced itself from former KKK member David Duke when he ran for governor on the Republican ticket, and Republican senator Trent Lott was forced to step down as majority leader after saying that the country would have been better off had Strom Thurmond won the 1948 election (Edsall 2002). In 2005 Republican National Committee chairman Ken Mehlman apologized to the NAACP for the GOP's Southern strategy saying, "Some Republicans gave up on winning the African American vote, looking the other way or trying to benefit politically from racial polarization. I am here today as the Republican chairman to tell you we were wrong" (Allen 2005).

To be sure, many white Americans continue to hold conservative racial policy preferences. The 2004 NES indicates that most white Democrats support the Republican Party position on affirmative action.[3] Likewise, state-level ballot initiatives banning affirmative action in employment, education, and public-contracting decisions have easily won electoral support. But with the realignment of many racially conservative Democrats to the Republican Party, and with the increased potential for a backlash, Republicans have turned their attention to other potentially persuadable voters. Discussing the 1984 Reagan electoral strategy, Atwater explained that "we must remember the fundamentals of Southern politics with an electorate divided into three groups: country clubbers (Republican), populists ('usually Democratic: will swing to the GOP under the right circumstances'), and blacks (Democratic). . . . We must assemble coalitions in every Southern state largely based on the country clubbers and the populists" (Brady 1997, 117–118). In his memoirs, Richard Nixon explained that "the Republican counterstrategy was clear. . . . We should aim our strategy primarily at disaffected Democrats, and blue-collar workers, and at working-class white ethnics. We should set out to capture the vote of the forty-seven-year-old Dayton housewife" (Nixon 1978, 491).[4]

GOP strategists decided that cultural issues could potentially bridge the country clubbers and populists. The abortion debate, the quickly rising divorce rate, and other societal problems brought attention to issues that continue to split Democrats in the contemporary American electorate. Attempting to reach socially conservative Democrats, Republican candidates began to emphasize social issues like school prayer, flag burning, pornography, and gay rights. The motivation behind a campaign emphasis on such issues was confirmed by Chris Henick, the RNC's Southern political director during the late 1980s, who explained that linking [Michael] Dukakis and the Democrats to "opposition to certain anti-pornography laws and to prayer in the schools provide ideal 'wedge issues' to encourage moderate-to-conservative Democrats to abandon their party" (Edsall 1988).[5] In his 1988 nomination speech, George H. W. Bush ran through a litany of wedge issues that might divide the traditional Democratic coalition:

> Should public school teachers be required to lead our children in the pledge of allegiance? My opponent says no—and I say yes. Should society be allowed to impose the death penalty on those who commit crimes of extraordinary cruelty and violence? My opponent says no—but I say yes. And should our children have the right to say a voluntary prayer, or even observe a moment of silence in the schools? My opponent says no—but I say yes. And should, should free men and women have the right to own a gun to protect their home? My opponent says no—but I say yes. And is it right to believe in the sanctity of life and protect the lives of innocent children? My opponent says no—but I say yes.[6]

A content analysis of campaign news coverage by the *New York Times,* shown in Figure 21-1, indicates the increasing focus on moral issues in presidential elections as news coverage of racial issues declined.[7] Beginning in 1984 the percentage of articles discussing morality outnumbered the percentage of articles addressing race—and the focus on moral issues continued through the 2004 presidential contest.

Perhaps ironically, cultural issues are now the primary issues on which Republican candidates attempt to appeal to minority voters. For example, in the 2000 election, candidate George W. Bush emphasized policies like faith-based initiatives and school vouchers when he spoke to African American audiences. At a conference held by the National Urban League during the 2004 presidential contest, President Bush encouraged the predominantly black audience to consider voting Republican: "If you believe the institutions of marriage and family are worth defending and need defending today, [then] take a look at my agenda." Following a round of applause, President Bush continued, "If you believe in building a culture of life in America, take a look at my agenda."[8]

The Effects of Racial and Moral Cross-Pressures over Time

To examine the role of racial and moral cross-pressures over time, we rely on the closed-ended policy questions in the NES cumulative file. We again estimate

Figure 21-1 Racial and Moral Issues as Percentage of Campaign News
Coverage

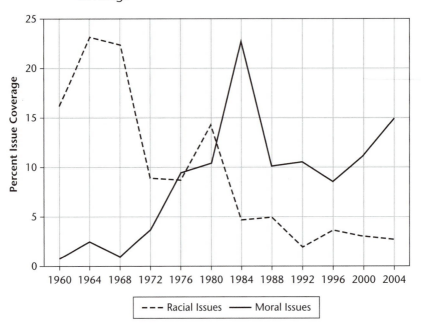

Note: Figure shows the percent of *New York Times* general election campaign coverage devoted to racial and moral issues, 1960–2004. Data provided by Lee Sigelman and Emmett Buell.

the substantive effect of racial and moral cross-pressures on the probability that a Democrat voted for the Republican presidential candidate in each of the last eleven presidential campaigns, reported in Figure 21-2.[9] These results follow the general pattern that we would expect given the strategic campaign decisions we have discussed throughout this chapter [of Hillygus and Shields 2008]. Those who are highly cross-pressured on racial issues were much more likely to defect in the 1960s–1980s, compared to those not cross-pressured, while racial policy incongruence has little impact in recent years. In contrast, Democrats highly cross-pressured on social issues, like abortion, were more likely to defect in recent years compared to the 1980s (when questions were first asked). It was with the 1992 presidential election that the effect of moral cross-pressures exceeded the effect of racial cross-pressures, perhaps reflecting the prominence of moral criticisms of then-candidate Bill Clinton.

There is little doubt that race was central to the early transformation of the South, but the importance of race in American attitudes and behavior in the later part of the twentieth century has been a topic of considerable debate. Some scholars have argued that racial issues no longer explain voting behavior by the 1970s, while others contend it remains an important predictor of vote choice.[10] Alan

Figure 21-2 Effect of Racial and Moral Cross-pressures on the Predicted Probability of Defection, 1964–2004

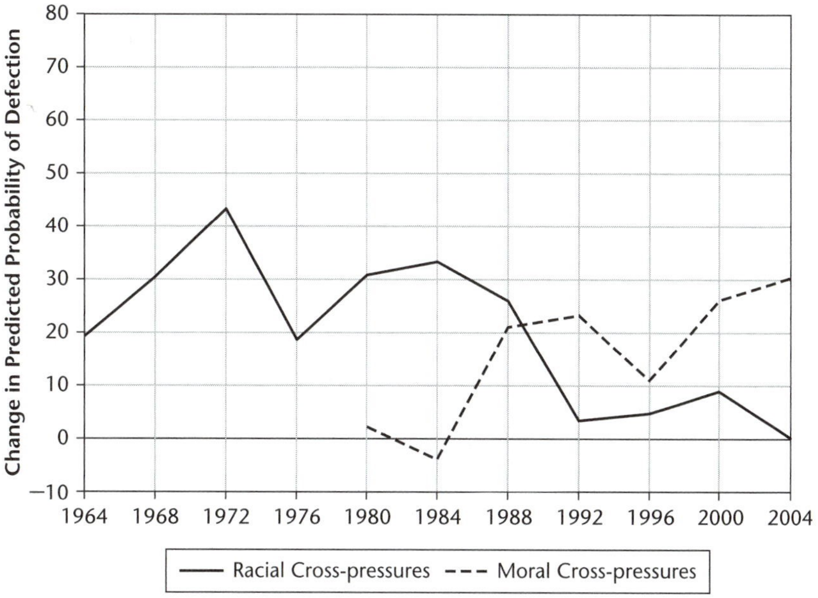

Note: Figure indicates that the impact of racial cross-pressures has declined in recent years, while the impact of moral cross-pressures has increased. Reported is the change in the predicted probability of defection between highly cross-pressured white Democrats and congruent Democrats, holding constant all other variables in the model. Data source is the American National Election Study cumulative file.

Abramowitz concludes, for instance, that "attitudes toward racial issues had a negligible impact on voting decisions" by the late 1980s (1994, 21). Our findings suggest that the extent to which voters weighed racial policies in their vote decisions has depended on the particular campaign context. When presidential candidates took divergent positions on questions of race and were willing to emphasize those differences in their campaigns, voters' racial attitudes played a stronger role in their decision-making processes. In recent elections, Republican candidates have been more likely to focus their strategic efforts on winning over culturally conservative Democrats, and we see those efforts reflected in the behavior of Democrats who face inconsistent policy positions on social and moral issues.

Notes

1. Just over 20 percent of Democratic respondents who defected and voted for Nixon in 1972 changed their party identification in the 1976 wave of the panel study.

2. Arguments about the reasons for the change in Democratic Party identification across the South range from in-migration of Republican Party industrialists, cohort replacements with younger more conservative voters, the efforts of religious groups across the South, ideological decisions among voters to align themselves with the Republican Party, an extension of elite conflict among some voters, etc. For extensive reviews, see Green et al. (2002).

3. On the other hand, racial policies do not seem to be a great concern to white Democrats today—not a single Democrat volunteered a racial issue as a reason for disliking John Kerry or the Democrats in 2004.

4. This strategy could be traced to Scammon and Wattenberg (1970).

5. Certainly there are still campaign appearances of racially charged political messages, such as the classic Willie Horton ad.

6. The full transcript of the speech is available online through the American Presidency Project (www.presidencyucsb.edu).

7. More detailed information about the data coding can be found in Sigelman and Buell (2004). This estimate likely underestimates news coverage of racial issues in 1976 because coding was limited to the general-election campaign. During the primary season, George Wallace's candidacy as a Democratic hopeful helped to focus attention on the busing issue in particular. For instance, Nixon made more than eleven television statements about the busing issue between January and September alone (compiled from www.presidency.ucsb.edu). After Wallace was shot in May 1972, the focus on the busing issue declined somewhat.

8. The White House, 23 July 2004. President emphasizes minority entrepreneurship at Urban League. Remarks by the president to the 2004 National Urban League Conference. Washington, D.C.: Retrieved 10 November 2005.

9. [In Hillygus and Shields 2008,] [s]ee appendix 1 for issues included by year, and appendix 3 for full results. Reported are the changes in the predicted probability of moving from 0 to 75 percent (95th percentile) on the policy incongruence scale, holding other variables at their global means or modes from the earliest survey year. The results are substantively similar, albeit muted, if we also control for retrospective evaluations of the national economy, ideology, attitudes toward Vietnam, and strength of partisanship.

10. For example, see Valentino and Sears (2005). For arguments that race was less important see Shafer and Johnston (2006) [of which chap. 2 is reprinted in this volume, chap. 19].

References

Abelson, Robert P. 1968. *Theories of Cognitive Consistency: A Sourcebook.* Chicago: Rand McNally.

Abelson, Robert P., and Ariel Levi. 1985. "Decision Making and Decision Theory." In *The Handbook of Social Psychology,* vol. 1, 3rd ed., ed. Gardner Lindzey and Elliot Aronson. New York: Random House.

Abelson, Robert P, Elizabeth F. Loftus, and Anthony G. Greenwald. 1992. "Attempts to Improve the Accuracy of Self-Reports of Voting." In *Questions about Questions,* ed. Judith M. Tanur. New York: Russell Sage Foundation.

Abramowitz, Alan I. 1994. "Issue Evolution Reconsidered: Racial Attitudes and Partisanship in the U.S. Electorate." *American Journal of Political Science* 39: 1–24.

———. 2008. "Don't Blame Primary Voters for Polarization." *The Forum* 5(4): Article 4.

Abramowitz, Alan I., and H. Gibbs Knotts. 2006. "Ideological Realignment in the American Electorate: A Comparison of Northern and Southern White Voters in the Pre-Reagan, Reagan, and Post-Reagan Eras." *Politics and Policy* 34: 94–108.

Abramowitz, Alan I., and Kyle L. Saunders 1998. "Ideological Realignment in the U.S. Electorate." *Journal of Politics* 60: 634–652.

———. 2005. "Why Can't We All Just Get Along? The Reality of a Polarized America." *The Forum* 3(2): Article 1.

———. 2006. "Exploring the Bases of Partisanship in the American Electorate: Social Identity vs. Ideology." *Political Research Quarterly* 59: 175–187.

———. 2008. "Is Polarization a Myth?" *Journal of Politics* 70: 542–555.

Abramson, Paul R., and John H. Aldrich. 1982. "The Decline of Electoral Participation in America." *American Political Science Review* 76: 502–521.

Abramson, Paul R., John H. Aldrich, and David W. Rohde. 2007. *Change and Continuity in the 2004 and 2006 Elections.* Washington, D.C.: CQ Press.

Achen, Christopher. 1975. "Mass Political Attitudes and the Survey Response." *American Political Science Review* 69: 1218–1231.

———. 1983. "Towards Theories of Data: The State of Political Methodology." In *Political Science: The State of the Discipline,* ed. Ada W. Finifter. Washington, D.C.: American Political Science Association.

Achen, Christopher H., and Larry M. Bartels. 2006. "It Feels Like We're Thinking: The Rationalizing Voter and Electoral Democracy." Paper presented at the annual meeting of the American Political Science Association, Philadelphia.

Ackerman, Bruce A., and James S. Fishkin. 2004. *Deliberation Day.* New Haven, Conn.: Yale University Press.

Adams, Greg D. 1997. "Abortion: Evidence of Issue Evolution." *American Journal of Political Science* 41: 718–737.

Aistrup, Joseph A. 1996. *The Southern Strategy Revisited.* Lexington: University Press of Kentucky.

Aldrich, John H. 1995. *Why Parties? The Origin and Transformation of Party Politics in America.* Chicago: University of Chicago Press.

———. 2000. "Southern Politics in State and Nation." *Journal of Politics* 62: 643–670.

———. 2003. "Electoral Democracy during Politics as Usual—and Unusual." In *Electoral Democracy,* ed. Michael B. MacKuen and George Rabinowitz. Ann Arbor: University of Michigan Press.

Aldrich, John H., Mark M. Berger, and David W. Rohde. 1999. "The Historical Variability in Conditional Party Government, 1877–1986." Paper presented at a conference on the history of Congress. Stanford University, Palo Alto, Calif. January 14–15.

Aldrich, John H., and John D. Griffin. 2000. "Ambition in the South: The Emergence of Republican Electoral Support, 1948–1998." Paper presented at the 12th Biennial Symposium on Southern Politics, The Citadel, Charleston, S.C.

Aldrich, John H., and Richard G. Niemi. 1996. "The Sixth American Party System: Electoral Change, 1952–1992." In *Broken Contract?* ed. Stephen C. Craig. Boulder, Colo.: Westview.

Alford, Robert. 1963. *Party and Society: The Anglo-American Democracies.* Chicago: Rand McNally.

Allen, Mike. 2005. "RNC Chief to Say It Was 'Wrong' to Exploit Racial Conflict for Votes." *Washington Post,* 14 July, A4.

Althaus, Scott L. 1998. "Information Effects in Collective Preferences." *American Political Science Review* 92: 545–558.

———. 2003. *Collective Preferences in Democratic Politics.* New York: Cambridge University Press.

Alvarez, R. Michael, Jonathan Nagler, and Shaun Bowler. 2000. "Issues, Economics, and the Dynamics of Multiparty Elections: The British 1987 General Election." *American Political Science Review* 94: 131–149.

Alwin, Duane F., and Jon A. Krosnick. 1991. "Aging, Cohorts, and the Stability of Sociopolitical Orientations over the Life Span." *American Journal of Sociology* 97: 169–195.

"America's Civic Health Index: Broken Engagement." 2006. Washington, D.C.: National Conference on Citizenship.

Andersen, Robert, and Anthony Heath. 2002. "Class Matters: The Persisting Effects of Contextual Social Class on Individual Voting Behaviour in Britain, 1964–97." *European Sociological Review* 18: 125–138.

Anderson, Cameron D. 2006. "Economic Voting and Multilevel Governance: A Comparative Individual-Level Analysis." *American Journal of Political Science* 50: 449–463.

Anderson, Christopher J., Silvia M. Mendes, and Yuliya V. Tverdova. 2004. "Endogenous Economic Voting: Evidence from the 1997 British Election." *Electoral Studies* 23: 683–708.

Anderson, Richard B. 1997. "Electoral Competition and Southern State Legislatures: The Dynamics of Change." In *Southern Parties and Elections*, ed. Robert P. Steed, Laurence W. Moreland, and Tod A. Baker. Tuscaloosa: University of Alabama Press.

Andrews, William. 1966. "American Voting Participation." *Western Political Quarterly* 19: 636–652.

Ansolabehere, Stephen, and Shanto Iyengar. 1996. *Going Negative: How Attack Ads Shrink and Polarize the Electorate*. New York: Free Press.

Ansolabehere, Stephen, Jonathan Rodden, and James M. Snyder Jr. 2006. "Purple America." *Journal of Economic Perspectives* 20: 97–118.

———. 2008. "The Strength of Issues: Using Multiple Measures to Gauge Preference Stability, Ideological Constraint, and Issue Voting." *American Political Science Review* 102: 215–232.

Ansolabehere, Stephen, and James M. Snyder Jr. 2002. "The Incumbency Advantage in U.S. Elections: An Analysis of State and Federal Offices, 1942–2000." *Election Law Journal* 1: 313–338.

Ansolabehere, Stephen, and Charles H. Stewart III. 2005a. "Truth in Numbers." *Boston Review*. February/March, 30: 40.

———. 2005b. "Residual Votes Attributable to Technology." *Journal of Politics* 67: 365–389.

———. 2009. "Amazing Race: How Post-Racial Was Obama's Victory?" *Boston Review* January/February 2009 (http://bostonreview.net/BR34.1/ansolabehere_stewart.php).

Antista, Jonathan, Jenny Coukos, Michelle Desrosiers, Lauren Jewett, and Richard Niemi, 2010. "Newspaper Coverage of Presidential Campaigns from 1888–2008." Paper presented at the annual meeting of the Western Political Science Association, San Francisco, April 3, 2010.

Aronson, Elliot, Timothy D. Wilson, and Marilynn B. Brewer. 1998. "Experimentation in Social Psychology." In *The Handbook of Social Psychology*, 4th ed., ed. Daniel T. Gilbert, Susan T. Fiske, and Gardner Lindzey. Boston: McGraw-Hill.

Avey, Michael J. 1989. *The Demobilization of American Voters: A Comprehensive Theory of Voter Turnout*. New York: Greenwood.

Baldassarri, Delia, and Andrew Gelman. 2008. "Partisans without Constraint: Political Polarization and Trends in American Public Opinion." *American Journal of Sociology* 114: 408–446.

Banfield, Edward C. 1961. *Political Influence*. New York: Free Press.

Barker, David C., and Susan B. Hansen. 2005. "All Things Considered: Systematic Cognitive Processing and Electoral Decision-Making." *Journal of Politics* 67: 319–344.

Barker, David C., and James D. Tinnick III. 2006. "Competing Visions of Parental Roles and Ideological Constraint." *American Political Science Review* 100: 249–263.

Barnes, Samuel, Max Kaase, et al. 1979. *Political Action: Mass Participation in Five Western Democracies.* Beverly Hills, Calif.: Sage.

Barreto, Matt A., Fernando Guerra, Mara Marks, Stephen A. Nuño, and Nathan D. Woods. 2006. "Controversies in Exit Polling: Implementing a Racially Stratified Homogenous Precinct Approach." *PS: Political Science & Politics* 39: 477–483.

Barreto, Matt A., and Gary M. Segura. 2009. "Estimating the Effects of Traditional Predictors, Group Specific Forces, and Anti-Black Affect on 2008 Presidential Vote among Latinos and Non-Hispanic Whites." Paper presented at the Mershon Conference on the Transformative Election of 2008, Columbus, Ohio, Oct. 2–4.

Barro, Robert. 1973. "The Control of Politicians: An Economic Model." *Public Choice* 14: 19–42.

Bartels, Larry M. 1996. "Uninformed Votes: Information Effects in Presidential Elections." *American Journal of Political Science* 40: 194–230.

———. 2000. "Partisanship and Voting Behavior, 1952–1996." *American Journal of Political Science* 44: 35–50.

———. 2002. "Beyond the Running Tally: Partisan Bias in Political Perceptions." *Political Behavior* 24: 117–150.

———. 2006. "What's the Matter with *What's the Matter with Kansas?*" *Quarterly Journal of Political Science* 1: 201–226.

———. 2008. *Unequal Democracy: The Political Economy of the New Gilded Age.* Princeton, N.J.: Princeton University Press.

Bartels, Larry M., and Wendy M. Rahn. 2000. "Political Attitudes in the Post-Network Era." Paper presented at the annual meeting of the American Political Science Association, Washington.

Bartels, Larry M., and John Zaller. 2001. "Presidential Vote Models: A Recount." *PS: Politics & Political Science.* 34: 8–20.

Barwise, T. P., A. S. C. Ehrenberg, and G. J. Goodhardt. 1982. "Glued to the Box: Patterns of TV Repeat-Viewing." *Journal of Communication* 32: 22–29.

Basinger, Scott J., and Howard Lavine. 2005. "Ambivalence, Information, and Electoral Choice." *American Political Science Review* 99: 169–184.

Bass, Jack, and W. De Vries. 1976. *The Transformation of Southern Politics.* New York: Basic Books.

Baum, Matthew A. 2002. "Sex, Lies, and War: How Soft News Brings Foreign Policy to the Inattentive Public." *American Political Science Review* 96: 91–109.

———. 2003. *Soft News Goes to War: Public Opinion and American Foreign Policy in the New Media Age.* Princeton, N.J.: Princeton University Press.

———. 2005. "Talking the Vote: Why Presidential Candidates Hit the Talk Show Circuit." *American Journal of Political Science* 49: 213–234.

Baum, Matthew A., and Angela S. Jamison. 2006. "The Oprah Effect: How Soft News Helps Inattentive Citizens Vote Consistently." *Journal of Politics* 68: 946–959.

Baum, Matthew, and Samuel Kernell. 1999. "Has Cable Ended the Golden Age of Presidential Television?" *American Political Science Review* 93: 99–114.

Baybeck, Brady. 2006. "Sorting Out the Competing Effects of Racial Context." *Journal of Politics* 68: 386–396.

Beck, Nathaniel, and Jonathan N. Katz. 1995. "What to Do (and Not to Do) with Time-Series Cross-Section Data." *American Political Science Review* 89: 634–647.

———. 1996. "Nuisance vs. Substance: Specifying and Estimating Time-Series–Cross-Section Models." *Political Analysis* 6: 1–36.

Beck, Paul Allen. 1986. "Model Choice in Political Science: The Case of Voting Behavior Research, 1946–1975." In *Political Science: The Science of Politics*, ed. Herbert F. Weisberg. New York: Agathon.

———. 1997. *Party Politics in America*, 8th ed. New York: Longman.

Becker, Lee B., and Klaus Schoenbach. 1989. "When Media Content Diversifies: Anticipating Audience Behaviors." In *Audience Responses to Media Diversification: Coping with Plenty*, ed. Lee B. Becker and Klaus Schoenbach. Hillsdale, N.J.: Lawrence Erlbaum.

Bendor, Jonathan, and John G. Bullock. 2008. "Lethal Incompetence: Voters, Officials, and Systems." *Critical Review* 20: 1–23.

Bennett, Stephen Earl. N.d. "Has Democracy Survived Television? Jarol Manheim's Thesis Revisited." Typescript, University of Southern Indiana.

———. 1988. "'Know-Nothings' Revisited: The Meaning of Political Ignorance Today." *Social Science Quarterly* 69: 476–490.

Bennett, W. Lance. 1997. *News: The Politics of Illusion*, 3rd ed. New York: Longman.

———. 2003. "The Burglar Alarm that Just Keeps Ringing: A Response to Zaller." *Political Communication* 20: 131–138.

Bennett, W. Lance, and Robert Entman, eds. 2000. *Mediated Politics: Communication in the Future of Democracy*. Cambridge: Cambridge University Press.

Bentler, Peter M. 1995. *EQS: Structural Equations Program Manual.* Encino, Calif.: Multivariate Software.

Berinsky, Adam J. 1999. "The Two Faces of Public Opinion." *American Journal of Political Science* 43: 1209–1230.

———. 2005. "The Perverse Consequences of Electoral Reform in the United States." *American Politics Research* 33: 471–491.

Besley, Timothy and Stephen Coate. 2003. "Elected versus Appointed Regulators: Theory and Evidence." *Journal of the European Economic Association* 1: 1176–1206.

Bishop, Bill. 2004. "The Cost of Political Uniformity." *Austin American Statesman*, 8 April, Special Section: The Great Divide.

Black, Earl. 1976. *Southern Governors and Civil Rights.* Cambridge, Mass.: Harvard University Press.

Black, Earl, and Merle Black. 1987. *Politics and Society in the South.* Cambridge, Mass.: Harvard University Press.

———. 1992. *The Vital South: How Presidents Are Elected.* Cambridge, Mass.: Harvard University Press.

———. 2002. *The Rise of Southern Republicans.* Cambridge, Mass.: Harvard University Press.

———. 2007. *Divided America: The Ferocious Power Struggle in America Politics.* New York: Simon & Schuster.

Black, Merle. 1978. "Racial Composition of Congressional Districts and Support for Federal Voting Rights in the American South." *Social Science Quarterly* 59: 435–450.

———. 2004. "The Transformation of the Southern Democratic Party." *Journal of Politics* 66: 1001–1017.

Blais, André. 2007. "Turnout in Elections." In *The Oxford Handbook of Political Behavior,* ed. Russell J. Dalton and Hans-Dieter Klingemann. Oxford: Oxford University Press.

———. 2010. "Political Participation." In *Comparing Democracies 3: Elections and Voting in the 21st Century,* ed. Lawrence LeDuc, Richard G. Niemi, and Pippa Norris. London: Sage.

Blais, André, Elisabeth Gidengil, Neil Nevitte, and Richard Nadeau. 2004. "Where Does Turnout Decline Come From?" *European Journal of Political Research* 43: 221–236.

Bodenhausen, Galen V., and Meryl Lichtenstein. 1987. "Social Stereotypes and Information-Processing Strategies: The Impact of Task Complexity." *Journal of Personality and Social Psychology* 52: 871–880.

Bodenhausen, Galen V., and Robert S. Wyer. 1985. "Effects of Stereotypes on Decision Making and Information-Processing Strategies." *Journal of Personality and Social Psychology* 48: 267–282.

Bollen, Kenneth A. 1989. *Structural Equations with Latent Variables.* New York: Wiley.

Born, Richard. 2008. "Party Polarization and the Rise of Partisan Voting in U.S. House Elections." *American Politics Research* 36: 62–84.

Boulianne, Shelley. 2009. "Does Internet Use Affect Engagement? A Meta-Analysis of Research." *Political Communication* 26: 193–211.

Bowman, Gary. 1975. "Consumer Choice and Television." *Applied Economics* 7: 175–184.

Box-Steffensmeier, Janet M., and Suzanna De Boef. 2001. "Macropartisanship and Macroideology in the Sophisticated Electorate." *Journal of Politics* 63: 232–248.

Brader, Ted. 2006. *Campaigning for Hearts and Minds: How Emotional Appeals in Political Ads Work.* Chicago: University of Chicago Press.

Brady, Henry E., Kay Lehman Schlozman, Sidney Verba, and Laurel Elms. 2002. "Who Bowls? The (Un)Changing Stratification of Participation." In *Understanding Public Opinion,* 2nd ed., ed. Barbara Norrander and Clyde Wilcox. Washington, D.C.: CQ Press.

Brady, Henry E., and Paul M. Sniderman. 1985. "Attitude Attribution: A Group Basis for Political Reasoning." *American Political Science Review* 79: 1061–1078.

Brady, John. 1997. *Bad Boy: The Life and Politics of Lee Atwater.* Reading, Mass.: Addison-Wesley.

Brewer, Mark D. 2005. "The Rise of Partisanship and the Expansion of Partisan Conflict within the American Electorate." *Political Research Quarterly* 58: 219–229.

———. 2009. *Party Images in the American Electorate.* New York: Routledge.

Brewer, Mark D., and Jeffrey M. Stonecash. 2007. *Split: Class and Cultural Divides in American Politics.* Washington, D.C.: CQ Press.

———. 2009. *Dynamics of American Political Parties.* New York: Cambridge University Press.

Brians, Craig Leonard, and Bernard Grofman. 2001. "Election Day Registration's Effect on U.S. Voter Turnout." *Social Science Quarterly* 82: 170–183.

Brody, Richard A. 1978. "The Puzzle of Participation in America." In *The New American Political System,* ed. Anthony King. Washington, D.C.: American Enterprise Institute.

———. 1991. *Assessing the President: The Media, Elite Opinion, and Public Support.* Stanford, Calif.: Stanford University Press.

Brooks, Clem, Paul Nieuwbeerta, and Jeff Manza. 2006. "Cleavage-Based Voting Behavior in Cross-National Perspective: Evidence from Six Postwar Democracies." *Social Science Research* 35: 88–128.

Brooks, David. 2001. "One Nation, Slightly Divisible." *Atlantic Monthly* 288: 53–65.

Budge, Ian. 1999. "Party Policy and Ideology: Reversing the 1950s?" In *Critical Elections: British Parties and Voters in Long-Term Perspective,* ed. Geoffrey Evans and Pippa Norris. London: Sage.

Bullock, Charles S., III 1985. "Congressional Roll Call Voting in a Two-Party South." *Social Science Quarterly* 66: 789–804.

———. 2009. "Introduction: Southern Politics in the Twenty-First Century." In *The New Politics of the Old South,* 4th ed., ed. Charles S. Bullock III and Mark J. Rozell. Lanham, Md.: Rowman & Littlefield.

Bullock, Charles S., III and M.V. Hood III. 2006. "A Mile-Wide Gap: The Evolution of Hispanic Political Emergence in the Deep South." *Social Science Quarterly* 87: 1117–1135.

Bullock, Charles S., III and David J. Shafer. 1997. "Party Targeting and Electoral Success." *Legislative Studies Quarterly* 22: 573–584.

Burden, Barry C. 2000. "Voter Turnout and the National Election Studies." *Political Analysis* 8: 389–398.

———. 2004. "An Alternative Account of the 2004 Presidential Election." *The Forum* 2(4): Article 2.

Burden, Barry C. and David C. Kimball. 1999. "A New Approach to the Study of Ticket Splitting." *American Political Science Review* 92: 533–544.

———. 2002. *Why Americans Split Their Tickets: Campaigns, Competition, and Divided Government.* Ann Arbor: University of Michigan Press.

Burnham, Walter Dean. 1965. "The Changing Shape of the American Political Universe." *American Political Science Review* 59: 7–28.

———. 1987. "The Turnout Problem." In *Elections American Style,* ed. A. J. Reichley. Washington, D.C.: Brookings.

———. 2007. "Triumphs and Travails in the Study of American Voting Participation Rates, 1788–2006." *Journal of the Historical Society* 7: 505–519.

Burns, Nancy, Donald R. Kinder, Steven J. Rosenstone, Virginia Sapiro, and the National Election Studies. 2001. *American National Election Study, 2000: Pre- and Post-Election Study* [dataset]. Ann Arbor: University of Michigan, Center for Political Studies [producer and distributor].

Butler, David, and Donald E. Stokes. 1969. *Political Change in Britain.* New York: St. Martin's.

Campbell, Angus, Philip E. Converse, Warren E. Miller, and Donald E. Stokes. 1960. *The American Voter.* New York: Wiley.

Campbell, David E. 2002. "The Young and the Realigning: A Test of the Socialization Theory of Realignment." *Public Opinion Quarterly* 66: 209–234.

———. 2006. "Religious 'Threat' in Contemporary Presidential Elections." *Journal of Politics* 68: 104–115.

———. 2006. *Why We Vote: How Schools and Communities Shape Our Civic Life.* Princeton, N.J.: Princeton University Press.

Campbell, David E., and J. Quin Monson. 2008. "The Religion Card: Gay Marriage and the 2004 Presidential Election." *Public Opinion Quarterly* 72: 399–419.

Campbell, James E., ed. 2004. "Introduction—The 2004 Election Forecasts." *PS: Political Science & Politics* 37: 733–735.

———. 2008a. *The American Campaign: U.S. Presidential Campaigns and the National Vote,* 2nd ed. College Station: Texas A & M University Press.

———, ed. 2008b. "Symposium—Forecasting the 2008 National Elections." *PS: Political Science & Politics* 41: 679–682.

Caplan, Bryan. 2007. *The Myth of the Rational Voter: Why Democracies Choose Bad Policies.* Princeton, N.J.: Princeton University Press.

Carmines, Edward G., and James H. Kuklinski. 1990. "Incentives, Opportunities, and the Logic of Public Opinion in American Political Representation." In *Information and Democratic Processes,* ed. John A. Ferejohn and James H. Kuklinski. Urbana: University of Illinois Press.

Carmines, Edward G., and James A. Stimson. 1989. *Issue Evolution.* Princeton, N.J.: Princeton University Press.

Carmines, Edward G., and James Woods. 2002. "The Role of Party Activists in the Evolution of the Abortion Issue." *Political Behavior* 24: 361–377.

Carroll, John S., and Eric J. Johnson. 1990. *Decision Research: A Field Guide.* Beverly Hills, Calif.: Sage.

Carsey, Thomas M., and Geoffrey C. Layman. 2006. "Changing Sides or Changing Minds? Party Identification and Policy Preferences in the American Electorate." *American Journal of Political Science* 50: 464–477.

Cassel, Carol A., and Robert C. Luskin. 1988. "Simple Explanations of Turnout Decline." *American Political Science Review* 82: 1321–1330.

Cavanagh, Thomas E. 1981. "Changes in American Voter Turnout, 1964–1976." *Political Science Quarterly* 96: 53–65.

Chaiken, Shelley. 1980. "Heuristic versus Systematic Information Processing and the Use of Source versus Message Cues in Persuasion." *Journal of Personality and Social Psychology* 39: 752–766.

———. 1987. "The Heuristic Model of Persuasion." *In Social Influence: The Ontario Symposium,* vol 5., ed. Mark P. Zanna, J. M. Olson, and C. P. Herman. Hillsdale, N.J.: Lawrence Erlbaum.

Chong, Dennis, Herbert McClosky, and John Zaller. 1983. "Patterns of Support for Democratic and Capitalist Values." *British Journal of Political Science* 13: 401–440.

Chou, Chin-Ping, and Peter M. Bentler. 1995. "Estimates and Tests in Structural Equation Modeling." In *Structural Equation Modeling: Concepts, Issues, and Applications,* ed. Rick H. Hoyle. Thousand Oaks, Calif.: Sage.

Citrin, Jack, Eric Schickler, and John Sides. 2003. "What if Everyone Voted? Simulating the Impact of Increased Turnout in Senate Elections." *American Journal of Political Science* 47: 75–90.

The Civic Mission of Schools. 2003. New York and College Park, Md: Carnegie Corp. of New York and Center for Information & Research on Civic Learning and Engagement.

Clark, John A., and Brad Lockerbie. 1998. "Split-Partisan Identification." In *Party Activists in Southern Politics: Mirrors and Makers of Change,* ed. Charles D. Hadley and Lewis Bowman. Knoxville: University of Tennessee Press.

Clarke, Harold, Allan Kornberg, Thomas J. Scotto, Jason Reifler, David Sanders, Marianne C. Stewart, and Paul Whiteley. 2009. "Yes We Can! Valence Politics and Electoral Choice in America, 2008." Paper presented at the Mershon Conference on the Transformative Election of 2008, Columbus, Ohio, Oct. 2–4.

Clarke, Harold, Marianne C. Stewart, and Paul Whiteley. 1997. "Tory Trends: Party Identification and the Dynamics of Conservative Support Since 1992." *British Journal of Political Science* 27: 299–319.

Cobb, James C. 1999. *Redefining Southern Culture: Mind and Identity in the Modern South.* Athens: University of Georgia Press.

Cohen, Marty, David Karol, Hans Noel, and John Zaller. 2008. *The Party Decides: Presidential Nominations before and after Reform.* Chicago: University of Chicago Press.

Combs, Michael W., John R. Hibbing, and Susan Welch. 1984. "Black Constituents and Congressional Roll Call Votes." *Western Political Quarterly* 37: 424–434.

Conover, Pamela Johnston, and Stanley Feldman. 1984. "How People Organize Their Political World: A Schematic Model." *American Journal of Political Science* 28: 95–125.

————. 1986. "The Role of Inference in the Perception of Political Candidates." In *Political Cognition*, ed. Richard R. Lau and David O. Sears. Hillsdale, N.J.: Erlbaum.

————. 1989. "Candidate Perception in an Ambiguous World: Campaigns, Cues, and Inference Processes." *American Journal of Political Science* 33: 912–940.

Conover, Pamela Johnston, Stanley Feldman, and Kathleen Knight. 1986. "The Personal and Political Underpinnings of Economic Forecasts." *American Journal of Political Science* 31: 559–583.

Converse, Philip E. 1964. "The Nature of Belief Systems in Mass Publics." In *Ideology and Discontent*, ed. David Apter. New York: Free Press.

————. 1969. "Of Time and Partisan Stability." *Comparative Political Studies* 2: 139–171.

————. 1970. "Attitudes and Non-Attitudes: Continuation of a Dialogue." In *The Quantitative Analysis of Social Problems*, ed. Edward R. Tufte. Reading, Mass.: Addison-Wesley.

————. 1971. "Non-Voting among Young Adults in the United States." In *Political Parties and Political Behavior*, 2nd ed., ed. William J. Crotty, Donald M. Freeman, and Douglas S. Gatlin. Boston: Allyn and Bacon.

————. 1975. "Public Opinion and Voting Behavior." In *Handbook of Political Science*, vol. 4, ed. Fred I. Greenstein and Nelson W. Polsby. Reading, Mass.: Addison-Wesley.

————. 1976. *The Dynamics of Party Support*. Beverly Hills, Calif.: Sage.

————. 2006. "Democratic Theory and Electoral Reality." *Critical Review* 18: 297–329.

Converse, Philip E., and Roy Pierce. 1986. *Political Representation in France*. Cambridge, Mass.: Harvard University Press.

Cook, Fay Lomax, and Edith J. Barrett. 1992. *Support for the American Welfare State: The Views of Congress and the Public*. New York: Columbia University Press.

Cotter, Cornelius P., James L. Gibson, John F. Bibby, and Robert J. Huckshorn. 1984. *Party Organizations in American Politics*. New York: Praeger.

Cox, David R., and Nanny Wermuth. 1993. "Linear Dependencies Represented by Chain Graphs." *Statistical Science* 8: 204–218.

————. 1996. *Multivariate Dependencies: Models, Analysis, and Interpretation*. London: Chapman and Hill.

Craig, Stephen C. 1985. "The Decline of Partisanship in the United States: A Reexamination of the Neutrality Hypothesis." *Political Behavior* 7: 57–78.

Crewe, Ivor, and Martin Harrop, eds. 1989. *Political Communications: The General Election Campaign of 1987*. Cambridge: Cambridge University Press.

Crewe, Ivor, and Katarina Thomson, 1999. "Party Loyalties: Dealignment or Realignment?" In *Critical Elections: British Parties and Voters in Long-Term Perspective*, ed. Geoffrey Evans and Pippa Norris. London: Sage.

Curran, Patrick J., Stephen G. West, and John F. Finch. 1996. "The Robustness of Test Statistics to Nonnormality and Specification Error in Confirmatory Factor Analysis." *Psychological Methods* 1: 16–29.

Curtice, John, and Alison Park. 1999. "Region: New Labour, New Geography?" In *Critical Elections: British Parties and Voters in Long-Term Perspective,* ed. Geoffrey Evans and Pippa Norris. London: Sage.

Cutler, Fred. 2002. "The Simplest Shortcut of All: Sociodemographic Characteristics and Electoral Choice." *Journal of Politics* 64: 466–490.

Dahl, Robert A. 1961. *Who Governs?* New Haven, Conn.: Yale University Press.

Dalton, Russell J. 2002. *Citizen Politics: Public Opinion and Political Parties in Advanced Industrial Democracies.* New York: Chatham House.

———. 2004. *Democratic Challenges, Democratic Choices: The Erosion of Political Support in Advanced Industrial Democracies.* Oxford: Oxford University Press.

———. 2008. *Citizen Politics: Public Opinion and Political Parties in Advanced Industrial Democracies,* 5th ed. Washington, D.C.: CQ Press.

———. 2009. *The Good Citizen: How a Younger Generation is Reshaping American Politics,* rev. ed. Washington, D.C.: CQ Press.

———. 2010. "Ideology, Partisanship, and Democratic Development." In *Comparing Democracies 3: Elections and Voting in the 21st Century,* ed. Lawrence LeDuc, Richard G. Niemi, and Pippa Norris. London: Sage.

Dalton, Russell J., Ian McAllister, and Martin P. Wattenberg. 2001. "The Consequences of Partisan Dealignment." In *Parties without Partisans: Political Change in Advanced Industrial Democracies,* ed. Russell J. Dalton and Martin P. Wattenberg. Oxford: Oxford University Press.

David, Paul T. 1972. *Party Strength in the United States, 1872–1970.* Charlottesville: University of Virginia Press.

Davis, Darren W., and Brian D. Silver. 2003. "Stereotype Threat and Race of Interviewer Effects in a Survey on Political Knowledge." *American Journal of Political Science* 47: 33–45.

Davis, Richard. 2005. *Politics Online: Blogs, Chatrooms, and Discussion Groups in American Democracy.* New York: Routledge.

———. 2009. *Typing Politics: The Role of Blogs in American Politics.* Oxford: Oxford University Press.

Dawes, Robyn M. 1988. *Rational Choice in an Uncertain World.* New York: Harcourt Brace Jovanovich.

De Boef, Suzanna L., and Paul M. Kellstedt. 2004. "The Political (And Economic) Origins of Consumer Confidence." *American Journal of Political Science* 48: 633–649.

Delli Carpini, Michael X., and Scott Keeter. 1996. *What Americans Know about Politics and Why It Matters.* New Haven, Conn.: Yale University Press.

Demerath, N. J., III. 2005. "The Battle over a U.S. Culture War: A Note on Inflated Rhetoric vs. Inflamed Politics." *The Forum* 3(2): Article 6.

Denver, David. 1998. "The Government That Could Do No Right." In *New Labour Triumphs: Britain at the Polls*, ed. Anthony King. Chatham, N.J.: Chatham House Publishers.

DeSart, Jay A. 1995. "Information Processing and Partisan Neutrality: A Reexamination of the Party Decline Thesis." *Journal of Politics* 57: 776–795.

DiMaggio, Paul, John Evans, and Bethany Bryson. 1996. "Have Americans' Social Attitudes Become More Polarized?" *American Journal of Sociology* 102: 690–755.

Dionne. E. J., Jr. 1991. *Why Americans Hate Politics*. New York: Touchstone.

Dixit, Avinash and John Londregan. 1995. "Redistributive Politics and Economic Efficiency." *American Political Science Review.* 89: 856–866.

———. 1996. "The Determinants of Success of Special Interests in Redistributive Politics." *Journal of Politics* 58: 1132–1155.

Donovan, Todd, and Shaun Bowler. 2004. *Reforming the Republic: Democratic Institutions for the New America.* Upper Saddle River, N.J.: Pearson Prentice Hall.

Donovan, Todd, Caroline J. Tolbert, and Daniel A. Smith. 2008. "Priming Presidential Votes by Direct Democracy." *Journal of Politics* 70: 1217–1231.

Doppelt, Jack C., and Ellen Shearer. 1999. *Nonvoters: America's No-Shows.* Thousand Oaks, Calif.: Sage.

Downs, Anthony. 1957. *An Economic Theory of Democracy.* New York: Harper and Row.

Drasgow, Fritz, and Ruth Kanfer. 1985. "Equivalence of Psychological Measurement in Heterogeneous Populations." *Journal of Applied Psychology* 70: 662–680.

Druckman, James N. 2001. "The Implications of Framing Effects for Citizen Competence." *Political Behavior* 23: 225–256.

———. 2005. "Does Political Information Matter?" *Political Communication* 22: 515–519.

Druckman, James N., and Kjersten R. Nelson. 2003. "Framing and Deliberation: How Citizens' Conversations Limit Elite Influence." *American Journal of Political Science* 47: 729–745.

Duch, Raymond M., Harvey D. Palmer, and Christopher J. Anderson. 2000. "Heterogeneity in Perceptions of National Economic Conditions." *American Journal of Political Science* 44: 635–652.

Duch, Raymond M., and Randolph T. Stevenson. 2005. "Context and the Economic Vote: A Multilevel Analysis." *Political Analysis* 13: 387–409.

———. 2008. *The Economic Vote: How Political and Economic Institutions Condition Election Results.* New York: Cambridge University Press.

Duff, Brian, Michael J. Hanmer, Won-ho Park, and Ismail K. White. 2007. "Good Excuses: Understanding Who Votes with an Improved Turnout Question." *Public Opinion Quarterly* 71: 67–90.

Eagly, Alice H., and Shelly Chaiken. 1993. *The Psychology of Attitudes,* Fort Worth, Texas: Harcourt Brace Jovanovich.

Edsall, Thomas. 1988. "Why Bush Accentuates the Negative: Beyond Beating Dukakis, the GOP Aims at Permanent Political Change." *Washington Post,* 2 October, C1.

———. 2002. "Lott Decried for Part of Salute to Thurmond: GOP Senate Leader Hails Colleague's Run as Segregationist." *Washington Post,* 7 December, A6.

Elff, Martin, Thomas Gschwend, and Ron J. Johnston. 2008. "Ignoramus, Ignorabimus? On Uncertainty in Ecological Inference." *Political Analysis* 16: 70–92.

Enders, Craig K. 2001. "The Performance of the Full Information Maximum Likelihood Estimator in Multiple Regression Models with Missing Data." *Educational and Psychological Measurement* 61: 713–740.

Enders, Craig K., and Deborah L. Bandalos, 2001. "The Relative Performance of Full Information Maximum Likelihood Estimation for Missing Data in Structural Equation Models." *Structural Equation Modeling: A Multidisciplinary Journal* 8: 430–457.

Enelow, James M., and Melvin J. Hinich. 1984. *The Spatial Theory of Voting: An Introduction.* New York: Cambridge University Press.

Epstein, David, and Sharyn O'Halloran. 1999. "Measuring the Electoral and Policy Impact of Majority-Minority Voting Districts: Candidates of Choice, Equal Opportunity, and Representation." *American Journal of Political Science* 43: 367–395.

Epstein, Edward Jay. 1973. *News from Nowhere.* New York: Random House.

Erikson, Robert, and John H. Goldthorpe. 1992. *The Constant Flux: A Study of Class Mobility in Industrial Societies.* Oxford: Clarendon Press.

Erikson, Robert S., Michael B. MacKuen, and James A. Stimson. 1998. "What Moves Macropartisanship: A Response to Green, Palmquist, and Schickler." *American Political Science Review* 92: 901–912.

———. 2002. *The Macro Polity.* Cambridge: Cambridge University Press.

Eulau, Heinz. 1962. *Class and Party in the Eisenhower Years: Class Roles and Perspectives in the 1952 and 1956 Elections.* New York: Free Press.

Evans, Geoffrey. 1994. "Tactical Voting and Labour's Prospects." In *Labour's Last Chance?* ed. Anthony Heath, Roger Jowell, and John Curtice. Aldershot, Eng.: Dartmouth.

———. 1998. "Euroscepticism and Conservative Electoral Support: How an Asset Became a Liability." *British Journal of Political Science* 28: 573–590.

———. 1999. "Economic and Politics Revisited: Exploring the Decline in Conservative Support, 1992–95." *Political Studies* 47: 139–151.

Evans, Geoffrey, and Robert Andersen. 2004. "Do Issues Decide? Partisan Conditioning and Perceptions of Party Issue Positions across the Electoral Cycle." *British Elections and Parties Review* 14: 18–39.

————. 2006. "The Political Conditioning of Economic Perceptions." *Journal of Politics* 68: 194–207.

Evans, Geoffrey, John Curtice, and Pippa Norris. 1998. "New Labour, New Tactical Voting? The Causes and Consequences of Tactical Voting in the 1997 General Election." *British Elections and Parties Review* 8: 65–79.

Evans, Geoffrey, Anthony Heath, and Clive Payne. 1999. "Class: Labour as a Catch-All Party?" In *Critical Elections,* ed. Geoffrey Evans and Pippa Norris. London: Sage.

Evans, John H., Bethany Bryson, and Paul DiMaggio. 2001. "Opinion Polarization: Important Contributions, Necessary Limitations." *American Journal of Sociology* 106: 944–959.

Evans, John H., and Lisa M. Nunn. 2004. "The Deeper 'Culture Wars' Questions." *The Forum* 3 (2): Article 3.

————. 2006. "Geographic Polarization in Social Attitudes." Paper presented at the annual meeting of the American Sociological Association, Montreal Convention Center. www.allacademic.com/meta/p103658_index.html.

Eveland, William P., Jr. and Dietram A. Scheufele. 2000. "Connecting News Media Use with Gaps in Knowledge and Participation." *Political Communication* 17: 215–237.

Fair, Ray C. 2002. *Predicting Presidential Elections and Other Things.* Stanford, Calif.: Stanford University Press.

————. 2009. "Presidential and Congressional Vote-Share Equations." *American Journal of Political Science* 53: 55–72.

Farnsworth, Stephen J., and S. Robert Lichter. 2007. *The Nightly News Nightmare: Television's Coverage of U.S. Presidential Elections, 1988–2004.* Lanham, Md.: Rowman & Littlefield.

Feddersen, Timothy, Sean Gailmard, and Alvaro Sandroni. 2009. "Moral Bias in Large Elections: Theory and Experimental Evidence." *American Political Science Review* 103: 175–192.

Feldman, Stanley. 1988. "Structure and Consistency in Public Opinion: The Role of Core Beliefs and Values." *American Journal of Political Science* 32: 416–440.

Feldman, Stanley. 1989. "Measuring Issue Preferences: The Problem of Response Instability." In *Political Analysis: Volume 1,* ed., James A. Stimson. Ann Arbor: University of Michigan Press.

Feldman, Stanley, and Marco R. Steenbergen. 2001. "The Humanitarian Foundation of Public Support for Social Welfare. *American Journal of Political Science* 45: 658–677.

Feldman, Stanley, and John Zaller. 1992. "The Political Culture of Ambivalence: Ideological Responses to the Welfare State." *American Journal of Political Science* 36: 268–307.

Fenno, Richard F., Jr. 2000. *Congress at the Grassroots: Representational Change in the South, 1970–1998.* Chapel Hill: University of North Carolina Press.

Finkel, Steven E. 1995. *Causal Analysis with Panel Data.* Sage University Paper Series on Quantitative Applications in the Social Sciences, 07–105. Beverly Hills, Calif.: Sage.

Fiorina, Morris P. 1978. "Economic Retrospective Voting in American National Elections: A Micro-Analysis." *American Journal of Political Science* 22: 426–443.

———. 1981. *Retrospective Voting in American National Elections.* New Haven, Conn.: Yale University Press.

———. 1992. "An Era of Divided Government." *Political Science Quarterly* 107: 387–410.

———. 1996. *Divided Government,* 2nd ed. Needham Heights, Mass.: Allyn and Bacon.

———. 1999. "Extreme Voices: A Dark Side of Civic Engagement." In *Civic Engagement in American Democracy,* ed. Theda Skocpol and Morris P. Fiorina. Washington, D.C. and New York: Brookings; Russell Sage.

Fiorina, Morris P., and Samuel J. Abrams. 2008. "Political Polarization in the American Public." *Annual Review of Political Science* 11: 563–588.

———. 2009. *Disconnect: The Breakdown of Representation in American Politics.* Norman: University of Oklahoma Press.

Fiorina, Morris P., Samuel J. Abrams, and Jeremy C. Pope. 2005. *Culture War? The Myth of a Polarized America.* New York: Pearson Longman.

———. 2006. *Culture War? The Myth of a Polarized America,* 2nd ed. New York: Pearson Longman.

———. 2008. "Polarization in the American Public: Misconceptions and Misreadings." *Journal of Politics* 70: 556–560.

Fiorina, Morris P., and Matthew S. Levendusky. 2006. "Disconnected: The Political Class versus the People." In *Red and Blue Nation? Volume I—Characteristics and Causes of America's Polarized Politics,* ed. Pietro S. Nivola and David W. Brady. Stanford, Calif.: Hoover Institution.

Fishkin, James P. 1995. *The Voice of the People: Public Opinion and Democracy.* New Haven, Conn.: Yale University Press.

Fiske, Susan T. 1986. "Schema-Based versus Piecemeal Politics: A Patchwork Quilt, but Not a Blanket, of Evidence." In *Political Cognition: The 19th Annual Carnegie Symposium on Cognition,* ed. Richard R. Lau and David O. Sears. Hillsdale, N.J.: Lawrence Erlbaum.

Fiske, Susan T., and Shelley E. Taylor. 1991. *Social Cognition.* 2nd ed. New York: McGraw-Hill.

Fogarty, Brian J., Nathan J. Kelly, and H. Whitt Kilburn. 2005. "Issue Attitudes and Survey Continuity Across Interview Mode in the 2000 NES." *Political Analysis* 13: 95–108.

Ford, J. Kevin, Neal Schmitt, Susan L. Schechtman, Brian M. Hults, and Mary L. Doherty. 1989. "Process Tracing Methods: Contributions, Problems, and Neglected Research Questions." *Organizational Behavior and Human Decision Processes* 43: 75–117.

Fortier, John C. 2006. *Absentee and Early Voting: Trends, Promises, and Perils.* Washington, D.C.: AEI Press.

Fournier, Patrick. 2006. "The Impact of Campaigns on Discrepancies, Errors, and Biases in Voting Behavior." In *Capturing Campaign Effects,* ed. Henry E. Brady and Richard Johnston. Ann Arbor: University of Michigan Press.

Frank, Thomas. 2004. *What's The Matter with Kansas?* New York: Metropolitan Books.

Franklin, Mark N. 1985. *The Decline of Class Voting in Britain.* Oxford: Oxford University Press.

———. 2004. *Voter Turnout and the Dynamics of Electoral Competition in Established Democracies Since 1945.* Cambridge: Cambridge University Press.

Franklin, Mark N., and Wolfgang P. Hirczy de Miño. 1998. "Separated Powers, Divided Government, and Turnout in U.S. Presidential Elections." *American Journal of Political Science* 42: 316–326.

Franklin, Mark N., and Christopher Wlezien, eds. 2002. *The Future of Election Studies.* Amsterdam: Pergamon.

Franz, Michael M., Paul B. Freedman, Kenneth M. Goldstein, and Travis N. Ridout. 2007. *Campaign Advertising and American Democracy.* Philadelphia: Temple University Press.

Freedman, Paul B., Michael M. Franz, and Kenneth M. Goldstein. 2004. "Campaign Advertising and Democratic Citizenship." *American Journal of Political Science* 48: 723–741.

Friedman, Jeffrey. 2006. "Public Competence in Normative and Positive Theory: Neglected Implications of 'The Nature of Belief Systems in Mass Publics.'" *Critical Review* 18: 1–44.

Funk, Carolyn L. 1999. "Bringing the Candidate into Models of Candidate Evaluation." *Journal of Politics* 61: 700–720.

Funk, Carolyn L., and Patricia A. García-Monet. 1997. "The Relationship between Personal and National Concerns in Public Perceptions about the Economy." *Political Research Quarterly* 50: 317–342.

Gaines, Brian J., James H. Kuklinski, and Paul J. Quirk. 2007. "The Logic of the Survey Experiment Reexamined." *Political Analysis* 15: 1–20.

Gaines, Brian J., James H. Kuklinski, Paul J. Quirk, Buddy Peyton, and Jay Verkuilen. 2007. "Same Facts, Different Interpretations: Partisan Motivation and Opinion on Iraq." *Journal of Politics* 69: 957–974.

Gamm, Gerald H. 1989. *The Making of New Deal Democrats: Voting Behavior and Realignment in Boston, 1920–1940.* Chicago: University of Chicago Press.

Gans, Herbert J. 1979. *Deciding What's News: A Study of CBS Evening News, NBC Nightly News, Newsweek, and Time.* New York: Pantheon Books.

Gavin, Neil T., and David Sanders. 1997. "The Economy and Voting." *Parliamentary Affairs* 50: 631–40.

Gaziano, Cecilie. 1997. "Forecast 2000: Widening Knowledge Gaps." *Journalism and Mass Communication Quarterly* 74: 237–264.

Geer, John G. 1992. "New Deal Issues and the American Electorate, 1952–1988." *Political Behavior* 14: 45–65.

———. 2002. "Parties and Partisanship: A Brief Introduction" (special issue). *Political Behavior* 24: 85–91.

———. 2006. *In Defense of Negativity: Attack Ads in Presidential Campaigns.* Chicago: University of Chicago Press.

Gelman, Andrew, David Park, Boris Shor, Joseph Bafumi, and Jeronimo Cortina. 2008. *Red State, Blue State, Rich State, Poor State.* Princeton, N.J.: Princeton University Press.

Gerber, Alan S., and Donald P. Green. 1999. "Misperceptions about Perceptual Bias." *Annual Review of Political Science* 2: 189–210.

———. 2000. "The Effects of Canvassing, Direct Mail, and Telephone Contact on Voter Turnout: A Field Experiment." *American Political Science Review* 94: 653–663.

Gerber Alan S., Donald P. Green, and Christopher W. Larimer. 2008. "Social Pressure and Vote Turnout: Evidence from a Large-Scale Field Experiment." *American Political Science Review* 102: 33–48.

Gerber, Alan S., and Gregory A. Huber. 2009. "Partisanship and Economic Behavior: Do Partisan Differences in Economic Forecasts Predict Real Economic Behavior?" *American Political Science Review* 103: 407–426.

Gerber, Elisabeth R., and Justin H. Phillips. 2003. "Development Ballot Measures, Interest Group Endorsements, and the Political Geography of Growth Preferences." *American Journal of Political Science* 47: 625–639.

GfK Roper Public Affairs. 2006. *Final Report: National Geographic–Roper Public Affairs 2006 Geographic Literacy Survey.* Washington, D.C.: National Geographic Society. www.nationalgeographic.com/roper2006/pdf/FINALReport-2006GeogLitsurvey.pdf.

Gidengil, Elisabeth, André Blais, Neil Nevitte, and Richard Nadeau. 2003. "Turned Off or Tuned Out? Youth Participation in Politics." *Electoral Insight* (published by Elections Canada), July.

———. 2004. *Citizens.* Vancouver: UBC Press.

Gilens, Martin. 1999. *Why Americans Hate Welfare.* Chicago: University of Chicago Press.

———. 2001. "Political Ignorance and Collective Policy Preferences." *American Political Science Review* 95: 379–396.

———. 2005. "Inequality and Democratic Responsiveness." *Public Opinion Quarterly* 69: 778–796.

Gilens, Martin, Lynn Vavreck, and Martin Cohen. 2004. "See Spot Run: The Rise of Advertising, the Decline of News, and the American Public's Perceptions of Presidential Candidates, 1952–2000." Paper presented at the annual meeting of the Midwest Political Science Association.

———. 2007. "The Mass Media and the Public's Assessments of Presidential Candidates, 1952–2000." *Journal of Politics* 69: 1160–1175.

Giles, Micheal W. 1977. "Percent Black and Racial Hostility: An Old Assumption Revisited." *Social Science Quarterly* 70: 820–835.

Giles, Micheal W., and Melanie A. Buckner. 1993. "David Duke and Black Threat: An Old Hypothesis Revisited." *Journal of Politics* 55: 702–713.

———. 1996. "Comment." *Journal of Politics* 58: 1171–1180.

Giles, Micheal W., and Arthur Evans. 1986. "The Power Approach to Intergroup Hostility." *Journal of Conflict Resolution* 30: 469–486.

Giles, Micheal W., and Kaenan Hertz. 1994. "Racial Threat and Partisan Identification." *American Political Science Review* 88: 317–326.

Gillig, Paulette M., and Anthony G. Greenwald. 1974. "Is it Time to Lay the 'Sleeper Effect' to Rest?" *Journal of Personality and Social Psychology* 29: 132–139.

Glaeser, E. L., and B. A. Ward. 2006. "Myths and Realities of American Political Geography." Harvard Institute of Economic Research Discussion Paper No. 2100. Typescript. Available at SSRN: http://ssrn.com/abstract=874977.

Glaser, James M. 1994. "Back to the Black Belt: Racial Environment and White Racial Attitudes in the South." *Journal of Politics* 56: 21–41.

———. 1996. *Race, Campaign Politics, and the Realignment in the South.* New Haven, Conn.: Yale University Press.

———. 2005. *The Hand of the Past in Contemporary Southern Politics.* New Haven, Conn.: Yale University Press.

Gober, Patricia. 1993. "Americans on the Move." *Population Bulletin* 48: 1–48.

Godbout, Jean-François, and Éric Bélanger. 2007. "Economic Voting and Political Sophistication in the United States." *Political Research Quarterly* 60: 541–554.

Goldstein, Kenneth M., and Paul Freedman. 2002. "Campaign Advertising and Voter Turnout: New Evidence for a Stimulation Effect." *Journal of Politics* 64: 721–740.

Gomez, Brad T., and J. Matthew Wilson. 2001. "Political Sophistication and Economic Voting in the American Electorate: A Theory of Heterogeneous Attribution." *American Journal of Political Science* 45: 899–914.

———. 2006. "Cognitive Heterogeneity and Economic Voting: A Comparative Analysis of Four Democratic Electorates." *American Journal of Political Science* 50: 127–145.

———. 2007. "Economic Voting and Political Sophistication: Defending Heterogeneous Attribution." *Political Research Quarterly* 60: 555–558.

Gordon, Stacy B., and Gary M. Segura. 1997. "Cross-National Variation in the Political Sophistication of Individuals: Capability or Choice?" *Journal of Politics* 59: 126–147.

Goren, Paul. 2001. "Core Principles and Policy Reasoning in Mass Publics: A Test of Two Theories." *British Journal of Political Science* 31: 159–177.

———. 2004. "Political Sophistication and Policy Reasoning: A Reconsideration." *American Journal of Political Science* 48: 462–478.

————. 2005. "Party Identification and Core Political Values." *American Journal of Political Science* 49: 881–96.

————. Forthcoming. *On Voter Competence.* New York: Oxford University Press.

Graber, Doris A. 1984. *Processing the News: How People Tame the Information Tide.* New York: Longman.

————. 1988. *Processing the News: How People Tame the Information Tide,* 2nd ed. New York: Longman.

————. 1997. *Mass Media and American Politics,* 5th ed. Washington, D.C.: CQ Press.

Graefe, Andreas, J. Scott Armstrong, Alfred G. Cuzán, and Randall J. Jones Jr. 2009. "Combining Forecasts of the 2008 Election: The Pollyvote." *Foresight* 12: 41–42.

Grafstein, Robert. 2005. "The Impact of Employment Status on Voting Behavior." *Journal of Politics* 67: 804–824.

Green, Donald P., and Alan S. Gerber. 2004. *Get Out the Vote! How to Increase Voter Turnout.* Washington, D.C.: Brookings.

Green, Donald P., and Bradley Palmquist. 1990. "Of Artifacts and Partisan Instability." *American Journal of Political Science* 34: 872–902.

Green, Donald P., Bradley Palmquist, and Eric Schickler. 1998. "Macropartisanship: A Replication and Critique." *American Political Science Review* 92: 883–899.

————. 2000. "The Coming Democratic Realignment." *PS: Political Science & Politics* 33: 199–200.

————. 2002. *Partisan Hearts and Minds: Political Parties and the Social Identities of Voters.* New Haven, Conn.: Yale University Press.

Green, John C. 2007. *The Faith Factor: How Religion Influences American Elections.* Westport, Conn.: Praeger.

Green, John C., James L. Guth, Corwin E. Smidt, and Lyman A. Kellstedt. 1996. *Religion and the Culture Wars.* New York: Rowman & Littlefield.

Green, John C., Lyman A. Kellstedt, Corwin E. Smidt, James L. Guth. 1998. "The Soul of the South: Religion and the New Electoral Order." In *The New Politics of the Old South,* ed. Charles S. Bullock III and M. J. Rozell. New York: Rowman & Littlefield.

————. 2009. "The Soul of the South: Religion and Southern Politics in the New Millennium." In *The New Politics of the Old South,* 4th ed., ed. Charles S. Bullock III and Mark J. Rozell. Lanham, Md.: Rowman & Littlefield.

Greenberg, Stanley. 2004. *The Two Americas: Our Current Political Deadlock and How to Break It.* New York: Thomas Dunne Books.

Greene, Steven. 2002. "The Social-Psychological Measurement of Partisanship." *Political Behavior* 24: 171–197.

Greene, W. H. 2000. *Econometric Analysis,* 4th ed. New York: Prentice Hall.

Griffin, John D., and Brian Newman. 2005. "Are Voters Better Represented?" *Journal of Politics* 67: 1206–1227.

Grofman, Bernard, Robert Griffin, and Amihai Glazer. 1992. "The Effect of Black Population on Electing Democrats and Liberals to the House of Representatives." *Legislative Studies Quarterly* 17: 365–379.

Gujarati, D. N. 1988. *Basic Econometrics*, 2nd ed. New York: McGraw-Hill.

Guth, James L. 2005. "Southern Baptist Clergy, the Christian Right, and Political Activism in the South." In *Politics and Religion in the White South*, ed. Glenn Feldman. Lexington: University Press of Kentucky.

Hacker, Jacob, and Paul Pierson. 2005. "Abandoning the Middle: The Revealing Case of the Bush Tax Cuts." *Perspectives on Politics* 3: 33–53.

Hadley, Arthur Twining, Frederick T. Steeper, and Felicity V. Swayze. 1978. *The Empty Polling Booth.* Englewood Cliffs, N.J.: Prentice-Hall.

Hajnal, Zoltan. 2006. *Changing White Attitudes toward Black Political Leadership.* New York: Cambridge University Press.

———. 2010. *America's Uneven Democracy: Race, Turnout, and Representation in City Politics.* Cambridge: Cambridge University Press.

Haller, H. Brandon, and Helmut Norpoth. 1997. "Reality Bites: News Exposure and Economic Opinion." *Public Opinion Quarterly* 61: 555–575.

Hamill, Ruth, and Milton Lodge. 1986. "Cognitive Consequences of Political Sophistication." In *Political Cognition*, ed. Richard R. Lau and David O. Sears. Hillsdale, N.J.: Erlbaum.

Hamill, Ruth, Milton Lodge, and Frederick Blake. 1985. "The Breadth, Depth, and Utility of Class, Partisan, and Ideological Schemata." *American Journal of Political Science* 29: 850–870.

Hamilton, James T. 2003. *All the News That's Fit to Sell: How the Market Transforms Information into News.* Princeton, N.J.: Princeton University Press.

Hampson, Rick. 1998. "The Invisible Voter Is Everywhere." *USA Today,* October 28, 1998, p. 1A.

Hanmer, Michael J. 2009. *Discount Voting: Voter Registration Reforms and Their Effects.* New York: Cambridge University Press.

Harris, Fredrick C., Valeria Sinclair-Chapman, and Brian D. McKenzie. 2006. *Countervailing Forces in African-American Civic Activism, 1973–1994.* New York: Cambridge University Press.

Hayes, Danny, and Seth C. McKee. 2008. "Toward a One-Party South?" *American Politics Research* 36: 3–32.

Heard, Alexander. 1952. *A Two-Party South?* Chapel Hill: University of North Carolina Press.

Heath, Anthony, Roger Jowell, and John Curtice, eds. 2001. *The Rise of New Labour: Party Policies and Voter Choices.* Oxford: Oxford University Press.

Heeter, Carrie. 1985. "Program Selection with Abundance of Choice: A Process Model." *Human Communication Research* 12: 126–152.

Heise, David R. 1970. "Causal Inference from Panel Data." *Sociological Methodology* 2: 3–27.

Hellwig, Timothy T. 2001. "Interdependence, Government Constraints, and Economic Voting." *Journal of Politics* 63: 1141–1162.

Henn, Matt, Mark Weinstein, and Sarah Forrest. 2005. "Uninterested Youth? Young People's Attitudes towards Party Politics in Britain." *Political Studies* 53: 556–578.

Herstein, John A. 1981. "Keeping the Voter's Limits in Mind: A Cognitive Process Analysis of Decision Making in Voting." *Journal of Personality and Social Psychology* 40: 843–861.

Hetherington, Marc J. 1996. "The Media's Role in Forming Voters' National Economic Evaluations in 1992." *American Journal of Political Science* 40: 372–395.

———. 1999. "The Effect of Political Trust on the Presidential Vote: 1968–96." *American Political Science Review* 93: 311–326.

———. 2001. "Resurgent Mass Partisanship: The Role of Elite Polarization." *American Political Science Review* 95: 619–631.

———. 2005. *Why Trust Matters: Declining Political Trust and the Demise of American Liberalism.* Princeton, N.J.: Princeton University Press.

———. 2009. "Putting Polarization in Perspective." *British Journal of Political Science* 39: 413–448.

Hetherington, Marc J., and Jonathan Weiler. 2009. *Authoritarianism and Polarization in American Politics.* New York: Cambridge University Press.

Hibbing, John R., and Elizabeth Theiss-Morse. 1995. *Congress as Public Enemy: Public Attitudes toward American Political Institutions.* New York: Cambridge University Press.

———. 2002. *Stealth Democracy: Americans' Beliefs about How Government Should Work.* New York: Cambridge University Press.

Hicks, Alexander H., and Duane H. Swank. 1992. "Politics, Institutions, and Welfare Spending in Industrialized Democracies, 1960–1982." *American Political Science Review* 86: 658–674.

Highton, Benjamin. 2009. "Revisiting the Relationship between Educational Attainment and Political Sophistication." *Journal of Politics* 71: 1564–1576.

Highton, Benjamin, and Raymond E. Wolfinger. 1998. "Estimating the Effects of the National Voter Registration Act of 1993." *Political Behavior* 20: 79–104.

Hillygus, D. Sunshine, and Michael Henderson. 2010. "Valence and Positional Issues in the 2008 Presidential Election: The Nuances of Economic Voting." *Journal of Elections, Public Opinion, and Voting* 20: 241–269.

Hillygus, D. Sunshine, and Todd G. Shields. 2005. "Moral Issues and Voter Decision Making in the 2004 Presidential Election." *PS: Political Science & Politics* 38: 201–209.

———. 2008. *The Persuadable Voter: Wedge Issues in Presidential Campaigns.* Princeton, N.J.: Princeton University Press.

Hindman, Matthew. 2009. *The Myth of Digital Democracy.* Princeton, N.J.: Princeton University Press.

Hinich, Melvin J. and Michael C. Munger. 1994. *Ideology and the Theory of Political Choice.* Ann Arbor: University of Michigan Press.

Ho, Daniel E., Kosuke Imai, Gary King, and Elizabeth A. Stuart. 2007. "Matching as Nonparametric Preprocessing for Reducing Model Dependence in Parametric Causal Inference." *Political Analysis* 15: 199–236.

Holbrook, Thomas M. 2009. "Economic Considerations and the 2008 Presidential Election." *PS: Political Science & Politics* 42: 473–478.

Hood, M. V., III, Quentin Kidd, and Irwin L. Morris. 1999. "Of Byrd[s] and Bumpers: Using Democratic Senators to Analyze Political Change in the South, 1960–1995." *American Journal of Political Science* 43: 465–487.

———. 2004. "The Reintroduction of the *Elephas Maximus* to the Southern United States: The Rise of Republican State Parties, 1960 to 2000." *American Politics Research* 32: 68–101.

———. 2008. "Two Sides of the Same Coin? Employing Granger Causality Tests in a Time Series Cross-Section Framework." *Political Analysis* 16: 324–344.

Hood, M. V., III and Seth C. McKee. 2010. "What Made Carolina Blue? Immigration and the 2008 North Carolina Presidential Vote." *American Politics Research* 38: 266–302.

Howe, Paul. 2003. "Electoral Participation and the Knowledge Deficit." *Electoral Insight* 5: 20– 25.

Hu, Li-Tze, and Peter M. Bentler. 1995. "Evaluating Model Fit." In *Structural Equation Modeling: Concepts, Issues, and Applications,* ed. Rick H. Hoyle. Thousand Oaks, Calif.: Sage.

Huckfeldt, Robert, Edward G. Carmines, Jeffery J. Mondak, and Eric Zeemering. 2007. "Information, Activation, and Electoral Competition in the 2002 Congressional Elections." *Journal of Politics* 69: 798–812.

Huckfeldt, Robert, Paul E. Johnson, and John Sprague. 2002. "Political Environments, Political Dynamics, and the Survival of Disagreement." *Journal of Politics* 64: 1–21.

Hunter, James Davison. 1991. *Culture Wars: The Struggle to Define America.* New York: BasicBooks.

———. 1995. *Before the Shooting Begins: Searching for Democracy in America's Culture War.* New York: Free Press.

Hurwitz, Jon, and Mark Peffley. 1987. "How Are Foreign Policy Attitudes Structured? A Hierarchical Model." *American Political Science Review* 81: 1099–1120.

———. 1990. "Public Images of the Soviet Union: The Impact on Foreign Policy Attitudes." *Journal of Politics* 52: 3–28.

Hutchings, Vincent L., Nicholas A. Valentino, Tasha S. Philpot, and Ismail K. White. 2004. "The Compassion Strategy: Race and the Gender Gap in Campaign 2000." *Public Opinion Quarterly* 68: 512–541.

Inglehart, Ronald. 1990. *Culture Shift in Advanced Industrial Society.* Princeton, N.J.: Princeton University Press.

————. 1997. *Modernization and Postmodernization: Cultural, Economic, and Political Change in 43 Societies.* Princeton, N.J.: Princeton University Press.

————. 1999. "Postmodernization Erodes Respect for Authority, but Increases Support for Democracy." In *Critical Citizens: Global Support for Democratic Government,* ed. Pippa Norris. Oxford: Oxford University Press.

Iyengar, Shanto. 1990. "Shortcuts to Political Knowledge: The Role of Selective Attention and Accessibility." In *Information and Democratic Processes,* ed. John A. Ferejohn and James H. Kuklinski. Urbana: University of Illinois Press.

Jackman, Simon, and Lynn Vavreck. 2010. "Primary Politics: The Effects of Race, Gender, and Party in the 2008 Democratic Primary." *Journal of Elections, Public Opinion, and Parties* 20: 153–186.

Jacobs, Lawrence R., and Benjamin I. Page. 2005. "Who Influences U.S. Foreign Policy?" *American Political Science Review* 99: 107–123.

Jacobson, Gary C. 2000. "Party Polarization in National Politics: The Electoral Connection." In *Polarized Politics: Congress and the President in a Partisan Era,* ed. Jon Bond and Richard Fleisher, Washington, D.C.: CQ Press.

————. 2004. "Partisan and Ideological Polarization in the California Electorate." *State Politics and Policy Quarterly* 4: 113–139.

————. 2005. "Polarized Politics and the 2004 Congressional and Presidential Elections." *Political Science Quarterly* 120: 199–218.

————. 2007. *A Divider, Not a Uniter: George W. Bush and the American People.* New York: Pearson Longman.

Jacoby, Jacob, James Jaccard, Alfred Kuss, Tracy Troutman, and David Mazursky. 1987. "New Directions in Behavioral Process Research: Implications for Social Psychology." *Journal of Experimental Social Psychology* 23: 146–175.

Jacoby, William G. 1988. "The Impact of Party Identification on Issue Attitudes." *American Journal of Political Science* 32: 643–661.

————. 2006. "Value Choices and American Public Opinion." *American Journal of Political Science* 50: 706–723.

Jaffe, Natalie. 1978. "Appendix B: Attitudes toward Public Welfare Programs and Recipients in the United States." In *Welfare: The Elusive Consensus,* ed. Lester M. Salamon. New York: Praeger.

Jelen, Ted G. 2006. "Reflections on Scholarship in Religion and Southern Politics." In *Writing Southern Politics: Contemporary Interpretations and Future Directions,* ed. Robert P. Steed and Laurence W. Moreland. Lexington: University Press of Kentucky.

Jelen, Ted G., and Clyde Wilcox. 2003. "Causes and Consequences of Public Attitudes toward Abortion: A Review and Research Agenda." *Political Research Quarterly* 56: 489–500.

Jennings, M. Kent. 1992. "Ideological Thinking among Mass Publics and Political Elites." *Public Opinion Quarterly* 56: 419–441.

Jerit, Jennifer, Jason Barabas, and Toby Bolsen. 2006. "Citizens, Knowledge, and the Information Environment." *American Journal of Political Science* 50: 266–282.

Jervis, Robert.1986. "Representativeness in Foreign Policy Judgments." *Political Psychology* 7: 483–505.

Jewett, A. W. 1997. *Partisan Change in Southern State Legislatures.* Unpublished doctoral dissertation, Florida State University, Tallahassee.

Johnson, Dirk. 1998. "The 1998 Campaign: The Electorate; Bored, Dispirited, Disgusted, Most Won't Vote." *New York Times,* November 3, 1999, p. 1A.

Johnson, Janet, and H. T. Reynolds. 2008. *Political Science Research Methods,* 6th ed. Washington, D.C.: CQ Press.

Johnston, Richard, Michael Hagen, and Kathleen Hall Jamieson. 2004. *The 2000 Presidential Election and the Foundations of Party Politics.* Cambridge: Cambridge University Press.

Johnston, Richard, Emily Thorson, and Andrew Gooch. 2010. "The Economy and the Dynamics of the 2008 Presidential Campaign: Evidence from the NAES." *Journal of Elections, Public Opinion, and Parties* 20: 271–289.

Johnston, Ron, Charles Pattie, Daniel Dorling, Iain MacAllister, Helena Tunstall, and David Rossiter. 2000. "Local Context, Retrospective Economic Evaluations, and Voting: The 1997 General Election in England and Wales." *Political Behavior* 22: 121–143.

Jones, David R., and Monika L. McDermott. 2009. *Americans, Congress, and Democratic Responsiveness.* Ann Arbor: University of Michigan Press.

Joslyn, Mark R. 2003. "The Determinants and Consequences of Recall Error about Gulf War Preferences." *American Journal of Political Science* 47: 440–452.

Jost, John T. 2006. "The End of the End of Ideology." *American Psychologist* 61: 651–670.

Kahneman, Daniel, Paul Slovic, and Amos Tversky, eds. 1982. *Judgement under Uncertainty: Heuristics and Biases.* New York: Cambridge.

Kahneman, Daniel, and Amos Tversky. 1972. "Subjective Probability: A Judgment of Representativeness." *Cognitive Psychology* 3: 430–454.

Kam, Cindy D. 2006. "Political Campaigns and Open-Minded Thinking." *Journal of Politics* 68: 931–945.

———. 2007. "When Duty Calls, Do Citizens Answer?" *Journal of Politics* 69: 17–29.

Katz, Richard S. 2001. "Are Cleavages Frozen in the English-Speaking Democracies?" In *Party Systems and Voter Alignments Revisited,* ed. L. Karvonen and S. Kuhnle. New York: Routledge.

Keefe, William J. 1998. *Parties, Politics, and Public Policy in America,* 8th ed. Washington, D.C.: CQ Press.

Keeter, Scott, and Harry Wilson. 1986. "Natural Treatment and Control Settings for Research on the Effects of Television." *Communication Research* 13: 37–53.

Keith, Bruce, E., David B. Magleby, Candice J. Nelson, Elizabeth Orr, Mark C. Westlye, and Raymond E. Wolfinger. 1992. *The Myth of the Independent Voter.* Berkeley: University of California Press.

Kellstedt, Lyman. A. 1989. "Evangelicals and Political Realignment." In *Contemporary Evangelical Political Involvement,* ed. Corwin E. Smidt. Lanham, Md.: University Press of America.

Kellstedt, Lyman A., James L. Guth, John C. Green, and Corwin E. Smidt. 2007. "The Soul of the South: Religion and Southern Politics in the Twenty-First Century." In *The New Politics of the Old South*, 3rd ed., ed. Charles S. Bullock III and Mark J. Rozell. Lanham, Md.: Rowman & Littlefield.

Kessel, John H., and Herbert F. Weisberg. 1999. "Comparing Models of the Vote: The Answers Depend on the Questions." In *Reelection 1996: How Americans Voted*, ed. Herbert F. Weisberg and Janet M. Box-Steffensmeier. New York: Chatham House.

Key, V. O., Jr. 1949. *Southern Politics in State and Nation.* New York: Knopf.

———. 1955. "A Theory of Critical Elections." *Journal of Politics* 17: 3–18.

———. 1959. "Secular Realignment and the Party System." *Journal of Politics* 21: 198–210.

———. 1966. *The Responsible Electorate: Rationality in Presidential Voting, 1936–1960.* Cambridge: Harvard University Press.

Keyssar, Alexander. 2000. *The Right to Vote: The Contested History of Democracy in the United States.* New York: Basic Books.

———. 2009. *The Right to Vote: The Contested History of Democracy in the United States,* rev. ed. New York: Basic Books.

Kiewiet, D. Roderick. 1983. *Macroeconomics and Micropolitics: The Electoral Effects of Economic Issues.* Chicago: University of Chicago Press.

Killian, Mitchell, and Clyde Wilcox. 2008. "Do Abortion Attitudes Lead to Party Switching?" *Political Research Quarterly* 61: 561–573.

Kinder, Donald R. 1986. "Presidential Character Revisited." In *Political Cognitions,* ed. Richard R. Lau and David Sears. Hillsdale, N.J.: Lawrence Erlbaum.

Kinder, Donald R., and D. Roderick Kiewiet. 1981. "Sociotropic Politics: The American Case." *British Journal of Political Science* 11: 129–161.

Kinder, Donald R., and Lynn M. Sanders. 1996. *Divided by Color.* Chicago: University of Chicago Press.

Kinder, Donald R., and David O. Sears. 1985. "Public Opinion and Political Action." In *Handbook of Social Psychology,* vol. 2, 3rd ed., ed. Gardner Lindzey and Elliot Aronson. New York: Random House.

King, David C. 1997. "The Polarization of American Parties and Mistrust of Government." In *Why People Don't Trust Government,* ed. Joseph S. Nye, Jr., Philip D. Zelikow, and David C. King. Cambridge, Mass.: Harvard University Press.

King, Gary, Michael Tomz, and Jason Wittenberg. 2000. "Making the Most of Statistical Analyses: Improving Interpretation and Presentation." *American Journal of Political Science* 44: 341–355.

Kirby, Emily Hoban, Karlo Barrios Marcelo, Joshua Gillerman, and Samantha Linkins. 2008. "The Youth Vote in the 2008 Primaries and Caucuses." Center for Information & Research on Civic Learning & Engagement (CIRCLE) Fact Sheet, www.civicyouth.org.

Klein, Paul. 1972. "The Television Audience and Program Mediocrity." In *Mass Media and Society,* ed. Alan Wells. Palo Alto: National Press Books.

Klingberg, Frank L. 1952. "The Historical Alternation of Moods in American Foreign Policy." *World Politics* 4: 239–273.

Klingemann, Hans-Dieter, Andrea Volkens, Judith Bara, Ian Budge, and Michael McDonald. 2006. *Mapping Policy Preferences II: Estimates for Parties, Electors, and Governments in Eastern Europe, European Union and OECD 1990–2003.* Oxford: Oxford University Press.

Klinkner, Phillip A. 2004a. "Red and Blue Scare: The Continuing Diversity of the American Electoral Landscape." *The Forum* 2(2). Article 2.

———. 2004b. "Counter Response from Klinkner to Bishop and Cushing." *The Forum* 2(2). Article 9.

Klinkner, Philip A., and Ann Hapanowicz. 2005. "Red and Blue Déjà Vu: Measuring Political Polarization in the 2004 Election." *The Forum* 3(2): Article 2.

Knack, Stephen. 1995. "Does 'Motor Voter' Work? Evidence from State-Level Data." *Journal of Politics* 57: 796–811.

———. 1999. "Drivers Wanted: Motor Voter and the Election of 1996." *PS: Political Science & Politics* 32: 237–243.

Knight, Kathleen 1986. "Judging Inflation and Unemployment: The Origins of Retrospective Evaluations." *Journal of Politics* 48: 565–588.

———. 2006. "Transformations of the Concept of Ideology in the Twentieth Century." *American Political Science Review* 100: 619–626.

Knuckey, Jonathan. 2005. "Racial Resentment and the Changing Partisanship of Southern Whites." *Party Politics* 11: 5–28.

———. 2006. "Explaining Recent Changes in the Partisan Identifications of Southern Whites." *Political Research Quarterly* 59: 57–70.

Knutsen, Oddbjørn. 2007. "The Decline of Social Class?" In *The Oxford Handbook of Political Behavior,* ed. Russell J. Dalton and Hans-Dieter Klingemann. New York: Oxford University Press.

Konda, Thomas M., and Lee Sigelman. 1987. "Public Evaluations of the American Parties, 1952–1984." *Journal of Politics* 49: 814–829.

Kousser, Thad, and Megan Mullin. 2007. "Does Voting by Mail Increase Participation? Using Matching to Analyze a Natural Experiment." *Political Analysis* 15: 428–445.

Krause, George A. 1997. "Voters, Information Heterogeneity, and the Dynamics of Aggregate Economic Expectations." *American Journal of Political Science* 41: 1170–1200.

Krosnick, Jon A., and Lin Chiat Chang. 2009. "National Surveys via RDD Telephone Interviewing versus the Internet: Comparing Sample Representativeness and Response Quality," *Public Opinion Quarterly* 73: 641–678.

Krosnick, Jon A., Arthur Lupia, Matthew DeBell, and Darrell Donakowski. 2008. "Problems with ANES Questions Measuring Political Knowledge." American National Election Studies, March 2008. www.electionstudies.org/announce/newsltr/20080324PoliticalKnowledgeMemo.pdf.

Krotki, Karol, and J. Michael Dennis. 2001. "Probability-Based Survey Research on the Internet." Paper presented at the 53rd Conference of the International Statistical Institute, Seoul, South Korea.

Krugman, Herbert E., and Eugene L. Hartley. 1970. "Passive Learning from Television." *Public Opinion Quarterly* 34: 184–190.

Kruse, Kevin M. 2005. *White Flight.* Princeton, N.J.: Princeton University Press.

Kuklinski, James H., Robert C. Luskin, and John Bolland. 1991. "Where Is the Schema? Going Beyond the "S" Word in Political Psychology." *American Political Science Review* 85: 1341–1356.

Kuklinski, James H., and Paul J. Quirk. 2000. "Reconsidering the Rational Public: Cognition, Heuristics, and Mass Opinion." In *Elements of Reason: Cognition, Choice, and the Bounds of Rationality,* ed. Arthur Lupia, Mathew D. McCubbins, and Samuel L. Popkin. New York: Cambridge University Press.

———. 2001. "Conceptual Foundations of Citizen Competence." *Political Behavior* 23: 285–311.

Kuklinski, James H., Paul J. Quirk, Jennifer Jerit, and Robert F. Rich. 2001. "The Political Environment and Citizen Competence." *American Journal of Political Science* 45: 410–424.

Kuklinski, James H., Paul J. Quirk, Jennifer Jerit, David Schwieder, and Robert F. Rich. 2000. "Misinformation and the Currency of Democratic Citizenship." *Journal of Politics* 62: 790–816.

Kuklinski, James H., Paul J. Quirk, and Buddy Peyton. 2008. "Issues, Information Flows, and Cognitive Capacities: Democratic Citizenship in a Global Era." In *International Perspectives on Contemporary Democracy,* ed. Peter F. Nardulli. Champaign: University of Illinois Press.

Kumkale, G. Tarcan, and Dolores Albarracín. 2004. "The Sleeper Effect in Persuasion: A Meta-Analytic Review." *Psychological Bulletin* 130: 143–172.

Kurtz, Karl T., Bruce Cain, and Richard G. Niemi, eds. 2007. *Institutional Change in American Politics: The Case of Term Limits.* Ann Arbor: University of Michigan Press.

Kwak, Nojin. 1999. "Revisiting the Knowledge Gap Hypothesis: Education, Motivation, and Media Use." *Communication Research* 26: 385–413.

Ladd, Everett Carll. 1982. *Where Have All the Voters Gone? The Fracturing of America's Political Parties.* New York: Norton.

Ladd, Everett Carll, and Charles D. Hadley. 1975. *Transformations of the American Party System.* New York: Norton.

Ladner, Matthew, and Christopher Wlezien. 2007. "Partisan Preferences, Electoral Prospects, and Economic Expectations." *Comparative Political Studies* 40: 571–596.

Lakoff, George. 2002. *Moral Politics: How Liberals and Conservatives Think.* Chicago: University of Chicago Press.

Lamis, Alexander P. 1988. *The Two-Party South.* Oxford: Oxford University Press.

———, ed. 1999. *Southern Politics in the 1990s.* Baton Rouge: Louisiana State University Press.

Langer, Gary, and Jon Cohen. 2005. "Voters and Values in the 2004 Election." *Public Opinion Quarterly* 69: 744–759.

Lassen, David Dreyer. 2005. "The Effect of Information on Voter Turnout: Evidence from a Natural Experiment." *American Journal of Political Science* 49: 103–118.

Lassiter, Matthew D. 2006. *The Silent Majority: Suburban Politics in the Sunbelt South.* Princeton, N.J.: Princeton University Press.

Lau, Richard R. 1986. "Political Schemata, Candidate Evaluations, and Voting Behavior." In *Political Cognition,* ed. Richard R. Lau and David O. Sears. Hillsdale, N.J.: Lawrence Erlbaum.

———. 1989. "Construct Accessibility and Electoral Choice." *Political Behavior* 11: 5–32.

———. 1992. "Searchable Information during an Election Campaign." Unpublished manuscript, Rutgers University.

———. 1995. "Information Search during an Election Campaign: Introducing a Process Tracing Methodology to Political Science." In *Political Judgment: Structure and Process,* ed. Milton Lodge and Kathleen McGraw. Ann Arbor: University of Michigan Press.

Lau, Richard R., David J. Andersen, and David P. Redlawsk. 2008. "An Exploration of Correct Voting in Recent U.S. Presidential Elections." *American Journal of Political Science* 52: 395–411.

Lau, Richard R., and Ralph Erber. 1985. "An Information Processing Perspective on Political Sophistication." In *Mass Media and Political Thought,* ed. Sidney Klaus and Richard Perloff. Beverly Hills, Calif.: Sage.

Lau, Richard R., and David P. Redlawsk. 1997. "Voting Correctly." *American Political Science Review* 91: 585–599.

———. 2001a. "Advantages and Disadvantages of Cognitive Heuristics in Political Decision Making." *American Journal of Political Science* 45: 951–971.

———. 2001b. "An Experimental Study of Information Search, Memory, and Decision Making during a Political Campaign." In *Citizens and Politics: Perspectives from Political Psychology,* ed. James Kuklinski. Cambridge: Cambridge University Press.

———. 2006. *How Voters Decide: Information Processing during Election Campaigns.* New York: Cambridge University Press.

Lau, Richard R., and David O. Sears, eds. 1986. *Political Cognition.* Hillsdale, N.J.: Lawrence Erlbaum.

Laver, Michael, Kenneth Benoit, and John Garry. 2003. "Estimating the Policy Positions of Political Actors Using Words as Data." *American Political Science Review* 97: 311–331.

Lavine, Howard, Cynthia J. Thomsen, and Marti Hope Gonzales. 1997. "The Development of Interattitudinal Consistency: The Shared Consequences Model." *Journal of Personality and Social Psychology* 72: 735–749.

Layman, Geoffrey C. 1997. "Religion and Political Behavior in the United States: The Impact of Beliefs, Affiliations, and Commitment from 1980 to 1994." *Public Opinion Quarterly* 61: 288–316.

———. 2001. *The Great Divide: Religious and Cultural Conflict in American Party Politics.* New York: Columbia University Press.

Layman, Geoffrey C., and Edward G. Carmines. 1997. "Cultural Conflict in American Politics: Religious Traditionalism, Postmaterialism, and U.S. Political Behavior." *Journal of Politics* 59: 751–777.

Layman, Geoffrey C., and Thomas M. Carsey. 2002. "Party Polarization and 'Conflict Extension' in the American Electorate." *American Journal of Political Science* 46: 786–802.

Layman, Geoffrey C., Thomas M. Carsey, and Juliana Menasce Horowitz. 2006. "Party Polarization in American Politics." *Annual Review of Political Science* 9: 83–110.

Layman, Geoffrey C., and John C. Green. 2006. "Wars and Rumours of Wars: The Contexts of Cultural Conflict in American Political Behaviour." *British Journal of Political Science* 36: 61–89.

Lazarsfeld, Paul, Bernard Berelson, and Hazel Gaudet. 1948. *The People's Choice.* New York: Columbia University Press.

Lee, Woojin, and John Roemer. 2005. "Values and Politics in the U.S.: An Equilibrium Analysis of the 2004 Election." Working Paper 2005–08, University of Massachusetts, Amherst, Department of Economics.

Leege, David C., Kenneth D. Wald, Brian S. Krueger, and Paul D. Mueller. 2002. *The Politics of Cultural Differences: Social Change and Voter Mobilization Strategies in the Post–New Deal Period.* Princeton, N.J.: Princeton University Press.

Lehmann, Donald R. 1971. "Television Show Preference: Application of a Choice Model." *Journal of Marketing Research* 8: 47–55.

Leighley, Jan E., and Jonathan Nagler. 2007. "Unions, Voter Turnout, and Class Bias in the U.S. Electorate, 1964–2004." *Journal of Politics* 69: 430–441.

Levendusky, Matthew. 2006. "Sorting: Explaining Change in the U.S. Electorate." Unpublished Ph.D. dissertation. Stanford University.

———. 2009a. "The Microfoundations of Mass Polarization." *Political Analysis* 17: 162–176.

———. 2009b. *The Partisan Sort: How Liberals Became Democrats and Conservatives Became Republicans.* Chicago: University of Chicago Press.

Levin, A., C. Lin, and C. J. Chu. 2001. "Unit Root Tests in Panel Data: Asymptotic and Finite-Sample Properties." *Journal of Econometrics* 108: 1–24.

Levine, Peter. 2007. *The Future of Democracy: Developing the Next Generation of American Citizens.* Medford, Mass: Tufts University Press.

Lewis, Gregory B. 2005. "Same-Sex Marriage and the 2004 Presidential Election." *PS: Political Science & Politics* 38: 195–199.

Lewis-Beck, Michael, William Jacoby, Helmut Norpoth, and Herbert F. Weisberg. 2008. *The American Voter Revisited.* Ann Arbor: University of Michigan Press.

Lewis-Beck, Michael S., and Richard Nadeau. 2009. "Obama and the Economy in 2008." *PS: Political Science & Politics* 42: 479–483.

Lewis-Beck, Michael, Richard Nadeau, and Angelo Elias. 2008. "Economics, Party, and the Vote: Causality Issues and Panel Data." *American Journal of Political Science* 52: 84–95.

Lewis-Beck, Michael S., and Mary Stegmaier. 2000. "Economic Determinants of Electoral Outcomes." *Annual Review of Political Science* 3: 183–219.

———. 2007. "Economic Models of Voting." In *The Oxford Handbook of Political Behavior,* ed. Russell J. Dalton and Hans-Dieter Klingemann. New York: Oxford University Press.

Lewis-Beck, Michael S., and Charles Tien. 2008. "The Job of President and the Jobs Model Forecast: Obama for '08?" *PS: Political Science & Politics* 41: 687–690.

Lijphart, Arend. 1997. "Unequal Participation: Democracy's Unsolved Dilemma." *American Political Science Review* 91: 1–14.

Lindaman, Kara, and Donald P. Haider-Markel. 2002. "Issue Evolution, Political Parties, and the Culture Wars." *Political Research Quarterly* 55: 91–110.

Lindbeck, Assar, and Jörgen W. Weibull. 1987. "Balanced-Budget Redistribution as the Outcome of Political Competition." *Public Choice* 52: 273–297.

Linn, Suzanna, Jonathan Moody, and Stephanie Asper. 2009. "Explaining the Horse Race of 2008." *PS: Political Science & Politics* 42: 459–465.

Lipset, Seymour Martin. 1981. *Political Man: The Social Bases of Politics.* Baltimore: Johns Hopkins University Press.

Lipset, Seymour Martin, and Stein Rokkan. 1967a. "Cleavage Structures, Party Systems, and Voter Alignments: An Introduction." In *Party Systems and Voter Alignments: Cross-National Perspectives,* ed. Seymour Martin Lipset and Stein Rokkan. New York: Free Press.

———. 1967b. *Party Systems and Voter Alignments.* New York: The Free Press.

Listhaug, Ola, and Lars Grønflaten. 2007. "Civic Decline? Trends in Political Involvement and Participation in Norway, 1965–2001." *Scandinavian Political Studies* 30: 272–299.

Lockerbie, Brad. 2008. *Do Voters Look to the Future? Economics and Elections.* Albany: State University of New York Press.

Lodge, Milton G., and Ruth Hamill. 1986. "A Partisan Schema for Political Information Processing." *American Political Science Review* 80: 505–519.

Lodge, Milton, Kathleen M. McGraw, and Patrick Stroh. 1989. "An Impression-Driven Model of Candidate Evaluation." *American Political Science Review* 83: 399–420.

Lodge, Milton, Marco R. Steenbergen, and Shawn Brau. 1995. "The Responsive Voter: Campaign Information and the Dynamics of Candidate Evaluation." *American Political Science Review* 89: 309–326.

Lodge, Milton, and Charles S. Taber. 2000. "Three Steps toward a Theory of Motivated Political Reasoning." In *Elements of Reason: Cognition, Choice, and the Bounds of Rationality,* ed. Arthur Lupia, Mathew D. McCubbins, and Samuel L. Popkin. London: Cambridge University Press.

"Lone Star Rising, A Special Report on Texas." 2009. *The Economist,* July 11–17.

LoSciuto, Leonard A. 1972. "A National Inventory of Television Viewing Behavior." In *Television and Social Behavior. Television in Day-to-Day Life: Patterns of Use,* ed. Eli A. Rubinstein, George A. Comstock and John P. Murray. Washington, D.C.: U.S. Government Printing Office.

Lowndes, Joseph E. 2008. *From the New Deal to the New Right.* New Haven, Conn.: Yale University Press.

Lublin, David. 2004. *The Republican South.* Princeton, N.J.: Princeton University Press.

Lublin, David, and D. Stephen Voss. 2000. "Racial Redistricting and Realignment in Southern State Legislatures." *American Journal of Political Science* 44: 792–810.

————. 2003. "The Missing Middle: Why Median-Voter Theory Can't Save Democrats from Singing the Boll-Weevil Blues." *Journal of Politics* 65: 227–237.

Lupia, Arthur. 1994. "Shortcuts versus Encyclopedias: Information and Voting Behavior in California Insurance Reform Elections." *American Political Science Review* 88: 63–76.

————. 2006. "How Elitism Undermines the Study of Voter Competence." *Critical Review* 18: 217–232.

Lupia, Arthur, and Mathew D. McCubbins. 1998. *The Democratic Dilemma: Can Citizens Learn What They Need to Know?* Cambridge: Cambridge University Press.

Luskin, Robert C. 1987. "Measuring Political Sophistication." *American Journal of Political Science* 31: 856–899.

————. 2000. "From Denial to Extenuation (and Finally Beyond): Political Sophistication and Citizen Performance." In *Thinking about Political Psychology,* ed. James H. Kuklinski. New York: Cambridge University Press.

————. 2002. "Political Psychology, Political Behavior, and Politics: Questions of Aggregation, Causal Distance, and Taste." In *Thinking about Political Psychology,* ed. James H. Kuklinski. New York: Cambridge University Press.

Luskin, Robert C., James S. Fishkin, and Roger Jowell. 2002. "Considered Opinions: Deliberative Polling in the U.K." *British Journal of Political Science* 32: 455–487.

Lusztig, Michael, and J. Matthew Wilson. 2005. "A New Right? Moral Issues and Partisan Change in Canada." *Social Science Quarterly* 86: 109–128.

Lyons, William, and Robert Alexander. 2000. "A Tale of Two Electorates: Generational Replacement and the Decline of Voting in Presidential Elections." *Journal of Politics* 62: 1014–1034.

Macdonald, Kenneth, and Anthony Heath. 1997. "Pooling Cross-Sections: A Comment on Price and Sanders." *Political Studies* 45: 928–941.

Macedo, Stephen, et al. 2005. *Democracy at Risk: How Political Choices Undermine Citizen Participation, and What We Can Do about It.* Washington, D.C.: Brookings.

MacKuen, Michael B., Robert S. Erikson, and James A. Stimson. 1989. "Macropartisanship." *American Political Science Review* 83: 1125–1142.

————. 1992. "Peasants or Bankers? The American Electorate and the U.S. Economy." *American Political Science Review* 86: 597–611.

Maggiotto, Michael A., and Gary D. Wekkin. 2000. *Partisan Linkages in Southern Politics.* Knoxville: University of Tennessee Press.

Mair, Peter, and Ingrid van Biezen. 2001. "Party Membership in Twenty European Democracies, 1980–2000." *Party Politics* 7: 5–22.

Malhotra, Neil, and Jon A. Krosnick. 2007. "The Effect of Survey Mode and Sampling on Inferences about Political Attitudes and Behavior: Comparing the 2000 and 2004 ANES to Internet Surveys with Nonprobability Samples." *Political Analysis* 15: 286–323.

Manza, Jeff, and Christopher Uggen. 2006. *Locked Out: Felon Disenfranchisement and American Democracy.* New York: Oxford University Press.

Marcus, George E. 1988. "The Structure of Emotional Response: 1984 Presidential Candidates." *American Political Science Review* 82: 737–761.

Marcus, George, and Michael MacKuen. 1993. "Anxiety, Enthusiasm, and the Vote: The Emotional Underpinnings of Learning and Involvement during Presidential Campaigns." *American Political Science Review* 87: 672–685.

Marcus, George E., W. Russell Neuman, and Michael MacKuen. 2000. *Affective Intelligence and Political Judgment.* Chicago: University of Chicago Press.

Markus, Gregory B. 1982. "Political Attitudes during an Election Year: A Report on the 1980 NES Panel Study." *American Political Science Review* 76: 538–560.

———. 1988. "The Impact of Personal and National Economic Conditions on the Presidential Vote: A Pooled Cross-Sectional Analysis." *American Journal of Political Science* 32: 137–154.

Martin, Paul S. 2003. "Voting's Rewards: Voter Turnout, Attentive Publics, and Congressional Allocation of Federal Money." *American Journal of Political Science* 47: 110–127.

Martinez, Michael D., and David Hill. 1999. "Did Motor Voter Work?" *American Politics Quarterly* 27: 296–315.

"Massachusetts Senate Election: Youth Turnout Was Just 15%, Compared to 57% for Older Citizens; Young Voters Favored Coakley." Center for Information & Research on Civic Learning & Engagement (CIRCLE), www.civicyouth.org.

Matthews, Donald R., and James W. Prothro. 1966. *Negroes and the New Southern Politics.* New York: Harcourt, Brace, & World.

Mayer, William G. 2009. "The Divided Democrats Revisited." Paper presented at the annual meeting of the American Political Science Association, Toronto, September 2–6.

McCarty, Nolan, Keith T. Poole, and Howard Rosenthal. 1997. *Income Redistribution and the Realignment of American Politics.* Washington D.C.: AEI Press.

———. 2006. *Polarized America: The Dance of Ideology and Unequal Riches.* Cambridge: MIT Press.

McDermott, Monika L. 2005. "Candidate Occupations and Voter Information Shortcuts." *Journal of Politics* 67: 201–219.

McDonald, Michael P. 2002. "The Turnout Rate among Eligible Voters for U.S. States, 1980–2000." *State Politics and Policy Quarterly* 2: 199–212.

———. 2003. "On the Over-Report Bias of the National Election Study." *Political Analysis* 11: 180–186.

———. 2004. "Up, Up and Away! Voter Participation in the 2004 Presidential Election." *The Forum* 2(4): Article 4.

———. 2007. "The True Electorate: A Cross-Validation of Voter File and Election Poll Demographics." *Public Opinion Quarterly* 71: 588–602.

———. 2009. "2008 Current Population Survey Voting and Registration Supplement," http://elections.gmu.edu/CPS_2008.html, last updated November 20.

———. 2010. "2008 Current Population Survey Voting and Registration Supplement." United States Elections Project. http://elections.gmu.edu/CPS_2008.html.

McDonald, Michael P., and Samuel Popkin. 2001. "The Myth of the Vanishing Voter." *American Political Science Review* 95: 963–974.

McDonald, Michael P., and Thomas Schaller. 2009. "Voter Mobilization in the 2008 Presidential Election." In *The Change Election: Money, Mobilization and Persuasion in the 2008 Federal Elections,* ed. David Magleby. Washington, D.C.: Pew Monograph.

McKee, Seth C. 2009. *Republican Ascendancy in Southern U.S. House Elections.* Boulder, Colo.: Westview.

McKee, Seth C., and David Hill. 2009. "The New Democratic Majority: Who Voted in the 2008 Presidential Election?" Paper presented at the annual meeting of the American Political Science Association. Toronto, September 2–6.

McKelvey, Richard D, and Peter C. Ordeshook. 1985. "Elections with Limited Information: A Fulfilled Expectations Model Using Contemporaneous Poll and Endorsement Data as Information Sources." *Journal of Economic Theory* 36: 55–85.

Meffert, Michael G., Helmut Norpoth, and Anirudh V. S. Ruhil. 2001. "Realignment and Macropartisanship." *American Political Science Review* 95: 953–962.

Meltzer, Allan, and Scott Richard. 1981. "A Rational Theory of the Size of Government." *Journal of Political Economy* 89: 914–927.

Mendelberg, Tali. 2001. *The Race Card: Campaign Strategy, Implicit Messages and the Norm of Equity.* Princeton, N.J.: Princeton University Press.

Mermin, Jonathan. 1999. *Debating War and Peace: Media Coverage of U.S. Intervention in the Post-Vietnam Era.* Princeton, N.J.: Princeton University Press.

Merrill, Samuel, III, Bernard Grofman, and Thomas L. Brunell. 2008. "Cycles in American National Electoral Politics, 1854–2006: Statistical Evidence and an Explanatory Model." *American Political Science Review* 102: 1–17.

Miller, Arthur H., and Martin P. Wattenberg. 1981. "Policy and Performance Voting in the 1980 Election." Paper presented at the annual meeting of the American Political Science Association, New York.

Miller, Arthur H., Martin P. Wattenberg, and Oksana Malanchuk. 1986. "Schematic Assessments of Presidential Candidates." *American Political Science Review* 80: 521–540.

Miller, Gary, and Norman Schofield. 2003. "Activists and Partisan Realignment in the United States." *American Political Science Review* 97: 245–260.

Miller, Joanne, and Jon Krosnick. 2000. "New Media Impact on the Ingredients of Presidential Evaluations: Politically Knowledgeable Citizens are Guided by a Trusted Source." *American Journal of Political Science* 44: 301–315.

Miller, Nicholas R. 1986. "Information, Electorates, and Democracy: Some Extensions and Interpretations of the Condorcet Jury Theorem." In *Information Pooling and Group Decision Making*, ed. Bernard Grofman and Guillermo Owen. Greenwich: JAI.

Miller, Warren E. 1991. "Party Identification, Realignment, and Party Voting: Back to the Basics." *American Political Science Review* 85: 557–568.

———. 1992. "The Puzzle Transformed: Explaining Declining Turnout." *Political Behavior* 14: 1–43.

———. 1998. "Party Identification and the Electorate of the 1990s." In *The Parties Respond: Changes in American Parties and Campaigns*, 3rd ed., ed. L. Sandy Maisel. Boulder, Colo.: Westview.

———. 1999. "Temporal Order and Causal Inference." *Political Analysis* 8: 119–140.

Miller, Warren E., and J. Merrill Shanks. 1996. *The New American Voter*. Cambridge, Mass.: Harvard University Press.

Milner, Henry. 2002. *Civic Literacy: How Informed Citizens Make Democracy Work*. Hanover, N.H.: University Press of New England.

Mindich, David T. Z. 2005. *Tuned Out: Why Americans Under 40 Don't Follow the News*. New York: Oxford University Press.

Mintz, Alex, Nehemia Geva, Steven B. Redd, and Amy Carnes. 1997. "The Effect of Dynamic and Static Choice Sets on Political Decision Making: An Analysis Using the Decision Board Platform." *American Political Science Review* 91: 553–566.

Mochmann, Ekkehard, Ingvill C. Oedegaard, and Reiner Mauer. 1998. *Inventory of National Election Studies in Europe 1945–1995*. Bergisch Gladbach: Edwin Ferger Verlag.

Mondak, Jeffery J. 1993. "Public Opinion and Heuristic Processing of Source Cues." *Political Behavior* 15: 167–192.

———. 1999. "Reconsidering the Measurement of Political Knowledge." *Political Analysis* 8: 57–82.

———. 2001. "Developing Valid Knowledge Scales." *American Journal of Political Science* 45: 224–238.

Monroe, Burt L., and Philip A. Schrodt. 2008. "Introduction to the Special Issue: The Statistical Analysis of Political Text." *Political Analysis* 16: 351–355.

Morin, Richard, and Claudia Deane. 2000. "As Turnout Falls, Apathy Emerges as Driving Force." *Washington Post*, November 4, 2000, p. 1A.

Mueller, Dennis C. 2003. *Public Choice III.* Cambridge: Cambridge University Press.

Mulligan, Kenneth. 2008. "The 'Myth' of Moral Values Voting in the 2004 Presidential Election." *PS: Political Science & Politics* 41: 109–114.

Mutz, Diana. 1992. "Impersonal Influence: Effects of Representations of Public Opinion on Political Attitudes." *Political Behavior* 14: 89–122.

———. 1998. *Impersonal Influence: How Perceptions of Mass Collectives Affect Political Attitudes.* Cambridge: Cambridge University Press.

———. 2002. "Cross-Cutting Social Networks: Testing Democratic Theory in Practice." *American Political Science Review* 96: 111–126.

Mutz, Diana C., and Paul S. Martin. 2001. "Facilitating Communication across Lines of Political Difference: The Role of the Mass Media." *American Political Science Review* 95: 97–113.

Mutz, Diana C., and Jeffery J. Mondak. 1997. "Dimensions of Sociotropic Behavior: Group-Based Judgments of Fairness and Well-Being." *American Journal of Political Science* 41: 284–308.

Myerson, Roger B. 1995. "Analysis of Democratic Institutions: Structure, Conduct and Performance." *Journal of Economic Perspectives* 9: 77–89.

Nadeau, Richard, Richard G. Niemi, David P. Fan, and Timothy Amato. 1999. "Elite Economic Forecasts, Economic News, Mass Economic Judgments, and Presidential Approval." *Journal of Politics* 61: 109–135.

Nadeau, Richard, Richard G. Niemi, Harold W. Stanley, and Jean-François Godbout. 2004. "Class, Party, and South/Non-South Differences: An Update." *American Politics Research* 32: 52–67.

Nadeau, Richard, Richard G. Niemi, and Antoine Yoshinaka. 2002. "A Cross-National Analysis of Economic Voting: Taking Account of the Political Context across Time and Nations." *Electoral Studies* 21: 403–423.

Nadeau, Richard, and Harold W. Stanley. 1993. "Class Polarization in Partisanship among Native Southern Whites, 1952–90." *American Journal of Political Science* 37: 900–919.

National Standards for Civics and Government. 1994. Calabasas, Calif.: Center for Civic Education.

National Telecommunications and Information Administration. 2002. *A Nation Online: How Americans Are Expanding Their Use of the Internet.* Washington, D.C.: U.S. Department of Commerce.

Negroponte, Nicholas. 1995. *Being Digital.* New York: Knopf.

Neuman, W. Russell. 1976. "Patterns of Recall among Television News Viewers." *Public Opinion Quarterly* 40: 115–123.

———. 1986. *The Paradox of Mass Politics: Knowledge and Opinion in the American Electorate.* Cambridge, Mass.: Harvard University Press.

———. 1996. "Political Communication Infrastructure." *The Annals of the American Academy of Political and Social Science* 546: 9–21.

Neuman, W. Russell, Marion R. Just, and Ann N. Crigler. 1992. *Common Knowledge: News and the Construction of Political Meaning.* Chicago: University of Chicago Press.

Nicholson, Stephen P. 2003. "The Political Environment and Ballot Proposition Awareness." *American Journal of Political Science* 47: 403–410.

———. 2005. *Voting the Agenda: Candidates, Elections, and Ballot Propositions.* Princeton, N.J.: Princeton University Press.

Nie, Norman H., Sidney Verba, and John R. Petrocik. 1976, 1979. *The Changing American Voter.* Cambridge, Mass.: Harvard University Press.

Niemi, Richard G., and M. Kent Jennings. 1991. "Issues and Inheritance in the Formation of Party Identification." *American Journal of Political Science* 35: 970–988.

Niemi, Richard G., Kent Portney, and David King. 2008. "Sampling Young Adults: Internet Surveys and Inferences about the Political Engagement of College Students." Paper presented at the annual meeting of the American Political Science Association, Boston.

Niemi, Richard G., and Herbert F. Weisberg, eds. 1976. *Controversies in American Voting Behavior.* San Francisco: W. H. Freeman.

———. 1993a. *Classics in Voting Behavior.* Washington, D.C.: CQ Press.

———. 1993b. *Controversies in American Voting Behavior,* 3rd ed. Washington, D.C.: CQ Press.

———. 2001. *Controversies in American Voting Behavior,* 4th ed. Washington, D.C.: CQ Press.

Nisbett, Richard E., and Lee Ross. 1980. *Human Inference: Strategies and Shortcomings of Social Judgment.* Englewood Cliffs, N.J.: Prentice-Hall.

Nisbett, Richard E., and Timothy D. Wilson. 1977. "Telling More Than We Can Know: Verbal Reports on Mental Processes." *Psychological Review* 84: 231–259.

Nixon, Richard. 1978. *RN: The Memoirs of Richard Nixon.* New York: Grosset & Dunlap.

Norpoth, Helmut and Milton Lodge. 1985. "The Difference between Attitudes and Nonattitudes in the Mass Public: Just Measurement?" *American Journal of Political Science* 29: 291–307.

Norpoth, Helmut, and Andrew H. Sidman. 2007. "Mission Accomplished: The Wartime Election of 2004." *Political Behavior* 29: 175–195.

Norris, Pippa. 2000. *A Virtuous Cycle: Political Communications in Postindustrial Societies.* Cambridge: Cambridge University Press.

———. 2002. *Democratic Phoenix: Reinventing Political Activism.* Cambridge: Cambridge University Press.

Nye, M. A., and Charles S. Bullock III. 1993. "Civil Rights Support: A Comparison of Southern and Border State Representatives." *Legislative Studies Quarterly* 17: 81–94.

Offe, Claus, and Susanne Fuchs. 2002. "A Decline of Social Capital? The German Case." In *Democracies in Flux: The Evolution of Social Capital in Contemporary Society,* ed. Robert D. Putnam. Oxford: Oxford University Press.

Ostrom, Charles W., Jr. 1978. *Time Series Analysis: Regression Techniques.* Beverly Hills, Calif.: Sage.

Ottati, Victor C. 1990. "Determinants of Political Judgments: The Joint Influence of Normative and Heuristic Rules of Inference. *Political Behavior* 12: 159–179.

Ottati, Victor C., Martin Fishbein, and S. E. Middlestadt.1988. "Determinants of Voters' Beliefs about the Candidates' Stands on the Issues: The Role of Evaluative Bias Heuristics and the Candidates' Expressed Message." *Journal of Personality and Social Psychology* 55: 517–529.

Page, Benjamin I. 1978. *Choices and Echoes in Presidential Elections: Rational Man and Electoral Democracy.* Chicago: University of Chicago Press.

Page, Benjamin I., and Robert Y. Shapiro. 1992. *The Rational Public: Fifty Years of Trends in Americans' Policy Preferences.* Chicago: University of Chicago Press.

Palfrey, Thomas R., and Keith T. Poole. 1987. "The Relationship between Information, Ideology, and Voting Behavior." *American Journal of Political Science* 31: 511–530.

Palmer, Harvey. 1995. "Effects of Authoritarian and Libertarian Values on Conservative and Labour Party Support in Great Britain." *European Journal of Political Research* 27: 273–292.

Patterson, Thomas E. 1980. *The Mass Media Election: How Americans Choose Their President.* New York: Praeger.

———. 1993. *Out of Order.* New York: Vintage.

———. 2000. "Doing Well and Doing Good." Research Report. Cambridge, Mass.: Joan Shorenstein Center on the Press, Politics and Public Policy. Harvard University.

———. 2002. *The Vanishing Voter: Public Involvement in an Age of Uncertainty.* New York: Knopf.

———. 2003. "The Search for a Standard: Markets and the Media." *Political Communication* 20: 139–143.

Pattie, Charles, Ron Johnston, and David Sanders. 1999. "On Babies and Bathwater: A Comment on Evans' 'Economics and Politics Revisited,'" *Political Studies* 47: 918–932.

Payne, John W., James R. Bettman, and Eric J. Johnson. 1992. "Behavioral Decision Research: A Constructive Processing Perspective." *Annual Review of Psychology* 43: 87–131.

———. 1993. *The Adaptive Decision Maker.* Cambridge: Cambridge University Press.

Perlmutter, David D. 2008. *Blogwars.* Oxford: Oxford University Press.

Perlstein, Rick. 2001. *Before the Storm: Barry Goldwater and the Unmaking of the American Consensus.* New York: Hill and Wang.

Persily, Nathaniel, Stephen Ansolabehere, and Charles Stewart III. 2010. "Race, Region, and Vote Choice in the 2008 Election: Implications for the Future of the Voting Rights Act." *Harvard Law Review* 123: 1386–1436.

Persson, Torsten, Gerard Roland, and Guido Tabellini. 2000. "Comparative Politics and Public Finance." *Journal of Political Economy* 108: 1121–1161.

Persson, Torsten, and Guido Tabellini. 2000. *Political Economics: Explaining Economic Policy.* Cambridge, Mass.: MIT Press.

Petrocik, John R. 1987. "Realignment: New Party Coalitions and the Nationalization of the South." *Journal of Politics* 49: 347–375.

———. 1996. "Issue Ownership in Presidential Elections, with a 1980 Case Study." *American Journal of Political Science* 40: 825–850.

Petrocik, John R., and Scott W. Desposato. 1998. "The Partisan Consequences of Majority-Minority Redistricting in the South, 1992 and 1994." *Journal of Politics* 60: 613–633.

Petty, Richard E., and John T. Cacioppo. 1986. *Communication and Persuasion: Central and Peripheral Routes to Attitude Change.* New York: Springer-Verlag.

Pew Research Center for the People and the Press. 2007. "Trends in Political Values and Core Attitudes: 1987–2007. Political Landscape More Favorable To Democrats." News Release. March 22, 2007.

Piven, Frances Fox, and Richard A. Cloward. 1988. *Why Americans Don't Vote.* New York: Pantheon.

Plissner, Martin, and Warren Mitofsky. 1981. "What If They Held an Election and Nobody Came?" *Public Opinion* 4(1): 50–51.

Polsby, Nelson W. 1997. "A Revolution in Congress?" Inaugural Lecture, Oxford University.

———. 2004. *How Congress Evolves.* New York: Oxford University Press.

Poole, Keith T. 1998. "Recovering a Basic Space from a Set of Issue Scales." *American Journal of Political Science* 42: 954–993.

Poole, Keith T., and Howard Rosenthal. 1997. *Congress: A Political–Economic History of Roll Call Voting.* New York: Oxford University Press.

———. 2001. "D-Nominate After 10 Years: A Comparative Update to Congress: A Political-Economic History of Roll-Call Voting." *Legislative Studies Quarterly* 26: 5–29.

———. 2007. *Ideology and Congress,* 2nd ed. New Brunswick, N.J.: Transaction.

Popkin, Samuel L. 1994. *The Reasoning Voter: Communication and Persuasion in Presidential Campaigns,* 2nd ed. Chicago: University of Chicago Press.

———. 2006. "The Factual Basis of 'Belief Systems': A Reassessment." *Critical Review* 18: 233–254.

Potthoff, Richard F., and Michael C. Munger. 2005. "Voter Uncertainty Can Produce Preferences with More than One Peak, but Not Preference Cycles: A Clue to the Fate of Ross Perot?" *Journal of Politics* 67: 429–453.

Powell, G. Bingham Jr. 1986. "American Voter Turnout in Comparative Perspective." *American Political Science Review* 80: 17–43.

Presser, Stanley, and Michael Traugott. 1992. "Little White Lies and Social Science Models: Correlated Response Errors in a Panel Study of Voting." *Public Opinion Quarterly* 56: 77–86.

Price, Simon, and David Sanders. 1995. "Economic Expectations and Voting Intentions in the UK, 1979–87: A Pooled Cross-Section Analysis." *Political Studies* 43: 451–471.

———. 1997. "Pooling Cross-Sections: A Response to Macdonald and Heath." *Political Studies* 45: 942–946.

Price, Vincent, and John Zaller. 1993. "Who Gets the News? Alternative Measures of News Reception and Their Implications for Research." *Public Opinion Quarterly* 57: 133–164.

Prior, Markus. 2003. "Any Good News in Soft News?" *Political Communication* 20: 149–172.

———. 2005. "News vs. Entertainment: How Increasing Media Choice Widens Gaps in Political Knowledge and Turnout." *American Journal of Political Science* 49: 577–592.

———. 2007. *Post-Broadcast Democracy: How Media Choice Increases Inequality in Political Involvement and Polarizes Elections.* Cambridge: Cambridge University Press.

Putnam, Robert D. 2000. *Bowling Alone: The Collapse and Revival of American Community.* New York: Simon & Schuster.

Putz, David W. 2002. "Partisan Conversion in the 1990s: Ideological Realignment Meets Measurement Theory." *Journal of Politics* 64: 1199–1209.

Quattrone, George A. and Amos Tversky. 1988. "Contrasting Rational and Psychological Analyses of Political Choice." *American Political Science Review* 82: 719–736.

Rabinowitz, George, and Stuart Elaine Macdonald. 1989. "A Directional Theory of Issue Voting." *American Political Science Review* 83: 93–121.

Rahn, Wendy M. 1993. "The Role of Partisan Stereotypes in Information Processing about Political Candidates." *American Journal of Political Science* 37: 472–496.

Rahn, Wendy M., Jon A. Krosnick, and Marijke Breuning. 1994. "Rationalization and Derivation Processes in Survey Studies of Political Candidate Evaluation." *American Journal of Political Science* 38: 582–600.

Redlawsk, David P. 2001a. "You Must Remember This: A Test of the On-Line Model of Voting." *Journal of Politics* 63: 29–58.

———. 2001b. "Implications of Motivated Reasoning for Voter Information Processing." Paper presented at the annual meeting of the Midwest Political Science Association.

———. 2002. "Hot Cognition or Cool Consideration? Testing the Effects of Motivated Reasoning on Political Decision Making." *Journal of Politics* 64: 1021–1044.

Reise, Steven P., Keith Widaman, and Robin H. Pugh. 1993. "Confirmatory Factor Analysis and Item Response Theory: Two Approaches for Exploring Measurement Equivalence." *Psychological Bulletin* 114: 552–566.

Rhodes, Terrel L. 2000. *Republicans in the South: Voting for the State House, Voting for the White House.* Westport, Conn.: Praeger.

Riggle, Ellen D. B., and Mitzi M. S. Johnson. 1996. "Age Differences in Political Decision Making: Strategies for Evaluating Political Candidates." *Political Behavior* 18: 99–118.

Riggle, Ellen D., Victor Ottati, Robert S. Wyer, James Kuklinski, and Norbert Schwarz. 1992. "Bases of Political Judgments: The Role of Stereotypic and Nonstereotypic Information." *Political Behavior* 14: 67–87.

Riker, William H. 1982. *Liberalism against Populism.* San Francisco: Freeman.

Riker, William H., and Peter C. Ordeshook. 1968. "A Theory of the Calculus of Voting." *American Political Science Review* 62: 25–42.

Roberts, Kevin W. S. 1977. "Voting over Income Tax Schedules." *Journal of Public Economics* 8: 329–340.

Roemer, John E. 1998. "Why the Poor do Not Expropriate the Rich: An Old Argument in New Garb." *Journal of Public Economics* 70: 399–424.

Rohde, David W. 1991a. *Parties and Leaders in the Postreform House.* Chicago: University of Chicago Press.

———. 1991b. "'Something's Happening Here; What It Is Ain't Exactly Clear': Southern Democrats in the House of Representatives." In *Home Style and Washington Work: Studies of Congressional Politics,* ed. Morris P. Fiorina, David W. Rohde, and Richard F. Fenno. Ann Arbor: University of Michigan Press.

Romer, Daniel, Kate Kenski, Kenneth Winneg, Christopher Adasiewicz, and Kathleen Hall Jamieson. 2006. *Capturing Campaign Dynamics 2000 and 2004.* Philadelphia: University of Pennsylvania Press.

Romer, Thomas. 1975. "Individual Welfare, Majority Voting, and the Properties of a Linear Income Tax." *Journal of Public Economics* 4: 163–185.

Rosenberg, Shawn W., Shulamit Kahn, and Tuy Tran. 1991. "Creating a Political Image: Shaping Appearance and Manipulating the Vote." *Political Behavior* 13: 345–367.

Rosenstone, Steven J., Roy L. Behr, and Edward H. Lazarus. 1996. *Third Parties in America: Citizen Response to Major Party Failure,* 2nd ed. Princeton, N.J.: Princeton University Press.

Rosenstone, Steven J., and John Mark Hansen. 1993. *Mobilization, Participation, and Democracy in America.* New York: Macmillan.

Rosenthal, Cindy S. 2005. "Local Politics: A Different Front in the Culture War?" *The Forum* 3(2): Article 5.

Rothstein, Bo. 2002. "Sweden: Social Capital in the Social Democratic State." In *Democracies in Flux: The Evolution of Social Capital in Contemporary Society,* ed. Robert D. Putnam. Oxford: Oxford University Press.

Rubin, Alan M. 1984. "Ritualized and Instrumental Television Viewing." *Journal of Communication* 34: 67–77.

Rucht, Dieter. 2007. "The Spread of Protest Politics." In *The Oxford Handbook of Political Behavior,* ed. Russell J. Dalton and Hans-Dieter Klingemann. Oxford: Oxford University Press.

Rudolph, Thomas J. 2006. "Triangulating Political Responsibility: The Motivated Formation of Responsibility Judgments." *Political Psychology* 27: 99–122.

Sanbonmatsu, Kira. 2002. "Gender Stereotypes and Vote Choice." *American Journal of Political Science* 46: 20–34.

———. 2003. "Political Knowledge and Gender Stereotypes." *American Politics Research* 31: 575–594.

Sanders, David. 1996. "Economic Performance, Management Competence, and the Outcome of the Next General Election." *Political Studies* 44: 203–231.

———. 1999a. "Conservative Incompetence, Labour Responsibility, and the Feelgood Factor: Why the Economy Failed to Save the Conservatives in 1997." *Electoral Studies* 18: 251–270.

———. 1999b. "The Impact of Left-Right Ideology." In *Critical Elections: British Parties and Voters in Long-Term Perspective,* ed. Geoffrey Evans and Pippa Norris. London: Sage.

Sanders, David, and Neil T. Gavin. 2004. "Television News, Economic Perceptions and Political Preferences in Britain, 1997–2001." *Journal of Politics* 66: 1245–1266.

Sanders, David, and Simon Price. 1995. "Party Support and Economic Perceptions in the UK 1979–87: A Two-Level Approach." In *The British Elections and Parties Yearbook, 1994,* ed. Colin Rallings, David M. Farrell, David Denver, and David Broughton. London: Frank Cass.

Sapiro, Virginia, Steven J. Rosenstone, Warren E. Miller, and the American National Election Studies. 1997. *1948–1996 Cumulative Data File* [dataset]. Ann Arbor: University of Michigan, Center for Political Studies [producer and distributor].

Sarbaugh-Thompson, Marjorie, Lyke Thompson, Charles D. Elder, John Strate, and Richard C. Elling. 2004. *Political and Institutional Effects of Term Limits.* New York: Palgrave Macmillan.

Saunders, Kyle L., and Alan I. Abramowitz. 2004. "Ideological Realignment and Active Partisans in the American Electorate." *American Politics Research* 32: 285–309.

Scammon, Richard, and Ben Wattenberg. 1970. *The Real Majority.* New York: Coward-McCann.

Scarrow, Susan E. 2007. "Political Activism and Party Members." In *The Oxford Handbook of Political Behavior,* ed. Russell J. Dalton and Hans-Dieter Klingemann. Oxford: Oxford University Press.

Schaffner, Brian F. 2005. "Priming Gender: Campaigning on Women's Issues in U.S. Senate Elections." *American Journal of Political Science* 49: 803–817.

Schaller, Thomas F. 2006. *Whistling Past Dixie.* New York: Simon & Schuster.

Schattschneider, E. E. 1975. *The Semisovereign People: A Realist's View of Democracy in America,* 2nd ed. New York: Holt, Rinehart, & Winston.

Scher, Richard K. 1997. *Politics in the New South: Republicanism, Race, and Leadership in the Twentieth Century,* 2nd ed. Armonk, N.Y.: M. E. Sharpe.

Schickler, Eric, and Donald Green. 1997. "The Stability of Party Identification in Western Democracies: Results from Eight Panel Surveys." *Comparative Political Studies* 30: 450–483.

Schofield, Norman, and Gary Miller. 2007. "Elections and Activist Coalitions in the United States." *American Journal of Political Science* 51: 518–531.

Scholz, John T. 1998. "Trust and Taxpaying: Testing the Heuristic Approach to Collective Action." *American Journal of Political Science* 42: 398–417.

Schudson, Michael. 1998. *The Good Citizen: A History of American Civic Life.* New York: Free Press.

Schumpeter, Joseph. 1942. *Capitalism, Socialism, and Democracy.* New York: Harper and Brothers.

Sears, David O., P. J. Henry, and Rick Kosterman. 2000. "Egalitarian Values and Contemporary Racial Politics." In *Racialized Politics,* ed. David O. Sears, Jim Sidanius, and Lawrence Bobo. Chicago: University of Chicago Press

Shafer, Byron E., and William J. M. Claggett. 1995. *The Two Majorities: The Issue Context of Modern American Politics.* Baltimore: Johns Hopkins University Press.

Shafer, Byron E., and Richard Johnston. 2001. "The Transformation of Southern Politics Revisited: The House of Representatives as a Window." *British Journal of Political Science* 31: 601–625.

———. 2006. *The End of Southern Exceptionalism.* Cambridge, Mass.: Harvard University Press.

Shaffer, Stephen D. 1981. "A Multivariate Explanation of Decreasing Turnout in Presidential Elections, 1960–1976." *American Journal of Political Science* 25: 68–95.

Shani, Danielle. 2006. "Knowing Your Colors: Can Knowledge Correct for Partisan Bias in Political Perceptions?" Paper presented at the annual meeting of the Midwest Political Science Association, Chicago.

Shapiro, Robert Y., and John M. Young. 1989. "Public Opinion and the Welfare State: The United States in Comparative Perspective." *Political Science Quarterly* 104: 59–89.

Shapiro, Walter. 2005. "What's the Matter with Central Park West?" *Atlantic Monthly* March, 295: 46.

Shaw, Daron R. 1999. "The Effect of TV Ads and Candidate Appearances on Statewide Presidential Votes, 1988–96." *American Political Science Review* 93: 345–361.

———. 2006. *The Race to 270: The Electoral College and the Campaign Strategies of 2000 and 2004.* Chicago: University of Chicago Press.

Shogan, Robert. 2002. *War without End: Cultural Conflict and the Struggle for America's Political Future.* Boulder, Colo.: Westview.

Shotts, Kenneth W. 2003. "Does Racial Redistricting Cause Conservative Policy Outcomes? Policy Preferences of Southern Representatives in the 1980s and 1990s." *Journal of Politics* 65: 216–226.

Sigelman, Lee, and Emmett Buell. 2004. "Avoidance or Engagement? Issue Convergence in U.S. Presidential Campaigns, 1960–2000." *American Journal of Political Science* 48: 650–661.

Sigelman, Lee, and David Bullock. 1991. "Candidates, Issues, Horse Races, and Hoopla: Presidential Campaign Coverage, 1888–1988." *American Politics Quarterly* 19: 5–32.

Silver, Brian D., Barbara A. Anderson, and Paul R. Abramson. 1986. "Who Overreports Voting?" *American Political Science Review* 80: 613–624.

Simon, Herbert A. 1957. *Models of Man: Social and Rational.* New York: Wiley.

———. 1985. "Human Nature in Politics: The Dialogue of Psychology with Political Science." *American Political Science Review* 79: 293–304.

Skocpol, Theda. 1999. "Advocates without Members: The Recent Transformation of American Civic Life." In *Civic Engagement in American Democracy*, ed. Theda Skocpol and Morris P. Fiorina. Washington, D.C. and New York: Brookings; Russell Sage.

———. 2003. *Diminished Democracy: From Membership to Management in American Civic Life.* Norman: University of Oklahoma Press.

Skowronek, Stephen. 1993. *The Politics Presidents Make: Leadership from John Adams to George Bush.* Cambridge, Mass.: Belknap Press.

———. 2008. *Presidential Leadership in Political Time: Reprise and Reappraisal.* Lawrence: University Press of Kansas.

Smith, Alastair. 2009. *Election Timing.* Cambridge: Cambridge University Press.

Smith, Eric R. A. N. 1989. *The Unchanging American Voter.* Berkeley: University of California Press.

Smith, Mark A. 2007. *The Right Talk: How Conservatives Transformed the Great Society into the Economic Society.* Princeton, N.J.: Princeton University Press.

Sneider, Daniel. 1996. "Do Low Turnouts Show Contempt? Or Contentment?" *The Christian Science Monitor*, November 6, 1996, p. 1, International.

Sniderman, Paul M. 1993. "The New Look in Public Opinion Research." In *Political Science: The State of the Discipline* I., ed. Ada W. Finifter. Washington, D.C.: American Political Science Association.

Sniderman, Paul M., Richard A. Brody, and Philip E. Tetlock. 1991. *Reasoning and Choice: Explorations in Political Psychology.* New York: Cambridge University Press.

Sniderman, Paul M., Michael G. Hagen, Philip E. Tetlock, and Henry E. Brady. 1986. "Reasoning Chains: Causal Models of Policy Reasoning in Mass Publics." *British Journal of Political Science* 16: 405–430.

Sniderman, Paul M., Thomas Piazza, Philip E. Tetlock, and Ann Kendrick. 1991. "The New Racism." *American Journal of Political Science* 35: 423–447.

Sniderman, Paul M., and Philip E. Tetlock. 1986. "Symbolic Racism: Problems of Motive Attribution in Political Analysis." *Journal of Social Issues* 42: 129–150.

Sosna, M. 1987. "More Important Than the Civil War? The Impact of World War II on the South." In *Perspectives on the American South: An Annual Review of Society, Politics, and Culture*, vol. 4, ed. James C. Cobb and Charles R. Wilson. New York: Gordon and Breach.

Stanga, John E., and James F. Sheffield. 1987. "The Myth of Zero Partisanship: Attitudes toward the American Political Parties." *American Journal of Political Science* 31: 821–855.

Stanley, Harold. 2008. "Hispanics in the South." Keynote address at the biennial meeting of the Citadel Symposium on Southern Politics. Charleston, SC.

Stanley, Harold W., and David S. Castle. 1988. "Partisan Changes in the South: Making Sense of Scholarly Dissonance." In *The South's New Politics: Realignment and Dealignment*, ed. Robert H. Swansbrough and David M. Brodsky. Columbia: University of South Carolina Press.

Stanley, Harold W., and Richard G. Niemi. 2006. "Partisanship, Party Coalitions, and Group Support, 1952–2004." *Presidential Studies Quarterly* 36: 172–188.

———, eds. 2010. *Vital Statistics on American Politics 2009–2010*. Washington, D.C.: CQ Press.

Stimson, James A. 1975. "Belief Systems: Constraint, Complexity, and the 1972 Election." *American Journal of Political Science* 19: 393–417.

———. 2004. *Tides of Consent: How Public Opinion Shapes American Politics*. New York: Cambridge University Press.

Stoker, Laura, and M. Kent Jennings. 2008. "Of Time and the Development of Partisan Polarization." *American Journal of Political Science* 52: 619–635.

Stokes, Donald E. 1966a. "Party Loyalty and the Likelihood of Deviating Elections." In *Elections and the Political Order*. Angus Campbell, Phillip Converse, Warren Miller, Donald Stokes. New York: Wiley.

———. 1966b. "Some Dynamic Elements of Contests for the Presidency." *American Political Science Review* 60: 19–28.

Stolle, Dietlind, Marc Hooghe, and Michele Micheletti. 2005. "Politics in the Supermarket: Political Consumerism as a Form of Political Participation." *International Political Science Review* 26: 245–269.

Stonecash, Jeffrey M. 2000. *Class and Party in American Politics*. Boulder, Colo.: Westview.

Stonecash, Jeffrey M., Mark D. Brewer, and Mack D. Mariani. 2003. *Diverging Parties: Social Change, Realignment and Party Polarization*. Boulder, Colo.: Westview.

Streb, Matthew J. 2008. *Rethinking American Electoral Democracy*. New York: Routledge.

Strong, Donald S. 1955. "The Presidential Election in the South, 1952." *Journal of Politics* 17: 343–389.

———. 1960. *Urban Republicanism in the South*. Tuscaloosa: University of Alabama, Bureau of Public Administration.

Sturgis, Patrick. 2003. "Knowledge and Collective Preferences: A Comparison of Two Approaches to Estimating the Opinions of a Better Informed Public." *Sociological Methods and Research* 31: 453–485.

Sturgis, Patrick, Nick Allum, and Patten Smith. 2008. "An Experiment on the Measurement of Political Knowledge in Surveys." *Public Opinion Quarterly* 72: 90–102.

Sundquist, James L. 1983. *Dynamics of the Party System: Alignment and Realignment of Political Parties in the United States.* Washington, D.C.: Brookings Institution.

Sunstein, Cass R. 2001. *Republic.Com 2.0.* Princeton, N.J.: Princeton University Press.

Taber, Charles S., and Milton Lodge. 2006. "Motivated Skepticism in the Evaluation of Political Beliefs." *American Journal of Political Science* 50: 755–769.

Tarman, Christopher, and David O. Sears. 2005. "The Conceptualization and Measurement of Symbolic Racism." *Journal of Politics* 67: 731–761.

Teixeira, Ruy A. 1987. *Why Americans Don't Vote: Turnout Decline in the United States, 1960–1984.* New York: Greenwood.

———. 1992. *The Disappearing American Voter.* Washington, D.C.: Brookings.

Tesler, Michael, and David O. Sears. 2009. "The Two Sides of Symbolic Racism: Explaining the Effects of Racial Resentment in the Primaries and General Election." Paper presented at the Mershon Conference on the Transformative Election of 2008, Columbus, Ohio, Oct. 2–4.

———. Forthcoming. *Obama for President: Watershed to a Post-Racial Era?* Chicago: University of Chicago Press.

Thomassen, Jacques. 1976. "Party Identification as a Cross-National Concept." In *Party Identification and Beyond,* ed. Ian Budge, Ivor Crewe, and Dennis Farlie. London: Wiley.

Thomson, Katarina. 2001. "Appendix. The British Election Surveys, 1979–1997." In *The Rise of New Labour: Party Policies and Voter Choices,* ed. Anthony Heath, Roger Jowell, and John Curtice. Oxford: Oxford University Press.

Tichenor, Philip J., George A. Donohue, and Calice A. Olien. 1970. "Mass Flow and Differential Growth in Knowledge." *Public Opinion Quarterly* 34: 149–170.

Tindall, George B. 1972. *The Disruption of the Solid South.* Athens: University of Georgia Press.

Tingsten, Herbert. 1937. *Political Behavior: Studies in Election Statistics.* Totowa, N.J.: Bedminster Press.

Tomz, Michael, and Robert P. Van Houweling. 2003. "How Does Voting Equipment Affect the Racial Gap in Voided Ballots?" *American Journal of Political Science* 47: 46–60.

———. 2009. "The Electoral Implications of Candidate Ambiguity." *American Political Science Review* 103: 83–98.

Traugott. Michael W. 2004. "Why Electoral Reform Has Failed: If You Build It, Will They Come?" In *Rethinking the Vote: The Politics and Prospects of American Election Reform,* ed. Ann N. Crigler, Marion R. Just, and Edward J. McCaffery. New York: Oxford University Press.

U.S. Census Bureau. Current Population Survey. Table 4b. Reported Voting and Registration of the Voting-Age Population, by Sex, Race and Hispanic Origin, for States: November 2008. Internet Release Date: February 2009.

U.S. Census Bureau. Table 3: Annual Estimates of the Resident Population by Sex, Race, and Hispanic Origin: April 1, 2000 to July 1, 2008 (SC-EST2008–03–01). Release Date: May 14, 2009.

U.S. General Accounting Office. 1997. "2000 Census: Progress Made on Design but Risks Remain." Washington, D.C.: U.S. Government Printing Office.

Van Deth, Jan W., José Ramón Montero, and Anders Westholm. 2007. *Citizenship and Involvement in European Democracies: A Comparative Analysis.* London: Routledge.

Valentino, Nicholas A., Vincent L. Hutchings, and Ismail K. White. 2002. "Cues that Matter: How Political Ads Prime Racial Attitudes during Campaigns." *American Political Science Review* 96: 75–90.

Valentino, Nicholas A., and David O. Sears. 2005. "Old Times There Are Not Forgotten: Race and Partisan Realignment in the Contemporary South." *American Journal of Political Science* 49: 672–688.

Vavreck, Lynn. 2009. *The Message Matters: The Economy and Presidential Campaigns.* Princeton, N.J.: Princeton University Press.

Vavreck, Lynn, and Douglas Rivers. 2008. "The 2006 Cooperative Congressional Election Study." *Journal of Elections, Public Opinion and Parties* 18: 355–366.

Verba, Sidney, Kay Lehman Schlozman, and Henry E. Brady. 1995. *Voice and Equality: Civic Voluntarism in American Politics.* Cambridge, Mass.: Harvard University Press.

Viswanath, Kasisomayajula, and John R. Finnegan, Jr. 1996. "The Knowledge Gap Hypothesis: Twenty-Five Years Later." In *Communication Yearbook,* ed. Brant Burleson. Thousand Oaks, Calif.: Sage.

"Volunteer Growth in America: A Review of Trends Since 1974." 2006. Washington, D.C.: Corporation for National and Community Service.

Voss, D. Stephen. 1996. "Beyond Racial Threat: Failure of an Old Hypothesis in the New South." *Journal of Politics* 58: 1156–1170.

Wald, Kenneth D., and Allison Calhoun-Brown. 2006. *Religion and Politics in the United States,* 5th ed. Lanham, Md.: Rowman & Littlefield.

Walsh, Andrew D. 2000. *Religion, Economics, and Public Policy: Ironies, Tragedies, and Absurdities of the Contemporary Culture Wars.* Westport, Conn.: Praeger.

Wattenberg, Ben J. 1995. *Values Matter Most: How Republicans or Democrats or a Third Party Can Win and Renew the American Way of Life.* New York: Free Press.

Wattenberg, Martin P. 1984. *The Decline of American Political Parties, 1952–1980.* Cambridge, Mass.: Harvard University Press.

———. 1990. *The Decline of American Political Parties, 1952–1988.* Cambridge, Mass.: Harvard University Press.

———. 1994. *The Decline of American Political Parties, 1952–1992.* Cambridge, Mass.: Harvard University Press.

————. 1996. *The Decline of American Political Parties, 1952–1994.* Cambridge, Mass.: Harvard University Press.

————. 1998. *The Decline of American Political Parties, 1952–1996.* Cambridge, Mass.: Harvard University Press.

————. 2002. *Where Have All the Voters Gone?* Cambridge, Mass.: Harvard University Press.

————. 2008. *Is Voting for Young People?* New York: Pearson Longman.

Weatherford, M. Stephen. 1978. "Economic Conditions and Electoral Outcomes: Class Differences in the Political Response to Recession." *American Journal of Political Science* 22: 917–938.

Webb, Paul, and David M. Farrell. 1999. "Party Members and Ideological Change." In *Critical Elections: British Parties and Voters in Long-Term Perspective,* ed. Geoffrey Evans and Pippa Norris. London: Sage.

Webster, James G. 1984. "Cable Television's Impact on Audience for Local News." *Journalism Quarterly* 61: 419–422.

Webster, James G., and Gregory D. Newton. 1988. "Structural Determinants of the Television News Audience." *Journal of Broadcasting & Electronic Media* 32: 381–389.

Weisberg, Herbert F. 2002. "Partisanship and Incumbency in Presidential Elections." *Political Behavior* 24: 339–60.

————. 2005a. "The Structure and Effects of Moral Predispositions in Contemporary American Politics." *Journal of Politics* 67: 646–668.

————. 2005b. *The Total Survey Error Approach: A Guide to the New Science of Survey Research.* Chicago: University of Chicago Press.

Weisberg, Herbert F., and Dino P. Christenson. 2007. "Changing Horses in Wartime? The 2004 Presidential Election." *Political Behavior* 29: 279–304.

Weisberg, Herbert F., and Christopher J. Devine. 2010a. "Party Defection and Change in the 2008 U.S. Presidential Election." *Journal of Elections, Public Opinion, and Parties* 20: 213–240.

————. 2010b. "Racial Attitude Effects on Voting in the 2008 Presidential Election." *Electoral Studies,* forthcoming.

Weisberg, Herbert F., and Jerrold G. Rusk. 1970. "Dimensions of Candidate Evaluations." *American Political Science Review* 64: 1167–1185.

Wheaton, Blair, Bengt Muthen, Duane E. Alwin, and Gene F. Summers. 1977. "Assessing Reliability and Stability in Panel Models." *Sociological Methodology* 8: 84–136.

Whitby, Kenny J. 1985. "Effects of the Interaction between Race and Urbanization on Votes of Southern Congressmen." *Legislative Studies Quarterly* 10: 505–517.

White, John Kenneth. 2003. *The Values Divide.* New York: Chatham House.

Wickham-Jones, Mark. 1997. "How the Conservatives Lost the Economic Argument." In *Labour's Landslide: The British General Election 1997,* ed. Andrew Geddes and Jonathan Tonge. Manchester: Manchester University Press.

Wilcox, Clyde. 2000. *Onward Christian Soldiers?,* 2nd ed. Boulder, Colo.: Westview.

Wilcox, Nathaniel T., and Christopher Wlezien. 1993. "The Contamination of Responses to Survey Items: Economic Perceptions and Political Judgments." *Political Analysis* 5: 181–213.

Williams, Rhys H. 1997. *Cultural Wars in American Politics: Critical Reviews of a Popular Myth*. New York: De Gruyter.

Wittkopf, Eugene. 1990. *Faces of Internationalism*. Durham: Duke University Press.

Wittman, Donald A. 1989. "Why Democracies Produce Efficient Results." *Journal of Political Economy* 97: 1395–1424.

Wlezien, Christopher. 2001. "On Forecasting the Presidential Vote." *PS: Political Science & Politics* 34: 25–31.

Wlezien, Christopher, Mark Franklin, and Daniel Twiggs. 1997. "Economic Perceptions and Vote Choice: Disentangling the Endogeneity." *Political Behavior* 19: 7–17.

Wright, Gerald C. 1977. "Contextual Models of Electoral Behavior: The Southern Wallace Vote." *American Political Science Review* 71: 497–508.

———. 1993. "Errors in Measuring Vote Choice in the National Election Studies, 1952–88." *American Journal of Political Science* 37: 291–316.

Wright, Gerald C., Robert S. Erikson, and John P. McIver. 1985. "Measuring State Partisanship and Ideology with Survey Data." *Journal of Politics* 47: 469–489.

Wright, Gerald C., and Brian F. Schaffner. 2002. "The Influence of Party: Evidence from the State Legislatures." *American Political Science Review* 96: 367–379.

Youn, Sug-Min. 1994. "Program Type Preference and Program Choice in a Multichannel Situation." *Journal of Broadcasting & Electronic Media* 38: 465–475.

Young, Dannagal G. 2006. "Late-Night Comedy and the Salience of the Candidates' Caricatured Traits in the 2000 Election." *Mass Communication and Society* 9: 339–366.

Zaller, John. 1985. "Proposal for the Measurement of Political Information. Report to the NES Board of Overseers." Center for Political Studies, University of Michigan.

———. 1992. *The Nature and Origins of Mass Opinion*. New York: Cambridge University Press.

———. 2003. "A New Standard of News Quality: Burglar Alarms for the Monitorial Citizen." *Political Communication* 20: 109–130.

———. 2004. "Floating Voters in U.S. Presidential Elections, 1948–2000." In *Studies in Public Opinion*, ed. Willem E. Saris and Paul M. Sniderman. Princeton, N.J.: Princeton University Press.

Zaller, John R., and Stanley Feldman. 1992. "A Simple Theory of the Survey Response: Answering Questions versus Revealing Preferences." *American Journal of Political Science* 36: 579–616

Zhao, Xinshu, and Steven H. Chaffee. 1995. "Campaign Advertisements versus Television News as Sources of Political Issue Information." *Public Opinion Quarterly* 59: 41–65.

Zukin, Cliff, Scott Keeter, Molly Andolina, Krista Jenkins, and Michael X. Delli Carpini. 2006. *A New Engagement? Political Participation, Civic Life, and the Changing American Citizen.* Oxford: Oxford University Press.

Zukin, Cliff, and Robin Snyder. 1984. "Passive Learning: When the Media Environment Is the Message." *Public Opinion Quarterly* 48: 629–638.

Name Index

✧ ✧ ✧

Subject Index

✧ ✧ ✧

461

Credits

✧ ✧ ✧

Chapter 3

From Markus Prior, "News vs. Entertainment: How Increasing Media Choice Widens Gaps in Political Knowledge and Turnout," *American Journal of Political Science* 49, no. 3 (July 2005): 577–592. Copyright © 2005 by the Midwest Political Science Association. Reprinted by permission of John Wiley and Sons.

Chapter 6

From Matthew A. Baum and Angela S. Jamison, "The *Oprah* Effect: How Soft News Helps Inattentive Citizens Vote Consistently," *Journal of Politics* 68, no. 4 (November 2006): 946–959. Copyright © 2006 Southern Political Science Association. Reprinted with the permission of Cambridge University Press.

Chapter 7

From Richard R. Lau and David P. Redlawsk, "Advantages and Disadvantages of Cognitive Heuristics in Political Decision Making," *American Journal of Political Science* 45, no. 4 (October 2001): 951–971. Copyright © 2001 by the Midwest Political Science Association. Reprinted by permission of John Wiley and Sons.

Chapter 8

From Paul Goren, "Political Sophistication and Policy Reasoning: A Reconsideration," *American Journal of Political Science* 48, no. 3 (July 2004): 462–478. Copyright © 2004 by the Midwest Political Science Association. Reprinted by permission of John Wiley and Sons.

Chapter 10

From Geoffrey Evans and Robert Andersen, "The Political Conditioning of Economic Perceptions," *Journal of Politics* 68, no. 1 (February 2006): 194–207. Copyright © 2006 Southern Political Science Association. Reprinted with the permission of Cambridge University Press.

Chapter 11

From Stephen Ansolabehere, Jonathan Rodden, and James M. Snyder Jr., "Purple America," *Journal of Economic Perspectives* 20, no. 2 (Spring 2006): 97–118. Reprinted by permission of the American Economic Association and the authors.

Chapter 13

From Marc Hetherington, "Resurgent Mass Partisanship: The Role of Elite Polarization," *American Political Science Review* 95, no. 3 (September 2001): 619–631. Copyright © 2001 by the American Political Science Association. Reprinted with the permission of Cambridge University Press.

Chapter 14

From Alan I. Abramowitz and Kyle L. Saunders, "Is Polarization a Myth?" *Journal of Politics* 70, no. 2 (April 2008): 542–555. Copyright © 2008 Southern Political Science Association. Reprinted with the permission of Cambridge University Press.

Chapter 15

From Morris P. Fiorina, Samuel J. Abrams, and Jeremy C. Pope, "Polarization in the American Public: Misconceptions and Misreadings," *Journal of Politics* 70, no. 2 (April 2008): 556–560. Copyright © 2008 Southern Political Science Association. Reprinted with the permission of Cambridge University Press.

Chapter 19

Reprinted by permission of the publisher from *The End of Southern Exceptionalism: Class, Race, and Partisan Change in the Postwar South* by Byron E. Shafer and Richard Johnston, 22–50, Cambridge, Mass.: Harvard University Press. Copyright © 2006 by the President and Fellows of Harvard College.

Chapter 20

From M. V. Hood III, Quentin Kidd, and Irwin L. Morris, "The Reintroduction of the *Elephas Maximus* to the Southern United States: The Rise of Republican State Parties, 1960 to 2000," *American Politics Research* 32, no. 1 (January 2004): 68–101. Copyright © 2004 SAGE Publications. Reprinted by permission of SAGE Publications, Inc.

Chapter 21

From D. Sunshine Hillygus and Todd G. Shields, *The Persuadable Voter: Wedge Issues in Presidential Campaigns.* Copyright © 2008 by Princeton University Press. Reprinted by permission of Princeton University Press.